The New Apple II User's Guide

The New Apple II User's Guide

David Finnigan

The New Apple II User's Guide
David Finnigan

ISBN-10: 0615639879

ISBN-13: 978-0-615-63987-1

This book was prepared using Adobe software products on Macintosh computers. The display face is Futura. Text is in Bookman Old Style.

Published by Mac GUI
Lincoln, IL

Acknowledgements

This book became reality with the help of many different people, both directly and indirectly. I've tried to get most of the names down, but if I left you out, I apologize now!

Thanks goes out to Glenn Jones, who donated an Uthernet card to help me write Chapter 10. Joe DeHoff, Larry M. Keeran, Jeremy Moskowitz, George Rentovich, and Peter Wong also deserve thanks for sending me their extra Apple II hardware and manuals, which have really helped me grow in my knowledge of the system. I'm just carrying the torch.

Chapter 10 was further helped along by Ewen Wannop, who provided a copy of Spectrum and SIS, as well as pre-release copies of SNAP and SAFE2. Geoff Weiss also answered my questions about SIS.

Special thanks goes to the three-man technical review team of Glenn Jones, Michael J. Mahon, and Ewen Wannop. Their knowledge and sharp eyes much improved the manuscript.

I'd also like to thank all of the regulars on comp.sys.apple2 for being helpful, knowledgeable, and at times, witty: Tony Cianfaglione, Kevin Dady, David Empson, Sean Fahey, Egan Ford, Ken Gagne, Bill Garber, Steven Hirsch, Hugh Hood, Richard Jackson, Matt J, Alex Lee, James Littlejohn, Mike Maginnis, Michael J. Mahon, Bill Martens, John B. Matthews, Steve Nickolas, Dean Phares, Brendan R, Andrew Roughan, David Schmidt, Oliver Schmidt, Eric Shepherd, Mike Stephens, Mike T, Linards Ticmanis, Antoine Vignau, Mike Willegal, Peter Wong, Nick, and many others. They've been great at answering my many questions.

Thank you to everyone who keeps the Apple II hobby alive by contributing his knowledge, developing hardware or software, writing books or articles, or just using and experimenting with the Apple. Thirty years later, there is still so much to be accomplished.

Finally, this book wouldn't exist without the magic of one Steve Wozniak and his Apple II computer. Thanks.

Table of Contents

Chapter 3 : Beginning BASIC 65

Chapter 4 : Advanced BASIC 89

Chapter 8 : Graphics and Sound 293

Chapter 9 : Printing 353

Chapter 11 : Machine Language Monitor 435

Chapter 12 : The IIgs and GS/OS 471

Introduction

Why still use the Apple? You might get asked this question. There are a number of reasons why. The Apple remains, as it ever was, a machine simple enough that it can be entirely understood by a single person. It remains, as it ever was, a machine on which one can learn to program. There is no fear of breaking the machine by experimenting, or with a program gone wrong. The fundamentals of programming can be learned from BASIC, and the Apple also has further languages available to it, such as C, Pascal, and assembly. Some people may have grown up with an Apple, perhaps having used one in school. Thus there is the nostalgia factor, especially with the old games and early memories.

Perhaps the most remarkable thing about the Apple II is that after three decades, it's still not finished yet. Or in other words, not everything that can be accomplished, has been accomplished. It wasn't finished when the Macintosh superseded it in 1984, and it wasn't finished when Apple Computer finally discontinued the Apple II family in 1993. Even today, the Apple II continues on. What does this mean? It means that the Apple still has opportunities for its users. That means you! There are still so many programs to be written, experiments to be conducted, and adventures to be had.

About This Book

This book is a modern-day replacement for the published Apple guides of years gone by. If you've just recently obtained your Apple II, chances are that you obtained little or no documentation on how to use it. Back when the Apple was new, book stores and computer shops contained shelves of books on using and programming the Apple II. Not so anymore.

The book you have now is written with both the beginner and the expert in mind, and covers all models of Apple II, as well as the latest developments since the past 20 years. The newcomer will receive all of the training that he needs to master the Apple II, whereas the expert can use this book as a reference to refresh his memory on many diverse topics.

Who This Book is for

If you are reading this, then this book is probably for you. If you're new to the Apple II, then this book contains everything you need to know to get started. If you're an Apple old timer, but haven't used one in a while, then this book should help refresh your memory. For everyone else, if you enjoy reading material about the Apple, then this book is also for you.

Little to no assumptions are made about the reader's existing Apple knowledge. As long as you have at least a basic understanding of a modern day computer system, then you will find the Apple to be no more difficult to comprehend. Detailed instructions, and figures where necessary, are provided to aid in understanding.

Companion Web Site

This book has its own web site where you may get access to additional information and resources, as well as the example BASIC programs presented in the book. If you'd like, you can even email the author to send him your questions, praise, and comments. The URL is:

`http://macgui.com/newa2guide/`

The companion web site contains links to other great Apple II sites, including hardware and software vendors. One such site is Mac GUI Vault, a comprehensive source for Apple II materials. The Vault includes over 25,000 software files, a photo gallery, a collection of over 1,000 text and PDF files, and an archive of more than one million Usenet articles dating back to the early 1980s.

The URL for Mac GUI Vault is:

`http://macgui.com/vault/`

Apple II Emulators

If you do not own a physical Apple II machine, but instead use an emulator, the content in this book is no less relevant, except for passages which describe setup and physical aspects of the computer. Emulator users should refer to the program's documentation for assistance in the startup and configuration of the emulated Apple II.

If you have neither a physical Apple II computer, nor an emulator, then the end of Chapter 1 lists some tips for purchasing a used Apple computer, as well as emulators for Macintosh and Windows. Visit the companion web site for links to these emulators.

Organization

This book is organized into four main sections. The first is an introduction to the world of Apple II. It explains the Apple II system, its peripherals, how to set them up, and basic means of operation. Chapters 1 and 2 make up this section. The second part, which consists of Chapters 3 through 9, is concerned with programming the Apple in BASIC. The third part, Chapters 10 to 12, are specialized chapters that deal with specific applications on the Apple II. The fourth and final part is the appendices and glossary, which serve as a general reference guide to a number of topics.

The flow of this book is such that it can easily be read sequentially starting at Chapter 1 and finishing at the end. If you are a novice to the Apple II, then it is suggested that you approach the book in this manner. However, each chapter can stand on its own, and readers with varying levels of experience can choose to start in at whichever chapter grabs his or her interest.

Conventions Used

New and important terms will be introduced in *italic type* when they are defined. Most, if not all, of these terms also appear in the Glossary.

Screen output, as well as commands which should be typed on the Apple appear in a `fixed-width face`.

Keys on the keyboard will be displayed in SMALL CAPS.

At various points in the book, you will be instructed to press various key combinations. These involve holding down one or more keys while pressing and releasing a final key, then releasing the remaining keys. Key combinations are indicated with a hyphen and must be pressed in the order that they appear, from left to right. For example, CONTROL-G means to hold down the CONTROL key, press and release G, then release the CONTROL key. CONTROL-SHIFT-RESET means to hold down the CONTROL and SHIFT keys, press and release RESET, then release the CONTROL and SHIFT keys.

Without further ado, let's begin at the beginning!

Chapter 1 : Meeting Your Apple

This chapter will explain the main components of the Apple computer system. You will learn to identify what model of Apple you have, as well as the parts which make it up. Not every system is alike; not every system consists of the same components. However, this chapter will cover the most common components and peripherals which the beginning Apple user is likely to have. At the end is a summary of significant advances in the Apple II world over the past 20 years.

About the Apple

If you're used to modern-day computer systems, then many aspects of the Apple will seem novel to you: there is no built-in hard drive, there is no video card needed, a programming language and rudimentary operating system are built-in, and for the most part, you won't be using a mouse.

Yes, this is the Apple II: a computer first released in the late 70's that became wildly popular because it had built-in color graphics, sound, game paddles, and the BASIC programming language. You will learn about all of these features in this book.

Since then, six or seven different models of Apple have been released. Each one has features unique to it, though for the most part, all Apples behave the same way.

Identify Your Apple

The first step to take is to identify what model of Apple you have. This is important to do now, because while many techniques remain the same among varieties of Apple, there are some key differences. These differences will be duly noted in this guide so you can read the material which applies to your specific kind of Apple. Fortunately, all models of Apple II come with a nameplate or badge that serves as a fairly accurate means of identification.

The Apple II, Apple II Plus, and Apple IIe

If your Apple resembles a typewriter and has slotted vents in the sides, then you have either an Apple II, an Apple II Plus, or an Apple IIe. The original model of Apple II was produced from 1977 until about 1980. There are not many of them left in the world, so you would do well to hang on to it.

The second model, known as the Apple II Plus, was manufactured from 1979 to 1983. The Apple II Plus is quite similar to the original Apple II, except that it has some modifications which make using the disk drive more convenient, as well as having a newer version of BASIC built-in.

The final model in this set, the Apple IIe, is the longest-lived model of Apple, and was produced from 1983 to 1993, with a few revisions in-between. The most significant revision to the IIe is known as the *Enhanced IIe*, released in 1985. The Enhanced IIe includes additional features and options which became standard with the release of the Apple IIc in 1984. These features include an upgraded processor (the 65C02), MouseText characters, and firmware updates. Most Apple IIe computers are of the Enhanced variety.

The final revision of IIe, the Platinum IIe, debuted in 1987. It is an Enhanced IIe that comes in a slightly redesigned case, its keyboard featuring an updated layout as well as a numeric keypad.

The Apple IIc and Apple IIc Plus

Two models of Apple look like bulky laptops without an LCD screen. These are the IIc and IIc Plus. The IIc, released in 1984, has a large 5.25" floppy disk drive on the right-hand side. The IIc Plus, introduced in 1988, has a smaller, 3.5" disk drive on that side, and sports a faster processor. The IIc and IIc Plus have much in common with the Enhanced IIe, as they all share the same processor and similar firmware.

Figure 1-1. The Apple II Plus and Apple IIe

Figure 1-2. The Apple IIc

Figure 1-3. An Apple IIgs system

The Apple IIgs

Finally, if your Apple II looks like a vaguely modern yet quaint desktop box, then you likely have an Apple IIgs. The Apple IIgs was first produced in 1986 and underwent two revisions. The first release, named ROM 00, is not compatible with some software later released for the IIgs, and isn't very common. The next revision, ROM 01, is compatible with the widest range of software, and is also the most common IIgs revision. The final revision, the ROM 3, includes more built-in memory than the previous two versions, as well as several other improvements.

The Apple IIe Card

In 1991, Apple Computer introduced the Apple IIe Card, essentially an enhanced Apple IIe that worked inside of a Macintosh computer. Primarily intended to ease schools' transitions from Apple II to Macintosh, the IIe Card allowed the Macintosh LC, and other models, to run most Apple II software.

The Apple IIe Card featured a 65C02 processor and 256K of RAM built-in. Furthermore, the Macintosh host computer allowed the Apple IIe access to a clock, 1.44 MB SuperDrive, SCSI hard drive, mouse, two serial ports, 80 columns video, AppleShare networking, and 1 MB additional RAM. A port on the IIe Card allowed a joystick, an 800K UniDisk drive, and up to two 5.25" drives to be connected.

In essence, the Apple IIe Card is similar to using an emulator, except that some functions, such as disk access, are still handled by physical equipment. For the purposes of this book, think of the Apple IIe Card as an Apple IIc Plus. Its firmware and built-in hardware make it a close equivalent.

Apples in Disguise

In most cases, what's printed on the lid or case of the Apple is enough to identify it, but there is also the possibility that the original lid has been substituted for a different one, or even that the computer inside the case has been upgraded. To name some examples, an Apple IIgs could be inside of a IIe case, and an Apple II could have its original lid and case, but be upgraded to a II Plus.

Timeline

In terms of features added, where later models have the same features, as well as new ones, compared to previous models, a timeline of Apple computers would look like this:

1. Apple II (1977)
2. Apple II Plus
3. Apple IIe (unenhanced)
4. Apple IIc
5. Apple IIe (Enhanced)
6. Apple IIc Plus
7. Apple IIgs

Which Model is Best?

This is a question which comes up fairly often, and which can be the subject of intense debate. However, the answer is simple: it depends on what you, the user, need. If you're beginning on the Apple system, then the IIgs is a good choice, since it has the most features built-in and the greatest compatibility. The IIe is also an excellent machine, though it does not have as many built-in features compared to the IIgs. The IIc and IIc Plus are distinctive for the built-in disk drive, which can come in quite handy, but are limited by lack of expansion slots.

The Keyboard

All models of Apple except for the IIgs have a built-in, typewriter-style keyboard. The Apple IIgs differs in that its keyboard is not built into the case, but is instead detached. If you have an Apple IIgs or a Platinum IIe, then there is also a numeric keypad on the right-hand side. An external numeric keypad is an optional add-on for the Apple II, II Plus, and earlier IIe models.

Most of the keys should be familiar to you: letters and numbers, the SPACE BAR, and the SHIFT keys. Others are unique to the Apple.

The earliest models of Apple, the II and II Plus, only type uppercase letters. Starting with the IIe, lowercase became a built-in option. Therefore, the SHIFT key on the Apple II and II Plus is only used to produce the upper character on the numeric and alphabetic keys, with one exception. The G key has the word BELL printed above it, but SHIFT-G does not make a bell on the screen. Read on to find out what this key's alternate use is.

Special Keys Common to All Models

Each model of Apple II has a keyboard with a different set of special keys. However, some keys are common among all models.

CONTROL or CTRL - This key is used in conjunction with another key to send a certain signal or command to the Apple. For example, CONTROL-G makes a beep. To use this key, hold down the CONTROL key, then press a letter or number key. Finally, release both keys.

ESCAPE or ESC - If you become stuck in a program, you may try pressing the ESCAPE key to exit from it. Other programs require one to press ESCAPE to cancel the current operation. In addition, the ESCAPE key is used in cursor-control movements known as Escape key sequences. These are explained in Chapter 2.

RESET - Pressing the RESET key will end whatever program is currently running and return control of the Apple to the keyboard. On the earliest models of Apple, a press of the RESET key alone would do the trick. With newer models, the CONTROL key must be held down while the RESET key is pressed. This combination is a requirement that was designed to avoid accidental resets of the Apple.

LEFT ARROW and RIGHT ARROW - These keys are also used to control the screen cursor. On the earliest models of Apple, the II and II Plus, the LEFT ARROW key is the only way to back up and correct a typing mistake. The Apple IIe and later models also have up and down arrows.

Special Keys on the Apple II and II Plus

The only unique key on these models is the REPT key, which stands for "repeat." This key is used to automatically repeat another key. For example, to back the cursor over many spaces, hold down REPT and the LEFT ARROW key simultaneously. Release both keys when the cursor has moved to the desired position. The REPT key has no effect when used with the RESET, CTRL, ESC, or SHIFT keys. On some models of Apple II, pressing REPT by itself will repeat the most recently-typed key exactly once.

Special Keys on the Apple IIe and IIc

The Apple IIe introduced not only a keyboard that could produce lowercase letters, but also nine new keys. Some of these keys merely add more symbols to the typist. The rest are special keys. The Apple IIc has exactly the same keyboard layout. On the IIc, the switch labeled "Keyboard" is used to switch the key layout between Qwerty and Dvorak. The Platinum IIe has a larger keyboard, as it includes a numeric keypad, and some of the key positions have been changed. Except for those two changes, the Platinum IIe keyboard features no other differences.

TAB - This key's function is identical to the tab key on a typewriter. It indents the cursor to the next tab stop. Programs must be written to take advantage of the TAB key, however. Typically, these are word processing programs. Notably, the version of BASIC provided with the early Apple IIe and IIc does not recognize TAB.

DELETE - The DELETE key is an alternative to using the LEFT ARROW key to correct mistakes. As with the TAB key, programs must be written to make use of it, and BASIC on the early models of IIe and IIc does not recognize the DELETE key.

OPEN-APPLE - The OPEN-APPLE key, located on the left of the SPACE BAR on the IIe and IIc, is similar in purpose to the CONTROL key. It can be used in conjunction with another key to send a command to a program. When held down in association with the CONTROL and RESET keys, the IIe will do a full restart as if you had flipped the power switch off and on. Finally, the OPEN-APPLE key is connected to paddle button 0, so it can be used for gaming.

SOLID-APPLE - The SOLID-APPLE key is the twin of the OPEN-APPLE key. When used with CONTROL-RESET, it triggers the IIe self-test routine. The OPEN-APPLE key is also connected to paddle button 1. Sometimes this key is referred to as the CLOSED-APPLE key.

Figure 1-4. The Apple II and II Plus keyboard

Figure 1-5. The Apple IIe keyboard

Figure 1-6. The Apple IIc keyboard

CAPS LOCK - When in the depressed position, the Apple keyboard will only produce uppercase letters. Many older programs, including BASIC on the unenhanced Apple IIe, only recognize commands entered in uppercase.

Special Keys on the Apple IIc Plus and IIgs

These two models of Apple were the last to be produced, and therefore have the most amount of keys. The same keys from the IIe and IIc are included, with two exceptions: the OPEN-APPLE key has been turned into the COMMAND key; the SOLID-APPLE key became the OPTION key.

The RESET key on the Apple IIgs keyboard is adorned with a left-facing triangle. This key, located at the top left of the keyboard, is used as part of a key combination to simulate a power cycle (flipping the power switch off then on).

Taking the Lid Off

If you have an Apple IIc or IIc Plus, then you unfortunately are going to have to miss out on this section. Like today's laptop computers, the IIc models are not made to be opened and looked at. You can if you really want to, but for the beginning Apple II user, there is no advantage to doing so.

To take the lid off an Apple II, II Plus, or IIe, simply pop up the tabs on the left and right sides of the back of the case. Lift up the lid slightly, and slide it toward the keyboard. Finally, pull it away from the computer. If the lid will not budge, take a close look at the back of the Apple and see if there is a screw or two holding down the lid. If so, remove them.

With an Apple IIgs, there are two plastic tabs on the left and right sides of the back. Press these tabs inward, and lift up the case from the back. Be sure to do this slowly, since the plastic is quite old and may be brittle by now. If the case will not come off, check the back for any screws, and remove them if found.

You have now successfully exposed your Apple's interior!

Figure 1-7. The Apple IIgs keyboard

If there's a lot of dust down in there, do your best to blow it out. A few major components you should see include the power supply on the left, the RAM chips near the front, the expansion slots to the back, and many other small integrated circuit chips abound. The Apple II and II Plus have over 100 chips laid out in a grid. The later models, the IIe and IIgs, have far fewer– less than half that amount. One of these chips is responsible for acting as the Apple's "brain." It's the microprocessor, or CPU (Central Processing Unit), and is called either a 6502, 65C02, or 65C816, depending on what model of Apple you have.

Direct your attention to the rectangular slots at the back of the motherboard. If you have an Apple IIgs, then it is possible that all seven of them are empty.

As it turns out, a lot of common functionality which was provided by expansion cards is built in to the IIgs. However, if you have any older model of Apple II, then there should be at least one card there, maybe even two.

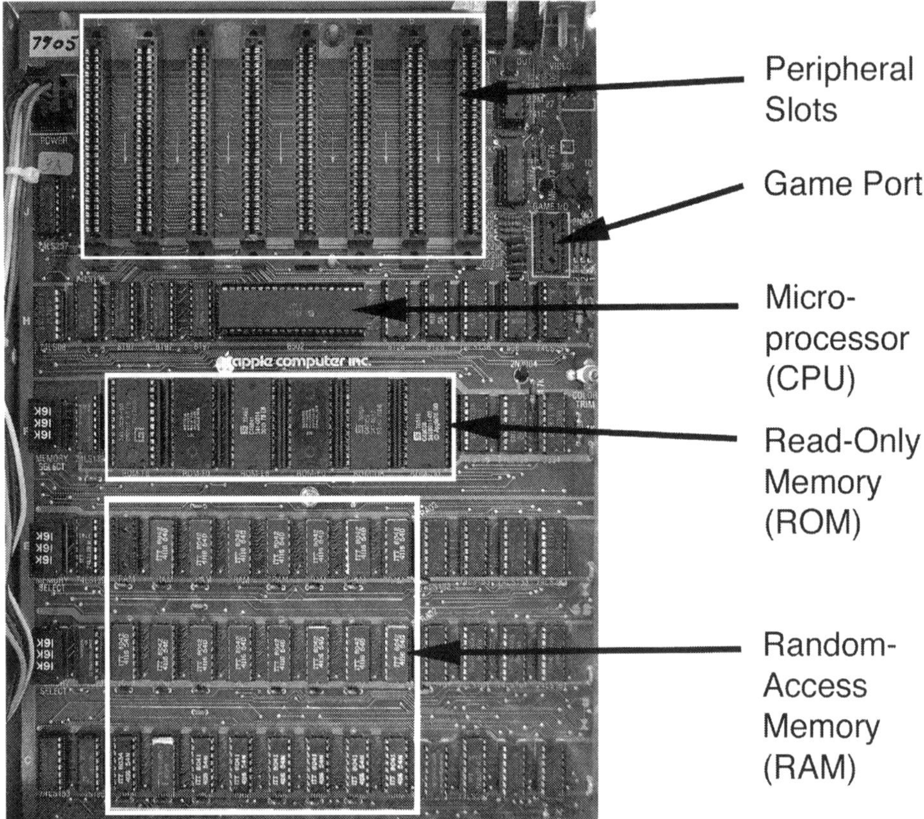

Figure 1-8. The Apple II and II Plus motherboard

Memory

Unless you have an Apple IIgs, or a souped-up IIe, your Apple's memory is measured in *kilobytes*, a term often abbreviated as K or KB. 1K is equal to 1,024 bytes. The byte is the smallest unit of memory, capable of storing exactly one character. Most Apples have 128K of total memory. However, if you have an original Apple II or II Plus, your computer likely has either 48 or 64 kilobytes of memory. In those two models, the Apple Language Card is used to provide an additional 16 kilobytes of RAM, thus giving 64 kilobytes in total.

As you no doubt know, the computer uses its *memory* to store both the program which you are currently using, such as a word processor, and the data that the program is currently working with, such as a letter. The larger the program and data are, the more memory required.

To add a slight twist to things, the Apple has two types of memory. One type, just mentioned, is known as *RAM*, which stands for Random Access Memory. RAM is used to store data which will change, such as programs and the data being used in a program. The contents of RAM are not permanent! When the power is switched off, the Apple "forgets" everything in its random access memory.

The second type of memory has a similar acronym, *ROM*, meaning Read-Only Memory. Another term for ROM is *firmware*. ROM is nearly the exact opposite of RAM: its contents never change, and they are permanent no matter if the Apple is on or off. What gets stored in ROM are programs and helper functions which never need to change. The BASIC programming language, which you will learn about in Chapter 3, is one example of a program stored in ROM.

The Apple Language Card, shown in Figure 1-9, adds both types of memory to an Apple II or II Plus: 16 kilobytes of additional RAM and 2 kilobytes of ROM.

Figure 1-9. The Apple Language Card in an Apple II or II Plus

Peripheral Expansion Cards

Every model of Apple except for the IIc and IIc Plus has a number of *expansion slots* at the back of the motherboard. In these slots are placed various *peripheral cards* which add functionality to the Apple II, similar to PCI cards in today's computers. Hardly anyone runs an Apple without any cards, for even features which one might take for granted today, such as the disk drive, require an expansion card in most models of Apple.

During the course of its life, several hundred peripheral expansion cards were manufactured for the Apple II series, and a handful still are produced today.

Card Name	Compatible with	Typical Slot	Description
Apple 5.25" Controller Card	All Apples*	5 or 6	Connects to the newer-style Apple 5.25" drives.
AppleMouse Card	All Apples*	4	Enables mouse support for programs that include it.
Disk II Controller Card	All Apples	6	Connects to the older-style Disk II 5.25" drives.
Extended 80-column Card	IIe	Aux	Allows the IIe to display 80 columns of text and adds 64K of additional memory.
Grappler+ Printer Interface Card	All Apples	1	Allows a variety of printers to be connected to the Apple.
Language Card	II, II Plus	0	Adds an additional 16K of RAM, and the Autostart ROM to the Apple.
Super Serial Card	All Apples*	1 or 2	Connects to a range of serial devices, such as printers, modems, and other computers.

* not needed on the IIgs, but can be used if desired

Table 1-1. Some common peripheral cards

An entire book could be dedicated to describing the many types of cards available: disk controllers, printing, modems, memory expansion, video display, input, networking and communications, and many others.

Shown in Figure 1-10 are several peripheral expansion cards. From left to right, top to bottom, they are: AppleMouse Card, Extended 80-column Card, Super Serial Card, Grappler+, Disk II Controller, and Apple 5.25" Controller.

All models of Apple with slots contain seven general-purpose slots and one specialized slot. In the Apple IIe and IIgs, the slots are numbered starting with slot 1 at the left, and the Apple II and II Plus start with slot 0 being at the left. All three models of Apple end with slot 7 being rightmost. For the most part, a card which is compatible with the general-purpose slots may be inserted into any of them and will work properly. However, over the years, a set of conventions developed for what types of cards go into which slots.

For example, the floppy disk card usually goes in slot 6. A hard disk controller is generally placed in slot 7. A printer card typically occupies slot 1. A modem customarily takes up slot 2. Some cards were designed only to work in a certain slot.

The eighth slot, the special slot, is located nearest to the power supply, on the left, in the Apple II, II Plus, and American IIe. In the IIgs, the eighth slot is located on the right side of the motherboard, near the front.

In the European version of the Apple IIe, the slot is located near the center of the motherboard, directly in front of slot 3. In the Apple II and II Plus, this slot is called slot 0. In the IIe and IIgs, it is referred to as the *Auxiliary* or "Aux" slot. The majority of cards designed for this special slot are those that provide memory expansion; the typical expansion card will not work in this slot.

In Table 1-1 is a brief description of some Apple II peripheral cards. For brevity, this table only covers a few of the more popular and common cards. In the table, "All Apples" should be interpreted to mean "All Apples which can accept peripheral cards."

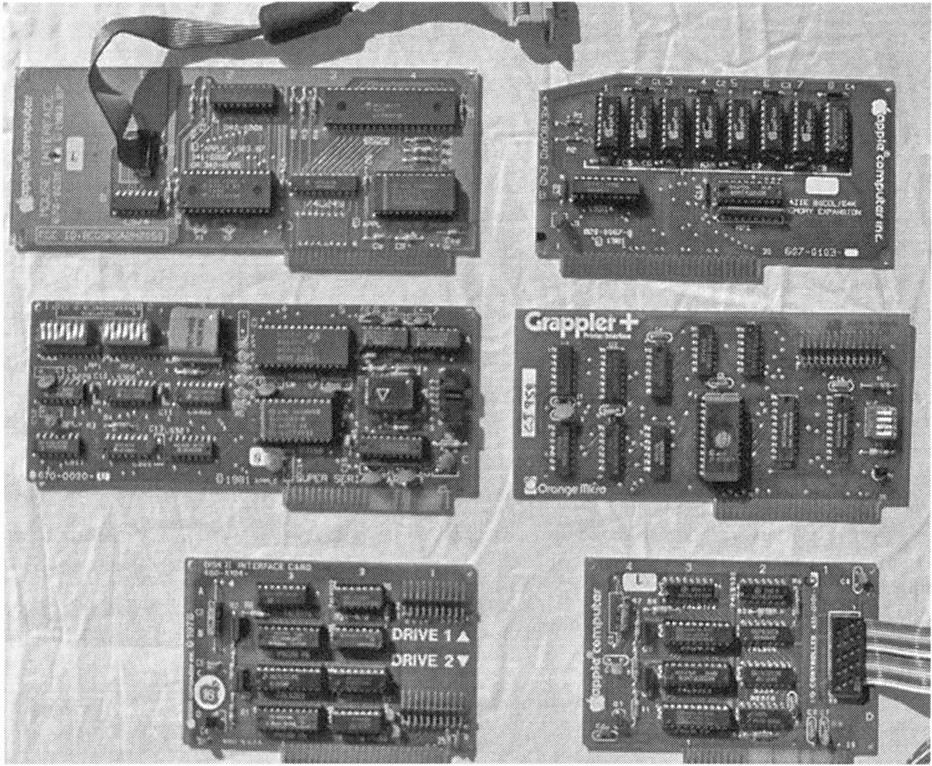

Figure 1-10. Several common peripheral expansion cards

Software

Software is what makes your Apple do something useful; it's the set of instructions which the Apple follows. There are two main types of software: operating systems, and application programs. Your Apple needs both to be of any use to you.

An *operating system* takes care of the most basic functions of the computer, such as keyboard entry, screen display, and management of the disk drive. Your Apple already comes with an operating system built into its ROM, known as the *Monitor*. The Monitor takes care of the keyboard and screen, and allows you to look at and modify the Apple's memory, as well as load and execute programs. A further operating system, known as *DOS*, is responsible for managing data on a disk drive. DOS, which stands for

Disk Operating System, must be loaded into your Apple before a disk may be used.

The second type of software, known as *applications,* is what you use to perform everyday tasks on the Apple, such as typing a letter, managing a database, designing graphics, or even just playing a game. Applications software relies on the operating system to function. Without an operating system, you would have a hard time running an application program.

Over the thirty-five years of its life, more than 10,000 application programs have been written for the Apple II series. Therefore, it is quite likely that the program you're looking for has already been written. However, if you need something specialized, you can program the Apple to do it. Later chapters in this book will instruct you on how to write your own programs.

Generally speaking, all software for the Apple is compatible with all models. There are some exceptions, though. The IIgs in particular is the biggest exception. Software written specifically for the Apple IIgs cannot run on any older Apple, such as the IIc or IIe. However, the Apple IIgs is compatible with nearly all older software. The small number of programs which won't work on newer models of Apple are generally incompatible because they make use of clever programming tricks that weren't officially supported by Apple Computer. In addition, some software written after 1984 that takes advantage of the 65C02 processor will not work on older models of Apple IIe, II Plus, and original Apple II which only have the 6502 CPU. When run on an incompatible Apple, these programs will typically display an error message such as "Requires an Enhanced IIe."

Disks

If you're not using cassette tapes to load and store your programs and data, then you'll use a disk system instead. It is not necessary to have a disk drive and disks to use the Apple, but it's the most common and convenient arrangement. There are a few different types of disks which can be used with the Apple. Most disk systems are removable, that is, you can use more than one disk with them. Expanding your storage is as easy as getting another disk to put your data on. Some other disk systems are fixed. They cannot be so easily expanded, but there is nothing to insert or remove. Fixed disk systems typically store 10 to 30 times as much as data as removable disk systems.

5.25" Disks

These disks are so named because they are exactly 5 1/4 inches square. They are made up of a plastic jacket that encloses a round magnetic recording surface. An oval cutout allows access to the recording surface while a circular hole in the middle enables a motor to spin the inner disk surface. The disk surface is divided into a scheme of tracks and sectors; these terms will be described later in this chapter.

With the exception of the Apple IIgs and the IIc Plus, the 5.25" disk is by far the most common type of disk for the Apple. A large percentage of the world's Apple II data is stored on this type of disk.

The original disk system for the Apple II was released in 1978 and was called the Disk II. It could store up to 116,480 bytes of data on a removable disk in the 13 sector format. A later upgrade allowed the disk to store 143,360 bytes of information, or 140K, called the 16 sector format. It is extremely unlikely that you will come across the earlier, 13 sector type of disk.

The Apple II uses a peculiar formatting scheme for its 5.25" disks that makes them completely incompatible with other models of computers, such as IBM PCs and the Macintosh.

One advantage of this peculiar scheme is that both sides of the disk may be used to store data, effectively doubling the capacity of the disk. To use the second side of the disk, simply cut a notch on the right side of the disk jacket and flip the disk over. Such a disk is called a *flippy disk*.

A disadvantage of 5.25" disks is that they are vulnerable to dust, dirt, and other contaminants. They are also rather flexible, which can cause harm to them. For these reasons, 5.25" disks should always be stored in a protective paper disk sleeve when not in use.

Figure 1-11. The Disk II system, including drive, controller, and diskette

Disks should be kept away from magnets, extreme temperatures, and other adverse conditions. If properly taken care of, the data on 5.25" disks can last for as long as two decades.

3.5" Disks

Unless you have an Apple IIgs or IIc Plus, the 3.5" disk is not commonly used. The Apple II, II Plus, and IIe, all require a special expansion card that was not as popular as the 5.25" disk card. Early models of Apple IIc cannot use a 3.5" disk drive at all, though later revisions can. Despite that, the 3.5" disk format is superior to that of the 5.25" disk in that it can store roughly 5 times as much data: up to 800K on a double-sided disk. The 3.5" disk is enclosed in a rigid shell which makes it more secure than the flexible 5.25" disk. Older models of Macintosh computers (made before 1999) with a built-in floppy disk drive can read and write 3.5" Apple II disks. PCs generally cannot.

Two models of 3.5" disk drive were popular with the Apple: the *UniDisk*, and the *Apple 3.5"* drive. The UniDisk is the older of the two and was originally intended for the Apple IIe and IIc. It has on-board logic which regulates the high-speed flow of data, slowing it down for the Apple. The newer model, the Apple 3.5" drive, was designed for the Apple IIgs and operates at a much faster speed.

The two disk drives look similar, but there are some differences: the UniDisk is distinctly whiter in color and the emergency eject hole is below the eject button. On the bottom of both disk drives is a label which identifies the device by name.

The Apple IIc Plus has a built-in 3.5" disk drive, and the Apple IIgs has a disk port which can power up to four 3.5" drives. On later revisions of the IIc, the UniDisk can be plugged directly into the disk port. For other models of Apple, a UniDisk card is required to attach a 3.5" UniDisk drive. Since not many of these cards were sold when they were new, there are not many of them around today.

A final type of 3.5" disk drive is available for the Apple II: the *SuperDrive*, first introduced with the Macintosh SE/30 in 1989. The SuperDrive can read and write high-density (1.44 MB) and double-density (800K and 720K) Apple II, Macintosh, and PC disks. The SuperDrive requires a special controller card; both card and drive are quite expensive and hard to find these days.

Figure 1-12. At left, the UniDisk, right, the Apple 3.5" drive

Hard Disks

Another popular type of disk system for users with a lot of data is a *hard disk*, sometimes referred to as a *Winchester* or *fixed disk*. Hard disks are high-capacity, low-maintenance disk systems which consist of a disk that is sealed inside a case. There are no disks to swap out, and no fear of damaging a disk with dust or dirt. Hard disks range in capacity from 5,120 kilobytes to 32,768 kilobytes and more.

Since hard disks do not involve a removable disk, some models are internal, fitting entirely within the Apple II case. Others are external, and connect to an interface card within the Apple.

Recently, some new developments in hard disk technology have resulted in the release of IDE controller cards and Compact Flash adapters. The advantage of these two media is that they can be connected to a modern PC or Macintosh, where special software may then be used to view and modify the disk contents. The downside to these new types of hard disks is expense; they typically cost two to three times as much as traditional forms of storage.

How Disks Work

Except for Compact Flash (CF), all disk systems use a spinning magnetic disk to store and retrieve data. To facilitate access for the Apple, disks are divided using a system of tracks and sectors. A sector represents the smallest unit of data which may be stored on a disk. Many sectors together make up a track. Tracks run in concentric circles from the outer edge of the disk to the inside edge. They are similar to grooves on a phonograph record, except that they are not connected in a spiral.

To speed up access to the data on a disk, the Apple II keeps a *catalog*. The catalog is a listing of all files on the disk and the location of each one, just like a library card catalog. To read data from a file, the Apple first consults the catalog entry for the file, then gets the track and sectors where the file is stored. Finally, the disk drive reads the appropriate sectors and sends the data to the Apple.

Where to Get Disks

If you have been to a computer store recently, then you probably didn't see any 5.25" disks for sale, and you may not have seen any 3.5" disks either. Unfortunately, magnetic computer disks are becoming harder and harder to find.

Likely what will end up as the best solution for you is to buy "new old stock," that is, disks which are still shrink-wrapped in their box after all these years, but were never sold. Several online web sites sell these disks.

When buying 5.25" disks, be sure to get double-sided, double-density (DS/DD) disks. If you end up with high-density disks (HD), they will not work with your Apple. Do not buy them.

For 3.5" disks, you should be on the lookout for double-sided, 720K disks. In a pinch, 1.44 MB high-density 3.5" disks will work, but they may not be reliable when formatted for 800K in the UniDisk or Apple 3.5" drives. The reliability is subject to debate: the author of this book has several HD disks that he had formatted as 800K for use with an Apple IIgs several years ago, and which still hold their data today.

Hand Controls

In some cases, it may be convenient to send input to the Apple by means other than the keyboard. Three such methods are typically available on Apple II systems: a joystick, game paddles, and a mouse. Collectively, these are known as *hand controls*. Not every Apple system will have hand controls; they are largely optional.

Joystick and Paddles

Every model of Apple II can use a joystick or *game paddles* for gaming and all other manner of analog input. You are probably familiar with a joystick, but may be wondering what "game paddles" are. The term goes back to 1977 when the first-ever Apple II game, Breakout, was written. As you may recall, Breakout involves a paddle which moves left and right to deflect a ball upward to break bricks.

Figure 1-13. Game paddles and joystick

The device used to control the on-screen movement of the paddle was therefore also called a paddle. Put simply, the paddle is a large knob with a button. They come in pairs and are attached to the same cable. In typical computer counting fashion, they are labeled 0 and 1. It is possible to have a third paddle, number 2, but it is rare to do so. Later on, Apple Computer started calling the game paddles "hand controls" instead.

Mouse

You are probably familiar with the computer mouse. It's a small device which fits in your hand. One rolls it across a flat surface to move an on-screen pointer. A button on the mouse is used to make selections and execute commands, similar to pressing the RETURN key on the keyboard. Moving the pointer over different areas of the screen, such as a menu, allows you to issue commands without having to use the keyboard. The mouse can also be used for gaming and producing graphics.

The Apple IIgs has a built-in port called ADB to which the keyboard, mouse, and other input devices may be attached. The Apple IIc and IIc Plus have a combination mouse and game port, meaning that it is not possible to have both a mouse and a joystick or game paddles connected. The use of a mouse on an Apple II, II Plus, or IIe requires an AppleMouse peripheral card which is typically installed in slot 4.

The ADB mouse used with the Apple IIgs is not compatible with any other model of Apple. Likewise, the AppleMouse IIe and Mouse IIc cannot be used with the Apple IIgs unless the AppleMouse peripheral card is installed.

Except for the Apple IIgs, it is fairly uncommon to have a mouse connected to an Apple. The device, which debuted on the Macintosh in 1984, never really caught on with the earlier Apple II systems.

Printer

A printer is useful for obtaining hardcopy output of your work on the Apple. It is especially advantageous for reading long documents, such as program listings. With the right type of printer, your Apple can also reproduce graphics, such as pictures, diagrams, and greeting cards.

There are two main types of printers: letter-quality and dot-matrix. Letter-quality printers use a better print-head which produces crisper type that looks as good as a typewriter. Dot-matrix printers produce output which is of lesser quality compared to a letter-quality printer, but have the advantage of being more versatile: they can print graphics.

Many different types of printers were manufactured for use with the Apple II over the years. A popular printer for the Apple II is the Apple ImageWriter II. The ImageWriter II is a dot-matrix printer and can even print in color with the appropriate ribbon.

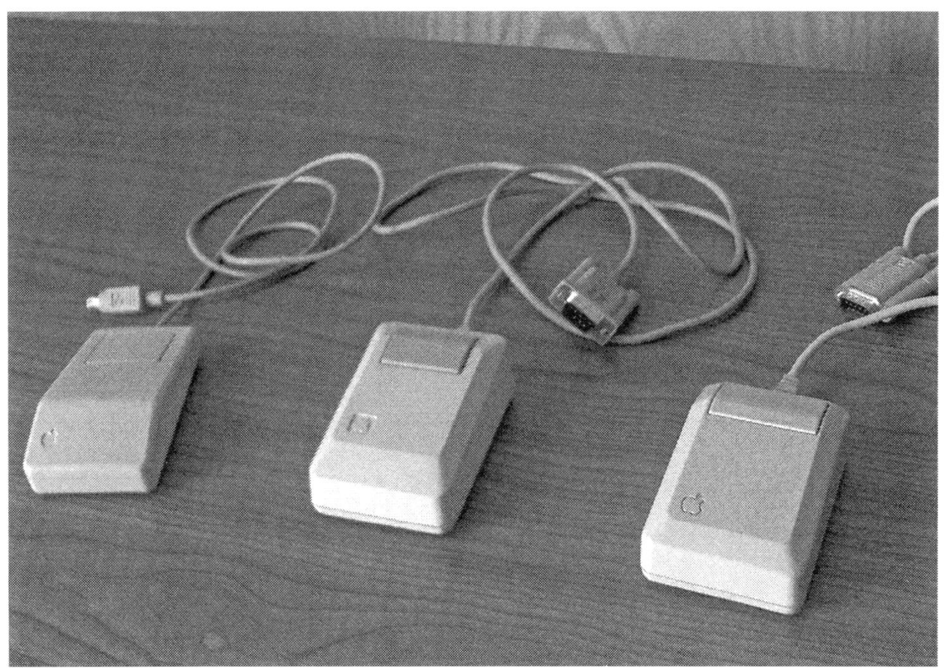

Figure 1-14. Left to right: IIgs Mouse, AppleMouse IIe, Mouse IIc

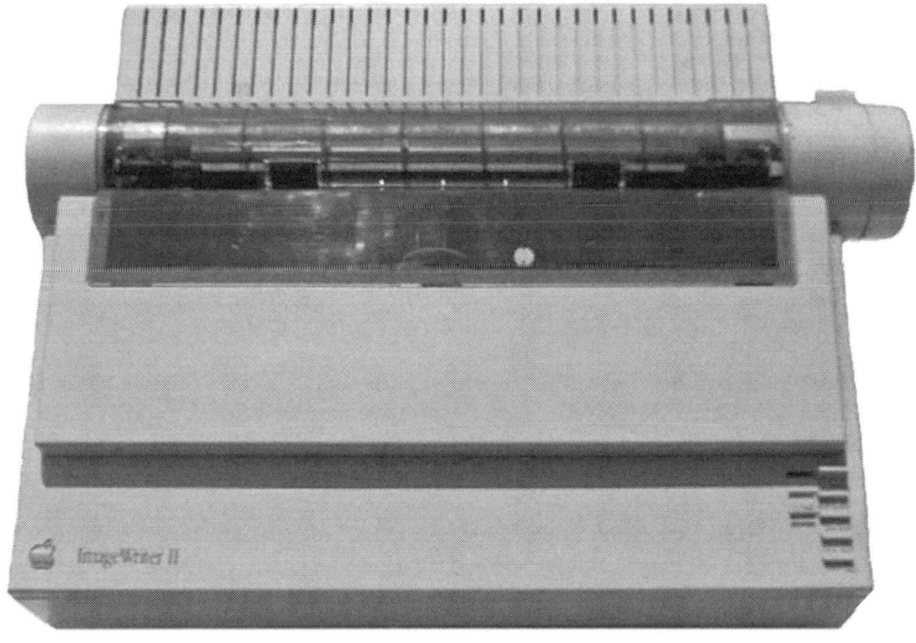

Figure 1-15. The Apple ImageWriter II printer

Printer Connections

Printers connect to the Apple using one of two methods: serial or parallel. The technical details of the two methods are beyond the scope of this chapter, but suffice it to say, you will need to obtain an appropriate printer expansion card for your type of printer. The ImageWriter II happens to use a serial connection. Fortunately, the Apple IIc, IIc Plus, and IIgs all have a built-in serial port. These models of Apple will need a parallel card if the printer's connection is parallel, however. The Apple II, II Plus, and IIe do not have any built-in printer connection, and will need an expansion card no matter what type of printer you have.

Printer Buffers

Ordinarily, when you send a document to be printed, the Apple II cannot do anything else until the entire document has finished. With a small, one page document, this may not seem like a burden, but with a longer document, you may not want to have your Apple tied up with printing.

The solution is an add-on called a *printer buffer*. The buffer stores the information sent from the Apple II such that the printer can access it without holding up the computer. Some printer cards, such as certain models of the Grappler card, have a buffer built-in to them. In other cases, the buffer is part of the printer, such as the 32K memory option for the ImageWriter II.

Tips for Buying an Apple

If you're inheriting someone's Apple, then you should be grateful to accept whatever it is that you're given. However, if you have decided to go out and spend money, then you should aim to get a good system that won't require you to obtain more parts or cause you a headache to get running. Of course, every Apple will function quite well without any add-ons or cards, but its capabilities will be rather limited. Therefore, it is best if the Apple that you are considering buying meets the following minimum requirements.

For all models of Apple, except for the IIc, IIc Plus, and IIgs, you will want to make sure that there is a disk controller card provided; either a Disk II controller card, or the newer Apple 5.25" card. For all models of Apple except for the IIc and IIc Plus, you will want to have at least one 5.25" drive, but two are better.

For the Apple II and II Plus, be sure that it has the full 48K of RAM on the motherboard. It's rare these days to find one that doesn't. You will also want to get one that has the Language Card installed. This card, shown in Figure 1-9, is distinctive in that it is installed in slot 0, and has a cable that connects to where a RAM chip would go on the motherboard. Do not buy an Apple II or II Plus that is missing a RAM chip unless you are receiving a Language Card too. An 80-column card is desirable to have with the II and II Plus. Check for one in slot 3; a popular 80-column card of the day was the Videx Videoterm.

When purchasing an Apple IIe, make sure that it has an Extended 80-column text card (or compatible) installed in the Aux slot. It is also preferable to obtain an Enhanced IIe, since it will be compatible with a wider range of software. The Enhanced IIe typically has black-lettered keys, and may have a sticker that says "Enhanced" on the power light.

Since the Apple IIc requires an external power brick, be sure to buy one with a power supply, and make sure that the power supply is working. The Apple IIc Plus uses a conventional electrical plug, meaning that you do not have to worry about the external supply. Early models of the Apple IIc had design faults and firmware limitations that make them less desirable. In particular, the original revision of the IIc could not use a 3.5" UniDisk drive, and had problematic serial ports.

If you are buying an Apple IIgs, try to avoid the original ROM 00 model. These are typically found in the Limited Edition Woz case. Also, make sure that the IIgs has an Apple Memory Expansion card (or compatible) installed. The IIgs should come with at least one Apple 5.25" drive and one Apple 3.5" drive.

Other useful things to have include a Super Serial Card for the II, II Plus, and IIe; a video monitor with composite input; and a supply of floppy disks that match your Apple's disk drive.

Testing an Apple

You should always obtain verification that the Apple is working before you buy it. Some sellers may claim that they are "unable to test it," usually because they don't have a monitor or a disk. Don't settle for that. It is simple enough to test an Apple with no disk or monitor. Simply instruct the seller to do the following:

1.) Plug in the Apple and turn it on. It should beep and the power light should be lit.

2.) Press CONTROL-RESET. The Apple will beep again. If there is a CAPS LOCK key, make sure that it is depressed. If an original Apple II with Integer BASIC is being tested, then press CONTROL-B and RETURN, instead of CONTROL-RESET. The Apple will not beep after CONTROL-B.

3.) Type the following two lines, remembering to press RETURN after each line:

```
0 CALL-198:GOTO 0
RUN
```

This short BASIC program will make the Apple beep continuously. Once this test has been passed, the Apple may be switched off, and there is little doubt that it is working properly. This test is not absolutely conclusive; there could be other problems with the computer, or the speaker may not be working, but it is better than no test at all.

If you find a seller who is unwilling or unable to perform these three simple procedures, then perhaps you should save your money and buy from someone else.

Improvements Over the Past 20 Years

This section is mainly for the old-timers who are rediscovering the Apple II from the good old days. Here are just a few of the developments which have taken place since the early 1990s, when the II line was discontinued.

Accelerators

Using a replacement oscillator crystal, the TransWarp GS can be accelerated up to 10 MHz. A group known as BrainSystems is working on new accelerator technology to push the IIgs up to 30 MHz.

Emulators

Several excellent emulators for both Mac OS X and Windows are available. Virtual][and Sweet16 provide highly accurate emulation of the Apple IIe and IIgs, respectively, on Mac OS X. AppleWin, for Windows, also provides competent emulation. All three of these emulators are regularly updated.

Mass Storage

There are now a few different IDE and CompactFlash cards available whose capacity and reliability far exceed all previous forms of storage. The FocusDrive, released in 1994, was the first popular IDE card for the Apple. Now there is also the MicroDrive and CFFA cards, both of which offer potentially gigabytes of storage on a CompactFlash card or USB flash drive. Cédric Peltier is working on an external hard drive for the IIc, IIc Plus, and IIgs which should be available when you read this book.

Networking

The first Ethernet card for Apple II was released in 2000, called the LANceGS. Another Ethernet card, called the Uthernet, was released later, around 2005. Both cards are capable of 10 Mbps communication.

Two open source TCP/IP stacks are readily available for the Apple. The first, Marinetti, written by Richard Bennett, is for the Apple IIgs. The second, Contiki, was ported to the Apple IIe by Oliver Schmidt, and is in fact an entire operating system.

Parallel Computing

Michael J. Mahon has devised a novel form of networking using the Apple II game socket, which he calls NadaNet. Using a cluster of Apple IIe computers, he has even written parallel computing applications. He has provided full schematics and source code on-line.

Programming Languages

David Schmenk gained fame in 2010 for writing a Java Virtual Machine (JVM) called VM02 that will run on any model of Apple with at least 64K of RAM. He is currently working on a system known as PLASMA that is a hybrid virtual machine, combining a 6502 assembler and a high-level language that is similar to C.

Chapter 2 : Setting Up the Apple

In this chapter, you will learn how to set up your Apple II system and how to plug in all of the components. If you have just bought an Apple II from eBay or at a bargain shop, you may not have been told how to set it all up. If you inherited your Apple from a friend or family member, then he or she may have been kind enough to set it up for you, but probably did not provide explicit instructions.

Whatever the case may be, this chapter will introduce you to the basics of setting up a working Apple II system. You will then learn how to turn on the Apple and use the keyboard. Finally, you will learn about the cursor, command prompts, and how to edit on-screen text which you have typed.

Plugging In

Except for the Apple IIgs, which has an external keyboard and mouse, there is very little to plug in for a minimal Apple II system.

Remember to always turn off your Apple before connecting or disconnecting any peripheral card, cable, or wire! Otherwise, you may cause serious, often permanent damage.

IIgs Keyboard

If you have any model of Apple II other than a IIgs, you will notice that the keyboard is built in. If your Apple does happen to be a IIgs, then you should have with it a cable and keyboard. The cable is known as *ADB*, which stands for Apple Desktop Bus. If you do not have a keyboard cable, then you may substitute an S-Video cable instead. The IIgs has its own unique keyboard, but any other ADB keyboard will also work, such as those intended for older Macintosh computers.

Figure 2-1. Connecting the keyboard to the IIgs

Figure 2-2. Back panel ports on the Apple IIgs

The ADB port is on the back of the Apple IIgs, the farthest to the right as you face the back. It is marked with a three-branches symbol. Plug one end of the keyboard cable into the port, and the other end into the similarly marked port on the keyboard.

The Apple IIgs has several other backside ports beside ADB. From left to right, the ports on the back of the IIgs are: mono headphones, modem, printer, game (joystick), disk, RGB monitor, composite monitor, and ADB. The disk port is also known as the SmartPort.

Mouse

If you have an Apple IIgs, then you should have also received a mouse with it. This mouse also uses the Apple Desktop Bus system. Plug the end of the mouse cord into the other port on the keyboard.

If you have an Apple IIc or IIc Plus, you may have received an Apple Mouse to go with it. The use of mice with models of Apple other than the IIgs is uncommon, since not much software was written to use the mouse.

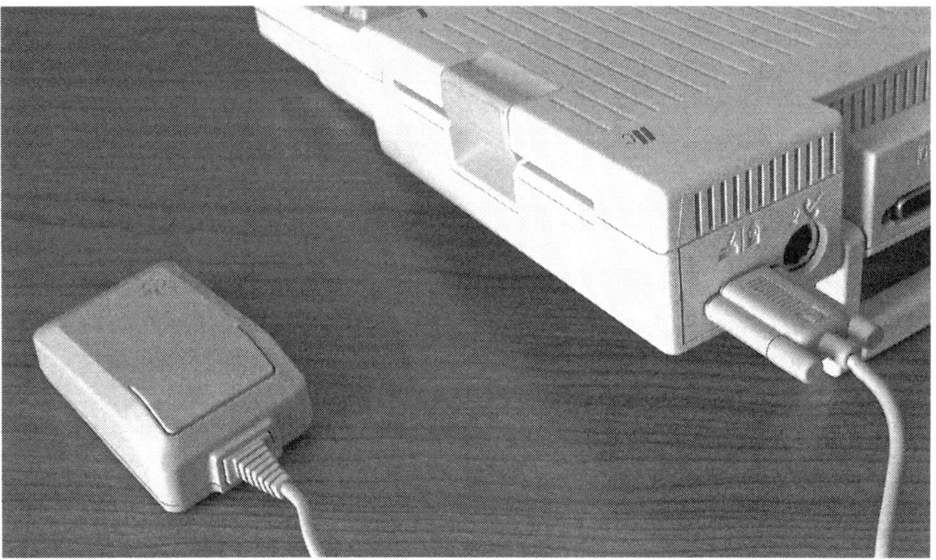

Figure 2-3. Mouse connected to the Apple IIc

The mouse port on the back of the IIc and IIc Plus is located at the left and is marked with both a mouse and a joystick symbol. It is shared with the joystick, so you can have either a mouse or joystick connected, but not both. Simply connect the mouse there and remember to tighten the thumbscrews.

For the standard Apple II, Apple II Plus, and Apple IIe computers, a Mouse Interface card is required. This card is usually inserted into slot 4 and has a connector which protrudes through an opening in the back of the case. Connect the AppleMouse to the DB-9 connector on this card.

Make sure that you have a clean and large enough area on your desk or work space to roll the mouse around. It is recommended to use a mouse pad, both to give better traction for the mouse ball, and to cut down on the dirt and debris which can enter the mouse.

Monitor

To be able to see what your Apple is doing, you need to connect either a television set, a video monitor, or an Apple monitor. These days, the difference between the connection of a television set and a video monitor may be minimal. If you take a look at the back of your Apple, you will find an RCA video jack. Back when the Apple II was new, this RCA composite video connector would have been used only with high-end, expensive monitors. Today, it is rare to find a television set that does not have an RCA jack built-in. Therefore, you may connect your television to this jack with a standard, yellow RCA cable. A dedicated video monitor, on the other hand, will afford a higher picture quality than an ordinary television.

The composite video signal generated by American Apples is NTSC, but it has some irregularities about it. Older television sets and monitors with analog tuners should have little trouble displaying the picture. Modern sets, such as flat-panel LCD displays with digital synchronization logic, may be incompatible with the Apple II. You will have to test and find out what works.

The Apple IIgs composite video jack behaves a bit differently compared to that of other Apple models in that it does not always display color. Specifically, when the Apple IIgs is in text mode, the composite video jack switches to a grayscale video signal in order to increase text legibility. Otherwise, the display will be in color for any of the Apple graphics modes.

The most common way to connect a television set back when the Apple was new was to use an RF modulator. This device would connect to a set of four video pins inside the Apple II. The video signal would then be broadcasted on either UHF channels 3 or 4, or VHF channels 33 or 34. These days, however, the need for such a device is uncommon. In addition, the picture quality is reduced: the Apple is capable of producing a much finer video picture than the television is capable of displaying.

A popular RF modulator solution was the Sup-R-Mod II. This modulator connected to the auxiliary video connector in the Apple II, II Plus, or IIe, and provided an RCA phono cable to connect to a TV switch box. The switch box allowed the television to receive either antenna broadcast or Apple video from the RF modulator. The Apple video was typically on VHF channel 33.

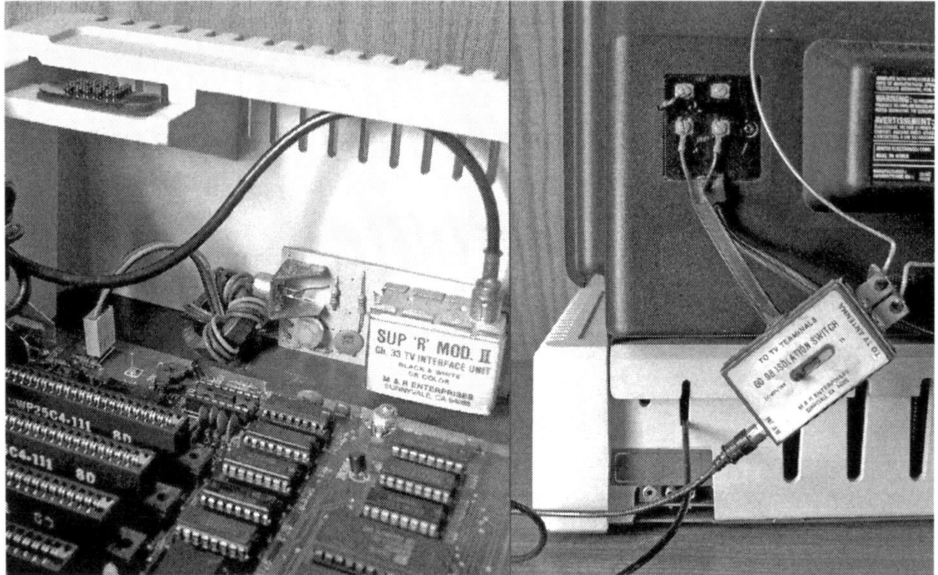

Figure 2-4. RF modulator and switch box (Apple II Plus shown)

The final way to show video from your Apple is to use an Apple monitor. The Apple monitor for the IIgs is RGB and connects to the RGB port on the back of the Apple. This monitor happens to accept only an analog RGB signal. Apple Computer sold an earlier RGB monitor that took a digital signal; this older monitor will not function on the IIgs.

If you are familiar with older Macintosh computers, specifically those manufactured before 1999, you may notice that the IIgs monitor cable is the same as is used on Macintosh computers, a DB-15. Unfortunately, the similarities end there: no Macintosh monitor is compatible with the IIgs, nor can the IIgs monitor be used on any Macintosh computer.

The Apple IIc and IIc Plus also have a specialized monitor port that is only compatible with the IIc RF adapter and the IIc Flat Panel Display.

Apple monitors for other varieties of Apple all connect to the RCA video jack and will work on any model of Apple.

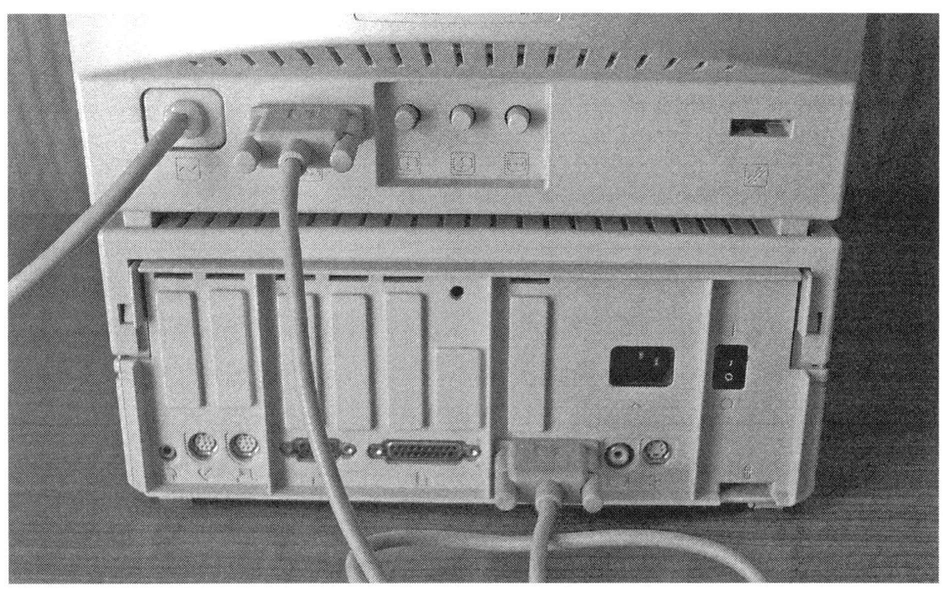

Figure 2-5. Apple IIgs RGB Monitor connection

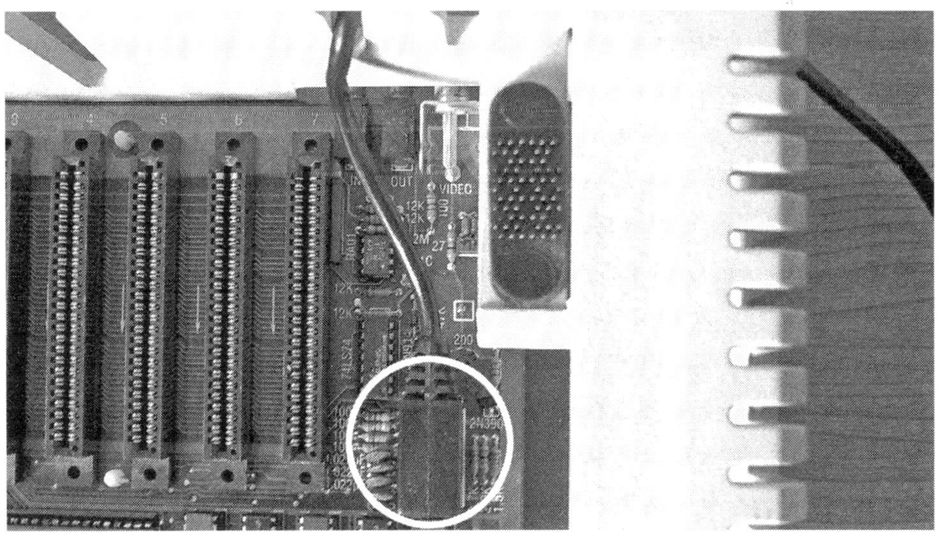

Figure 2-6. 16-pin game plug in socket (II Plus shown)

Joystick or Game Paddles

The Apple IIe, IIc, IIc Plus, and IIgs all have a DB-9 game port on the back panel. You may connect either a joystick or the game paddles to this port. If the set of paddles or joystick is old enough to have a 16-pin DIP plug, then you will need a 16-pin DIP to DB-9 adapter for it.

The older models, the Apple II and II Plus, do not have such a port. Instead, one must connect the game controls to a special 16-pin socket inside the case. The Apple IIe and IIgs also have this socket. Consult Table 2-1 for information on which models have which port or socket. The socket is typically of white plastic (though it may be black in older Apples) and is located near the back of the motherboard, on the right-hand side. On the Apple IIgs, it is near the center of the motherboard.

The 16 pins that fit into this socket are especially fragile. Be sure that you have them all lined up so that they don't get bent when you make the connection. For the Apple II, II Plus, and IIe, you must orient the plug such that the wire is pointing toward the back of the Apple's case. The DIP socket in the Apple IIgs is rotated 180 degrees around, so make sure that the cable is coming out toward the front of the case.

Model	Game Port	Game Socket
Apple II		X
Apple II Plus		X
Apple IIe	X	X
Apple IIc	X	
Apple IIc Plus	X	
Apple IIgs	X	X

Table 2-1. Table of Apple models with game ports or game sockets

Figure 2-7. The game I/O socket in the Apple IIe

Cassette Tape Recorder

If you have an Apple II, II Plus, or IIe, then you can connect a cassette tape recorder. Instead of recording and playing back music, the Apple will use cassettes to record and play back computer programs and data.

A tape recorder is both optional and obsolete, having become so in 1978 when the Apple disk drive was released. The only practical reason to use a cassette recorder with your Apple is if you do not have a disk drive or other means of storing and recalling programs. Of course, if you just want to know what cassette storage was like, or if you want to relive the bad old days, that is a perfectly acceptable reason.

The two cassette tape jacks are 3.5 mm miniature phono plugs, and are located at the left-hand side on the back of the Apple. The Apple II and II Plus have them labeled as “In” and “Out.” On the Apple IIe, they are labeled with a cassette tape picture and an arrow. In both cases, the labels are relative to the Apple.

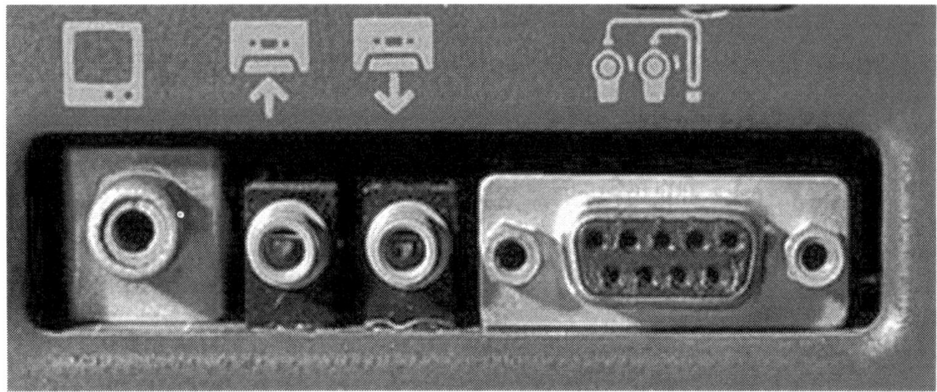

Figure 2-8. Back-panel ports on the Apple IIe

On the tape recorder, identify the Mic. or Microphone jack and the Monitor or Headphone jack. The microphone jack connects to the Out jack. On the IIe, that is the icon with the arrow pointing to the cassette tape. Finally, connect the remaining two jacks. The audio signal is mono, so virtually any mini-phono cable will suffice. Ideally, two cables are preferred, but in a pinch, if you only have one, you could switch between jacks as needed. It is extremely unlikely that the Apple will be both playing and recording a cassette tape at the same time.

In order for the Apple to be able to properly "hear" the cassette tape, adjustment of the tone and volume knobs will be required. It is also a good idea to make sure that the cassette tape recorder itself is in good condition– heads aligned, cleaned, and so forth.

You may be wondering if another sonic device may be substituted in place of the cassette recorder. In theory, yes. You may experiment on your own with other such devices as an iPod, digital recorder, PC, or wax cylinder apparatus.

Adjusting the Cassette Playback Volume

The volume at which the cassette player plays back the tape must be set at a certain level. If the volume is too high, the Apple will hear a distorted version, and if it is too low, the Apple will not hear anything. Playback volume only matters, obviously, when playing back a tape, not when recording it. Unfortunately, the only method of adjusting the playback volume is by trial and error.

If you do not have any Apple tapes, then you will have to make one. Follow the instructions in Chapter 11, in the section Saving Memory to Tape. The example shown there is fine to use for making your first cassette recording.

Once you have a good tape recording, rewind the tape and start by setting the volume low, and try to read in the tape (again, see the appropriate section in Chapter 11 for instructions). If it was successful, the Apple will beep twice and no error message or other indicator will appear on the screen. Mark this volume setting and do not change it! Otherwise, if an error message did appear on the screen, turn the volume up a bit and try again. Keep doing so until the tape loads successfully.

Disk Drive

If your Apple came with a disk drive (and most do) then you already have one of the two components needed to use 5.25" or 3.5" floppy disks to store your data and programs. The second component needed is a controller card, which is also typically found in every Apple these days—it's built in to the IIc, IIc Plus, and IIgs.

The instructions for connecting a disk drive vary depending on what model of Apple you have.

Connecting a Disk Drive to the Apple II, II Plus, and IIe

The most common type of storage for these three models is the 5.25" disk. There are two types of 5.25" disk: the older Disk II system, and the newer Apple 5.25" Disk system. Both systems have their own controller card and disk drive mechanism; neither one is interchangeable (though the removable disks are).

If you haven't already, check slot 6 for a small card with two sets of connectors. Figure 2-9 shows this card. This is the Disk II controller card and it can control either one or two Disk II drives. If instead you find a card with a ribbon cable permanently attached to it, which ends with a DB-19 connector, then that is most likely the newer Apple 5.25" controller card. To connect a Disk II drive to the Disk II controller card, first make sure that the Apple is switched off, then gently remove the card from its slot, being careful to grasp it only by the edges.

Now, on the back of a Disk II drive is a ribbon cable with a small rectangular connector. The Apple IIe has a number of rectangular cutouts on its back panel. You should thread the ribbon cable through one of the cutouts before connecting it to the controller card. The Apple II and II Plus have tall vertical openings in the back panel. You should arrange the ribbon cable so that it lays flat over the space between the openings. Replacing the Apple II lid will clamp the cable to hold it in place.

This is important: pay attention when you are connecting the cable! If you misalign the pins and turn on the Apple, you could destroy the card and/or the disk drive. When connecting the cable to the controller card, the cable should come away from the card. Otherwise, you have connected it backwards and may cause permanent damage if you turn on the Apple. Be careful.

If you only have one Disk II drive, plug its cable into the set of pins marked Drive 1 on the controller card. If you have two drives, then you should plug in both to their respective set of pins. When you are finished, plug the Disk II controller card back into slot 6 and replace the Apple II lid.

The Apple 5.25" Disk system is simpler to connect, since it does not require the Apple's lid to be removed, and there is no worry about misaligning the pins. Simply connect the disk drive plug to the appropriate port on the back of your Apple. The first disk drive plugged into the card is always Drive 1. If you have two disk drives, then connect the second drive to the port on the back of the first one, thus making it Drive 2. Be sure not to connect more than two Apple 5.25" Disk drives to a single card!

Your disk drives are likely labeled Drive 1 and Drive 2. Electrically speaking, the disk drives are identical. You could plug the drive marked 2 into the Drive 1 plug, but why? The labels are for your convenience.

Note that some 5.25" Drives may be labeled as "A" and "B." These two letters are the equivalent of 1 and 2, respectively. The norm is to refer to the drives by number, and the majority of Apple software, manuals, and users do so.

Figure 2-9. Connecting the Disk II to the controller card

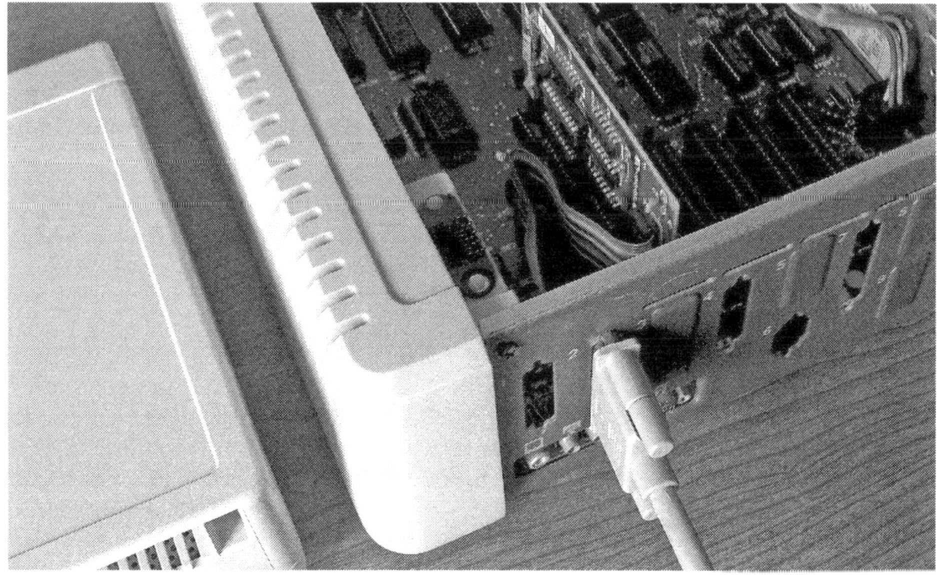

Figure 2-10. Connecting an Apple 5.25" drive to the IIe

Connecting a Disk Drive to the Apple IIc

Your Apple IIc has a built-in 5.25" disk drive on the right hand side. You don't need to connect another disk drive unless you prefer to have two, or use a program that requires a second disk drive. When programs refer to Drive 1 or Drive 2, the internal drive is always 1, and the external drive, if connected, is 2.

Disk drives should be connected to the disk port on the back of the Apple IIc. Every version of the Apple IIc supports one external 5.25" drive. Only the original version of the IIc cannot use a UniDisk 3.5" drive. Refer to Appendix F for information on how to identify your Apple IIc version.

Connecting a Disk Drive to the Apple IIc Plus

Your Apple IIc Plus has a built-in 3.5" disk drive on the right-hand side. Therefore, unless you would like to have a second disk drive, or use a program which uses two disk drives, there is no immediate need to attach another one.

The internal 3.5" disk drive is assigned to slot 5. A second 3.5" drive will also be assigned to slot 5. Up to two more 3.5" drives may be connected (totaling four), and they are assigned to slot 2.

Any 5.25" drives attached will be assigned to slot 6.

Any combination of UniDisk 3.5", Apple 5.25", and Apple 3.5" drives may be connected to the IIc Plus as long as there are no more than three drives attached. If both 5.25" and 3.5" drives are connected, the 3.5" drives must be connected *before* the 5.25" drives.

Connecting a Disk Drive to the Apple IIgs

Your Apple IIgs has a built-in disk controller and a port for it, known as the SmartPort, on the back of the computer. To connect a disk drive, simply match its plug with the appropriate port on the back of the IIgs. Both the plug and the port will be marked with the same icon depicting a floppy disk.

The IIgs can have up to four disk drives connected to its SmartPort, a technique known as *daisy-chaining.*

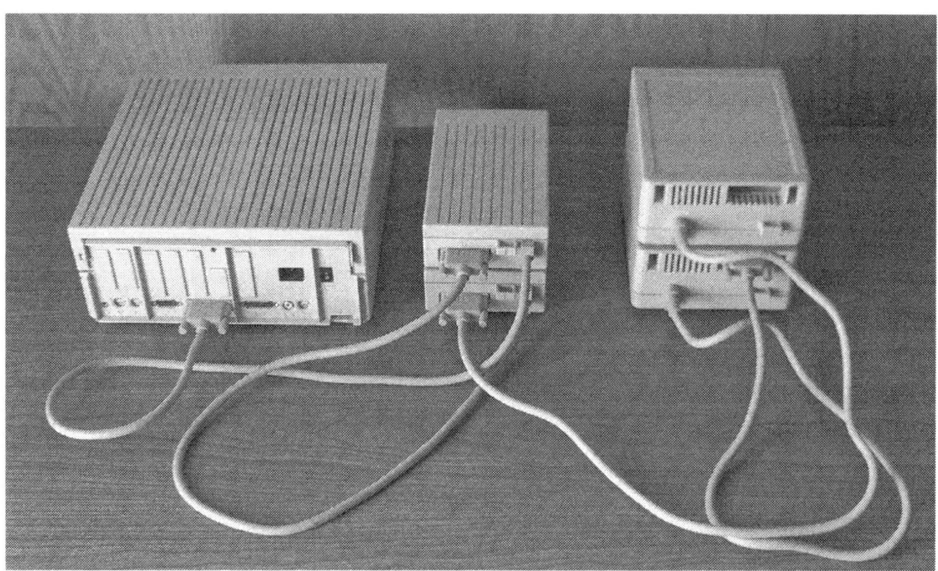

Figure 2-11. Daisy-chaining disk drives on the Apple IIgs

The first disk drive plugs directly into the IIgs, and a second disk drive plugs into a port on the first disk drive. The first disk drive plugged in becomes Drive 1, and the second one becomes Drive 2.

The IIgs can support both 3.5" and 5.25" disk drives, however, the 3.5" drives must be connected before the 5.25" drives in the chain. You may have at most two 5.25" drives and two 3.5" drives simultaneously connected to the IIgs disk port (see Figure 2-11). The 5.25" drives are assigned to slot 6, the 3.5" drives to slot 5.

If you are using both Apple 3.5" and UniDisk 3.5" drives, the UniDisk drives must be connected after the Apple 3.5" drives.

Printer

If you have a printer that uses a serial connection, such as the ImageWriter II, you will need a serial cable. You will also need a serial interface card, such as the Super Serial Card, for the Apple II, II Plus, and IIe. Depending on what model of Apple you have, the cable required will differ. Figure 2-12 shows the cable required for an Apple IIc Plus or IIgs, and Figure 2-13 shows the cable required when using a Super Serial Card with the Apple II, II Plus, or IIe. The Apple IIc requires a DIN-8 cable that looks like a larger version of the cable shown in Figure 2-12.

Once the correct cable has been chosen, setup for the Apple IIc Plus and IIgs is straightforward: both include a built-in printer port marked with an ImageWriter II icon. Plug one end of the cable into this port, and the other end into the port on the ImageWriter II. See Figure 2-14 for the connection between the Apple IIgs and the ImageWriter II.

You will need to install a Super Serial Card for the Apple II, II Plus, or IIe. This card is typically installed in slot 1. You may need to adjust some settings on the Super Serial Card before you install it into the Apple; see Chapter 9 for instructions. A DB-25 port attaches to the Super Serial Card. Plug the large end of the printer cable to this port, then plug the other end into the ImageWriter II, as shown in Figure 2-15.

If your printer uses a parallel connection, you will need a parallel cable and printer interface card. The Grappler is a popular interface card for parallel printers.

Figure 2-12. System/Peripheral-8 Cable for the Apple IIc Plus and IIgs

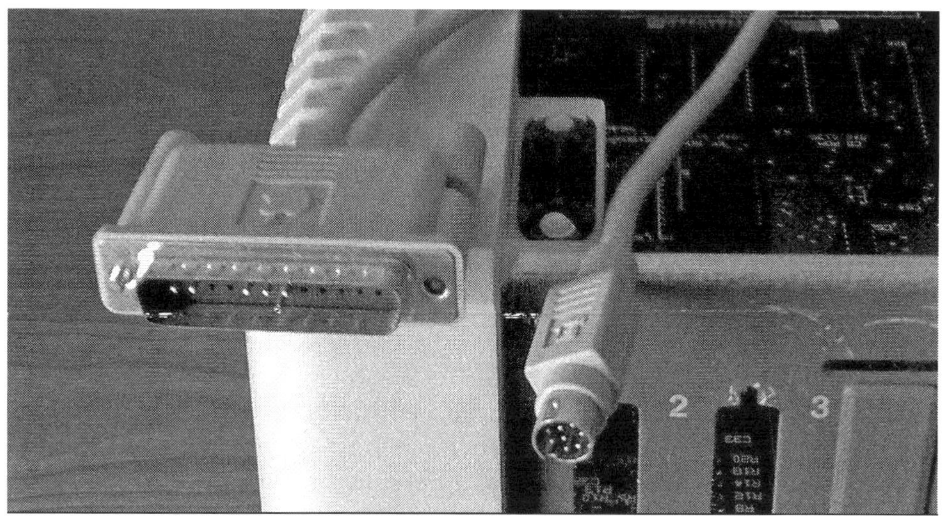

Figure 2-13. Apple IIe Printer-8 Cable for the Apple II, II Plus, and IIe

Figure 2-14. ImageWriter II connected to the Apple IIgs

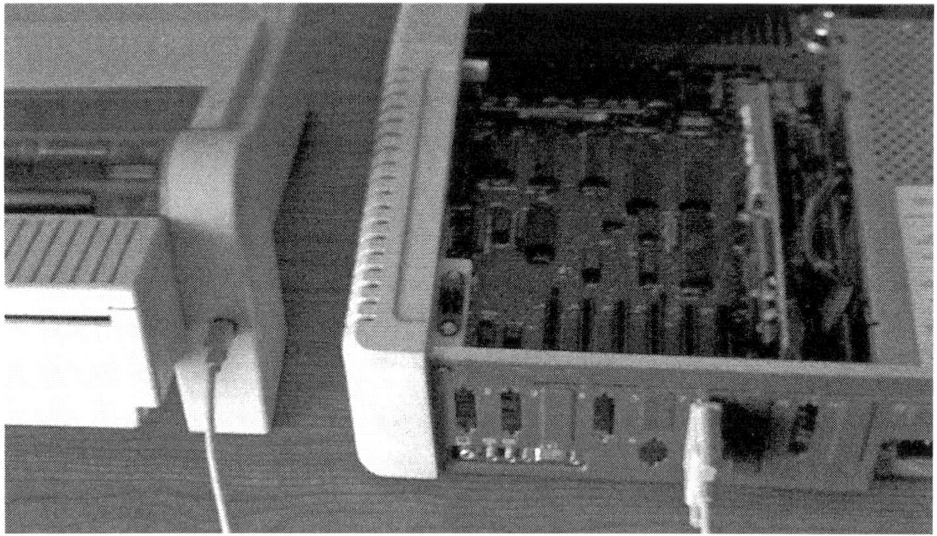

Figure 2-15. ImageWriter II connected to the Apple II, II Plus, or IIe (IIe shown)

Power Cord

All models of Apple II except for the IIc use a standard computer power cord. Look at the back of the machine, on the right-hand side, and plug it in there. The Apple IIc uses an external power supply known colloquially as the "brick-on-a-leash." You have probably seen modern-day laptop computers with a similar, albeit smaller, power supply.

Beware: unlike today's computer power supplies, those of the Apple II are not "international." That is, an American Apple made for 110 volts will not tolerate 220 volt French current, for example. If your Apple is not native to your country, be safe and use an electrical transformer! The consequences can be dire: crack, pop, dead Apple!

Powering Up

Each model of Apple has a distinctive startup screen that can be used to identify which model you have. Compared to today's computer startup screens, the Apple II screen is rather spartan.

First switch on the television or monitor connected to the Apple. When you're ready and facing the computer, reach around the left side of the Apple and flip the power switch upward. You should immediately hear a beep and see the Power On light. The light is located at the bottom-left of the keyboard on the Apple II, II Plus, IIe; it is located at the top-right of the keyboard on the IIc and IIc Plus. On the IIgs, the power light is on the front of the main computer unit and is colored green. If you have an original Apple II, II Plus, or IIe, there is a small chance that the light bulb could be burnt out. The IIc, IIc Plus, and IIgs all use an LED power light that is virtually immortal.

Depending on what model of Apple you have and what is connected to it, a few different things could happen after you switch on the power and hear the beep.

If you have the original model of Apple II, without a Language Card in slot 0, then you will be greeted with a screen full of garbage characters or question marks. Press the RESET key once and you should see an asterisk at the bottom of the screen and a flashing cursor. You are in the Machine Language Monitor, and the Apple is waiting for your command. Press CONTROL-B and then RETURN.

If you have an Apple II Plus or original model II with Language Card, then you should see the title "APPLE][" printed at the top-center of the screen. Press CONTROL-RESET (hold down the CONTROL key, press the RESET key, then release the CONTROL key) and a right-bracket character and flashing cursor will appear at the bottom of the screen, prompting you for input.

Older models of Apple IIe will display "Apple][" at the top of the screen using lowercase lettering. Newer versions of IIe, known as the *Enhanced IIe*, will say "Apple //e" instead. Press CONTROL-RESET to get a right-bracket symbol and a flashing checkerboard cursor.

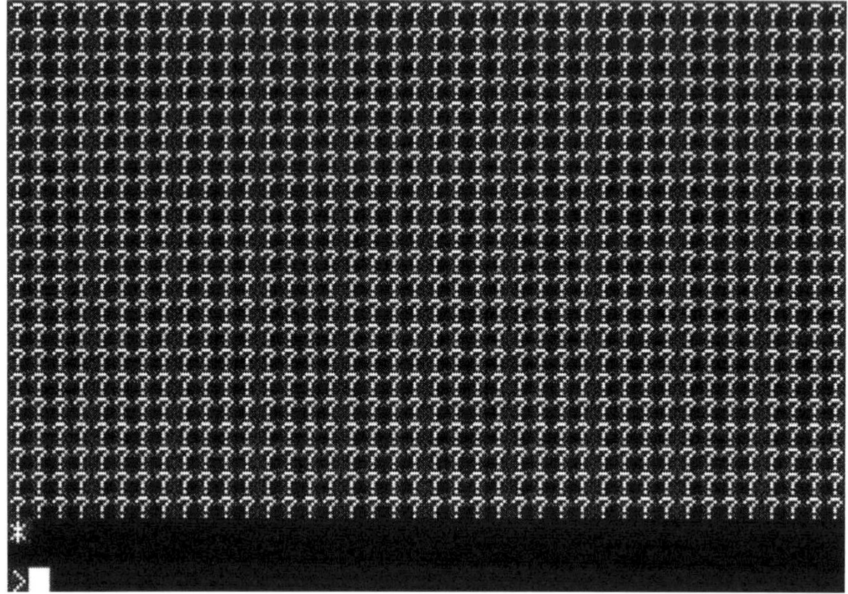

Figure 2-16. The Apple II after startup and CONTROL-B

Figure 2-17. Apple II Plus and early model IIe startup screen

Figure 2-18. Enhanced Apple IIe startup screen

The Apple IIc behaves in a similar fashion to the IIe. It will print "Apple //c" at the top center of the screen. After a moment, it will then display "Check Disk Drive" at the bottom center. Press CONTROL-RESET to get into BASIC.

The Apple IIc Plus has a built-in accelerator that is always active unless you hold down the ESCAPE key while powering on the computer. Doing so will reduce the speed down to 1 MHz, which may be required for some older programs or games.

Finally, the Apple IIgs has the most elaborate startup screen of all. The IIgs prints its name at the top of the screen, and a copyright notice near the bottom, along with the ROM version. There were three versions of IIgs ROM: 00, 01 and 3. The most common ROM version is 01. The original ROM version, 00, is quite old and unlikely to be found in your Apple IIgs. After a moment, the screen will clear and the message "Check startup device!" will appear, with an Apple logo zooming back and forth across the screen (For a fun surprise, press COMMAND-CONTROL-SHIFT-OPTION-N). Press CONTROL-RESET to get a command prompt. Remember that on the IIgs, the RESET key is at the top left and has a left-facing triangle on it.

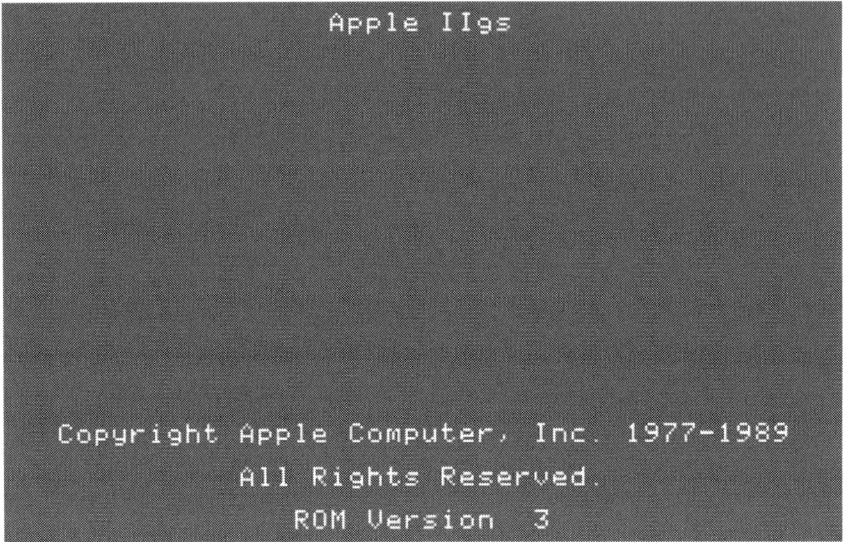

Figure 2-19. The Apple IIgs startup screen

If your Apple has a disk drive, then the activity indicator light should have come on, unless you have an old model of Apple II that starts up in the Monitor (Figure 2-16). Even if more than one disk drive is connected, only one will light up. Don't worry; the other drive or drives are likely just fine. The 5.25" disk drive will make a loud racket for a few moments, then settle down to a softer whir. The Apple is looking for a startup disk in the drive; since you probably didn't put one in, pressing CONTROL-RESET will abort the attempt at disk startup.

At this point you should try striking some keys to make sure that the keyboard is working OK. It doesn't matter what you type; you can't break the Apple by merely typing nonsense on it.

After typing something, such as your name, press RETURN, and the Apple II should beep. A "Syntax error" message should also appear, notifying you that the Apple wasn't able to make head or tails of what you typed.

Soon, you'll learn a whole range of commands to type which the Apple can understand.

Starting from a Disk

If your Apple has a disk drive, then you may have some disks to go with it. There are two main types of disk drives: 3.5" and 5.25". Check to make sure that you have the right kind of disks for your drive.

All models of Apple except for the very oldest will automatically try to look for a startup disk when first powered on. The search starts at the disk controller in slot 7 and proceeds down to slot 1. Slots without a disk drive controller are ignored. Only Drive 1 of each slot will be checked. If you have a System Master or equivalent disk, try inserting it into the disk drive and powering on the Apple. If you are using a 5.25" disk, don't forget to close the drive door by pressing down on the lever. It is normal for the 5.25" disk drive to make loud noises at first.

Chapter 7 contains all the rest of the information needed to use the disk drive with the Apple.

Adjusting the Speaker Volume

Unfortunately, owners of the Apple II, II Plus, and IIe must get used to the speaker's fixed setting: loud. The only way to disable the sound is to open the case and disconnect the speaker wire.

Starting with the Apple IIc, a volume control was finally made available for the built-in speaker. While the Apple IIc offers a physical control, a knob on the left side, the IIgs speaker volume is controlled via a built-in Control Panel setting. See Chapter 12, the IIgs chapter, for full instructions on how to adjust the volume. The Apple IIc Plus has a volume slider located just above the keyboard, near the RESET key.

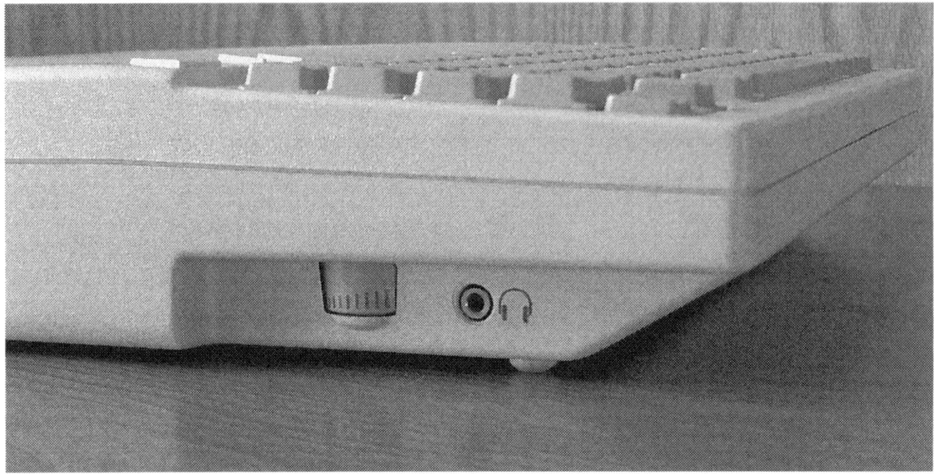

Figure 2-20. Volume control and headphone jack on the IIc

A Word About Prompts

The *prompt* character always appears at the left edge of the screen, and is followed by a flashing cursor and the characters that you've typed. The prompt serves to remind you what mode the Apple is in. The *mode* defines what sort of commands that the Apple expects to receive from you.

When you are finished typing, you must press the RETURN key to let the Apple know that you are ready for it to process what you typed. Otherwise, the Apple will wait patiently, forever. Your commands, or instructions, to the Apple may be up to 255 characters in length. Starting with the 240th character, the Apple will beep after every keystroke as a warning to let you know that you are close to the limit. Once you type the 256th character, the Apple beeps for a final time and gives up: it ignores everything that you typed, forcing you to start over.

If you're using the original model of Apple II and the prompt character is an asterisk, some of the things you typed may have caused the computer to print some information on the screen. While you don't need to worry too much about it now, you're in a mode called the Monitor. Every Apple has this mode, but only the original Apple II starts up in it. Press CONTROL-B, then RETURN, to get into BASIC mode from the Monitor.

Other models of Apple start up in BASIC mode, which usually presents a different prompt and expects different commands. For example, the commands for the Monitor are typically just one letter and are quite different from BASIC commands.

Table 2-2 has a list of command prompts and what mode they indicate.

In this book, many illustrated examples will show a prompt symbol as the leftmost character. Remember that the Apple provides this character for you; you should not type it yourself!

Prompt symbol	Mode	Description
*	Monitor	This is the low-level "inspector" mode of the Apple. You can do things such as change memory values, and execute machine language programs.
>	Integer BASIC	This is the standard BASIC for the original model of Apple II.
]	Applesoft BASIC	The Apple II Plus and all later models have this version of BASIC built in.
?	BASIC Input	A BASIC program is requesting some data from you.
!	Mini-Assembler	The original Apple II, later models of IIe and IIc, the IIc Plus, and IIgs all have this built into the Monitor. The assembler facilitates entry of assembly language programs. Assembly language is faster and more powerful than BASIC, but far less user-friendly.

Table 2-2. Table of common command prompts

Getting Familiar with the Keyboard

A flashing symbol known as the *cursor* will always mark your place when typing. When you type a letter, digit, or symbol, it will appear where the cursor was, and the cursor will advance one space to the right. When the cursor reaches the rightmost edge of the screen, it will drop down to the next line and appear at the left, allowing you to continue typing.

Pressing the LEFT ARROW key will cause the cursor to back up one space, making the Apple "forget" the character which was just skipped over. You can then type a different key, or instead press the RIGHT ARROW key. The RIGHT ARROW has the opposite effect as the LEFT ARROW: it causes the cursor to move to the right, and the character which it passes over is once again acknowledged by the Apple.

At this point, you should practice using the keyboard and moving the cursor around. Use the LEFT ARROW key to back up and correct a mistake. Use the RIGHT ARROW key to move forward and continue typing.

In this example, the underlined character indicates where the cursor is. The bracket (which may be a > on an older model of Apple) is provided by the Apple; you don't need to type it. First, enter the following:

```
]I USE AN APPLEE_
```

As you should notice, there is a mistake: an extra *E* at the end of APPLE. To correct it, press the LEFT ARROW key once. The cursor moves to the left and the line now looks like:

```
]I USE AN APPLEE
```

The cursor is now directly on the superfluous *E*. As far as the Apple is concerned, that *E* is not part of the line which you typed. Sure, it appears on the screen, but press RETURN to see the results.

```
]I USE AN APPLE
```

The extra *E* vanishes, leaving the correct spelling. The Apple will also beep with an error message, but that is immaterial to this example on cursor usage. The important part to remember is that you should make sure that the cursor always appears *after* the text which you want the Apple to accept as your command. If you go back to correct a wrong character and forget to use the RIGHT ARROW key to move the cursor to the end of your line, the Apple will truncate the line, and you will likely get a syntax error.

Using Escape Key Sequences

There is also a way to move the cursor without causing the Apple to "forget" or "remember" any characters at all. Pressing ESCAPE, then either I, J, K, or M will move the cursor up, left, right, or down, respectively. This is known as *Escape mode*. You should note that these keys are arranged in roughly a cross shape on the keyboard. Doing this will allow you to correct any text on the screen, or insert text in between other characters. Press ESCAPE again, or any other key (except for SHIFT, CONTROL, CAPS LOCK, OPEN-APPLE, or CLOSED-APPLE), to leave Escape mode and resume normal typing.

On the Enhanced IIe and newer models of Apple, the four directional arrow keys may also be used to move the cursor while in Escape mode.

If you have the original Apple II without a Language Card or Autostart ROM, however, the cursor control keys are rather less intuitive. They are instead A, B, C, and D, which move the cursor right, left, down, and up, respectively. As a mnemonic, think of "advance" for A, and "backspace" for B. In addition, ESCAPE must be pressed every time before using a cursor movement key. Once the cursor has been moved, the Apple II leaves Escape mode. Therefore, to move the cursor one space down and one space left requires the following key sequence: ESCAPE, C, ESCAPE, B. Be sure to use the appropriate Escape key sequences for your Apple when reading the following sections.

Adding Text to a Line

Unfortunately, the Apple can't add text in between existing characters of a line by merely shunting them apart to make way for the new characters. Instead, you must use the Escape key cursor movement controls to add text to a line.

To learn this feature, start by typing the following line, but don't press RETURN at the end!

```
]PRINT "I LOVE PIE"
```

Unfortunately, there is a problem: you meant to say Apple pie! Without retyping the entire line, here is how to add the word APPLE. First, press the LEFT ARROW key four times. The cursor should be on the P, as shown:

```
]PRINT "I LOVE PIE"
```

Now press the ESCAPE key, then press the letter I. The cursor moves one line up, above the letter P. You are currently in Escape mode. The cursor can be moved anywhere on the screen without affecting the current line. To resume typing, press ESCAPE again. This causes the Apple to leave Escape mode. Type the word APPLE, then press the SPACE BAR. The screen should now look like this

```
               APPLE _
]PRINT "I LOVE PIE"
```

What the Apple currently has in its memory is the phrase "I LOVE APPLE ." At this point, you could type the final word PIE and press RETURN, but let's not, and instead use another Escape key sequence to get more practice.

To complete the line, press the ESCAPE key again. Press M to move the cursor down one line, then press the J key six times, so that the cursor is on the *P* in PIE, like so

```
               APPLE
]PRINT "I LOVE PIE"
```

Press the ESCAPE key for the final time. Now press the RIGHT ARROW key four times so that the cursor appears just after the final quotation mark. You've just copied the word back into the Apple's memory. Press RETURN to see your results.

```
                  APPLE
]PRINT "I LOVE PIE"
I LOVE APPLE PIE
```

If you followed the instructions perfectly, the correct phrase should appear as intended.

You may be thinking that this is overkill—it would be quicker to just retype the line. You're probably right for this scenario, but if you have a line that is over 100 characters long, would you want to use this method to correct a mistake, or would you want to retype it all again? What are the chances that you won't make another mistake when retyping the line?

Removing Text from a Line

To do the opposite, to remove characters from a line, requires a similar pattern of steps. Remember that if you have the original Apple II, your Escape key method works differently.

To follow along in this example, start by typing the following line on your Apple. Do not press RETURN at the end.

```
]PRINT "I AM NOT A CROOK"
```

Now that it's been done, we want to remove the word "NOT" without having to retype the entire line. Here's how to do it. First, press the LEFT ARROW key thirteen times. The cursor should be on the space directly after the word "AM." What you've done has made the Apple forget about the words "NOT A CROOK."

```
]PRINT "I AM_NOT A CROOK"
```

At this point, press the ESCAPE key to enter Escape mode.

Press the K key four times, such that the cursor is right on the space after the word "NOT," as illustrated:

```
]PRINT "I AM NOT_A CROOK"
```

What you have done is to "float" the cursor over the word "NOT" without having the Apple retype it in memory. It is still shown on the screen, but as far as the Apple is concerned, it is not a part of the line that you have entered thus far.

Finally, press the ESCAPE key to exit Escape mode, then press the RIGHT ARROW key nine times so that it is right after the last quotation mark, like so:

```
]PRINT "I AM NOT A CROOK"_
```

You have traced over the words "A CROOK," causing the Apple to remember them again. The results of your effort are not visible until you press RETURN. Do so now. If everything went correctly, your screen should look like this:

```
]PRINT "I AM NOT A CROOK"_
I AM A CROOK
```

You made the Apple completely forget about the word "NOT."

Three More Line Editing Commands

These final three commands are much simpler than the Escape key sequence. If you decide that the line you've typed is no good, you can make the Apple ignore what you typed by pressing CONTROL-X. The Apple will print a backslash (\) to show that the line has been canceled, and will then move the cursor down to a new line. The Apple will have forgotten all about what you typed.

To delete everything from the current cursor position to the end of the line, press the ESCAPE key, then press the E key. This technique can be used to either remove superfluous characters at the end of the line before pressing RETURN, or to change the final part of a line by removing the unwanted characters at the end of it.

Finally, to erase everything on the screen from the current cursor position to the bottom of the screen, press ESCAPE, then F.

Be sure to try all three of these commands so you understand how they work.

Avoiding Getting Roasted with Reset

You may skip this section unless you have an original model Apple II or the Apple II Plus, and it will reset with a press of the RESET key alone. Take a moment to examine your Apple's keyboard. Notice anything exceptional about the placement of the RESET key with respect to the RETURN key? Yes, that's right! One slip of the finger and boom! Roasted! You may be able to recover some of what you were working on, but chances are, you'll have to start over.

Fortunately, there are two common methods to make accidental resets and roasting less common. The first method involves removing the RESET key cap. The second method involves setting a keyboard slide switch.

Figure 2-21. Location of the keyboard reset slide switch

First, a word about keyboards on the old Apples. The very first style of keyboard has a raised power light that looks like a key cap, and the entire keyboard is one component. The newer style of keyboard has a distinct power light and is made of two components. If you have the newer style of keyboard, then there may be a slide switch to control behavior of the RESET key. The older keyboard has no such switch.

If you do have the newer keyboard, which should be all models of Apple II Plus, and some II models, then your keyboard should have a switch to control the RESET key. Take the lid off of your Apple and peer beneath the keyboard. This switch is black, and it is located directly underneath the "3" and "4" keys, and above the "B" printed on the motherboard. When the switch is on the left, you must press CONTROL-RESET to reset the Apple. This is the recommended position. With the switch to the right, then the RESET key alone will reset the Apple. This position is not recommended.

If your Apple will reset with just a press of the RESET key, and you were not able to find a slide switch, then you probably have one of the older keyboards that is permanently set to allow single-key resets. You might notice that the RESET key has a bit of a stiffer feel to it, that more pressure is required to press it. This is likely due to a spring that is under the key cap. You can use a screwdriver to gently remove the key cap. At this point, you can either put the key cap in a safe place, such as inside the Apple case, or put a rubber washer on the key stem, then replace the key cap. Either option will suitably reduce the likelihood of someone accidentally striking the RESET key during a critical moment.

Simulating a Restart

The Apple IIe and all newer machines have a three-key combination that simulates the effect of switching the power switch off and on. For the IIe and IIc, this key combination is OPEN-APPLE-CONTROL-RESET (Remember that OPEN-APPLE is the key to the left of the SPACE BAR). For the IIc Plus and IIgs, it is COMMAND-CONTROL-RESET. Recall that the RESET key on the IIgs keyboard is the one in the top center, marked with a leftward-pointing triangle.

The Apple's memory will be cleared out, and it will act just as if you had turned on the power for the first time. The Apple II and II Plus do not have this feature; the RESET key operates a bit differently and is generally used to return the Apple either to the Monitor or to the BASIC prompt.

When you're satisfied with your ability to type and edit text, and move the cursor around, it's time to get started with something useful: programming in BASIC!

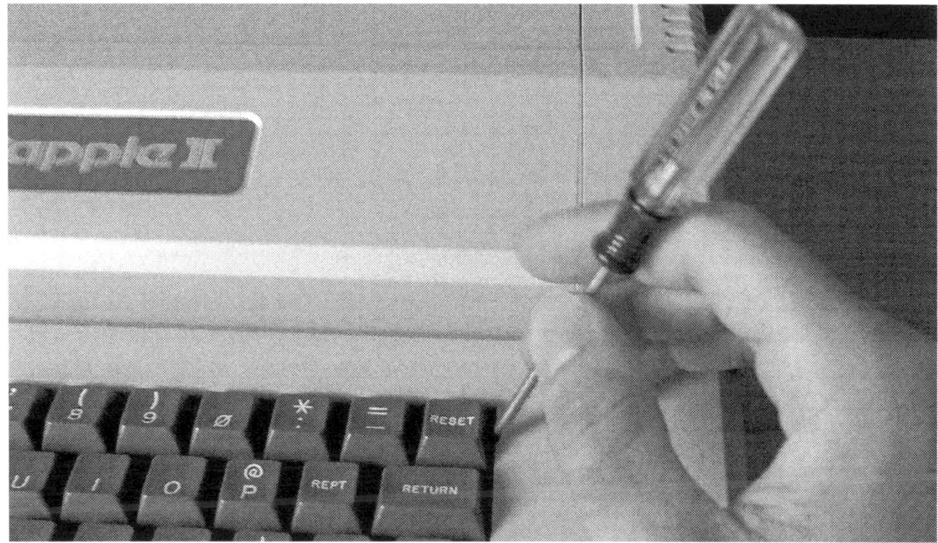

Figure 2-22. Removing the RESET keycap

Chapter 3 : Beginning BASIC

This chapter will teach you the basics of programming, starting off with a few fundamental ideas. You will then learn about the two different types of BASIC on the Apple and how to distinguish them. The rest of the chapter will then be devoted to learning enough commands to make a simple, yet functional BASIC program.

If you wish to learn BASIC, it is imperative that you follow along with the examples in this book, and then experiment on your own. You cannot learn a programming language by just reading and memorizing; you must practice it too.

About BASIC

If you're interested in programming your Apple, then BASIC is likely the first language that you'll use. It comes built into every Apple computer. BASIC stands for Beginner's All-purpose Symbolic Instruction Code and was developed at Dartmouth University in the 1960s. Using English words, BASIC is easy to learn, even by those with no previous programming experience.

If you're used to other high-level languages such as C, Java, or Pascal, then you'll find that BASIC is quite a bit different. It is not a structured language. Instead, BASIC uses line numbers to separate program statements.

Programs, Statements, and Commands

In case you are new to programming computers, there are a few basic terms to learn first. What you will be doing in this chapter is writing what is known as a computer program. A *program* is a set of instructions which are followed exactly by the computer to carry out a task. The shortest program consists of just one instruction, but as you might guess, it wouldn't be very useful. The longest programs for the Apple contain many thousands of instructions.

Taken by themselves, these instructions are formally known as *statements*. An example of a statement is one which multiplies two numbers and stores the result. A further statement could then print the stored product on the screen. A statement makes up just a small part of a program, but if even one critical statement is wrong or missing, the program will not perform as desired.

A statement usually includes a *command*, an operation for the computer to perform. In BASIC, a command is always a single English word or abbreviation. Take, for example, a command to display a number that was stored earlier. By itself, this command is not a statement, since it is missing a critical component: the number to be displayed. It has no meaning otherwise. Once these pieces are brought together, the command becomes part of a meaningful statement.

Syntax

Just like human languages such as English and French have rules of grammar which should be followed, so too do computer languages have such a grammar, known as *syntax*. The main difference is that if you make a small mistake while speaking a language, odds are that the other person will be able to compensate and still understand what you mean. The Apple can do no such thing. To a computer, there are only two results: right and wrong. Either you have entered a command correctly, or you have not.

Fortunately for you, BASIC is based on commands which are common English words or abbreviations. Therefore, with the exception of typographical errors, you should have little or no trouble with syntax errors after you have had some practice.

The Two BASICs

In the course of the Apple II's life, two major versions of BASIC were released. The first, available on the original model of Apple II, is known as *Integer BASIC*. If you recall from Chapter 1, its prompt is a > character. Integer BASIC was written by Steve Wozniak mostly for gaming purposes, but is not limited to just games. As a result of it only handling integer (whole) numbers, it is quite speedy. Starting with the Apple II Plus, Integer BASIC no longer came built-in as a standard option. Therefore, Integer BASIC is less commonly used.

The other version of BASIC is known as *Applesoft*. It is somewhat slower than Integer BASIC, but has more features, such as support for floating point (decimal) numbers, and high-resolution graphics. These features make it suited to many scientific, business, and mathematical applications. Applesoft is built in to the Apple II Plus and all later models and is far more common than Integer BASIC. It is available as an option on the original model of Apple II. The Applesoft prompt character is a] symbol.

Differences between the two versions of BASIC will be pointed out where they exist. In the absence of such documentation, one may assume that the two BASICs behave identically.

Getting into BASIC

Before you can start telling your Apple what to do in the BASIC language, you need to get into the BASIC mode. The process to do so varies by type of Apple. First, if any disk drives are connected to your Apple, make sure that there aren't any disks in them, and turn on your monitor (or television) and Apple II. While first learning BASIC, you won't be using the Apple disk system.

If you have an original model Apple II which starts in the Monitor, press CONTROL-B and then RETURN to enter Integer BASIC. As soon as you press RETURN, a > prompt will appear.

For all other models of Apple II, press CONTROL-RESET to enter Applesoft BASIC. The] prompt will appear.

All examples shown will use the square bracket prompt of Applesoft BASIC, unless the information applies only to Integer BASIC, in which case the angle bracket will be shown.

Switching to Integer BASIC

To switch from Applesoft to Integer BASIC, type INT, followed by RETURN. The Applesoft prompt will be replaced with the Integer BASIC greater-than bracket (>). Integer BASIC must be available on your model of Apple in one of three ways:

- Built-in to the motherboard ROMs
- Located on an Apple Firmware (ROM) card
- Loaded from DOS 3.3 to an Apple Language Card.

The first method is only available on the original model of Apple II. The second method is restricted to the Apple II Plus. Finally, the third method, using a Language Card, can be used with any model of Apple. Integer BASIC cannot be used with ProDOS on any model of Apple. See Chapter 7 for an explanation of DOS 3.3 and ProDOS.

Use the FP command (which is short for floating point) to return to Applesoft.

Upper Versus Lowercase

Unfortunately, there can be quite a bit of confusion for the new Apple II user as whether to use uppercase or lowercase letters when typing commands.

This problem arose in 1983, with the introduction of the Apple IIe. Before then, the two earlier models of Apple, the II and II Plus, had keyboards which could only type capital letters. The SHIFT key existed only to produce the upper symbol on a key cap with two symbols, such as the P key, or the number keys. There was absolutely no way to get lowercase letters without performing a hardware modification to the computer. Therefore, the vast majority of software operated in, and expected commands in, uppercase only.

Then everything changed when the Apple IIe was released. It was the first model of Apple to have a built-in keyboard capable of typing both lower and uppercase letters on screen. However, the generation of software written before it expected only uppercase commands. Even the BASIC included with the original model of Apple IIe expected commands to be in uppercase. Therefore, the user of the Apple IIe typically operated it with the CAPS LOCK key depressed.

Later on, when further models of Apple were introduced, lowercase became standard, and thus more common. The built-in BASIC in the later revisions of Apple IIe, as well as all revisions of the IIc, IIc Plus, and IIgs, can accept commands in either upper or lowercase. To summarize, the only model of Apple whose keyboard can generate lowercase letters, but whose BASIC only accepts uppercase is the standard, unenhanced Apple IIe.

To make things simpler for all models of Apple, this book will show examples in uppercase only. It is recommended that users of an unenhanced Apple IIe make sure that the CAPS LOCK key is depressed.

Your First BASIC Command

Now it's time to learn and type your first BASIC command. If you have an unenhanced Apple IIe (that prints "Apple][" at startup), be sure that the CAPS LOCK key is depressed. Now, type:

```
]NEW
```

and press RETURN. Remember that either the angle bracket (>) or square bracket (]) is provided on screen for you; do not type it yourself. The bracket is merely shown in these examples to illustrate what the final screen line should look like. If everything went correctly, it should appear as if nothing happened. The Apple will print another prompt and flash the cursor at you.

However, something in fact did happen. The command NEW tells the Apple that you intend to start a new BASIC program. If any BASIC program was already in memory, it will be discarded. The Apple can only have one BASIC program in its RAM (memory) at a time. If you forgot to type NEW, and an old program was already in memory, your new program could get mixed in with the old one. Since there wasn't already a program in the Apple this time, typing NEW here was a mere formality, but it's a good habit to get into.

Errors

The Apple is not shy when it comes to telling if you've done something that it cannot understand. If you enter a command and the Apple beeps and shows either:

`*** SYNTAX ERR` (Integer BASIC)

or

`?SYNTAX ERROR` (Applesoft)

on the screen, then it means that you entered something which the Apple couldn't comprehend, known as making a *syntax error*. If you've been experimenting on your own, then you have probably already received this error message. BASIC on the Apple only understands a limited, predefined set of words. It will not recognize any synonyms or other command words. Once you've learned the BASIC commands and functions, the most likely cause of a syntax error is a typing mistake. Simply retype the line and try again.

On the other hand, if you make a logic error, the Apple will never notice. It can only detect syntax errors. As an example, if you mean to multiply two numbers but type an addition sign instead of multiplication, it is up to you to detect and correct this mistake.

Printing Text on Screen

If you weren't too impressed with your first command, this next one should be better: it at least has visible results! One of the most common ways that computers communicate with humans is to display text, whether it be the results of a calculation, or a prompt to enter in some data, or merely instruction on how to use the program.

In the case of BASIC, the command to display something on the screen is called PRINT. The name of this command is a throwback from the old days when computers would display output on an actual line-printer or teletype, instead of a display screen.

To try out your first PRINT command, type the following:

```
]PRINT "HELLO, WORLD!"
```

and press RETURN. The Apple should respond by displaying the phrase "HELLO, WORLD!" on the screen (without the quotes). If not, check your typing and reenter the line (remember that you don't need to type the] symbol).

Congratulations, you've just written your first line of BASIC! Notice that only the text in between the quotes is displayed. The quotes themselves are not part of the subsequent output.

Now enter this line:

```
]10 PRINT "HELLO, WORLD!"
```

When you press RETURN, the Apple *won't* print anything on the screen. What happened? Here's what this line, or statement, means. To begin, it has two parts: a line number, and a command.

The line number in this example is 10. All BASIC programs must have line numbers, which can range from 0 to 32767 in Integer BASIC, and 0 to 63999 in Applesoft. The Apple will run a program from the lowest line number to the highest, unless told otherwise by a command.

You may be wondering about the first two commands you entered, NEW and PRINT, both of which did not have a line number. This leads us to the next part.

Immediate Versus Deferred Execution

When you typed the NEW command, the Apple II instantly executed it by clearing out any existing program. In other words, the command was executed immediately. Likewise, with the first PRINT statement, the line was executed as soon as you pressed RETURN. This is called *immediate execution*.

However, when you typed the line 10 PRINT "HELLO, WORLD" the Apple did not actually execute that command. Instead, the computer saved it in memory, allowing you to execute it and any other commands you entered at a later time. This is an example of *deferred execution*: storing a set of statements (also known as a program) to be executed later. Every proper BASIC program is made up of one or more numbered lines of deferred execution commands. Sometimes you will see the term “programmed mode” used in place of “deferred execution”; they mean the same thing.

In many cases, BASIC commands can be used in both the immediate and deferred execution modes. The PRINT command is one example. Other commands do not make sense if used in the opposite mode, and the Apple will not allow them.

The Rest of the PRINT Command

Now, let's take a look at the final two parts of the PRINT command which you just entered.

After the line number comes the actual command itself. In this case, it's PRINT, telling the Apple to display some information. How does it know what to display? Well, the third and final part of the statement is the answer. The argument to the command is "HELLO, WORLD!" The Apple takes everything between the quotation marks and displays it on the screen when this command is executed.

What happens when you type a PRINT command with no argument? Try it. The Apple just prints a blank line.

Printing Numbers and Calculations

The PRINT command can do more than just write text onto the screen. It can also display numerals and mathematical expressions, such as in the following examples:

```
]PRINT 10 - 3
7

]PRINT 2*8
16

]PRINT -115 + 200
85

]PRINT 64/2
32

]PRINT "12*6"
12*6
```

Pay close attention to the last line. If you type an expression in quotation marks, the Apple does not evaluate it. Instead, it just prints it as if it were any other ordinary text. You must remember this distinction, unless you really do want to print an expression and not the results of it.

In every other case, the Apple prints the results of the mathematical expression on the next line. However, there are some limitations to what the Apple can compute in BASIC mode.

Integer BASIC supports a numerical range of -32767 to +32767. Therefore, attempting a calculation such as the following will result in an error:

```
>PRINT 32767+1
*** >32767 ERR

>PRINT 5/0
*** >32767 ERR
```

As its name suggests, Integer BASIC cannot deal with non-integral numbers (decimal numbers having a fractional part, such as 2.5). The following examples illustrate this limitation:

```
>PRINT 5/2
2

>PRINT 1 + 0.5
*** SYNTAX ERR
```

In the first case, the Apple discards the remainder instead of displaying the true value of 2.5. The number is not rounded. In the second case, Integer BASIC cannot accept decimals, so the entire line is rejected as having a syntax error.

Applesoft does not deal with fractions such as 1/4, but it can work with the decimal equivalent, such as 0.25. Furthermore, it is limited to a total of nine significant digits in all fractional numbers which it displays. This includes all significant digits after the decimal point, and not just the whole number part.

```
]PRINT 3.141592653589793
3.14159266
```

Despite this limitation, Applesoft is superior to Integer BASIC in that it can handle numbers of much greater magnitude than 32,767.

```
]PRINT 3.141 * (500 ^ 2)
785250.002

]PRINT 785250.002 ^ 3
4.84198945E+17
```

Applesoft represents large numbers using scientific notation, as shown in the previous example. In case you are unfamiliar with this form of notation, one simply takes the value after the *E* (known as the exponent) and moves the decimal point by that many places. A positive number means that the decimal point is to be moved to the right, whereas a negative number dictates that the decimal point be moved to the left.

Thus, 4.84198945E+17 is written in standard form notation as 484,198,945,000,000,000.

The range for exponents is E-38 to E+38.

Combining Calculations and Characters

If you would like a PRINT line to show both characters, such as some tcxt, as well as a calculation, you may separate the two using a semicolon, like so:

```
]PRINT 365-120;" DAYS LEFT IN THE YEAR"
245 DAYS LEFT IN THE YEAR
```

You can append many more characters and calculations to a single line. Remember that letters and numbers which should be displayed literally ("as-is") must be placed within quotation marks.

```
]PRINT "I AM ";365*28;" DAYS OLD AND ";6
*12;" INCHES TALL."
I AM 10220 DAYS OLD AND 72 INCHES TALL.
```

In Applesoft, using the semicolon to join parts in a PRINT statement is optional.

A Shorter PRINT Command

Applesoft has a convenient shortcut for PRINT, a command that gets used fairly often. If you want to cut down on the amount of typing you do, you'll appreciate this alternative. Anywhere you want to type the PRINT command, type a single question mark (?) instead. You'll save four letters of typing. Here are a few examples of its usage:

```
]?"VENI, VEDI, VICI"
VENI, VEDI, VICI

]?10*24
240
```

The question mark syntax can be used in both deferred and immediate mode execution. When you LIST your program (this command will be explained shortly), the question mark will be converted to a PRINT command.

Finishing the Program with END

Now that you have a one-line program, it is time to finish it off with a final line. The END command is required in Integer BASIC, but is optional in Applesoft. Whenever the Apple encounters END, it stops running your program and returns to the BASIC prompt.

To add an END command to your first program, type

```
]20 END
```

and press RETURN. You now have a simple, yet complete BASIC program.

If you don't put an END command in your program, then Applesoft will stop when it runs out of lines to execute. Integer BASIC will also stop under the same condition, but it will also return a *** NO END ERR message.

Running Your Program

So far you have a program with two lines of instructions. Can you guess what command to enter to run it and see the results?

Type

```
]RUN
```

and press RETURN. By now, you should realize that every line typed on the Apple must be completed with a tap of the RETURN key. In future, this direction will not be explicitly given. If the Apple does not appear to be responding to your command, perhaps you have forgotten to press RETURN!

If all went well, your efforts will be rewarded with the line “HELLO, WORLD!” and another command prompt. You can type RUN again if you wish, and the Apple will execute the program once more. The Apple II won’t ever get tired of running your program over and over.

If nothing happens, it may be that you did not type in line 10 from a few sections ago, or that you typed NEW at some point, thus obliterating it. To recover, type the entire program again:

```
10 PRINT "HELLO, WORLD!"
20 END
```

And then RUN it again:

```
]RUN
HELLO, WORLD!

]
```

Examining the Program

By now, there is likely a whole mess of program lines and output lines on your screen. To make matters worse, some of the program lines could have changed from what is shown on the screen if you retyped them. The solution is to ask the Apple to print the current *program listing*. The command to do so is called LIST. Try it now to see what your program looks like:

```
]LIST
```

The LIST command always prints what the program currently looks like, and always in ascending line order. Even if one were to type line 20 first, then line 10, internally, the Apple rearranges those lines in correct order. The LIST command always reflects the proper order.

Often times, a program will contain more lines than may be shown on the screen at one time. The LIST command can accept some arguments to limit its output and solve this problem.

To list just one line, type LIST and the desired line number, as demonstrated:

```
]LIST 10
```

To list a sequential range of lines, separate the starting and ending line numbers with a comma as in this example:

```
]LIST 10,20
```

In Applesoft, two additional listing modes are available.

To list all lines starting from the beginning up to a certain line number, type a comma, then the final line number. The Apple will list all program lines up to and including the line number that you entered.

```
]LIST ,20
```

This list mode may be simulated in Integer BASIC by typing a zero before the comma.

Finally, to list all lines after a certain line number, type the line number, then a comma. The Apple will start the listing with the line number that you entered, and stop with the last program line.

```
]LIST 10,
```

In Applesoft, a hyphen (-) may be used in place of a comma in the LIST command. It has the same effect.

Sometimes you may want to abort the listing of a rather long program. To do so in Applesoft, press CONTROL-C. The one drawback to this method is that there is no easy way to immediately continue listing the program from where it was stopped. Integer BASIC does not have a way to abort the program listing.

You may find that the earlier lines in a long program pass by too quickly for you to read. Fortunately, the Apple II Plus and all later models support a listing pause feature. To pause the output of a program listing, press CONTROL-S. The Apple will wait for as long as you need to read the lines on the screen. When you're ready for the rest of the program listing, press any key, such as the SPACE BAR (or CONTROL-S again) to resume.

Modifying the Program

Let's say that you want the program to print something different. How about your name? To revise the program, you can either change existing lines, add more lines, or delete lines.

Changing Lines

To change a line, merely retype the entire line. Alternatively, if the line is especially long, you could make good use of the Escape key sequences covered near the end of Chapter 2 to correct it.

In this case, let's have the Apple print your name. Type line number 10, a quotation mark, your name, and a final quotation mark. The line in my program looks like:

```
]10 PRINT "DAVID FINNIGAN"
```

Type RUN to see the new results. If you successfully changed line 10 by retyping it, the Apple should now display only your name.

Adding Lines

You may add new lines to a program at any time, and in any order. You do not have to enter lines sequentially. The Apple will always arrange the lines in the proper order when it displays the program listing or when it executes the program.

In this example, five program lines are entered out of sequence:

```
]20 PRINT "AS HE FISHED HIS"

]10 PRINT "BOTHER, SAID POOH,"

]40 PRINT "HONEY JAR."

]50 END

]30 PRINT "DISKETTES FROM THE"
```

However, when the program is listed, the lines are in the right order:

```
]LIST

 10  PRINT "BOTHER, SAID POOH,"
 20  PRINT "AS HE FISHED HIS"
 30  PRINT "DISKETTES FROM THE"
 40  PRINT "HONEY JAR."
 50  END
```

Notice that the line numbers are incremented by 10. Allowing this space in numbering makes inserting additional lines convenient.

Deleting Lines

To delete a line, simply type its number followed by the RETURN key. This will replace the existing line with a blank which effectively obliterates it. To verify, use the LIST command, and notice that the line no longer appears, as in this example:

```
]NEW
]50 PRINT "BLUETS AND GRANOLA BARS"
]60 PRINT "MAKE A"
]70 PRINT "CHEWY"
]80 PRINT "SNACK"
]90 END
```

First, five new lines are added. Then line 70 is deleted:

```
]70
```

Now listing the program will show that line 70 is indeed gone:

```
]LIST

 50  PRINT "BLUETS AND GRANOLA BA
     RS"
 60  PRINT "MAKE A"
 80  PRINT "SNACK"
 90  END
```

To efficiently remove a block of lines, use the DEL command, such as in this continuation of the previous example:

```
]DEL 60,80

]LIST

 50  PRINT "BLUETS AND GRANOLA BA
     RS"
 90  END
```

In this example, all line numbers between, and including, 60 to 80 are removed. Even if the range specifies line numbers which do not cxist, BASIC takes no exception.

About Program Writer

The limitations of the Apple's small screen and line-editing commands make writing and modifying a large program cumbersome. Program Writer, written by Alan Bird, and formerly published by Beagle Bros, is a utility program designed to make the task of BASIC programming easier. Program Writer features an interface that works like a conventional word processor, allowing automatic line numbering, full screen scrolling and copy-paste functionality.

Putting Multiple Statements on One Line

Sometimes you may find it convenient to place more than one statement on a line, such as if you wish to conserve line numbers, or if the statements are closely related. The one pitfall to this practice is that editing such a line becomes more burdensome. In Applesoft and Integer BASIC, the syntax to add additional statements is the same. Use the colon (:) to separate statements, such as in this example:

```
]10 PRINT "NOTHING" : PRINT "IS REAL"

]RUN
NOTHING
IS REAL

]
```

Remember that you only need to type the line number once. Afterward, type the desired statement, then a colon, and the next statement. You may, of course, have more than two statements on a line, but there are some limits.

In Applesoft, the colon syntax can be used in both immediate and deferred execution modes. The maximum line length is 255 characters, which will place a limit on how many statements can be in a single line.

Integer BASIC restricts such syntax to deferred mode only, meaning that you can only combine BASIC statements in your program, and not when issuing immediate commands. Integer BASIC also has a stricter limit on the maximum number of statements which may be placed on a single line. The line limit is around 150 characters, but the exact limit depends on the sort of commands involved. Some experimentation on your part will reveal what these limits are.

Adding Comments to a Program

Your first few BASIC programs will be short, and it is unlikely that you will not understand what they are doing. However, long BASIC programs will almost certainly introduce more complexity. To help the programmer, *comments* or *remarks* may be added to a BASIC program. Comments should be used to explain what certain lines of a program are expected to do, or what input should be expected from the user.

To add a comment, use the REM command:

```
]30 REM THIS IS A PROGRAM COMMENT
```

Program comments can appear anywhere and on any line in a program, but typically they are placed just before the line that they describe. If you include a REM command as part of a multiple-statement line, you should add it as the last statement. If you decide to share your program with other people, they will likely appreciate it if you include comments, especially if they try to modify your program. Adding comments will also help you remember what different parts of your program do if you come back to work on the program months or years later.

The Apple does not pay any attention to your comments; when executing your program, it will skip over them as if they were never there. Keep this in mind when using the colon to place multiple statements on one line: be sure that any REM is the last statement on the line.

Clearing the Screen

Running your program and using PRINT statements likely made a lot of text on your screen, not all of which was related. Fortunately, there is an easy way to clean the screen and begin with a "blank slate," so to speak. In Applesoft, the HOME command will clear the screen and return the cursor to the upper-left corner, known as the *home position*. Integer BASIC does not have a HOME command, instead you must use CALL -936, which has the same effect.

Both HOME and CALL -936 can be used in either immediate mode, or as part of your program. It's good to get into the habit of beginning your program by clearing the screen, since you don't know what the user was doing beforehand that may have cluttered it.

A final method of clearing the screen is by an Escape sequence. Press ESCAPE, then type an @ (on the Apple II and II Plus, an @ is generated by typing SHIFT-P). This too will clear the screen, leaving just a flashing cursor at top left. The one difference with this method is that it cannot be used as part of a program.

Automatic Line Numbering

Integer BASIC has a handy feature that when enabled, can automatically number each successive line for you. To enable this feature, use the AUTO command, such as in this example:

```
>AUTO 10
```

When you press RETURN, the Apple will have started the next line with 10 for you. When you type your statement and press RETURN, the next line will be numbered 20.

By default, the line numbering interval is 10. If you would like to use a different interval, then you must provide it as a second argument, like so:

```
>AUTO 100, 5
```

In this example, the Apple II will start numbering your program at line number 100, and will advance by 5 every time you enter a valid line.

The Apple II will not increment the line number if you enter an invalid line, such as one with a syntax error, or a blank line. Instead, the Apple will print the same line number again, allowing you to retype the line.

To stop the Apple from automatically numbering each line, first press CONTROL-X to cancel the current line. Finally, use the MAN command to resume manual line numbering.

Saving and Loading Programs

While your first few BASIC programs probably won't be worth saving, you will no doubt conceive of others which you do wish to keep. There are two methods to save a program: on tape, and on disk.

Saving on Tape

Saving a program to tape is rather old-fashioned, but still works. You must have a cassette tape recorder properly connected to your Apple; see Chapter 2 for setup details. When you are ready to save your program, make sure that you have a cassette tape loaded in the recorder. Type the following command, but *do not* press RETURN:

```
]SAVE
```

At the cassette recorder, press the Record and Play buttons. Now press RETURN on the Apple keyboard. After a few seconds, the Apple will beep. Then, after a few more seconds, the Apple will beep again and the BASIC prompt will return. At this point, you may press Stop on the recorder; your Apple has finished. It is convenient to use the cassette recorder's tape counter to track the positions of multiple programs on a tape.

Saving on Disk

To save a program on disk, which is faster and more convenient than tape, you must have first started a Disk Operating System, DOS or ProDOS. For instructions on this procedure, see Chapter 7. If you load DOS or ProDOS with a BASIC program in memory, that BASIC program will be destroyed!

Using a disk allows you to file your programs by name. The format for the SAVE command is similar to that for saving on tape, except that you must specify a filename, such as in this example:

```
]SAVE MYPROGRAM
```

Entering that command will place a file named MYPROGRAM on your disk containing a copy of your program. The copy of the BASIC program in memory remains unmodified. Depending on what version of operating system you're using, the filename may have some restrictions. Again, take a look at Chapter 7 for the full details on using the disk.

Be aware: if a file with the same name already exists when you SAVE your program, it will be overwritten! The Apple will not warn you that a file already exists, nor will it ask for confirmation to overwrite the previous file.

Loading from Tape

To load an existing program from tape, first position the cassette tape to the beginning of your program. If you are unsure of where your program begins, play back and listen to the tape. When you hear a steady tone, that marks the beginning of your program. Stop the tape. Make sure that the cassette tape recorder is properly attached to your Apple; see Chapter 2 for details.

At the Apple, type in the following, but *do not* press RETURN:

```
]LOAD
```

Press Play on the cassette recorder, then press RETURN on the Apple keyboard. A few seconds will pass as the Apple listens to the steady tone marking the beginning of your saved program. After that, the Apple will beep, and your program will be read into memory. Finally, if all went well, the Apple will beep again, and the cursor will reappear. Type RUN to start your program, or LIST to see if it was loaded correctly.

If you get an error, rewind the tape, adjust the volume control, and try again. The volume control should be set to around 50-70% of maximum. It can take a few tries to successfully load a tape. Once you have successfully loaded a tape, you should not need to adjust the tape recorder's volume settings anymore.

Loading from Disk

Loading programs from disk is far quicker and more convenient than loading from cassette tape. First, you must have started the disk operating system, either DOS 3.3 or ProDOS. Chances are, the disk on which your program is stored already has an operating system on it. For more details on starting DOS, see Chapter 7.

Once DOS is loaded into your Apple, you can use one of two commands:

```
]RUN MYPROGRAM
```

This will load and then run a program named MYPROGRAM from the disk. Alternatively, if you do not want a program to start running, say if you want to LIST and edit it, use the following command:

```
]LOAD MYPROGRAM
```

This will load the file named MYPROGRAM into memory, overwriting any existing BASIC program. There you may LIST or RUN it, and resume working on it as usual.

If you get a FILE NOT FOUND error, then check your spelling; you may have mistyped the filename. Alternatively, it could be that the file does not exist on the disk; you may have inserted the wrong disk. Finally, if you get a FILE TYPE MISMATCH error, then you have tried to load a file that is not a BASIC program.

Use the CATALOG command to get a listing of each file and its file type present on the disk. Again, see Chapter 7 for full instructions on these procedures.

Listing Programs on a Disk

All of the files saved on a disk are listed in the disk's catalog. After the operating system is loaded, type the following:

```
]CATALOG
```

to list the files saved on the disk. ProDOS will allow you to type CAT instead, which will yield a more compact listing. On a DOS 3.3 disk with more than 18 files the listing will pause to give you time to read it. Press RETURN to see the rest of the files.

Chapter 4 : Advanced BASIC

In this chapter you will learn further BASIC commands that will make your programs far more useful and interesting, such as how to alter the flow of execution, how to get input from the user, and how to use looping to make efficient algorithms. You will also learn about variables, which include integers, real numbers, and strings.

Strings

In computer language, a *string* is any literal representation of a number, letter, or any other symbol. Both Applesoft and Integer BASIC strings can be anywhere from 0 to 255 characters in length. A string with 0 characters is given a special name, the *null string*. The previous chapter had many examples with strings: any PRINT statement which had quotation marks was using a string.

Some examples of valid strings are:

```
"CRANBERRY SAUCE"
"USE THE FORMULA X=3.14*R^2"
"1600 PENNSYLVANIA AVENUE"
"128"
```

Even if a string is made up of nothing but numbers, or any other valid mathematical expression such as those shown in Chapter 3, the Apple does not evaluate it. You cannot add, subtract, multiply, or perform any other mathematical operation on a string.

On the other hand, strings are quite versatile in that they can contain just about every character which you can type on your Apple's keyboard, with a few exceptions. Some of these exceptions include the arrow keys, ESCAPE, RETURN, CONTROL-H, CONTROL-M, CONTROL-U, and CONTROL-X. These characters cannot be included in a string because they either alter the cursor or cancel the line that you're typing.

Strings can even contain *nonprinting characters*, characters that when typed, do not appear on the screen. One such character is the Bell, produced by pressing CONTROL-G. Try this example:

```
]PRINT ""
```

In between the quotation marks, press CONTROL-G a few times. Each time you press CONTROL-G, the Apple speaker beeps, and an invisible *control character* is added to the string. When you type the final quotation mark and press RETURN, the Apple speaker will beep as many times as you originally pressed CONTROL-G. This technique can be put to use in your programs to provide an auditory alert to the user. Most other control characters are, however, both invisible and inaudible.

The Apple can only store numbers in its memory. Therefore, each letter that you type is automatically converted to a number using the *ASCII* system. For example, A becomes 65, B becomes 66, and so on. When displaying letters on screen from memory, the Apple reverses the process. A chart of character conversions is located in Appendix E.

Numbers

As you saw in the previous chapter, the Apple II is quite capable of dealing with two types of numbers: integers and real numbers. *Integers* are whole numbers without any fractional part, whereas *real numbers*, sometimes known as *floating point numbers*, can have a fractional part.

When entering numbers into the Apple, you must not use commas, or any other form of thousands separator. For example, to enter one million, you must type 1000000, and not 1,000,000.

Integers

An integer is a number with no fractional part. This sort of number is the only type that Integer BASIC can deal with. Integers can be either positive (+) or negative (-). If you don't give a sign, then it is assumed that the number is positive. Applesoft can use integers as well. Both versions of BASIC limit integers to the range of -32767 to +32767. Some examples of integers are:

```
0
1
-15
26890
67
```

Real Numbers

The set of real numbers includes both integers, as well as numbers with a fractional part. Like integers, real numbers can be either positive (+) or negative (-), and unsigned numbers are assumed to be positive. Only Applesoft can manage the full set of real numbers. The following are all examples of real numbers:

```
400
-12.67
0
-19
391.0004
76
```

Scientific Notation

Applesoft represents numbers having more than 9 digits in front of the decimal point using a method known as *scientific notation.* This type of notation, explained earlier in Chapter 3, consists of a coefficient and an exponent, separated by an *E.*

Scientific notation only expresses a number by a power of 10, such as 100 or 1000. The range of numbers using scientific notation is the same as that of real numbers. In scientific notation, this range is -1E+38 to +1E+38.

Rounding

Applesoft rounds any numbers with more than 9 digits, as shown in these examples:

```
]PRINT 98765432101
9.87654321E+10

]PRINT -1122334455667788
-1.12233446E+15

]PRINT 9900000000.12345
9.9E+09

]PRINT -49999999.85
-49999999.9
```

Fractional numbers are also held to similar bounds, with the difference that the nine digits of precision do not include any leading zeros to the right of the decimal point. Here are two examples:

```
]PRINT .9876543210
.987654321

]PRINT 0.00000000050000001234
5.00000013E-10
```

Variables

So far, all of our programs have dealt with *constants*, values that never change. To really take advantage of the power of the Apple II, a program can make use of *variables*. If you have studied algebra, then you ought to be familiar with the concept of variables, often represented with a letter such as *x* or *y*. If not, then think of variables as a box with a name attached to it. The contents of the box may change, hence making it variable, but the name does not. Therefore, we can call on the name in our programs, and always get back the current contents stored under that name.

A variable's name should be logical, chosen to describe its function in the program. The first few examples in this chapter show single-letter variable names because the programs are fairly trivial and easy to understand. Larger programs that you write, and later examples, should use descriptive names.

On the Apple, variables can contain both strings and numbers. However, one variable may only contain one type of data. In other words, a variable which was initially assigned a string cannot be assigned an integer later on. Despite this limitation, a variable can be changed at will and it can contain any legal value.

Variable Names in Integer BASIC

Integer BASIC dictates that all variable names start with a letter, and be no longer than 100 characters. Symbols other than letters and numbers may not be used. If a variable is to hold a string value, then its name must end with a $ (pronounced as *string*). In addition, you must dictate the maximum length of the string using the DIM command, which is explained later on. Here are some examples of legal Integer BASIC variable names:

OUTPUT
NAME$
SCORE2

Some illegal Integer BASIC variable names follow:

2REPORT
PASS$WORD
OUTPUT!

A variable's type is also part of what the Apple uses to determine if a variable name is already used. Therefore, these two variable names are distinct and separate of each other:

WEEK
WEEK$

Variable Names in Applesoft

Applesoft variable names are not quite as flexible as those in Integer BASIC. The main difference is that Applesoft only recognizes the first two letters of a variable name. Further characters are not considered. Therefore, the following variable names are identical in Applesoft:

MOUSE
MONTH

SCORE
SCREEN

In addition, Applesoft supports three types of variables. Real numbers do not have any suffix, integers have a % suffix, and strings have a $ suffix. As with Integer BASIC, the suffix is taken into account when evaluating a variable name. Therefore, these three variables are all distinct:

DAY
DAY%
DAY$

Reserved Words

Some words cannot be used as part of a variable name, because they are BASIC commands. Unfortunately, neither Applesoft nor Integer can tell the difference between a word intended as a command, such as PRINT, and a word intended as a variable name.

In Integer BASIC, variable names may not contain AND, AT, MOD, OR, STEP, or THEN. Furthermore, Integer BASIC variable names may not begin with END, LET, or REM.

Arrays

Put simply, an *array* is a table of variables that are all related in some manner. When they are in an array, variables are known as *array elements*. The array itself is given an *array name*, which follows the same rules as variable names.

Some examples of arrays include a list of basketball scores, monthly revenue for a business, and a to-do list. These are all lists of information, which is exactly what an array is designed to store.

In Applesoft, an array can contain any legal value: string, integer, or real, but every value in the array must be of the same type. In Integer BASIC, only numbers may be used in arrays.

Values in arrays are stored and retrieved using an *index number*. This number marks a place in the array. The simplest array is a flat list, and is called *one-dimensional*. Figure 4-1 is an illustration of such an array.

This array contains four values: 42, 51, 39, and 76. To access or modify any of these values, its corresponding index number must be specified. In this case, 42 has an index number of 0. The index number for 51 is 1. Without an index number, the Apple would not know which value in the array you mean to access.

Index Number	**Value**
0	42
1	51
2	39
3	76

Figure 4-1. A one-dimensional array

Index Number	0	1	2	3
0	15	37	21	85
1	60	31	44	78
2	59	20	38	56

Figure 4-2. A two-dimensional array

In Applesoft, arrays can also be multidimensional, or have more than one dimension. Figure 4-2 is an example of a two-dimensional array. It is arranged much like the grid on a map.

This array is more complex in that each of the 12 values requires not one, but two index numbers to be specified. For example, to access the slot holding the value of 20, index numbers 2 and 1 must be given. Applesoft arrays may have up to 88 dimensions.

Notice that all arrays start with zero. This is due to the fact that computers start counting with zero, while humans generally start at 1.

Here is an example program that uses a string array TD$ in Applesoft to store a short to-do list:

```
10 REM TO-DO LIST
15 REM ASSIGN ARRAY ELEMENTS
20 TD$(0) = "BRUSH FACE"
30 TD$(1) = "WASH TEETH"
40 TD$(2) = "EVAPORATE THEATER"
50 REM NOW PRINT EACH ITEM
60 HOME : PRINT "TO-DO LIST:" : PRINT
70 PRINT "FIRST, YOU MUST ";TD$(0)
80 PRINT "THEN, ";TD$(1)
90 PRINT "FINALLY, ";TD$(2)
100 END
```

Lines 20, 30, and 40 assign a string value to array index numbers 0, 1, and 2, respectively. Each array element is then printed on the screen on lines 70 through 90. Notice that the array index number is enclosed in parentheses. It is legal to provide a constant (as is done in this program), a variable, or an expression.

Array Dimensions

An array which has not been dimensioned will only be able to hold up to 11 elements. In order to use an array with more than 11 elements in your program, you should define its maximum size, known as its *dimension*. To do so, use the DIM command. Because arrays start at zero, the array will hold always one more value than the number given in the DIM command. For example, this statement will create an array which has room for 11 string elements:

```
]DIM AR$(10)
```

The argument in parentheses is not the total number of values which the array may hold, but rather is the largest index number of the array. More than one array may be dimensioned using a single DIM command; the only limitation is the program line length. This example dimensions a string array, an integer array, and a real array each with a maximum of 10 total elements:

```
]DIM A$(9), A%(9), A(9)
```

Separate each array to be dimensioned with a comma.

A multi-dimensional array in Applesoft is declared like so:

```
]DIM TD$(20,14)
```

This line creates a two-dimensional string array, TD$, which can hold 21 elements in one dimension, and 15 elements in the other. To make an array with more dimensions, simply separate additional values with commas between the parentheses.

The limit to the size of an array, in terms of how many values it can hold, is limited only by the available memory of the Apple. There is no fixed limit.

Redimensioning Arrays

To redimension an array means to change its size in terms of the number of elements that it can contain. In most cases, this is not allowed. In Applesoft, once an array has been dimensioned during the execution of a program, it cannot be redimensioned until the next time that the program is run. Attempting to do so will yield an error. An array can be dimensioned just once in a program, and that is it. Here is an example of an Applesoft program which attempts to redimension an array, and the error message that results:

```
10  DIM A(5)
20  DIM A(10)

]RUN

?REDIM'D ARRAY ERROR IN 20
```

In Integer BASIC, the rules are a bit different: it is possible to redimension an array, but only under very strict conditions. Only the most recently defined variable may be redimensioned. The following two programs demonstrate legal and illegal attempts at redimensioning an array in Integer BASIC:

```
>10 A = 5
>20 DIM B(15)
>30 DIM C(3)
>40 B(0) = A
>50 DIM C(10)
>60 END
>RUN

>
```

This first program runs successfully (it does not produce any output). The next program illustrates a failed attempt to redimension an array:

```
>10 DIM A(15)
```

```
>20 DIM C(3)
>30 B = 5
>40 C(0) = A
>50 DIM A(20)
>60 END
>RUN
*** DIM ERR
STOPPED AT 50
>
```

A *** DIM ERR was caused because both array C and variable B were defined after array A, therefore array A cannot be redimensioned. Moreover, since variable B is the most recently defined variable, the dimensions of neither array A nor array C may be altered. This limitation on redimensioning applies to both integer arrays and strings.

Expressions

Expressions offer a way to take one or more variables and constants and combine them to get new results. Some of the simplest expressions have already been covered in this book, such as addition:

```
]PRINT 5 + 2
```

This mathematical expression, following the PRINT statement, directs the Apple to take two constants, 5 and 2, and compute the sum.

Similarly, this statement tells the Apple to add and print the values of variables X and Y:

```
]PRINT X + Y
```

In both of these examples, the plus sign designates addition. The technical term for the plus sign is *operator*. More specifically, it is an *arithmetic operator*, since it directs the Apple to perform the arithmetic operation of addition. Other familiar operators include the minus sign (-) for subtraction, the slash (/) for division, and the asterisk (*) for multiplication.

You are quite likely to be familiar with these four basic operators. However, the Apple has other operators which aren't immediately apparent. These operators include *string operators*, *relational operators*, and *Boolean operators*. Fortunately, these operators are also easy to use after some explanation and examples.

Order of Operations

Every operator in an expression is evaluated in a predetermined order by the Apple. This is known as the order, or precedence, of operations. Without any assistance from you, the Apple will always evaluate expressions from left-to-right, following this procedure. However, you may easily override the standard order if you so desire.

Changing the Order of Operations

There may be times when the Apple's default order of operations does not suit you. In that case, you may override it. To do so, the use of parentheses in expressions is required. The Apple uses the nesting of parentheses to determine order: innermost operations are performed first. The following example illustrates the effects of using parentheses to determine the order of operations:

```
]PRINT 5*2+1
11
```

In this first example, the Apple multiplies 5 and 2 to get 10, then adds 1 to make 11. However, the next example uses parentheses to alter the order of operations:

```
]PRINT 5*(2+1)
15
```

Here, the Apple first adds 2 and 1 to get 3, then multiplies 3 and 5 to get 15.

String Concatenation

Concatenation is a technical word meaning “to join.” Both Applesoft and Integer BASIC allow you to join two or more strings together to form a longer string. To do so in Applesoft, use the plus (+) sign, like this:

```
]PRINT "IPSO"+"FACTO"
IPSOFACTO

]PRINT "MON "+"TAILLEUR "+"EST "+"RICHE"
MON TAILLEUR EST RICHE
```

Applesoft strings can range from 0 to 255 characters in length. The concatenated string may not exceed these limits.

String concatenation may also be used with string variables. The following program and figure illustrate this concept:

```
]LIST

 10 A$ = "MAMAN "
 20 B$ = "EST "
 30 C$ = "MORTE."
 40  REM  JOIN THESE TO MAKE D$
 50 D$ = A$ + B$ + C$
 60  PRINT D$
 70  END

]RUN
MAMAN EST MORTE.
```

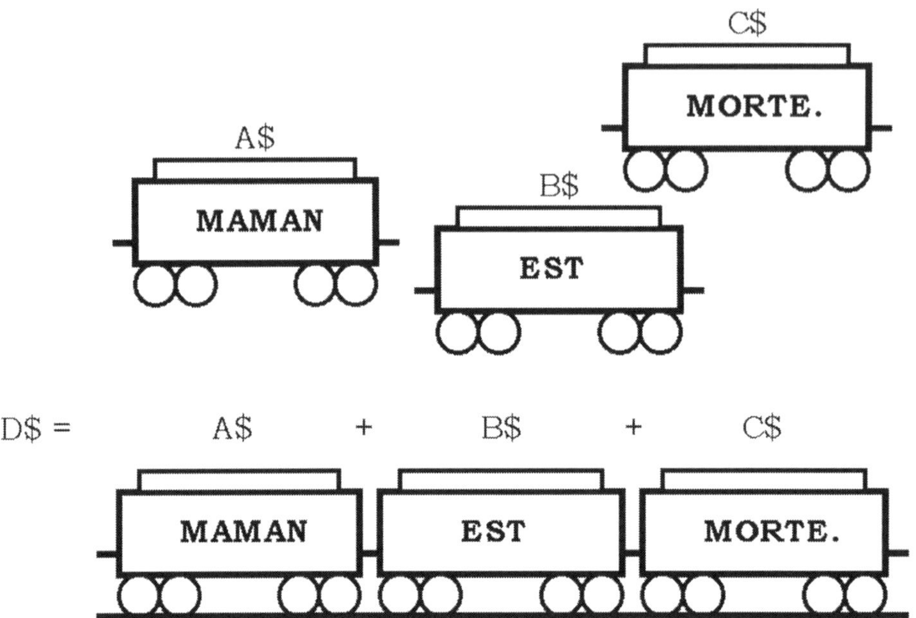

Figure 4-3. String Concatenation visualized using train cars

Once a concatenated string has been formed, it is no longer associated with its constituents. That is to say, in the previous example, if A$, B$, or C$ were modified, that modification would have no effect on D$.

Integer Expressions

This type of mathematical expression involves one or more integers and returns a single integer. Both constants and variables may be used. If you want to mix both reals and integers in an expression, see the heading "Mixed-type Expressions" which is coming up.

All integer expressions make use of five operators: plus (+) for addition, minus (-) for subtraction and negative numbers, asterisk (*) for multiplication, slash (/) for division, and the carat (^) for exponentiation. Expressions are evaluated using the following order of precedence: negative numbers (unary minus), exponentiation, multiplication and division, then addition and subtraction. Expressions are parsed from left to right to determine the order of operators with equal precedence.

Following are some examples of integer expressions in Applesoft:

256*2^3	equals	2048
3+5*-8/4	equals	-7
A%*B%	equals	the value of A% times the value of B%
5/4+5	equals	6 (the decimal part remains)

Here are some examples in Integer BASIC:

50 + 25 / 5	equals	55
1+5^3	equals	126
A*B+3	equals	3 plus the product of A and B
5/4+5	equals	6 (the decimal part is ignored)

Integer BASIC includes one additional operator which is exclusive to it: modulus. This operator returns the remainder of a division operation. For example, 8 modulo 3 is 2. Here are some other examples:

6 MOD 3	equals	0
4 MOD 7	equals	4
9 MOD 6	equals	3
10 MOD A	equals	10 modulo the value of A

Real Expressions

In Applesoft only, you may also use real numbers in expressions. The syntax and operators are exactly the same as Integer expressions, except that a real number is returned as the result. The order of operation is also the same, with negation first, then exponentiation, multiplication and division, and lastly addition and subtraction.

Following are some examples of Applesoft real expressions:

45.3 + 4^3	equals	109.3
0.5 + (7/2)^2	equals	12.75
9 - (X / 3.14 + Y)	equals	The quotient of the value of X divided by 3.14, plus the value of Y, all subtracted from 9
6.2 + 3.8	equals	10

Relational Expressions

With relational operators you can compare two values and see how they relate, such as if one is greater, lesser, or equal to the other. The values being compared may come from a constant, a variable, or an expression, however there are some limitations in Integer BASIC. The comparisons include testing a first number to find if it is equal to, not equal to, greater than, less than, greater than or equal to, or less than or equal to, a second number. If you choose to compare a string value, then you must compare it to a second string. Except for this restriction, you may freely mix any other type of number in a comparison.

If the comparison is true, for example if you want to test if a number is greater than another, and it indeed is, then the result will be a 1. Otherwise, if not, then the result of the relational expression is 0, for false.

The symbols used for relational operations in Applesoft and Integer BASIC are fairly similar, as Table 4-1 shows; Applesoft allows some variation with a few of the comparison symbols. Relational operators all have the same precedence: they are merely evaluated from left to right.

Here are a few examples of relational expressions:

1 = 0	equals	0 (false)
5 = 4+1	equals	1 (true)
20 < 40	equals	1 (true)
4 <= 2	equals	0 (false)
"GO" <> "GO"	equals	0 (false)
(A - B) = 3	equals	if the difference of A and B is 3, then the result is 1 (true). If not, then the result is 0 (false).

If you find that the result of either 0 or 1 is confusing, remember that these two numbers stand for false and true, respectively. The Apple is merely evaluating the truth of falsehood of the expression. For instance, in the first example, does 1 equal 0? No, that's false. So the Apple returns 0 to mean "false." In the second example, does 5 equal the sum of 4 and 1? Yes, that is true. So the Apple returns a 1 to mean "true."

Applesoft Operator	Comparison	Integer BASIC Operator
>	Greater Than	>
<	Less Than	<
=	Equals	=
<> or ><	Not Equal	# or <>
>= or =>	Greater Than or Equal	>=
<= or =<	Less Than or Equal	<=

Table 4-1. Relational Operators

String Comparisons

String comparisons are done character-by-character, going from left to right, and by assigning each letter or other character a numeric value. This value happens to be the character's ASCII code. Therefore, A<B<C<D, and so on. See ASCII Value Chart in Appendix E for a full list of codes.

For two strings to be equal, they must be of the same length, and contain the same characters in the same order. For example, the strings "TAR" and "RAT," even though they are composed of the same length and letters, are unequal because the letters are in a different sequence.

Applesoft can test if a string is greater than or less than another string, but Integer BASIC cannot. In Applesoft, "AA" is less than "AB" because even though the first two letters are the same, when comparing the second letters, the ASCII code for A, 65, is less than the code for B, 66. Integer BASIC can only test for equality or inequality of two strings.

Boolean Expressions

Boolean expressions are named after George Boole and include the following operators: AND, OR, NOT, and EXCLUSIVE OR. Both Applesoft and Integer BASIC understand the first three. A Boolean expression will always evaluate to be true or false. The Apple represents true by returning a 1, and false by returning a 0. This is the same behavior as for relational expressions, and in fact, Boolean and relational expressions are often used together. Also like relational operators, all Boolean operators have equal precedence; they are evaluated in order from left to right. Table 4-2 contains what is known as a *truth table*, the result of each Boolean operator.

The AND operator evaluates true if and only if all values are nonzero (true). Try these three examples:

```
]PRINT 1 AND 1
1

]PRINT 1 AND 0
0

]PRINT 0 AND 0 AND 0
0
```

The OR operator evaluates true if at least one of the values is nonzero, as demonstrated by these examples:

```
]PRINT 1 OR 0
1

]PRINT 0 OR 0
0
```

NOT returns *true* if the expression that it evaluates is *not true*. If you're having trouble visualizing its operation, try looking at and running this simple program:

```
10 INPUT A
20 IF NOT (A = 3) THEN 40
30 PRINT "YOU DID TYPE A 3." : GOTO 50
40 PRINT "YOU DID NOT TYPE A 3."
50 END
```

First Value	Operator	Second Value	Result
T	AND	T	T
T	AND	F	F
F	AND	T	F
F	AND	F	F
T	OR	T	T
T	OR	F	T
F	OR	T	T
F	OR	F	F
(none)	NOT	T	F
(none)	NOT	F	T

Table 4-2. Boolean Expression Truth Table

All of the main action in this program happens on line 20. First off, the Apple knows what is true and what is false, but only when it comes to numbers. If you, for example, typed a 2 at the input prompt, the Apple knows that 2 does not equal 3. Therefore, the expression in the parentheses evaluates to false. Next, the Apple evaluates the expression "NOT false." In English, such an expression would just be a longer way of saying "true." The Apple follows the same logic, and jumps to line 40 to tell you that you, in fact, did not type a 3.

Mixed-type Expressions

There may be times when you wish to compare two or more variables of a differing type, for example, a real with an integer in Applesoft. To do so, the Apple must convert all numeric values to the real type before performing any calculations. Since strings cannot be reasonably converted to numeric values, their use is illegal in any real, integer, or Boolean expression.

Strings may only be used in string comparison or relational expressions.

The precedence of operations becomes more complicated in a mixed-type expression. Any quantity within parentheses is evaluated first. If parentheses are nested, then the innermost ones are calculated first, proceeding on to the outermost set. The remaining arithmetic expressions are then evaluated, followed by relational expressions, and then logical expressions.

A relational expression can be used as part of a real or integer expression since it returns 1 or 0 if the relationship is true or false.

When it comes time to assign the final value of the expression, Applesoft sets the numeric type to whatever is most appropriate for the situation. For example, if the result of the expression is to be assigned to an integer variable, then the result is converted to an integer.

If Applesoft must convert a real number to an integer, it does so by dropping the fractional part and rounding to the next lower whole number. This process is known as *truncation*, and here are some examples:

2.5 truncates to 2
6.06 truncates to 6
-7.5 truncates to -8

Assigning Values

Variables whose values never change severely limit the usefulness of a program. To assign or change the value of a variable, simply name the variable, add an equal sign, and then enter the new value. The new value can be supplied as either a constant or a mathematical expression. One variable may even be set using the value of another variable.

This following program demonstrates the different ways of assigning values to variables. Before you type it in and run it on the Apple, mentally evaluate it to predict what the printed values of C and D will be.

```
10 A = 5
20 B = A
30 C = B + A
40 D = C + 5
50 PRINT C
60 PRINT D
70 END
```

If you prefer, you can also use the LET command to assign values, but its use is optional. Here are lines 10 through 40 of the previous program rewritten to use LET:

```
10 LET A = 5
20 LET B = A
30 LET C = B + A
40 LET D = C + 5
```

A variable may be incremented in the following fashion:

```
50 A = A + 1
```

Mathematically, this is nonsense. Variable A cannot equal itself plus 1. The explanation is that the equal sign serves as a symbol of assignment, not as a test for equality. The LET keyword makes this distinction clearer. In this line, the variable A is assigned its current value plus 1, thus incrementing it.

To assign a value to a string variable, enclose the value in quotes ("), like in this example string variable assignment:

```
]400 B$ = "ALEA JACTA EST..."
```

This causes string variable B$ to store the words ALEA JACTA EST, followed by three periods.

The null (empty) string is one which contains no characters. To make a null string, simply type two quotation marks with nothing in between, like so:

```
]NULL$ = ""
```

The value assigned to a numeric value can be the result of an expression, such as in this example statement:

```
]100 X = 100 + (25/5)
```

Executing that line will give the value of 105 to variable X, but one might as well just type 105 in that case. Using expressions to assign a value is more useful if the expression includes one or more other variables or functions.

Because an array holds more than one value, you must declare the array index which will hold a particular value.

The following program assigns two values to a numeric array, N, and three values to a string array, S:

```
10 N(1) = 3
20 N(2) = 5
30 S$(1) = "DESCARTES"
40 S$(2) = "PASCAL"
50 S$(3) = "FERMAT"
```

If you were to run this program, then type PRINT S$(2), you would get back PASCAL. Since a BASIC program can have more than one statement on a line, separated by colons, the variable assignments of this program could be simplified to two lines, as follows:

```
]10 N(1) = 3 : N(2) = 5

]20 S$(1) = "DESCARTES" : S$(2) = "PASCAL" : S$(3) =
"FERMAT"
```

Computing an Average

The following program uses two different variable assignment techniques to compute the average of three numeric variables, A, B, and C. The computed average is stored in variable D:

```
5 REM DEFINE THE VARIABLES
10 LET A = 7
```

```
20 LET B = 5
30 LET C = 3
40 REM COMPUTE AVERAGE
50 LET D = (A + B + C) / 3
60 REM PRINT RESULT
70 PRINT D
```

When you run this program, you should get a result of 5. The parentheses in line 50 are used to ensure that the three values are added first, then finally divided by 3; otherwise you would get an incorrect result of 13.

Remember that using the LET keyword to assign a value to a variable is optional. You can use it or not depending on your preference. For example, without using LET, line 10 would become:

```
10 A = 7
```

DATA and READ Statements

If you have a block of data which is constantly in use in your program and you don't wish to manually assign it to variables or an array, then you can use the DATA and READ statements to have the Apple do it for you.

In Integer BASIC, DATA is restricted to numeric values only. In Applesoft, DATA can be either numeric or string. The READ statement must use a variable whose type matches the data type. The following example illustrates a DATA statement which provides three numeric values:

```
110 DATA 10, 15, 20
```

Notice that the values are entered sequentially and are separated by a comma. While the data values themselves have no order in which they must appear (it is up to the programmer to determine the order), the Apple always reads in values in the order that they appear in your program. You may use more than one DATA statement line if you have more data than will fit on one line. Traditionally, DATA statements are placed at the very end of the program, but they can be interspersed wherever you desire.

To use these data in a program and assign them to an array, the READ statement is used. READ implements what is known as a *pointer*, a way for the Apple to mark its place when sequentially reading in the data. READ must be used with one or more variable names. For each variable given in a READ command, and each successive READ command executed in your program, the pointer is incremented to the next data element.

The following program demonstrates the use of DATA and READ:

```
10 REM READ IN FIRST DATA ELEMENT
20 REM AND ASSIGN IT TO VARIABLE A
30 READ A
40 PRINT "FIRST DATA IS: "; A
50 REM NOW READ THE NEXT TWO ELEMENTS
60 REM AND ASSIGN THEM TO VARIABLES B AND C
70 READ B,C
80 PRINT "NEXT NUMBERS ARE ";B
90 PRINT "AND ";C
110 END
120 REM HERE COMES THE DATA
130 REM NOTE THAT DATA CAN BE PLACED
140 REM AFTER THE END STATEMENT
150 DATA 6, 8
160 DATA 9
```

When you run the program, you should see the numbers 6, 8 and 9. Even though there are two DATA statements, all data in a program gets grouped into the same "stack." The two DATA statements could have been consolidated into one, but were meant to demonstrate this point. In this program, the Apple sees the following set of data:

6
8
9

The data pointer is initialized to point to 6, so when the first READ statement on line 30 is executed, variable A receives the value of 6. The pointer is then incremented to point to 8. The READ statement on line 70 has two variables, so the pointer is incremented twice. At this point, the data pointer is past the end of the data.

What would happen if you tried to READ again? To find out, add this line to the program and run it again:

```
100 READ D
```

The modified program should give the following result:

```
]RUN
FIRST DATA IS: 6
NEXT NUMBERS ARE 8
AND 9

?OUT OF DATA ERROR IN 100
]
```

Because the data pointer was at the end, there was no more data for the READ statement to fetch. It is the programmer's job to ensure that the program does not read past the end of the data. To reset the pointer back to the start of the data, use the RESTORE command.

Clearing Variables

Both versions of BASIC, Applesoft and Integer, include a method of reseting every variable at once. All numeric variables and array elements will be set to 0, and all string variables and array elements will be set to null.

In Applesoft, this function is performed with the CLEAR command, which also resets the DATA pointer. CLEAR can be used in both programmed and immediate modes.

To reset all variables in Integer BASIC, use the CLR command. Unfortunately, this command is limited in that it may only be used in immediate mode, and not in any program. Here is a demonstration:

```
>A=123

>PRINT A
```

```
123

>CLR
>PRINT A
0
```

Displaying Values

The PRINT statement allows you to display the contents of any variable or array in your program. You have a few options relating to format when using PRINT.

The PRINT statement is flexible in that it can display any mixture of constants and variables, such as in this example:

```
]10 A = 2
]20 B$ = "APPLE"
]30 PRINT 4;" PEOPLE HAVE AN ";B$;A

]RUN
4 PEOPLE HAVE AN APPLE2
```

PRINT Format

If PRINT is used with multiple values, it will ordinarily just display the values in sequence, with no spacing in between, followed by a new line after the last one. However, there are two formatting options which may be used instead.

Typing a comma will cause the following output to be tabbed over one field when displayed on the screen. Putting a semicolon at the end of a PRINT will eliminate the new line that is customarily added.

Try these examples:

```
]PRINT 31,41,59
31              41              59
```

```
]PRINT "PI";"DAY";
PIDAY
```

Entering Values

Your programs can quite easily accept user input using the INPUT command. With INPUT, the Apple will pause the program and prompt the user for either a number or a string. When the user has supplied satisfactory input, it is assigned to a variable and the program resumes. If not, the Apple prompts the user again.

The following is a program which prompts the user to enter a number, assigns that number to variable A, then prints variable A:

```
]10 PRINT "ENTER A NUMBER"
]20 INPUT A
]30 PRINT A
]40 END

]RUN
ENTER A NUMBER
?50
50
```

Line 20 contains the INPUT statement that stops the program and waits for the user to respond. The Apple prints a question mark (?) on a new line to signal the user. Following the word INPUT must be a variable name to which the user input is assigned. This variable's type declares the legal values which the user may enter. In this program, if the user were to enter anything other than digits, a ?REENTER message would appear and the user would be prompted again. Integer BASIC will display the message RETYPE LINE and reissue the prompt.

The next program demonstrates the use of a string INPUT statement:

```
]10 PRINT "TYPE YOUR NAME"
]20 INPUT NAME$
```

```
]30 PRINT "HELLO, ";NAME$
]40 END


]RUN
TYPE YOUR NAME
?DAVID
HELLO, DAVID
```

String input has a few limitations. One of them is that a comma cannot be entered. That is because a comma is used to separate multiple input values in Applesoft.

One INPUT statement can be used to request more than one piece of input from the user. In this example, two variables, X and Y, are to be supplied by the user. The program is run twice, demonstrating two different ways of entering the data.

```
]10 PRINT "TYPE A MAP COORDINATE"
]20 INPUT X,Y
]30 PRINT "YOU TYPED ";X;",";Y
]40 END

]RUN
TYPE A MAP COORDINATE
?4,5
YOU TYPED 4,5

]RUN
TYPE A MAP COORDINATE
?5
??4
YOU TYPED 5,4
```

The two input variables need not be of the same type, as shown in this program:

```
10 PRINT "TYPE YOUR NAME AND AGE"
20 INPUT NAME$,AGE
```

```
30 PRINT "HELLO, ";NAME$;", AGED ";AGE
40 END
```

Entering string values in Integer BASIC works a bit differently compared to Applesoft. First, the question mark prompt is not displayed. It is up to the programmer to display a prompt, if desired. Second, since the length of string variables must be declared in advance, attempting to enter a string longer than the variable's length will result in a *** STR OVFL ERR message.

Finally, you may not enter multiple string inputs on the same line, as you can with Applesoft. This is because Integer BASIC does not recognize the comma as separating the input; instead, the comma is a valid character for string input.

INPUT Statement Prompts

With an ordinary INPUT statement, the prompt is always a question mark, and it is up to the programmer to use a PRINT statement to tell the user what data the program expects. However, both Applesoft and Integer BASIC offer a way to combine these two statements into one. The syntax differs slightly.

In Applesoft, you may place your desired prompt in quotation marks, then type a semicolon before the variable, as in this example:

```
]10 INPUT "ENTER YOUR NAME: ";N$
]20 PRINT "HELLO, ";N$
]30 END

]RUN
ENTER YOUR NAME: DAVID
HELLO, DAVID
```

Notice that Applesoft does not automatically append a question mark (?) to your input prompt. You are free to include a question mark, or any other symbol, if you so desire.

The Integer BASIC version differs slightly in two ways: first, the prompt and variable name are separated by a comma, and second, a question mark is printed after your prompt if the input expected is numeric. In other words, you only get a question mark if you are not using a string variable to store the input.

Here is the Integer BASIC version of the same program above:

```
>5 DIM N$(30)
>10 INPUT "ENTER YOUR NAME: ",N$
>20 PRINT "HELLO, ";N$
>30 END
>RUN
ENTER YOUR NAME: DAVID

HELLO, DAVID
```

If this program were changed to accept a number, such as the user's age, then the Apple would automatically add a question mark to the prompt string.

Functions

Functions perform a certain operation on a given *argument*, or input value, and then return a value based on that input and the function's operation. Both Applesoft and Integer BASIC have a variety of built-in mathematical and string-related functions, and you may even define your own functions in Applesoft. Some of these functions operate on numbers, such as the SQR function for computing square roots. Other functions, such as LEFT$, which returns the leftmost characters of a string, deal with strings.

BASIC functions must always be called with one or more operands (another term for arguments) enclosed in a pair of parentheses. The operand may be a variable, a constant, or the result of an expression. Functions may be used in any BASIC expression in the same way that you would use a constant or variable.

Appendix B contains the entire set of Applesoft and Integer BASIC functions.

Substring Functions

A *substring* is one part of a larger string. For example, given the string "DIAMOND," the following are all valid substrings:

DIA
MOND
IAM
D

Ideally, a substring must contain at least one character and be less than the total length of the original string. Two or more characters must be consecutive. That is, "DAD" is not a valid substring of "DIAMOND."

To get a substring of the leftmost characters of a string, use the LEFT$ function, as demonstrated:

```
]PRINT LEFT$("PUBLIUS",3)
PUB
```

In this example, the three leftmost characters of the string PUBLIUS are printed on screen. Specifying a substring of an equal or greater amount of characters has no effect other than to return the original string value:

```
]PRINT LEFT$("FEDERALIST",11)
FEDERALIST
```

However, specifying a substring length less than or equal to 0 produces an error:

```
]PRINT LEFT$("SOCIALIST",0)

?ILLEGAL QUANTITY ERROR
```

Conversely, to get the rightmost characters of a string, use the RIGHT$ function. It operates in a similar manner to LEFT$:

```
]PRINT RIGHT$("COMMON",3)
MON
```

The same restrictions apply to RIGHT$: a 0 substring is not allowed, and specifying a value equal to or greater than the length of the string has no effect.

The string supplied may be a variable or a concatenation; a constant value is not required.

Finally, to get a substring with arbitrary bounds, use the MID$ function. This function takes two parameters in addition to the string value. The first is the starting position, and the second is the total number of characters to return. Here are some examples of the function in action:

```
]PRINT MID$("SENSE",2,4)
ENSE

]PRINT MID$("COMMON SENSE",5,2)
ON

]PRINT MID$("COMMON SENSE",4,6)
MON SE
```

As you can see, the MID$ function takes the first number as the position of the starting character, and continues rightward across the string for the amount of characters specified by the second number.

Unfortunately, Integer BASIC does not have any substring functions, though there are still ways to simulate them. To do so, you must act as if the string variable is a two-dimensional array, and specify a starting character position and the number of characters to be extracted, as shown in this example:

```
10 DIM A$(10),B$(4)
20 A$ = "CHARACTERS"
30 B$ = A$(1,4)
40 PRINT B$
50 END
```

The notation on line 30 with the parentheses sets B$ to be equal to the first four characters of A$. It looks like the same syntax for accessing an array, but as you may recall, there are no string arrays in Integer BASIC.

Integer BASIC String Concatenation

Unlike Applesoft, Integer BASIC does not use the plus sign (+) to concatenate strings. Instead, use a semicolon, like so:

```
>PRINT "JAMES ";"MADISON"
JAMES MADISON
```

To concatenate string variables, a bit more work is required. In Integer BASIC, when a string variable is dimensioned, it can hold any number of characters less than or equal to that dimension. For example, a string dimensioned to 10 total characters could be only 6 characters long. The total characters currently in a string is known as the string's length, and can be found using the LEN function, as shown in this example:

```
10 DIM A$(10) : REM MAKE A$ HOLD AT MOST 10 CHARACTERS
20 A$ = "PAPERS" : REM ASSIGN A VALUE TO THE STRING
30 PRINT LEN(A$) : REM PRINT STRING LENGTH
40 END
```

When you run this program, you should get back 6, as expected. A$ has room for 10 total characters, is currently using 6, and has room for 4 more.

The way to concatenate two strings in Integer BASIC is to first dimension a string that is large enough to hold both strings. Then the length of the first string must be computed using LEN. Finally, the second string must be added on to the first, but after the last character of the first string. The last character happens to be LEN + 1.

This next program demonstrates string concatenation in Integer BASIC:

```
10 REM DIMENSION FIRST STRING VARIABLE LARGE
20 REM ENOUGH TO HOLD BOTH STRINGS
30 DIM A$(25)
```

```
40 A$ = "FEDERALIST"
50 REM NOW, HERE IS THE SECOND STRING
60 DIM B$(10)
70 B$ = " PAPERS"
80 REM WE WANT TO ADD B$ AFTER THE END OF A$
90 REM THAT HAPPENS TO BE LEN(A$) + 1
100 A$( LEN(A$) + 1) = B$
110 REM NOW PRINT THE RESULT
120 PRINT A$
130 END
```

ASCII Conversion Functions

In Applesoft, the CHR$ function may be used to convert an ASCII code number into its respective character. To do so, wrap the desired ASCII number in parentheses. Try the following examples:

```
]PRINT CHR$(7)

]PRINT CHR$(20)

]PRINT CHR$(65)
```

The first example prints the Bell character, which is invisible, though it causes the Apple speaker to beep. The third example prints a space, and the final example prints an A.

See Appendix E for the full ASCII character code table. Remember that BASIC uses decimal notation for ASCII codes, not hex.

To perform the opposite operation, to get the ASCII code for a specified character, use the ASC function. ASC takes a string and returns its ASCII code number. If the string contains more than one character, then only the first character is evaluated.

```
]PRINT ASC("B")
66
```

ASC is available in both Applesoft and Integer BASIC.

Defining Your Own Functions

In Applesoft, if your program frequently makes use of a specific mathematical calculation, then you can define it as a *user function* and use the function throughout your program. User functions may only operate on numbers; string functions may not be defined. To define a function, use the following syntax:

DEF FN *name* (*argument*) = *expression*

This syntax creates a function with a single argument. The mathematical expression of the function must follow the equal sign, and use of the argument is optional. Function names follow the same rules as variable names: in Applesoft, only the first two characters are significant, though longer function names are permissible. A function may be redefined later on in the program by giving its name again.

Here is an example of a simple function named A that takes an argument X and returns the square of X:

```
DEF FN A(X) = X^2
```

All functions must take one and only one argument as an input. In this case, the input is assigned to variable X. However, the argument does not need to be used in the argument's definition, as shown in this example:

```
DEF FN TWO(X) = 1 + 1
```

This trivial function always returns 2. The argument provided to this function must be a legal value, even though it is not used in the function.

In addition, function definitions may contain variables used elsewhere in the program, as well as the results of other functions. The following program defines two functions which take advantage of these features:

```
10 B = 3
20 A - 5
30 DEF FN C(Y) = Y + COS(A + 40)
```

```
40 DEF FN D(X) = C(2) + A^2
```

To call a user defined function in your program, use the following syntax:

FN *name* (*expression*)

To add on to the previous program, here is how to call the two functions C and D and display the result with a PRINT statement:

```
]50 PRINT FN C(2)

]60 PRINT FN D(1)
```

Line 50 calls function C with an argument of 2, meaning that the Y variable in the function definition holds a 2. Function D is called on line 60 with an argument of 1. However, function D does not make use of its argument, so the 1 is discarded.

You should get the following output after typing RUN:

```
]RUN
2.52532199
25
```

Like any built-in function, the results of user functions may also be assigned to a variable, or used as part of an expression elsewhere in your program.

As you might expect, a user function must be defined before it may be called. More precisely, the program line which defines the function must be executed before any line which calls the function. Attempting to do otherwise will yield an ?UNDEF'D FUNCTION ERROR.

Function Nesting

Functions can be nested within each other, or in other words, the output of one function may be used as the argument (input) of a secondary function. Doing this saves space; otherwise, a variable would have to be used to store the result of the first function. Here are two simple examples:

```
]PRINT LOG(SIN(3))
-1.95814463
```

```
]10 INPUT X
]20 PRINT SQR(COS(X))
]30 END
```

Nested functions are executed in order from innermost to outermost. In the first example, the SIN function is executed, and the result is then returned to the LOG function for computation. Similarly, in the second example, the cosine of X is first computed, then returned as input to the square root function, and the result is finally printed on screen.

Functions may be nested in both immediate and deferred execution modes. Deferred execution mode with PRINT is a great way to experiment and see the results of nested functions.

Random Numbers

Strictly speaking, the Apple can't generate truly random numbers. Instead, Applesoft and Integer BASIC both have a function called RND which is suitable for generating pseudo-random numbers. These numbers aren't quite as random as true random numbers, but in any case, this RND function should suffice.

RND works a bit differently in the two versions of BASIC. In Applesoft, supplying RND with an argument greater than zero will return a random floating point number between 0 and 1. If the argument to RND is 0, then the last random number generated will be returned. This feature could be used if you do not want to allocate another variable to store the random number. Finally, giving a negative argument will "seed" the random number generator, leading to a repeatable sequence of random numbers. This could be useful for testing a program that makes use of RND.

At first, the default behavior of RND may seem unintuitive. It generates a decimal number between 0 and 1. Usually, you will want to generate a random number within a certain range, such as from 0 to 10. To do so, multiply the output of RND by the top range desired, then convert the result to an integer with the INT function. To set a lower limit, just add that bottom range to the result.

The following program simulates the roll of a 6-sided die:

```
10 R = INT(RND(1) * 6) + 1
20 PRINT R
```

Line 10 calls the RND function with a lower range of 1 and an upper range of 6. Remember that the lower range is not the argument passed to RND, but is instead the number added to the result generated by RND.

In Integer BASIC, the RND function generates a random integer between 0 and one less than the given argument. Thus, in Integer:

```
>PRINT RND(6)
```

will randomly print either a 0, 1, 2, 3, 4, or 5. To simulate a die roll in Integer BASIC, run the following program:

```
10 R = RND(6) + 1
20 PRINT R
30 END
```

As with the Applesoft version of the die rolling program, a 1 is added to the result to avoid rolling a zero.

Chapter 5 : Program Design and Control

When your programs get larger, it becomes more important that they are logically organized and efficient. This chapter will teach new BASIC commands and theory on organizing and designing the layout and structure of larger programs, as well as how to alter the flow of program execution.

Lastly, this chapter will explain low-level programming techniques that allow direct access to any area of the Apple's memory, as well as how to debug a program.

Jumping Around with Branches

So far, any program you devise using the commands you have learned up until now will execute in one order: the order in which the lines are numbered. However, you will hardly find many programs which always execute sequentially. Most programs use a statement known as a *branch*, a means to tell the computer to continue not to the next line number, but instead to the line number indicated as part of the branch statement.

The GOTO Statement

GOTO is the most elementary type of branch statement: it merely specifies a line number which should be executed next. This is known more precisely as an *unconditional branch*, since the branch is always followed.

Here is a simple program that uses GOTO. Notice that one of the program lines is never executed when the program is run:

```
10 PRINT "DAFFY"
20 GOTO 40
30 PRINT "DONALD"
40 PRINT "DUCK"
50 END
```

In this program, the GOTO statement on line 20 tells the Apple not to proceed to line 30, as it would ordinarily, but instead to line 40. The result is that the name DAFFY DUCK is printed on the screen; DONALD is left out entirely.

Let's take a look at another, more complicated program which uses GOTO:

```
10 GOTO 90
20 GOTO 70
30 GOTO 50
40 GOTO 110
50 PRINT "C"
60 GOTO 40
70 PRINT "B"
80 GOTO 30
90 PRINT "A"
100 GOTO 20
110 END
```

Can you predict in which order the letters will be printed before running this program? The secret is in the carefully planned GOTO statements. Admittedly, this program is rather complex for a beginner. You may wish to trace it with your finger as you mentally run through it. Amazingly, the letters are printed in alphabetical order: A, B, C.

The BASIC line numbers will be executed by the Apple in this order: 10, 90, 100, 20, 70, 80, 30, 50, 60, 40, 110. Every statement gets executed, but not necessarily in the order in which it appears in the program listing. The diagram in Figure 5-1 shows conceptually what is going on for the first two GOTO statements.

The Apple sees that the first GOTO statement on line 10 says to go to line 90. The Apple branches to line 90 and prints an A. The following line, 100, tells the Apple to branch up to line 20.

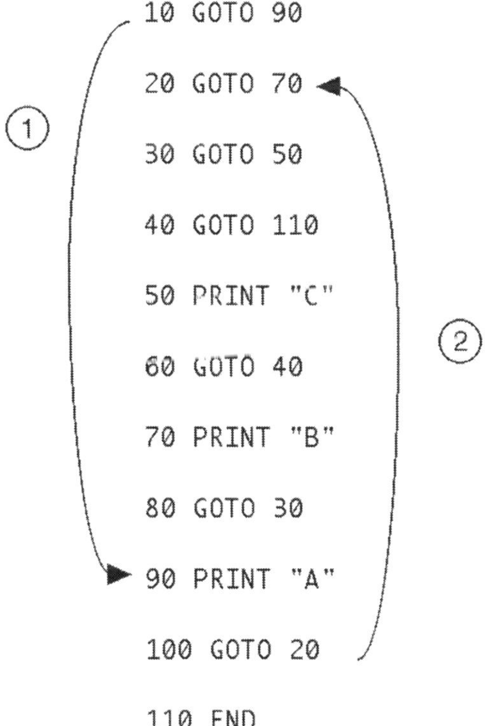

Figure 5-1. The GOTO statement in action

The GOTO statement can also be used to create what is known as an *infinite loop*, a condition wherein the Apple executes the same instructions over and over again until you force it to stop. The following program demonstrates an infinite loop:

```
]10 PRINT "ANOTHER ROUND!"
]20 GOTO 10
]30 END
```

The END statement on line 30 will never be executed. To stop this runaway program, press CONTROL-C. As you can imagine, an infinite loop is generally an undesirable feature in a program.

Computed GOTO Statement

While the line number of a GOTO statement must always exist in the program, it does not have to be supplied as a constant value. Instead, it can be the result of a mathematical computation. Here is an example of such a statement. This Integer BASIC program accepts a number between 1 and 5, then jumps to the line number using the formula *number x 100.* See what happens when you enter a number that is out of the specified range.

```
>10 PRINT "ENTER A NUMBER FROM 1-5"
>20 INPUT A
>30 REM COMPUTED GOTO STATEMENT HERE
>40 GOTO A * 100
>100 PRINT "BANANA"
>110 END
>200 PRINT "APPLE"
>210 END
>300 PRINT "ORANGE"
>310 END
>400 PRINT "PEAR"
>410 END
>500 PRINT "TOMATO"
>510 END
```

The computed GOTO statement is on line 40. It merely takes the current value of variable A, multiplies it by 100, and then jumps to the line number which equals the result. If variable A were 2, then the GOTO would point to line 200.

The syntax for a computed GOTO statement differs slightly in Applesoft, which uses ON-GOTO. The syntax is as follows:

ON *expression* GOTO *list of line numbers*

The result of the expression should be in the range of 1 to however many line numbers are given. Consider this example:

```
ON X GOTO 40,60,80
```

If X were 1, then the program would branch to line 40. If X were 2, then line 60 would be executed next, and if X were 3, then the GOTO would lead to line 80. If X happened to be less than 1 or greater than 3, then the GOTO would be ignored, and the next program line would be executed instead. However, if X evaluated to less than 0 or greater than 255, the Apple will respond with an ?ILLEGAL QUANTITY ERROR message. You can have as many line numbers after the GOTO as will fit on a program line.

Loops

A *loop* is a controlled method of executing one or more commands a certain number of times. There are always three parts to a loop: the *condition*, the *index counter*, and a *next* command.

The condition indicates how many times the loop should be executed, and under what circumstances should it be stopped. The index counter is a variable which serves to keep track of how many times the loop has been executed. The NEXT command marks the loop boundary; when it is reached, the loop condition is evaluated again to determine if the loop should be executed again.

A loop can be constructed using GOTO statements, but making sure that the loop only occurs a certain number of times takes extra work for the programmer. Therefore, Applesoft and Integer BASIC offer syntax which makes using loops easier for the programmer.

The FOR-NEXT Syntax

To make a loop, start off with a FOR command and an index variable. Traditionally, the variable name I is used, standing for "index." The index variable is used to count how many iterations, or cycles, of the loop have occurred.

Afterward follows the condition of the loop, that is to say, how long should the loop continue. This part consists of two numbers separated by the TO keyword. The first number indicates the starting value for the index counter. The second number indicates the maximum loop counter value. When the index counter meets or exceeds this maximum value, the loop is terminated.

Generally, the loop index counter increments by one each time the loop is completed. However, to alter it, say to make the counter increment by two each time, the optional STEP keyword is used.

Here is the full syntax of a FOR statement:

FOR *index* = *start* TO *end* STEP *increment*

In the syntax example, *start*, *end*, and *increment* can be supplied as either constants, variables, or the result of an expression. It is recommended that either constants or variables be used, since the expression must be evaluated every time the loop is executed, thus slowing down that section of your program. The line with the FOR statement is known as the loop declaration.

Following is the body of the loop, those program lines that should be executed within the loop. The body should consist of one or more lines.

The end of the loop should contain a NEXT command followed by the index variable.

This next example illustrates a simple program which produces a multiplication table for the number nine. The loop starts at one and goes on to 10. Once 10 is printed, the loop terminates, since the index counter reaches 11, and that is larger than 10.

```
]10 PRINT "MULT. TABLE FOR 9"
```

```
]20 FOR I = 1 TO 10

]30 PRINT "9 X ";I;" = ";9*I

]40 NEXT I

]50 END

]RUN
MULT. TABLE FOR 9
9 X 1 = 9
9 X 2 = 18
9 X 3 = 27
9 X 4 = 36
9 X 5 = 45
9 X 6 = 54
9 X 7 = 63
9 X 8 = 72
9 X 9 = 81
9 X 10 = 90
```

In this program, the loop declaration is on line 20, the loop body on line 30, and the end of the loop is marked on line 40.

Because the index variable I behaves like any ordinary variable, it can be used elsewhere in the program. In this case, it is both displayed and multiplied by 9 as part of the program output on line 30. To make the multiplication table extend to 20 and increment by three, alter line 20 to the following:

```
]20 FOR I = 1 TO 20 STEP 3
```

The output then looks like:

```
]RUN
MULT. TABLE FOR 9
9 X 1 = 9
9 X 4 = 36
9 X 7 = 63
```

```
9 X 10 = 90
9 X 13 = 117
9 X 16 = 144
9 X 19 = 171
```

Is this what you expected? Since the loop starts at one, not zero, the multiplication table is not showing multiples of three, but rather is starting with one and adding three each time. To instead show 3, 6, 9, 12, etc., make one more change to line 20. Turn the 1 to a 0 and RUN the program once more:

```
]20 FOR I = 0 TO 20 STEP 3
```

```
]RUN
MULT. TABLE FOR 9
9 X 0 = 0
9 X 3 = 27
9 X 6 = 54
9 X 9 = 81
9 X 12 = 108
9 X 15 = 135
9 X 18 = 162
```

Backward Loops

So far, we have only seen a loop run in one direction: forward, where the index variable is incremented each time. However, loops can also run backward as well, with the index variable decreasing. To do so requires the use of the STEP keyword. Following the previous multiplication example, once again alter line 20 like so:

```
]20 FOR I = 10 TO 0 STEP -1
```

What you have done is to start the index counter at 10, then decrement it by 1 each time the loop executes. Once the index counter is less than zero, the loop terminates. In this case, the index counter must be greater than the maximum index value for the loop to continue, not less than as before. RUN the program to see the multiplication table in reverse order.

It should be noted that the lines and instructions within the loop are not executed in reverse order; it is only the index variable which is affected.

Using Loops with Arrays

Loops are commonly used to access elements of an array. Since the index variable of a loop is nothing more than an ordinary variable, it may be used to store and fetch values from an array, such as in the following program. This program contains two loops: one runs forward to populate an array with values. The second loop runs backward to print out the stored values.

```
10 PRINT "ARRAY INDEX EXAMPLE"
20 DIM A(4)
30 FOR I = 0 TO 4
40 A(I) = (I+1)^2 :REM ASSIGN VALUES
50 NEXT I
60 REM NOW OUTPUT THE VALUES
70 FOR I = 4 TO 0 STEP -1
80 PRINT A(I)
90 NEXT I
100 END
```

Line 40 in the program assigns the value of I plus one raised to the second power to each of the five elements of array A. The PRINT statement on line 80 then shows the value of each element.

Nested Loops

One or more loops may be placed inside each other, known as *nested loops*. Each loop must have its own unique index variable. Traditionally, the outermost loop uses I, the next loop uses J, the third K.

When completing nested loops with the NEXT command, you must do so in opposite order that the loops were started. In other words, you cannot "tangle" the loops. The example in Figure 5-2 demonstrates proper loop nesting, where the ellipses represent program lines in the loop body that aren't relevant to this concept.

```
10 FOR I = 0 TO 20

...

50 FOR J = 5 TO 50 STEP 5

...

60 FOR K = 1 TO 6

...

100 NEXT K
110 NEXT J
120 NEXT I
```

Figure 5-2. Proper example of nested loops

```
10 FOR I = 1 TO 10

...

30 FOR J = 0 TO 256 STEP 2

...

70 NEXT I

...

150 NEXT J
```

Figure 5-3. Example of illegally nested loops

If you imagine the layers of loops as the layers in an onion or a sandwich, it may help you to visualize the concept. The K loop is the innermost layer, so it must be closed first, then J is in the middle, surrounding the K loop. Finally, the I loop makes the outermost layer, surrounding both the K and J loops.

Nested loops are most commonly used to access the elements of a two-dimensional array, an array that requires two index variables in order to return or set a value.

Computing Prime Numbers

A prime number, as you may recall, is one whose only factors are 1 and itself. Some examples of prime numbers are 2, 3, 5, 7, and 4691.

Let's suppose that we want to write an Applesoft program to compute all prime numbers up to a given integer. One method to do so is to start dividing the target number by 2, and checking if an integer was returned. If so, then a factor has been found, and the target number is not prime. If not, the divisor is incremented. This process keeps going until the divisor has reached the square root of the target. At this point, the target number must be prime. The Applesoft program that implements this algorithm might look something like this:

```
10 REM TESTING FOR PRIMES BY DIVISION
20 N = 0 : REM TARGET NUMBER
30 S = 0 : REM SQUARE OF TARGET
40 F = 2 : REM STARTING FACTOR

90 REM CLEAR SCREEN AND PROMPT USER
100 TEXT : HOME : INPUT "ENTER UPPER RANGE: ";R
110 REM START MAIN, OUTER LOOP TO UPPER RANGE
120 FOR N = 2 TO R
130 REM COMPUTE SQUARE ROOT OF TARGET
140 S = SQR(N)

150 REM INNER LOOP TESTS DIVISIONS
160 FOR F = 2 TO S
170 Q = N / F
180 REM WAS Q AN INTEGER?
```

```
190 IF Q = INT(Q) THEN 300
200 NEXT F

210 REM N MUST BE PRIME
220 PRINT N;", ";
300 REM Q WAS AN INTEGER, SO N IS NOT PRIME
310 REM RESET FACTOR F
320 F = 2
330 NEXT N
```

This program works by trial division. The user enters a number that is assigned to variable R to serve as the maximum range; the program will attempt to find all prime numbers up to R.

A main loop iterates over all integers between 2 and R. The square root of R is computed and stored in variable S on line 140. Then, an inner loop on line 160 tests all numbers from 2 up to S. If the quotient Q of the target number N divided by the factor F is an integer, then N is not prime. However, if none of the operations yield an integer, then N is indeed prime, because its only factors are 1 and itself.

You may notice that the only even prime number, 2, is not counted as prime by this program. This omission has to do with the testing for integers. Two divided by 2 returns 1, which is an integer, and the program therefore (incorrectly) marks 2 as not prime. Larger numbers take a longer amount of time, since there is a greater range of numbers to test. One way to improve this program would be to research a more efficient algorithm for finding prime numbers, and implement it in BASIC.

Subroutines: a Program Within a Program

All but the smallest of programs may be divided up into discrete components which do a specific task. Such a component may be identified as a *subroutine*, a smaller unit of a program. A subroutine is accessed by a branching statement, similar to GOTO.

Use subroutines when you have a certain function which needs to be performed at different points in your program. For example, if your program contains some lines of code which take an input as a variable, perform a calculation on that input, and then return the result, those lines of code could be made part of a subroutine.

The distinction between a subroutine and a GOTO statement is that the subroutine has more "intelligence"; it knows where to jump back once it is finished.

The GOSUB Statement

Subroutines are invoked with the GOSUB statement, and finished with the RETURN command. In programming jargon, the GOSUB statement *calls* the subroutine. When a subroutine has finished, program control is handed to the next statement after the GOSUB. The following example illustrates a program which makes use of a subroutine to perform a trivial mathematical calculation:

```
10 REM MULTIPLIER PROGRAM
20 LET A = 10
30 LET B = 5
40 GOSUB 90
50 LET A = 21
60 LET B = 17
70 GOSUB 90
80 END
90 REM THIS SUBROUTINE MULTIPLIES TWO NUMBERS AND PRINTS THE RESULT
100 LET C = A * B
110 PRINT A;" TIMES ";B;" IS ";C
120 RETURN
```

In this program, the subroutine consists of lines 90 to 120. The subroutine is called with a GOSUB on lines 40 and 70. In each instance that the subroutine is used, it always does the same calculation with the variables A and B. When it is finished, the subroutine returns the program to the line just after the GOSUB. RUNning the program produces the following output:

```
]RUN
10 TIMES 5 IS 50
```

```
21 TIMES 17 IS 357
```

For comparison, here is the same program written without using subroutines. Notice that it has repeated code; a benefit of subroutines is that they eliminate the need to duplicate existing lines of your program.

```
]LIST

 10  REM  MULTIPLIER PROGRAM WITH
     OUT SUBROUTINE
 20  LET A = 10
 30  LET B = 5
 40  LET C = A * B
 50  PRINT A;" TIMES ";B;" IS ";C
 60  LET A = 21
 70  LET B = 17
 80  LET C = A * B
 80  PRINT A;" TIMES ";B;" IS ";C
 90  END
```

All subroutines should end with a RETURN command. If not, the program may start executing program lines that weren't intended to be part of the subroutine. If the Apple encounters a RETURN command without having branched into a subroutine, an error will occur.

Dividing parts of a program into subroutines makes more sense in large programs consisting of many hundreds of lines. Later on in this book, much more complex programs will be shown that rely heavily on subroutines.

Exiting a Subroutine Early with POP

There may be times when you want a subroutine to be called and exited a bit differently than usual. In these cases, you would not want the subroutine to return to the next program line after it was called. These situations are handled with the use of the POP statement.

POP makes the Apple "forget" that it entered the most recent subroutine. In other words, execution will occur as normal, and your program is free to do as it pleases.

Here are two examples of this behavior. The first program demonstrates the usual use of a subroutine with GOSUB and RETURN:

```
10 PRINT "ASTERIX"
20 GOSUB 40
30 END
40 PRINT "OBELIX"
50 RETURN
60 PRINT "PANORAMIX"
```

If you examine this program, or type it and run it on your Apple, you will discover that it never gets to line 60. Now, let's alter this program, and substitute a POP statement in place of the RETURN on line 50:

```
]50 POP
```

```
]RUN
ASTERIX
OBELIX
PANORAMIX
```

The difference now is that line 60 is finally executed, because program execution never returns to line 30, as it did in the first version of the program. In short, POP is like a RETURN, with the exception that it does not take program execution back to the line following the original GOSUB. In other words, POP turns a GOSUB into a GOTO.

The most common use of POP is with GOTO to leave a subroutine early, or by a different means than usual. With this combination, you can call a particular subroutine at one place, and then have it branch off to somewhere completely different in your program.

One should be warned: it is generally not considered to be good programming style to make use of POP. Too liberal use of it can quickly render a program listing quite complicated and hard to follow. Therefore, one should avoid its use whenever possible. Chances are, you can restructure the relevant portions of the program instead of using POP.

Computed GOSUB Statement

The syntax for a computed GOSUB statement is the same as the respective syntax for a computed GOTO statement in Applesoft and Integer BASIC. In each subroutine, the statement executed after RETURN is always the one after the previous GOSUB. If no subroutine branch occurs, the program execution falls through to the next line, the same as with a computed GOTO. In both cases with the example program shown below, that line would be 50.

Here is a program in Applesoft that makes use of a computed GOSUB:

```
10 PRINT "TYPE 1, 2, OR 3"
20 INPUT A
30 ON A GOSUB 100,200,300
50 END
100 PRINT "ONE"
120 RETURN
200 PRINT "TWO"
220 RETURN
300 PRINT "THREE"
320 RETURN
```

This program could be modified for Integer BASIC by changing line 30 to:

```
30 GOSUB A * 100
```

If A is indeed 1, 2, or 3, the appropriate subroutine is executed, and the RETURN statement brings program execution back to line 50, which is an END. If A is greater than 3, then line 50 is immediately executed, and the program ends without branching to any subroutine.

Nested Subroutines

One subroutine may call another subroutine, known as a *nested subroutine.* Integer BASIC has a limit of 16 nested subroutines. Attempting a seventeenth will yield a *** 16 GOSUBS ERR. Applesoft has no such fixed limit, instead, the maximum nested subroutines is limited only by the amount of memory that your Apple has. When the Apple's memory is exhausted, an ?OUT OF MEMORY ERROR will be printed on the screen.

The final limitation on subroutines is that of *recursion*, wherein a subroutine calls itself, or a nested subroutine calls the initial subroutine. Neither version of BASIC on the Apple permits recursion.

Making Decisions with IF Statements

The IF statement can be used as a conditional branch, because the Apple only takes the branch if the specified conditions are met. Furthermore, the IF allows the program to make conditional execution. That is, the Apple will only execute the instructions *if* certain conditions are met. The IF statement follows this syntax:

IF *condition(s)* THEN *further statements*

Here is a simple example:

```
25 IF A = 3 THEN GOTO 300
```

The statement after THEN can be nearly anything: variable assignment, a GOTO or GOSUB, PRINT, or any function call.

In Applesoft, IF features a shortcut: if you want to have a GOTO branch, then you do not need to include the word GOTO; you may just use the line number, like so:

```
350 IF C$ = "START" THEN 60
```

If the IF condition evaluates to be true, then all statements on the same line, separated by a colon, will be executed. If the condition evaluates to false, then nothing else on that program line will be executed; the Apple will continue directly to the next line. In the previous example, if the value of C$ was *not* START, then the next line after 350 would be executed. Otherwise, if the value of C$ was START, then the Apple would branch back to line 60.

An IF statement may contain more than one condition, such as in this case:

```
IF AGE > 16 AND WEIGHT < 80 THEN 200
```

Remember from Chapter 4 that the AND operator means that *both* expressions must be true. In this case, if AGE were 18, but WEIGHT 90, the branch to line 200 would *not* be taken, since only one of the conditions was met.

Stopping and Starting a Program

There are a variety of ways to stop a BASIC program. The easiest and most common method is to press CONTROL-C. If the program was expecting input, such as from an INPUT statement, you will need to press RETURN to get back to the BASIC prompt.

Both versions of BASIC will print the line number which was currently being executed when you pressed CONTROL-C. If the program stopped at line 10, then Integer BASIC will print the message STOPPED AT 10, while Applesoft will say BREAK IN 10.

In some situations, you may be able to continue the program using the CONT (Applesoft) or CON (Integer BASIC) commands.

Reset

Pressing the CONTROL-RESET key combination will also stop a running BASIC program. When reset, most models of Apple will jump to the BASIC prompt with the program and variables intact.

If you have an original model of Apple II which enters the Monitor when reset, you will have to press CONTROL-C, then RETURN, to get back to BASIC. This is known as "warm-start" because it returns you to BASIC with your program and its variables intact. The other method is to press CONTROL-B instead of CONTROL-C. This is called "cold-start" because your program and all variables are eliminated as if the Apple had just been switched on.

The END Statement

Using the END statement is the most common way of halting a BASIC program when it has reached its natural ending point. END does not print out any message or status; it merely terminates the program and returns the user to the BASIC prompt.

In Applesoft, END is optional. Program execution will continue until there are no more lines to execute. However, END is required in Integer BASIC. If an Integer BASIC program runs out of lines to execute before reaching an END, the error message *** NO END ERR will be printed, and the program stops.

The STOP Statement

If the Apple comes across a STOP statement when running an Applesoft program, it will print the line number at which the STOP was located, then halt execution. The behavior is similar to that of pressing CONTROL-C.

STOP is primarily used for debugging a program. You can insert a STOP statement at a certain place in your code, then PRINT out the variables to check what the values are. You may then resume the program, if you wish, with the CONT command.

The WAIT Statement

In Applesoft, you can cause a program to halt until a specified memory location contains a certain value. This functionality is most useful for waiting on peripheral devices attached to your Apple. The syntax for WAIT is:

WAIT *memory location, value*

Appendix B contains a better description of how to use the WAIT statement.

Low-level Programming

As you become more proficient with BASIC, eventually you may start to reach some limitations of what you can do with the built-in commands and functions. In these instances, you will need to combine BASIC and machine language. Fortunately, there are easy ways to do so.

Accessing Memory

With BASIC, you have access to most of the Apple's entire range of memory. In total, there are 65,536 locations of memory accessible to your BASIC programs. Later Apples, the IIe, IIc, IIc Plus, and IIgs, have one or more banks of memory, but this additional memory cannot be used by BASIC.

Not all of these memory locations are RAM. Some are connected to the Apple's peripherals, such as the speaker, game paddles, and cards connected to slots. Other locations are ROM, and can only be read, not modified.

Still other locations are what is known as a *soft-switch*. A soft-switch affects the behavior of the Apple, and may be "thrown" by accessing its memory location. For example, one soft-switch controls whether the Apple's screen is in text mode or low-resolution graphics mode. This soft-switch is set automatically when you use certain BASIC commands. Most soft-switches have no dedicated BASIC command; you must know their location and set them yourself.

PEEK and POKE

With the PEEK and POKE statements, you may access, and set, respectively, any of the Apple's 65,536 memory locations. This includes reading and storing values in the Apple's memory, controlling peripheral devices, and setting soft-switches.

PEEK is used to read a memory location, and optionally assign its contents to a variable. For example,

```
A = PEEK(33)
```

would assign the contents of memory location 33 to the variable A. PEEK always returns an integer in the range of 0 to 255.

PEEK can also be used to access the Apple's hardware, for example. Try this short program:

```
10 FOR X = 0 TO 5 : NEXT X
20 A = PEEK(-16336)
30 GOTO 10
```

What happens when you run this program? Well, you should hear the results. Memory location -16336 governs the Apple's speaker.

You may be wondering why a negative number is used. If you recall, Integer BASIC cannot handle numbers greater than 32,767. As it turns out, the memory location for the speaker in hex is $C030. BASIC uses decimal notation, so this hex number becomes 49,200 in decimal. Unfortunately, that's too large for Integer BASIC, and if you tried it, you'd get an error. The solution is to subtract 65,536 from 49,200, which will yield a negative number. This number is perfectly acceptable to Integer BASIC, and it will know what to do with it. Applesoft does not have this limitation, meaning that you can use either form, -16336 or 49200.

POKE is the opposite of PEEK, and is used to store a value in any of the Apple's memory locations. Due to the nature of the Apple's hardware, a POKE command accesses the memory location *twice*: once as a read operation, and then a final time to store the value. This fact has no relevance except for with soft-switches. Using POKE on a soft-switch will trigger the switch twice.

The following program line causes the number 65 (which happens to be the ASCII code for the letter A) to be stored in memory location 768:

```
10 POKE 768,65
```

Since the Apple is an 8-bit computer, the largest value that will fit in any one memory location is one byte, whose allowed range is 0 to 255. To store a number greater than 255 requires more than one byte, or memory location, in the Apple's memory.

As mentioned earlier, some of the memory locations are read-only (ROM). Attempting to POKE a value to one of these locations has no effect.

If you're having trouble figuring out ways to use PEEK and POKE, then have a look at Appendix C. It contains several tables of useful PEEKs and POKEs, sorted by function.

Accessing Machine Language Programs

Any machine language routine may be accessed from BASIC with the CALL statement. For example, the routine to clear a screen may be accessed with the statement:

```
CALL -936
```

CALL uses the same "negative notation" as do PEEK and POKE.

Numbers can be hard to remember, especially ones which you do not use so often. CALL can accept a variable in place of a numeric constant. This can help make your program more readable and remind you of what each CALL statement does.

```
10 CLRSCRN = -936
20 CALL CLRSCRN
```

Program Debugging

A *bug* is a mistake in a program, such as an error in logic, or a wrong variable name. Bugs cause a program to work improperly in some or all situations. Unfortunately, the larger the program, the more bugs that are likely to be in it.

The process of correcting these mistakes is known as *debugging.* BASIC comes with a few ways to make debugging easier on the programmer.

Debugging with PRINT

PRINT has two very useful debugging applications: the first is to print the value of a variable, and the second is to report the current line number.

In the first application, it may be that you've tracked a bug down to a variable having the wrong value. You would then use PRINT at strategic locations to display the target variable on screen. Doing so would help you pinpoint the area of your program where the bug occurs.

The second application is useful if you have identified a section of code in your program as having a bug. You can insert some new lines with PRINT statements that print their line number, such as:

```
1000 PRINT "1000"

... BUGGY SECTION OF CODE ...

1230 PRINT "1230"
```

You can then move the PRINT statements around to narrow down the range of lines which may have a bug, until you finally deduce the line or lines which have the problem.

PRINT can also be used for audible debugging, which is useful if you do not want screen display to be altered. Merely PRINT a CONTROL-G followed by a semicolon, like so:

```
31 PRINT ""; : REM CONTROL-G IN QUOTES
```

The Apple will beep, leaving the screen display unaltered. This is another good way to determine which sections of your program are being executed, and when.

Examining Execution with TRACE

TRACE will display the number of every program line on screen as it is executed. This command can be useful when debugging a program with conditional GOTO or GOSUB statements: you can tell which branch the program took. Conversely, the output of

TRACE can help you deduce which program lines are *not* being executed.

Unfortunately, TRACE gets a bit bothersome in loops, such as FOR loops, as it prints the line number of every line as it is executed, on every iteration of the loop.

Following is a short demonstration on the use and effects of TRACE. A new program is keyed in, then TRACE is entered in immediate mode before RUNning the program:

```
]10 A = PEEK -16336
]20 FOR X = 0 TO 2
]30 PRINT "GOOD MORNING!"
]40 NEXT X
]50 PRINT "TO YOU"
]60 END

]TRACE

]RUN
#10 #20 #30 GOOD MORNING!
#40 #30 GOOD MORNING!
#40 #30 GOOD MORNING!
#40 #50 TO YOU
#60
]
```

The effects of TRACE are canceled with the NOTRACE command.

One possible application of TRACE stems from the fact that both it and its companion, NOTRACE, may be used as part of your program. Therefore, it is not necessary to have the trace on throughout the duration of your program. Instead, you may insert a line to activate TRACE before a certain section of code which you wish to debug, observe its output, and then have a further line with NOTRACE when your program has gotten out of the certain section of code.

The DSP Command

Integer BASIC incorporates the DSP command, which is a useful debugging tool. DSP is short for display, and is used with a variable name. Once activated, every time the given variable changes, the variable name and its new value are printed on the screen. Unfortunately, Applesoft does not have a DSP command.

Here is an example of DSP in action:

```
>LIST
    0 DSP A
   10 A=0
   20 INPUT A
   30 FOR X=0 TO 2
   40 LET A=A+X
   50 NEXT X
   60 PRINT A
   70 END

>RUN
#10 A=0
?6
#20 A=6
#40 A=6
#40 A=7
#40 A=9
9

>
```

Line 0 activates the DSP feature for the variable A, which happens to be the only variable in this program. From that point on, every time that the value of A changes, the line number and the new value are printed in the format:

#{line} {variable}={value}

Notice that this report is only printed when the variable changes, not whenever it is referenced, such as on line 60, which merely displays the value of A.

To track the changes of more than one program variable, you may use multiple DSP statements, or you can separate multiple variable names with a comma.

To turn off the display of variable changes, use the NO DSP command. This command can even be used as part of your program, to only show changes in certain sections of code.

Chapter 6 : Input and Output Formatting

By now, you should be familiar with the Apple's most common form of input: the keyboard. However, there are many more ways to get data into the Apple to be used by your programs. The first part of this chapter will cover the mouse and game controllers, as well as alternative forms of keyboard input. The concept of a "user-friendly" program will be introduced, showing both examples and guidelines on making programs that are easy to use and understand.

Putting data into the Apple is rather pointless if there is no way to get it back out in a reasonable format. The second part of this chapter deals with data formatting, making it easy for humans to comprehend.

Programming the Apple Mouse II

A small device which is rolled across a flat surface to make selections and issue commands, the mouse is quite commonly found attached to computers, sometimes including the Apple II. Moving the mouse causes an on screen pointer to move in the same direction. A button on the mouse can be used in one of two ways: either a click (a single press and release of the button) while the mouse is stationary, to signal a command; or the button may be held down while moving the mouse, known as *dragging,* to signal a different type of action.

Just attaching the mouse to the Apple won't automatically allow any program to use it. Instead, programs must be written with the mouse in mind, and the program must take care of keeping the on screen pointer updated when the mouse is moved, as well as responding to mouse clicks and drags. Furthermore, not all programs may use the mouse in the same way, for example, a program is not required to make use of a pointer.

Setup

As explained in Chapter 1, the mouse is not so commonly found on models of Apple other than the IIgs. However, every Apple has the opportunity to accept input using this device. See Chapter 2 for full details on how the mouse connects to your Apple; some models require a mouse interface card be installed first.

If you have an Apple II, II Plus, or IIe, the mouse card is typically installed in slot 4, though it will work in any of the six other slots. For the Apple IIc, IIc Plus, and IIgs, the "virtual" mouse card is located in slot 4. Later versions of the IIc (the platinum, Memory Expansion Card revision) have the mouse card in slot 7 instead of 4.

Activating the Mouse

Before your program can use the mouse for input, the mouse must be "switched on" and initialized. It is sufficient to send an ASCII byte 1 to the mouse card to do this. To do so, you must "wake up" the mouse by using the PR statement and then printing the correct byte. If you are using DOS or ProDOS, you must send a Control-D before the PR. The following code does all of this:

```
]10 PRINT CHR$(4);"PR#4" : PRINT CHR$(1)
```

Remember: if your mouse card is not in slot 4, change the number to the correct slot. If you have not loaded DOS or ProDOS, then leave off the "PRINT CHR$(4);" beginning part, thus making the line look like this:

```
]10 PR#4 : PRINT CHR$(1)
```

After running this line of code, it will appear that nothing has happened. To fully test out the mouse, reset the Apple, then type in this short program:

```
10 PRINT CHR$(4);"PR#4" : PRINT CHR$(1)
20 PRINT CHR$(4);"PR#0" : PRINT CHR$(4);"IN#4"
30 INPUT "";X,Y,S
40 PRINT X,Y,S
50 GOTO 30
```

Run this program, then move the mouse around and press the mouse button to observe the effects of the on-screen numbers. Press CONTROL-RESET to stop this program.

As is easy to deduce, the numbers in the first two columns indicate the X and Y coordinates of the mouse. The coordinate range for both axes is 0 to 1023, with the upper-left corner of the screen being 0,0. The final number is the status of the mouse button; its range is 1 to 4. The following table lists all possible status values.

Status	Current Reading	Last Reading
1	Pressed	Pressed
2	Pressed	Released
3	Released	Pressed
4	Released	Released

Table 6-1. Mouse button status

The status digit becomes negative if any key on the Apple's keyboard is held down. To change it back to positive, use this POKE statement:

```
]POKE (-16368,0)
```

Deactivating the Mouse

When your program is done using the mouse, you can disable it with the following line:

```
PRINT CHR$(4);"PR#4" : PRINT CHR$(0)
```

This sends the mouse ASCII byte 0, which is the code to turn it off. Afterward, it is a good idea to change input and output back to the keyboard and video screen, respectively. The following line accomplishes this task:

```
PRINT CHR$(4);"IN#0" : PRINT CHR$(4);"PR#0"
```

Using the Mouse

The mouse can serve several different uses in a program, such as by cycling through menu options, making a text selection in a word processing program, or creating a graphic in a drawing program.

The next two sections demonstrate two particular applications of the mouse: a pointer, and a menu. These example programs are ultimately meant to be used as part of a larger program.

Displaying a Pointer

Unfortunately, merely activating the mouse does not cause a pointer to appear on the screen. It is up to us, as programmers, to manage it.

Fortunately, however, the theory of managing a pointer is fairly simple. We need merely keep track of three things: the X-coordinate of the pointer, the Y-coordinate, and the screen element on which the pointer is currently resting. Since the pointer will cover up whatever element is underneath it, we need a way to save that element to a memory location, then restore it when the pointer moves away.

There is one problem to be overcome: the range of the mouse X and Y coordinates is 0 to 1023, while the 40 column text screen only has 40 columns and 24 rows. Thus, the mouse coordinates must be scaled to fit the text screen boundaries. There are two methods of doing so. The first method is to scale down the mouse coordinates by dividing the mouse range by the screen range. There are 1024 positions for the mouse, but only 24 rows, so 1024 divided by 24 yields a scale factor of 42.67 for the Y-coordinate, and 25.6 (1024 / 40) for the X-coordinate. The second method is to track relative motion of the mouse compared to its last position. For example, if the mouse were moved 20 units to the left, then the cursor on screen would be moved 1 position left. Both methods have advantages and disadvantages. Using absolute scaling, the first method, is simple, but may require excessive mouse movement.

A small BASIC program which accomplishes all of these requirements of displaying a pointer on the screen might look like this:

```
10 REM MOUSE POINTER DEMO
20 TEXT : HOME : REM CLEAR SCREEN
30 P$ = "@" : REM CHARACTER TO USE FOR POINTER
40 PX = 1 : PY = 1 : REM POINTER COORDINATES
50 OX = 1 : OY = 1 : REM OLD COORDINATES
60 CC$ = " " : REM COVERED CHARACTER
70 D$ = CHR$(4)
85 T = 25

100 REM POPULATE SCREEN WITH SOME LETTERS
110 FOR I = 0 TO T
120 X = INT((RND(1) * 39))+1 : Y = INT((RND(1) *
23))+1
130 C$ = CHR$((RND(1) * 26) + 65)
140 HTAB(X) : VTAB(Y) : PRINT C$;
150 NEXT I : PRINT

200 PRINT D$;"PR#4" : REM TALK TO MOUSE
```

```
210 PRINT CHR$(1) : REM TURN ON MOUSE
220 PRINT D$;"PR#0" : REM SWITCH BACK TO SCREEN
230 PRINT D$;"IN#4" : REM GET INPUT FROM MOUSE

300 VTAB 23 : HTAB 39
310 INPUT "";X,Y,S : REM GET MOUSE COORDS AND STATUS
315 PX = INT((X / 25.6) + 1) : PY = INT((Y / 42.67) +
1)
320 IF PX = OX AND PY = OY THEN 300 : REM DID POINTER
MOVE?
325 REM GET CHARACTER AT NEW COORD
330 NC$ = CHR$(SCRN(PX-1, 2*(PY-1))+16*SCRN(PX-
1,2*(PY-1)+1))
335 REM DRAW POINTER AT NEW COORD
340 VTAB PY : HTAB PX : PRINT P$;
345 REM RESTORE CHARACTER AT OLD COORD
350 VTAB OY : HTAB OX : PRINT CC$; : REM ERASE OLD
CURSOR
355 REM SET OLD COORDS = NEW COORDS
360 OX = PX : OY = PY
365 REM SET OLD CHAR
370 CC$ = NC$
380 GOTO 300
```

This program first places 25 random letters around the text screen. These are the elements over which the pointer may pass. The rest of the program keeps track of moving the pointer around the screen, covering up any letter, and then restoring it if necessary. The pointer's location on the screen is tracked using absolute coordinates, scaled down to match the dimensions of the text screen.

Lines 20 through 85 set up the initial program values. The text screen is activated and cleared, then the character that will represent the pointer is declared. Pointer coordinates, both old and new, are set to 1, which is in the upper-left corner of the screen. D$ is set to be the DOS attention character, the character that signifies a DOS command. If you have not loaded DOS or ProDOS (see Chapter 7 for full details on DOS), then you will have to change some program lines, namely, lines 200, 220, and 230.

The loop on lines 110 through 150 is responsible for generating T random letters at random locations on the screen. T is set to 25 on line 85. Line 120 first generates a random X and Y coordinate, after which line 130 generates a random letter of the alphabet (see Chapter 4 for an overview of random number generation in BASIC). Finally, line 140 moves the cursor to the (X, Y) coordinate and prints the random letter.

The final phase of program setup is to establish communication with the mouse. The mouse must first be activated, then the Apple must be instructed to take all input from the mouse. These lines are written assuming that DOS or ProDOS has been loaded into the Apple. If not, change those lines to the following:

```
200 PR#4 : REM TALK TO MOUSE
210 PRINT CHR$(1) : REM TURN ON MOUSE
220 PR#0 : REM SWITCH BACK TO SCREEN
230 IN#4 : REM GET INPUT FROM MOUSE
```

Line 200 redirects program output to the peripheral card located in slot 4. That should be the mouse in a standard Apple configuration. To activate the mouse, the program must send it the ASCII code 1. Line 210 takes care of this step. Next, line 220 redirects output back to the screen, and finally line 230 tells the Apple to take input from the mouse instead of the keyboard.

After all this preparation, the main program loop begins at line 300, devoted to moving the pointer around the screen. The program follows a fairly simple algorithm:

1. Get new mouse coordinates.
2. Get screen character at new coordinates.
3. Draw pointer at new coordinates.
4. Restore character at old coordinates.
5. Set old coordinates equal to new coordinates.
6. Begin again at step 1.

Line 300 accounts for a side-effect of the INPUT statement that would result in a blank line being shown. The INPUT statement on line 310 queries the mouse for its current X and Y location, and button status, S. S is not used in this program, only the coordinates are. Line 315 scales the mouse coordinates to make them acceptable for the screen. Finally, line 320 checks to see if the pointer moved by comparing the new coordinates with the old coordinates. If the pointer did move, the program continues onward.

Line 320 examines the screen to record the character at the new pointer coordinates. This action is performed by a new BASIC command, SCRN. SCRN is actually a graphics command, and is covered in Chapter 8. As it so happens, when used with the text screen, SCRN can be used to return the character at screen location (X, Y) by way of the following expression:

CHR$(SCRN(X-1, 2*(Y-1))+16*SCRN(X-1,2*(Y-1)+1))

After the character at the new coordinates is saved to variable NC$, the pointer is promptly written over it by line 340.

Line 350 then restores the old character on which the pointer previously rested. The old coordinates are then set to the new coordinates, the saved screen character is transferred to become the old screen character on line 370, and the loop begins again.

Mouse-driven Menu

This short BASIC program will show how to use the mouse to make a menu for your own program. Moving the mouse will highlight each entry in turn; clicking the button will select the currently highlighted menu item. The highlighting is done using the INVERSE command which is explained later in this chapter. The mouse is tracked using relative movement rather than absolute coordinates.

```
10 REM MOUSE MENU DEMO
15 D$ = CHR$(4)
20 REM FIRST MAKE THE MENU CHOICES
20 T = 5 : REM NUMBER OF CHOICES
30 DIM M$(T+1) : REM ARRAY OF CHOICES
40 S = 0 : REM CURRENT SELECTION
50 REM NOW READ IN DATA STATEMENTS
60 FOR I = 0 TO T
70 READ M$(I)
80 IF M$(I) = "0" THEN 100
```

```
90 NEXT I
100 HOME : PRINT "WHERE DO YOU WANT TO GO?"
110 REM DRAW ALL CHOICES
120 FOR I = 0 TO T - 1
130 VTAB (3 + (I*2)) : PRINT M$(I)
140 NEXT I
150 REM TURN ON THE MOUSE
160 PRINT D$;"PR#4" : REM SEND OUTPUT TO MOUSE
170 PRINT CHR$(1)
180 PRINT D$;"PR#0"
190 REM NOW WE BEGIN THE MAIN LOOP
200 REM GET CURRENT MOUSE DATA
210 OY = Y
220 PRINT D$;"IN#4" : REM GET INTPUT FROM MOUSE
225 VTAB 23 : HTAB 39
230 INPUT "";X,Y,B : REM GET X,Y COORD AND BUTTON
235 Y = 1023 - Y : REM INVERT Y COORDINATE
240 PRINT D$;"IN#0" : REM STOP GETTING INPUT FROM
MOUSE
250 REM CHECK MOUSE BUTTON
260 IF B = 1 THEN 450
270 REM NOW CHECK FOR MOUSE MOVEMENT
280 IF (OY - Y) < -5 OR (OY - Y) > 5 THEN 300: REM
MOVE
290 GOTO 210
300 REM CHECK IF WE ARE AT THE EDGE
310 IF (S = 0 AND (OY - Y) < -5) OR (S = T-1 AND (OY -
Y) > 5) THEN 210
320 REM NO, SO REDRAW THE OLD SELECTION
330 VTAB (3 + (S*2))
340 PRINT M$(S)
350 REM NOW GET MOVEMENT DIRECTION
360 IF (OY - Y) < -5 AND S > 0 THEN S = (S - 1)
370 IF (OY - Y) > 5 AND S < T-1 THEN S = (S + 1)
380 REM REDRAW THE CURRENT SELECTION
390 VTAB (3 + (S*2))
400 INVERSE
```

```
410 PRINT M$(S)
420 NORMAL
430 GOTO 210
440 REM PRINT THE SELECTION AND END
450 HOME : PRINT "OK, LET'S GO TO "; M$(S)
460 END
500 REM THESE ARE THE MENU CHOICES
510 REM WE USE 0 TO INDICATE END
520 DATA "CHICAGO", "NEW YORK"
530 DATA "PARIS", "LONDON"
540 DATA "BERLIN", "0"
```

Lines 20 through 90 initialize the variables used for the program. Variable T contains the total number of menu choices, which is 5. M$ is a string array for each menu item. It is dimensioned to hold T + 1 elements. S is the current selection. Its value should always be in the range of 1 to T. The menu elements are read into array M$ from DATA statements in a loop spanning lines 60 to 90.

Once M$ is prepared, lines 120 through 140 display the menu choices on the screen. Line 130 uses VTAB to control vertical spacing and make sure that each menu item is separated by a blank line.

Lines 160 and 170 activate the mouse, first by directing output to slot 4, where the mouse is located, and then sending the activation code to it. Line 180 returns output to the screen, where it will remain for the rest of the program.

Line 210 starts the main event loop of the program. The object is to compare the current mouse reading with the previous mouse value, and see whether the mouse was moved up or down. If the mouse was moved, the menu selection is changed appropriately. Finally, if the mouse button is pressed, then the current menu selection is made, and the program ends.

Variable OY stores the old (previous) mouse value. It is copied from variable Y, which is the current mouse value, on line 210. Lines 220 through 235 poll the mouse for its current values: position and button status. Line 225 is necessary due to the carriage return automatically generated by INPUT. Line 235 inverts the mouse Y position, the one used for highlighting menu entries. It makes sure that moving the mouse downward also moves the current selection downward.

Line 260 checks to see if the mouse button was pressed. If so, the program jumps to line 450 where the current selection is printed, and the program ends. Otherwise, line 280 checks to see if the mouse has moved more than five spaces from its old position. If not, program control returns to the top of the loop to read the mouse again. Otherwise, the menu selection may be changed.

If the mouse has been moved, control branches to line 310, to check if the current menu selection is the first or last option. If so, it is possible that the menu selection will not be updated, such as if it would move above the first option, for example.

Line 330 redraws the current menu selection in normal text, in preparation for a different menu item to be selected. Notice that the formula in VTAB is the same as on line 130. Lines 360 and 370 test for which direction the mouse was moved, and increment or decrement S as appropriate. Finally, lines 390 through 410 draw the new menu selection in highlighted style, while lines 420 and 430 return the text style back to normal and jump back to the top of the loop to poll the mouse again.

Programming the Game Controllers

The game controllers, either a single joystick or a pair of paddles, are easier to program than the mouse, and offer similar functionality. A single game paddle has an input range of 0 to 255 as well as a single push button. A joystick is really just two paddles put together, offering the same range in the X and Y coordinates, and it typically has two buttons.

On a paddle, rotating the knob from left to right increases the value. The knob happens to be a variable resistor, much like the volume knob on a stereo system. The Apple hardware allows for a maximum of four paddles, numbered 0 through 3. Their value is accessed using the PDL function in BASIC, like so:

```
10 PRINT PDL(0)
```

This line, when executed in immediate mode, will print the current value of paddle number zero. Try this short program and experiment with twisting the paddle knob or moving the joystick to see how it affects the values on screen:

```
10 PRINT PDL(0)
20 GOTO 10
```

Similarly, the second paddle is accessed using PDL(1). Most systems have just two paddles, 0 and 1. A joystick counts as two paddles, where the X coordinate is typically paddle 0, and Y is paddle 1.

There is a quirk that one should be aware of when reading two paddle inputs consecutively: the reading of the first paddle may affect the reading of the second paddle. The solution is to allow several program lines between paddle readings, or to place an empty FOR loop with about 10 iterations in between the PDL functions.

The paddle button is quite simple: it is either pressed, or it is not. There is no dedicated BASIC statement to get its value, so one must use PEEK instead. The Apple allows for three paddle buttons, and the locations are as follows: -16287, -16286, and -16285, for buttons 0, 1, and 2, respectively. If the button has been pressed, then the value returned from PEEK will be greater than 127.

Paddle-driven Menu

The following program demonstrates how to use the paddle for a menu system in a BASIC program. Turning the knob will highlight each menu choice in turn. The command used to highlight the text is explained later in this chapter. Pressing the button will select the currently highlighted item.

```
10 REM PADDLE MENU DEMO
20 REM FIRST MAKE THE MENU CHOICES
20 T = 5 : REM NUMBER OF CHOICES
30 DIM M$(T+1) : REM ARRAY OF CHOICES
40 S = 0 : REM CURRENT SELECTION
50 REM NOW READ IN DATA STATEMENTS
```

```
60 FOR I = 0 TO T
70 READ M$(I)
80 IF M$(I) = "0" THEN 100
90 NEXT I
100 HOME : PRINT "WHERE DO YOU WANT TO GO?"
110 REM DRAW ALL CHOICES
120 FOR I = 0 TO T - 1
130 VTAB (3 + (I*2)) : PRINT M$(I)
140 NEXT I
150 REM NOW WE BEGIN THE MAIN LOOP
160 REM CHECK FOR BUTTON PRESS
170 IF PEEK(-16287) > 127 THEN 400
180 REM NOW CHECK FOR PADDLE MOVEMENT
190 X = PDL(0)
200 IF X < 110 OR X > 140 THEN 230: REM MOVE
210 GOTO 170
220 REM CHECK IF WE ARE AT THE EDGE
230 IF (S = 0 AND X < 110) OR (S = T-1 AND X > 140)
THEN 170
240 REM NO, SO REDRAW THE OLD SELECTION
250 VTAB (3 + (S*2))
260 PRINT M$(S)
270 REM NOW GET MOVEMENT DIRECTION
280 IF X < 110 AND S > 0 THEN S = (S - 1)
290 IF X > 140 AND S < T-1 THEN S = (S + 1)
300 REM REDRAW THE CURRENT SELECTION
310 VTAB (3 + (S*2))
320 INVERSE
330 PRINT M$(S)
340 NORMAL
350 GOTO 170
400 REM PRINT THE SELECTION AND END
410 HOME : PRINT "OK, LET'S GO TO "; M$(S)
420 END
500 REM THESE ARE THE MENU CHOICES
510 REM WE USE 0 TO INDICATE END
520 DATA "CHICAGO", "NEW YORK"
```

```
530 DATA "PARIS", "LONDON"
540 DATA "BERLIN", "0"
```

This program has one small flaw: the first choice (Chicago) is not automatically highlighted when the menu is first printed on screen. See if you can come up with a simple solution to fix it.

User-friendly Input

As a programmer, you should have a good idea of what your program is looking for when it comes to input. A user, however, didn't write the program, and may not always know right away what is expected. Therefore, it is the programmer's job to make the program intuitive and easy to figure out. Such a program is deemed *user-friendly*. A user-friendly program informs the user as to exactly what input is expected, and gives a helpful error message when invalid data is received. On the other hand, a user-hostile program does not provide clear direction for input, and gives cryptic error messages (or none at all) when illegal input is met with.

Here is an example of a user-friendly program:

```
10 REM USER-FRIENDLY PROGRAM
20 INPUT "PLEASE ENTER A NUMBER FROM 5 TO 10: ";N
30 IF N < 5 THEN PRINT "THAT NUMBER WAS TOO SMALL; TRY
AGAIN" : GOTO 20
40 IF N > 10 THEN PRINT "THAT NUMBER WAS TOO LARGE;
TRY AGAIN" : GOTO 20
50 PRINT "THANK YOU."
```

The program first informs the user what to enter: a number from 5 to 10. It then checks the input to make sure that it is within range. If not, the program tells the user what was wrong, and prompts again. Otherwise, the program acknowledges the correct input. This is the type of program which users do like.

Now, here is the opposite example, a user-hostile program:

```
10 REM USER-HOSTILE PROGRAM
20 INPUT "TYPE THE INPUT ";N
```

```
30 IF N < 5 OR IF N > 10 THEN PRINT "WRONG INPUT!" :
END
50 END
```

This program is user-hostile because it does not define what "the input" exactly is. Furthermore, when incorrect input is given, the program gives an unhelpful error message and then terminates. If correct input is given, the program makes no acknowledgement of it. This is the type of program which users do not like.

Notice that the user-friendly program is longer and has more checks than the user-hostile program. This additional length is one of the tradeoffs in making an easy-to-use program: it's more work for the programmer to make the user experience smoother. You may have to compromise on some degree of friendliness, unless you don't mind all of the extra work.

Alternate Ways to Read the Keyboard

As it turns out, there is an alternative method of detecting key strokes. This method is to use PEEK(-16384). That location will contain the code for the key that was most recently typed. If the value returned from PEEK is 127 or less, then no key was pressed. Subtracting 128 from the value returned from PEEK will yield the ASCII code of the key that was pressed. One may then use CHR$ to translate the code back into its respective character.

If you use this method of reading the keyboard, then you should be sure to clear the keyboard with POKE -16368,0. If you fail to do this operation, then successive reads of the keyboard will always return the same value, even if a different key was pressed. Note that you only need to perform this operation if the value returned by PEEK(-16384) was greater than 127. Otherwise, no key was pressed, therefore there is no reason to clear the keyboard.

This simple example demonstrates the use of PEEK and POKE to read the keyboard:

```
10 X =  PEEK ( - 16384) : REM READ KEYBOARD
20  IF X < 128 THEN  GOTO 10 : REM WAS A KEY PRESSED?
30  PRINT "YOU TYPED: ";
```

```
40  PRINT  CHR$ (X - 128) : REM PRINT ASCII CHARACTER
50  POKE  - 16368,0 : REM CLEAR KEYBOARD
60  GOTO 10
```

Try removing line 50, then see what happens when you run this program again. As a second experiment, try changing the GOTO in line 20 to point to line 50 instead of 10. This will cause the keyboard to be cleared no matter if a key was pressed or not. See how it affects the program when run. Press CONTROL-C to stop the program.

The GET Statement

If INPUT doesn't offer enough control, but reading the keyboard directly using PEEK and POKE is overkill, then the GET statement is a middle-ground between the two methods. GET halts the program until the user types something, like INPUT, but it only accepts a single character at a time, like using PEEK(-16384).

GET accepts either a string or numeric variable, and expects the user's key press to match that variable's type. Here is an example using GET with a string variable:

```
10 GET A$
```

Since GET accepts only one character at a time, there is no need to press RETURN. In addition, GET does not show the character on the screen, nor does it display a prompt. This allows the programmer extra flexibility: the program can be made to display a prompt and the character with PRINT, or not.

GET is useful as a way to pause a program, such as to allow the user to read instructional text on the screen, or some other resultant output of your program. Using GET with a "throwaway" string variable will allow the user to press nearly any key, including the SPACE BAR or RETURN, to continue the program.

The following short program demonstrates the use of GET with a numeric variable:

```
10 PRINT "ENTER A NUMBER FROM 0 TO 9"
20 GET N
```

```
30 IF N < 0 OR N > 9 THEN GOTO 10
40 PRINT "YOU CHOSE: "; N
50 END
```

Try entering a letter or nondigit symbol. The Apple reports a ?SYNTAX ERROR and the program ends. GET is more commonly used with string variables than with numeric variables, and this is one reason why. (Recall that with INPUT, entering data of the wrong type will prompt the user to reenter, instead of halting the program.)

GET could also be used as the basis of an "enter anything" subroutine. The INPUT statement is limited in that it cannot accept some characters, such as the comma. GET knows no such limitations, as shown in this program example:

```
10 REM SIMPLE ENTER ANYTHING ROUTINE
20 I$ = "" : REM STRING TO HOLD INPUT
30 PRINT "TYPE ANYTHING, THEN PRESS RETURN"
40 GET C$
50 IF ASC(C$) = 13 THEN GOTO 100 : REM CHECK FOR RE-
TURN
60 I$ = I$ + C$ : REM ADD THIS CHARACTER TO INPUT
70 PRINT C$; : REM AND SHOW IT ON THE SCREEN
80 GOTO 40
100 PRINT : PRINT "YOU SAID: " : PRINT I$
110 END
```

This program will accept up to 255 characters (the maximum length of a string variable) until the user presses RETURN. The characters will be displayed as typed, and then the final string will be printed at the end.

Text Styles

Typical text output from the Apple is white on black (or if you have a IIgs, it may be white on blue). This is defined as the normal text style. However, if you followed the paddle-driven and mouse-driven menu programs, you discovered that there is another style: inverse. Inverse is exactly the complement of normal. It's black on white, great for highlighting some important text on the screen.

The final text style is flashing: alternating between normal and inverse styles approximately two to three times per second. This text style should be used most infrequently, and only for dire warnings to the user of a program; injudicious use may induce headaches!

Text styles have a few eccentricities on the earlier Apple models. For starters, lowercase text in 80-column mode will not flash on the IIe. When 40-column mode is active on the IIe, flashing lowercase letters will appear instead as nonsense characters.

Applesoft has built-in commands to set all three text styles, but Integer BASIC does not. Table 6-2 shows the relationship between each text style and the appropriate Applesoft and Integer BASIC command to activate it.

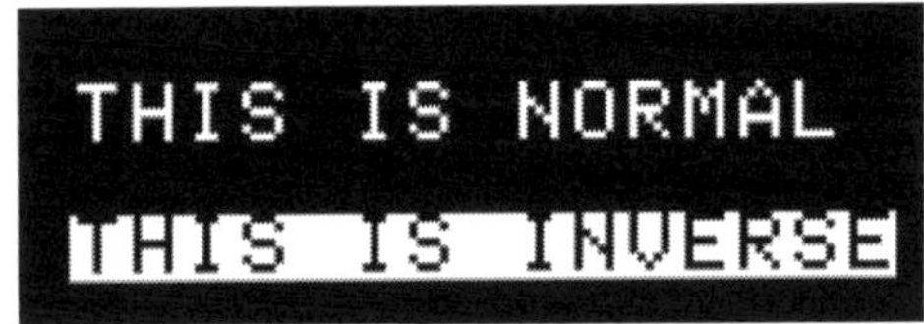

Figure 6-1. Normal and inverse text styles

Text style	Applesoft	Integer BASIC
Normal	NORMAL	POKE 50,255
Inverse	INVERSE	POKE 50,63
Flashing	FLASH	POKE 50,127

Table 6-2. Text styles and how to invoke them

The following program illustrates the use of all three text styles in Applesoft:

```
10 HOME : REM CLEAR TEXT SCREEN
20 NORMAL : REM SET NORMAL TEXT STYLE
30 PRINT : PRINT "THIS IS NORMAL"
40 PRINT
50 INVERSE : REM SET INVERSE TEXT STYLE
60 PRINT "THIS IS INVERSE"
70 PRINT
80 FLASH : REM SET FLASHING TEXT STYLE
90 PRINT "THIS IS FLASHING"
100 NORMAL : REM BACK TO NORMAL AGAIN
110 END
```

Try removing line 100, running the program again, and seeing what happens afterward.

Setting a text style affects all future text displayed on the screen, even if it's not from your program. If your program ends in inverse text mode, then you'll get an inverse prompt, listing your program will result in inverse text, etc. Also know that there is no single command to change the style of existing text on the screen. The text style commands only affect text displayed *after* the command is given.

Setting Text Speed

In Applesoft only, you may set the rate at which new characters appear on the screen with the SPEED command. Setting the speed doesn't just affect the output from PRINT statements, but rather all output is affected, including error messages and program listings.

Speed takes a numeric value from 0 to 255, where 0 is the slowest possible rate, and 255 is the fastest:

```
]SPEED = 140
```

The SPEED command could be useful with a peripheral device which cannot accept data at the full rate possible by the Apple.

For example, some older printers or modems may require a reduced data rate.

Control Characters

Control characters are so named because they don't appear on the screen, yet they control some behavior of the Apple, such as moving the cursor, setting 80 columns mode, or making the speaker beep. Control characters are not recopied when using the RIGHT ARROW key to pass the cursor over text on the screen.

Control characters are the first 32 ASCII codes, numbering from 0 to 31. CHR$ is typically used to produce a control character in a program, though control characters may also be typed from the keyboard using the CONTROL key. For example, CHR$(7) will beep the speaker, and CHR$(10) will move the cursor down. Control characters are unique in that unless the control character is designed to move the cursor (such as ASCII code 8), printing a control character will not affect the cursor, because the character is invisible and does not appear on the screen. Many control characters only have effect when the 80 column screen is active. Table 6-3 lists each ASCII control code and its effect.

Screen Formatting

One of the challenges and goals of a program is to present its results in a format that is most appropriate and easily understood by the user. Fortunately, Applesoft and Integer BASIC present the programmer with a number of tools and ways to accomplish this goal.

The best way to display one type of data may be inherently horizontal in layout, thus making a longer screen line length desirable. If your Apple II contains 80-column firmware, then BASIC can switch the video screen to allow longer lines. Other data may be more columnar in format, thus making it desirable to align the data elements by decimal point, or in columns. BASIC also has commands which can be used to achieve these formatting goals.

ASCII Code	Effect in 80 Columns	40 Columns
4*	Deactivate control characters except codes 5, 7, 8, 10, and 13	None
5*	Reactivate control characters	None
7	Beep the speaker	Same
8	Move cursor left	Same
10	Move cursor down	Same
11	Clear from cursor to end of text window	None
12	Clear text window	None
13	Carriage return	Same
14	Set normal video	None
15	Set inverse video	None
17	Set active-40 mode	None
18	Set active-80 mode	None
21	Deactivate 80-column card	None
22	Scroll down one line	None
23	Scroll up one line	None
24*	Deactivate Mousetext	None
25	Move cursor home	None
26	Clear cursor line	None
27*	Activate Mousetext	None
28	Move cursor right	None
29	Clear from cursor to end of display line	None

* Requires Enhanced IIe or newer Apple

Table 6-3. Text screen control characters

The main tool in screen formatting is the ability to exactly position and control the cursor. Printed output always appears at the next space indicated by the cursor, and the cursor advances for each character in turn. There are ways to change this behavior, and BASIC offers a number of them.

Screen Line Length

Every Apple computer can display screen lines of up to 40 characters, typically called a 40-column display. The Apple II, II Plus, and IIe require an 80-column adapter card to display more than 40 columns, but the IIc, IIc Plus, and IIgs have 80-columns capability built-in. When the Apple is first switched on, the display is set for 40 columns (as an exception, the IIgs can be configured through the Control Panel to start in 80 columns mode). To activate 80-column display, you must type PR#3 in immediate mode. This command also works as part of a program.

If you're using an original Apple II or the II Plus, your 80-columns card may need to be connected to the display screen. If you enter PR#3, and the cursor disappears but otherwise the screen appears frozen (nothing typed on the keyboard will appear), then you likely need to manually connect the display screen to the 80-column card.

If the Apple is booted in DOS 3.3 or ProDOS, then the special control character whose ASCII code is 4 must be prefixed to the PR#3 command when it is used in a program. This sequence must be a PRINT statement in your program:

```
]10 PRINT CHR$(4);"PR#3" : REM SWITCH TO 80-COLUMNS
```

This ASCII code lets the Apple know to interpret what follows in the PRINT statement as a command to the operating system. The operating system then knows to activate the 80-column adapter in the Apple. If your Apple cannot display 80 columns, then it will hang up, forcing you to press CONTROL-RESET. Similarly, if your 80-column card is installed in a slot other than 3, be sure to substitute the correct slot number in the PR# command. The Apple IIe, IIc, IIc Plus, and IIgs all have their 80-column adapter installed in slot 3. The Apple IIe is exceptional in that it also requires an 80-column card be installed in the Aux slot.

The last PRINT statement issued in your program must have been one that ended with a new line, otherwise the PR#3 command will not work. To ensure correct behavior, it is wise to put an empty PRINT statement before the one that issues the 80-columns command. Otherwise, it is possible to disconnect the operating system, or cause the Apple to hang.

It is also common practice to assign CHR$(4) to the variable D$, and use the variable instead. The letter D is used because ASCII code 4 is generated by pressing CONTROL-D on the keyboard. Here is the same program as above, but modified with the two enhancements:

```
]10 D$ = CHR$(4) : REM ASSIGN CONTROL-D
]20 PRINT : PRINT D$;"PR#3" : REM SWITCH TO 80-COLUMNS
```

Integer BASIC does not have the CHR$ function, therefore you must type CONTROL-D in between quotes, like so:

```
>10 D$ = "" : REM CONTROL-D BETWEEN QUOTES
```

Lastly, it is possible for the 80-column adapter in your Apple to be active, yet only display 40 columns. This is known as *active 40* mode. Alternatively, when the 80-column adapter is displaying the full 80 columns, as it does when first activated, it is called *active 80*. To switch to active 40 mode, print CHR$(17). To return to active 80, print CHR$(18). Finally, to disable the 80-column adapter entirely, returning the Apple to 40-column display, print a CHR$(21).

The cursor provides an indication whether the 80-column firmware is active or not. If the cursor is blinking, then the 80-column firmware is inactive, otherwise, if the cursor does not blink, then likely the screen is in 80-columns mode.

The Apple IIc 80/40 Switch

The Apple IIc has a switch located above the keyboard that can be set by the user to indicate to the program which screen line length is preferred. The switch merely sets a bit in memory; it is up to the programmer to take advantage of the switch. In other words, the 80/40 switch does not have implicit control over the Apple's 80-column firmware.

The status of the switch can be ascertained by examining memory location 49248 ($C060 in hexadecimal). If the value is greater than 127, the switch is down. Otherwise the switch is up. A program can check this memory location and make a decision whether to enable or disable the 80-column firmware.

The following Applesoft program reads the status of the 80/40 switch and activates 80-columns mode if the switch is down:

```
5 D$ = CHR$(4)
10 TEXT : HOME
15 PRINT CHR$(21) : REM DEACTIVATE 80-COLS FIRMWARE
20 PRINT "SET THE IIC 80/40 SWITCH, "
25 PRINT "THEN PRESS RETURN."
30 GET A$ : PRINT
40 SW = PEEK(49248) : REM READ SWITCH SETTING
50 IF SW > 127 THEN PRINT D$;"PR#3" : PRINT "80-
COLUMNS ACTIVE" : END
60 PRINT "40-COLUMNS STILL ACTIVE"
70 END
```

Controlling Vertical Spacing

Every time you press RETURN, a new line is created, and the cursor moves down to that new line. This is the same behavior from a PRINT statement. The reason for this behavior is that PRINT follows the output with ASCII code 13, a control character that forces the cursor to move down a line and back to the left margin of the text window. When the cursor reaches the bottom of the text window, there is no more room for it to go, so instead the topmost line is pushed off the screen. This program gives an example:

```
10 HOME
20 C$ = "A"
30 PRINT "FIRST LINE"
40 FOR X = 1 TO 23
50 PRINT C$
60 NEXT
70 GOTO 70
```

The program first clears the screen using HOME, then prints "FIRST LINE," followed by 23 lines of the letter "A." This makes 24 lines of text in total, which is the maximum that can be displayed on the screen. However, when you run the program, you'll see that the first line disappears! This is because each PRINT statement is followed by a carriage return, and when the last line reaches the bottom of the screen, the next carriage return pushes the first line off, even though there was nothing more to print: the last line is empty. Press CONTROL-C to stop this program.

Fortunately, appending a semicolon to the end of a PRINT statement suppresses the carriage return. However, even using a semicolon is not foolproof. Try this program:

```
10 HOME
20 C$ = "GINGER"
30 FOR X = 1 TO 133
40 PRINT C$;
50 NEXT
60 END
```

The Apple's screen will fill up with the word "GINGER," but look at the right margin: the Apple still managed to put in some carriage returns, even though the PRINT statement had a semicolon.

If the cursor reaches the right side of the text window, it will automatically move down to the next line, no matter if the PRINT statement contains a semicolon or not. Otherwise, text written past the edge of the screen would be lost. This behavior is inherent to the Apple; it cannot be changed in BASIC.

Aligning by Column

This simplest method to align text in a column can be employed by using a comma in a PRINT statement. The comma will align text with one of three tab stops on the screen.

```
]PRINT "A","B"
A               B

]PRINT "A","B","C"
A               B               C

]PRINT ,"A","B"
                A               B

]PRINT ,,"A"
                                A

]PRINT "A",,"B"
A                               B

]
```

Figure 6-2. Various tab stops using the comma

The first two tab stops are of the same size, and can contain up to 16 characters. The third tab stop has room for at most 8 printing positions. The first tab stop starts at the left edge of the text window and is always available. The second tab stop is only available if the nothing was printed at the end of the first tab stop, in the sixteenth space. The final tab stop may only be used if nothing was printed in positions 24 through 32 of the second tab field. Integer BASIC has five tab stops on a 40 column screen, each wide enough for 8 characters. They are located at columns 1, 9, 17, 25, and 33.

The following program uses commas to align two columns of unit conversions:

```
10 PRINT "KILOGRAMS","POUNDS"
20 FOR K = 1 TO 10 STEP 0.5
30 P = K * 2.2 : REM CONVERT TO POUNDS
40 PRINT K,P
50 NEXT K
60 END
```

Whenever Applesoft or Integer BASIC comes across a comma in a print statement, it moves the cursor to the next tab stop (using spaces) before printing the next value, thus causing the display to align in columns.

On older Apple models, the II, II Plus, and unenhanced IIe, using commas in PRINT statements does not work correctly in 80-columns mode. There will only be two tab stops, one at column 1, and the second at column 9 in Integer BASIC or column 17 in Applesoft. On the Enhanced IIe and all newer Apples, tabbing with commas behaves as expected on the 80-column screen.

```
]RUN
KILOGRAMS        POUNDS
1                2.2
1.5              3.3
2                4.4
2.5              5.5
3                6.6
3.5              7.7
4                8.8
4.5              9.9
5                11
5.5              12.1
6                13.2
6.5              14.3
7                15.4
7.5              16.5
8                17.6
8.5              18.7
9                19.8
9.5              20.9
10               22

]
```

Figure 6-3. Columnar output from using commas

Using TAB

The TAB command is used in conjunction with PRINT to move the cursor some number of spaces to the right. The argument given to TAB must be greater than the current cursor position, otherwise the cursor will not be affected; TAB does not move the cursor to the left. If the cursor ends up past the line limit, then it is wrapped around down to the next line and appears at the left.

TAB is an alternative to using the comma in a PRINT statement: TAB allows the programmer to set the columns in which output is to be aligned, whereas the comma does not. TAB numbers the screen columns from 1 to 40, where 1 is the leftmost column, and 40 is the right margin.

```
]PRINT TAB(20);"MOVE ON OVER"
```

TAB works on an 80-column screen, allowing columns 41 to 80 to be specified, but its behavior is slightly unpredictable on the original Apple II, II Plus, and unenhanced IIe.

The following program is the same as shown earlier, except that it is modified to use TAB instead of commas in PRINT statements:

```
10 PRINT TAB(6); "KILOGRAMS";TAB(18);"POUNDS"
20 FOR K = 1 TO 10 STEP 0.5
30 PRINT TAB(8);K;
40 P = K * 2.2 : REM CONVERT TO POUNDS
50 PRINT TAB(20);P
60 NEXT K
70 END
```

Note that the trailing semicolon on line 30 is used to suppress a new line from being printed on the screen.

In Applesoft, TAB is a function which *must* be used in a PRINT statement. Integer BASIC also has TAB, but it is a statement that moves the cursor to an absolute position on the line; it is not restricted to PRINT.

```
]RUN
     KILOGRAMS    POUNDS
       1            2.2
       1.5          3.3
       2            4.4
       2.5          5.5
       3            6.6
       3.5          7.7
       4            8.8
       4.5          9.9
       5            11
       5.5          12.1
       6            13.2
       6.5          14.3
       7            15.4
       7.5          16.5
       8            17.6
       8.5          18.7
       9            19.8
       9.5          20.9
       10           22

]
```

Figure 6-4. Columnar output with the TAB function

Aligning by Decimal Point

Often it improves readability by aligning a column of numbers by decimal point. BASIC provides no built-in functionality for such alignment, but it is still possible to achieve. It will first be necessary to find the length of each number when printed on the screen. The LEN function will work, but only on strings. Therefore, the STR$ function will be used to convert the decimal number to a string. Finally, the location of the decimal point must be determined by finding the length of the integer portion of the number as provided by the Applesoft INT function.

Remember that the number's length that it takes up on the screen will also include the decimal point and any numbers following it, so do plan for the longest-possible number that your program could display.

The following program is the same mass-to-force convertor as seen previously, but modified to align both columns by decimal point:

```
10 PRINT TAB(6); "KILOGRAMS";TAB(22);"POUNDS"
20 FOR K = 1 TO 10 STEP 0.5
30 LN = LEN(STR$(INT(K))) : REM KILOS LENGTH
35 IF K < 1 THEN LN = 0
40 PRINT TAB(6); SPC(5 - LN + 1);K;
50 P = K * 2.2 : REM CONVERT TO POUNDS
60 LN = LEN(STR$(INT(P))) : REM POUNDS LENGTH
65 IF P < 1 THEN LN = 0
70 PRINT TAB(20);SPC(5 - LN + 1);P
80 NEXT K
90 END
```

Lines 30-40, and 60-70 contain the critical code needed for alignment by decimal point. Line 30 contains the code that implements the logic discussed a few paragraphs ago: it converts the kilograms value to an integer, then converts the integer to a string, then computes the length of that string in variable LN. Line 35 handles the case where a value is less than 1, and therefore has no number in front of the decimal point. It makes sure that there is an extra space added to make up for the missing zero. The next line uses SPC to right-align the integer portion of the number by taking the total width designated for the column, 5, subtracting LN, and adding 1. The addition of 1 is to guarantee that a minimum of one space is inserted, in case the number's length is also 5.

Right-aligned Text

Ordinarily, text on the screen is left-aligned. However, with a bit of thought, and use of some Applesoft functions, it is simple to right-align text from a PRINT statement.

```
]RUN
      KILOGRAMS          POUNDS
           1               2.2
           1.5             3.3
           2               4.4
           2.5             5.5
           3               6.6
           3.5             7.7
           4               8.8
           4.5             9.9
           5              11
           5.5            12.1
           6              13.2
           6.5            14.3
           7              15.4
           7.5            16.5
           8              17.6
           8.5            18.7
           9              19.8
           9.5            20.9
          10              22

]
```

Figure 6-5. Decimal-aligned output

The key is by clever use of the SPC and LEN functions. SPC, which is short for "space," prints a number of spaces given as its argument. LEN, short for "length," returns the length of its given string argument.

To align text to the right, one needs to display a number of spaces before the text itself. This number of spaces should be equal to the total width of the screen (either 40 or 80 columns) minus the length of the text to be printed. The following program contains a string array with 5 elements. Line 90 computes the number of spaces needed to right-align the text on a 40-column display screen:

```
10 DIM A$(5)
20 A$(0) = "HERE IS SOME TEXT."
30 A$(1) = "AND MORE."
40 A$(2) = "THIS IS A LONGER LINE..."
50 A$(3) = "SHORT."
60 A$(4) = "DONE :-)"
70 FOR X = 0 TO 4
80 REM COMPUTE SPACING AMOUNT
90 PRINT  SPC( 40 -  LEN (A$(X)));A$(X)
100 NEXT X
```

Changing the Text Window

When you first switch on the Apple II and begin typing, all output appears in a window whose size is the same as the display screen. A window can be thought of as the frame in which text appears, and forms the borders around it.

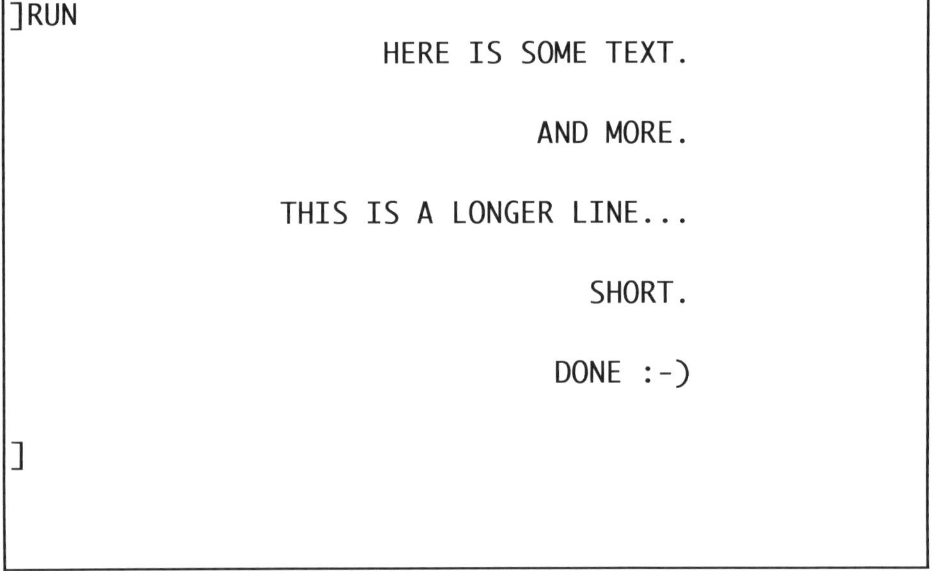

Figure 6-6. Right-aligned text

Dimension	Address	Range
Left Margin	32	0-39 or 0-79
Width	33	1-40 or 1-80
Top Margin	34	0-24
Bottom Margin	35	0-24

Table 6-4. Text window dimensions

Four memory locations in the Apple control the four corners and, therefore, dimensions of the text window. These locations are 32, 33, 34, and 35 ($20, $21, $22, and $23 in hex) representing the left edge, width, top edge, and bottom edge, respectively. When the Apple is first turned on, or if the TEXT command is given, these values are initialized to take up the entire screen. Left margin is set to 0, width to 40, top margin to 0, and bottom margin to 24.

Use PEEK to read the value of any of the window dimensions, and POKE to set a new value. Table 6-4 shows the acceptable range for each dimension. The ranges for left margin and width depend on whether the screen is in 40 or 80-columns mode. Attempting to POKE a value outside of a range will likely crash the Apple or destroy part of your program.

Second, it is imperative that the bottom and top margin not cross. In other words, the top margin should not be set below the bottom margin, nor should the bottom margin be set above the top margin. When setting the top and bottom margins, a value of 0 indicates the topmost line of the screen, and 24 indicates the bottom line.

For example, entering:

```
]POKE 35,20 : REM SET BOTTOM DIMENSION

]CALL -936 : REM HOME THE CURSOR
```

will move the bottom margin up four lines and ensure that the cursor is within the new window dimensions.

When changing the window dimensions, the cursor is not automatically relocated within them. If the cursor is outside of the new dimensions, you should reposition it using HOME or the appropriate combination of HTAB and VTAB.

Any text outside of the window will be preserved, impervious to the effects of PRINT, HOME, CALL -936, and ESCAPE-@.

Controlling the Cursor

In many programs, the programmer is free to let the cursor take care of itself. The cursor continues to mark the placement of the next character, and will advance forward and to the next line as necessary. However, with a few simple commands, control of the cursor may be assumed, allowing varied screen output, such as overwriting, centered text, and columns. These commands, HTAB and VTAB, offer much more flexibility than using semicolons, commas, or the TAB function in PRINT statements.

HTAB is used to move the cursor horizontally in Applesoft. In Integer BASIC, this command is called TAB, though it has the same behavior. Likewise, VTAB is used to move the cursor vertically. Integer BASIC also has the VTAB command. These two commands allow the programmer to position the cursor at any place on the screen. VTAB takes a row number, and HTAB (or TAB in Integer BASIC) requires a column number. Both values specify an absolute position, starting from the top-left corner of the screen.

Here is an Applesoft program that makes use of HTAB and VTAB to print a short message on the screen:

```
10 HOME
20 INPUT "ROW? ";ROW
30 INPUT "COLUMN? ";COL
40 VTAB ROW : HTAB COL
50 PRINT "OVER HERE!"
60 END
```

VTAB works with row numbers 1 to 24, where 1 is the topmost line of the screen, and 24 is the very bottom. Attempting to specify a number outside of this range will yield an ?ILLEGAL QUANTITY error.

The effects of HTAB differ depending on two factors: what model of Apple you're using, and whether nor not the 80-column card is active. On all models of Apple, when the screen is in 40 columns mode, HTAB will accept a single numeric parameter from 1 to 40, where 1 is the leftmost column, and 40 the rightmost. Attempting to use a number less than 1 will result in an error, but giving a number greater than 40 will cause the cursor to wrap around to the next line. For example, HTAB 43 will leave the cursor in the third column of the next line.

When HTAB is used in 80-column mode, the model of Apple determines its effects. On an original Apple II, the II Plus, and standard IIe, HTAB cannot be used to position the cursor in columns 41 to 80 of the screen. On the Enhanced IIe and later models, this limitation was fixed. On the earlier models, you must POKE location 36 with the desired column number, from 0 to 79, to overcome the limitation of HTAB. This method will work on any model of Apple.

Here is a modified version of the previous program that will work with the 80-column screen on any model of Apple, using the POKE technique:

```
10 PRINT CHR$(4);"PR#3" : REM ACTIVATE 80-COLS
20 HOME
30 INPUT "ROW? ";ROW
40 INPUT "COLUMN? ";COL
50 VTAB ROW : POKE 36, COL - 1
60 PRINT "OVER HERE!"
70 END
```

Be careful not to POKE a value greater than the current screen width (either 40 or 80) into location 36. If you do, it could cause your program to crash. Note that when using the POKE method, the leftmost column is 0 and rightmost is 79, instead of 1 to 80.

As a final method of moving the cursor, Applesoft programs may use the CHR$ function to print the cursor movement ASCII characters, the same as generated by pressing the LEFT ARROW or DOWN ARROW on the keyboard. Recall that these characters do not affect the other characters that they move across. Use CHR$(8) to backspace the cursor and CHR$(10) to move it down one line.

Finding the Cursor Position

The cursor may move all around the screen, but the Apple always knows its exact location. The POS function in Applesoft returns the cursor's horizontal position as it moves from left to right across the current screen line. Since POS is a function, it requires a single numeric operand, but that operand is not used (though it must be legal). Unlike the other screen commands such as HTAB and TAB, POS numbers the columns from 0 to 39 instead of 1 to 40. Column 0 is the left edge of the screen, and 39 is the right side. Here is a program that shows POS in use:

```
5 REM PRINT A LINE
10 PRINT "TU ES PETRUS";
20 REM NOW FIND THE CURSOR POSITION
30 COLUMN = POS(0) + 1
40 PRINT : PRINT "CURSOR IS AT COLUMN "; COLUMN
50 END
```

POS is used on line 30, and 1 is added to its result to start the column numbering at the more familiar 1 (instead of 0). Running the program will inform the user that the cursor is at position 13, the space right after the "S" in "PETRUS."

POS is usually used in conjunction with HTAB, such as if the programmer wishes to overwrite existing text on a screen line by backing up the cursor.

Alternatively, one may use PEEK(36) to find the current cursor column. Likewise, to find the current cursor row, use PEEK(37). It will return a number between 0 and 23, representing top and bottom of the screen, respectively.

Using MouseText

MouseText is an alternate character set that made its debut in 1984 with the Apple IIc. The Enhanced IIe, the IIc Plus, and IIgs also have MouseText. MouseText resides in the video ROM of these newer Apples and serves as a means of creating a Graphical User Interface (GUI) on the text screen, specifically for use with the mouse. The only three models which cannot use MouseText are the original II, II Plus, and unenhanced IIe.

The MouseText set consists of 33 graphical characters that can be used in a variety of ways. Two of these characters, F and G, were changed for the IIgs. On all other models of Apple, these two characters form a running man; on the IIgs, they are an inverse carriage return symbol, and striped title bar, respectively. On older Apples that don't have MouseText, all of these characters will look like various capital letters and punctuation marks.

To activate MouseText, follow these steps:

- First, ensure that the 80-column display is active.
- Use INVERSE to set inverse display style.
- Use CHR$(27) or an equivalent to print ASCII code 27.

Finally, you may print the character codes which correspond to the desired MouseText graphics, listed in Table 6-5.

Some MouseText characters can be combined to produce a composite graphic:

- F and G to make a running man
- V and W to make a gray line
- X and Y to make a folder
- Z and ^ to make a box with a dot.

When MouseText is active, all screen output is affected, even keys that you type during program input. To return to inverse style, use PRINT CHR$(24) to issue the control character whose ASCII code is 24. This disables MouseText and allows inverse uppercase letters and other symbols to be displayed. To return to the usual text style, type NORMAL.

Mousetext Character	Normal Character	Mousetext Character	Normal Character
	@		P
	A		Q
	B		R
	C		S
	D		T
	E		U
	F*		V
	G*		W
	H		X
	I		Y
	J		Z
	K		[
	L		\
	M		]
	N		^
	O		_

* Graphic is changed on the Apple IIgs

Table 6-5. MouseText graphics characters

The following two Applesoft lines will activate MouseText, draw the two characters that represent a folder, and return to normal:

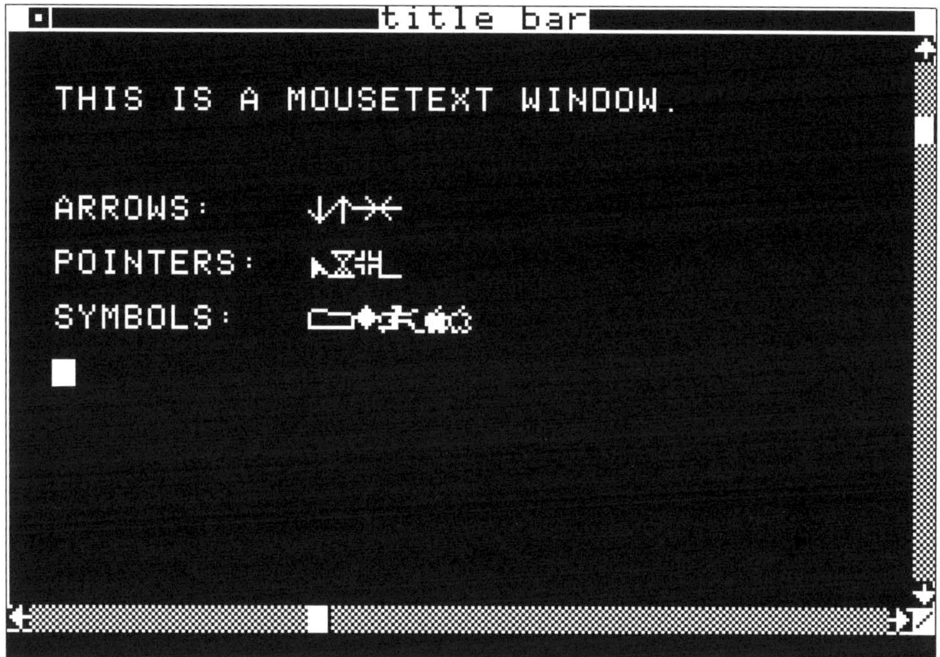

Figure 6-7. MouseText Sampler program

```
]PR#3 : REM SWITCH TO 80-COLUMNS
]INVERSE : PRINT CHR$(27);"XY";CHR$(24) : NORMAL
```

If you were to then type PR#0, you would see that the folder graphic had returned to a flashing X and Y.

MouseText Sampler

The following Applesoft program gives a sample of what MouseText can be used to create. Figure 6-7 shows what it would display on the screen.

```
10 REM MOUSETEXT SAMPLER
20 REM FOR APPLE IIC, IIC PLUS,
30 REM ENHANCED IIE, AND IIGS

40 PRINT CHR$(4);"PR#3" : REM ACTIVATE 80-COLUMNS CARD
50 AM$ = CHR$(27) : REM ACTIVATE MOUSETEXT
60 PRINT CHR$(17) : REM CHANGE TO ACTIVE-40
```

```
70 AN$ = CHR$(24) : REM ACTIVATE NORMAL TEXT

100 REM DRAW TITLE BAR
110 INVERSE : PRINT AM$
120 HTAB 1 : VTAB 1
130 FOR I = 1 TO 40
140 PRINT "\";
150 NEXT I
160 HTAB 1 : VTAB 1
170 PRINT AN$;" ";AM$;"^";
180 HTAB 17
190 PRINT AN$;"title bar";
200 HTAB 40
210 PRINT " ";

300 REM DRAW VERTICAL SCROLL BAR
310 INVERSE : PRINT AM$;
320 FOR I = 3 TO 22
330 HTAB 40 : VTAB I
340 PRINT "W";
350 NEXT I
360 HTAB 40 : VTAB 2
370 PRINT "R";
380 HTAB 40 : VTAB 5
390 PRINT "N";
400 HTAB 40 : VTAB 22
410 PRINT "Q";

500 REM DRAW HORIZONTAL SCROLL BAR
510 HTAB 2 : VTAB 23
520 FOR I = 2 TO 19
530 PRINT "VW";
540 NEXT I
550 PRINT "VP/";
560 VTAB 23 : HTAB 14
570 PRINT "N";
580 VTAB 23 : HTAB 1
```

```
590 PRINT "O";

600 REM DRAW LEFT EDGE OF WINDOW
610 FOR I = 2 TO 22
620 HTAB 1 : VTAB I
630 PRINT "_";
640 NEXT I

700 REM PRINT VARIOUS LABELS
710 NORMAL : PRINT AN$;
720 VTAB 4 : HTAB 3
730 PRINT "THIS IS A MOUSETEXT WINDOW.";
740 VTAB 8 : HTAB 3
750 PRINT "ARROWS:";
760 VTAB 10 : HTAB 3
770 PRINT "POINTERS:";
780 VTAB 12 : HTAB 3
790 PRINT "SYMBOLS:";

800 REM DRAW ARROWS
810 INVERSE : PRINT AM$;
820 VTAB 8 : HTAB 14
830 PRINT "JKUH";
840 VTAB 10 : HTAB 14
850 PRINT "BC]T";
860 VTAB 12 : HTAB 14
870 PRINT "XY[FG@A";
880 NORMAL
890 PRINT AN$;

900 VTAB 14 : HTAB 3
910 GET A$
920 END
```

Entering Phone Numbers

How exactly to handle phone numbers is a problem that many programmers eventually have to deal with. One of the issues is that countries tend to each have their own preferred format, and some people from the same country will even use differing formats. Of course, the simplest solution is to do nothing and just accept whatever the user enters and trust that it is a valid number. Another solution is to pick a format and enforce it. This program will choose the latter option.

In this example program, the American 10-digit format (222-555-1212) will be used, but the format is stored as a string and can easily be edited to whatever is appropriate for your locality. The format string works as a template, where "X" represents a digit, and all other characters are displayed "as-is." Thus, the format string:

(XXX) - XXX - XXXX

Would allow for the following number:

(222) - 555 - 1212

A cursor marks where the next digit will appear, and is advanced upon entry of each digit. The LEFT and RIGHT ARROW keys serve to move the cursor back or forward to correct a typing mistake. When finished entering the number, the user presses RETURN, and the entire phone number is passed as an array. Here is the program:

```
10 REM PROGRAM TO ENTER PHONE NUMBERS
20 HOME
30 PRINT "PLEASE ENTER A PHONE NUMBER:"
40 GOSUB 15000 : REM PHONE NUMBER INPUT ROUTINE
50 PRINT : PRINT "YOU ENTERED: "
60 GOSUB 14000 : REM PHONE NUMBER PRINT ROUTINE
100 END

14000 REM SUBROUTINE TO OUTPUT PHONE NUMBER
```

```
14020 REM FORMAT STRING
14030 REM X'S ARE SPACES FOR A NUMBER, ALL OTHER CHAR-
ACTERS
14040 REM WILL BE SHOWN "AS-IS"
14050 F$ = "(XXX) - XXX - XXXX"
14060 DC = 0
14070 FOR I = 1 TO LEN(F$)
14080 C$ = MID$(F$,I,1)
14090 IF C$ = "X" THEN DC = DC + 1 : PRINT PN(DC);
14100 IF C$ <> "X" THEN PRINT C$; : REM PRINT ALL
OTHER CHARS
14110 NEXT I
14120 RETURN

15000 REM SUBROUTINE TO ENTER PHONE NUMBER
15020 REM FORMAT STRING
15030 REM X'S ARE SPACES FOR A NUMBER, ALL OTHER CHAR-
ACTERS
15040 REM WILL BE SHOWN "AS-IS"
15050 F$ = "(XXX) - XXX - XXXX"
15060 DC = 0 : REM DIGIT COUNT
15070 BL$ = CHR$(95) : REM CHARACTER TO REPRESENT A
BLANK
15080 DIM PS(LEN(F$) + 1) : REM ARRAY OF DIGIT POSI-
TIONS
15090 PO = 1 : REM CURRENT CURSOR POSITION

15100 REM FIRST WE NEED TO GET DIGIT COUNT
15105 REM AND WE CAN ALSO OUTPUT THE FORMAT
15110 FOR I = 1 TO LEN(F$)
15120 C$ = MID$(F$,I,1)
15125 REM CHECK IF THIS CHARACTER IS AN X
15130 IF C$ = "X" THEN DC = DC + 1 : PS(DC) = I :
PRINT BL$;
15140 IF C$ <> "X" THEN PRINT C$; : REM PRINT ALL
OTHER CHARS
15150 NEXT I
```

```
15160 PS(DC + 1) = LEN(F$) + 1 : REM ADD ONE MORE
SPACE AT THE END

15200 REM CREATE THE PHONE NUMBER ARRAY
15210 DIM PN(DC)
15220 FOR I = 1 TO DC
15230 PN(I) = -1 : REM MAKE ALL ELEMENTS -1
15240 NEXT I
15250 REM MOVE CURSOR TO FIRST DIGIT POSITION
15260 GOTO 15680

15300 REM START MAIN LOOP
15310 C = PEEK(-16384) : REM READ KEYBOARD
15320 IF C < 128 THEN 15310 : CHECK FOR KEY PRESS
15330 POKE -16368,0 : REM RESET KEYBOARD STROBE
15335 REM KEY MUST HAVE BEEN A DIGIT, CR, OR L/R ARROW
15340 C = C - 128
15350 IF (C < 48 OR C > 57) AND C <> 8 AND C <> 13 AND
C <> 21 THEN CALL -198 : GOTO 15310
15360 REM TEST FOR A RETURN
15370 IF C = 13 THEN GOTO 15510
15380 REM TEST FOR LEFT OR RIGHT ARROW
15390 IF C = 8 OR C = 21 THEN GOTO 15610

15395 REM HANDLE INPUT OF A DIGIT
15400 C = C - 48 : REM CONVERT ASCII TO DIGIT
15410 IF PO <= DC THEN PN(PO) = C : REM STORE DIGIT
15420 VTAB(PEEK(37)+1) : HTAB(PS(PO)) : PRINT C;
15430 REM ADVANCE CURSOR POSITION IF NOT AT END
15440 IF PO < DC THEN PO = PO + 1 : GOTO 15690
15445 REM ALL DIGITS ENTERED
15450 VTAB(PEEK(37)+1) : HTAB(PS(PO)) : PRINT PN(PO);
15460 PO = PO + 1 : GOTO 15690

15500 REM CHECK FOR ALL DIGITS ENTERED
15510 FOR I = 1 TO DC
15520 IF PN(I) = -1 THEN CALL -198 : GOTO 15310
```

```
15530 NEXT I
15540 RETURN

15600 REM GO BACK OR FORWARD
15610 IF C = 8 AND PO <= 1 THEN CALL -198 : GOTO 15310
15620 IF C = 21 AND PO > DC THEN CALL -198 : GOTO
15310
15625 REM REPLACE MISSING DIGIT
15630 VTAB(PEEK(37)+1) : HTAB(PS(PO))
15640 IF PO > DC THEN PRINT " "; : GOTO 15670
15650 IF PN(PO) = -1 THEN PRINT BL$; : GOTO 15670
15660 PRINT PN(PO);
15670 IF C = 8 THEN PO = PO - 1 : GOTO 15690
15680 IF C = 21 THEN PO = PO + 1
15685 REM DRAW CURSOR AT NEW POSITION
15690 VTAB(PEEK(37)+1) : HTAB(PS(PO)) : FLASH : PRINT
" "; : NORMAL
15700 GOTO 15310
```

This program consists of three parts: a beginning section that calls two subroutines: one to enter a phone number, and the second to display the number. The remaining two parts are those subroutines.

The first subroutine takes a phone number as an array of digits, in variable PN, and displays it according to the format described in F$. Any "X" characters in F$ are replaced with the corresponding digit from PN, and all other characters are shown without change. The subroutine then places a cursor at the first space for a digit and waits for user input. Numeric input will advance the cursor, and the LEFT and RIGHT ARROW keys can be used to move the cursor. Finally, pressing RETURN will submit the entered phone number.

The subroutine starts work on lines 15050 to 15090 by initializing and setting a few variables: format, digit count, blank, position, and current position. The position array is dimensioned to be the length of format plus 1. This allows the cursor to move one space after the format string, as well as allowing for the case where all characters in the format string represent an input digit.

Variable	Full Name	Purpose	Lines Used
BL$	Blank	Character to represent a blank where a digit may be entered.	15070, 15650
C	Input Character	Hold character read from keyboard.	15310, 15320, 15340, 15350, 15370, 15390, 15400, 15410, 15420, 15610, 15620,15670, 15680
C$	String Character	Hold individual character from F$.	15120, 15130, 15140
DC	Digit Count	Store maximum digits in phone number.	15060, 15130, 15160, 15210, 15220, 15410, 15440, 15510, 15620, 15640
F$	Format	Format of phone number.	15050, 15080, 15110, 15120, 15160
PN	Phone Number	Store digits of phone number.	15210, 15230, 15410, 15520, 15650, 15660
PO	Current Position	Hold current cursor position.	15090, 15410, 15420, 15440, 15450, 15460, 15630, 15640, 15650, 15660, 25670, 15680, 15690
PS	Positions	Hold positions of digits.	15080, 15130, 15160, 15420, 15450, 15630, 15690

Table 6-6. Variables used in phone input subroutine

The next step is to count how many digits are expected to make up the phone number, and where they are located in the format string. This is done by a loop that starts at line 15110. The loop iterates over each character in F$, and line 15120 extracts each character into C$ for analysis. If C$ is an "X," then the digit count DC is incremented, the digit's location is stored in array PS, and BL$ is printed to indicate a blank. If C$ is not an "X," then it is merely printed. After the loop is finished, at line 15160, one extra space for the cursor is added to PS, set to be the space just after the format string. This is to prevent the cursor from potentially obscuring the last digit in the phone number by allowing the cursor to move to the right.

Next, the phone number array is initialized by first dimensioning array PN to hold DC elements, and then by setting each array element to -1 to indicate that no digit has yet been entered. Line 15260 moves the cursor to the first digit position, and the main loop starts.

The subroutine's main loop checks the keyboard for a key press, then decides what to do. Line 15310 checks the keyboard and assigns the result to variable C. If C is greater than 127, then a key has been pressed. If so, line 15330 resets the keyboard strobe, and line 15340 subtracts 128 from C to get the ASCII code. Line 15350 checks if the code was any of the following: the digits 0 to 9, the LEFT ARROW key, the RETURN key, or the RIGHT ARROW key. If the ASCII code C was not any of these, then the Apple speaker is beeped, and the subroutine checks the keyboard again. Lines 15370 and 15390 make the appropriate branches for the RETURN, LEFT, and RIGHT ARROW keys.

If C is a digit, then execution passes on to line 15400 where C is converted from an ASCII code into an ordinary digit. This is done by subtracting 48 from C, knowing that 48 is the code for 0, 49 indicates 1, 50 means 2, and so on. The current cursor position is verified to make sure that it is less than the digit count. If it were greater than DC, then that would mean that an extra digit could get stored after the end of the format string or phone number array. Otherwise, the digit is stored in the appropriate element number of array PN, based on the current cursor position. The digit is then printed in the correct screen column and row by the logic on line 15420. First, the cursor is moved to the correct row by PEEKing at memory location 37 which contains the current cursor row number. Then the cursor is moved horizontally to the correct screen column by getting the value in PS that corresponds to the current cursor position in the phone number. Finally, the digit is printed to the screen.

If this digit entered was not the last on the line, then position PO is incremented, and the subroutine jumps to line 15690 to draw the cursor in its next position. Otherwise, the last digit is printed, and the cursor is advanced to the space right after the end of the format string.

Lines 15510 through 15540 handle a press of the RETURN key when the user is finished typing the phone number. Every element of array PN is checked to make sure that it does not contain a -1. If it does, then not all of the digits have been entered, therefore the Apple's speaker is beeped, and control returns to the start of the main loop. Otherwise, the subroutine returns back to the calling program with the phone number stored in array PN.

Cursor movement is managed by lines 15610 to 15700. The cursor is restricted to moving only to places where a digit may be entered, or the space right after the end of the format string. These locations are stored in PS, which associates a position number with a screen column number. Lines 15610 and 15620 first check to make sure that the cursor won't end up before the first digit or after the final position.

When the cursor moves, the character that it was covering must be replaced. This character is either a blank from BL$, a space, or a digit. Line 15630 moves the printing cursor to the correct screen row and column, and lines 15640 through 15660 determine what character will be printed there. If the cursor position is past the end of the format string, as tested for on line 15640, then a space is printed. If the digit in the phone number for that position had not been entered, then BL$ is printed. Otherwise, the phone digit for that position is printed.

Line 15670 decrements PO if the LEFT ARROW key was pressed, and line 15680 increments PO if the RIGHT ARROW was pressed. Finally, line 15690 prints the cursor, a flashing space, at the correct position, and the subroutine jumps back to read the keyboard again.

This subroutine has room for two possible improvements. The first would be to change the cursor behavior. As it stands, if the cursor is on a space where a digit has already been entered, the digit is obscured. Instead, the subroutine should be changed to show a flashing version of the existing digit as the cursor, or a flashing space if there is no digit yet entered. The second improvement would be to allow for multiple format strings based on a selected country. For example, a variable CO could hold a number representing a country, and F$ would be changed to reflect the telephone number format of that country.

Chapter 7 : The Disk System

A *disk* is the square plastic object which has inside of it a round, magnetic recording surface. Disks are inserted into a *disk drive*, a mechanism which can access the data stored on a disk. Data stored on a disk are organized into logical collections known as *files*. Finally, a system program known as the *Disk Operating System* (DOS) manages the task of storing and retrieving your data.

There are two major Disk Operating Systems used on the Apple: DOS 3.3 and ProDOS. This chapter will cover both versions and will explain how to use a disk to save and load programs and files, as well as get a listing of all files on a disk, and modify, rename, and delete those files. For the sake of brevity, the term DOS will be used when explaining functions that apply to both DOS 3.3 and ProDOS.

Furthermore, this chapter will explain how to use sequential and random-access text files with your BASIC programs to quickly store and retrieve data.

Basics of the Disk

Disk storage is called "random-access" because it is possible for the computer to jump to any section of the disk and retrieve the data stored there. This is in opposition to cassette tape storage, which is known as "sequential-access." It is up to you, Ô user, to manually advance or rewind the tape to the correct starting position.

Disks also offer another advantage to cassette tape storage, and that is the concept of the *file*. A file is a single collection of data: a program, a letter, a picture, or any other type of data consumed or produced on the Apple. Files are stored and retrieved using a *filename*. Filenames are the label by which you store your data.

Taking Care of Your Disks

The disks that you use with your Apple can be damaged and rendered unusable if you do not take good care of them. 5.25" disks are especially susceptible. Although they are commonly referred to as floppy disks, actually bending them will damage them. Do not touch the plastic recording surface that is visible through the oval cutout. Do not leave disks in extreme heat or cold. Keep all disks away from magnetic fields, such as those present in telephones and large CRT displays. When labeling a 5.25" disk, use only a felt-tip pen, and do not press too hard. It is best to write the label separately, then attach it to the disk.

3.5" disks are sturdier, but still require care. They have a metal shutter to protect the recording surface, and you should not open it. Keep them away from heat, cold, and magnets. It is safe to use any type of pen to label 3.5" disks, since the hard plastic shell protects the recording surface.

Disks which have been well-kept can last for over two decades.

The IIgs System

If you have an Apple IIgs-specific disk, please also read Chapter 12, which contains specialized coverage of the Apple IIgs operating system. This chapter covers only the older disk operating systems which work on all other models of Apple, including the IIgs.

DOS and ProDOS Basics

Though DOS and ProDOS share many features, they also have a few major differences. In general, though, both disk operating systems allow you to store both programs and data files on a disk using a filename. This name is a way for you to easily identify what sort of content a file contains.

The two operating systems share a similar set of commands for listing the contents of a disk, known as the catalog, as well as opening, saving, renaming, and deleting files. These commands can be incorporated into your BASIC program, or they can be used in immediate execution mode, outside of a BASIC program. In many ways, DOS and ProDOS act as extensions to BASIC.

One main difference between the two systems is that DOS 3.3 only works on 5.25" disks, whereas ProDOS may be used with any disk system for the Apple: 3.5", 5.25", and hard disks.

In this chapter, the term *DOS* will be used to refer to both DOS 3.3 and ProDOS, whereas *DOS 3.3* is used explicitly to mean DOS 3.3, and not ProDOS.

ProDOS Compatibility

Whereas every Apple can run DOS 3.3, not all versions of ProDOS are compatible with all models of Apple. If you have an Enhanced Apple IIe, IIc, IIc Plus, or IIgs, then you can skip this part. Your Apple can run all versions of ProDOS.

If you have an Apple II or II Plus without a Language Card, then you can only run the earliest versions of ProDOS, 1.0 and 1.0.1, and you cannot use the ProDOS BASIC interpreter. All later versions of ProDOS require 64 kilobytes of RAM provided by the Language Card (remember that the Language Card is built-in to the Apple IIe, IIc, IIc Plus, and IIgs).

Starting with ProDOS 2.0, the 6502 processor is no longer supported. This means that the original Apple II, II Plus, and unenhanced IIe cannot use the newest versions of ProDOS unless they have received a CPU upgrade.

Older Versions of DOS 3.3

Versions of DOS before 3.3 used a different disk formatting scheme involving 13 sectors per track instead of 16. These versions, 3.2.1, 3.2, and 3.1, were current until summer 1980 when DOS 3.3 was issued. The change to 16 sectors required an upgraded Disk II controller card that could no longer read the older disk format. The result is that most disk drives today cannot directly read these older DOS disks.

Fortunately, there is a solution. On the DOS 3.3 System Master is a program called BOOT13. It works by overriding the newer disk controller code with the older 13 sector code. To boot a 13 sector disk, boot the DOS 3.3 System Master disk and type BRUN BOOT13. When the program is loaded, type the desired disk slot number. Insert the 13 sector disk into drive 1 of that slot, then press RETURN. The disk will then boot, allowing you to CATALOG it and RUN or BRUN the desired programs.

Inserting and Removing Disks

The general procedure for inserting and removing disks in a disk drive is the same, but it varies depending on the type of disk drive that is in use. If you have a hard disk drive system, then there is no disk to insert or remove; it is permanently fixed within the system.

In both disk systems, inserting a disk causes the disk head (responsible for reading and writing data) to rest on the disk surface. If a disk is not actively being used in the drive (such as if the Apple is powered off), it should be removed to avoid prolonged stationary contact with the drive head. With 3.5" disks, this involves ejecting the disk entirely. With 5.25" disks, only the drive door need be opened.

Figure 7-1. Inserting a 5.25" disk into the Disk II

In any case, it is a good idea to get into the habit of putting disks away where they belong when you are finished, instead of leaving them in the drive.

5.25" Disks

These larger, old-style disks must be inserted label side up, and with the oval-shaped cutout facing the opening of the disk drive. First, make sure that the disk drive door is open. For the Disk II, lift up the plastic lever. For all other models of disk drives, press in on the center piece, and a spring should pull it up out of the way.

Check to make sure that there is not already another disk inserted into the drive. If there is, grasp it and carefully pull it straight out, taking care not to bend it.

To insert a disk, hold it with your thumb over the label, and your forefinger beneath it. Gently push the disk into the disk drive.

There may be some resistance. Do not force it, as the disk is flexible and may be easily damaged.

Once the disk is entirely in the drive opening, press down on the drive door lever. Do not forget this last step. If you do not close the drive door, then the disk drive cannot read from the disk, and the Apple will think that you have not inserted any disk.

To remove the disk, first make sure that the red light on the front of the drive is off. Then open the drive door and pull out the disk. If you remove a disk while the light is on, there is a good chance that data may have been destroyed on the disk. Usually, this means that you can reuse the disk, but you probably won't get your original data back.

3.5″ Disks

These disks are of a newer design. They have a hard plastic shell, a shutter, and the drives do not have a door. Hold the disk label side up with the metal shutter facing the drive. Place your thumb over the label and your forefinger beneath it. Push the disk into the drive until it "clicks" in.

To remove the disk, press the eject button on the right-hand side of the disk drive. The disk should automatically be partially ejected. Pull it out the rest of the way. The 3.5" disk drive has smart electronics which will not eject the disk until the red light is off, meaning that it is harder to accidentally destroy data while the disk is in use.

Should a disk ever become stuck or refuse to eject, you may carefully insert a straightened paper clip into the emergency eject hole located near the eject button. Carefully push the paperclip in until the disk pops out.

Protecting Disks

There may be times when you want to ensure that the contents of a disk are not modified or erased. To do so, you must protect the disk by using a notch or tab. The exact procedure differs by type of disk.

Figure 7-2. Inserting a 3.5" disk into the Apple 3.5" disk drive

5.25" Disks

These disks employ a cutout notch on side of the disk to enable write-access, meaning that the disk contents may be modified. To protect the disk, cover this notch with a bit of tape. If the disk has two notches, then the notch on the right-hand side affects the face-up side of the disk.

3.5" Disks

These disks have a more convenient form of protection. They have a plastic tab which is a part of the disk's shell. When the tab is covering the hole, then the disk contents may be modified; it is not protected. When the tab is slid back to expose the hole, the disk is then write-protected; it may not be modified.

Figure 7-3. 5.25" disk and location of write-protect notch

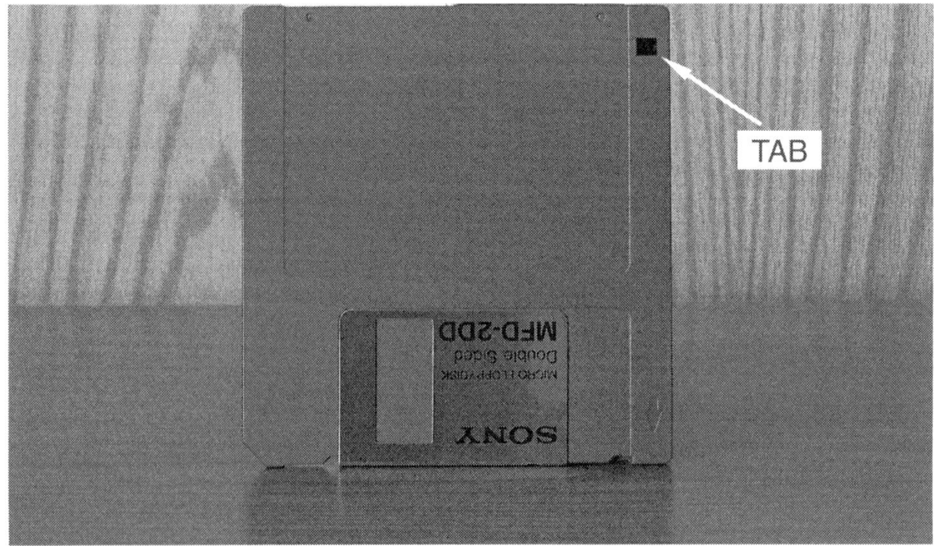

Figure 7-4. 3.5" disk and location of write-protect tab

Booting DOS

DOS is not built-in to your Apple. Instead, it must be loaded into memory each time that the Apple is started up, a process termed *booting.* As it turns out, the instructions which let your Apple use a disk are stored on disk too.

Almost every model of Apple has what is known as the Autostart ROM. This ROM enables the Apple II to automatically boot from a disk when the power is turned on. If your model of Apple is the Apple II Plus, IIe, IIc, IIc Plus, or IIgs, then you have the Autostart ROM. All that you need to do to boot DOS is to insert the disk into the drive, then switch on your Apple.

If you have the original model of Apple II, then there is a chance that your computer does not have the Autostart ROM. The easy way to verify is to switch on your Apple and see if the disk drive light comes on and the motor starts spinning. If not, then you do not have Autostart. Instead, to boot a disk, you will need to type the slot number where the disk controller card is located, CONTROL-K, then press RETURN. This command will only work from the Monitor, whose prompt is an asterisk (*).

For all models of Apple, it is important to take note that you may only boot from drive one, and never from drive two.

To boot a disk when the Apple is already turned on and in either Applesoft or Integer BASIC mode, you may use the BASIC command PR. For example, if your 5.25" disk controller card is in the usual slot 6, type the following:

```
]PR#6
```

That should start drive one spinning, and if a good disk is inserted, some whirring and clacking noises will sound as DOS is loaded into the Apple's memory. When more than one disk drive is connected to a controller card, then only the first one will ever boot.

3.5" disk drives are typically connected to slot 5. Any 3.5" drives connected to the Apple IIgs are assigned to this slot number.

The internal 3.5" disk drive on the IIc Plus is also assigned to slot 5. Type PR#5 to start up from the 3.5" drive.

If your IIgs startup disk normally starts with a pale blue screen and the message "Welcome to the IIgs," press COMMAND-CONTROL-RESET, then hold down the 8 key while starting up. Release the key when you see the title "PRODOS BASIC" at the top of the screen. This command will signal the IIgs to enter into ProDOS.

Depending on what model of Apple you have, and what version of DOS is being booted, you may get one of the following screens.

If you get an error message such as UNABLE TO LOAD PRODOS, or if the disk spins with no further activity, there are several possible reasons:

- If it is a 5.25" drive, the door could be left open. Close it.
- If you get an error message, the disk may not function as a startup disk. Try another disk.
- If it is a 5.25" drive, the disk could be 13 sector. Try the BOOT13 program described earlier.
- If nothing at all happens, the disk may be blank, or otherwise not able to startup the Apple. Try another disk.

If you are in a situation where you do not have any usable startup disks for your Apple, consult Appendix D. Therein is described a program which can create a startup disk.

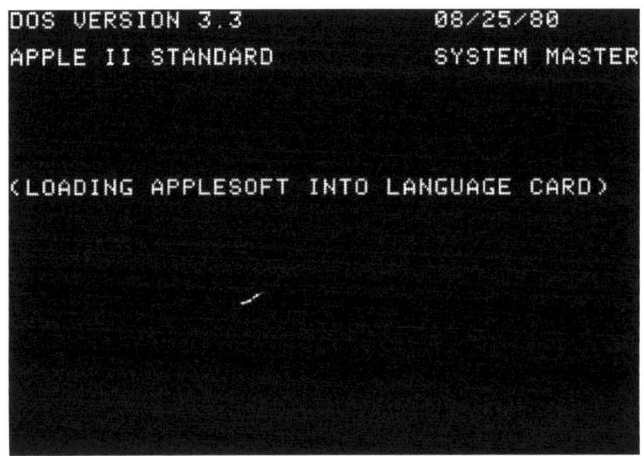

Figure 7-5. DOS 3.3 on the Apple II, with Language Card

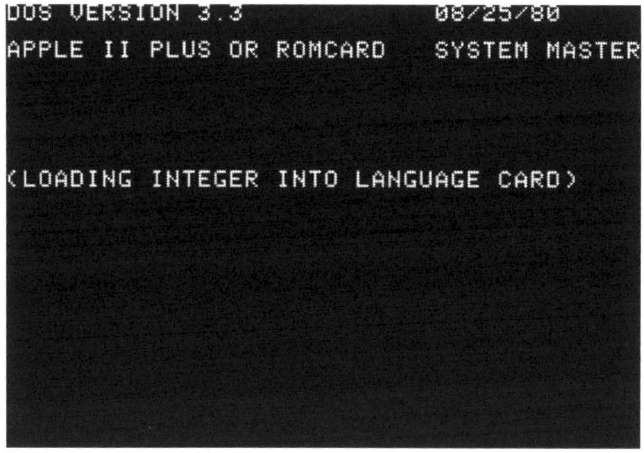

Figure 7-6. DOS 3.3 on the II Plus or IIe, with Language Card

Figure 7-7. DOS 3.3 on the Apple IIe

Figure 7-8. ProDOS 8 on the Enhanced IIe, IIc, IIc Plus, or IIgs

Getting Connected with DOS

If you use an Apple II long enough, you will eventually come across such phrases as "doing such-and-such may disconnect DOS," or, "to exit and reconnect DOS, follow these steps." To the new Apple user, these terms may not make sense.

DOS acts as an extension to BASIC. The simplest explanation is that it merely adds additional commands for working with disks. To do so, DOS needs to make some changes to your Apple. These changes involve redirecting input to the DOS command interpreter. DOS first examines input to see if it is a command that it recognizes, such as CATALOG. If so, DOS takes care of performing the correct operation. If not, DOS hands the command over to the BASIC interpreter. If the BASIC interpreter does not understand what you've typed, then you get a syntax error. Under ProDOS, the file named BASIC.SYSTEM is responsible for connecting Applesoft and the disk operating system; DOS 3.3 can connect with both Integer BASIC and Applesoft, and the support for doing so is built-in.

The area of memory that DOS modifies to receive commands is known as the input switch. When you first power on your Apple, the input switch is set to send all commands that you type to BASIC. It turns out that it is possible for this input switch to be changed back to the default, such as by resetting the Apple, or by running a program that modifies it.

If the input switch is changed, then DOS no longer receives commands, and DOS is therefore said to be disconnected. DOS could still exist in memory, but it never gets a chance to do anything. One way to reconnect DOS is to boot the disk again, but this might be inconvenient.

Fortunately, there is a simpler solution. You can, in most cases, reconnect DOS without having to reset or reboot a disk. To do so, enter the Monitor by typing CALL -151, and type the following:

```
*3D0G
```

When you press RETURN, you will end up back at the BASIC prompt. To test if DOS was successfully reconnected, type a DOS command, such as CATALOG.

Specifying the Slot, Drive, and Volume

In DOS 3.3 and ProDOS, disk access commands will operate on the most recently used drive. However, if you have more than one drive, then you can access any disk in a drive using its slot, drive, and volume number, or any combination of those three.

The arguments are S, D, and V, and they follow after the unique arguments given for each command. For example,

```
]CATALOG ,D2
```

will print the catalog of the disk in drive 2 of the most recently accessed slot number. Whereas

```
]CATALOG ,S5,D2,V254
```

will print the catalog of the disk in drive 2 of slot 5 whose volume number is 254.

ProDOS does not use a volume number, therefore you cannot use the V argument. However, specifying slot and drive number will still work.

The leading comma after the DOS command is optional in DOS 3.3, but is required for ProDOS.

Listing the Contents of a Disk

Every disk contains a catalog of files on it. Logically enough, the DOS command to display this listing is CATALOG. Under ProDOS, there are two catalog formats, short and extended. The short form is displayed with the CAT command, while the extended format is shown with CATALOG. The extended format requires the 80-column screen to be active for best results.

```
]CATALOG

DISK VOLUME 254

*A 006 HELLO
*I 018 ANIMALS
*T 003 APPLE PROMS
*I 006 APPLESOFT
*I 026 APPLEVISION
*I 017 BIORHYTHM
*B 010 BOOT13
*A 006 BRIAN'S THEME
*B 003 CHAIN
*I 009 COLOR DEMO
*A 009 COLOR DEMOSOFT
*I 009 COPY
*B 003 COPY.OBJ0
*A 009 COPYA
*A 010 EXEC DEMO
*B 020 FID
*B 050 FPBASIC
*B 050 INTBASIC
```

Figure 7-9. DOS 3.3 catalog listing of the System Master disk

```
]CAT

/USERS.DISK

 NAME              TYPE  BLOCKS  MODIFIED

*PRODOS             SYS      30  18-SEP-84
*BASIC.SYSTEM       SYS      21  18-JUN-84
*FILER              SYS      51  18-JUN-84
*CONVERT            SYS      42   5-FEB-85
*STARTUP            BAS      24  26-JUL-84
*MOIRE              BAS       3  15-OCT-83
*HYPNOSIS           BAS       3  15-OCT-83
*ANIMALS            BAS      10  15-OCT-83

BLOCKS FREE:   89      BLOCKS USED:   191

]
```

Figure 7-10. ProDOS short catalog of the ProDOS User's Disk

Indicator	Type
A	Applesoft program
B	Binary
I	Integer BASIC program
T	ASCII text file
*	File is locked

Table 7-1. DOS 3.3 file types

The DOS 3.3 Catalog

The DOS 3.3 catalog is rather quite simple: first, the disk volume number is displayed at the top of the screen. The volume number is a method for programs to identify a disk. Instead of supplying a name, you may supply a number. By default, a disk will have a volume number of 254, and you will find that most disks have this default number.

The listing of files follows afterward, made in three columns. The first column shows two pieces of information: the file's status, and its type. In DOS 3.3, a file has either one of two statuses: either it is locked, or it is unlocked. A locked file may not be deleted, renamed, or modified, and will be indicated with an asterisk. As you can see in Figure 7-9, all the files on this disk are locked. A file which is unlocked will not have an asterisk, instead a blank space will be shown. The single letter indicates the file's type. The file type indicates what sort of data the file contains: an Applesoft program, ASCII text, or a binary image, as some examples. Table 7-1 shows four common file types in DOS 3.3.

The second, middle column, displays a file's size in number of sectors on disk. The smallest file always takes 1 sector of space. If a file becomes greater in size than 255 sectors, the number starts back again at zero, thereby showing an incorrect sector count. Since a sector represents 256 bytes, a file's size in bytes can be found by multiplying its sector count by 256. For example, a file of 50 sectors uses 12,800 bytes of storage, or 12.5 kilobytes on disk.

The final column is the file's name. In DOS 3.3, filenames can contain any ASCII character, even control characters, and range from 1 to 30 characters in length. The name must start with a letter, however.

If a DOS 3.3 disk has more than 18 files, the Apple will pause before displaying the nineteenth and further files. You must press a key to see the rest of the catalog.

The ProDOS Catalog

The short catalog format in ProDOS shows all of the same information as does the catalog in DOS 3.3, with some additional details. Since ProDOS disks are identified by a name, not a number, the disk name is shown first. ProDOS also uses an asterisk to indicate locked files, but it uses a three letter code to indicate file type.

Filenames in ProDOS are restricted more so than DOS 3.3 names. In ProDOS, a filename must start with a letter, be no longer than 15 characters, and may only contain letters, numbers, and periods.

The size of files on ProDOS disks is given in terms of blocks, not sectors. A ProDOS block typically represents 512 bytes of data. ProDOS does not have the "255 wraparound" bug that the DOS 3.3 catalog has.

If you have an Apple IIgs, or a clock card installed in your Apple, ProDOS will keep track of the date and time when a file was created and modified. Only the file's modification date and time is reported in the short catalog format; the dates and times of both are shown in the extended listing.

Finally, the ProDOS listing shows the disk use statistics: blocks free and blocks used. Blocks free indicates how much space is left on the disk to store files. Blocks used represents how much disk space is being used to hold the files. Determining a disk's total capacity is as simple as adding the two figures. A 5.25" disk typically has a capacity of 280 blocks, a 3.5" disk has 1,600, and hard disks have several thousand blocks. The maximum capacity of any ProDOS disk is 65,536 blocks, or 32 MB.

Preparing a New Disk

To prepare a new disk for use, it must be initialized. The initialization process lays down a "grid" that helps the disk drive plan out where each file may reside. In doing so, any data that was already on a disk gets overwritten. Therefore, you should be careful not to accidentally initialize a disk with valuable data on it.

In DOS 3.3, initialization is performed with the INIT command. ProDOS does not have a built-in method to initialize a disk; instead, you must use a utility program, such as the one provided on the ProDOS User's Disk.

INIT in DOS 3.3

Preparing a new disk is fairly straightforward, though there is a bit of terminology involved. DOS 3.3 disks can be either one of two types: slave or master. A slave disk is one that has just been initialized. A slave diskette may only be used on an Apple system with as much or more RAM than the system used to initialize it. In other words, if one were to initialize a DOS 3.3 disk on an Apple II Plus with 48K of RAM, that disk could not be used on an Apple II with only 32K of RAM. However, the opposite would work: a disk from a 32K system would work on a 48K system. A master disk does not have this memory size restriction: a master disk created on any Apple system will work with any Apple. A slave disk can be turned into a master disk using the MASTER CREATE program on the DOS 3.3 System Master disk.

The distinction between slave and master disks is largely irrelevant these days. DOS 3.3 will work on models of Apple with as little as 16 kilobytes of RAM. Only two models of Apple, the II and II Plus, can even be configured with less than 48K of RAM, and it is extremely rare to find such configurations.

The second part of initializing a disk involves the greeting program. This program is always the first to run when a disk is booted. It must be either an Applesoft program or an Integer BASIC program. By convention, the greeting program is named HELLO, but you could give it any name that you want. Once a disk has been initialized, the name of the greeting program that DOS looks for cannot be changed. In other words, while you could rename or outright delete the greeting program, there is no way to make DOS use a file with a different name as the greeting program without reinitializing the disk.

The current BASIC program in memory is always used as the greeting program when initializing a disk. Following is an example of a typical greeting program, in Applesoft:

```
10 HOME
20 PRINT "DISK INITIALIZED ON DATE"
30 PRINT "BY NAME"
40 D$ = CHR$(4)
50 PRINT D$;"CATALOG"
```

You can use this program as a model for your own disks. Make sure to type in the current date and your name. Tradition also dictated that the RAM size of your Apple (20K, 32K, 48K, etc) be entered too, but that is mostly unnecessary, for the reason stated earlier.

Once you have the program in memory, RUN it to make sure that it operates as you expect. Once satisfied, type:

```
INIT HELLO
```

The disk drive will spin and whir for a while. Finally, the In Use light will go out, and the motor will stop spinning. Your disk has been initialized and now contains your greeting program. Boot it to make sure that everything worked. If you used the example program above, you should get the date, your name, and the disk catalog on screen.

Format in ProDOS

To format a ProDOS disk requires a disk utility program. One such program, the ProDOS Filer, is provided on the ProDOS User's Disk. If you do not have this disk, you could buy it online from Syndicomm.

Otherwise, perhaps you may have one of the following disks which too include a ProDOS initialization function:

- AppleWorks
- ShrinkIt
- ProSel
- ADT
- Copy II Plus.

The ProDOS Filer will be covered here. Each program above will have a format command that may work a bit differently, but should produce the same result.

To use the Filer to format a disk, launch it, then press V at the main menu. The Volume commands sub-menu will appear. The Format option is at the top. Press F. At this point, you should be at the Format a Volume screen, and you should remove your disk for safety.

Enter the slot and drive number to format, or just press RETURN to select the default, which is the same drive that you used to start the Filer (probably slot 6, drive 1). Afterward, you are prompted to enter a volume name. This name must adhere to the ProDOS file naming conventions: 15 characters total, beginning with a letter, and limited to A-Z, 0-9, and the period. Insert the disk to be formatted, then press RETURN when you are finished. There is no confirmation, so be sure that you have the correct disk inserted, and that you entered the volume name correctly (though you can change the name later if you want).

The formatting will take a few moments, and then the Apple will announce when it is finished.

Because formatting ProDOS disks takes more time and is not as convenient as in DOS 3.3, it is a good idea to always keep a stock of formatted disks on hand. It would be quite bothersome to be stuck in a program, unable to save your work because your last disk was full and you lacked a fresh disk.

ProDOS Directories

One of the major improvements that ProDOS offers over the old DOS 3.3 system is the concept of a folder hierarchy. In DOS 3.3, all of your files appeared in one "flat" listing in the disk catalog. There was no way to organize files into logical groups.

ProDOS introduced the idea of folders. A folder is a named container for files. For example, on one disk, you could have two folders: LETTERS, and REPORTS. Within these two folders, you could then have any number of business letters and financial reports, respectively. Folders may also contain other folders; in this case, you could have the LETTERS and REPORTS folders organized by year, where each year gets its own folder. This structure is known as a folder hierarchy. It is useful for keeping catalog listings concise, and your files organized.

Instead of *folder*, you may see the technical terms *directory* or *subdirctory* used instead. All three terms mean the same thing in ProDOS.

Every ProDOS disk has at least one directory, known as the *volume directory*, because it contains files and directories that are not located in any other directory on the disk. The volume directory is sometimes also called the root directory (using a tree analogy). Capable of holding up to 51 files and directories, the volume directory is always referred to as either a single slash (/) or a slash preceding the disk's name.

Changing Directories

ProDOS has a concept of a current working directory. When you type CAT, this is the directory whose catalog is listed, and it is the directory that ProDOS searches when you tell your Apple to LOAD or RUN a program. To change into a different directory, use the PREFIX command, followed by the directory name. Nested directories are separated by a / (slash) character. If you type PREFIX by itself, you will get the name of the current working directory.

As an example, imagine a disk named WORK that has two directories, one inside the other:

REPORTS
URGENT

The URGENT directory is located inside the REPORTS directory, and REPORTS is located in the volume directory.

Now, when you are at the volume directory, you may change into the REPORTS directory by typing:

```
PREFIX REPORTS
```

You may then change into the URGENT directory by typing:

```
PREFIX URGENT
```

Doing so relies on the use of a relative pathname for specifying the new prefix. The Apple takes the current prefix, which was /WORK/REPORTS/ and appends the specified prefix, URGENT.

You can, however, change directly into the URGENT directory by using either method:

```
PREFIX /WORK/REPORTS/URGENT
```

or

```
PREFIX REPORTS/URGENT
```

The first method can be recognized as an absolute path because it begins with a slash. This form will ensure that the correct directory is selected even if the current prefix is located on a different disk. The second method uses a relative path, this time from the volume directory of the WORK disk.

Creating Directories

Making new directories is accomplished with the CREATE command. Simply type the path at which the new directory should be located, followed by the directory name, such as:

```
CREATE /WORK/REPORTS/TOP.SECRET
```

which would create a subdirectory called TOP.SECRET in the REPORTS directory on the disk named WORK. As soon as the directory is created, it can be used to store BASIC programs, directories, and other files. If a file or directory with that name already exists, then a DUPLICATE FILE NAME error will result.

Deleting Files

To remove an old file that you no longer want, use the DELETE command. Only files that are unlocked (shown without an asterisk in the catalog) may be deleted. Attempting to delete a locked file will result in a FILE LOCKED error. The command syntax is:

DELETE *filename*

Be careful, as there is no confirmation when deleting a file. There exist some utilities to undelete a file, but it is better not to have to use them. Deleting a file does not immediately remove its data from the disk; it only clears its catalog entry. The space which the file occupied on disk is marked as free, and new data may be written over it at any time.

Locking and Unlocking Files

Locking a file gives it the following characteristics:

- The file's name may not be changed.
- The file may not be deleted.
- The file's contents may not be changed.

It is most useful to lock a file which is both important and unlikely to change, such as the BASIC greeting program, or a machine language binary program.

Use the LOCK command to lock a file:

LOCK *filename*

In ProDOS, the *filename* can be specified as a partial or full pathname as well. A ProDOS directory can be locked, meaning that it cannot be deleted or renamed, but its contents may still be modified (that is, files may be added to or deleted from the locked directory).

Conversely, unlocking a file frees the restrictions on it. To unlock a file, use the UNLOCK command.

As with most DOS commands, both LOCK and UNLOCK can be used with a slot and drive number, and a volume number in DOS 3.3.

Renaming Files

If you decide that a file's present name is no longer suitable, you may change it with the RENAME command. Recall the naming limitations stated earlier: any character, with a maximum of 30 characters for DOS 3.3; and only letters, numbers and periods, with a maximum of 15 characters for ProDOS. RENAME is used with the old name, followed by a comma and the new name, such as:

```
RENAME OLDNAME, NEWNAME
```

In DOS 3.3, it is possible to give more than one file the same name by renaming. This leads to confusion, as it is difficult to predict which file will be affected by subsequent DOS commands. ProDOS eliminates this potential mishap, and will respond with a DUPLICATE FILE NAME error.

Verifying Files

Occasionally, the disk on which a file is stored may get a physical defect or other damage which would prevent the file from being successfully read by the disk drive. To check for such an occurrence, the VERIFY command may be used with a filename.

VERIFY works by merely reading the file from disk. If there are no errors encountered, then no message is returned. However, if there is a problem, then an I/O ERROR message is printed on screen.

Typing VERIFY in ProDOS without a filename yields an Apple Computer copyright message.

Copying Disks

Neither ProDOS nor DOS 3.3 contain any built-in commands for copying entire disks or copying specific files on a disk.

DOS 3.3 provides a program known as COPYA that can copy an entire disk. This is an Applesoft BASIC program; the Integer version is known as COPY. Both programs come on the DOS 3.3 System Master disk. Alternatively, you may use the FID program, described later in this chapter, to copy entire disks or individual files (as well as perform many other disk-related tasks).

For ProDOS disks, the FILER utility provides a convenient method of copying one or more files, or even an entire disk. It too is explained later in this chapter, since it has many more features than just disk copying.

Some disks may be copy-protected, that is, they are formatted in a clever way to prevent unauthorized duplication. Disks typically were copy-protected to prevent copyright infringement. None of the standard DOS 3.3 or ProDOS disk copying programs will serve to effectively duplicate such a disk. The copy may appear to have completed successfully, but the duplicate will likely fail. Always test the newly copied disk before assuming that it works.

Converting from DOS 3.3 to ProDOS

Disks initialized under DOS 3.3 and disks initialized with ProDOS are not directly compatible. That is, a ProDOS disk may not be cataloged or have files loaded from it under DOS 3.3, and vice-versa.

Fortunately, a few specialized utility programs do exist which can perform the task of copying files from one system to the other. One such program is the ProDOS Converter, which is located on the ProDOS User's Disk. Boot this disk, then once the main menu is loaded, press C to access the Converter.

The Converter only has just a few options on its main screen. When it first starts, it is set to convert from DOS 3.3 to ProDOS. Press R to reverse direction.

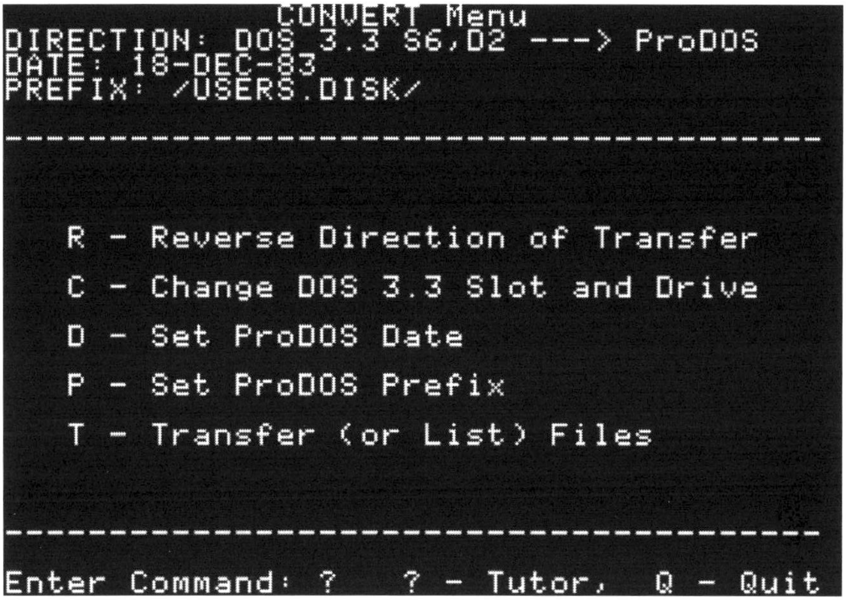

```
           CONVERT Menu
DIRECTION: DOS 3.3 S6,D2 ---> ProDOS
DATE: 18-DEC-83
PREFIX: /USERS.DISK/
---------------------------------------

   R - Reverse Direction of Transfer

   C - Change DOS 3.3 Slot and Drive

   D - Set ProDOS Date

   P - Set ProDOS Prefix

   T - Transfer (or List) Files

---------------------------------------
Enter Command: ?   ? - Tutor,  Q - Quit
```

Figure 7-11. The ProDOS Convert Menu

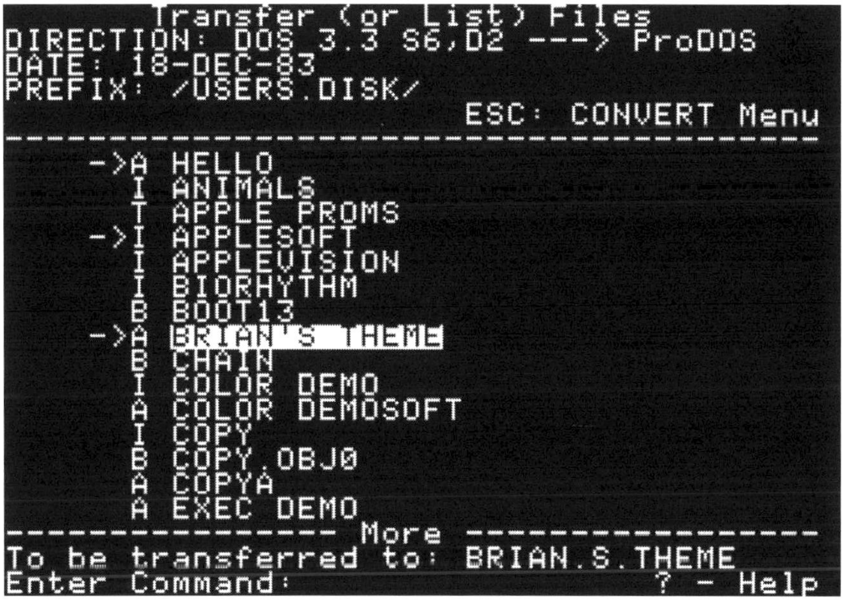

```
       Transfer (or List) Files
DIRECTION: DOS 3.3 S6,D2 ---> ProDOS
DATE: 18-DEC-83
PREFIX: /USERS.DISK/
                    ESC: CONVERT Menu
---------------------------------------
    ->A HELLO
      I ANIMALS
      T APPLE PROMS
    ->I APPLESOFT
      I APPLEVISION
      I BIORHYTHM
      B BOOT13
    ->A BRIAN'S THEME
      B CHAIN
      I COLOR DEMO
      A COLOR DEMOSOFT
      I COPY
      B COPY.OBJ0
      A COPYA
      A EXEC DEMO
--------------- More ------------------
To be transferred to: BRIAN.S.THEME
Enter Command:                ? - Help
```

Figure 7-12. Choosing files to convert

The DOS 3.3 slot and drive number are first set to Drive 2 of the slot from which ProDOS was booted. If your Apple only has one disk drive, or if you wish to use a different slot or drive number, press C to change them.

The date, which should be current if your Apple has a clock card (or is a IIgs, which has a built-in clock), can be changed by pressing D. This is the date which will be applied to ProDOS files as they are converted from DOS 3.3, since the latter operating system does not record file dates. Finally, the ProDOS prefix may be set by typing P.

Transferring Files

Once the desired parameters are set, press T to choose which files to transfer. You may press RETURN to see a list of files on the current disk. When prompted for files, there are two wild card characters which may be used to match multiple filenames. These two characters are the question mark (?) and the equals sign (=). A wild card can be used to match one or more characters in a filename. Only one wild card may be used at a time. For example, entering KED= would match a file named KEDLESTON, and entering =WICK would match a file named HARDWICK. One may also enter a specific filename to transfer just that particular file.

When using the ? wild card, files matching the given filename will be shown on a list. You must then select each file that you wish to transfer by highlighting its name on the list and then pressing the SPACE BAR. Use the LEFT or UP ARROW on the keyboard to move up the list, and use the RIGHT or DOWN ARROW to move down. To deselect a file, highlight it and press the SPACE BAR again.

If you entered an exact filename or used the = wild card, the Converter will attempt to transfer the file or matching files immediately. Otherwise, when you have marked all the files desired for conversion, press RETURN. Pressing ESCAPE will cancel conversion.

Some file types cannot be transferred at all. ProDOS directories are not allowed to be transferred, as DOS 3.3 has no concept of a directory. Furthermore, file types BIN, $F*n*, REL, and VAR cannot be converted to DOS 3.3. While DOS 3.3 Integer files (type I) may be transferred to ProDOS, they may not be executed, since Integer BASIC programs are incompatible with ProDOS.

The rules for ProDOS filenames are stricter than for DOS 3.3. Any spaces, punctuation, and other symbols are changed to periods, and names longer than 15 characters are truncated. When selecting a file, the Converter will show the modified filename near the bottom of the screen. When converting to DOS 3.3, however, all ProDOS filenames are legal DOS 3.3 names.

You may run into issues with the ProDOS volume directory filling up. A DOS 3.3 disk catalog has enough room to hold 105 files, but the equivalent for ProDOS, the volume directory, is limited to less than half this figure, only 51 files. If you are converting a large number of DOS 3.3 files, the way to avoid this limitation is to create a ProDOS subdirectory, and use the PREFIX command to send all converted files there. A ProDOS directory can hold any number files, limited only by the free space on the disk.

It is important to realize that the conversion process merely transfers the file to a new disk. While text files generally do not require any further modification, most programs, especially those that use disk commands, will need to be changed in order to run properly under the new operating system. Do not expect to be able to transfer a BASIC program that uses the disk and expect it to work right away.

Quitting the Program

To exit the Conversion program, press the ESCAPE key until the main menu appears (shown in Figure 7-11). There, press Q to Quit. Enter the name of the next program to run, or press RETURN to accept the provided entry, which will usually lead to the Applesoft BASIC prompt.

Using the FocusDrive

The FocusDrive is an innovative "hard drive on a card" peripheral, first introduced in the mid 1990s. Today it is sold by 16Sector, operated by Tony Diaz. It uses an IDE interface to a hard drive, or, with the use of an IDE-to-Compact Flash adapter, a Compact Flash card. Hard disk storage is many times faster and offers a much greater capacity compared to traditional storage on 3.5" or

5.25" disks. Once you get used to the speed and convenience, you'll be amazed that you were ever able to manage without it.

Because there is nothing to plug in, insert, or attach to the FocusDrive once it has been configured, it is simple to setup and install. It will work on all models of Apple (except for the IIc and IIc Plus of course, because they don't have slots). In an Enhanced Apple IIe or Apple IIgs, the FocusDrive will automatically start up the Apple, similar to a 5.25" or 3.5" disk.

The FocusDrive uses a 44-pin mini IDE connector, the same as used on 2.5" laptop hard drives. The Connor CP-2064 miniature hard drive is known to work well with the FocusDrive, and will provide 60 MB of storage.

Alternatively, with the addition of a 44-pin IDE to CompactFlash adapter, a CompactFlash card can be connected, offering faster solid-state storage compared to a traditional hard disk. Cards with a capacity of 64, 128, or 256 MB are inexpensive and well-suited to the Apple.

Low-level Formatting

Though the FocusDrive will operate in both a IIe and a IIgs, the formatting utility for it, the Focus Formatter, is written for the IIgs. This program performs the low-level format and partitioning, which should only need to be done once.

If it should happen that you do not have an Apple IIgs available, you can order the FocusDrive to come pre-formatted for Apple IIe, with the ProDOS operating system pre-installed too.

Other Hard Disk Systems

Of course, the FocusDrive isn't the only hard disk system currently sold for the Apple. There is also the MicroDrive and CFFA, both of which use Compact Flash cards for storage.

Richard Dreher created the CFFA as a personal project in 2002. The card is ProDOS 8 and GS/OS compatible, and is designed to work in all models of Apple with slots.

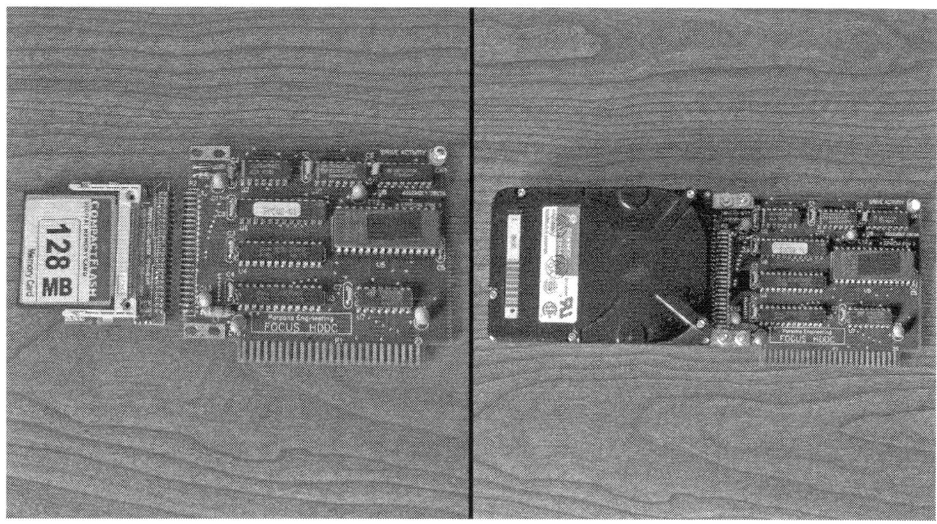

Figure 7-13. FocusDrive with Compact Flash (left) and hard drive (right)

The newest version of the card, the CFFA3000, should be available as you read this book. It will support operating systems other than ProDOS, emulate a Disk II drive, and have a USB port for USB flash drives.

The advantages of these three hard disk systems are speed and convenience. With no moving parts, access to data is much quicker than with a magnetic disk. Since Compact Flash cards and USB flash drives are easily removable, they can be loaded into a modern-day PC or Macintosh for fast transfer of programs and documents.

Programming Data Files

DOS and ProDOS both deal with a number of different file types. Some files are for storing BASIC programs, and other files are for machine language programs. A third type of file, known as the text file, can contain nearly any kind of data, and more importantly, can be read and used in a BASIC program.

Communicating with DOS

When used with an Applesoft or Integer BASIC program, DOS is invoked by a special ASCII character known as Control-D, whose code is 4. This ASCII code must be used before every DOS command in a BASIC program, as part of a PRINT statement.

The most common procedure is to create a variable D$ which contains a Control-D. In Applesoft, this task is accomplished with the following line:

```
]10 D$ = CHR$(4)
```

Integer BASIC lacks a CHR$ function, so one must define a string variable and type CONTROL-D between the quotes, like so:

```
>10 D$ = "" : REM CONTROL-D BETWEEN QUOTES
```

When typing this line, type the first set of quotation marks, then press CONTROL-D, then type the final set of quotation marks. Remember that control characters never appear on the screen, so it will look like there is nothing between the quotation marks. This method may also be used in Applesoft.

Following is a program that will print the disk catalog:

```
10 REM PRINT DISK CATALOG
20 D$ = CHR$(4): REM CONTROL-D
30 PRINT D$;"CATALOG"
40 END
```

The PRINT statement on line 30 issues the DOS Catalog command. Only one DOS command may be used in a single PRINT statement, and it must be preceded with a Control-D. Furthermore, a carriage return (ASCII code 13) must have been sent immediately before the Control-D.

Now you may write a program that uses RENAME, DELETE, and any of the other DOS commands that you learned earlier in this chapter.

The Null DOS Command

The shortest DOS command consists of just a Control-D by itself, and is known as the "null" or "empty" command:

```
5 D$ = CHR$(4)
10 PRINT D$
```

The null command is typically used to cancel the effects of a previous DOS command, as you will learn shortly.

Records and Fields

As already explained, a *file* is a named collection of data, represented on disk as a sequence of bytes. Remember that a byte is the smallest unit of memory that can contain a single ASCII character, such as a letter or number. Data within a DOS file are grouped into *records*, a logical unit of data. Records are constituted by one or more *fields*, representing one item of data. Sometimes the term "field" is used to refer to an entire record. In this case, it means a record that contains exactly one field of data.

As an analogy, a library card catalog could be represented by a file. The individual cards would make up the records for each book; the information about each book, the title, subject, author, and so on, would each be a field of every record.

DOS automatically manages files and records, but it leaves some decisions on the organization of fields within a record up to the programmer. By default, every field is terminated by a carriage return character. However, it possible for a programmer to use another character, such as a comma, to separate units of data within a field. A comma is most practical, since it corresponds with the BASIC convention of separating multiple INPUT variables with a comma.

The Two Types of Files

DOS offers two types of data files: sequential and random-access. Both are made up of one or more fields, however, the manner in which your programs may access the fields differs. Each record in a random-access file acts like a separate sequential text file. A program may read the records in a random-access file in any order, whereas the fields in a sequential file must always be read in order, starting from the first field.

Sequential files are best used when the data stored within them is often read in order, and when that data does not need to be updated or revised. Random-access files work well to represent a database or card catalog: the individual records may be rapidly accessed and easily updated. Sequential files typically make more efficient use of disk space, whereas random-access files often waste some space.

File Buffers

Both ProDOS and DOS 3.3 work efficiently with data files by using a buffer. The *file buffer* is an area of memory used to hold part of the data read from or to be written to the disk. In order to reduce the number of times that the disk must be accessed, modifications to a file are first performed in memory on the buffer, then later written to disk, thus increasing the speed of the program. Likewise, when reading from disk, a large block of data is read into memory, from which a program may then read as much or as little as necessary.

With ProDOS, as many as eight file buffers may be allocated, meaning that at most eight files may be open at a time. ProDOS manages these buffers automatically. DOS 3.3, however, only reserves space for three file buffers. The MAXFILES command will allow for more, up to 16 open files at a time. Exact use of MAXFILES is covered later in this chapter.

Using Sequential Files

Sequential files are quite simple to use, and there are only four commands to know. Imagine a sequential file as a scroll of paper. Reaching later sections of the scroll can only be achieved by seeking past the earlier sections. Since a scroll is just one long page, there is no way to easily access individual sections. Adding on to the end of the scroll is the easiest way to enter additional information. A sequential file in DOS acts much like this scroll analogy.

In a sequential text file, each item of data is called a *field*. A field is made up of a series of ASCII characters terminated by a carriage return character, ASCII code 13. The fields are stored sequentially in the file, each following the preceding field's return character. The fields may each be of differing lengths.

Opening Sequential Files

As explained earlier, after a program opens a file, the contents of the file are read from the disk into a buffer, and changes to the file are made to the buffer before being finally written back to the disk.

Opening a file is the first step toward reading or writing it. Afterward, the program must locate the desired field. The OPEN command will open a file, creating it if it does not exist:

```
10 PRINT CHR$(4);"OPEN MYFILE"
```

As with all disk commands, a CONTROL-D, or ASCII character 4, must be given before each command word.

DOS is now prepared to read from the beginning of MYFILE.

Like most DOS commands, a slot and drive number may be specified in both DOS 3.3 and ProDOS. Additionally, in DOS 3.3 only, a Volume number may be provided. The following line opens a file named STOURHEAD from a disk in slot 5, drive 2 (assume that a CONTROL-D was assigned earlier to D$):

```
15 PRINT D$;"OPEN STOURHEAD,S5,D2"
```

With ProDOS, the Apple will search the volume directory for the filename. If the PREFIX command was used earlier, the prefix directory will be searched instead. Alternatively, a full pathname may be specified.

After a ProDOS file is successfully opened, it must always be referred to in the same way, even if the the PREFIX command is used. As an example, if a file is opened by giving its entire pathname, then that the same string must always be used. Alternatively, if a file was opened by giving only its name, then only the name must be used. The way that a file is referred to may be changed the next time that it is opened.

Writing Sequential Files

To write to a file, the program must tell BASIC to redirect all PRINT statements to DOS. DOS then takes the output of PRINT and adds it to the file buffer. The WRITE command effects this redirection:

```
20 PRINT CHR$(4);"WRITE MYFILE"
```

WRITE may only be used in programmed mode as part of a BASIC program. Attempting to use the WRITE command in immediate mode will cause a NOT DIRECT COMMAND error message to appear.

Since it is possible to have more than one file open at a time, you must specify to which file you wish the writes be applied. Once a WRITE command is issued to DOS, all screen output will be written to the specified file, unless any of the following events occur:

- An INPUT statement is executed
- Any DOS command is issued
- The Apple is reset
- A DOS error occurs.

In DOS 3.3, even INPUT statement prompts and the text of error messages can be written to an open file. The program will stop after an error occurs, however. ProDOS fixes these deficiencies: it prevents INPUT prompts and error messages from being written to a file. Just like DOS 3.3, a ProDOS error causes the program to terminate without closing the file. Type CLOSE in immediate mode to close all open files.

Furthermore, a program running under DOS 3.3 should take care not to send inverse or flashing characters to a disk file, as they are not properly accepted. ProDOS works around the problem by converting all text to the normal style.

You may also designate a byte offset at which to begin writing, such as in this example:

```
100 PRINT D$;"WRITE DATAFILE, B40"
```

This line will start writing to DATAFILE beginning at the fortieth byte. Writing at arbitrary byte locations within a sequential text file is quite dangerous unless you already have a firm structure in mind for the file. Otherwise, it is too easy to miscalculate and unintentionally write over other data.

DOS maintains a file pointer for every open file. The pointer marks the next location at which data will be read or written, and it is advanced each time a byte is read or written. Since the file pointer can only be moved forward, it is necessary to close and reopen the file to access earlier fields.

Here is an example program that will WRITE some words to a text file. Another program, shown a bit later, will read these words back into memory.

```
10 REM SEQUENTIAL FILE DEMO 1
20 D$ = CHR$(4) : REM CONTROL-D
30 REM OPEN THE TEXT FILE, CREATING IT IF IT DOES NOT
EXIST
40 PRINT D$;"OPEN WORDS"
50 REM TELL THE APPLE TO WRITE TO THIS FILE
60 PRINT D$;"WRITE WORDS"
70 REM WRITE SOME WORDS
80 PRINT "TEMPUS" : PRINT "FUGIT"
90 PRINT "MEMENTO" : PRINT "MORI"
100 REM NOW CLOSE THE FILE
110 PRINT D$;"CLOSE WORDS"
120 END
```

After you RUN this program, type CAT (for ProDOS) or CATALOG (for either operating system). You should see a new file named WORDS. It contains the four words that this BASIC program wrote. The WRITE command on line 60 forced the output from the four PRINT statements on lines 80 and 90 to go to the text file instead of the screen. The CLOSE command (to be fully explained a bit later) on line 110 closed the WORDS file, thus signaling the end of writing.

Since without given any direction, WRITE will always begin writing from the beginning of the file, each time this program is run, the four words are overwritten. This is not an issue because exactly the same data is being written. What becomes a problem, however, is when differing data is overwritten in a sequential file. This can quite easily cause a field to become partially overwritten, where some of the old data becomes attached to the end of the new data. Later, we will see a DOS command that automatically starts writing at the end of a sequential file, thus avoiding this problem.

Separating Fields

It is important that fields be properly separated from each other when written to a disk file. If not, an INPUT statement could read more than one value at a time into a variable, thus running the data together. Remember that the carriage return character serves as the field separator for text files.

PRINT will always add a carriage return unless it is terminated with a semicolon. Therefore, it is best to put the data for each field into its own PRINT statement, and then be sure that each PRINT does not end with a semicolon.

The following PRINT statement will write two values both to one field because it uses a semicolon between the values:

```
20 PRINT "STRATFORD";86
```

Likewise, even though there are two PRINT statements in this next example, again only one field will be written, since the first PRINT statement ends with a semicolon:

```
30 PRINT "STRATFORD";
40 PRINT 86
```

Finally, the two lines in this example will create two separate fields for the data:

```
30 PRINT "STRATFORD"
40 PRINT 86
```

Notice that the semicolon at the end of line 30 was removed. Both PRINT statements end with a carriage return character, thus separating the fields.

Overwriting a File

In some cases it is simpler to overwrite an entire sequential text file instead of having to manage WRITE statements to avoid mixing old and new data.

DOS lacks an explicit command to overwrite a file, but the effect may be achieved by first deleting the file. However, a problem arises if the program is run for the first time and the file does not exist: DOS will present a FILE NOT FOUND error when attempting to delete the file.

The solution is to execute the following DOS commands in sequence:

```
OPEN
DELETE
OPEN
```

The first OPEN serves to create the file if it does not exist. Then the file may be deleted, since it surely exists. If the program must read the existing data from the file, it should do so *before* the DELETE command is issued. The second OPEN command creates a new, blank file.

A program may then issue a WRITE command, confident that the new data will not be mixed in with any existing data.

Closing Sequential Files

Closing a file informs DOS that the program is done reading or making changes to that file. Any changes that were in the file buffer are committed to disk, and the area of memory for the buffer is released for use by another file or program. The example program shown earlier used CLOSE. Here is another example using CLOSE:

```
50 PRINT CHR$(4);"CLOSE MYFILE"
```

In this example, the file named MYFILE will be closed. In ProDOS, the filename or path must be given exactly as it was when the file was first opened.

Closing a file that was never opened causes no error, but if a program fails to close a file that had changes made to it, then some data may be lost.

To close all open files, issue the CLOSE command with no filename argument, as shown:

```
60 PRINT CHR$(4);"CLOSE"
```

Neither slot, drive, nor volume numbers are allowed in a CLOSE command. DOS remembers these values; the file name alone will suffice.

CLOSE can also be used in immediate mode.

Reading Sequential Files

The READ command instructs DOS to fill subsequent BASIC INPUTs (or GETs in Applesoft) with characters from the current text file. To read from a file, it must be OPENed first. After reading is finished, the file should be CLOSEd.

When a READ command is executed, an INPUT or GET statement should follow immediately. The READ command is terminated by any further DOS command in a PRINT statement, even an “empty” DOS command.

The syntax for READ is the same as for WRITE, as shown in this example:

```
80 PRINT CHR$(4);"READ MY.LIPS”
```

The filename used with READ must be the same name that was originally used with OPEN. READ may be used only in programmed mode, preceded by the usual ASCII character 4, just like WRITE. Attempting to issue a READ command in immediate mode will lead to a NOT DIRECT COMMAND error.

Beware that stopping a READ in Applesoft using CONTROL-C will cause an endless loop of REENTER messages. Press CONTROL-RESET to return to the Applesoft prompt.

Like WRITE, READ may also be used with a byte argument to start reading from that byte in the file. In this example, the next INPUT statement will start reading from the twenty-third byte and stop before the beginning of the next field from the file ORDERS:

```
PRINT CHR$(4);"READ ORDERS, B22”
```

The first byte in a file is always byte 0, and this is where all READs start from if the B argument is not specified.

Remember the program earlier that wrote some words to a text file? Here is the program that will read them back to display on the screen:

```
10 REM SEQUENTIAL FILE DEMO 2
20 D$ = CHR$(4) : REM CONTROL-D
30 REM OPEN THE TEXT FILE, CREATING IT IF IT DOES NOT
EXIST
40 PRINT D$;"OPEN WORDS"
50 REM TELL THE APPLE TO READ FROM THIS FILE
60 PRINT D$;"READ WORDS"
70 REM READ SOME WORDS
80 FOR I = 1 TO 4
90 INPUT W$ : REM READ WORD FROM NEXT FIELD
100 PRINT W$
110 NEXT I
120 REM NOW CLOSE THE FILE
130 PRINT D$;"CLOSE WORDS"
140 END
```

```
]RUN

TEMPUS
```

```
FUGIT
MEMENTO
MORI

]
```

The program uses a FOR-NEXT loop to call the INPUT statement four times. Because of the READ command given on line 60, the INPUT statement (line 90) takes control from the disk file, not the keyboard.

As an experiment, try altering the FOR loop on line 80 to make it run to 5, that is:

```
80 FOR I = 1 TO 5
```

Run the program and see what happens.

Detecting the End of a File

Trying to READ past the end of a file leads to an END OF DATA error in both ProDOS and DOS 3.3. As this error causes program execution to halt, it is desirable to detect the condition ahead of time and CLOSE the file.

The solution in Applesoft is to intercept the error, handle it as necessary, then continue program execution. The Applesoft statement to intercept errors is ONERR GOTO, which like an ordinary GOTO, accepts a line number to which Applesoft will branch. This statement should be used as early as possible within a program, such as shown:

```
15 ONERR GOTO 10000
```

It is common practice to place an ONERR GOTO statement in the beginning part of a program, during the initialization phase. The lines starting at 10000, in this example, should contain BASIC statements to get the error number and decide what to do.

Every DOS and ProDOS error may be identified by number. For example, error number 5 means End of Data. Error numbers are listed in Appendix I. An Applesoft program may determine the error number by examining memory location 222 with a PEEK statement.

Once the error number is determined, it is usually enough information for the error-handling routine to take appropriate action. Additionally, the line number at which the error occurred may be determined with a line like the following:

```
10010 EL = PEEK(218)+PEEK(219)*256
```

Knowledge of the line number is useful if a program deals with more than one file at various sections. The program can take different steps depending on at which line number the error occurred.

Once the error routine is finished, there are three methods to return to the usual program. Alternatively, an END statement could be used if resuming the program proves to be impractical. A GOTO, ON GOTO, or a RESUME statement can each be used to return to the main program. The RESUME statement is useful in that it causes an automatic branch back to the line number where the error originally occurred.

To deactivate the effects of ONERR GOTO, thus sending error control back to Applesoft, use POKE 216,0. Doing so will cause Applesoft to report the error and halt program execution, as usual, for any future errors.

The following program features an error-handling routine which can detect several different errors, including END OF DATA:

```
10 REM PROGRAM SHOWING ONERR GOTO USE
20 ONERR GOTO 500 : REM SET ERROR HANDLER
30 D$ = CHR$(4) : REM ASSIGN DOS COMMAND PREFIX
40 PRINT D$;"OPEN DATAFILE"
50 PRINT D$;"READ DATAFILE"
60 INPUT A$
70 PRINT A$
80 GOTO 60
90 END
```

```
500 REM ERROR HANDLER STARTS HERE
510 EC = PEEK(222) : REM GET ERROR CODE NUMBER
520 EL = PEEK(218)+PEEK(219)*256 : REM GET ERROR LINE
NUMBER
530 REM CHECK FOR END OF DATA
540 IF EC = 8 THEN GOTO 600 : REM I/O ERROR
550 IF EC = 23 THEN GOTO 650 : REM NO BUFFERS
560 IF EC = 5 AND EL = 60 THEN GOTO 700
570 REM SOME OTHER ERROR OCCURRED
580 POKE 216,0 : REM DISABLE ONERR GOTO
590 RESUME : REM RETURN TO PROGRAM AND HALT

600 PRINT "AN I/O ERROR OCCURRED!"
610 GOTO 700
650 PRINT "NO BUFFERS AVAILABLE!"
700 PRINT D$;"CLOSE DATAFILE" : REM CLOSE THE FILE
710 GOTO 90 : REM END
```

This program is designed to read and print as many lines as are contained in the file named DATAFILE. The error-handling routine is set up on line 20 with the ONERR GOTO statement. The routine itself begins at line 500. First it obtains the error code number and line number by the PEEK statements on lines 510 and 520. Three error conditions are tested on lines 540, 550, and 560: I/O Error, No Buffers Available, and End of Data, respectively. If none of these errors occurred, line 580 removes the error handling routine, and program execution resumes again. This time, however, the default Applesoft error handler will run, and the program will terminate. All errors except the end of data error print an error message. Finally, line 700 closes the file and ends the program.

Unfortunately, Integer BASIC does not have any provision for allowing a custom error-handling routine. There are two workaround methods. One is to use the first field to store the total number of fields. The first INPUT statement then reads this value to a variable, and uses a counter to read only the exact number of fields. The second method is to store a unique value as the very last character of the file. This value, which could be any ASCII character, or a string of characters, should never appear elsewhere in the file. When a program reads the file back into memory, it should check for this trailing value. These two methods can also be used in Applesoft programs.

Problems with ONERR GOTO

With the standard Apple II, II Plus, and IIe, ONERR GOTO can lead to some problems in a limited number of cases. Note that on the Enhanced IIe and later models, these problems have been fixed.

If TRACE mode is active, or in a program containing a PRINT statement, ONERR GOTO will terminate the Applesoft program and transfer control to the Machine Language Monitor after 43 errors occur. This problem does not happen if RESUME is used with errors generated from an INPUT statement. However, if GOTO is used instead of RESUME with an INPUT error, the Apple will switch back to the Monitor after the 87th error. From the Monitor, one must type CONTROL-C and press RETURN to enter the Applesoft prompt with the program intact.

Furthermore, if ONERR GOTO is used with a RESUME statement to handle errors from using GET, the program will "hang" after two consecutive GET errors. To recover the Apple, press CONTROL-RESET. If the Applesoft prompt does not appear, press CONTROL-C and RETURN. Using GOTO instead of RESUME can avoid the problem with GET.

Some of these problems can be prevented with the aid of a short machine language subroutine. This subroutine must be called at the beginning of your error-handling routine. While not built-in to the Apple, the routine is fairly short, and can be entered from your BASIC program.

The following code will place the machine language routine into memory starting at location 768. This code need only be executed once at the beginning of the program. However, the error-handling routine must always perform a CALL 768 command when it intercepts an error.

```
380 POKE 768,104 : POKE 769,168 : POKE 770,104 : POKE
771,166 : POKE 772,223 : POKE 773,154 : POKE 774,72 :
POKE 775,152 : POKE 776,72 : POKE 777,96
```

Change the line number, 380, to one that is convenient for your program. This subroutine fixes some of the problems with PRINT and ?OUT OF MEMORY ERROR messages.

If you were to use this machine language program with the error handler shown just previously, you would add the following line to the error handling section:

```
505 CALL 768
```

Appending to a Sequential File

The WRITE command can be used to start writing a file either at the beginning or at any arbitrary byte position. The APPEND command is useful for it allows data to be added at the end of a file. When the APPEND command is executed, the data pointer for writing is set to one byte beyond the last byte in the file. This allows a program to safely add new data to the end of a file without worrying about overwriting any existing data.

A WRITE command should immediately follow APPEND. Attempting to READ will cause an END OF DATA error message. With ProDOS, APPEND automatically executes the necessary WRITE command. To cancel writing, issue the null ("empty") DOS command.

The syntax for APPEND should be familiar:

APPEND *filename*

as in

```
APPEND WORDS
```

Drive and slot numbers can also be provided in ProDOS and DOS 3.3, and in DOS 3.3 only, the volume number too.

Even if a file is locked, using APPEND will not cause an error. It is only upon an attempt to WRITE that the FILE LOCKED message will appear.

With DOS 3.3, the filename used with APPEND should already exist on the disk; if it does not, a FILE NOT FOUND error will occur. Unlike OPEN, APPEND will not automatically create a file.

The APPEND command *should not* be preceded or followed by an OPEN command; APPEND opens the file as part of its execution. Issuing an OPEN command after APPEND will reset the data pointer, thus defeating the purpose of using APPEND.

The following Applesoft program uses APPEND to add two additional strings, "INSIGNIFICANT" and "TWADDLE" to the end of the sequential text file named WORDS. The two new strings will be added as two new fields in the file.

```
10 REM APPEND DEMO
20 D$ = CHR$(4) : REM CONTROL-D
30 PRINT D$;"APPEND WORDS" : REM OPEN WORDS AND SEEK
TO END
40 PRINT D$;"WRITE WORDS" : REM WRITE TO FILE
50 PRINT "INSIGNIFICANT"
60 PRINT "TWADDLE"
70 PRINT D$;"CLOSE WORDS" : REM CLOSE THE FILE
80 END
```

Seeking in a Sequential File

The data pointer for an open file may be set to any field through the POSITION command. This operation allows a file to be read or written starting at any field number.

Here is an example of using POSITION:

```
POSITION WORDS, R1
```

This command positions the data pointer for the file named WORDS at field number 1. Since the fields are numbered starting from 0, this field is actually the second field in the file (which, if you recall, contains the string "FUGIT"). Subsequent READ or WRITE commands will now start at this point in the file. In ProDOS, the letter F, for field, can be substituted in place of R. It has the same effect.

The value for R must be greater than or equal to 0, and less than or equal to the last field in the file. Furthermore, R stands for relative field number; it only moves the data pointer forward counting from the current field pointer, never backward. If a second POSITION command were to be executed with R1, then the data pointer would be incremented to field number 2, the third field in the text file.

When R is 0, the next command will operate on the current field. When R is 1, the next command will skip over the current field and work on the following one. If R is 2, then two fields will be skipped over, and so on.

Since POSITION, like any other DOS command, cancels a READ or WRITE, it must be used *before* the intended READ or WRITE.

DOS performs a linear seek through the text file to find the field specified by POSITION. This process is performed by scanning each byte in the file, looking for the *n*th return character, where *n* is the number given for R. If during its scan of the file, a null byte (ASCII code 0) is encountered, an END OF DATA error message is immediately returned.

In ProDOS only, the READ command can be used with a field number. The following example skips over the first three fields in the file WORDS. The next INPUT will then start reading at the fourth field:

```
200 PRINT CHR$(4);"READ WORDS,F3"
```

The ProDOS WRITE command also supports exactly the same field parameter. Unfortunately, DOS 3.3 does not have the option to specify a field number when reading or writing.

Reading from ProDOS Directories

A directory in ProDOS is treated just like any other sequential file—it can be opened and its contents read. Doing so returns the catalog information on each file in the directory. The following program shows how:

```
5 D$ = CHR$ (4)
10 INPUT "WHICH DIRECTORY? ";DI$
```

```
20 PRINT D$;"OPEN ";DI$;", TDIR"
30 PRINT D$;"READ ";DI$
40 INPUT DN$ : REM DIRECTORY NAME
50 INPUT TI$ : REM TITLE LINE
60 INPUT BL$ : REM BLANK LINE
65 PRINT DN$ : PRINT TI$ : PRINT
70 INPUT DL$ : REM DIRECTORY LINE
75 PRINT DL$
80 IF DL$ <> "" THEN 70
90 INPUT BU$ : REM BLOCK USE
95 PRINT BU$
100 PRINT D$;"CLOSE ";DI$
```

The first three lines are always the directory name, title line, and a blank line, respectively. Following are the catalog entries, ending with a blank line. The final line is the block use information for the disk. When you run this program and enter a directory name, the screen output should look the same as when the CATALOG command is used.

Word Processing Program

One obvious use of the disk is to store text files whose contents represent material that could be produced by a word processor: letters, stories, reports, and other such documents.

Word processing programs are typically quite complex, but this one will be simpler, supporting only just a few features. It will show a main menu when first started that will allow the user to start a new document or edit an existing one. A save option will write the current document to disk as a sequential text file, after asking for a name.

If the Apple running the program has TAB and DELETE keys (every model except the original II and II Plus), they will serve to indent text by adding 8 spaces, and move the cursor back, respectively.

Chapter 9 will show an improvement to the program that will allow for a document to be printed on a printer attached to the Apple II.

Here is the program listing:

```
10 REM WORD PROCESSING PROGRAM
15 ONERR GOTO 10000 : REM ERROR HANDLER
20 REM DEFINE VARIABLES
30 D$ = CHR$(4) : REM CONTROL-D
35 IF PEEK(977) <> 0 THEN PRINT D$;"MAXFILES 1"
40 IB$ = "" : REM INPUT BUFFER
50 DIM DL$(70, 80) : REM ARRAY HOLDING EACH DOCUMENT
LINE
60 LC = 1 : REM TOTAL LINE COUNTER
65 SL% = 1 : REM SCREEN LINE POINTER
70 CL = 1 : REM CURRENT LINE POINTER
75 TL = 1 : REM TOP LINE POINTER (FOR SCROLLING)
80 SL = 40 : REM SCREEN LENGTH (40 OR 80 COLS)
85 MO$ = "" : REM CURRENT PROGRAM MODE
90 CP = 1 : REM CURSOR POSITION
95 FI$ = "" : REM FILE NAME

100 REM PRINT MAIN SCREEN
105 PRINT CHR$(21) : REM FORCE 40-COLUMN DISPLAY
110 HOME : PRINT "WORD PROCESSOR" : PRINT : PRINT
120 PRINT "CHOOSE AN OPTION:"
130 PRINT : INVERSE : PRINT "N"; : NORMAL
140 PRINT "EW DOCUMENT": PRINT : INVERSE
150 PRINT "L"; : NORMAL : PRINT "OAD DOCUMENT"
160 PRINT : INVERSE : PRINT "Q"; : NORMAL
170 PRINT "UIT" : PRINT

220 REM GET USER CHOICE
230 INPUT "";A$ : D$ = CHR$(4)
240 IF A$ <> "N" AND A$ <> "L" AND A$ <> "Q" THEN 230
260 IF A$ = "N" THEN GOSUB 1000
270 IF A$ = "L" THEN MO$ = "L" : GOSUB 2000
290 IF A$ = "Q" THEN GOTO 4000
300 GOTO 110
```

```
1000 REM CREATE A NEW DOCUMENT
1005 HOME : INVERSE : PRINT " " : NORMAL
1010 FI$ = ""
1015 GOSUB 5520

2000 REM LOAD AN EXISTING DOCUMENT
2010 REM ASK FOR FILE NAME
2020 HOME : INPUT "LOAD WHICH DOCUMENT? ";FI$
2030 IF FI$ = "" THEN RETURN
2035 HOME
2040 REM CHECK IF FILE EXISTS
2050 PRINT : PRINT D$;"RENAME ";FI$;",";FI$
2060 REM NOW TRY TO OPEN THE FILE
2070 PRINT : PRINT D$;"OPEN ";FI$
2080 PRINT : PRINT D$;"READ ";FI$
2180 REM READ TOTAL LINES
2190 INPUT "";LC%
2200 REM READ LINES INTO DL ARRAY
2210 FOR I = 1 TO LC%
2215 INPUT "";LI$ : IF LI$ = "" THEN 2235
2220 FOR J = 1 TO LEN(LI$)
2225 C = ASC(MID$(LI$,J,1)) : GOSUB 8715
2230 NEXT J
2235 IF I <> LC% THEN GOSUB 9510
2240 NEXT I
2250 PRINT D$ : REM CANCEL DOS COMMAND
2260 PRINT D$;"CLOSE ";FI$
2280 REM ENTER INTO MAIN EVENT LOOP
2290 GOSUB 5520

4000 REM QUIT THE PROGRAM
4010 REM MAKE SURE THE FILE IS CLOSED
4020 IF FI$ <> "" THEN PRINT D$;"CLOSE ";FI$
4030 HOME : END

5000 REM SCREEN DISPLAY SUBROUTINE
```

```
5010 REM RESPONSIBLE FOR DISPLAYING LINES OF TEXT ON
SCREEN
5020 REM BY DOING A COMPLETE REDRAW
5030 HOME
5040 REM CALCULATE RANGE OF LINES TO DISPLAY
5050 RE = TL + 23 : IF RE > LC THEN RE = LC
5060 LC% = 1 : REM REDRAW LINE COUNTER
5200 FOR I = (TL) TO (RE) : REM PARENS NEEDED FOR RE-
SERVED WORDS
5205 FOR J = 1 TO SL : REM PRINT A ROW
5210 VTAB(LC%) : HTAB(J) : PRINT DL$(I,J);
5215 NEXT J : REM NEXT CHAR IN ROW
5220 LC% = LC% + 1 : IF LC% > 24 THEN LC% = 24
5225 NEXT I : REM NEXT ROW
5230 RETURN

5500 REM MAIN EVENT LOOP
5510 REM LISTENS FOR KEY PRESSES AND DECIDES WHAT TO
DO
5520 C = PEEK(-16384) : REM READ KEYBOARD
5530 IF C < 128 THEN 5520 : CHECK FOR KEY PRESS
5540 POKE -16368,0 : REM RESET KEYBOARD STROBE
5545 C = C - 128 : REM CONVERT TO ASCII CODE
5550 IF C = 17 THEN GOSUB 4020 : REM CTRL-Q, QUIT
5555 IF C = 9 THEN GOSUB 6000 : REM CTRL-I, TAB
5560 IF C = 19 THEN GOSUB 7000 : REM CTRL-S, SAVE
5565 IF C = 1 OR C = 26 THEN GOSUB 8000 : REM CTRL-A,
CTRL-Z UP/DOWN CURSOR
5570 IF C = 8 OR C = 21 THEN GOSUB 9000 : REM LEFT,
RIGHT CURSOR
5575 IF C = 11 OR C = 10 THEN GOSUB 8000 : REM UP,
DOWN CURSOR
5580 IF C = 13 THEN GOSUB 9500 : REM CARRIAGE RETURN
5585 IF C = 27 THEN GOSUB 6500 : REM ESCAPE, HELP MENU
5590 IF C = 127 THEN GOSUB 8500 : REM DELETE
5591 IF C = 18 THEN GOSUB 5030 : GOSUB 9050 : REM RE-
DRAW
```

```
5595 GOSUB 8700 : REM ADD A CHARACTER
5600 GOTO 5520

6000 REM INSERT A TAB (8 SPACES)
6005 TL% = SL - CP : REM TAB LENGTH
6010 IF TL% > 8 THEN TL% = 8
6015 FOR X = 1 TO TL%
6020 C = ASC(" ") : REM SPACE
6025 GOSUB 8715 : REM ADD CHARACTER
6030 NEXT X
6040 RETURN

6500 REM SHOW A HELP MENU THAT LISTS COMMANDS
6505 REM SET TEXT WINDOW
6510 POKE 32,INT((SL - 28) / 2) : POKE 34,6
6512 HTAB 1 : VTAB 6
6515 FOR X = 1 TO 27 : PRINT "=";: NEXT X : PRINT
6520 PRINT "|";: PRINT SPC(4);: PRINT "COMMAND REFER-
ENCE";: PRINT SPC(4); : PRINT "|"
6525 PRINT "|";: PRINT SPC(25);: PRINT "|"
6530 PRINT "| CTRL-Q : QUIT";: PRINT SPC(11);: PRINT
"|"
6535 PRINT "| CTRL-I : TAB (8 SPACES) |"
6540 PRINT "| CTRL-S : SAVE";: PRINT SPC(11);: PRINT
"|"
6545 PRINT "| CTRL-A : CURSOR UP";: PRINT
SPC(6);:PRINT "|"
6550 PRINT "| CTRL-Z : CURSOR DOWN";: PRINT SPC(4);:
PRINT "|"
6555 PRINT "|";: PRINT SPC(25);: PRINT "|"
6560 PRINT "|  PRESS ESC TO CONTINUE  |"
6565 FOR X = 1 TO 27 : PRINT "=";: NEXT X
6570 REM WAIT FOR ESC KEYPRESS
6575 C = PEEK(-16384) : REM READ KEYBOARD
6580 IF C < 128 THEN 6575 : CHECK FOR KEY PRESS
6585 POKE -16368,0 : REM RESET KEYBOARD STROBE
6590 C = C - 128 : REM CONVERT TO ASCII CODE
```

```
6595 IF C <> 27 THEN GOTO 6575
6600 REM RESET TEXT WINDOW
6605 POKE 32,0 : POKE 34,0 : POKE 33,SL
6610 GOSUB 5030 : REM REDRAW SCREEN
6620 GOSUB 9050 : REM FLASH CURSOR
6650 RETURN

7000 REM SAVE DOCUMENT
7010 REM ASK FOR NAME IF NONE, OTHERWISE WRITE OUT
LINES
7015 IF FI$ = "" THEN PRINT CHR$(7) : GOTO 7100
7020 PRINT : PRINT D$;"OPEN ";FI$ : PRINT D$;"CLOSE
";FI$
7025 PRINT D$;"DELETE ";FI$ : REM TRUNCATE THE FILE
7030 PRINT D$;"OPEN ";FI$
7045 PRINT D$;"WRITE ";FI$ : REM START WRITING TO FILE
7050 PRINT LC : REM TOTAL LINES
7060 FOR I = 1 TO LC
7065 FOR J = 1 TO SL : REM PRINT A ROW
7070 PRINT DL$(I,J);
7075 NEXT J : REM NEXT CHAR IN ROW
7080 PRINT : NEXT I : REM NEXT ROW
7085 PRINT : PRINT D$;"CLOSE ";FI$ : REM CLOSE THE
FILE
7090 GOTO 7190 : REM RETURN FROM SAVING
7100 REM ASK FOR NAME
7105 VTAB 1 : HTAB 1 : INVERSE : PRINT "NAME"; : NOR-
MAL
7110 PRINT SPC(20); : HTAB 5 : INPUT FI$
7120 IF LEN(FI$) > 15 THEN GOTO 7105
7125 GOTO 7020 : REM GO SAVE NOW
7190 PRINT : PRINT D$;"CLOSE ";FI$
7195 GOSUB 5030 : GOSUB 9050 : REM REDRAW SCREEN
7200 RETURN

8000 REM MOVE CURSOR UP OR DOWN
```

```
8005 IF (C = 1 OR C = 11) AND CL = 1 THEN RETURN : REM
AT TOP
8010 IF (C = 26 OR C = 10) AND CL >= LC THEN RETURN :
REM AT BOTTOM
8015 REM REPLACE CHARACTER UNDER CURSOR
8020 C$ = DL$(CL,CP) : IF C$ = "" THEN C$ = " "
8025 HTAB(CP) : VTAB(SL%) : PRINT C$;
8030 IF (C = 26 OR C = 10) AND CL < 70 THEN GOTO 8040
: REM MOVE DOWN
8035 IF (C = 1 OR C = 11) THEN CL = CL - 1 : GOTO 8055
: REM MOVE UP
8040 CL = CL + 1 : SL% = SL% + 1 : REM INCR. SCREEN
LINE
8045 IF SL% > 24 THEN SL% = 24 : TL = TL + 1 : GOSUB
5030 : REM REDRAW
8050 GOTO 8070
8055 SL% = SL% - 1 : REM DECR. SCREEN LINE
8060 IF SL% < 1 THEN SL% = 1 : TL = TL - 1 : GOSUB
5030 : REM REDRAW

8070 REM PUT CURSOR AFTER CHARACTER
8075 C$ = DL$(CL,CP) : IF C$ = "" THEN CP = CP - 1 :
IF CP > 0 THEN GOTO 8045 REM CHECK LEFT
8080 IF C$ <> "" OR CP <= 1 THEN GOTO 8090
8085 GOTO 8075 : REM CHECK NEXT POSITION
8090 REM DRAW CURSOR AT NEW POSITION
8095 IF CP < 1 THEN CP = 1 : C$ = DL$(CL,CP)
8100 IF C$ = "" THEN C$ = " "
8105 FLASH : VTAB(SL%) : HTAB(CP) : PRINT C$; : NORMAL
8110 RETURN

8500 REM DELETE KEY
8505 C = 8 : GOSUB 9005 : REM TREAT AS LEFT-ARROW FOR
NOW
8600 RETURN

8700 REM ADD A CHARACTER
```

```
8710 REM CHECK IF CHARACTER IS PRINTABLE
8715 IF C < 32 OR C > 126 THEN RETURN : REM NOT PRINT-
ABLE
8720 IF CP > SL THEN RETURN : REM AT END OF LINE?
8725 DL$(CL, CP) = CHR$(C) : REM ADD CHARACTER TO LINE
8730 C = 21 : REM MOVE CURSOR TO RIGHT
8735 GOSUB 9000 : REM INCREMENT CURSOR POSITION
8740 RETURN

9000 REM MOVE CURSOR LEFT OR RIGHT
9005 IF CP < 2 AND C = 8 THEN RETURN : REM CURSOR AL-
READY AT LEFT
9010 IF (CP >= SL OR DL$(CL,CP) = "" ) AND C = 21 THEN
RETURN : REM CURSOR ALREADY AT RIGHT
9015 REM REPLACE CHARACTER UNDER CURSOR
9020 C$ = DL$(CL,CP) : IF C$ = "" THEN C$ = " "
9025 HTAB(CP) : VTAB(SL%) : PRINT C$;
9030 REM MOVE CURSOR
9035 IF C = 8 THEN CP = CP - 1 : REM TO LEFT
9040 IF C = 21 THEN CP = CP + 1 : REM TO RIGHT
9045 REM DRAW CURSOR AT NEW POSITION
9050 C$ = DL$(CL,CP) : IF C$ = "" THEN C$ = " "
9055 FLASH : VTAB(SL%) : HTAB(CP) : PRINT C$; : NORMAL
9100 RETURN

9500 REM CARRIAGE RETURN
9505 REM REPLACE CHARACTER UNDER CURSOR
9510 C$ = DL$(CL,CP) : IF C$ = "" THEN C$ = " "
9515 HTAB(CP) : VTAB(SL%) : PRINT C$;
9520 IF CL < 70 THEN CL = CL + 1 : REM DROP DOWN A
LINE
9525 CP = 1 : REM MOVE CURSOR TO LEFT EDGE OF SCREEN
9530 SL% = SL% + 1 : REM INCR. SCREEN LINE
9535 IF SL% > 24 THEN SL% = 24 : TL = TL + 1 : GOSUB
5030 : REM REDRAW
9550 IF CL > LC THEN LC = LC + 1 : REM INCREASE LINE
COUNT
```

```
9555 GOSUB 9050 : REM FLASH CURSOR WITHOUT MOVING IT
9600 RETURN

10000 REM ERROR HANDLER FOR DOS
10010 X = PEEK(222) : REM GET ERROR CODE
10020 IF X = 6 OR X = 13 OR X = 10 THEN PRINT : PRINT
"THE FILE NAMED "; FI$; " ";
10030 IF X = 6 THEN GOTO 10100 : REM FILE NOT FOUND
10040 IF X = 13 THEN GOTO 10200 : REM FILE TYPE MIS-
MATCH
10050 IF X = 10 THEN GOTO 10300 : REM FILE LOCKED
10060 PRINT "AN UNEXPECTED ERROR HAS OCCURRED, CODE
";X
10065 PRINT "ON LINE: "; : L=PEEK(219)*256+PEEK(218) :
PRINT L
10070 END
10100 REM FILE NOT FOUND
10110 PRINT "DOES NOT EXIST."
10120 GOTO 10400
10200 REM FILE TYPE MISMATCH
10210 PRINT "IS NOT A TEXT FILE."
10220 GOTO 10400
10300 PRINT "IS LOCKED."
10400 PRINT "PRESS RETURN TO CONTINUE..."
10410 GET A$ : PRINT : REM NEED A PRINT AFTER GET FOR
DOS
10420 IF MO$ = "L" THEN GOTO 110
10430 RESUME
```

Above all, this program exemplifies the sheer folly of trying to write a word processing program in BASIC. Except when running on an Apple IIc Plus or IIgs, the program is unacceptably slow. Word processing programs are best written in assembly language.

Largely what makes this program slow is that instead of relying on the built-in, assembly language code to accept key presses and update the screen, the program is doing it all by itself. Unfortunately, BASIC is a lot slower than assembly language.

However, in terms of functionality, this word processing program is equal to the task.

Since this program must operate under both DOS 3.3 and ProDOS, it is written using only the features shared between the two systems, as best as possible. One notable exception is the use of MAXFILES on line 35, a command that will make more memory available to the word processing program. Under ProDOS, using this command will cause a SYNTAX ERROR. The solution is to check if ProDOS is running by PEEKing at memory location 977 ($3D1 in hex). If it's a 0, then ProDOS is running and MAXFILES should not be used. Otherwise, it will be 191, signifying that DOS 3.3 is active.

The program uses an error handler located at lines 10000-10430 to handle a few common errors which may arise. The error handler comes in handy when checking if a file exists before trying to load it, on line 2050. The technique is to perform an operation on the file that will not change the file if it in fact exists. Renaming a file with the same name accomplishes this task. If the file doesn't exist, then the error handler steps in and informs the user.

Once it is determined that a file exists, loading it into memory consists of a few more steps, all located on lines 2070-2260. First, DOS is told to OPEN then READ from the file. The first line of every file contains the total number of text lines. The INPUT statement on line 2190 reads this value. The quote marks and semicolon before the variable name are used to suppress the question mark that may appear under ProDOS.

Once the total number of lines is known, a FOR-NEXT loop is used to read each line into LI$. An inner loop then works over each character in LI$, adding it to the document. This progress is visible on-screen, as if invisible hands were retyping your document.

When the entire file is read from the disk, the file is CLOSEd on line 2260.

Saving the file, on lines 7000-7200, works similarly, though in the opposite direction. If a new document was started which has never been saved, the user is asked to supply a filename, FI$. Otherwise, if the document was previously loaded from disk or saved, the contents of FI$ are used as the filename without prompting the user.

To prevent any stale data from getting mixed into the new disk file, the old file is first created on line 7020, then DELETEd on line 7025. The WRITE command is next used to tell DOS to send data to the file. First the total line count is written to the file, followed by each character from the document, in a nested loop. On line 7190, the file is CLOSEd, thus ensuring that its memory buffer is written out to disk.

Most of the program lines deal with accepting keyboard input and moving the cursor. Nearly all of these techniques come from earlier chapters in this book, especially Chapters 5 and 6.

Using Random-Access Files

A random-access data file may be thought of as a book with pages. The book makes up the file, and each page, being numbered and of the same size, forms each record. Having numbered pages allows for random-access: any page may be instantly selected in any sequence.

Though random-access files have one great advantage over sequential files: increased speed when accessing records, there is one disadvantage. In order to gain an increase in speed, each record must be exactly the same size. This forces you, the programmer, to plan for the maximum length of data that will be expected to fit in each record. Records with too much data must be truncated, and records that are shorter than the maximum length will waste some disk space.

A random-access file is best suited for database-type applications which require fast access to various records of data, and which need to efficiently update specific records.

For the BASIC programmer, a random-access file is used much the same as a sequential text file: it must be opened and closed as usual. The main difference is that the record size must be specified when opening the file, and READ and WRITE commands must be given a record number parameter. Each record behaves like an independent sequential text file.

Opening Random-Access Files

A random-access file is opened much like a sequential file, with the exception that an additional parameter to specify the record length is necessary. It is important that a random-access file always be opened with the same record length; doing otherwise will almost certainly lead to data corruption or loss.

The L parameter specifies record length, as shown in this example:

```
5 D$ = CHR$(4)
10 PRINT D$;"OPEN RANDOM,L100"
```

Line 10 opens a random-access file named RANDOM with a record length of 100 bytes. This length means that each record may use no more than 100 bytes of space in the file. If a record uses fewer bytes, then the remainder will be filled with null values.

The record length L must be in the range of 1 to 32767 in DOS 3.3, and 1 to 65535 in ProDOS. If no value is specified, then the length is assumed to be 1.

As stated previously, it is imperative that a random-access file always be opened with the same record length. This length should be part of the program's documentation, as it is impossible to determine the length of a record in a DOS 3.3 file otherwise. Fortunately, ProDOS stores the record length in the file's catalog entry. The CATALOG command will display the length.

One way to store the file's record length in DOS 3.3 is to include it as part of the file's name, such as:

```
DATABASE.L120
SCORES(L20)
CALENDAR-L45
```

Placing the record length in the filename is purely for human convenience; the Apple has no way of knowing what the record length is supposed to be. Even in ProDOS, which stores the original record length, the Apple will not object to a random-access file being opened with differing record lengths.

Writing Random-Access Files

Since random-access files work on the concept of multiple records, writing requires a record number, R, be specified. Otherwise, the procedure for writing to a random-access file is the same as for a sequential-access file. The WRITE command is used with a filename and a record number. If no record number is specified, the default value of 0 is used, indicating the first record of the file.

The following example writes to the second record of a file named SCORES:

```
20 PRINT D$;"WRITE SCORES, R1"
```

Notice that the record number, 1, is preceded by an R. As with sequential files, the filename specified by WRITE must have been previously opened.

A WRITE command used with a random-access file in ProDOS may also specify a field within the record number at which to start writing. Use F*n* to specify a field.

A byte parameter, B, may be provided to start writing at a specific byte offset within a record. When omitted, B is assumed to be 0, the start of the record. The following line starts writing at byte 20 of record 5:

```
30 PRINT D$;"WRITE SCORES, R5, B20"
```

One should take care when using the byte parameter, as it can lead to corrupted data if poorly used. A programmer should make sure that his random-access file is well thought-out and planned before using byte offsets.

POSITION can also be used to move the byte pointer further ahead in a record. As with sequential files, POSITION may only advance the pointer, and then only by a relative offset. Since POSITION cancels a WRITE command, another WRITE (without a parameter) must be issued to resume writing.

If a record is longer than the number of bytes specified by the length parameter L when the file is opened, some records may be partially overwritten or merged, leading to unpredictable results.

The final carriage return character is also counted as part of the record's length. The programmer must take precaution to not write a record longer than the record length L, including the carriage return. Otherwise, the data will spill into the next record, leading to data corruption. For example, if the record length for a file is 250, your program must write no more than 249 characters (bytes) to each record, for the 250th byte is occupied by a carriage return.

To cancel a WRITE operation, simply issue any DOS command (such as the null command). WRITE is also cancelled by an INPUT statement.

Closing Random-Access Files

Closing a random-access file requires exactly the same procedure as is used for sequential text files, explained earlier in this chapter. Use the CLOSE command plus a filename. Executing CLOSE with no filename will close all open files.

Remember that changes to a file will not be written to disk unless the file is first closed. Failure to do so could lead to data loss.

Reading Random-Access Files

With a random-access file, reading works much the same as with a sequential text file, except that a record number, R, is required. Using the record number moves the data pointer to the beginning of that record, ready for reading.

The following example illustrates the syntax:

```
READ ABOOK,R2
```

The filename is specified first, in this example, ABOOK. The record number follows the R. In this case, reading will begin at record 2, actually the third record in the file (because records are numbered starting from 0).

As with sequential text files, after a READ command is issued, all subsequent INPUT and GET statements will take data from the disk file instead of the keyboard. In Applesoft, GET may be used to read one byte at a time from a record, whereas INPUT in Applesoft and Integer BASIC will read an entire field at a time from a record.

Reading from the disk continues until another DOS command is issued, including the null command.

A byte parameter, B, may be specified to start reading at a certain byte position of the record, as in this example:

```
READ ABOOK,R2,B25
```

Here, reading will begin at byte 25 of record 2 from the file ABOOK.

A READ command used with a random-access file in ProDOS may also specify a field within the record number at which to start reading. Use F*n* to specify a field.

End of File and Missing Records

It is possible to write noncontiguous records to a random-access file. For example, a file could contain records numbering 1, 2, and 10. In this case, the end of the file would be declared after record 10.

Behavior differs between DOS 3.3 and ProDOS when an attempt is made to read past the end of a file, in this case, any record number greater than 10. ProDOS returns with a Range Error, code 2, whereas DOS 3.3 presents an End of Data error, code 5.

Likewise, DOS 3.3 also returns an End of Data error if a program tries to read a record that was never written (such as record number 4 in this example). When an End of Data error occurs, DOS 3.3 sets the random-access record length to 1.

Under ProDOS, attempting to read a nonexistent record can also cause an End of Data error (code number 5). It is possible in some cases for no error to occur; this will cause the first field read to be empty.

Forcing ProDOS to Write to Disk

As explained earlier, when a WRITE command is issued in ProDOS, the changes are not immediately written to the disk. Instead, they linger in a memory buffer for some time. In some cases, it may be desired to have data immediately written to the disk, such as if power failure is a concern (because data in RAM disappears when the power is removed).

The ProDOS FLUSH command can be used to help prevent data loss. It will immediately write the changes from a memory buffer to the file on disk. Following is an example:

```
50 PRINT CHR$(4);"FLUSH WORDS"
```

Using FLUSH without a file or path name will cause the buffers of all open files to be written to disk.

Constant use of FLUSH will slow down a program, but this decrease in performance may be a worthwhile price to pay in exchange for greater data security.

DOS 3.3 does not have a FLUSH command. The only way to force the file buffer to be written to disk is to close the file.

A Database Program Using Random-Access Files

Using a random-access file to create a database program is one of the things that many programmers do when learning about this type of file.

This program will start out quite simply: it will store a name and a description in each record. The program will allow the user to add, modify, and delete records, as well as list all records at once and search by name for a record.

The first step is to plan how the data will be stored in the random-access text file. The name field will allow up to 20 characters, and the description field should hold 255 characters. Since it will be possible to delete records, a byte could be reserved to store the record's status. However, an easier method in this case would be simply to check if the name field is empty. If so, then we assume that the record is deleted (or never existed).

The total record length should now be calculated. Each field, of which there are two, is to be separated with a carriage return. The final field will also end with a carriage return. Therefore, the total record length is:

20 + 1 + 255 + 1 = 277 bytes

The first record, number 0, of the file will contain the total number of records. After that will follow the real records containing names and descriptions.

Here is the program, which will work both on DOS 3.3 and ProDOS:

```
10 REM SIMPLE DATABASE PROGRAM
15 FI$ = "DATABASE" : REM FILE NAME
20 RS% = 277 : REM RECORD LENGTH
25 D$ = CHR$(4)
30 SE$ = "" : REM SEARCH STRING
40 NE = 0 : RFM NEW FILE FLAG
45 TR = 0 : REM TOTAL RECORDS
50 RN = 0 : REM RECORD NUMBER
60 MR = 100 : REM MAXIMUM RECORD NUMBER
65 ED = 0 : REM END OF DATA FLAG
70 ONERR GOTO 10000

100 REM PROGRAM SETUP
105 GOSUB 300
110 PRINT CHR$(21) : HOME : REM CLEAR SCREEN
120 PRINT SPC(8);"SIMPLE DATABASE PROGRAM" : PRINT
125 PRINT TR;" RECORD(S) IN DATABASE" : PRINT
130 PRINT "1) ADD A RECORD"
```

```
135 PRINT "2) DELETE A RECORD"
140 PRINT "3) MODIFY A RECORD"
145 PRINT "4) LIST ALL RECORDS"
150 PRINT "5) SEARCH FOR RECORD"
155 PRINT "6) QUIT"
160 PRINT : INPUT "YOUR CHOICE? ";C$
165 C = INT(VAL(C$)) : IF C < 0 OR C > 6 THEN 160
170 ON C GOSUB 400,500,600,700,800,900
175 GOTO 110 : REM INVALID CHOICE

300 REM PREPARE DATABASE FILE
305 REM CHECK IF IT EXISTS
310 IF NE = 0 THEN PRINT D$;"RENAME ";FI$;",";FI$
320 PRINT D$;"OPEN ";FI$;",L";RS% : REM OPEN DATABASE
325 IF NE = 0 THEN GOTO 340
330 PRINT D$;"WRITE ";FI$ : REM WRITE INITIAL RECORD
335 PRINT 0 : PRINT D$ : NE = 0 : GOTO 355
340 PRINT D$;"READ ";FI$
345 VTAB 23 : HTAB 39
350 IF ED = 0 THEN INPUT ""; TR
355 PRINT D$;"CLOSE ";F$ : RETURN

400 REM ADD A RECORD
405 HOME : PRINT "ADD A RECORD" : PRINT
410 INPUT "NAME? ";NI$
411 IF NI$ = "" OR LEN(NI$) > 20 THEN PRINT "ENTER 1-
20 CHARS!" :GOTO 410
415 PRINT : INPUT "DESCRIPTION? ";DI$
420 PRINT : PRINT "ADDING RECORD..."
425 GOSUB 1005 : REM FIND FREE RECORD
426 PRINT D$;"OPEN ";FI$;",L";RS%
430 PRINT D$;"WRITE ";FI$;",R";RN
435 PRINT NI$ : PRINT DI$
438 PRINT D$
440 TR = TR + 1 : REM INCREMENT TOTAL RECORDS
445 PRINT D$;"WRITE ";FI$;",R0"
450 PRINT TR : REM WRITE TOTAL RECORDS
```

```
455 PRINT D$;"CLOSE ";FI$ : REM CANCEL WRITING
460 PRINT : PRINT "RECORD ADDED SUCCESSFULLY."
465 PRINT "PRESS ANY KEY TO CONTINUE..." : GET A$
470 RETURN

500 REM DELETE A RECORD
510 HOME
515 IF TR = 0 THEN PRINT "NO RECORDS!" : GET A$ : RETURN
520 INPUT "DELETE WHICH RECORD NUMBER? ";DR
525 IF DR < 1 THEN GOTO 520
530 PRINT D$;"OPEN ";FI$;",L";RS%
535 REM TRY TO READ THE REQUESTED RECORD
540 PRINT D$;"READ ";FI$;",R";DR
545 IF ED = 0 THEN INPUT "";NA$
550 IF ED = 1 OR NA$ = "" THEN GOTO 580 : REM RECORD DID NOT EXIST
555 PRINT D$;"WRITE ";FI$;",R";DR
560 PRINT : PRINT : TR = TR - 1 : REM DELETE THE RECORD
565 PRINT D$;"WRITE ";FI$;",R0" : PRINT TR : REM UPDATE TR
570 PRINT D$;"CLOSE ";FI$ : PRINT "RECORD DELETED." : GOTO 590
580 ED = 0 : PRINT D$;"CLOSE ";FI$
585 PRINT "RECORD DID NOT EXIST!"
590 GET A$ : RETURN

600 REM MODIFY A RECORD
605 HOME
610 IF TR = 0 THEN PRINT "NO RECORDS!" : GET A$ : RETURN
615 INPUT "MODIFY WHICH RECORD NUMBER? ";RM
620 IF RM < 1 THEN GOTO 520
625 PRINT D$;"OPEN ";FI$;",L";RS%
630 REM TRY TO READ THE REQUESTED RECORD
635 PRINT D$;"READ ";FI$;",R";RM
```

```
640 IF ED = 0 THEN INPUT "";NA$,DE$ : PRINT D$
645 IF ED = 1 OR NA$ = "" THEN GOTO 685 : REM RECORD
DID NOT EXIST
650 PRINT "NAME: ";NA$ : PRINT "DESCRIPTION: ";DE$
655 INPUT "ENTER NEW NAME: ";NN$
660 IF NN$ = "" OR LEN(NN$) > 20 THEN PRINT "ENTER 1-
20 CHARS!" : GOTO 655
665 INPUT "ENTER NEW DESCRIPTION: ";ND$
670 PRINT D$;"WRITE ";FI$;",R";RM
675 PRINT NN$ : PRINT ND$ : PRINT D$;"CLOSE ";FI$
680 PRINT "RECORD MODIFIED." : GOTO 690
685 ED = 0 : PRINT D$;"CLOSE ";FI$ : PRINT "RECORD DID
NOT EXIST!"
690 GET A$ : RETURN

700 REM LIST ALL RECORDS
705 HOME
710 IF TR = 0 THEN PRINT "NO RECORDS!" : GET A$ : RE-
TURN
715 C = 0 : RN = 0
716 PRINT D$;"OPEN ";FI$;",L";RS%
720 IF C = TR THEN 765
725 RN = RN + 1
730 IF ED = 0 THEN PRINT D$;"READ ";FI$;",R";RN
735 IF ED = 1 THEN GOTO 765 : REM REACHED END OF FILE
745 IF ED = 0 THEN INPUT "";NA$
750 PRINT D$ : REM STOP READING
751 IF ED = 1 THEN GOTO 765
755 IF NA$ = "" THEN GOTO 720
760 PRINT RN;") ";NA$ : C = C + 1 : GOTO  720
765 PRINT D$;"CLOSE ";FI$
770 PRINT "PRESS ANY KEY TO CONTINUE..." : GET A$
775 RETURN

800 REM SEARCH FOR RECORDS
805 HOME
```

```
810 IF TR = 0 THEN PRINT "NO RECORDS!" : GET A$ : RE-
TURN
815 INPUT "SEARCH FOR NAME: ";SS$ : C = 0
820 IF SS$ = "" OR LEN(SS$) > 20 THEN PRINT "ENTER 1-
20 CHARS!" : GOTO 815
825 PRINT D$;"OPEN ";FI$;",L";RS% : RN = 1 : REM OPEN
DATABASE
830 IF ED = 0 THEN PRINT D$;"READ ";FI$;",R";RN : REM
READ RECORD
835 IF ED = 1 THEN ED = 0 : RN = RN + 1 : GOTO 830 :
REM SKIP RECORD
840 IF ED = 0 THEN INPUT "";NA$ : PRINT D$ : REM READ
NAME
845 IF NA$ = "" THEN ED = 0 : RN = RN + 1 : GOTO 830
850 IF LEFT$(NA$, LEN(SS$)) = SS$ THEN PRINT RN;")
";NA$
855 RN = RN + 1 : C = C + 1 : ED = 0 : IF C = TR THEN
GOTO 865
860 GOTO 830
865 PRINT D$;"CLOSE ";FI$ : ED = 0
870 PRINT "SEARCH COMPLETE." : GET A$ : RETURN

900 REM QUIT
905 PRINT D$;"CLOSE ";FI$ : REM CLOSE THE DATABASE
910 END

1000 REM FIND A FREE RECORD
1005 IF TR = 0 THEN RN = 1 : RETURN
1008 PRINT D$;"OPEN ";FI$;",L";RS% : REM OPEN DATABASE
1010 FOR RN = 1 TO MR
1015 IF ED = 0 THEN PRINT D$;"READ ";FI$;",R";RN : REM
READ RECORD
1020 IF ED = 1 THEN ED = 0 : GOTO 1050 : REM FOUND A
RECORD
1025 IF ED = 0 THEN INPUT "";NA$ : REM READ NAME
1030 PRINT D$ : IF ED = 1 THEN ED = 0 : GOTO 1050 :
REM FOUND A RECORD
```

```
1035 IF NA$ = "" THEN ED = 0 : GOTO 1050 : REM FOUND A
RECORD
1040 NEXT RN : REM CHECK NEXT
1045 PRINT "ERROR: NO FREE RECORDS!" : GOTO 905
1050 PRINT D$;"CLOSE ";FI$ : RETURN

10000 REM ERROR HANDLER FOR DOS
10010 X = PEEK(222) : REM GET ERROR CODE
10020 IF X = 13 OR X = 10 THEN PRINT : PRINT "THE FILE
NAMED "; FI$; " ";
10030 IF X = 6 THEN NE = 1 : GOTO 10105 : REM FILE NOT
FOUND
10035 IF X = 2 OR X = 5 THEN ED = 1 : RESUME : REM END
OF DATA
10040 IF X = 13 THEN GOTO 10200 : REM FILE TYPE MIS-
MATCH
10050 IF X = 10 THEN GOTO 10300 : REM FILE LOCKED
10055 IF X = 254 THEN PRINT "ENTER A NUMBER" : RESUME
10060 PRINT "AN UNEXPECTED ERROR HAS OCCURRED, CODE
";X
10065 PRINT "ON LINE: "; : L=PEEK(219)*256+PEEK(218) :
PRINT L
10070 END
10105 PRINT D$ : PRINT "END OF DATA"
10120 RESUME
10200 REM FILE TYPE MISMATCH
10210 PRINT "IS NOT A TEXT FILE."
10220 GOTO 10400
10300 PRINT "IS LOCKED."
10400 PRINT "PRESS RETURN TO CONTINUE..."
10410 GET A$ : PRINT : REM NEED A PRINT AFTER GET FOR
DOS
10430 RESUME
```

The program is written to be modular: it consists of an initialization sequence, a main menu, and many subroutines to carry out the various operations.

Program initialization (lines 15-105) declares many variables that will be used later in the program, and sets the error handler. The subroutine called on line 105 checks the database file, creating it if it does not exist. The RENAME operation is used to check if the file exists without altering it if it does.

The next section of the program from lines 110 to 175 displays the main menu and prompts the user for a selection. The input is changed from a string to an integer in order to trap any errors and make the input handler more robust. Depending on the input, the program branches to one of six subroutines.

All of the subroutines OPEN the DATABASE file (whose name is defined by FI$), then CLOSE it when finished. Doing so causes overhead in the form of more disk accesses, but the benefit is that the DATABASE file is guaranteed to be up to date after every operation— data left in the memory buffer will be written to the disk.

Some of the notable algorithms include Search for Records at line 800 and Find a Free Record at line 1000.

The Search for Records algorithm takes an input search string, SS$, and matches it against each name in the database. For example, a search string of "SA" would match both "SARAH" and "SAM," but not "AILSA." Matching records are printed with their record number, while all other records are ignored. When the total number of records examined equals the total record count, TR, the search is complete.

The name matching is performed on line 850 with a combination of the LEFT$ and LEN functions. The characters of each record are truncated from the right, leaving only as many characters as were specified in the search string.

The algorithm to find a free record works similarly to the record search algorithm, except that it is looking for records with an empty name field, indicating a deleted record. If none are found, the next, unused, record number is returned.

The error handler at line 10000 is critical to the operation of this program. It catches the most common type of error, End of Data, and sets variable ED to 1 if such an error occurs. The various subroutines make decisions based on ED and reset its value back to 0 for next time.

Setting DOS 3.3 File Buffers

When DOS 3.3 opens a file, it reserves 595 bytes of memory for use as the file's buffer. When DOS 3.3 is booted, it reserves enough memory for three file buffers, meaning that a program may open at most three files at a time. To open more files concurrently, or to free some memory for other use, the MAXFILES command is used. MAXFILES will accept a whole number from 1 to 16 indicating the total number of file buffers to reserve. Only DOS 3.3 has a MAXFILES command; ProDOS manages file buffers dynamically. The following line will reserve five buffers:

```
]MAXFILES 5
```

Every DOS 3.3 command, except for IN#, PR#, and MAXFILES, requires a buffer to operate. Therefore, if you had as many files opened as specified by MAXFILES, (in this case, five) and then attempted to execute a DOS 3.3 command such as LOCK or RENAME, the program would receive a NO BUFFERS AVAILABLE error from DOS 3.3.

Executing MAXFILES in immediate mode will destroy an Integer BASIC program, and will scramble Applesoft strings. Thus, you should execute the MAXFILES command before loading or running any BASIC program. Additionally, MAXFILES disables the RENUMBER program.

In Applesoft only, MAXFILES may be used as part of a program only if it is the first instruction in the program (REM statements do not count as instructions). If MAXFILES is used anywhere later in the program, it will cause parts of the program to behave incorrectly, such as GOSUB and GOTO commands. As with any DOS command, MAXFILES must be prefixed by a CONTROL-D (ASCII character 4), as demonstrated:

```
10 REM SET MAXFILES IN A PROGRAM
20 PRINT CHR$(4);"MAXFILES 5"
30 REM BEGIN REST OF PROGRAM...
```

MAXFILES cannot be used as part of an Integer BASIC program, nor should it be used with ProDOS.

Automating the Apple

Sequential text files can be used to give a script to the Apple. The Apple will execute each command in the script to the best of its ability, just as if you had typed each successive command at the keyboard. The command for such automation is called EXEC, short for execute. The EXEC command is used similar to RUN, except that a text file is expected to contain keyboard commands or BASIC program lines

EXEC files are read line-by-line. When the end of a line is met with, signifying a press of the RETURN key, the line is then executed as either a BASIC or DOS command, or as a BASIC program line. Once the end of the file is reached, processing stops and the BASIC prompt reappears. Illegal commands that generate a SYNTAX ERROR will not stop the EXEC file; the next line is merely read and executed.

CONTROL-C will not work to interrupt an EXEC file. However, if a program is running while the EXEC file is open, pressing CONTROL-C will abort the program, and the remainder of the EXEC file typically will not be processed.

An EXEC file may call on another EXEC file, however, the first EXEC file will be CLOSEd. Only one EXEC file may be open and active at a time.

However, if an EXEC file RUNs a program, control will return to the EXEC file when the program terminates. The following EXEC line will then be executed.

Furthermore, if the running program contains any INPUT statements, the input will be taken from the next line in the EXEC file, and not from the keyboard. To further complicate matters, if the next line of the EXEC file that is being used for the INPUT happens to be a DOS command, that command will be executed before the program continues. This is a useful feature to have in some cases, such as in automated testing of a program, but it can be troublesome at other times.

Lastly, an EXEC file may be started at an absolute line number with the R parameter, as in this example:

```
]EXEC AUTOFILE, R2
```

R0 indicates the first line of the text file, R1 the second, and so on. If the line number specified by R is greater than the total number of lines, then nothing will happen. In ProDOS, the letter F may be used to specify the starting line, instead of R.

Creating an EXEC File

Making an EXEC file is as simple as writing a BASIC program that opens a sequential text file, prints the desired commands, then closes it.

Here is an Applesoft program that writes to a file named EXECME. The commands that will be written to the file are on lines 50 to 70:

```
5 REM CREATE AN EXEC FILE
10 D$ = CHR$(4) : REM CTRL-D
20 PRINT D$;"OPEN EXECME"
30 PRINT D$;"WRITE EXECME"
40 REM HERE ARE THE COMMANDS FOR THE FILE
50 PRINT "CATALOG"
60 PRINT "LIST"
70 PRINT "RUN HELLO"
80 PRINT D$;"CLOSE EXECME"
90 END
```

Notice that the commands which will be entered into the EXECME file are *not* preceded with a Control-D from D$. This is because the EXEC command takes care of adding a Control-D automatically.

Run this program, then type EXEC EXECME. You should get a disk catalog, a listing of this program, then the HELLO program on the disk should run (if it exists).

Listing a Program to a Text File

The EXEC command has another powerful function: the ability to list a BASIC program to a text file, then restore it later. This feature can be used to:

- Convert an Integer BASIC program to Applesoft.
- Renumber parts of a program.
- Include one or more common subroutines into a program.
- Join two or more programs.
- Repair a program that has become partially damaged.

The following program will list itself into a text file when run starting from line 300:

```
10 REM SELF-LISTING PROGRAM
20 PRINT "HELLO"
30 END
300 REM LIST TO FILE
301 D$ = CHR$(4) : REM CONTROL-D
302 PRINT D$;"OPEN LISTING"
303 PRINT D$;"WRITE LISTING"
304 POKE 33,30
305 LIST 10,30
306 PRINT D$;"CLOSE LISTING"
307 TEXT : END
```

```
]RUN 300
```

The LIST command on line 305 contains the line numbers of the program that will appear in the text file named LISTING. These lines can be placed at the end of a program in memory, or anywhere in the program that has free space for additional lines. One could even compress the lines down to one.

The resulting text file will have the program lines, complete with numbers. When the file is used with EXEC, those lines will be entered into memory, the same as if they had been typed from the keyboard. The program lines can then be LISTed, modified, and RUN. EXEC also has the added advantage over LOAD and RUN (with a filename) in that it does not obliterate the existing program in memory.

MAXFILES and Integer BASIC Programs

MAXFILES cannot be used in an Integer BASIC program without erasing it. However, there is a workaround to use MAXFILES by way of an EXEC file. First, follow the instructions given earlier to create an EXEC file. In this example, the EXEC file will be named SET MAXFILES.

SET MAXFILES should have the following command lines to allow for four open files at once:

```
MAXFILES 4
LOAD MYPROGRAM
DEL 5,10
RUN
```

These commands will first set MAXFILES to 4, then load the program named MYPROGRAM from disk. Be sure to substitute the correct program name for your case.

The first few lines of MYPROGRAM should be as follows:

```
5 PRINT "(Control-D)EXEC SET MAXFILES"
10 END
20 REM BEGIN PROGRAM HERE
```

Note that on line 5, the (Control-D) should be substituted with a CONTROL-D typed from the keyboard. This will ensure that the contents of the PRINT statement are interpreted as a DOS command.

When finished, running MYPROGRAM will EXEC the SET MAXFILES program, which will in turn set MAXFILES, delete the first two lines, then run MYPROGRAM.

Working with Binary Files

So far, you have seen two of the three major types of files: BASIC and text. The third file is known as the binary type, and it is used to contain raw data that can be loaded to and from the Apple's memory. A binary file can contain any sort of data: high-resolution or low-resolution graphics, digitized sounds, programs, and databases are just a few of the examples.

In a ProDOS disk catalog, binary files are identified by the BIN file type, whereas DOS 3.3 represents binary files with a letter B.

Just as the three DOS commands for working with BASIC commands are RUN, LOAD, and SAVE, the commands for manipulating binary files are similar: BRUN, BLOAD, and BSAVE. In ProDOS, the BLOAD and BSAVE commands can be used with files of any type.

Running Programs

Some binary files contain a program, written in assembly language, that may be loaded into the Apple's memory and executed, similar to a BASIC program. The BRUN command does this. The syntax of BRUN is quite similar to RUN. For its most basic use, simply type BRUN and the filename, such as:

```
]BRUN PROGRAM
```

to load and execute a binary file named PROGRAM from the disk. The file should contain a machine language program that was saved previously using BSAVE. Ordinarily, the machine language program will be loaded and started at the same memory address at which it was originally BSAVEd.

Specifying an address with the A parameter will instead load and execute the program at that given location. The address may be specified in decimal or hexadecimal. If using hexadecimal, type a dollar sign ($) before the address. The following two examples both load and execute a file at location $300:

```
]BRUN PROGRAM, A768
]BRUN PROGRAM, A$300
```

As with most DOS commands, BRUN can also accept slot, drive, and in DOS 3.3, volume number parameters.

ProDOS adds three additional parameters, E, L, and T. The first two parameters are mutually exclusive: they cannot be used together. T specifies a file type used to load and run any file. L specifies a length in number of bytes to load into memory. E specifies an ending memory location; the file contents will not be loaded into memory after this address.

After the file is loaded into memory, a machine language jump instruction is issued to the first address of the file. The machine language program can return to ProDOS by issuing an RTS, or in DOS 3.3, a JMP to the warm-start location $3D0.

Attempting to BRUN a file that is not a machine language program will have unpredictable results, including causing the Apple to lock up. Press CONTROL-RESET to restart the Apple.

Loading a Binary File into Memory

The BLOAD command will restore a binary file from disk back into memory. When supplied with only a filename, BLOAD will load the file into the same memory locations as it was originally saved. However, with the optional A (address) parameter, BLOAD can load the binary data starting at any memory location. Following is an example of BLOAD in DOS 3.3:

```
BLOAD FILENAME,A768,D2,S5
```

ProDOS adds four additional options to BLOAD: T for type, E for ending memory location, B for starting byte, and L for length. Options E and L are mutually exclusive and cannot be used together.

The type option specifies file type. This option allows a file other than a binary to be loaded to memory. If the type is not specified, the file must be a binary (BIN) file.

The byte parameter B will start loading the file at the specified byte offset from the file's beginning. Length L will terminate loading after a specified number of bytes are in memory. Alternatively, an ending address may be specified with E. File loading will cease once this address is reached.

The A and E parameters may be given in hexadecimal notation if preceded with a dollar sign ($).

Saving Memory to a Binary File

Any data in the Apple's memory may be committed to disk to be used later. This data includes the text screen, graphics, machine language programs, and any other memory. The BSAVE command is used to save memory to disk. It has additional options in ProDOS, but for both operating systems, it accepts a starting address and a length. The following line will save the 1,024 bytes of memory starting at location $400 to the file named TEXTSCR:

```
]BSAVE TEXTSCR, A$400, L$400
```

The A stands for address, the starting address of the block of memory, which in this case is $400 (decimal 1024). The L stands for length, the number of bytes after the starting address to save. In this case, hexadecimal values were used, prefixed by a dollar sign ($). If you wish to use a decimal value, do not type the dollar sign. Hex and decimal notation can be mixed in the same command, for example, one could denote the address in decimal, and the length in hexadecimal.

The file length L must be in the range 0 to 65535 for ProDOS and 1 to 32767 with DOS 3.3. Alternatively, in ProDOS, an ending memory location may be specified instead of a length. Use the E parameter, as in this example:

```
]BSAVE BIN.FILE,A768,E777
```

This command will save memory from locations 768 to 777 to a file named BIN.FILE.

The ProDOS BSAVE normally starts saving at the beginning of the file, just like the DOS 3.3 BSAVE. To skip ahead some number of bytes, use the byte offset parameter B. Note that this parameter skips bytes when writing the file, not bytes from memory (in other words, everything from the specified memory range is still written to the file, just not right at the beginning of the file). The following command writes exactly the same data as the previous command, except that it skips over the first 25 bytes of the file before writing:

```
]BSAVE BIN.FILE,A768,E777,B25
```

The final parameter allowed in ProDOS for BSAVE allows the file type to be specified. Specify the desired file type with T. Table 7-2 lists several common ProDOS file type codes that can be used. It is up to the user to ensure that the file type specified agrees with the type of data that is being saved to disk. If no type is specified, the file will be of type BIN.

Running any File with the Dash

ProDOS has a "smart run" command, also known as the dash command because it consists of a single dash (-). This command will automatically detect the file type and issue the appropriate run command. It works with BASIC programs, EXEC files, machine language programs, and ProDOS System programs. Here is an example:

```
]-STARTUP
```

The dash command does not have any options other than filename, drive, and slot number.

File Code	Type Meaning
DIR	Directory
TXT	Human-readable text
BAS	Applesoft BASIC program
VAR	Applesoft BASIC variables
BIN	Machine program or data
REL	Relocatable machine code
$F*n*	User-defined file type number *n*
SYS	ProDOS System program or data

Table 7-2. ProDOS file type codes

Tracing DOS 3.3 Commands

Just as Applesoft and Integer BASIC have a TRACE command that shows each line number as it is executed, so too does DOS 3.3 have such a command. DOS 3.3's trace command is called MON, short for MONitor, and it will provide an on-screen record of all disk commands and data being transferred. MON accepts three parameters, as follows:

```
]MON C I O
```

Each letter corresponds to a certain type of information that can be displayed. Letter C is for disk commands; I is for input, data being read from the disk; and O is for output, data being written to disk. Any combination of these parameters may be specified: only disk commands, or just input and output without disk commands, for example.

The NOMON command cancels the display from MON. In addition to NOMON, the effects of MON are completely stopped by the INT and FP commands, as well as whenever DOS 3.3 is restarted. NOMON uses the same parameters as MON, and these parameters may be given in any sequence and combination, as in the following two examples:

```
]NOMON C
```

```
]NOMON C I O
```

The first line will halt the display of disk commands only, whereas the second line will stop all display from MON.

The parameters for both MON and NOMON may be provided in any order, and can be separated by a space or a comma. At least one parameter must be supplied, otherwise the command will not have any effect.

Managing DOS 3.3 Disks with FID

The FID program, which stands for FIle Developer, allows you to easily perform common management tasks on DOS 3.3 disks, such as cataloging, copying, locking, unlocking, and deleting files. It also allows disk copying with only one drive.

FID requires Applesoft and at least 32K of RAM to operate, meaning that it will work on just about any model of Apple.

Starting FID

FID is located on the DOS 3.3 System Master disk. To start it, boot DOS 3.3 and type:

```
]BRUN FID
```

Some DOS System Master disks may have a BASIC program named FILEM. If you RUN FILEM, it should also start FID.

Once the program is started, you will be treated to the FID main menu, as shown in Figure 7-14. It lists all commands that the program will perform. To choose a command, type its number and press RETURN.

Using Wild Cards in Filenames

Since most of the FID commands operate on files, you will typically be prompted to enter a filename. You may enter a filename as usual, just like when using any other DOS command, or you can enter a "wild card." The wild card character, an equal sign (=), will match any character. For example, if you entered:

```
MAR=
```

files whose names were MARCH, MARRY, and MARBLE would all be matched.

The wild card can be used in any position of the filename, and you can even use multiple wild cards. To match every filename, enter the wild card character by itself.

```
****************************************
*         APPLE ][ FILE DEVELOPER      *
*                                      *
*            FID VERSION M             *
*                                      *
*  COPYRIGHT 1979 APPLE COMPUTER INC.  *
****************************************

CHOOSE ONE OF THE FOLLOWING OPTIONS

        <1>   COPY FILES
        <2>   CATALOG
        <3>   SPACE ON DISK
        <4>   UNLOCK FILES
        <5>   LOCK FILES
        <6>   DELETE FILES
        <7>   RESET SLOT & DRIVE
        <8>   VERIFY FILES
        <9>   QUIT

WHICH WOULD YOU LIKE?
```

Figure 7-14. FID main menu

If you do end up using a wild card in a filename, FID will ask "DO YOU WANT PROMPTING?" This is a chance to allow you to exclude certain files from being matched by the wild card. If you do intend to match all files, type an N for no. Otherwise, type a Y for Yes. Now with each file, FID will ask you to verify each filename before it is operated on. For each file, you may type a Y to continue the operation, or an N to exclude that file.

To abort the operation, type a Q when prompted.

Setting Slot and Drive Number

The first time that you choose a command that operates on a disk or disk file, FID will prompt you for a source slot and drive number. Afterward, these values will be used for each successive command until you reset them using option 7 from the main menu.

Take care to enter a slot number that has a disk controller card in it. If the Apple tries to access a slot with the wrong card or no card at all, the FID program could crash.

Copying Files

FID can copy files and entire disks using a one- or two-disk Apple system. From the main menu, type 1. When prompted, enter the source and destination slot and drive numbers. The source is the original disk to be copied, and the destination is the disk that will receive the copy.

If the source and destination slot and drive numbers are identical, then FID assumes that a single-drive copy is to take place, and you will be prompted when to change disks.

In any case, you will next be prompted for a filename. Enter a single filename to copy one file, or use a wild card to match multiple files. You can also copy the entire disk by entering a single = for the filename.

After entering the filename, the Apple will prompt you to insert the source and destination disks as appropriate. If a file with the same name already exists on the destination disk, then the Apple will ask if you wish to overwrite it or choose a new name for the destination copy. You can also cancel the copying by pressing ESCAPE or CONTROL-C.

If no matching files were found to copy, then a NO FILES SELECTED error will occur. Otherwise, if at least one file was found to be copied, the message DONE will be printed on the screen. Press RETURN to continue with FID.

Cataloging a Disk

To examine the files on a disk, type 2. If you have not already set a slot and drive number, you will be prompted for them now.

The catalog listing provided by FID is identical to what you would get by typing CATALOG from the BASIC prompt, as described earlier in this chapter.

Reporting Free Space on a Disk

DOS 3.3 lacks a command to show the free sectors on a disk. Fortunately, FID can perform the task. Press 3 to get a report on the number of free (unused) and used sectors on a disk.

Unlocking and Locking Files

The command to unlock files, 4, and the command to lock files, 5, are both used in the same way. First you will be prompted for a filename. If the name entered is invalid, you will be prompted again. You will then be given a chance to insert a disk. Press RETURN once the correct disk is in place to continue with the operation.

If you entered a filename which does not exist on the disk, FID will print a NO FILES SELECTED error on the screen. Press RETURN to abort the procedure and return to the main menu.

Deleting Files

To delete one or more files from a disk, choose the Delete Files option, number 6 from the menu.

When prompted, enter a filename. Remember that you can use = as a wild card to match more than one file. If at least one file was successfully deleted, the message <DONE> will appear. Otherwise, if no files were deleted, the message NO FILES SELECTED will be presented. Attempting to delete a locked file will return a FILE LOCKED error.

Resetting Slot and Drive Number

To change the default slot and drive number, choose option 7 from the main menu. The next time that you use a command that asks for a slot and drive number, such as CATALOG, you will be prompted to enter them.

Verify Files

The Verify command, number 8, in FID is analogous to the DOS 3.3 VERIFY command. It will handle all types of files, reading them in from disk to check for I/O errors.

Enter a filename when prompted, then press RETURN. Upon successful verification of a file, its name will be printed followed by the word DONE.

If a file fails the verification, meaning that it can't be read from disk, then an I/O ERROR message will appear.

Exiting the FID Program

Type 9 to quit the FID Program and return to the BASIC prompt.

Recovering from Errors

If there is an error while FID is working, such as during a file copy or when locking or unlocking a file, a message will be displayed, and the operation terminated. Errors during file copying are rather more problematic due to the possibility of half-written, possibly corrupted files. If FID was performing a file copy operation, it is likely that a bogus file will have been copied to the destination disk. This file will be shorter than the original, thus incomplete, and should be deleted immediately before taking any further action.

FID will display an error message for common errors such as DISK FULL, DISK WRITE PROTECTED, FILE LOCKED, and I/O ERROR. For all other, less common DOS errors, FID will report just the error number.

Managing ProDOS Disks with the Filer

The Filer program is the ProDOS equivalent to FID in DOS 3.3. It is designed to be user-friendly and includes built-in help screens which explain every command and menu.

```
****************************************
*                                      *
*    APPLE'S PRODOS SYSTEM UTILITIES   *
*                                      *
*           FILER VERSION 1.1          *
*                                      *
*  COPYRIGHT APPLE COMPUTER,  1983-84  *
*                                      *
****************************************

           ? - TUTOR

           F - FILE COMMANDS

           V - VOLUME COMMANDS

           D - CONFIGURATION DEFAULTS

           Q - QUIT

PLEASE SELECT AN OPTION:
```

Figure 7-15. The ProDOS Filer main menu

The ProDOS Filer is located on the ProDOS User's Disk. Boot this disk, then press F at the title screen to access the Filer.

The main menu has options to describe its commands, work on individual files, work on entire disks, set default options, or exit the program.

File Commands

All of these commands work on one or more files. When prompted to enter a filename or pathname, it is possible to enter a wild card character, ? or =, to match more than one file. The difference between the two is that the ? wild card causes the program to ask for confirmation for each file matched, whereas the = wild card acts on every matching name without confirmation.

Furthermore, the current ProDOS prefix will be added to the beginning of every pathname unless the pathname begins with a slash (/) character.

Option L for List ProDOS Directory works like the CAT command. Simply enter a path to get a listing of files in that directory. If there are more than 18 files, the listing will be separated into pages of 18 files at a time.

Copying one or more files is possible with option C. A file can be copied to a different directory on the same disk, or to an entirely new disk. Copying files to a second disk is possible even if your Apple has only one disk drive; if so, you will be prompted to swap disks when necessary. The ProDOS Filer will not overwrite existing files in the destination directory without first asking for confirmation.

Option D, for delete, allows any number of files to be deleted from a disk. Doing so releases storage space on the disk to make room for other files. A ProDOS subdirectory can also be deleted, but only if it does not contain any other files.

To check if the contents of two ProDOS files are identical, use the Compare Files command, option K. If the two files match, the message COMPARE COMPLETE appears, otherwise the message FILES DO NOT MATCH will appear.

Locking and unlocking files is accomplished with option A, the Alter Write-Protection command. When a file is locked, it may not be deleted, renamed, or changed. After specifying one or more filenames, the Filer will ask LOCK FILES? Press Y to lock the files, or N to unlock them.

The name of a file or directory may be changed using the Rename Files command, option R. When choosing a new name for a file, a file with that name must not already exist in the same directory.

Menu option M allows the creation of a ProDOS subdirectory. The directory will be created at the given pathname. As with most commands, the ProDOS prefix is automatically added to the beginning of the pathname.

To set the ProDOS prefix, use option P. The current ProDOS prefix will be shown. It may be modified using the LEFT ARROW and RIGHT ARROW keys. After entering the desired prefix, press RETURN to set it.

Volume Commands

The volume commands operate on an entire ProDOS disk. Remember that in most cases, the term "volume" is just another name for a disk. Press V from the Filer main menu to access these commands.

Apart from the Tutor option, there are seven commands for working with entire volumes.

The first option, F, is for formatting a volume. Formatting, sometimes also called initializing, is used to prepare a new disk for use with ProDOS. All data on the disk are destroyed, and the scheme of tracks and sectors is prepared on the disk surface.

The format option can be used only to make ProDOS disks, not DOS 3.3 disks. Furthermore, a newly formatted disk will not work as a startup disk. It must have a copy of the PRODOS file placed on it in the volume directory.

To format a disk, place the desired disk into a drive. Enter the slot and number of that drive, then enter a name for the disk. The disk name is restricted to the same rules as for naming ProDOS files: it must start with a letter, be no longer than 15 characters, and include only letters, numbers, and periods.

As a safety precaution, if the disk inserted is already a valid ProDOS disk, you will be asked for confirmation before formatting it.

Formatting a disk takes about 30 seconds. When it is finished, the message FORMAT COMPLETE appears near the bottom of the screen.

Copying an entire disk is performed with the Copy command, option C. This command is valuable, as it allows one to make backup copies of disks containing important work and programs.

Copying a disk naturally requires a source (original) disk and a destination (target) disk to receive the copy. To guard against "operator error," the source disk should be write-protected. For a 5.25" disk, write protecting involves covering the notch. A 3.5" disk is write-protected when the plastic tab is *not* covering the square hole at the top-right corner. The destination disk should not be write-protected. Furthermore, it need not even be formatted; the copy process automatically formats the target disk.

Copying is faster if two disk drives are used, though if your Apple has only one, the source and destination can be the same. Specify the slot and drive numbers for each by typing the desired number and pressing RETURN.

If the same slot and drive number were specified for source and destination, the Filer will ask you to place the source disk in the drive. You will then be prompted to enter a new volume name. To accept the default, which is the name of the destination, simply press RETURN. Otherwise, you may enter a new name and then press RETURN.

When using two disk drives, duplication will begin immediately after entering a new volume name. Be sure to insert the source and destination disks into their correct drives.

The Apple will prompt you to swap disks when appropriate if you're using just one drive. The Apple will alternate between reading a portion of the source disk into memory, then writing that bit of data back to the destination disk. This pattern continues until the entire disk is copied.

If any disk error occurs, such as an I/O error, or if you left a drive door open, the copy procedure will be terminated. A partially copied destination disk will be left with the name PARTIALCOPYDISK. You will have to begin again if you still wish to duplicate the source disk.

To display some information about all disks currently available to the Apple, choose option L to display (list) online volumes. An online volume is any disk that is currently inserted in a disk drive. The slot, drive number, and volume name of all online volumes are displayed.

Like a ProDOS file, a volume's name may also be changed with option R, Rename volume. Simply enter the slot and drive number containing the volume name to change, then enter a new name. The existing name will be displayed, allowing you to easily modify it. Press RETURN when finished to rename.

Defects on the recording surface of a disk can lead to data loss. Option D, Detect bad blocks, scans a disk for such defects. If the disk does not contain any defective blocks, then the message 0 BAD BLOCKS is shown. Otherwise, the Apple reports a list of bad blocks.

If a disk has bad blocks, its files should be immediately copied to a new disk. The bad disk can then be formatted. The bad blocks will be marked as unusable during the formatting process.

Option B, Block allocation, displays disk usage. Three figures are provided: number of blocks used to store files, number of blocks currently free for storage, and total number of blocks on the volume.

Two disks may be tested with option K, Compare Volumes, to see if their contents are identical. If so, the message COMPARE COMPLETE will appear. If the same slot and drive numbers were entered, the Apple will prompt you to swap disks when it is necessary to do so.

Default Options

From the Filer main menu, choosing option D for Configuration Defaults will allow you to set the default source slot and drive, and default destination slot and drive. These values will be provided automatically in any screen that uses them, such as when copying a disk. Furthermore, all Filer output may be sent to both screen and printer, or screen only. There is also a way to restore the default parameters if so desired.

Exiting the Filer

Choosing Quit from the main menu will lead you to a screen asking for the name of a program to run next. Usually, BASIC.SYSTEM is already entered; pressing RETURN will then take you to the Applesoft prompt. Alternatively, you may enter any valid pathname and press RETURN to start another program.

Chapter 8 : Graphics and Sound

One of the selling points of the original Apple II back in 1977 was the fact that it had easy-to-program color graphics support built into its BASIC. The Apple has integral color capabilities: all that you need is a color monitor or television. The graphics screen can even be used to create simple animation.

With BASIC, programming the Apple for graphics is fairly straightforward. Both Applesoft and Integer BASIC have a number of built-in commands to set colors, plot points, and draw lines. This chapter will show how to create bar charts, polygons, and a simple sketch pad program.

The last part of this chapter will explain how to control the Apple's speaker to produce all manner of blips, squawks, and tones. A music-generating program makes it easy to play songs on the Apple.

Low-Resolution and High-Resolution

There are two different types of graphics screen modes on the Apple: low-resolution, and high-resolution. These modes are sometimes referred to as *low-res* and *high-res* for short.

The *low-resolution* screen is divided into 40 rows by 40 columns of rectangular blocks. There are 16 colors which may be shown, including black.

The *high-resolution* screen allows more exact graphics, at the expense of having fewer colors available. Its size is 280 by 160. The number of colors available, however, is a mere six.

Both of these modes, by default, leave room for four lines of text at the bottom of the screen. It is possible to trade off these four lines in exchange for additional drawing area.

Low-Resolution Example

Here is a program which demonstrates the use of the low-resolution screen. Don't worry about understanding all of the new commands right now, as they will be explained shortly.

```
5 GR
10 X = 0:C = 0:R = 0
20 FOR C = 0 TO 39
30 FOR R = 0 TO 39
40 PLOT C,R
50 NEXT R
60 X = X + 1
70 COLOR= X
80 NEXT C
90 END
```

This program will generate a screen similar to what is shown in Figure 8-1, except that if you have a color monitor or TV, you'll get to see 15 different colors instead of shades of gray.

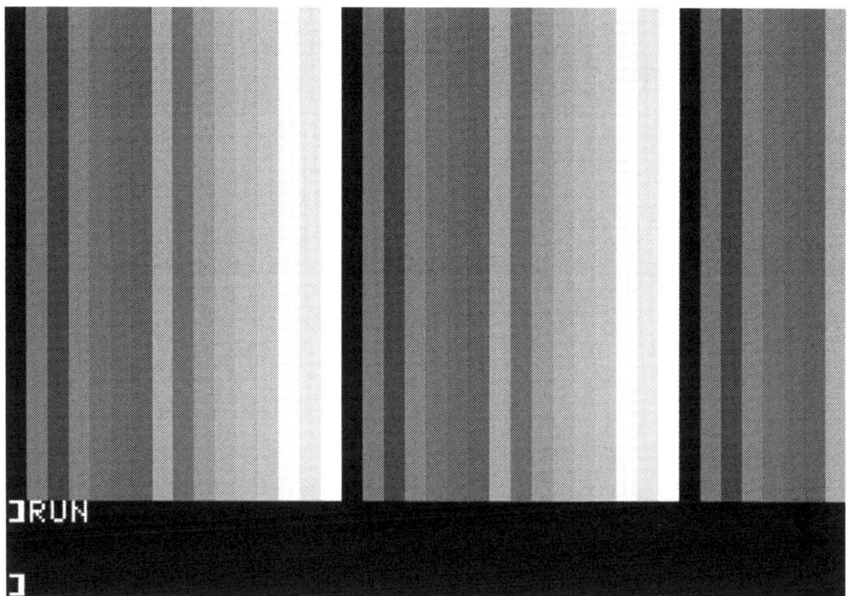

Figure 8-1. An example of the low-resolution screen

Switching Between Text and Graphics Modes

The Apple has two display modes: text and graphics. When you first start up your Apple, it will be in text mode. Most programs that you write in BASIC will be text-only. To tell the Apple to switch into graphics mode, you must give it the appropriate command.

As it turns out, since there are two graphics modes, there are two commands for accessing them. We are first going to cover low-resolution mode.

If you typed in and ran the BASIC program above, you should have several colored bars at the top of the screen, and a prompt at the bottom. Your Apple is in graphics mode, and the four lines at the bottom are reserved for text. Type the following command:

```
]TEXT
```

Now you should see that the colored bars have been replaced with various symbols, some of which may flashing. This behavior is due to where the Apple stores the data for the text and graphics screen. Indeed, it uses the very same memory locations!

Now type this command:

```
]GR
```

You should see the top portion of the screen get wiped out to black. Again, your Apple is in low-resolution graphics mode.

The BASIC command GR is used to enter low-resolution graphics mode. The top portion of the screen is used for graphics, while four lines at the bottom are reserved for text. GR automatically sets the text window.

GR always clears the screen to black. If the Apple is already in low-resolution graphics mode, GR can be used any number of times to clear the screen. Note that GR only clears the graphics screen, not the four-line text window.

Getting Some Extra Drawing Room

Ordinarily, the low-resolution graphics mode provided by GR leaves room for some text down at the bottom of the screen. If you'd rather have additional drawing space, issue this POKE command:

```
]POKE -16302,0
```

This will expand the drawing screen to 40 columns by 48 rows, giving you eight additional blocks, vertically. Note that this POKE command will only work after the GR command has been issued. Executing GR *after* this POKE will undo its effects.

If there was any text at the bottom of the screen, it will be converted to graphics dots. To clear the entire 48-row graphics screen, issue the following command:

```
]CALL -1998
```

These two commands are best suited for programmed mode, since in immediate mode, the Applesoft prompt and any text on the screen will be displayed as colored blocks (the prompt will be a yellow block, for example).

Restoring the Text Screen

As explained earlier, the TEXT command is one way to change the Apple back to full text mode. Since this command does not clear the screen, the contents of whatever was on the graphics screen will be converted to various ASCII characters. In Applesoft, use the HOME command to clear the screen of these characters. In both versions of BASIC, CALL -936 will also perform the same function as HOME.

To reverse the effects of the POKE command described in the previous section, issue the following POKE:

```
]POKE -16301,0
```

This POKE command restores the graphics mode to mixed text and graphics, leaving the bottom four lines of the screen for text.

Setting Colors

If you were to draw an image on screen right now, you wouldn't be able to see it. Why not? Because the default color is black, and the screen is already black! To fix this, make use of the COLOR command, such as in this example:

```
]COLOR = 1
```

There are 16 colors in total, numbered from 0 to 15. Zero is black, 1 is magenta, 2 is blue, and so on. See Table 8-1 or the Low-Resolution Colors table in Appendix E for the full listing, or experiment on your own to discover which number equals which color. While each color has an official name, the appearance of each color is subject to the controls on your monitor or television set. For example, magenta often looks more like a red. Furthermore, a black-and-white set will show shades of gray.

Number	Color	Number	Color
0	Black	8	Brown
1	Magenta	9	Orange
2	Dark Blue	10	Gray
3	Light Purple	11	Pink
4	Dark Green	12	Green
5	Gray	13	Yellow
6	Medium Blue	14	Aqua
7	Light Blue	15	White

Table 8-1. Low-Resolution colors

Every time that GR is executed, the color setting is changed back to 0 (for black).

Plotting on the Screen

Now that you have the Apple in graphics mode, and a favorite color set, it's time to draw something on the screen. The command for this action is called PLOT, and it takes two numeric arguments, separated by a comma:

```
]PLOT 1,1
```

The PLOT command always makes a rectangle with the last color chosen with the COLOR command. The first argument is the X-coordinate, and the second argument is the Y-coordinate. If you type this command, and you picked a color that isn't black, then you should see a small rectangle in the upper-left hand corner of your screen. As with most all BASIC commands, you can use any mixture of constants, variables, or expressions for the two coordinates.

Look at Figure 8-2 to help you understand the coordinate system. As you can see, the upper-left corner is (0, 0) and the lower-right corner is (39, 47).

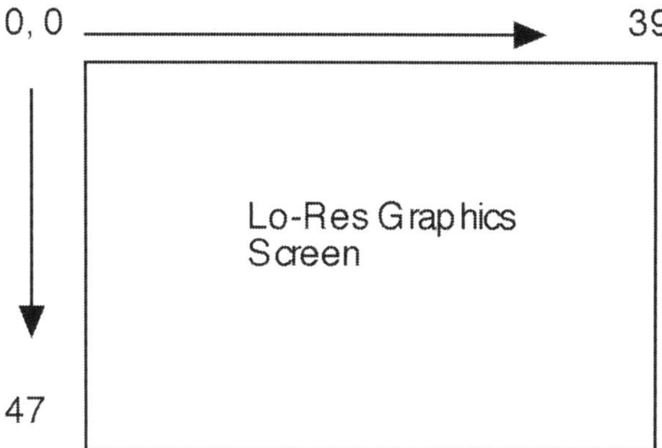

Figure 8-2. Low-Resolution graphics screen coordinates

Attempting to PLOT outside of these boundaries will result in an ?ILLEGAL QUANTITY ERROR from Applesoft, and a *** RANGE ERR from Integer BASIC.

Note that if you did not follow the tip in "Getting Some Extra Drawing Room," you will cut into the four lines of text if you attempt to plot in the Y range of 40 to 47. This will not cause an error, but you probably wouldn't want it to happen. If the screen is mixed graphics and text, as is the default, then the Y limit becomes the same as X, 39. Experiment on your own so you can learn firsthand the effects of PLOT.

Now you can go back and reexamine the Low-Resolution Example shown at the beginning of this chapter; you should have a better time understanding how it works now.

A Simple Drawing Program

One of the first programs that many people write to take advantage of the Apple's low-resolution graphics is a simple drawing program. The numbers at the top of the keyboard will allow the user to select a color. The letter keys IJKL will move the "pencil" around the screen, and the space bar will toggle the pencil between draw and no draw modes. This way, the artist can move the pencil without making any mark on the screen.

The following program illustrates one way to turn the Apple screen into a drawing pad. When you are finished running the program, press CONTROL-C to exit.

```
10 REM SIMPLE DRAWING PROGRAM
20 TEXT : HOME : REM CLEAR SCREEN
25 REM SET INITIAL VARIABLES
30 X = 0 : REM X-POSITION OF PENCIL
40 Y = 0 : REM Y-POSITION OF PENCIL
50 D = 1 : REM ARE WE IN DRAW MODE?
60 M = 0 : REM DID THE PENCIL MOVE?

65 REM PRINT INTRO SCREEN
70 HTAB(9) : PRINT "SIMPLE DRAWING PROGRAM
80 PRINT : PRINT "USE THE IJKL KEYS TO MOVE YOUR PEN-
CIL."
90 PRINT "PRESS SPACE BAR TO TOGGLE DRAW/NO DRAW."
100 PRINT "PRESS A NUMBER KEY TO CHANGE COLOR."
110 PRINT : PRINT "PRESS RETURN TO BEGIN..."
120 GET A$ : REM DUMMY VARIABLE TO MAKE A PAUSE
130 GR : REM SET LO-RES GRAPHICS MODE
140 COLOR = 1 : REM SET INITIAL COLOR

200 REM BEGIN MAIN PROGRAM
210 C = PEEK(-16384) : REM GET INPUT KEY
215 IF C < 128 THEN 210 : REM NO KEY PRESSED
220 POKE -16368,0 : REM CLEAR KEYBOARD STROBE
225 LET C = C - 128 : REM CONVERT TO ASCII CODE
230 REM CHECK FOR IJKL PENCIL MOVEMENT
235 IF C = 73 OR C = 105 THEN Y = Y - 1 : M = 1 : IF Y
< 0 THEN Y = 39
240 IF C = 75 OR C = 107 THEN Y = Y + 1 : M = 1 : IF Y
> 39 THEN Y = 0
250 IF C = 74 OR C = 106 THEN X = X - 1 : M = 1 : IF X
< 0 THEN X = 39
260 IF C = 76 OR C = 108 THEN X = X + 1 : M = 1 : IF X
> 39 THEN X = 0
270 REM DID WE MOVE?
```

```
280 IF M = 0 THEN GOTO 320 : REM NO, SO MOVE ON
290 IF D = 1 THEN PLOT X,Y : REM WE MOVED, SO MAKE A
MARK
300 M = 0 : REM RESET THE DID WE MOVE FLAG

310 REM CHECK FOR DRAW TOGGLE
320 IF C = 32 AND D = 0 THEN D = 1 : GOTO 340
330 IF C = 32 AND D = 1 THEN D = 0 : REM TURN OFF
DRAWING

340 REM NOW CHECK FOR A COLOR
350 IF C >= 48 AND C <= 57 THEN COLOR = C - 48

400 GOTO 210
```

Lines 10 through 60 clear the screen and set the initial variables. X and Y are used to hold the corresponding coordinates of the pencil's on-screen location. D and M are each used as a *flag*, a variable that is merely used to keep track of a specific condition. In this case, D is the drawing flag. When D = 0, moving the pencil will not make any marks on the screen, but when D = 1, the pencil will draw on the screen. M is used in a similar fashion: when it is equal to 1, it means that one of the keys was used to move the pencil. Otherwise, no movement occurred.

Lines 65 through 110 print the introduction screen that tells how to use the program. Line 120 uses GET with a dummy variable just to make a pause, allowing the user to read the text. Low-resolution graphics mode is set on line 130, and a starting color (red) is set on line 140.

Line 210 starts the main event loop of the program, the place where all the action happens. First, the keyboard is queried with PEEK to get the ASCII code of the most recently-pressed key. This code is saved in variable C for later use. Line 220 performs the slightly obscure, yet necessary, function of clearing the keyboard strobe. While the technical details are a bit beyond this discussion, suffice it to say, if you didn't clear the keyboard strobe, line 210 would always return the same ASCII code, even if you pressed different keys on the keyboard. This method of reading the keyboard was covered in Chapter 6.

With variable C containing the key code pressed, the next lines keep track of checking what action to take. Lines 235 through 260 manage pencil movement, and all have the same format. In the example of line 235, it checks for both lowercase and uppercase letter I. This allows the program to work on all Apple keyboards, no matter if Caps Lock is down or not. If variable C indicates that the letter I was pressed, then Y is decremented, moving the pencil up a square. The movement flag is set to indicate that the pencil did move, and if Y became negative, the pencil is "wrapped around" to the other side of the screen. The next three lines check for movement in the other three directions.

Lines 280 and 290 check if the pencil should make a mark or not. On line 280, if the movement flag was not set, program control skips over to line 320; no mark is made on the screen because the pencil did not move. Line 290 checks the drawing flag, D. If D is 1, then a mark is made on the screen. Line 300 then resets the movement flag back to 0.

Lines 320 and 330 implement the flip-flop drawing toggle, activated with a press of the SPACE BAR (which is ASCII code 32). If the SPACE BAR is pressed, and the draw flag was previously 0, then the flag becomes 1. If the SPACE BAR was pressed and the draw flag was set to 1, then it now becomes 0.

Line 350 performs a bit of an optimization. Since the 10 numerals all have ASCII codes in one contiguous range, C is first checked to see if it is within that range, which is 48 to 57. You might think at first that the ASCII codes for numbers would be the number itself, but that is not true. Number 0 has ASCII code 48, 1 is 49, and so on to number 9, which is 57. The rest of line 350 makes a quick translation from ASCII code to color number. The COLOR command expects a number from 0 to 15. We adjust for this offset by taking C, the ASCII code, and subtracting the lowest ASCII value, 48. This procedure makes the color number correspond to the number pressed on the keyboard. For example, pressing the 1 key generates an ASCII code of 49. Forty-nine minus 48 is 1, and color number 1 happens to be red.

Line 400 completes the main event loop, taking program control back up to line 210 to wait for the user's next key press.

Though this program does a fairly good job of turning the Apple screen into a sketch pad, it could use some improvements. One of these would be to implement a cursor to show the position of the pencil when drawing mode is off. This cursor could be white to stand out against the black background. To implement such a feature, you will need to save the color of the square where the cursor is about to move. Save it to a variable with the SCRN command (covered later in this chapter), then when the cursor moves off that square, PLOT the color back, and repeat the process again until drawing mode is turned on again. Remember that when drawing mode is turned back on, you will also need to restore the color underneath the cursor.

A second improvement to this program would be to allow for the full 16 low-resolution color palette, perhaps by using other keys to select the remaining six. Examine the ASCII Values chart in Appendix E to see what characters correspond to ASCII codes 58 through 63. Then extend the range in line 350.

Drawing Lines

While a line could be constructed from a series of PLOT commands, doing so would be tedious and use up many BASIC statements. Two commands are provided to aid in the plotting of horizontal and vertical lines. Appropriately, they are named HLIN and VLIN, respectively.

Horizontal Lines

While one could use multiple PLOT commands in a loop to plot a horizontal line, there is a more efficient way. The HLIN command to draw a horizontal line has this syntax:

HLIN *column1*, *column2* AT *row*

The first two arguments control the length of the line by indicating between which two columns the line should be drawn, and the final argument controls the vertical position of the line. The range for column 1 and column 2 is 0 to 39. The leftmost side of the screen is column 0. Row 0 is the top of the screen. For example, to draw a line across the entire screen, vertically positioned at the bottom, use this statement:

```
]HLIN 0,39 AT 39
```

The following will draw a short line in the middle of the screen:

```
]HLIN 18,23 AT 20
```

As with PLOT, the line color is dictated by the most recently issued COLOR statement. In Applesoft, it does not matter which column argument is greater. The following two statements draw the same line:

```
]HLIN 1,5 AT 10
]HLIN 5,1 AT 10
```

Vertical Lines

Drawing vertical lines is performed with the VLIN command, which has a similar syntax to HLIN:

VLIN *row1*, *row2* AT *column*

The first two arguments control the height of the line by dictating between which two rows the line should be drawn, and the final argument sets the horizontal position of the line. VLIN has the same characteristics and restrictions as HLIN. A row number must be from 0 to 39, and the column is restricted to the range 0 to 47.

The following statement will draw a short line near the left edge of the screen:

```
]VLIN 8,14 AT 3
```

Setting Background Color

Either of the two line-drawing commands may be used in a loop to clear the entire screen to a solid color. This method is a way to work around the limitation that GR only clears the screen to black.

The following program uses HLIN to clear the screen to each color in sequence:

```
10 REM LOW-RESOLUTION BACKGROUND COLOR
15 GR : REM SET LOW-RESOLUTION GFX
20 C = 0 : REM COLOR CHOICE
30 COLOR = C : REM SET COLOR
40 GOSUB 100 : REM CLEAR BACKGROUND
45 C = C + 1 : REM SELECT NEXT COLOR
50 IF C = 16 THEN C = 0 : REM RESET COLOR
55 FOR I = 0 TO 1000 : NEXT I : REM DELAY
60 GOTO 30

100 REM SUBROUTINE TO CLEAR SCREEN
110 REM COLOR MUST BE ALREADY SET
120 FOR I = 0 TO 39
130 HLIN 0,39 AT I
140 NEXT I
150 RETURN
```

This program uses an infinite loop consisting of lines 30 to 60 for iterating over each color choice. Line 55 implements a short delay using any empty FOR-NEXT loop. Press CONTROL-C to halt the program when you're finished with it. The screen is cleared using a convenient subroutine that starts on line 100. The subroutine uses HLIN in a loop on line 130 to clear the entire screen to the color last set using COLOR. This subroutine could be easily incorporated into any other program.

Drawing Diagonal Lines

BASIC doesn't have any built-in command to draw diagonal lines. Here is a program that demonstrates the use of the PLOT command inside of a loop to generate two intersecting diagonal lines. The color for each block is chosen randomly.

```
5 REM DIAGONAL LINES PROGRAM
10 GR : REM SET LO-RES GFX MODE
```

```
20 FOR I = 0 TO 39 : REM START OUR LOOP
25 REM PICK A COLOR AT RANDOM
30 COLOR = RND(1) * 16 + 1
35 REM THIS PLOT GOES FROM TOP LEFT TO BOTTOM RIGHT
40 PLOT I,I
45 REM THIS PLOT GOES FROM BOTTOM LEFT TO TOP RIGHT
50 PLOT I,39 - I
70 NEXT I : REM COMPLETE THE LOOP
80 END
```

To run this program in Integer BASIC, change line 30 to the following:

```
30 COLOR = RND(16) + 1
```

Determining Screen Color

The Apple can return the color of any point on the low-resolution graphics screen by way of the SCRN command. SCRN takes an X and Y coordinate, and then returns a number from 0 to 15 depending on what color is located at those coordinates. The X coordinate must be in the range of 0 to 39, and Y must be 0 through 47.

The following line will assign the color of the dot at (12, 20) to variable CO:

```
]CO = SCRN(12,20)
```

The parentheses around the coordinates for SCRN must not be omitted; otherwise, the Apple will think that you are trying to use a variable named SCRN.

The following example demonstrates the use of SCRN in immediate mode Applesoft:

```
]GR
]COLOR = 4
]PLOT 1,1
```

```
]PRINT SCRN(1,1)
```

The Apple replies back:

```
4
```

which indeed is the very same color plotted at (1, 1).

High-Resolution Graphics

The Apple high-resolution graphics mode affords a larger canvas allowing for more detailed renderings, at the expense of having fewer colors available. The high-resolution screen can display a total of 53,760 dots in an area of 280 dots wide and 192 dots high.

Most of the high-resolution commands are similar to their low-resolution counterparts, except that they start with H. While low-resolution graphics are fairly straightforward, high-resolution graphics mode has a few quirks, all of which will be explained. Unfortunately, only Applesoft BASIC has built-in support for high-resolution graphics. Integer BASIC programs can use high-resolution graphics, but there are no dedicated commands for doing so. Instead, one must use POKE and CALL statements.

Switching to High-Resolution Mode

The Applesoft command HGR sets high-resolution mode with four lines of text at the bottom of the screen. The graphics area of 280 by 160 is cleared to black.

The text window dimensions are left as they were from text mode, except that the top 20 lines are now "behind" the graphics screen. The cursor, and any other text, are still there. To make using the text lines more convenient, set the top line of the text window by using POKE 34,20.

As with low-resolution graphics mode, the four lines of text may be exchanged for a larger graphics area by using POKE -16302,0 *after* HGR is executed. The statement POKE -16301,0 will restore the text area, as will executing HGR again (though HGR will always clear the graphics screen too).

The usual TEXT command can be used to switch back to full-screen text mode, or GR for low-resolution graphics.

High-Resolution Colors

As already mentioned, the high-resolution color selection is quite limited. Most all Apples offer a choice of six distinct colors. Very old Apples (probably not yours) only allow four. These colors are green, orange, violet, blue, black, and white. Two of these colors appear twice: black and white. There are two different "types" of black and white, making the total color selection eight. This is just the first of the high-resolution mode's many eccentricities.

The Applesoft HCOLOR command sets the high-resolution plotting color according to a given number from 0 to 7. See the High-Resolution Colors chart in Appendix E for a table of colors and corresponding number. This statement sets the high-resolution color to green:

```
]HCOLOR = 1
```

HCOLOR can also use a variable or the results of an expression to set color, as in this example:

```
]C = 4

]HCOLOR = C + 1
```

This will set the high-resolution color to orange.

HCOLOR can only be used to control the color of the *next* dot to be plotted on the high-resolution graphics screen. It has no effect on existing dots, or on the low-resolution screen.

Color Quirks

The high-resolution graphics mode has a number of color quirks which stem from the manner in which the Apple stores the graphics screen in its memory. One byte of memory is used to store 7 distinct dots for the screen using 7 bits from the byte. The eighth bit is used to select the colors of those 7 dots. In all, 40 bytes of memory are used to display one line on the screen.

The eighth bit of each screen byte is not displayed. As stated, it is used to select colors. There are two color palettes: violet-green, and orange-blue. If any of the seven bits are set to 0 (off), they will always appear as a black dot. However, if a bit is set to 1 (on), its color depends on both its location on the screen and the state of the eighth bit.

If the eighth bit is set to 1, then the color palette of blue and orange is used. Otherwise, green and violet are used.

The following rules take effect:

1. Black dots are always available, anywhere on the screen.
2. Violet and blue dots are only allowed in even screen columns.
3. Orange and green dots are only allowed in odd screen columns.
4. All 7 dots from a screen byte must be of the same color palette.
5. Any two horizontally adjacent dots will always appear as white.

High-Resolution Plotting

The high-resolution plotting command works differently compared to the low-resolution plot command. In addition to simply plotting a single point, it can also plot horizontal, vertical, and diagonal lines. Finally, you may also plot any polygonal shape. This is all done with the HPLOT command.

Because of its versatility, HPLOT has three different formats. The first is used to plot a single point:

HPLOT *x,y*

This will place a dot at the location specified by x and y.

The second format can be used to plot a line in any direction and of any length:

HPLOT TO *x,y*

Because HPLOT remembers the location of the last point drawn on the screen, this format will draw a line from that previous location to the location of x and y. HPLOT must have already been used for this format to have any effect.

The final way of using HPLOT offers a way to draw closed and open polygons whose vertices are at any coordinate location that you specify:

```
]HPLOT 50,20 TO 70,20 TO 70,80 TO 20,80 TO 50,20
```

This HPLOT command draws an irregular, four-sided polygon. Due to the color quirks explained earlier, the majority of the shape appears in white, but the right-side vertical line appears violet.

Setting a Background Color

Clearing the high-resolution graphics screen to any arbitrary color is more easily done than in low-resolution mode. A certain CALL statement will clear the entire screen to the color that was most recently used with HPLOT. The command is as follows:

```
]CALL -3082
```

Here is a short Applesoft program that illustrates its use:

```
10 REM SET HIGH-RES BG COLOR
20 HGR : REM SWITCH TO HIGH-RES GFX
30 HCOLOR = 3 : REM FIRST, SET AN HCOLOR
40 HPLOT 1,1 : REM SECOND, HPLOT ANYWHERE
50 CALL -3082 : REM NOW CLEAR THE SCREEN
60 END
```

When run, this program will change the background color to white, because that is the color specified by HCOLOR. The HPLOT point can be anywhere on the screen; as the entire screen is cleared to the last HCOLOR, its coordinates are immaterial.

Another CALL statement will always clear the screen to black. It is CALL -3086.

Plotting Bar Graphs

Displaying information using a bar graph is a great way to visualize the data. With BASIC and high-resolution graphics, making bar graphs is fairly simple. Let's write a program that will take a given series of values and generate the corresponding bar graph.

First, we need to define some requirements for this program:

- The user should be able to enter up to 20 numbers.
- The program will automatically determine the scale.
- The program will center the bar graph display.

Here is a BASIC program which satisfies all of these requirements:

```
10 REM BAR GRAPH PROGRAM
20 DIM D(19) : REM ALLOW FOR 20 VALUES
30 VNUM = 0 : REM NUMBER OF VALUES TO GRAPH
40 SH = 159 : REM MAX HEIGHT OF A BAR
50 MH = 0 : REM GREATEST VALUE ENTERED
60 CD = 0 : REM CENTERING DISTANCE

100 HOME : PRINT "BAR GRAPH PROGRAM" : PRINT
110 PRINT "ENTER UP TO 20 VALUES TO BE PLOTTED ON"
120 PRINT "A BAR GRAPH. IF YOU ENTER FEWER THAN"
130 PRINT "20, TYPE 'STOP' TO FINISH."
140 PRINT : PRINT "PRESS RETURN TO BEGIN."
150 GET A$ : REM DUMMY INPUT TO ALLOW USER TO READ
SCREEN

200 REM HERE WE GATHER THE VALUES TO BE GRAPHED
210 FOR I = 0 TO 19
220 INPUT A$
230 IF A$ = "STOP" THEN 300 : REM CHECK FOR STOP
240 A = VAL(A$) : REM CONVERT STRING TO INTEGER
250 D(I) = A : REM ADD THIS VALUE TO OUR ARRAY
260 IF A > MH THEN MH = A : REM IS IT A MAX VALUE?
270 NEXT I
```

```
300 VNUM = I : REM SET NUMBER OF VALUES ENTERED
310 IF VNUM = 0 THEN END : REM NO VALUES WERE ENTERED
320 HGR : REM CHANGE SCREEN TO HI-RES GFX
330 HCOLOR = 3 : REM SET PLOT COLOR
340 W = 7 : REM WIDTH OF BAR
350 SP = 6 : REM SPACING BETWEEN BARS
360 CD = (279 - ( (W + SP) * VNUM)) / 2 : REM CENTER-
ING

400 REM START PLOTTING THE BARS
410 FOR I = 0 TO (VNUM - 1)
420 H = SH - ((D(I) / MH) * SH) : REM HEIGHT OF BAR
430 SO = I * (SP + W) + 1 + CD : REM STARTING OFFSET
OF BAR
440 HPLOT SO,SH TO SO,H TO SO+W,H TO SO+W,SH TO SO,SH
450 NEXT I

500 END
```

Lines 10 through 60 set up the variables and array. Lines 100 through 150 clear the screen, display the program name and instructions, and wait for the user to press a key when he is done reading.

Lines 200 through 270 collect the values to be graphed. Line 220 takes a string, because the program needs to check for STOP if the user is done entering values. If the input was STOP, then the program jumps to line 300. Otherwise, the input is converted to an integer and added to the array.

Lines 300 through 360 do some necessary processing before the bar graph may be plotted. First the total number of bars is set, then the screen is switched to high-resolution mode, the plot color is set, and the centering distance is calculated. The formula for centering is fairly simple. First, the width and spacing of each bar are added together. Then that sum is subtracted from the screen width, which is 279. Finally, the result is divided by 2.

Lines 400 through 480 work on plotting each bar. The height of the bar is calculated on line 420 by taking its value divided by the greatest bar value, then multiplying by 160. Line 430 computes the horizontal offset of each bar, taking into account the centering distance, bar width and spacing, and total number of bars drawn thus far. Finally, line 440 plots the four points which define the rectangular bar.

This bar graphing program could be easily condensed down to one or two subroutines which could then be incorporated into a larger, more useful program.

Plotting Circles

BASIC does not have any built-in command to plot a circle, but using mathematics, one may do so with HPLOT. Let us recall two methods of plotting a circle:

First is the method involving the trigonometric functions, sine and cosine. If we take a point P anywhere on a circle with a radius of R, its X and Y coordinates may be determined as follows:

X = R * COS(P)
Y = R * SIN(P)

The trigonometric functions of Applesoft work in radians, not degrees. Recall that a circle has 2 pi radians all around, and that one radian is approximately 57.2957795 degrees.

To use this method of plotting a circle, we need merely step from 0 radians to 2 pi radians, and at small intervals, plot a point using the above formulas.

Here is an Applesoft program which plots a circle in this manner:

```
10 REM CIRCLE DEMO 1
20 PI = 3.14159265
30 CX = 110 : CY = 80 : REM CENTER COORDINATES
40 R = 60 : REM RADIUS
50 HGR : HCOLOR = 1 : REM SET GFX SCREEN AND COLOR
60 HPLOT CX + R, CY : REM PLOT INITIAL POINT
70 REM STEP FROM 0 TO 2 PI RADIANS TO PLOT THE CIRCLE
```

```
80 FOR P = 0 TO 2 * PI STEP PI / 60
90 X = R * COS(P) : REM COMPUTE X COORD
100 Y = R * SIN(P) * 6/7 : REM COMPUTE Y COORD + SKEW
110 HPLOT TO (CX + X), (CY - Y)
120 NEXT P
130 END
```

Incidentally, by changing just two lines, one can make the Apple plot a filled-in circle, or a disc. The changes involve plotting a line from the circle's center to its edge. Modify the program by typing in these lines:

```
]80 FOR P = 0 TO 2 * PI STEP PI / 176
]110 HPLOT CX,CY TO (CX + X), (CY - Y)
```

The change in step size on line 80 is necessary because a greater step size would lead to some holes in the disc. A downside is, however, an increase in plotting time; a 1 MHz Apple IIe takes about 28 seconds to plot the green disc.

The second method involves the definition of the unit circle, centered at (CX, CY). These two coordinates may be located anywhere

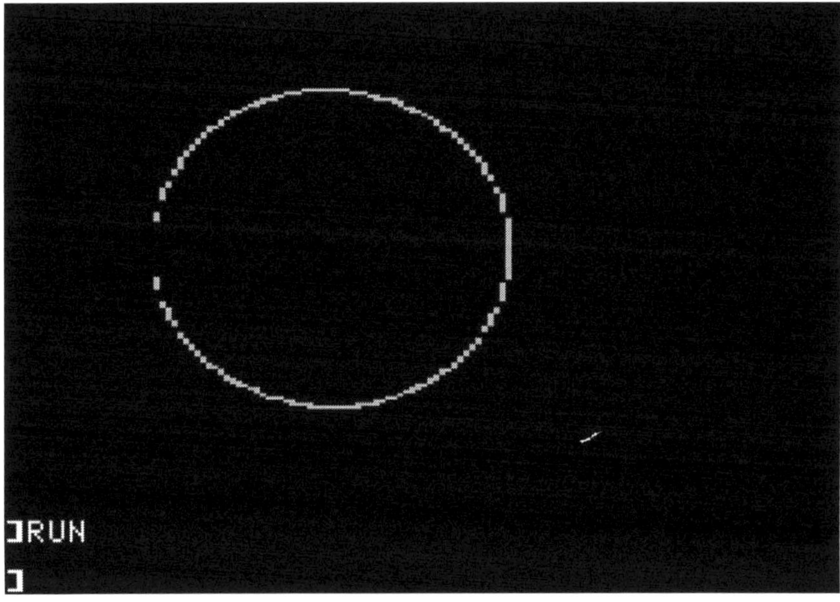

Figure 8-3. High-Resolution circle

on the high-resolution screen. The equation used to plot such a circle is as follows:

$R^2 = (PX - CX)^2 + (PY - CY)^2$

R represents the circle's radius. Coordinate pair (CX, CY) represents the center point about which the circle is drawn. The pair (PX, PY) represents a point on the circle.

Solving the equation for PX, we are left with:

$PX = CX \pm SQR(R^2-(PY-CY)^2)$

As you can see from this equation, PX will have two values: one for the left half of the circle, the other for the right.

This Applesoft program first plots the left half of the circle by calculating PX based on incrementing PY. It then switches over to the right half, decrementing PY.

```
10 REM CIRCLE DEMO 2
20 CX = 110 : CY = 80 : REM CENTER COORDINATES
30 R = 60 : REM RADIUS
40 RS = R^2 : REM RADIUS SQUARED
50 SN = -1 : REM SIGN
60 HGR : HCOLOR = 3: REM SET GFX SCREEN AND COLOR
70 HPLOT CX,CY - R : REM PLOT INITIAL POINT
80 PY = CY - R : REM INITIAL PY AT TOP OF CIRCLE
90 IF SN = -1 THEN PY - PY + 1 : REM LEFT HALF, INCRE-
MENT PY
95 IF SN = 1 THEN PY = PY - 1 : REM RIGHT HALF, DECRE-
MENT PY
100 PX = INT(SQR(ABS(RS - (PY - CY)^2))) * SN + CX :
REM CALCULATE POINTS
110 HPLOT TO PX,PY : REM PLOT POINT ON CIRCLE
120 IF PY = CY - R AND SN = 1 THEN END : REM DONE WITH
RIGHT HALF
130 IF PY = CY + R THEN SN = 1 : GOTO 90 : REM START
RIGHT HALF
140 GOTO 90 : REM GO DRAW NEXT POINT
```

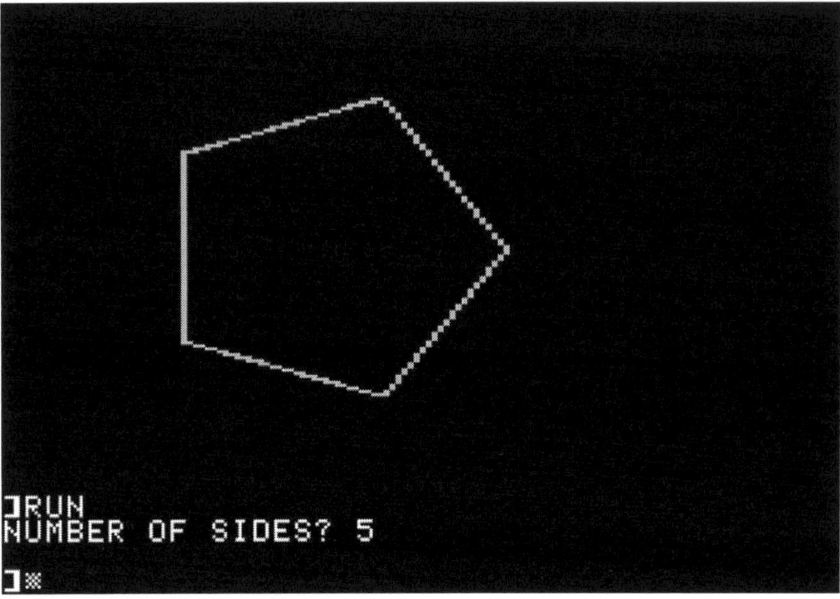

Figure 8-4. High-Resolution pentagon

Plotting Polygons

Using the first circle-plotting program as a prototype, it is possible to modify the program to produce many-sided regular polygons. A knowledge of geometry, specifically, the properties of polygons, is instructive. Recall that any regular polygon may be inscribed in a circle such that each of its vertices touch the circle. For example, a pentagon has five vertices that each touch the circle at five points evenly spaced about the circle.

Therefore, to plot a polygon, it is only necessary to plot the points (vertices) which touch the circle. HPLOT will automatically draw the line segments connecting each point.

One line is added:

```
15 INPUT "NUMBER OF SIDES? ";N
```

Line 15 asks the user to enter a number of sides for the polygon. Secondly, line 80 is modified to step the loop by 6.2831 / N.

Oddly, less precision is required for the step size. The final program is as follows:

```
10 REM POLYGON DEMO
15 INPUT "NUMBER OF SIDES? ";N
20 PI = 3.14159265
30 CX = 110 : CY = 80 : REM CENTER COORDINATES
40 R = 60 : REM RADIUS
50 HGR : HCOLOR = 1 : REM SET GFX SCREEN AND COLOR
60 HPLOT CX + R, CY : REM PLOT INITIAL POINT
70 REM STEP FROM 0 TO 2 PI RADIANS TO PLOT THE CIRCLE
80 FOR P = 0 TO 2 * PI STEP 6.283 / N
90 X = R * COS(P) : REM COMPUTE X COORD
100 Y = R * SIN(P) * 6/7 : REM COMPUTE Y COORD + SKEW
110 HPLOT TO (CX + X), (CY - Y)
120 NEXT P
130 END
```

Shape Tables

One of the unique features of the high-resolution graphics mode on the Apple is the ability to define a shape and then be able to recall it instantly. This shape could be anything which can be drawn on the screen: a circle, a square, a triangle, or even something more complex such as a house, a hot-air balloon or a sail boat. All of these things could be constructed using a number of HPLOT statements, however, shape tables offer some powerful features. The Apple can manipulate the shape by rotating it, scaling it, and drawing it in any high-resolution color. You can even do simple animation.

Shapes are stored in what is known as a *shape table*, a collection of one or more shapes stored in the Apple's memory. The shape table may also be saved to disk or cassette so you can easily use it again later.

The shape itself is defined as a series of vectors with two pieces of data: a direction, and whether or not to plot a point. Vector directions are constrained to the X and Y dimensions: up, down, left, and right. The vector does not have a defined magnitude, or any definition of length. You may assume, for sake of illustration, that each vector has a length of "1 unit." When it comes time to plot the shape on the screen, a scale factor determines the final length of each vector, and thus the size of the overall shape.

Unfortunately, with the power of shape tables comes complexity. Creating the shapes and entering them into memory will require some manual effort on your part. Luckily for you, though, this chapter will provide a BASIC program which should lighten the task.

Shapes can be used in both Applesoft and Integer BASIC programs, but only Applesoft has a range of built-in commands that simplify the use of shapes.

Creating a Shape by Hand

Creating a shape table "by hand" involves a few different steps. It's tedious, but fairly simple to learn after you have had some practice. As with BASIC programming, proficiency comes with experience.

The first step is to obtain some graph paper. The size of the grid does not matter. If you don't have graph paper, then ordinary paper will do; just make the grid lines using a pen and ruler.

For this first example, we will draw a simple shape, a triangle that is 7 blocks high and 8 blocks wide. Start drawing with the top of the triangle. Figure 8-5 shows what it should look like.

The next step is to break the shape down into a series of vectors. As mentioned earlier, these vectors are the steps required to draw the shape, and each vector contains two pieces of information: direction to move, and whether a point be plotted. Recall that the direction for a vector may be one of only up, down, left, or right.

For this shape, we will always plot a point and move, since it is a closed polygon. Later, you will see that there are more possibilities.

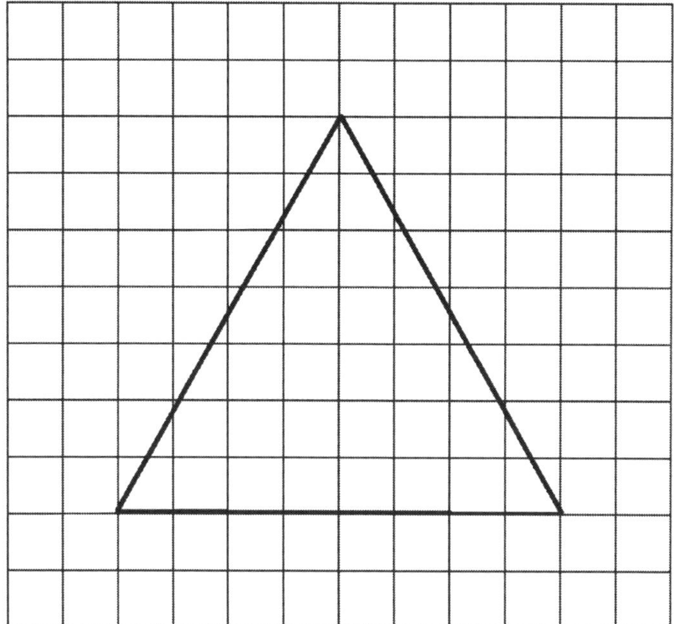

Figure 8-5. The triangle shape drawn on graph paper

There is no way to move diagonally, so the triangle must be simplified. We will also declare a starting point at the top, marked with a hollow circle. Each solid black dot in Figure 8-6 marks the starting point of each vector, and the arrow indicates direction. Movement proceeds clockwise, and there are 30 vectors in total.

The third step in creating a shape is to encode the vectors using a table. The code contains information about the vector, including its direction, and whether or not to plot a point. Begin at the starting vector, then follow the path around the shape until you end up at the beginning again. As you progress to each vector, write down a 1 if it plots a point, or a 0 if it does not. Since the triangle in this example is a closed polygon, every vector plots a point. Then, after each 1 or 0, write the vector direction. You can use L for left, R for right, U for up, and D for down. Table 8-2 shows this step completed for all 30 vectors.

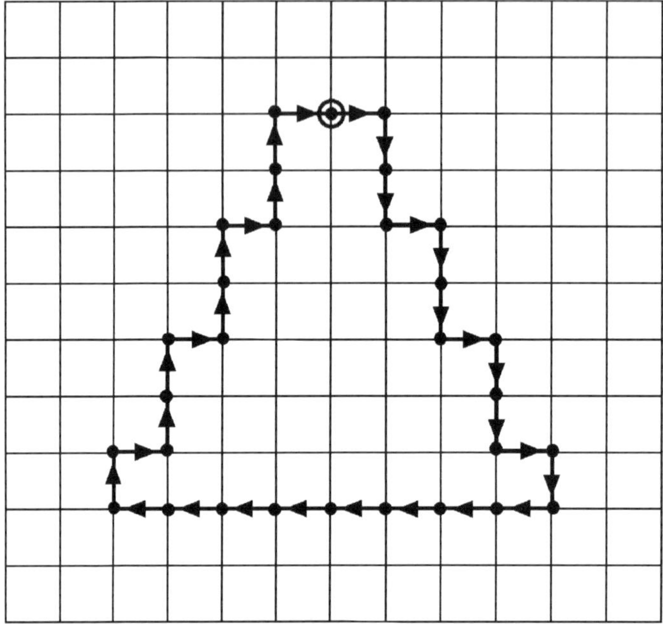

Figure 8-6. Triangle shape with vectors

1.) 1R	11.) 1D	21.) 1R
2.) 1D	12.) 1L	22.) 1U
3.) 1D	13.) 1L	23.) 1U
4.) 1R	14.) 1L	24.) 1R
5.) 1D	15.) 1L	25.) 1U
6.) 1D	16.) 1L	26.) 1U
7.) 1R	17.) 1L	27.) 1R
8.) 1D	18.) 1L	28.) 1U
9.) 1D	19.) 1L	29.) 1U
10.) 1R	20.) 1U	30.) 1R

Table 8-2. Table of vectors

The fourth step requires coding each of the vectors as a series of three binary digits. We've already written down one of these digits: whether or not a point will be plotted. The remaining two binary

Direction	Code
U	00
D	10
L	11
R	01

Table 8-3. Direction codes

digits are the direction code. Table 8-3 shows the code for each direction.

To code each of the vectors, take the first digit from the table of vectors (Table 8-2 for this example) and then look up the direction code in Table 8-3. For example, the first vector of the triangle shape becomes 101. Perform this step for each of the vectors so that you have a three-digit code for all of them.

Step five of creating a shape involves packing the binary vector codes into a byte. Since a byte is 8 bits, at minimum, two codes will fit in one byte, and the extra two bits may be set to 0. The only time that a third code could fit into a byte is if that code is for a nonplotting vector that is not moving up. In that case, enter only the two digits representing the vector's direction. The reason why you can't fit a nonplotting upward vector in the third slot of a byte is that the resulting vector code is 00, and zeros at the end of the byte are ignored by the Apple. If you find this rule confusing, you can always make do with putting just two vectors to a byte, no matter if they are nonplotting or not.

The first vector code in a pair uses the three rightmost digits in the byte, then the second vector code uses the next three. Finally, put a zero in each of the two leftmost positions. Repeat this step for each pair of vector codes. If you get to the end of the list and there is only one vector left, then fill the rest of the byte with zeros. The very last byte code of every shape must always consist of eight zeros. This final byte tells the Apple that it has reached the end of the shape. For example, the byte code for the first two vectors of the triangle would look like this:

```
00110101
```

Breaking it apart, it has two zeros at the left, as do all byte codes for just two vectors. Then the next three digits, 110, are for the second vector of 1D. The final three digits on the right, 101, are for the first vector, 1R.

Table 8-4 shows the binary vector code and completed shape bytes for all 30 vectors of the triangle.

Next, for step six, you must take the sequence of bytes which are in binary, and covert them to either hexadecimal or decimal. Which number base you use is determined by how you are going to enter the shape definition into the Apple's memory. If you are going to use the Machine Language Monitor (covered in Chapter 11) then you must convert to hex. For BASIC, you must use decimal notation. This chapter will assume that you are working in BASIC; a hexadecimal conversion table is provided in Appendix E for your convenience. Table 8-5 shows the resulting decimal values for each byte, suitable for use with the POKE statement in BASIC.

Step seven is to create a *shape table*, a directory that tells the Apple how many shapes you have defined, and where they are in memory. The directory, sometimes also called a *shape index*, can conceivably hold up to 255 distinct shape definitions, but for this example, only one will be used.

The index to the first shape definition is a two-byte offset from the start of the shape index to the start of the first shape definition. In this example, it will be 4. The offset is stored with the low-byte first, and the high-byte second. If the offset is $FF or less (255 or less, in decimal) then the high-byte is always 0, and the low-byte is the only value that matters. Otherwise, if the offset is some larger number, such as $100 or $2350, then the high-bytes would be $01 and $23, respectively, with the low-bytes being $00 and $50, respectively.

For a second shape, its offset is typically the sum of the offset for the first shape plus the length of the first shape's definition. This is only true if there are no gaps between the shape index and any of the shape definitions, which is the most common case.

Table 8-4. Vector binary codes and bytes

Binary Code	Byte
101	00110101
110	
110	00101110
101	
110	00110110
110	
101	00110101
110	
110	00101110
101	
110	00111110
111	
111	00111111
111	
111	00111111
111	
111	00111111
111	
111	00100111
100	
101	00100101
100	
100	00101100
101	

Binary Code	Byte
100	00100100
100	
101	00100101
100	
100	00101100
101	
	00000000

Table 8-4. Vector binary codes and bytes (*continued*)

53
46
54
53
46
62
63
63
63
39
37
44
36
37
44
0

Table 8-5. Decimal values for shape definition

It is most common for the shape definitions to immediately follow the shape index in memory, but this is not a requirement. The only restriction is that the shape definitions must all be located after the shape index. It is not allowed to have negative offsets.

Table 8-6 shows the shape index for this example shape.

1
0
4
0

Table 8-6. Decimal values for shape index

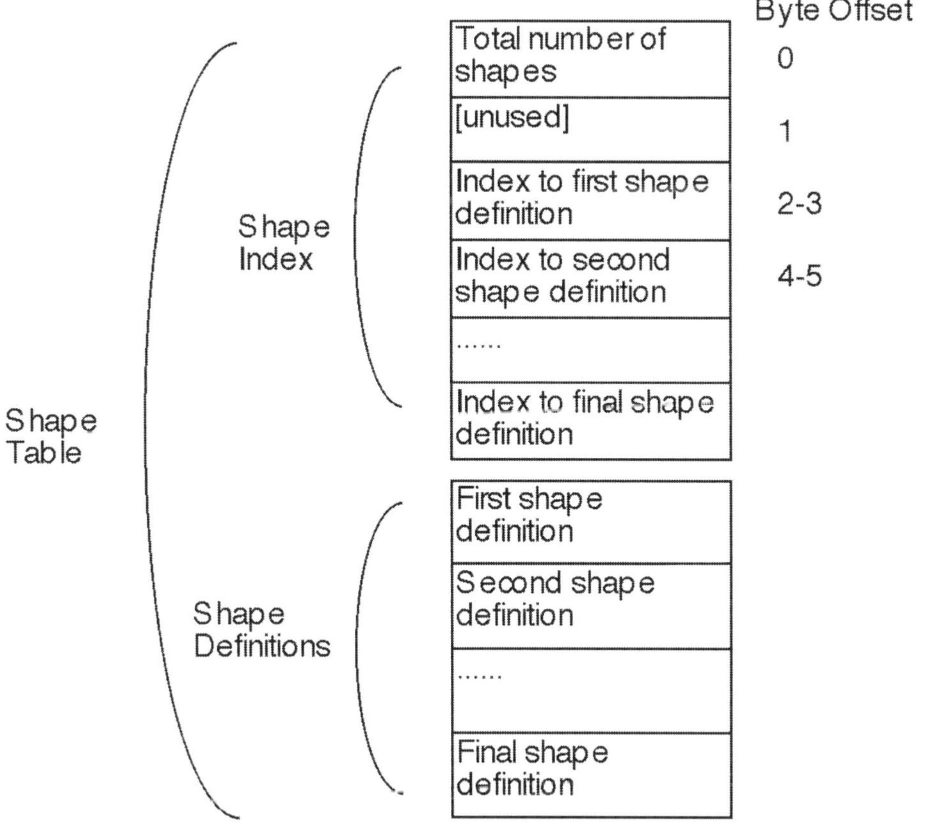

Figure 8-7. Format of shape table

Storing Shapes in Memory

Once you have obtained the sequence of bytes that composes a shape table, you must place it into an area of the Apple's memory. The location of the shape table must not be arbitrary; it must be an area not used by the operating system, BASIC, the text or graphics screens, or any other reserved area.

The most common place to locate shape tables is the range of memory starting at address 768 ($300 in hex). A sequence of POKE statements (see Chapter 5 for coverage of POKE) is all that is required to place the bytes of a shape table into memory.

The next step is to tell the Apple where to find your shape table. Both of these steps are quite straightforward and do not require any calculating. The Apple uses memory locations 232 and 233 ($E8 and $E9) to store the low and high-byte, respectively, of the beginning of the shape index, which is byte offset 0 in Figure 8-7.

It is convenient to place the bytes for a shape table into DATA statements. The DATA may then be READ and POKEd into memory with a loop, as shown:

```
10 REM POKE SHAPE TABLE INTO MEMORY
20 FOR I = 0 TO 19
30 READ B
40 POKE 768+I,B
50 NEXT I

500 REM SHAPE TABLE VALUES
510 DATA 1,0,4,0,53,46,54,53,46
520 DATA 62,63,63,63,39,37,44,36
530 DATA 37,44,0
```

This program places the 20 bytes of the shape table into memory starting at location 768. Two more POKE statements are required to set the address of the shape table:

```
60 REM SET SHAPE TABLE ADDRESS
70 POKE 232,0 : POKE 233,3
```

The decimal equivalent of 768 is $300. The low-byte is defined as the rightmost two digits, 00. These two digits are placed in location 232. The high-byte is the remaining 3. This value is placed in memory address 233.

The Apple now has the shape table in memory, and the location is set. The shape may now be plotted on the screen with the following lines:

```
100 HGR : REM SET HIGH-RES GFX
110 HCOLOR = 3 : REM SET COLOR
120 SCALE = 10 : REM SET SHAPE SIZE
130 ROT = 0 : REM SET SHAPE ROTATION
140 DRAW 1 AT 60,60 : REM PLOT SHAPE
```

Line 100 uses the familiar HGR command to activate high-resolution graphics mode and clear the screen to black. Line 110 then sets the color to white. The next three lines all contain new commands which are used exclusively for high-resolution shapes. All of these commands will be described in detail shortly.

The program in its entirety is:

```
10 REM POKE SHAPE TABLE INTO MEMORY
20 FOR I = 0 TO 19
30 READ B
40 POKE 768+I,B
50 NEXT I
60 REM SET SHAPE TABLE ADDRESS
70 POKE 232,0 : POKE 233,3

100 HGR : REM SET HIGH-RES GFX
110 HCOLOR = 3 : REM SET COLOR
120 SCALE = 10 : REM SET SHAPE SIZE
130 ROT = 0 : REM SET SHAPE ROTATION
140 DRAW 1 AT 60,60 : REM PLOT SHAPE

500 REM SHAPE TABLE VALUES
510 DATA 1,0,4,0,53,46,54,53,46
520 DATA 62,63,63,63,39,37,44,36
```

```
530 DATA 37,44,0
```

Run the program. A shape similar to that depicted in Figure 8-6 should appear in the lower-left region of the screen.

Saving a Shape Table to Disk

Saving a shape table to disk is convenient for larger tables that consume many bytes of memory. The BSAVE command, explained in Chapter 7, can be used to save a shape table to disk. Remember that either DOS 3.3 or ProDOS must be loaded into the Apple before BSAVE may be used. First, however, one must know the table's starting address and length. For example, to save a shape table that starts at location 768 and is 20 bytes long (such as the shape table used over the previous several pages of this chapter), use the following command:

```
BSAVE SHAPE, A768, L20
```

This will save the shape table to a file named SHAPE on the current disk.

A program can use DOS commands to load a shape table into memory from a disk file, instead of using POKE statements.

Loading a Shape Table from Disk

Loading a shape table from disk to memory is more straightforward than saving it. Simply BLOAD the appropriate file, and the Apple will take care of putting its contents at the correct memory locations. As with saving a shape table, DOS must be loaded before BLOAD may be used. For example, to load the file saved from the previous example, using this command:

```
BLOAD SHAPE
```

To load a shape table within a program, prefix the BLOAD command with a Control-D, as shown:

```
10 PRINT CHR$(4);"BLOAD SHAPE"
```

Recall that CHR$(4) produces the ASCII equivalent of Control-D, the character that signals a DOS command.

Be aware: using BLOAD does not restore the contents of memory locations 232 and 233, the area that the Apple uses to store the location of the shape table. Your program must POKE these locations with the correct values before attempting to use any high-resolution shapes.

Saving and Loading a Shape Table with Cassette Tape

Before the introduction of the disk system in 1978, shape tables were stored and recalled from cassette tape. Saving a shape table involves the knowledge of three details:

1. The starting address of the table
2. The ending address of the table
3. The total length of the table (the difference between 2 and 1).

These addresses and lengths must all be specified in hexadecimal notation. For the example shape shown earlier in this chapter, the starting address is $0300, the ending address is $031A, and the length is $001A.

Once you have obtained and calculated these three values, start by storing the length (the third value) in memory locations $0 and $1. Location $0 must contain the two digits on the right, and $1, the two digits on the left.

Enter the Monitor by typing CALL -151, and type the following:

```
0:1A 00
```

Once you press RETURN, the Apple will store the two bytes in memory locations $0 and $1.

The next step is to send the shape table information to the cassette tape. First ensure that the cassette recorder is properly connected and adjusted (see Chapter 2 for full details) and that a cassette tape is ready. Enter the following Monitor command, but be sure to start the cassette recording before you press RETURN:

```
0.1W 0300.031AW
```

This line is actually two commands in one: first the shape table length is written to tape, followed by the shape table. Once the Apple beeps for the second time and the flashing prompt reappears, you may press Stop on the recorder.

To load the shape table from tape, first rewind the tape, then press Play. If you are still in the Monitor, return to Applesoft by pressing CONTROL-C, then RETURN. Finally, type:

```
SHLOAD
```

After two beeps, press Stop on the recorder. The shape table is now back in the Apple's memory.

If you are using Integer BASIC, the instructions for saving the shape table will still work (since the Monitor is language-agnostic), however, Integer BASIC does not have an SHLOAD command. Instead, you will have to use the Monitor's cassette read command to read back the cassette tape into memory. Chapter 11 explains how to do so.

Shape Table Maker

Creating a shape table, especially the task of encoding the vectors, is a time-consuming and repetitive process, prone to error. It would be simpler to let the Apple take care of this task, and thus the following program will manage it. This program will accept a series of vectors, and will produce the corresponding shape bytes, ready for use in a BASIC program:

```
10 REM  SHAPE ENCODER
20 DIM V$(100)
30 HOME
40 PRINT  SPC( 14);"SHAPE ENCODER"
50 PRINT : PRINT "THIS PROGRAM WILL ALLOW YOU TO ENTER
UP TO 100 VECTORS";
60 PRINT " FOR A HI-RES SHAPE."
```

```
70 PRINT "IT WILL THEN DISPLAY THE ENCODED VECTORS IN
HEX OR DECIMAL."
80 PRINT : PRINT "FOR EACH VECTOR, ENTER:"
90 PRINT : PRINT "0 FOR NO PLOT"
100 PRINT "1 FOR PLOT"
110 PRINT : PRINT "U,D,L,R FOR UP, DOWN, LEFT, RIGHT"
120 PRINT : PRINT "EXAMPLE: 1U"
130 PRINT : PRINT "TYPE STOP WHEN FINISHED."
140 PRINT : PRINT : PRINT "PRESS RETURN TO BEGIN"
150 GET A$
160 HOME
170 INPUT I$
175 IF I$ = "STOP" OR COUNTER = 100 THEN  GOTO 250
180 IF LD$ = "0U" AND I$ = "0U" THEN PRINT
CHR$(7);"CANNOT MOVE UP TWICE WITHOUT PLOT!": GOTO 170
190 IF  LEFT$(I$,1) <> "1" AND LEFT$(I$,1) <> "0" THEN
PRINT CHR$ (7);"ENTER 1 OR 0 FOR PLOT OR NO PLOT!":
GOTO 170
200 IF  RIGHT$(I$,1) <> "U" AND RIGHT$(I$,1) <> "D"
AND RIGHT$(I$,1) <> "L" AND  RIGHT$(I$,1) <> "R" THEN
PRINT CHR$(7);"ENTER U,D,L,R FOR DIRECTION!": GOTO 170
210 LD$ = I$
220 V$(COUNT) = I$
230 COUNT = COUNT + 1
240 GOTO 170
250 REM  REVIEW THE VECTORS
260 INPUT "REVIEW THE VECTORS? ";A$
270 IF A$ = "N" OR A$ = "NO" THEN  GOTO 400
280 HOME
290 SPEED= 100
300 FOR I = 0 TO COUNTER
310 PRINT V$(I);"  ";
320 NEXT I
330 SPEED= 255
340 PRINT
400 INPUT "SHOW VECTORS IN HEX OR DECIMAL? ";A$
```

```
410 IF A$ <> "H" AND A$ <> "D" THEN  PRINT "TYPE H OR
D.": GOTO 400
415 SPEED = 150
420 REM  ENCODE THE SHAPES
430 FOR I = 0 TO COUNTER STEP 2
440 GOSUB 1010: REM COMPUTE VECTOR NUMBER
445 LB = B: REM  SAVE AS LOW-BYTE
450 REM GET NEXT VECTOR
455 I = I + 1:B = 0
460 IF V$(I) <> "" THEN  GOSUB 1010
465 I = I - 1
470 HB = B: REM  SAVE AS HIGH-BYTE
475 REM CHECK FOR A NON-PLOT BYTE
480 I = I + 2:B = 0
485 IF V$(I) <> "" THEN  GOSUB 1010
490 IF B > 0 AND B < 4 THEN NB = B: REM NO-PLOT BYTE
495 IF B = 0 OR B > 3 THEN I = I - 2
500 REM ASSEMBLE ALL BYTES
510 VB = LB + (HB * 08) + (NB * 64)
515 IF VB = 0 THEN  GOTO 600: REM END ON A 0 BYTE
520 B = LB = HB = NB = 0: REM RESET ALL BYTES
530 IF A$ = "D" THEN PRINT VB: GOTO 580
540 REM CONVERT DECIMAL TO HEX
550 HI% = VB / 16
555 LO% = VB - HI% * 16
560 REM ALIGN WITH ASCII TABLE FOR A-F
565 IF HI% > 9 THEN HI% = HI% + 7
570 IF LO% > 9 THEN LO% = LO% + 7
575 PRINT CHR$(HI% + 176); CHR$(LO% + 176): REM PRINT
HEX BYTE
580 NEXT I
600 PRINT 0: REM ALWAYS END WITH ZERO
999 SPEED = 255 : END
1000 REM CONVERT VECTOR TO A NUMBER
1010 DI$ = RIGHT$ (V$(I),1)
1015 IF DI$ = "U" THEN B = 0
1020 IF DI$ = "R" THEN B = 1
```

```
1025 IF DI$ = "D" THEN B = 2
1030 IF DI$ = "L" THEN B = 3
1035 IF  LEFT$ (V$(I),1) = "1" THEN B = B + 4
1040 RETURN
```

Note that this program only encodes shape vectors. It does not assemble the entire shape table, as it does not compute a shape directory, nor does it enter the shape into memory.

Drawing Shapes on Screen

Once a shape table is loaded into memory, and its starting address stored in locations 232, and 233, there are a few commands to control the shape's appearance as it is drawn on the screen. A high-resolution shape may be scaled and rotated before it is drawn. Always ensure that the Apple is in high-resolution mode before drawing a shape. In low-resolution or text mode, drawing a shape may produce garbage characters or blocks on the screen.

As mentioned earlier, these commands exist only in Applesoft.

Setting Scale

The relative size of a shape can be controlled by the SCALE command. Setting a scale determines how many screen dots make up each vector. The range for scale is 0 to 255. A SCALE value of 1 yields a 1:1 reproduction of the shape, wherein one point on the screen is equal to one vector of the shape. Setting SCALE equal to 0 will plot 256 dots for every vector of the shape, which is the maximum scale size.

The following line will set the scale for the next shape to be three points for every one vector:

```
]SCALE= 3
```

SCALE should be used before the shape is drawn on the screen, since once a shape is on the screen, its size cannot be changed.

Be aware that some shapes do not scale well; you may see gaps between vectors with large scales, or vectors that overlap with a small scale.

Drawing a Shape

The DRAW command is used to plot a shape on screen using the most recently-selected color, scale, and rotation. DRAW takes a shape number from 1 to 255 and an (X, Y) coordinate pair at which to begin the first vector of the shape. The X coordinate must be in the range 0 through 278, and Y must be from 0 to 191.

The following example will draw the first shape at screen coordinate (50, 60):

```
]DRAW 1 AT 50,60
```

If the coordinates are not specified, then the previously-given coordinates are used:

```
]DRAW 2
```

If this line were entered following the first, then the second shape from the table would also be plotted starting at screen location (50, 60).

As with most BASIC commands, both the shape number and the coordinates can be supplied as constants (as shown above), variables, or expressions.

If there is no shape table in memory, attempting to DRAW may hang the Apple. Press CONTROL-RESET to recover. Furthermore, this command should not be used outside of high-resolution graphics mode, as the Apple may write over your program.

Setting Rotation

A shape can be rotated clockwise by a certain degree before it is drawn on screen, using the ROT command. Curiously, the rotational values allowed by ROT are influenced by the shape's scale. A shape with a greater scale can be rotated to a greater number of

Color	XDRAW Color
Black	White
White	Black
Violet	Green
Green	Violet
Orange	Blue
Blue	Orange

Table 8-7. Complementary colors for XDRAW

intervals. The following line will plot a shape upside down by rotating it 180 degrees:

```
]ROT=32
```

There are 64 unique rotational points. When a shape's scale is 1, only four of these points are meaningful: 0, 16, 32, and 48, which correspond to 0, 90, 180, and 270 degrees, respectively. When the scale is 2, eight values are recognized. Unrecognized values, such as 5 when the scale is 1, will be rounded (usually down) to the nearest valid rotation point. For shapes having a scale of 5 or greater, all 64 rotational values may be used.

The value range for ROT runs from 0 to 255. If the value is greater than 64, it is interpreted as modulo 64. For example, ROT= 65 corresponds to ROT= 1, and ROT= 126 corresponds to ROT= 62.

Erasing Shapes

The XDRAW command can be used to erase a shape from the screen, leaving the background color in place. It works by plotting the complementary color of the shape. Table 8-7 lists all complementary colors.

XDRAW has the same syntax as DRAW: its plot coordinates may either be explicitly designated, or omitted to use the last coordinates given. This statement shows an example of XDRAW:

```
]XDRAW 1 AT 45,120
```

The XDRAW command is useful because it simplifies erasing a shape: simply use XDRAW to plot the shape on the screen, then use XDRAW again to erase it. XDRAW can be used to create high-resolution animations.

As with DRAW, XDRAW should only be used with a shape table that is properly loaded into memory, with high-resolution graphics mode active.

Shape Sampler Program

The following programs use shapes to generate interesting geometric patterns on the high-resolution screen:

```
10 REM SHAPE DEMO PROGRAM
20 REM POKE SHAPE TABLE INTO RAM
30 POKE 768,01 : POKE 769,00 : POKE 770,04 : POKE 771,00 : POKE 772,46 : POKE 773,04 : POKE 774,00
40 POKE 232,00 :  POKE 233,03 : REM TABLE ADDRESS
50 HGR : REM HIGH-RES GRAPHICS MODE
60 HCOLOR = 2 : REM SET COLOR
65 SCALE = 30 : REM SET SHAPE SCALE
70 FOR X = 20 TO 265 STEP 5
75 ROT = X - 20 : REM SET SHAPE ROTATION
80 DRAW 1 AT X,50
85 FOR Y = 1 TO 30 : NEXT Y : REM DELAY
86 IF X > 60 THEN HCOLOR = 6 : IF X > 120 THEN HCOLOR = 5
90 NEXT X
100 FOR X = 1 TO 3000 : NEXT X : REM DELAY
110 REM PART 2
120 CALL-3086 : REM CLEAR SCREEN
130 FOR X = 0 TO 40
135 HCOLOR = INT(RND(1) * 7)
140 SCALE = INT(RND(1) * 55) + 6
150 ROT = INT(RND(1) * 64)
```

```
160 DRAW 1 AT INT(RND(1) * 280), INT(RND(1) * 160)
170 NEXT X
```

This program uses just one shape, a square with only three sides. Line 30 POKEs the shape table into memory starting at location 768 ($300 hex), while line 40 sets the starting address of the table so that Applesoft knows where to find it.

Tic Tac Toe Game with Shapes

One simple, well-known game is that of Tic Tac Toe, or Naughts and Crosses in other parts of the world. The rules are simple: a grid of nine squares is made, and two players make their respective mark in turn, either an O or an X. The first player to have three of his mark in either a row, column, or diagonally, wins.

The Apple version of this game will pit the human player against a computer opponent. The computer will also keep track of the grid, marks, and winner. This game will naturally make use of high-resolution graphics, as well as shapes to represent the O and X.

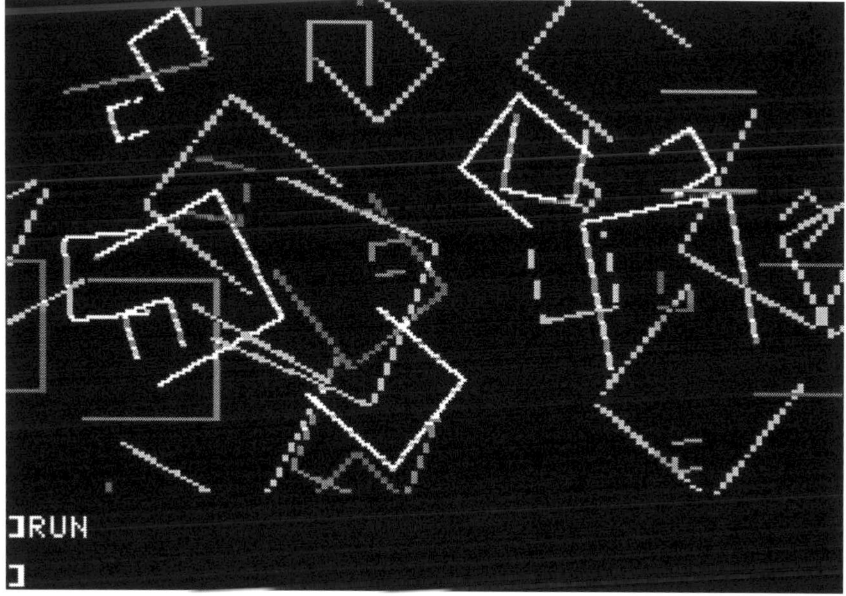

Figure 8-8. Part two of the shape sampler program

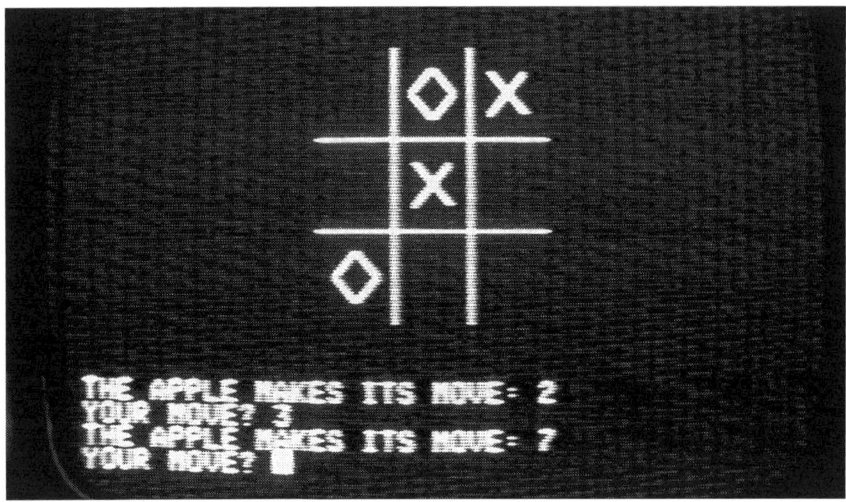

Figure 8-9. Playing the Tic Tac Toe game

To simplify the design of the program, the human player will always be X, and the Apple will always be O. A randomly-generated "coin toss" will determine who gets to move first.

The following program implements such a Tic Tac Toe game, where the computer's moves are random:

```
10 REM TIC TAC TOE WITH HI-RES SHAPES
20 REM INITIALIZE PROGRAM
30 REM LOAD SHAPE TABLE FROM DATA
40 READ L : REM GET SHAPE LENGTH
50 READ A : REM STARTING ADDRESS
100 REM LOAD SHAPE TABLE INTO RAM
110 FOR X = 1 TO L
120 READ B : REM READ SHAPE BYTE
130 POKE A,B : REM STORE SHAPE BYTE
140 A = A + 1 : REM INCREMENT ADDR
150 NEXT X
200 REM TELL APPLE WHERE TABLE IS
210 POKE 232,0 : POKE 233,3
230 REM INTRO SCREEN
240 HOME : PRINT SPC(14);"TIC TAC TOE"
```

```
250 PRINT : PRINT "YOU WILL PLAY A GAME OF TIC TAC
TOE"
260 PRINT "AGAINST THE APPLE COMPUTER."
270 PRINT "YOU ARE X, APPLE IS 0."
280 PRINT : PRINT "TO PLACE YOUR X, ENTER GRID NUM-
BER:"
290 PRINT " 1 2 3" : PRINT " 4 5 6" : PRINT " 7 8 9"
300 PRINT : PRINT "FLIP A COIN TO SEE WHO IS FIRST..."
310 REM GENERATE RANDOM NUMBER
320 C = INT(RND(1) * 2)
330 PRINT : IF C = 0 THEN PRINT "YOU GO FIRST" : GOTO
400
340 PRINT "APPLE GOES FIRST"
400 REM WAIT FOR KEY PRESS
410 PRINT : PRINT "PRESS RETURN TO BEGIN"
420 GET A$
450 REM INIT SCREEN
460 HGR : POKE 34,20 : HOME
470 REM DRAW GRID
480 HCOLOR = 3
490 HPLOT 95,81 TO 185,81 : HPLOT 95,111 TO 185,111
500 HPLOT 125,51 TO 125,141 : HPLOT 155,51 TO 155,141
520 REM LET FIRST PLAYER GO
530 IF C 0 THEN GOTO 600
540 IF C = 1 THEN GOTO 1000
600 REM MAKE PLAYER MOVE
610 INPUT "YOUR MOVE? ";M
620 IF M < 1 OR M > 9 THEN PRINT "PLEASE ENTER A GRID
NUMBER, 1-9" : GOTO 610
630 REM CHECK IF OK
635 G = M
640 GOSUB 11000
650 IF NOT OK THEN PRINT "YOU CANNOT MAKE A MARK
THERE" : GOTO 610
660 S = 1 : REM SET SHAPE TO X
670 GOSUB 10000 : REM DRAW X ON SCREEN
680 G$(G) = "X"
```

```
700 REM CHECK FOR GAME OVER
710 GOSUB 12000
1000 REM APPLE'S MOVE
1010 PRINT "THE APPLE MAKES ITS MOVE: ";
1020 REM GENERATE A RANDOM NUMBER
1030 M = INT(RND(1) * 9) + 1
1050 REM CHECK IF MOVE IS OK
1060 G = M
1070 GOSUB 11000
1080 IF NOT OK THEN GOTO 1030
1090 PRINT G : S = 2
1100 GOSUB 10000 : REM DRAW O ON SCREEN
1110 G$(M) = "O"
1200 GOSUB 12000 : REM CHECK FOR GAME OVER
1999 GOTO 600 : REM BACK TO PLAYER'S TURN
9000 DATA 16 : REM TOTAL SHAPE BYTES
9005 DATA 768 : REM STARTING ADDRESS
9010 DATA 2,0,6,0,10,0,156,173,35,0,40,54,63,36,5,0
10000 REM DRAW SHAPE
10010 REM S = SHAPE NUMBER
10020 REM G = GRID NUMBER
10100 IF S = 1 THEN SCALE= 10 : ROT= 8
10110 IF S = 2 THEN SCALE= 6 : ROT= 8
10120 REM COMPUTE GRID COORDS
10130 IF G = 1 OR G = 4 OR G = 7 THEN XX = 110 : GOTO
10200
10140 IF G = 2 OR G = 5 OR G = 8 THEN XX = 140 : GOTO
10200
10150 IF G = 3 OR G = 6 OR G = 9 THEN XX = 170
10200 IF G = 1 OR G = 2 OR G = 3 THEN YY = 66
10210 IF G = 4 OR G = 5 OR G = 6 THEN YY = 96
10220 IF G = 7 OR G = 8 OR G = 9 THEN YY = 126
10300 DRAW S AT XX,YY
10320 RETURN
11000 REM CHECK IF GRID IS TAKEN
11010 REM G = GRID NUMBER
11020 OK = (G$(G) <> "X" AND G$(G) <> "O")
```

```
11030 RETURN
12000 REM CHECK FOR WIN, LOSE, DRAW
12010 FOR X = 0 TO 1
12020 IF X = 0 THEN C$ = "X"
12030 IF X = 1 THEN C$ = "O"
12040 IF G$(1) = C$ AND G$(2) = C$ AND G$(3) = C$ THEN
GOTO 12200
12050 IF G$(4) = C$ AND G$(5) = C$ AND G$(6) = C$ THEN
GOTO 12200
12060 IF G$(7) = C$ AND G$(8) = C$ AND G$(9) = C$ THEN
GOTO 12200
12070 IF G$(1) = C$ AND G$(4) = C$ AND G$(7) = C$ THEN
GOTO 12200
12080 IF G$(2) = C$ AND G$(5) = C$ AND G$(8) = C$ THEN
GOTO 12200
12090 IF G$(3) = C$ AND G$(6) = C$ AND G$(9) = C$ THEN
GOTO 12200
12100 IF G$(1) = C$ AND G$(5) = C$ AND G$(9) = C$ THEN
GOTO 12200
12110 IF G$(7) = C$ AND G$(5) = C$ AND G$(3) = C$ THEN
GOTO 12200
12120 NEXT X
12130 REM CHECK FOR DRAW
12140 C = 0
12150 FOR X = 1 TO 9
12160 IF G$(X) ="X" OR G$(X) = "O" THEN C = C + 1
12170 NEXT X
12180 IF C = 9 THEN PRINT "GAME OVER! DRAW!" : GOTO
12300
12190 RETURN
12200 REM PRINT WINNER
12210 IF C$ = "X" THEN PRINT "YOU WON!" : GOTO 12300
12220 PRINT "THE APPLE WON!"
12300 POP
12400 INPUT "PLAY AGAIN? ";A$
12500 IF A$ = "Y" THEN GOTO 12520
12510 TEXT : HOME : END
```

```
12520 FOR X = 1 TO 9 : G$(X) = "" : NEXT X : GOTO 300
```

This program follows the general, overall form of first initializing the screen, loading the shape table, and presenting the explanatory text, then generating a random number to track who goes first. Moves are then checked against an array to see if the particular grid location has already been used. The appropriate high-resolution shape is then drawn on the screen to represent the player's move. After each player's turn, all possible winning scenarios (horizontal, vertical, and diagonal) are checked. Play continues until either player wins, or there is a draw.

The limitations of the Apple, in this case, its high-resolution shapes, force the programmer to come up with interesting solutions. The Tic Tac Toe game uses two shapes, an X and an O. Since the shape vectors limit one to using only two dimensions, some ingenuity had to be used. First of all, it is noted that an "X" is merely a cross (+) rotated 45 degrees. Therefore, the shape for the X is just an ordinary cross, and the ROT command is used to rotate it. Making a circular figure for the "O" would prove to be quite time-consuming. The solution employed here was to draw a square, and rotate it too, like the "X". The result is not quite as satisfactory, but is close enough to an "O" for the purposes of this game.

Lines 40 to 150 load the shape table into memory from DATA statements located on lines 9000 through 9010. The first two data elements are the shape table length and starting address, respectively. Lines 110 to 150 form a loop that reads in each successive byte, POKEs it into the correct memory address, and then increments the address for the next byte. Finally, line 210 POKEs the location of the shape table into the two zero-page memory addresses where the Apple knows to look for the shape table (such a memory address is known as a *vector*).

The next few lines, 240 to 300, clear the screen and print the introductory text for the game. To determine whether the Apple goes first or the human player goes first, a random number is generated whose range is 0 to 1, to simulate a coin flip. The results are then printed on the screen by line 330 or 340, depending on the outcome. The GET A$ on line 420 is used to pause the screen for as long as the user needs to read the text. The input to A$ is ignored.

Lines 460 to 500 set up the game screen. First, high-resolution graphics mode is activated, then the text window is adjusted to use the bottom four lines (for more information on the text window, see Chapter 6). Line 480 sets the high-resolution color, and lines 490 and 500 plot the Tic Tac Toe grid using HPLOT statements.

After the screen is prepared, the main game starts. Either the Apple or the human player starts first, and control flips between the two for each turn. The human player is asked to enter a grid number, whereas the Apple randomly generates a number. The number is then checked against the array G$ using a subroutine on line 11000. If the grid number is empty, then the move is OK. Otherwise, the player is prompted to enter a different number (if it is the Apple's turn, then another random number is generated). The correct shape is drawn on the screen using a subroutine at line 10000, and the G$ array is updated with the appropriate letter. After each turn, the third subroutine at 12000 checks for a winner or a tie game. A loop is used to save typing and lines when checking for "X" then "O". If a winning combination was found, C$ contains the name of the winning player, and it is printed on the screen. A draw is checked by summing up the nonempty elements of array G$. If the total is 9, then the game is a tie. The player is then asked whether he or she wishes to play again. If neither player has won yet, and the game is not a draw, then the next player takes a turn.

The Tic Tac Toe game could be improved by giving the Apple better strategy. As the game stands, the Apple's moves are entirely random. The algorithm could be improved by making the Apple first pick the center grid location, then the corners, and then the remaining locations. Alternatively, one could modify the game to allow two human players to take turns, instead of having one human play against the computer. The option for two humans could be picked at the introductory screen.

Other Graphics Modes

Double-high-resolution and super-high-resolution are two further graphics modes, introduced with the Apple IIe and Apple IIgs, respectively. Unfortunately, while these graphics modes offer additional colors and higher resolution, they are not accessible from the realm of BASIC. To make use of these other modes requires knowledge of assembly language, a topic that is beyond the scope of this book.

Sound

You should already know that the Apple can make sounds: it beeps on startup, and if you make a syntax error. However, the Apple's speaker has an entire range of noises, sounds, and tones that it can produce. These sonic effects can all be controlled from a BASIC program.

How the Speaker Works

The loudspeaker inside the Apple is rather quite simple: it is connected to a particular memory location. When this memory location is accessed, the speaker changes state: the speaker's cone either moves in, or it moves out. This action is sometimes referred to as "tweaking the speaker." Every other time that the speaker changes, a small click is produced. This click is caused by the speaker's cone movement creating a vibration in the air that is audible to your ear.

As you may know from the study of physics, a slower vibration creates a longer wave that has a lower pitch. Conversely, faster vibration creates a short, high-pitched wave. Knowing this, one can create any range of tones from the speaker, simply by varying the rate at which one tweaks the speaker.

To experience this speaker clicking on your own, enter the Monitor by typing CALL -151. Make sure that the room around you is quiet. When you see the asterisk prompt, enter C030. This is the hexadecimal memory location of the speaker. Depending on what state the speaker was already in, you either may or or may not have heard a soft click (or pop) after you pressed RETURN. Type C030 again. If you didn't hear a click the first time, then you should have heard one now. Every other time you type C030, you should hear a click. When you're finished experimenting, press CONTROL-C and RETURN to resume BASIC.

Tweaking the Speaker in BASIC

Tweaking the speaker is much the same in BASIC as it was in the Monitor, except that the PEEK function is used with the speaker's decimal location, -16336.

Try this short program:

```
0 A=PEEK(-16336) : GOTO 0
```

When you type RUN, you should hear a steady, medium-pitched tone coming from your Apple. If you are using Integer BASIC, this tone will be noticeably higher-pitched than the tone from Applesoft. This is because Integer BASIC executes at a greater speed than Applesoft, and being able to tweak the speaker more rapidly results in a high pitched tone. Press CONTROL-C to stop the program.

Unfortunately, this is one of the limitations of both versions of BASIC: their speed prevents them from being able to tweak the speaker fast enough to yield its full dynamic range. The tone produced by that program is the highest-possible tone that can be made solely from BASIC.

Varying the Pitch

This next program makes use of paddle 0 to introduce a variable delay in a FOR-NEXT loop, thus demonstrating how the speed at which the speaker is accessed determines its pitch:

```
10 FOR X = 0 TO PDL(0)
20 NEXT X
30 A = PEEK(-16336)
40 GOTO 10
```

Run this program, then try slowly turning the paddle knob (or joystick). Moving the paddle to the left should raise the pitch of the speaker, because the delay loop becomes shorter, whereas turning the knob to the right introduces a greater delay. When you're done, press CONTROL-C to stop the program.

Varying the Duration

The two programs shown so far both produced an unending tone. To instead produce a tone of finite duration, a second loop must be introduced. This loop will wrap around the inner loop that controls the speaker pitch. Following is a program which will prompt the user for a pitch and duration:

```
10 INPUT "PITCH (1-20)? "; P
20 INPUT "DURATION (1-100)? ";D
25 REM OUTER LOOP GOVERNS DURATION
30 FOR I = 0 TO D
40 A = PEEK(-16336)
45 REM INNER LOOP CONTROLS PITCH
50 FOR J = 0 TO P : NEXT J
60 NEXT I
70 GOTO 10
80 END
```

When you run this program, notice that the pitch is also a factor in the tone's duration. This is because it takes longer to produce a lower-pitched note due to the loop in line 50 having more iterations. Try it by first entering a pitch of 1, and then a pitch of 20, both with a duration of 10. The tone with a pitch of 20 lasts slightly longer than the tone with a pitch of 1.

Machine Language Speaker

As remarked earlier, BASIC is too slow to fully exploit the tonal range of the speaker. The solution is to use a program written in machine language to tweak the speaker. Machine language is the Apple's native tongue, and therefore it executes at a greater speed than any BASIC program. With such a program, BASIC will provide the pitch and duration parameters, and the program will take care of the rest.

The Speaker Subroutine

This speaker program will work as a subroutine to any BASIC program that you write. Its details are beyond the scope of this book, but suffice it to say, this program does its job, and most importantly, does it quickly.

```
* MACHINE LANGUAGE SPEAKER SUBROUTINE
* RELOCATED FROM THE "RED BOOK" TONE
* ROUTINE.
*
* USES ZERO-PAGE LOCATIONS 06 & 08
* 06: PITCH
* 08: DURATION
*
* USE FROM BASIC WITH CALL 768
*
* EQUATES
SPKR        EQU  $C030
PITCH       EQU  $06
DURATN      EQU  $08

            ORG  $300

*
* PROGRAM START
*
                 START      EQU   *
0300: AD 30 C0              LDA   SPKR  ; TWEAK SPEAKER
0303: 88         L1         DEY
0304: D0 04                 BNE   L2
0306: C6 08           DEC   DURATN
0308: F0 08           BEQ   END
030A: CA         L2   DEX
030B: D0 F6           BNE   L1
030D: A6 06           LDX   PITCH
030F: 4C 00 03        JMP   START
0312: 60         END  RTS
```

The subroutine occupies 19 bytes of memory from $0300 to $0312. Two zero-page memory locations, $06 and $08, are used to store the pitch and duration, respectively.

Before it can be used by a BASIC program, the subroutine must be placed into the Apple's memory. The following program lines use DATA and POKE statements to accomplish this task:

```
10 FOR I = 768 TO 786
20 READ B
30 POKE I,B
40 NEXT I
100 DATA 173, 48, 192, 136, 208, 4, 198, 8, 240
110 DATA 8, 202, 208, 246, 166, 6, 76, 0, 3, 96
```

Alternatively, the machine subroutine could be saved as a binary file with the following DOS command:

```
]BSAVE SPEAKER,A768,L19
```

The SPEAKER file could then be loaded back into memory with a BLOAD command at the beginning of a BASIC program.

The following program tests the speaker subroutine by stepping over each pitch:

```
5 REM LOAD SPEAKER SUBROUTINE
10 FOR I = 768 TO 786
20 READ B
30 POKE I,B
40 NEXT I
50 REM PLAY EACH PITCH
60 FOR P = 255 TO 0 STEP -1
70 POKE 8,15 : REM SET DURATION
80 POKE 6,P
90 CALL 768
95 NEXT P
100 DATA 173, 48, 192, 136, 208, 4, 198, 8, 240
110 DATA 8, 202, 208, 246, 166, 6, 76, 0, 3, 96
```

When RUN, this program will cause the Apple to rapidly emit an increasing sequence of notes. The range is much broader than the previous programs which relied entirely on BASIC.

Note that pitch increases as its value decreases. Curiously, however, pitch 0 is the *lowest*, not the highest pitch. This oddity is due to how the machine language routine was written.

Music Program

With the machine language speaker program, a music-playing program can be constructed. This program will take a sequence of values from DATA statements. The data will be broken up logically into pairs: the first value representing the duration, the second designating the pitch.

One component of the music program will be a BASIC subroutine that will simplify the task of calling the machine language subroutine. It will take the values of two BASIC variables, POKE them into memory, CALL the machine language subroutine, then return. Here it is:

```
500 REM MACHINE LANGUAGE INTERFACE SUBROUTINE
510 POKE 6,P : REM PITCH
520 POKE 8,D : REM DURATION
530 CALL 768 : REM PLAY THE NOTE
540 RETURN
```

As you can see, the subroutine expects the variables P and D to carry the pitch and duration, respectively, of the desired note.

The final program is as follows:

```
5 REM LOAD SPEAKER SUBROUTINE
10 FOR I = 768 TO 786
20 READ B
30 POKE I,B
40 NEXT I
50 DATA 173, 48, 192, 136, 208, 4, 198, 8, 240
60 DATA 8, 202, 208, 246, 166, 6, 76, 0, 3, 96
```

```
100 REM GET TOTAL NOTES
110 READ T
120 REM PLAY EACH NOTE
130 FOR I = 1 TO T
140 READ D : REM DURATION
150 READ P : REM PITCH
160 GOSUB 510 : REM CALL SPEAKER SUBROUTINE
170 NEXT I
180 END
200 REM NOTE DATA BEGINS HERE
210 REM FIRST DATA ELEMENT SHOULD BE TOTAL NOTES
220 DATA 6
230 DATA 60,20,60,20,70,20,160,30,175,27,180,32

500 REM MACHINE LANGUAGE INTERFACE SUBROUTINE
510 POKE 6,P : REM PITCH
520 POKE 8,D : REM DURATION
530 CALL 768 : REM PLAY THE NOTE
540 RETURN
```

A few notes from the first movement of Beethoven's Fifth Symphony should come out of the Apple's speaker when you run this program. Line 220 defines how many notes will be played, while line 230 contains the note data which is to be interpreted in pairs. To make the music program play other notes or songs, simply change the data statements on these two lines.

This music program and the machine language subroutine are not tuned to any particular scale. You will have to "play it by ear" to figure out which pitch values give melodious notes.

Another defect of this music program is that there is no way to have rests. One way to add this feature would be to modify the speaker interface subroutine at line 500 and add an IF statement to look for P = 0. When P is zero, the value of D could be used as part of an empty FOR-NEXT loop to create a delay. D should probably be multiplied by some constant in order to extend the range of rest durations. After the delay loop, the subroutine would immediately return instead of executing the CALL statement.

Sound on the Apple IIgs

The Apple IIgs is capable of a much broader range of sound: over 30 voices in either mono or stereo, thanks to its built-in Ensoniq synthesizer. Unfortunately, there is no way to program the synthesizer from BASIC.

Chapter 9 : Printing

When the Apple produces output, it usually shows up as text on the display screen. One drawback to this method is that the text is transitory; there isn't an easy way to obtain a permanent record of it. If you have a printer, your Apple can produce text and graphics on paper. Integrating printing into your BASIC programs is easy to do, since many of the screen commands will translate to the printer.

Printers typically are connected to a peripheral card in slot 1. A popular printer for the Apple II is the ImageWriter II, a printer capable of text and color graphics. This chapter will cover the basics of configuring and printing with the ImageWriter II.

Printer Cards

If you have an Apple II, II Plus, or IIe, then you will need a printer card installed in your Apple. A Super Serial Card is popularly used with the ImageWriter II. A card such as the Grappler+ is commonly found with the Epson series of printers. The printer card is typically installed in slot 1, and nearly all software written for the Apple will assume that it is located there.

Now if you have an Apple IIc, IIc Plus, or IIgs, then you are lucky: your model of Apple has a built-in printer card located in slot 1. This card will work with the ImageWriter II, and any other printer that utilizes a serial connection.

Configuring the Super Serial Card

If you have an Apple II, II Plus, or IIe, then you will need to configure your Super Serial Card in order for your commands to reach the printer. Configuring the Super Serial Card entails two simple procedures: setting two banks of DIP switches, and orienting a jumper block.

If your Super Serial Card is already installed in the Apple, (remember, slot 1 is recommended) then disconnect the DB-25 ribbon cable and carefully remove the card from its slot, leaving the connector behind.

The Super Serial Card has two sets of seven DIP switches that control how the card communicates with a connected device,

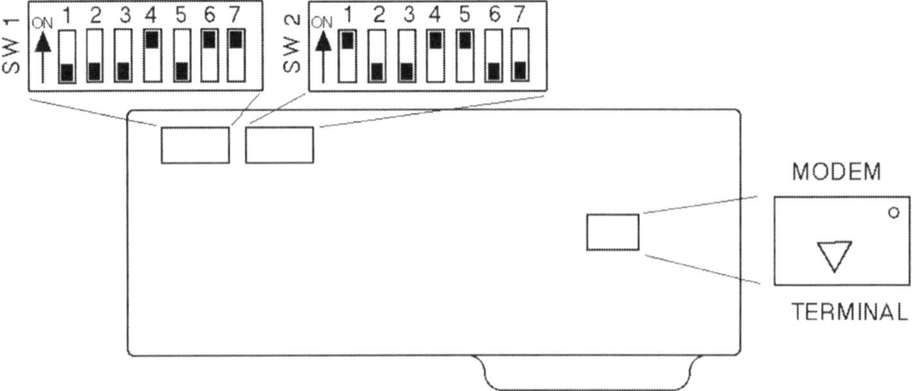

Figure 9-1. Super Serial Card configuration

Switch 1	Function	Switch 2	Function
1 Open	9600 baud	1 Closed	8 data, 1 stop bit
2 Open	9600 baud	2 Open	No delay
3 Open	9600 baud	3 Open	Line width 80/ video off
4 Closed	9600 baud	4 Closed	
5 Open	Printer mode	5 Closed	Linefeed after carriage return
6 Closed	Printer mode	6 Open	Interrupts off
7 Closed	Normal CTS	7 Open	Normal CTS

Table 9-1. Super Serial Card switch settings for ImageWriter II

in this case, the printer. See Table 9-1 for the switch settings and functions. Be sure to set the Super Serial Card's switches the same way.

Check the Modem/Terminal jumper block and see if the white triangle is pointing downward, toward the word Terminal. If it is, then you have nothing left to do. If not, you will need to gently pry it up with a small flat blade screwdriver or IC extractor, turn it around, then reseat it.

Once you have configured the two banks of switches and the jumper block, you may reattach the DB-25 ribbon cable and seat the Super Serial Card in slot 1 of your Apple. Be sure to install the card by gently rocking it front to back as you press the gold "fingers" into the Apple slot.

Finally, connect the serial cable from your printer to the DB-25 connector on the back of your Apple.

Using the ImageWriter II

The ImageWriter II is a popular printer that can be used both with the Apple II and the Macintosh. It happens to be one of the longest-running Apple products ever, having been manufactured from 1985 until 1996. Therefore, it is quite common and easy to obtain. Even better, the ribbons and supplies for it are still manufactured today.

Adding a Single Sheet of Paper

A single sheet of paper is added to the ImageWriter II in the same way that one would put paper in a typewriter. Make sure that the paper feed lever is set for friction feed, in the down position (see Figure 9-3).

Feed the paper down the back slot, around the platen, and back out the front slot. Align the left edge of the paper with the mark on the plastic housing. While still holding the paper, align the two ends as best as you can, then set the platen lever to hold the paper in place. If you have done everything correctly up to this point, then the paper should be straight, and will not go crooked.

For the final step, turn the platen knob, located on the right, to pull the paper back down until it is just below the plastic window. You can then adjust it how you like to set the top margin.

Alternatively, with the ImageWriter II powered on, pressing the Form Feed button will automatically load the paper to the correct printing position. This position is indicated by the red print line on the plastic paper guide. Be sure that the Select light is off, otherwise the Form Feed button will have no effect. Press the Select button to toggle the Select light.

With the front cover on and the paper properly loaded, the red Error light should not be on. If it is on, replace the front cover if you haven't, and check that the paper is rolled far enough into the printer.

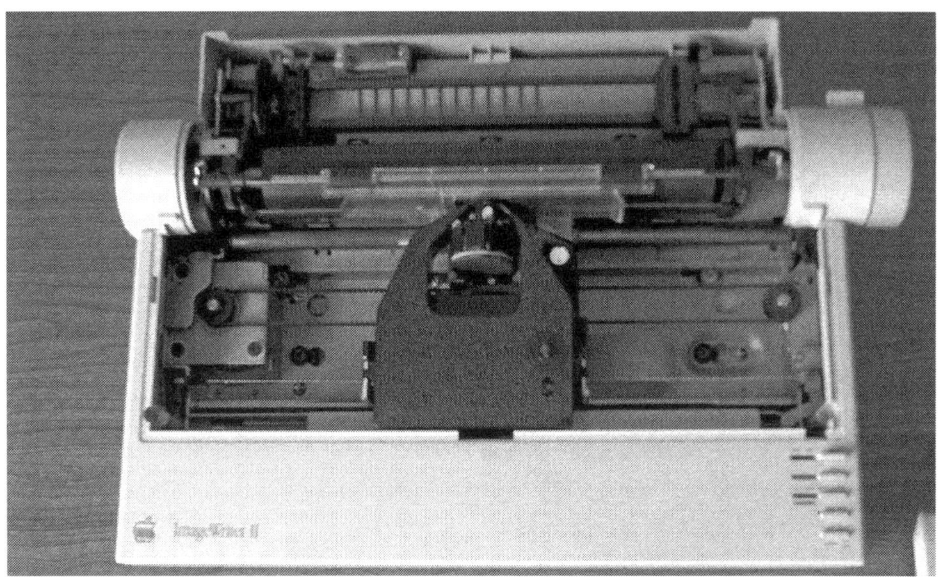

Figure 9-2. Interior of the ImageWriter II

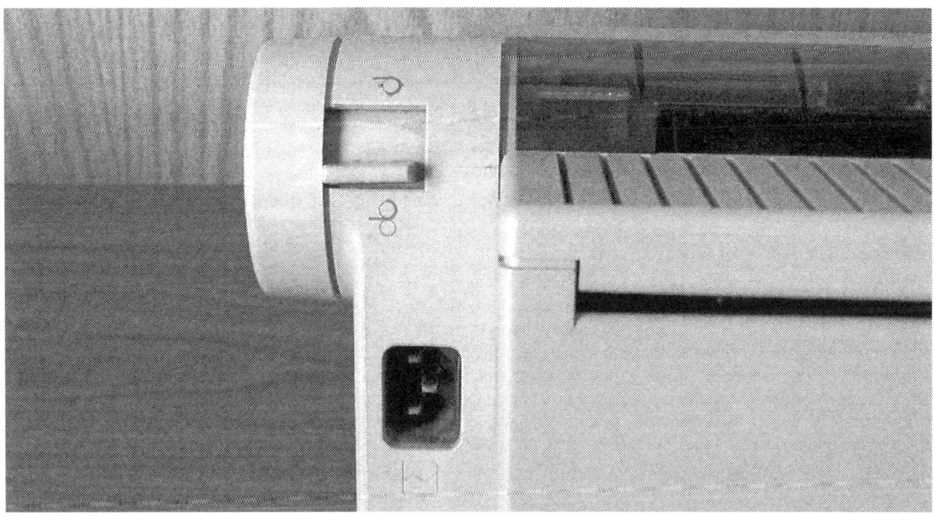

Figure 9-3. Paper feed lever set for friction feed

Adding Tractor Feed Paper

The most convenient type of paper to use with the ImageWriter II is tractor-fed paper, sometimes also called continuous or pin feed, which is distinctive for its perforated holes on the sides.

To load this kind of paper, pull off the smaller plastic cover on the back of the printer. On the left and right sides you should see the plastic pin and tread assemblies, known as the paper clamps (shown in Figure 9-4). These are movable to accommodate different paper widths. They may already be correctly set, but you should check them to make sure. To move them, pull up the lever, slide the clamp to the correct position, then press the lever back down to lock it in place. Make sure that the right paper clamp is aligned with the notch on the back of the ImageWriter II. This will ensure that the printing margin is 1/4" from the perforation.

Once you have the paper clamps properly aligned, pull open the top of each one, which is hinged. Align the sprocket holes of the paper with the pins on the two treads. Once you have everything in order, press the hinges back down on the treads. The paper should now be clamped down and secure (See Figure 9-5). Replace the plastic cover.

At this point, you should power on the ImageWriter II, and press

Figure 9-4. Locations of tractor hinge and lever

Figure 9-5. Paper clamped in tractor feed

the Form Feed button to advance the paper to the correct printing position. You should not need to make any further adjustments at all, at least until the paper runs out. The ImageWriter II is smart enough to know where one sheet of paper ends and the next begins.

Adjusting Paper Thickness

If you want to print on envelopes, or if you're using unusually thick cotton bond paper, you may need to adjust the ImageWriter II's paper thickness lever. Doing so will help prevent jams and other printing malfunctions.

The paper thickness lever is located inside the ImageWriter II, so you'll need to remove the front cover. See Figure 9-6 for the location (circled) of the lever.

The lever has four settings for different paper thicknesses. The topmost position is for a thickness of one sheet of paper, the next down is for two, then three, and then four. You should never use a form, label, or envelope that is thicker than four standard sheets of paper.

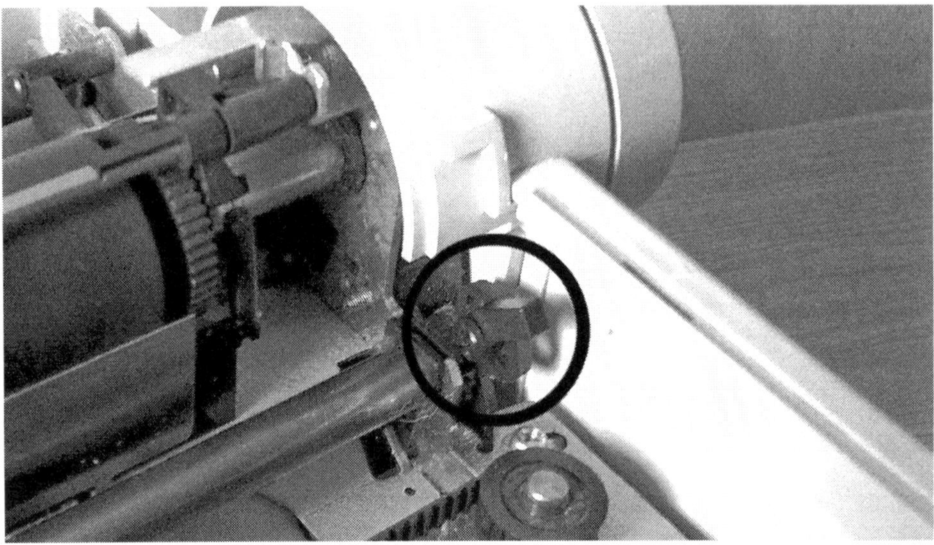

Figure 9-6. Location of the paper thickness lever

Clearing Paper Jams

Occasionally it may happen that the ImageWriter II pulls in more than one sheet of paper at a time, or pulls in a sheet crooked, or for some reason a sheet of paper gets stuck in the rollers. Any of these conditions is known as a paper jam, and it may cause the printer to stop and show the red Error light, or it may cause garbled output on crumpled paper.

The first thing to do when a paper jam occurs is to turn off the ImageWriter II right away using the power button. Then, take off the front cover and look inside. If you're using tractor feed paper, tear off the sheet that's connected to the rest of the ream. If the paper didn't make it in too far before jamming, you may be able to back it out using the large platen knob. Otherwise, you may have to pop open the paper bail that holds the paper in place, and attempt to pull out the jammed sheet.

Replacing the Ribbon

Replacing the ribbon in the ImageWriter II is a fairly simple procedure. First, make sure that the printer is switched off. Remove the lid and pull the print carriage over to the center.

The ribbon cartridge is held in place with a plastic tab, and the ribbon itself loops around the print head. Pull back the plastic tab to release the ribbon. Be sure to carefully pull the ribbon cartridge out so as to avoid damaging the print head or carriage.

When installing a new ribbon, you must ensure that the ribbon (the fabric which contains the printing ink) is run between the plastic ribbon guide and the clear paper guide. Press down on the cartridge to snap it into place, then rotate the small knob on the right side of the ribbon cartridge to tighten up any slack that may be in the ribbon.

Self-Test

The ImageWriter II has a built-in testing feature that will display some information about the printer's configuration, as well as all of the ASCII characters that the printer can produce.

To activate the test, first make sure that the printer has paper loaded into it. Turn the power off, if it isn't already, then hold down the Form Feed button as you turn the power back on. After a moment, the ImageWriter II should start printing the self-test. You may release the Form Feed button now. The test will continue forever, as long as there is still paper and power to the printer.

Troubleshooting

If you have the Super Serial Card installed, connected to the printer, and everything is turned on, yet you can't get the printer to print anything, the first thing to check should be the Super Serial Card configuration, especially the DIP switches. These switches can be confusing to set, since they may be labeled "Open" instead of "On." As it so happens, "Open" and "On" mean the opposite thing.

If you are certain that the Super Serial Card is configured and operating correctly, and that the cable connection is good, then there is a small chance that your ImageWriter II has an AppleTalk Option card installed. As long as this card is installed in your printer, the printer cannot be used when connected to a Super Serial Card.

Activating the Printer

The Apple II must be instructed to send output to the printer; it won't do so on its own just because there's a printer attached. Assuming that your printer card is located in slot 1, as is typical, this command will send all output to it:

```
]PR#1
```

Remember that the Apple IIc, IIc Plus, and IIgs have a built-in printer card, which happens to be located in "slot" number 1. For all other models of Apple, you will indeed require a printer card. Make sure that you type the correct slot number. Failure to do so, for example, by typing a slot number that is empty, may lock up the Apple, forcing you to press CONTROL-RESET.

Once you have executed this command, try typing some letters, and press RETURN. If all went well, the printer should come alive, and what you typed should appear on the paper. The Apple merely uses the printer as a substitute for the screen. All text that would ordinarily appear on the screen will be sent to the printer instead. This includes the output from CATALOG, INPUT, LIST, PRINT, and all other commands. At last, the BASIC PRINT statement is used in its literal sense.

If nothing is happening on the printer, check the following:

- Is the printer turned on?
- Does it have paper?
- Is it properly connected to the Apple or an interface card?
- Is the Select light on?

If you have an ImageWriter II, then you must have the lid on, the red Error light should be off, and the green Select light should be on. Press the Select button if it's not on.

Sending Text to the Screen and Printer

By setting switches or issuing commands to the Super Serial Card or Parallel Interface Card, you can cause program output to be both shown on the screen and printed on paper. When doing so, the printed line length is typically restricted to 40 columns, the same as the screen.

Commands to the Super Serial Card or Parallel Interface Card must be prefixed by ASCI code number 9. Sending this code signals the printer card that the next character or characters to follow are commands, and should not be printed on paper. Typing a CONTROL-I at the BASIC command prompt will also generate this ASCII code.

To stop screen display and change printer line width, execute the following command:

```
]PRINT CHR$(9);"80N"
```

CHR$(9) sends the ASCII code to get the printer card's attention. This command dictates that screen output will cease, printer output will continue, and subsequent printed lines will be 80 characters long. With the N command, you can change printer line length from 1 to 255 characters, but there are practical limitations: most printers cannot print more than 80 to 100 characters per line.

Another command will restart the screen display and change the printer line width to 40 characters. It is:

```
]PRINT CHR$(9);"I"
```

Again, CHR$(9) sends the ASCII code that tells the Super Serial Card or Parallel Interface Card that a command is about to follow. The I command instructs the printer card to print output and display it on the screen simultaneously.

If these commands are not registering with your printer, it could be that the printer card is set to accept a different ASCII code for commands. If this is the case, try using CHR$(1) instead of CHR$(9). If CHR$(1) works, use it instead wherever you see CHR$(9) later in this chapter. To produce this ASCII code at the BASIC prompt, type CONTROL-A.

When the Super Serial Card is in Communications mode, it expects commands to start with a CONTROL-A (ASCII code 1). In

Printer mode, the card expects commands to begin with CONTROL-I (ASCII code 9).

Printing a Disk Catalog

You may find it useful to keep a listing of the programs and data saved on a disk. Such a list could be kept in the paper disk sleeve for easy reference.

To print a disk catalog on the printer, first activate the printer by sending it a PR#1 command (replace the 1 if your printer card is in a different slot number). Then type CATALOG if you have DOS 3.3, or CAT, if you are using ProDOS, and press RETURN. The catalog listing will not appear on the screen, as is customary, but instead will be printed to paper. If you are using DOS 3.3, and the catalog has more than 18 files, then you will still need to press RETURN to get the remaining files printed. Type PR#0 to return back to screen output, then you may trim the catalog printout so that it will comfortably fit in a disk sleeve. As always, you may specify a pathname (if using ProDOS) or a slot and drive number with the catalog command, as described in Chapter 7.

Printing a Program Listing

Getting a copy of your BASIC program listing on paper is just as straightforward as getting a disk catalog listing. To do so, merely use the appropriate PR command, such as PR#1 for a printer connected to slot 1.

Then type LIST, and your program listing should appear on the printer. Type PR#0 to get back to the usual 40-column display screen (or PR#3 if you have an 80-column display). You can also print out partial listings by using the LIST command options detailed in Chapter 3.

Deactivating the Printer

To tell the Apple that you are finished printing is as simple as redirecting output back to the screen. This is accomplished by using the following command:

```
]PR#0
```

Ordinarily, the PR command is used with a slot number. However, this is the special exception: 0 doesn't refer to a slot in the Apple, rather it corresponds to the built-in keyboard and video screen.

If you have an 80-column card in your Apple II, II Plus, or IIe, or if you have any other model of Apple, then you may return to 80-column display with:

```
]PR#3
```

You may also send a command to the printer card to deactivate the printer. The following line will tell a Super Serial Card or Parallel Interface Card to stop printing:

```
]PRINT CHR$(9);"R"
```

Several other actions will also deactivate the printer, such as:

- Pressing CONTROL-RESET
- Booting DOS or ProDOS
- Running a program that uses the 80-column card.

Programming the Printer

Programming for the printer is much the same as programming for the screen. Output is still composed of lines, and there is still a cursor that moves. However, the cursor has some limitations imposed upon it: namely, it may only move downward and rightward. Some of the screen formatting tricks that you may have used to line up data will not work on the printer. For example, the VTAB command that will move the cursor to any vertical location on the screen has no effect on the printer.

Using the PR command, which itself is an abbreviation of PRINT, all PRINT statements and other subsequent program output can be sent to a printer. When the program is finished printing, PR#0 will deactivate the printer, directing output to the screen as usual (PR#3 will activate the 80-column card, if your Apple has one).

The following program prints two lines on the printer, using PR#1, and one line on the screen, using PR#0:

```
10 REM PRINTER OUTPUT DEMONSTRATION
20 PR#1 : REM SEND OUTPUT TO PRINTER IN SLOT 1
30 PRINT "IN FOURTEEN HUNDRED NINETY-TWO,"
40 PRINT "COLUMBUS SAILED THE OCEAN BLUE."
50 PR#0 : REM DEACTIVATE PRINTER
60 PRINT "AND NOW BACK TO NORMAL."
70 END
```

If DOS or ProDOS is active, using PR# could cause it to become disconnected (see Getting Connected with DOS in Chapter 7 for a full explanation of what "disconnected" means). When disconnected, you and your programs can no longer send commands to DOS, such as for loading or saving a program. The solution is to prefix the PR# command with the CONTROL-D character in a PRINT statement.

Here are the changes for the printer output demonstration program:

```
20 PRINT CHR$(4);"PR#1"
50 PRINT CHR$(4);"PR#0"
```

Alternatively, if you wanted to get back to the 80-columns screen, line 50 would become:

```
50 PRINT CHR$(4);"PR#3"
```

If you recall from Chapter 7, ASCII code 4 signals DOS that a disk command is about to follow. Instead of using CHR$(4) in Applesoft, you can make a variable D$ which contains a CONTROL-D character. In fact, this is the only method available in Integer BASIC, which lacks a CHR$ function:

```
15 D$ = "" : REM TYPE CONTROL-D BETWEEN QUOTES
20 PRINT D$;"PR#1"
50 PRINT D$;"PR#0"
```

Pressing CONTROL-D produces an invisible character on the screen, which is why the REM comment is there to remind you what is between the quotes.

Formatting Printer Output

Formatting output for the printer is quite similar to screen formatting covered in Chapter 6. The main exception is that the cursor is not free to move about anywhere on the printed page. More specifically, commas and TAB functions do not work correctly on the Super Serial Card or Parallel Interface Card. The alternative to these two methods of output formatting is use of the SPC function, which works just as well on the printer as it does on the screen.

This following program is an adaptation of an earlier screen formatting program from Chapter 6. With some changes, notably, converting HTAB to SPC, the same information is printed in the same format.

```
5 PRINT CHR$(21) : REM DISABLE 80-COLS CARD
6 PR#1 : REM ACTIVATE PRINTER
7 PRINT CHR$(9);"40N" : REM SET TO 40-COLS
10 PRINT SPC(6); "KILOGRAMS";SPC(4);"POUNDS"
20 FOR K = 1 TO 16
30 LN = LEN(STR$(INT(K))) : REM KILOS LENGTH
35 IF K < 1 AND K > 0 THEN LN = 0
40 PRINT SPC(7 - LN + 1);K;
50 P = K * 2.2 : REM CONVERT TO POUNDS
60 LN = LEN(STR$(INT(P))) : REM POUNDS LENGTH
65 IF P < 1 AND P > 0 THEN LN = 0
70 PRINT SPC(12 - LN + 1);P
80 NEXT K
90 PRINT CHR$(9);"R" : REM DISABLE PRINTER
```

Lines 5 through 7 prepare the Apple for printer output, and afterward, line 90 disables the printer and returns output to the screen.

HTAB in Applesoft, and its equivalent in Integer BASIC, TAB, can be used to move the cursor horizontally across the printed page, but only to the right. It is not possible to back up to what has already been printed on a line. If you are working with 80 columns or any value greater than 40, beware that the original Apple II, II Plus, and unenhanced IIe have an HTAB statement that only works with columns 1 through 40. If you wish to advance the cursor past column 40 on any of these models of Apple, you must use a POKE statement to place the desired column number in memory location 36. For example, POKE 36,41 will position the printer cursor to column 42. As with HTAB, POKE and TAB cannot be used to back the printer up to a column that it has already passed over in the current line.

Paging

Unless programmed to do otherwise, the printer will not make very intelligent page breaks. When left to its own devices, the printer tends to behave as though it were printing on a continuous spool of paper, making page breaks only when absolutely necessary. Therefore, it is up to the programmer to keep track of lines and page breaks to ensure that the printer output flows logically from page to page.

Fortunately, the method of doing so is not too difficult. The theory behind controlling page breaks is to count the number of lines which a program has produced, and take action when this count is at certain values.

The standard ImageWriter II configuration allows 66 lines to be printed on a standard, letter size sheet of paper, leaving no room for top or bottom margins. Most often, leaving some lines blank for the margins will be desired. Following is an Applesoft subroutine that keeps track of a printed line count, advancing to the next page when necessary:

```
12000 REM PRINTER PAGING SUBROUTINE
12001 REM INCREMENT LC% THEN CALL THIS SUBROUTINE
```

```
12010 IF LC% < 62 THEN RETURN : REM PRINTED ENOUGH
LINES YET?
12020 FOR X = 1 TO (69 - LC%) : REM PRINT BOTTOM MAR-
GIN
12030 PRINT : NEXT X
12040 LC% = 3 : RETURN : REM SET TOP MARGIN AND RETURN
```

The variable LC% (named for “line count”) is defined as an integer so as not to interfere with a main program variable name. It is up to the main program to increment this variable each time that a line is printed and then immediately call the subroutine.

As it stands, this subroutine will cause pages to have a top margin of four lines and a bottom margin of about three lines. To increase the top margin, decrease the value in line 12010. To increase the bottom margin, increase the value in line 12020.

Here is a program to demonstrate this paging subroutine. It will print three pages of lines.

```
5 PRINT CHR$(21)
10 PR#1
12 PRINT CHR$(9);"40N"
15 LC% = 0
20 PRINT "HERE IS THE HEADING"
25 LC% = LC% + 1 : GOSUB 12010
30 FOR I = 0 TO 170
40 PRINT "LINE "I
45 LC% = LC% + 1 : GOSUB 12010
50 NEXT I
60 PRINT CHR$(9);"R"
65 PR#0
70 END
```

Don’t forget to add the paging subroutine at the end before running this program.

Printer Control Characters

The Apple's text screen cannot show type styles such as italic, bold, or underline. Nor can it show condensed text, or text in a different face. Fortunately, printers such as the ImageWriter II can, with the use of certain control codes and Escape sequences. These codes are not like Escape key sequences used for editing on-screen text, even though they do involve the ESCAPE key. Instead they are so named because they start with the ASCII code for Escape (27, in decimal) to signal the printer that you mean to send it a control code, not something to display. For example, CONTROL-L means the same as pressing the Line Feed button on the ImageWriter II control panel, and ESCAPE-X will cause printed text to be underlined.

Control codes and Escape sequences can be sent from any BASIC program, or they can be typed directly on the keyboard, provided that you have set output to go to the printer with PR#1. Control characters do not appear on the printed page, even though they are issued with the PRINT command in BASIC.

Other control characters for the printer control the mechanics of printing, such as left margin, paper feed, and line spacing. These control characters are listed in the table below.

Setting Page Margins

Being able to dictate page margins to your printer is especially advantageous when using continuous, tractor-fed paper. By setting margins, one may control the length of the printed page.

When the ImageWriter II is first powered on, it assumes that the paper is positioned with the top edge just under the paper bail. For the duration that the printer remains on, it always calculates the top of the page from this point.

The ImageWriter II, if left to its own devices, knows how far to advance the paper such that page breaks occur at the bottom and top of each page, respectively. If there is human intervention, if someone were to, for example, manually advance the paper or press the Line Feed button, the printer's calculations would be thrown off, resulting in misplaced page breaks. The solution at present is to turn off the printer, adjust the paper as desired, then turn the printer back on.

Control Characters	Type Style
CHR$(27) + "n"	Extended (9 characters per inch)
CHR$(27) + "N"	Pica (10 cpi)
CHR$(27) + "E"	Elite (12 cpi)
CHR$(27) + "p"	Pica proportional (144 dots per inch)
CHR$(27) + "P"	Elite proportional (160 dpi)
CHR$(27) + "e"	Semicondensed (13.4 cpi)
CHR$(27) + "q"	Condensed (15 cpi)
CHR$(27) + "Q"	Ultracondensed (17 cpi)
CHR$(27) + CHR$(*n*)	Set spacing between proportional characters, where *n* is 1-9
CHR$(27) + "s" + CHR$(*n*)	For elite proportional style, separate adjacent characters with *n* dots of spacing, where *n* is 1-6
CHR$(14)	Begin headline style
CHR$(15)	End headline style
CHR$(27) + "X"	Begin underline style
CHR$(27) + "Y"	End underline style
CHR$(27) + "!"	Begin boldface style
CHR$(27) + CHR$(34)	End boldface style
CHR$(27) + "x"	Begin superscript style
CHR$(27) + "z"	End superscript style
CHR$(27) + "y"	Begin subscript style
CHR$(27) + "z"	End subscript style
CHR$(27) + "w"	Begin half-height style
CHR$(27) + "W"	End half-height style
CHR$(27) + "D" + CHR$(1) + CHR$(0)	Print slashed zeros
CHR$(27) + "Z" + CHR$(1) + CHR$(0)	Do not print slashed zeros
CHR$(27) + "c"	Return all styles and sizes to printer defaults

Table 9-2. ImageWriter II control characters for type styles

Control Characters	Function
CHR$(27) + “$”	Change to ASCII character set.
CHR$(27) + “&”	Change to MouseText character set.
CHR$(27) + “>”	Print left to right only.
CHR$(27) + “<“	Print bidirectionally.
CHR$(8) + “*c*”	Backspace, then print character *c*.
CHR$(12)	Feed to top of form.
CHR$(27) + “v”	Set top of form to current position.
CHR$(27) + “L*nnn*”	Set left margin to *nnn*.
CHR$(27) + “A”	Set line spacing to 6 lines per inch.
CHR$(27) + “B”	Set line spacing to 8 lpi.

Table 9-3. ImageWriter II control characters for general functions

As shown earlier, it is possible for a program to control the top and bottom margins of the paper. Unfortunately, this method tasks the programmer with managing the printed lines and margins. As luck would have it, the ImageWriter II supports several control characters for specifying page length. The length set by these characters remains in effect until the printer is powered off.

The margins will still be measured from wherever the ImageWriter II thinks the top of the paper is. That is to say, specifying a 1 inch margin with the top of the paper already 1 inch above the print line will result in an effective 2 inch margin.

Furthermore, the top margin affects the bottom margin by leaving less space on the paper. If the top margin were set to 1 inch, and a 2 inch bottom margin is desired, then the printer must be told to print a 3 inch bottom margin in order to account for the extra inch used at the top of the page.

Setting the left margin is rather simpler: one merely need specify the number of characters inward where printing should commence on each line.

The following program illustrates the use of control characters to set both top and left margins:

```
10 REM PAGE LENGTH WITH CTRL-CHARS
20 PRINT CHR$(21) : REM DISABLE 80-COLS
25 HOME
30 PRINT "IMAGEWRITER II PAGE MARGIN SETUP" : PRINT
40 INPUT "HOW WIDE SHOULD THE LEFT MARGIN BE? "; LM
50 PRINT : PRINT "TO SET THE TOP MARGIN, POSITION THE"
60 PRINT "PAPER AND PRESS ANY KEY WHEN READY."
70 GET A$ : REM WAIT FOR USER TO POSITION THE PAPER
80 PR#1 : REM TALK TO PRINTER
90 PRINT CHR$(9);"80N" : REM NO SCREEN ECHO
100 LM$ = STR$(LM) : REM CONVERT TO STRING
110 IF LM < 100 THEN LM$ = "0" + LM$ : REM PAD WITH
ZEROS
120 IF LM < 10 THEN LM$ = "0" + LM$
130 PRINT CHR$(27);CHR$(76);LM$ : REM SET LEFT MARGIN
140 PRINT CHR$(27);CHR$(118) : REM SET TOP MARGIN
150 PRINT CHR$(9);"R" : REM BACK TO SCREEN
160 PRINT : PRINT "THE MARGINS ARE NOW SET FOR PRINT-
ING."
170 END
```

Lines 20 through 70 prepare the program, print introductory text, and ask the user to enter a top and left margin. Lines 80 and 90 prepare the printer to receive its control characters. The value for left margin must be specified as a three-digit number, therefore lines 100 to 120 format it by prepending zeros as needed. Finally, lines 130 and 140 deliver the necessary control characters to the ImageWriter II and line 150 sends output back to the screen to tell the user that the page margins are now configured.

Print Subroutine for the Word Processor

A basic word processing program was demonstrated in Chapter 7. One notable feature that was missing was the ability to print a document.

The changes from the program as shown in Chapter 7 are surrounded with a box:

```
10 REM WORD PROCESSING PROGRAM
15 ONERR GOTO 10000 : REM ERROR HANDLER
20 REM DEFINE VARIABLES
30 D$ = CHR$(4) : REM CONTROL-D
35 IF PEEK(977) <> 0 THEN PRINT D$;"MAXFILES 1"
40 IB$ = "" : REM INPUT BUFFER
50 DIM DL$(70, 80) : REM ARRAY HOLDING EACH DOCUMENT
LINE
60 LC = 1 : REM TOTAL LINE COUNTER
65 SL% = 1 : REM SCREEN LINE POINTER
70 CL = 1 : REM CURRENT LINE POINTER
75 TL = 1 : REM TOP LINE POINTER (FOR SCROLLING)
80 SL = 40 : REM SCREEN LENGTH (40 OR 80 COLS)
85 MO$ = "" : REM CURRENT PROGRAM MODE
90 CP = 1 : REM CURSOR POSITION
95 FI$ = "" : REM FILE NAME

100 REM PRINT MAIN SCREEN
105 PRINT CHR$(21) : REM FORCE 40-COLUMN DISPLAY
110 HOME : PRINT "WORD PROCESSOR" : PRINT : PRINT
120 PRINT "CHOOSE AN OPTION:"
130 PRINT : INVERSE : PRINT "N"; : NORMAL
140 PRINT "EW DOCUMENT": PRINT : INVERSE
150 PRINT "L"; : NORMAL : PRINT "OAD DOCUMENT"
160 PRINT : INVERSE : PRINT "Q"; : NORMAL
170 PRINT "UIT" : PRINT

220 REM GET USER CHOICE
230 INPUT "";A$ : D$ = CHR$(4)
```

```
240 IF A$ <> "N" AND A$ <> "L" AND A$ <> "Q" THEN 230
260 IF A$ = "N" THEN GOSUB 1000
270 IF A$ = "L" THEN MO$ = "L" : GOSUB 2000
290 IF A$ = "Q" THEN GOTO 4000
300 GOTO 110

1000 REM CREATE A NEW DOCUMENT
1005 HOME : INVERSE : PRINT " " : NORMAL
1010 FI$ = ""
1015 GOSUB 5520

2000 REM LOAD AN EXISTING DOCUMENT
2010 REM ASK FOR FILE NAME
2020 HOME : INPUT "LOAD WHICH DOCUMENT? ";FI$
2030 IF FI$ = "" THEN RETURN
2035 HOME
2040 REM CHECK IF FILE EXISTS
2050 PRINT : PRINT D$;"RENAME ";FI$;",";FI$
2060 REM NOW TRY TO OPEN THE FILE
2070 PRINT : PRINT D$;"OPEN ";FI$
2080 PRINT : PRINT D$;"READ ";FI$
2180 REM READ TOTAL LINES
2190 INPUT "";LC%
2200 REM READ LINES INTO DL ARRAY
2210 FOR I = 1 TO LC%
2215 INPUT "";LI$ : IF LI$ = "" THEN 2235
2220 FOR J = 1 TO LEN(LI$)
2225 C = ASC(MID$(LI$,J,1)) : GOSUB 8715
2230 NEXT J
2235 IF I <> LC% THEN GOSUB 9510
2240 NEXT I
2250 PRINT D$ : REM CANCEL DOS COMMAND
2260 PRINT D$;"CLOSE ";FI$
2280 REM ENTER INTO MAIN EVENT LOOP
2290 GOSUB 5520
```

```
3000 REM PRINT DOCUMENT
3005 PRINT : PRINT D$;"PR#1" : REM ACTIVATE PRINTER
3010 PRINT CHR$(9);"40N"
3015 LC% = 0 : REM PRINTER LINE COUNTER
3020 FOR I = 1 TO LC
3030 FOR J = 1 TO SL : REM PRINT A ROW
3040 PRINT DL$(I,J);
3050 NEXT J : REM NEXT CHAR IN ROW
3060 PRINT : LC% = LC% + 1
3070 GOSUB 12010 : REM CHECK PRINTER LINE COUNTER
3080 NEXT I : REM NEXT ROW
3100 PRINT CHR$(9);"R" : REM DISABLE PRINTER
3110 PRINT D$;"PR#0"
3120 RETURN
```

```
4000 REM QUIT THE PROGRAM
4010 REM MAKE SURE THE FILE IS CLOSED
4020 IF FI$ <> "" THEN PRINT D$;"CLOSE ";FI$
4030 HOME : END

5000 REM SCREEN DISPLAY SUBROUTINE
5010 REM RESPONSIBLE FOR DISPLAYING LINES OF TEXT ON
SCREEN
5020 REM BY DOING A COMPLETE REDRAW
5030 HOME
5040 REM CALCULATE RANGE OF LINES TO DISPLAY
5050 RE = TL + 23 : IF RE > LC THEN RE = LC
5060 LC% = 1 : REM REDRAW LINE COUNTER
5200 FOR I = (TL) TO (RE) : REM PARENS NEEDED FOR RE-
SERVED WORDS
5205 FOR J = 1 TO SL : REM PRINT A ROW
5210 VTAB(LC%) : HTAB(J) : PRINT DL$(I,J);
5215 NEXT J : REM NEXT CHAR IN ROW
5220 LC% = LC% + 1 : IF LC% > 24 THEN LC% = 24
5225 NEXT I : REM NEXT ROW
5230 RETURN
```

```
5500 REM MAIN EVENT LOOP
5510 REM LISTENS FOR KEY PRESSES AND DECIDES WHAT TO
DO
5520 C = PEEK(-16384) : REM READ KEYBOARD
5530 IF C < 128 THEN 5520 : CHECK FOR KEY PRESS
5540 POKE -16368,0 : REM RESET KEYBOARD STROBE
5545 C = C - 128 : REM CONVERT TO ASCII CODE
5550 IF C = 17 THEN GOSUB 4020 : REM CTRL-Q, QUIT
```

```
5551 IF C = 16 THEN GOSUB 3000 : REM CTRL-P, PRINT
```

```
5555 IF C = 9 THEN GOSUB 6000 : REM CTRL-I, TAB
5560 IF C = 19 THEN GOSUB 7000 : REM CTRL-S, SAVE
5565 IF C = 1 OR C = 26 THEN GOSUB 8000 : REM CTRL-A,
CTRL-Z UP/DOWN CURSOR
5570 IF C = 8 OR C = 21 THEN GOSUB 9000 : REM LEFT,
RIGHT CURSOR
5575 IF C = 11 OR C = 10 THEN GOSUB 8000 : REM UP,
DOWN CURSOR
5580 IF C = 13 THEN GOSUB 9500 : REM CARRIAGE RETURN
5585 IF C = 27 THEN GOSUB 6500 : REM ESCAPE, HELP MENU
5590 IF C = 127 THEN GOSUB 8500 : REM DELETE
5591 IF C = 18 THEN GOSUB 5030 : GOSUB 9050 : REM RE-
DRAW
5595 GOSUB 8700 : REM ADD A CHARACTER
5600 GOTO 5520

6000 REM INSERT A TAB (8 SPACES)
6005 TL% = SL - CP : REM TAB LENGTH
6010 IF TL% > 8 THEN TL% = 8
6015 FOR X = 1 TO TL%
6020 C = ASC(" ") : REM SPACE
6025 GOSUB 8715 : REM ADD CHARACTER
6030 NEXT X
6040 RETURN

6500 REM SHOW A HELP MENU THAT LISTS COMMANDS
```

```
6505 REM SET TEXT WINDOW
6510 POKE 32,INT((SL - 28) / 2) : POKE 34,6
6512 HTAB 1 : VTAB 6
6515 FOR X = 1 TO 27 : PRINT "=";: NEXT X : PRINT
6520 PRINT "|";: PRINT SPC(4);: PRINT "COMMAND REFER-
ENCE";: PRINT SPC(4); : PRINT "|"
6525 PRINT "|";: PRINT SPC(25);: PRINT "|"
6530 PRINT "| CTRL-Q : QUIT";: PRINT SPC(11);: PRINT
"|"
6535 PRINT "| CTRL-I : TAB (8 SPACES) |"
6540 PRINT "| CTRL-S : SAVE";: PRINT SPC(11);: PRINT
"|"
6545 PRINT "| CTRL-A : CURSOR UP";: PRINT
SPC(6);:PRINT "|"
6550 PRINT "| CTRL-Z : CURSOR DOWN";: PRINT SPC(4);:
PRINT "|"
```

```
6551 PRINT "| CTRL-P : PRINT";: PRINT SPC(10);: PRINT
"|"
```

```
6555 PRINT "|";: PRINT SPC(25);: PRINT "|"
6560 PRINT "|  PRESS ESC TO CONTINUE  |"
6565 FOR X = 1 TO 27 : PRINT "=";: NEXT X
6570 REM WAIT FOR ESC KEYPRESS
6575 C = PEEK(-16384) : REM READ KEYBOARD
6580 IF C < 128 THEN 6575 : CHECK FOR KEY PRESS
6585 POKE -16368,0 : REM RESET KEYBOARD STROBE
6590 C = C - 128 : REM CONVERT TO ASCII CODE
6595 IF C <> 27 THEN GOTO 6575
6600 REM RESET TEXT WINDOW
6605 POKE 32,0 : POKE 34,0 : POKE 33,SL
6610 GOSUB 5030 : REM REDRAW SCREEN
6620 GOSUB 9050 : REM FLASH CURSOR
6650 RETURN

7000 REM SAVE DOCUMENT
```

```
7010 REM ASK FOR NAME IF NONE, OTHERWISE WRITE OUT
LINES
7015 IF FI$ = "" THEN PRINT CHR$(7) : GOTO 7100
7020 PRINT : PRINT D$;"OPEN ";FI$ : PRINT D$;"CLOSE
";FI$
7025 PRINT D$;"DELETE ";FI$ : REM TRUNCATE THE FILE
7030 PRINT D$;"OPEN ";FI$
7045 PRINT D$;"WRITE ";FI$ : REM START WRITING TO FILE
7050 PRINT LC : REM TOTAL LINES
7060 FOR I = 1 TO LC
7065 FOR J = 1 TO SL : REM PRINT A ROW
7070 PRINT DL$(I,J);
7075 NEXT J : REM NEXT CHAR IN ROW
7080 PRINT : NEXT I : REM NEXT ROW
7085 PRINT : PRINT D$;"CLOSE ";FI$ : REM CLOSE THE
FILE
7090 GOTO 7190 : REM RETURN FROM SAVING
7100 REM ASK FOR NAME
7105 VTAB 1 : HTAB 1 : INVERSE : PRINT "NAME"; : NOR-
MAL
7110 PRINT SPC(20); : HTAB 5 : INPUT FI$
7120 IF LEN(FI$) > 15 THEN GOTO 7105
7125 GOTO 7020 : REM GO SAVE NOW
7190 PRINT : PRINT D$;"CLOSE ";FI$
7195 GOSUB 5030 : GOSUB 9050 : REM REDRAW SCREEN
7200 RETURN

8000 REM MOVE CURSOR UP OR DOWN
8005 IF (C = 1 OR C = 11) AND CL = 1 THEN RETURN : REM
AT TOP
8010 IF (C = 26 OR C = 10) AND CL >= LC THEN RETURN :
REM AT BOTTOM
8015 REM REPLACE CHARACTER UNDER CURSOR
8020 C$ = DL$(CL,CP) : IF C$ = "" THEN C$ = " "
8025 HTAB(CP) : VTAB(SL%) : PRINT C$;
8030 IF (C = 26 OR C = 10) AND CL < 70 THEN GOTO 8040
: REM MOVE DOWN
```

```
8035 IF (C = 1 OR C = 11) THEN CL = CL - 1 : GOTO 8055
: REM MOVE UP
8040 CL = CL + 1 : SL% = SL% + 1 : REM INCR. SCREEN
LINE
8045 IF SL% > 24 THEN SL% = 24 : TL = TL + 1 : GOSUB
5030 : REM REDRAW
8050 GOTO 8070
8055 SL% = SL% - 1 : REM DECR. SCREEN LINE
8060 IF SL% < 1 THEN SL% = 1 : TL = TL - 1 : GOSUB
5030 : REM REDRAW

8070 REM PUT CURSOR AFTER CHARACTER
8075 C$ = DL$(CL,CP) : IF C$ = "" THEN CP = CP - 1 :
IF CP > 0 THEN GOTO 8045 REM CHECK LEFT
8080 IF C$ <> "" OR CP <= 1 THEN GOTO 8090
8085 GOTO 8075 : REM CHECK NEXT POSITION
8090 REM DRAW CURSOR AT NEW POSITION
8095 IF CP < 1 THEN CP = 1 : C$ = DL$(CL,CP)
8100 IF C$ = "" THEN C$ = " "
8105 FLASH : VTAB(SL%) : HTAB(CP) : PRINT C$; : NORMAL
8110 RETURN

8500 REM DELETE KEY
8505 C = 8 : GOSUB 9005 : REM TREAT AS LEFT-ARROW FOR
NOW
8600 RETURN

8700 REM ADD A CHARACTER
8710 REM CHECK IF CHARACTER IS PRINTABLE
8715 IF C < 32 OR C > 126 THEN RETURN : REM NOT PRINT-
ABLE
8720 IF CP > SL THEN RETURN : REM AT END OF LINE?
8725 DL$(CL, CP) = CHR$(C) : REM ADD CHARACTER TO LINE
8730 C = 21 : REM MOVE CURSOR TO RIGHT
8735 GOSUB 9000 : REM INCREMENT CURSOR POSITION
8740 RETURN
```

```
9000 REM MOVE CURSOR LEFT OR RIGHT
9005 IF CP < 2 AND C = 8 THEN RETURN : REM CURSOR AL-
READY AT LEFT
9010 IF (CP >= SL OR DL$(CL,CP) = "" ) AND C = 21 THEN
RETURN : REM CURSOR ALREADY AT RIGHT
9015 REM REPLACE CHARACTER UNDER CURSOR
9020 C$ = DL$(CL,CP) : IF C$ = "" THEN C$ = " "
9025 HTAB(CP) : VTAB(SL%) : PRINT C$;
9030 REM MOVE CURSOR
9035 IF C = 8 THEN CP = CP - 1 : REM TO LEFT
9040 IF C = 21 THEN CP = CP + 1 : REM TO RIGHT
9045 REM DRAW CURSOR AT NEW POSITION
9050 C$ = DL$(CL,CP) : IF C$ = "" THEN C$ = " "
9055 FLASH : VTAB(SL%) : HTAB(CP) : PRINT C$; : NORMAL
9100 RETURN

9500 REM CARRIAGE RETURN
9505 REM REPLACE CHARACTER UNDER CURSOR
9510 C$ = DL$(CL,CP) : IF C$ = "" THEN C$ = " "
9515 HTAB(CP) : VTAB(SL%) : PRINT C$;
9520 IF CL < 70 THEN CL = CL + 1 : REM DROP DOWN A
LINE
9525 CP = 1 : REM MOVE CURSOR TO LEFT EDGE OF SCREEN
9530 SL% = SL% + 1 : REM INCR. SCREEN LINE
9535 IF SL% > 24 THEN SL% = 24 : TL = TL + 1 : GOSUB
5030 : REM REDRAW
9550 IF CL > LC THEN LC = LC + 1 : REM INCREASE LINE
COUNT
9555 GOSUB 9050 : REM FLASH CURSOR WITHOUT MOVING IT
9600 RETURN

10000 REM ERROR HANDLER FOR DOS
10010 X = PEEK(222) : REM GET ERROR CODE
10020 IF X = 6 OR X = 13 OR X = 10 THEN PRINT : PRINT
"THE FILE NAMED "; FI$; " ";
10030 IF X = 6 THEN GOTO 10100 : REM FILE NOT FOUND
```

```
10040 IF X = 13 THEN GOTO 10200 : REM FILE TYPE MIS-
MATCH
10050 IF X = 10 THEN GOTO 10300 : REM FILE LOCKED
10060 PRINT "AN UNEXPECTED ERROR HAS OCCURRED, CODE
";X
10065 PRINT "ON LINE: "; : L=PEEK(219)*256+PEEK(218) :
PRINT L
10070 END
10100 REM FILE NOT FOUND
10110 PRINT "DOES NOT EXIST."
10120 GOTO 10400
10200 REM FILE TYPE MISMATCH
10210 PRINT "IS NOT A TEXT FILE."
10220 GOTO 10400
10300 PRINT "IS LOCKED."
10400 PRINT "PRESS RETURN TO CONTINUE..."
10410 GET A$ : PRINT : REM NEED A PRINT AFTER GET FOR
DOS
10420 IF MO$ = "L" THEN GOTO 110
10430 RESUME
```

```
12000 REM PRINTER PAGING SUBROUTINE
12001 REM INCREMENT LC% THEN CALL THIS SUBROUTINE
12010 IF LC% < 62 THEN RETURN : REM PRINTED ENOUGH
LINES YET?
12020 FOR X = 1 TO (69 - LC%) : REM PRINT BOTTOM MAR-
GIN
12030 PRINT : NEXT X
12040 LC% = 3 : RETURN : REM SET TOP MARGIN AND RE-
TURN
```

Due to the modular nature of the word processing program, the fact that it is made up of many subroutines, it was easy to add a printing feature.

First the main event loop at line 5500 was modified to recognize CONTROL-P (ASCII code 16) as the print command. For the user's benefit, the small help screen at line 6500 was also updated to reflect the addition of the new command.

The Printer Paging Subroutine at line 12000 should be familiar; it was introduced earlier in this chapter.

The main Print subroutine starts at line 3000. It begins by activating the peripheral card in slot 1, assuming it to be connected to a printer. The printer is then put into 40-column mode with no screen output (line 3010). LC%, the printer line counter used with the Printer Paging Subroutine, is initialized to 0. As each line of the document is sent to the printer in the FOR-NEXT loop, LC% is incremented and the paging subroutine is called.

When the entire document is printed, the printer is disabled and output is returned to the screen (lines 3100 and 3110).

One possible improvement to this subroutine would be to ask the user to specify a slot, in case the printer is not connected to slot 1. It may also be helpful to display an advisory "Now printing..." message, with advice to make sure that the printer is on, has paper, and that the Select light is on.

Chapter 10 : Networking

With a Super Serial Card, or any similar serial connection, the Apple II may be easily connected to other Apples, other devices, or even a global network such as the Internet. This chapter will describe the basics of allowing the Apple to communicate with other computers. First, a simple terminal example with the Super Serial Card will be shown, then the basics of AppleTalk networking will be covered, and finally several applications which utilize the Uthernet card and TCP/IP networking will be demonstrated. A novel form of networking for older Apple models will be introduced at the end of the chapter.

The Basics of Serial Communication

The word "serial" in serial communication comes from the fact that the data to be transmitted is arranged in a line, and transmitted one bit at a time. The idea can be likened to that of Morse Code, where each letter of a message is represented by a series of dots and dashes. Likewise, each byte of data is sent as a stream of ones and zeros down the wire.

There are a few different standards that govern serial data communications. The most common standard for the Apple is Electronic Industries Association (EIA) RS-232-C.

Getting Serial on Your Apple

If you have an Apple IIc, IIc Plus, or IIgs, then you are in luck: your model of Apple II has the necessary hardware for RS-232 serial communications built-in, with a port on the back.

However, if you have an Apple II, II Plus, or IIe, then you will need to install a peripheral card. The most popular such card was, and still is, the Super Serial Card. It's called "super" because it can handle a variety of communication speeds and modes. The Super Serial Card uses the RS-232-C standard, and it even imitates earlier serial cards from Apple Computer, such as the Apple II Serial Interface Card.

Scores of these cards were made and sold back in the day, and as a result, they are both common and inexpensive. If your Apple did not come with one installed, then you should be able to obtain a Super Serial Card inexpensively.

There were also some other serial cards manufactured, including an earlier Apple Serial Communications card, and third-party Super Serial compatibles. In general, you should avoid buying an older model card, and be sure to find out whether a third-party serial card is fully compatible. The rest of this chapter will be written assuming that you are using a Super Serial Card.

The Super Serial Card (or the equivalent which is built into the models of Apple mentioned earlier) is capable of two-way data communication between a number of devices including printers, modems, plotters, terminals, and other computers. The Super Serial Card can be programmed from BASIC, making it convenient and easy to use.

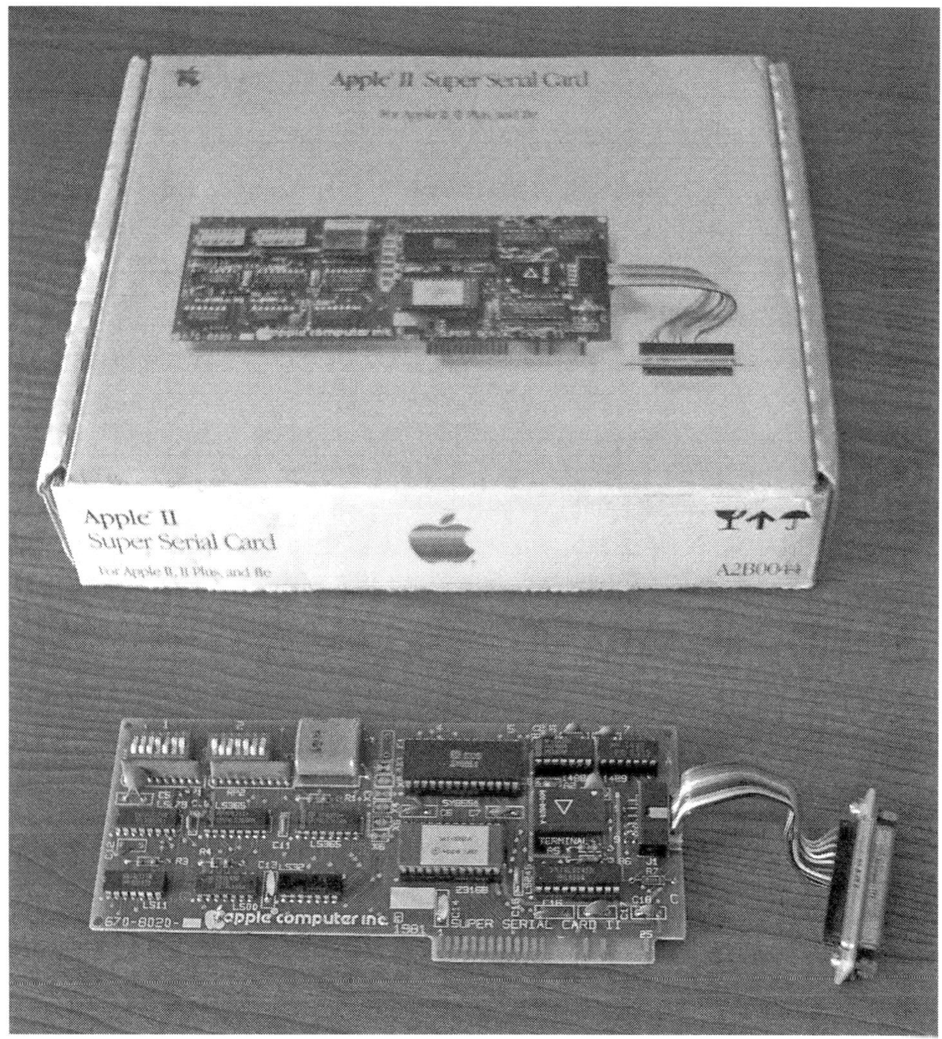

Figure 10-1. Super Serial Card and box

Configuring the Super Serial Card

You should first determine whether your Apple already has a serial card installed. As first explained in Chapter 1, serial cards are customarily found in either slot 1 or slot 2. Since a serial card requires a cable connection to be useful, there will be some wires coming from the card which connect to a port mounted on the back of the Apple case. If you can find no such card, then your

Apple probably did not come with a serial card, and you will have to install one.

The Super Serial Card has two groups of settings which may be changed: first is the row of DIP switches, and second is the MODEM eliminator block (sometimes referred to as the jumper block). The switches are located in the upper left corner, and are divided into two banks of seven. The MODEM eliminator block is in the center on the right, and has a triangle shape on it. This triangle will either point upward toward the word MODEM, or downward toward the word TERMINAL.

Choosing the Operating Mode

The Super Serial Card has two operating modes: Printer, and Communications. Printer mode is used to connect serial printers, as the name suggests, but is also used for any device that connects directly to the Apple, such as a terminal, a plotter, or another computer. The other mode, Communications, is used only for connecting a modem for a telephone line. You may also see the term "Modem Mode" used instead of Communications. The rest of this chapter will assume that you are using the Super Serial Card in printer mode, since it is the most common mode used today.

Setting the Jumper Block

To change the jumper block, it must be carefully pried up using a flathead screwdriver, rotated to the correct position, then reseated.

The jumper block should be positioned with the arrow pointing toward MODEM if such a device is to be connected to the Super Serial Card. If a printer or plotter is going to be connected, ensure that the block is pointing toward TERMINAL.

RS-232 signals were originally intended to be carried across telephone lines. However, if you wish to connect to a device in the same room, such as a printer or another computer, a null modem or modem eliminator is required. Setting the jumper block to the word TERMINAL acts as a modem eliminator. Using the modem eliminator reroutes some signals when a telephone line isn't being used.

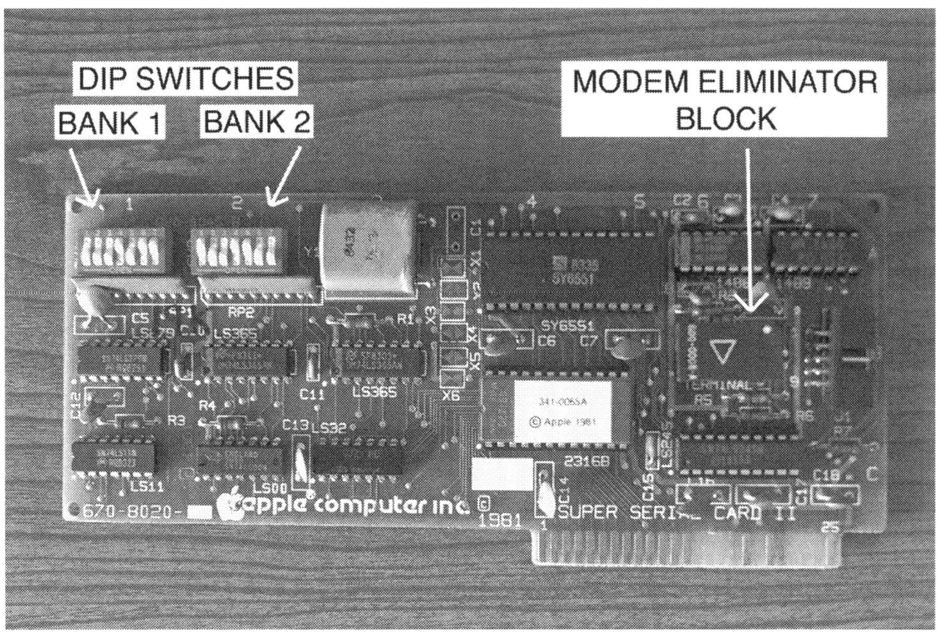

Figure 10-2. Super Serial Card showing locations of DIP switches and block

However, when the block is pointing toward MODEM, the Super Serial Card behaves as Data Terminal Equipment (DTE), able to talk to Data Communication Equipment (DCE), such as a modem connected to a telephone line.

Unless you are going to connect a modem to the Super Serial Card, the jumper block should be set to TERMINAL. This is the proper setting for printer mode.

Setting the Switches

The switches can be set using a paperclip, the tip of a ballpoint pen, or your fingernail. As mentioned earlier, there are two sets of switches. The set on the left is called SW1, and the other set is SW2.

Most of the switch settings can be overridden by using software commands from BASIC, or typing commands from the keyboard. The switches merely set the default settings for the Super Serial Card.

Mode	SW 1-5	SW 1-6
Printer	OFF	ON
Modem (Communications)	ON	ON

Table 10-1. Mode selection settings

SW1	Purpose	SW2	Purpose
1	Baud Rate	1	Stop Bits
2	Baud Rate	2	Delay after CR
3	Baud Rate	3	Line Width
4	Baud Rate	4	Line Width
5	Mode (Printer or Modem)	5	Line Feed
6	Mode (Printer or Modem)	6	Interrupts
7	RS-232-C Signals	7	RS-232-C Signals

Table 10-2. Super Serial Card switch settings for printer mode

Baud	SW 1-1	SW 1-2	SW 1-3	SW 1-4
300	ON	OFF	OFF	ON
1200	OFF	ON	ON	ON
9600	OFF	OFF	OFF	ON
19200	OFF	OFF	OFF	OFF

Table 10-3. Common baud rate switch settings

SW1	Purpose	SW2	Purpose
1	Baud Rate	1	Stop Bits
2	Baud Rate	2	Data Bits
3	Baud Rate	3	Parity
4	Baud Rate	4	Parity
5	Mode (Printer or Modem)	5	Line Feed
6	Mode (Printer or Modem)	6	Interrupts
7	RS-232-C Signals	7	RS-232-C Signals

Table 10-4. Super Serial Card switch settings for modem mode

Tables 10-1 to 10-4 should give you enough information to configure your Super Serial Card for connecting to another computer, the focus of this chapter. If you want to use a printer with the Super Serial Card, consult Chapter 9.

The first step for setting switches is to choose the operating mode for the Super Serial Card. If you're not using a modem, then you will be using printer mode; turn off SW 1-5 and on SW 1-6.

The next step is to choose the baud rate. The rate absolutely must match that of the other device. Otherwise, the signals will be garbled. The most common baud rates are 9600 and 19200. Pick a matching rate for both the Super Serial Card and the other device. Refer to Table 10-4 for the baud rate switch settings.

Finally, you must set the remainder of the switches. SW 2-1 is usually set ON for just one stop bit. Slower equipment, rarely used these days, may require two stop bits, accomplished by setting the switch to OFF.

SW 2-2 configures a delay after carriage return. Most equipment does not require a delay, so this switch can be set to OFF. Slower printers (again, uncommonly found these days) may need a delay, thus requiring the switch to be ON. In Modem Mode, SW 2-2 configures Data Bits. Set it to ON for 8 data bits or OFF for 7 bits (the most common setting).

Most printers and other equipment can manage 80 characters per line, so turn OFF SW 2-3 and ON SW 2-4. In Modem mode, parity is configured by these two switches. The common setting, no parity, is set with both switches 2-3 and 2-4 ON.

The Super Serial Card can be configured to generate line feeds if required. Set SW 2-5 to ON if needed, OFF if not.

Some programs on the Apple use interrupts for better data communication performance at higher baud rates. Check the program to find out if it uses interrupts; only a few programs do not. If the Super Serial Card should forward interrupts to the Apple, set SW 2-6 ON, otherwise, leave it OFF. The original Apple II, the II Plus, and the standard (unenhanced) IIe cannot properly handle interrupts, so SW 2-6 must be OFF at all times for these models of Apple.

Finally, switches 1-7 and 2-7 determine whether data will be exchanged using RS-232-C signals. This method is the most common, so in most cases, SW 1-7 should be ON and SW 2-7 OFF.

Installing the Super Serial Card

The Super Serial Card is installed the same way as any other peripheral expansion card: in one of the Apple's seven general-purpose slots. By tradition, the Super Serial Card is installed in one of two slots depending on its role. If the Super Serial Card is going to be connected to a printer, it is typically installed in slot 1. However, if the Super Serial Card is to work with a modem or other communications link, it is placed into slot 2.

The Super Serial Card should not be inserted into a slot until you have set its switches and MODEM eliminator block. As with any peripheral card, the Apple must be powered off before installing or removing the Super Serial Card. Once you have done so, insert the card into its slot by inserting the gold "fingers" on the card into the slot at an angle. Gently rock the card into position until it is securely seated in the slot.

Once the card is seated, the DB-25 port must be attached. The female end of the ribbon cable plugs into a male cable socket located just to the right of the MODEM eliminator block. The socket is keyed to prevent the cable from being plugged in upside down. Thread the ribbon cable through a convenient hole in the back of the Apple before attaching it to the cable socket.

Finally, the DB-25 port should be clamped to the Apple's case to prevent it from coming loose or ripping away. The Apple II and II Plus require a special clamping enclosure that slides down into one of the tall vertical slots. The Apple IIe, on the other hand, has a redesigned back that allows the DB-25 port to be attached with two screws.

Configuring the Apple IIgs Serial Ports

The Apple IIgs has the functionality of two Super Serial Cards attached to slots 1 and 2 in the form of its printer and modem ports, respectively. The settings for these two ports are governed by the Control Panel settings; there is no need to set switches or jumpers.

Access the Control Panel by pressing COMMAND-CONTROL-ESCAPE and choosing Control Panel from the Desk Accessories menu. From the Control Panel menu, select either Printer Port or Modem Port, depending on which port you are using. Make the appropriate changes and press RETURN when finished to save the settings.

Using the Apple as a Terminal

In the early days of computing, the computer was an enormous, room-sized machine kept running in the basement by a handful of computer scientists. The people who actually used the computer could be located nearby, or even in a different building. They communicated with the computer via a terminal. The terminal was not much more than a keyboard and display screen (or teletype); it didn't do any computing itself.

Likewise, the Apple can also act as a terminal for a larger computer system, such as a system running the UNIX operating system, or similar (this includes Linux and Mac OS X). All that is required for the Apple is a terminal emulator program and an appropriate connection to the remote computer. A null-modem cable is required for a direct serial connection. The Super Serial Card even allows two Apple II computers to communicate with each other.

The Super Serial Card provides a reliable connection, as does the printer port of the Apple IIc, IIc Plus, and IIgs. You will need to configure the operating system of the host machine to spawn a login shell (typically with getty) on the serial port, and have it operate at known baud rate, such as 1200. The exact details for this setup is beyond the scope of this book. The author has had good success using a 1998-model Power Macintosh G3 with Mac OS X 10.2 with both an Apple IIe and an Apple IIgs.

On the Apple side, make sure that the Super Serial Card is configured for the same baud rate. Once the hardware is configured, you will need a terminal emulator program. DCOM, written by James Hayes, is one such program, providing emulation of the VT100. Modem.MGR and ProTERM are other options. As a last resort, the Super Serial Card has built-in firmware that allows it to act as a dumb terminal.

Using DCOM

DCOM is a simple and straight-forward terminal emulator. It pretends to be a VT100 terminal operating at 1200 baud. It requires at minimum an Apple II Plus or IIe with an 80 columns card and a serial interface card (such as the Super Serial Card). In addition, the built-in hardware present in the Apple IIc and IIgs is supported. DCOM can be used with or without a modem.

When you first start DCOM, you will need to configure the terminal settings. Read over the introduction screens, then when prompted, press ESCAPE to run the configuration program.

The configuration program will ask you three or four questions about your Apple system.

The first question it will ask is "What 80 column card do you have?" If you are using an Apple IIe or IIgs, choose the option for Apple IIe in aux slot. If you are using an Apple IIc or IIc Plus, choose "//c built-in 80 column card." Otherwise, if you have an

Apple II or II Plus, choose the option that matches your installed 80 columns card.

The second question asked of you is "What serial card do you have?" A number of brands of serial card will be listed. Most likely, you are using the Super Serial Card with the Apple II, II Plus, or IIe. For the IIc, IIc Plus, and IIgs, choose "//c Serial Port."

If you chose one of the serial cards (not the serial port), then you will be asked to supply the slot number in which it is installed.

Finally, the configuration program will ask "What data comm. hardware do you have?" If you are using a modem, pick the option that matches. Otherwise, for a direct serial connection, choose "No modem."

Afterward, the program will confirm with you the selections that you made. If you made a mistake, press A to begin the configuration program again. Otherwise, press S to save the configuration to disk. The program will clear the screen and present a message that it is saving the driver settings. When prompted, press RETURN.

The introduction screens will appear again. Press RETURN at each screen. DCOM will then commence loading all of the necessary drivers. This process will take about 20 seconds. Once everything is loaded, the screen will clear again. The word "Go..." will appear at the upper-left-hand corner of the screen. Press the RETURN key.

If everything went well, you should see a login prompt sent from the host computer. Enter your username and password to log in. If the host operating system was configured correctly, the system should know that you are using a VT100 terminal. Try a few commands to make sure that they behave as expected. One thing that you may notice is the lag: at 1200 baud, screen updates will be slower than you are likely used to.

When you are finished, log out of the system as usual. You can then switch off the Apple if you are finished with it, or press CONTROL-RESET to run another program.

Figure 10-3. The DCOM VT100 terminal emulator running top

Troubleshooting

If garbage characters appear instead of a login prompt, then the baud rate is likely too fast or too slow. DCOM operates the Super Serial Card at 1200 baud. Ensure that the serial connection on the host computer is also configured for 1200 baud.

If nothing at all appears, then the following may be possible reasons:

- The host computer is not configured to spawn a login prompt.
- The serial card in the Apple is misconfigured.
- There is a problem with the physical cable connection.
- DCOM was misconfigured.

Networking with AppleTalk

There is only so much that can be done with a Super Serial Card when it comes to networking. The main limitation is only being able to connect two computers. AppleTalk was designed from the start to be able to network anywhere from two to ten (or even more) Apple II and Macintosh computers and printers. Only the Enhanced IIe and IIgs may use AppleTalk, but it's really most practical on the IIgs.

To make clear the terminology, *AppleTalk* is the networking protocol: the signals and commands that the computers send to each other. The cabling system that connects the computers is called *LocalTalk*. Finally, when a Macintosh hard disk is being shared across the network, the term for it is *AppleShare*.

The Apple IIe requires a peripheral card, the Apple Workstation Card, while AppleTalk support is built-in to the Apple IIgs, by way of its printer and modem ports. The Apple IIe Card, which requires a Macintosh to operate, also has the equivalent of the Apple Workstation Card built-in. Historically, only Apple II and Macintosh computers could be part of an AppleTalk network. However, even PCs may join in, as long as they are equipped with the appropriate hardware and software. A program called netatalk allows Linux-based PCs the ability to speak the AppleTalk protocol.

One of the principal uses of AppleTalk is AppleShare, a method of accessing files and folders over the network. AppleShare consists of at least one file server and one or more clients. The file server is typically a Macintosh computer that stores and shares information on its hard drive. The clients connect to the server to send and retrieve information over the network. It is even possible to run application programs directly from a file server.

To be clear, for Apple II family computers, AppleTalk only allows them to communicate as a client with an AppleTalk printer or a PC or Macintosh acting as an AppleShare file server. Apple II computers cannot use AppleTalk to directly communicate with each other.

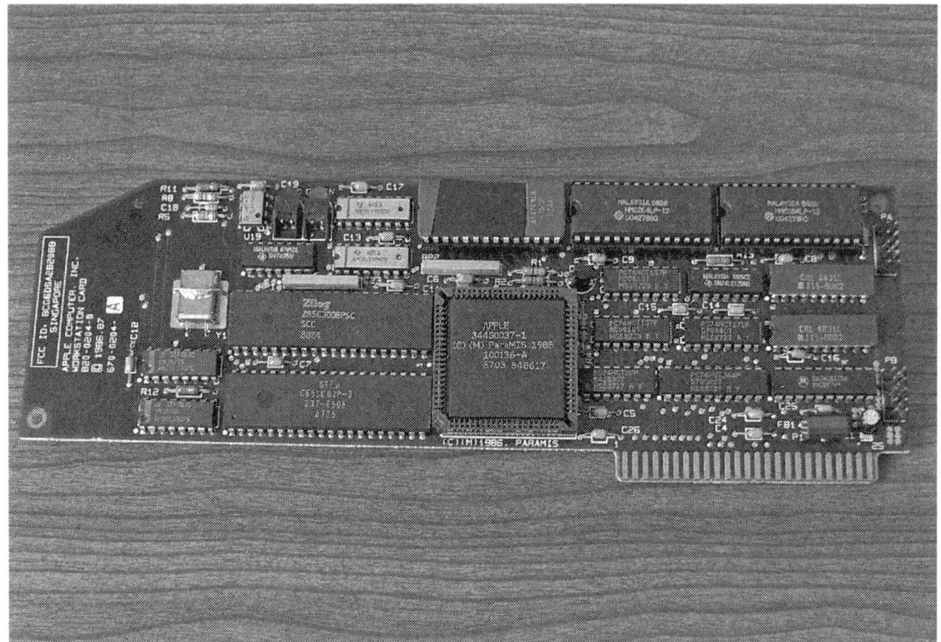

Figure 10-4. The Apple Workstation card

Connecting the Network

Unlike an Ethernet network, with which you may be more familiar, an AppleTalk network is bus-shaped. That is, instead of connecting the computers to a central hub as in Ethernet, all of the AppleTalk computers are connected linearly. The network must have two end-points, and is never circular or T-shaped.

The LocalTalk network connectors sold by Apple Computer were well-made, but quite expensive. Thus, a company called Farallon devised an inexpensive solution. PhoneNet, as their product was called, used ordinary four-wire telephone wiring in place of the more expensive cables sold by Apple. PhoneNet proved to be quite popular, many units were sold, and as a result, the connector boxes are quite easy to obtain today. Other companies also produced imitation PhoneNet connectors, as shown in Figure 10-5.

Connecting with PhoneNet is fairly straightforward. You will require one connector box for each device to be connected, and one telephone wire fewer than the total number of boxes. As an example, connecting two computers requires two PhoneNet boxes and one wire. Connecting five computers requires five boxes and four wires. First, connect a PhoneNet box to the Printer port of each computer or device (the general term for both is *node*). Then, identify the two end-points of the network. For a two-node network, as shown in Figure 10-6, both nodes are end nodes. A special terminating resistor must be inserted into one of the telephone jacks on the PhoneNet box on both of the end nodes. Finally, connect a telephone wire between the two remaining jacks. You have now constructed your network.

Figure 10-7 depicts a three-node network: an AppleTalk ImageWriter II is now a part of the original network, thus requiring an additional PhoneNet connector box and wire. The printer, on the left, and the Apple IIgs, on the right, constitute the two end-points of the network, and thus have the terminating resistor. The Macintosh, center, is connected to both the Apple IIgs and the AppleTalk ImageWriter II.

A common wiring problem when constructing PhoneNet networks is to mistakenly use two-wire phone cord, instead of four-wire. One of the key design features of PhoneNet is that it uses the

Figure 10-5. PhoneNet connectors

other two wires for network traffic that aren't used to carry a telephone call. Since standard telephones only use two wires out of the four, inexpensive phone cords will only have those two wires, and not the other two required for PhoneNet. Thus, no connection is made for the network. The solution is to check the phone cords carefully, and ensure that they all have four wires.

Mounting an AppleShare Volume on the IIgs

On the Apple IIgs, the AppleShare Control Panel is used to connect to an AppleShare server and select one or more volumes to mount. With GS/OS version 5.0.4, AppleShare 2.x is supported. System 6.x supports both AppleShare 3.x and 4.x.

From the Apple menu, choose Control Panels, then double-click the AppleShare icon. The AppleShare window will open, divided into two areas. One or more AppleShare servers should appear at the top of the window. If the AppleTalk network has any zones (yours likely will not), they will appear at the bottom.

Double-click the name of an AppleShare server to connect to it. The connection dialog box will appear. You can either log in as a guest or as a registered user. It is recommended that you log in as a registered user that you configured earlier on the AppleShare server. Enter the username and password and click OK.

If the server allows guest logins, the Guest radio button will be active; otherwise, it will be dimmed. To log in as a guest, press COMMAND-G, or click Guest and then click OK.

If the connection is successful, another dialog will appear listing one or more volumes available on the server. Click a volume name to select it. To select more than one, hold down the COMMAND key and click. If you would like to automatically mount a volume when the IIgs starts, click the checkbox next to its name.

The two radio buttons make subsequent log ins easier by automatically supplying either just your username, or both your username and password. If you are not concerned about security, then you can have the Apple save your username and password for convenience. When finished, click OK or press RETURN.

The dialog box will disappear, and the AppleShare window will be visible once more. Close its window and the Control Panel windows to return to the Program Launcher or Finder. You should see the mounted volume or volumes appear on the Finder desktop or the Launcher menu.

To unmount an AppleShare volume from the Finder, drag its icon to the Trash.

Mounting an AppleShare Volume on the IIe

Starting up over the network (described shortly) is perhaps the easiest way to mount an AppleShare volume on the IIe, as the startup volume is automatically mounted.

If the Apple IIe is to be started from a local disk, the Workstation disk has a File Server Log On program.

First, boot the Apple Workstation disk. When the menu appears, use the DOWN ARROW key to select File Server Log On, and press RETURN.

Skip to the next section, Logging On to the File Server, for the rest of the directions.

To log off from the AppleShare server, use the File Server Log Off program on the Workstation disk.

Starting Up Over the Network

With a Macintosh running AppleShare version 2 or 3, both the IIe and IIgs may netboot, that is, start up and load an operating system without requiring any disk drive. The Macintosh server must be configured to permit Apple II computers to start up over the network. It is possible to use the Apple without any local disks; all programs and documents are stored on the Macintosh server.

First, ensure that all devices on the network are properly connected as described in the previous section.

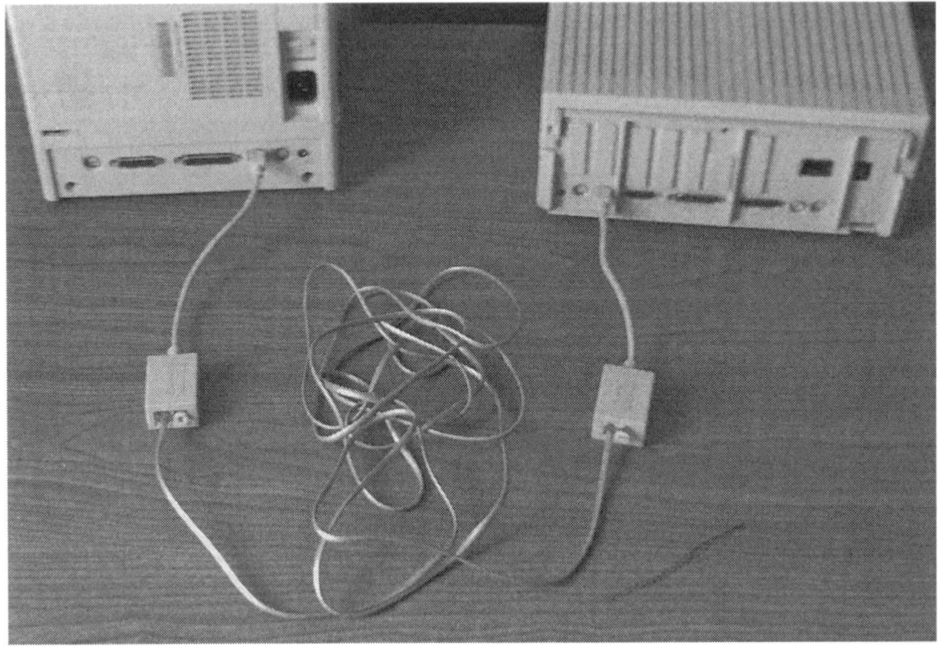

Figure 10-6. A two-node network of a Macintosh and an Apple IIgs

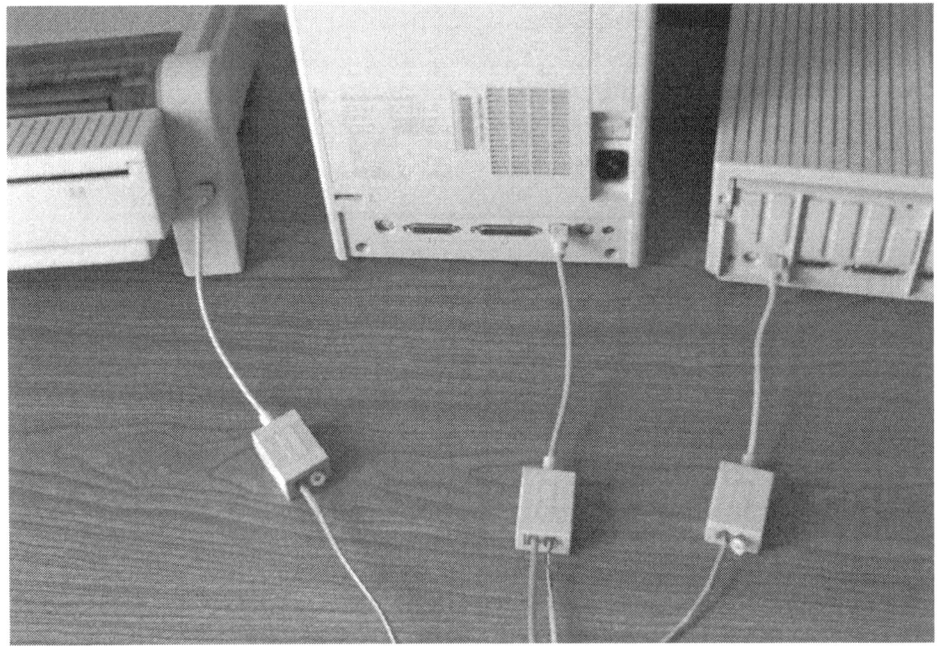

Figure 10-7. A three-node network, with an AppleTalk ImageWriter II

For the Apple IIgs, access the Control Panel by pressing COMMAND-CONTROL-ESCAPE, and select Slots. The necessary configuration differs depending on what revision of IIgs is in use. For a ROM 01 IIgs, slot 1 (the printer port) should be set to "Your Card," slot 7 must be set to "Built-in AppleTalk," and the Startup slot must also be set to "7." For the ROM 3 GS, both slots 1 and 7 must be set to "AppleTalk," with the StartUp slot set to "AppleTalk." At this point, the Apple IIgs is now properly configured to startup over the AppleTalk network. If the Macintosh server is also properly configured, restart the Apple IIgs to commence netboot.

For the Apple IIe, ensure that the Apple Workstation Card is installed in a slot higher than any disk controllers. It is typically installed in slot 7 for this purpose.

The netboot procedure is nearly identical for the Apple IIe and IIgs.

Restart the Apple. You will see some progress indicators and status messages as it receives its startup data from the AppleShare server.

After a moment, you will be prompted to log on to the file server.

Logging On to the File Server

If your network has no zones and only one file server, then you will bc treated to a login screen. Otherwise, you will be prompted to choose a network zone and file server, and then the login screen will appear.

You can either log in as a guest or as a registered user. It is recommended that you log in as a registered user that you configured earlier on the AppleShare server. Enter the username and password and click OK (or press RETURN).

If the AppleShare server has more than one volume, you will next be asked to select which other volumes you wish to mount. The startup volume is automatically mounted. To make a selection, use the UP and DOWN ARROW keys. To place a check mark next to a volume name, press the LEFT ARROW key or SPACE BAR. Press the LEFT ARROW key again to remove the mark. When you press RETURN, all check-marked volumes will be mounted.

The network startup program will then be launched. Depending on how the AppleShare user account was configured, it may be ProDOS BASIC, a program selector, or some other program.

If a complete copy of GS/OS is installed on the AppleShare server, the Apple IIgs can start up into the usual Finder program.

TCP/IP and Ethernet

One of the most exciting developments in the Apple II world in recent years is that of the Uthernet card, which adds an Ethernet port to the Apple. With an Uthernet, appropriate software, and a network connection, your Apple can go online to access email, IRC, and the World Wide Web.

So far, there are two models of Ethernet card available for Apple II: the LANceGS, and the Uthernet. The LANceGS card was introduced in 2000, and was intended specifically for the Apple IIgs. It is no longer produced. The Uthernet, still produced today, was released in 2005.

About the Uthernet Card

The Uthernet, designed by Glenn Jones of A2RetroSystems, is the most inexpensive and popular Ethernet card for the Apple. It will work in nearly every model of Apple (except for the IIc and IIc Plus), and is compatible with nearly all networking software. Programming the Uthernet is only possible in assembly language.

Unfortunately, the Uthernet card is not entirely compatible with all models of Apple II, II Plus, and IIe. It is really intended for the Enhanced IIe or the Apple IIgs. If you have an older, unenhanced IIe, or an Apple II or II Plus, then the Uthernet may not work reliably with your Apple. Contact Mr. Jones at A2RetroSystems before you purchase, and tell him what model of Apple you have.

The Uthernet is capable of 10 Mbps transmission speeds, though its actual speed will be limited by the processing speed of the Apple in which it is installed.

Figure 10-8. The Uthernet card

Installing Uthernet

Installing the Uthernet is fairly simple. It is an unusually small card, and you must take care to plug it in the right direction. By convention, the Uthernet is placed into slot 3, and it must be positioned with the RJ45 Ethernet jack facing the back of the Apple. Otherwise, the card is turned around, and you risk damaging the Uthernet, your Apple, or both.

The case of the II, II Plus, and IIe provides enough room for the Ethernet cable to come in through a back slot and connect into the Uthernet's jack. Unfortunately, the IIgs case is more cramped, and certain kinds of Ethernet cables, such as the "hooded" style, or those with a lot of plastic around the end, will not fit so comfortably.

Once you have the Uthernet installed in a slot, and the Ethernet cable attached, connect the other end of the cable to a hub, router, switch, or other computer. The Uthernet is a 10 Mbps device, so you must have a 10 Mbps hub, router, or switch, or an auto-sensing one. Once connected to the network, power on the Apple, and check that the orange link light is lit on the Uthernet. This means that the Ethernet connection is good.

Figure 10-9. The Uthernet installed in an Apple IIgs

Figure 10-10. The Uthernet installed in an Apple IIe

You may also see the green activity light flash briefly every so often. This indicates that your network hardware recognizes the Uthernet, and is attempting to send it Ethernet frames.

Figure 10-11. The Uthernet installed in an Apple II or II Plus

If the orange link light is not lit, check the following:

- Is the Uthernet card properly installed in the Apple?
- Is your Apple turned on?
- Is the Ethernet cable connected at both ends?
- Is the hub, switch, router, or computer into which the cable is plugged powered on?

Contiki

The Contiki Operating System is described as a "modern, Internet-enabled operating system and design environment." It was originally written by Adam Dunkels at the Swedish Institute of Computer Science. Oliver Schmidt is the man responsible for writing the Apple II version of Contiki.

There are two major versions of Contiki: version 1.3 has a cohesive, desktop interface and all of the applications are easily accessible. Contiki 2, however, drops the desktop interface, and instead leaves the applications to stand alone. With Contiki 2, pressing CONTROL-RESET will take you back to ProDOS (or the GS/OS desktop). Some of the Contiki 2 applications have more features than their version 1.3 counterparts.

Contiki requires an Enhanced Apple IIe or Apple IIgs. There are both 40 and 80-column versions available. Contiki may also be used with a mouse. This text will assume that a mouse is being used with Contiki, and will direct you to click on buttons and text fields. If you are using only a keyboard, use the TAB key to select fields and buttons. Press RETURN to activate a selected button.

Configuring Contiki

Before you can connect to the Internet, you must configure the TCP/IP settings in Contiki. Contiki offers both DHCP, which is automatic configuration, and manual IP configuration.

DHCP requires your network to have a suitably configured and active DHCP server. Most networks do have one, so you can usually assume that there is one available. DHCP works by having the client, in this case, the Apple with Uthernet, send out a broadcast message looking for a DHCP server. The DHCP server, if it exists, replies back with IP settings, including an address, that the client may then use. The client applies these settings and connects to the network. This entire process typically takes less than a second.

If you are not using DHCP, then you will have to manually supply an IP address, netmask, gateway, and DNS server.

Contiki 2.x has a standalone DHCP and network configuration program called DHCP.SYSTEM. Launch it, then either click the Request IP Address button, or fill in the fields yourself. Click Save & close when finished to save the settings and return to the previous program (typically the ProDOS program selector or the Finder).

To configure Contiki 1.3, start Contiki by launching the CONTIKI.SYSTEM program. Click the Directory at the bottom-right corner of the screen. If you are using DHCP, then click the DHCP client button. In the DHCP window, click Request address. In a few moments, the IP address, Netmask, and other fields should automatically be populated. If so, then you are finished. Click the X to close the window.

Otherwise, if DHCP configuration did not work, or if you are using manual network configuration, click the Configuration icon from the Directory window. Enter the IP address, Netmask, Gateway, and DNS server in the appropriate fields. Click Save & close when you are finished.

No matter which method you are using to configure Contiki, DHCP or manual, you should open the Configuration program and ensure that the LAN driver is set to Uther.drv if you are using the Uthernet card. Then make sure that the LAN slot is set to the slot in which the Uthernet is installed (typically slot 3). If you make any changes, remember to click Save & close.

Using the Contiki Web Browser

The Contiki Web Browser is quite simple to use. It will accept a URL to a web page, and will then download it and attempt to parse and format the HTML. It will not handle cookies, images, Javascript, forms, or any sort of multimedia or interactive content.

The Web Browser interface is divided vertically into three regions: button and address bar at top, web page content in the middle, and status bar at the bottom. There are four buttons to control the Web Browser's operation: Back, to go to the previously-loaded web page; Down, to scroll a web page; Stop, to cancel loading a web page; and Go, to start loading a URL entered in the address bar.

As remarked earlier, one may use the TAB key to select each button and the address bar in turn. Press RETURN to execute the command of the selected button. If your Apple has a mouse attached, remember that it may be used to click the buttons and select the address bar.

Due to the limited RAM of the Apple, scrolling is implemented using the Down button. When a web page is first loaded, the top of the page is shown. Clicking Down will reload the web page and scroll down to the next page. There is no way to scroll back up, except for to reload the top of the web page again by clicking the Go button.

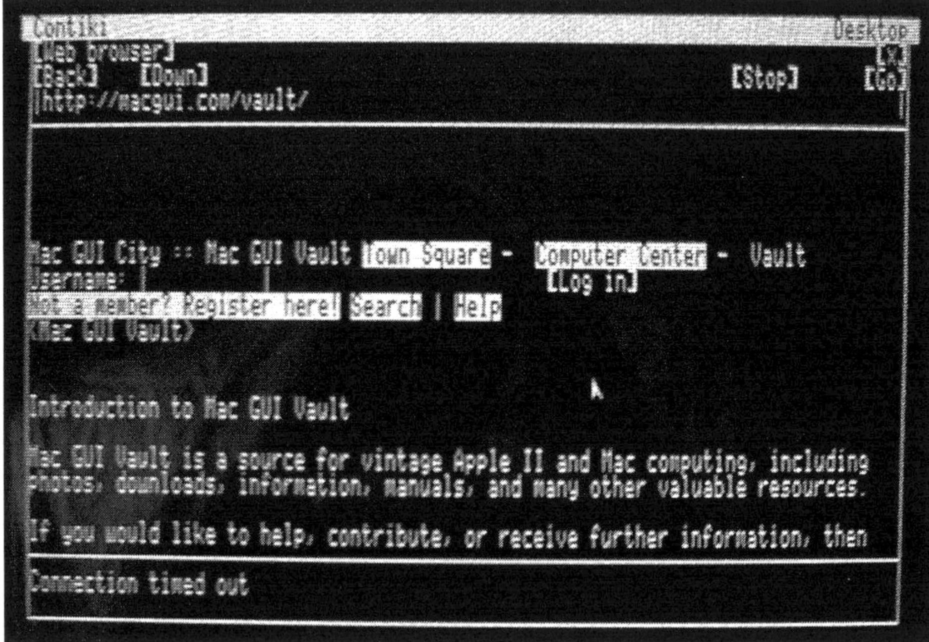

Figure 10-12. The Contiki 1.3 web browser

If the web page contains any hyperlinks, they will be highlighted, and can be selected and followed with the appropriate key presses (TAB and RETURN), or clicked on using the mouse.

Figure 10-12 shows the Contiki Web Browser loading a web page. Notice that the hyperlinks are highlighted with inverse text.

Downloading Files with the Contiki FTP Client

Contiki comes with a simple FTP client. Files may only be downloaded from the FTP server to the Apple; uploading is not supported. Furthermore, under Contiki 1.3, directories are ignored. Only files listed in the FTP user's home directory are accessible. The FTP client in Contiki 2.x can navigate directories.

Unfortunately, the Contiki FTP client does not support the PASV command. This limitation means that if your Apple is behind a firewall, it will likely be unable to communicate with any FTP server.

If you are using Contiki 1.3, click the Connection button to open the connection window. Contiki 2.x's FTP client starts with the connection window open. Enter the FTP server, username, and password, then click Connect.

The list of files on your Apple will appear at the left under the heading "Local files." At right should appear the files on the remote FTP server. Use the UP and DOWN ARROW keys to select a file from the server. If you are using Contiki 2.x, pressing the U key will load the parent directory and list its files.

To download a file, select its name then press RETURN. A dialog will open where you may edit the filename when it is downloaded to your Apple. Click Download file to start the process.

When you are finished with the FTP client, click the Quit button.

Chatting with the Contiki IRC Client

With the Contiki IRC client, you can participate in Internet Relay Chat with your Apple. To start IRC in Contiki 1.3, open the Directory, then choose the IRC client icon. For Contiki 2, launch the IRC.SYSTEM program.

You will be asked to supply the name of an IRC server and a nickname used to represent you when chatting. Do so, then click the Connect button. You will then see a screenful of messages from the IRC server. Depending on the server and nickname, you may be asked to enter a password to verify your authorization to use the nickname.

Otherwise, you may use standard IRC commands to find and join a channel (the IRC term for a chat room). Every IRC command is prefixed with a forward-slash (/). Common commands are: list, join, who, nick, privmsg, and quit.

To list all available channels on the IRC server, type the following command:

```
/list
```

The list of all channels will appear on the screen. There may be too many to show all at once. To filter out channels that don't have many active participants, use the -min parameter. For example, to only show channels with at least five participants, type the following:

```
/list -min 5
```

When you have found a channel that interests you, use the join command to participate in the chat. Channel names are always prefixed with a pound (#) symbol. The following command will let you join the apple2 channel:

```
/join #apple2
```

Once you have joined a channel, you may send chat messages to everyone else by simply typing whatever it is you wish to say. All messages are prefixed with the nickname of whomever sent them. It is customary to say "hi" or "hello" when you first join a channel. If there are others in the channel, they should greet you in return.

To get a list of all participants in a channel, use /who. You can also search for nicknames that match a given pattern using an asterisk (*). For example, this command would list all active nicknames starting with the letter d:

```
/who d*
```

To remind you of your nickname, use the nick command. When given a parameter, your nickname will be changed. For example, to change your nickname to "kilroy," type the following:

```
/nick kilroy
```

Ordinarily, the messages that you type are sent to all participants of a channel. To send a message to only one user in private, use /privmsg with the intended nickname and message. The following example will send a message of "hello" to the nickname "bob":

```
/privmsg bob hello
```

To quit IRC, use /quit. The others in the channel will be notified of your departure. To give a specific reason, type a message, such as:

```
/quit time for lunch
```

to let everyone know that you had to take a lunch break.

Marinetti

Marinetti is an open source TCP/IP networking stack for the Apple IIgs, written by Richard Bennett. It was first introduced in 1997, and the latest version is 3.0b3, released in July of 2006.

Several network connection methods, known as Link Layers, are supported by Marinetti, and are included by default. Most of these methods, which include PPP and SLIP, are for computers that only have a modem or direct serial connection. The most popular Link Layer today for Marinetti is the Uthernet ethernet card. Unfortunately, this Link Layer does not come as a part of the default Marinetti installation.

A number of Internet applications have been written for Marinetti, including:

- Two FTP clients
- Two Web browsers
- Several Telnet clients
- An Email client
- Two Web servers
- An NTP client
- An NNTP client
- An AIM client
- A Twitter client
- An SMS (text message) client.

Installing Marinetti

Marinetti is available online for download. Once downloaded, an installer application will place the necessary files into your System folder. When installation is finished, your IIgs must be restarted for Marinetti to become active.

A newer version, 3.0b3, of the TCPIP Init for Marinetti is available, though it is not included in the main installation package. This Init file must be downloaded separately, then copied to the System.Setup folder within the System folder. You must restart your Apple IIgs again for this Init to take effect.

Marinetti includes several files of documentation, as well as two demonstration programs: a Telnet client, and a Web server. You should read the documentation, but you should not try either of the applications until you have first configured Marinetti.

Installing the Uthernet Link Layer

The latest version of the Uthernet Link Layer for Marinetti is located at A2RetroSystems' Web site, and is version 1.0.1b5, as of this writing. Codeveloped by Ewen Wannop, the Uthernet Link Layer, like Marinetti itself, is also open source. Once you have the Link Layer copied to your Apple IIgs, unshrink it, then drag it into the TCPIP folder, located within the System folder. You will then have to restart the IIgs in order for the Link Layer to be recognized in the TCP/IP Control Panel.

Configuring Marinetti

All of the configuration options for Marinetti are managed in the TCP/IP Control Panel. Open this Control Panel by choosing Control Panels from the Apple menu. Scroll down the list until you see the TCP/IP icon. Select it, then click the Help button. Check the version number in the upper right corner to make sure that it is 3.0d4, then click OK. Next, open the TCP/IP Control Panel and verify that the Disconnect from network button is grayed out. If it is not, click it. You cannot change certain settings unless you are disconnected from the network.

Next, click the Setup connection button. A dialog with a number of options will appear, most of which are irrelevant at this point. At the bottom left is a popup menu for Link layer. Select Uthernet (or, if you are using a different connection method, select the appropriate one), then click the Configure button.

If your Uthernet card is not installed in slot 4, you will need to select the correct slot from the LAN Slot popup menu. If your network has a DHCP server (and most networks do), click the DHCP checkbox to have the remaining settings automatically configured for you. Click Save when you are finished.

If your network does not have a DHCP server, or if you want to manually configure the IP settings, you must fill in the IP Address, Netmask, and Gateway. If you need help entering these values, consult your network administrator. You may leave the MAC Address as-is; it will not need to be changed unless you have more than one Apple connected to the same network. Click Save when you are finished.

You will be returned to the Setup connection dialog box. Unless you are not using the Uthernet Link Layer, you may leave the Username and Password fields blank. If you did not check the DHCP box, then you may need to fill in the Primary and Secondary Domain Name Server IP addresses. Consult your network administrator if you do not know what these addresses are.

At this point, you can click OK to dismiss the dialog box, then click the Connect to network button. A connecting dialog will appear with some status messages. After a few moments, it should disappear, leaving you connected to the network and ready to try out the number of TCP/IP programs for the IIgs.

Spectrum

Spectrum, written by Ewen Wannop, is a telecommunications program for the IIgs. It can be used either with a serial connection, a modem, or with Marinetti and TCP/IP. The latest version is 2.5.3.

Spectrum requires an Apple IIgs running System 6 with at least 1 MB of memory and 1 3.5" disk drive (though a hard drive is recommended). A full installation of Spectrum consumes just under 3 MB of disk space.

According to the documentation, Spectrum is "a fully featured desktop telecommunications application for GS/OS, having an extremely powerful scripting language, supporting many features not found in other telecommunications applications." In short, it is easily the most accomplished telecomm program written for the Apple IIgs. The documentation that comes with Spectrum is quite extensive and in-depth: roughly 400 pages on every aspect of the program, including how to use the scripting language.

Installing Spectrum

Spectrum comes either on a single CD-ROM or on a set of six 3.5" floppy disks. If you are using the floppy disks, the installer is located on the disk simply named "Spectrum." This disk, which must be write-enabled, contains the Install program, a Read.Me.First file, and five other files and folders. If you are installing from the CD-ROM version of Spectrum, you will not need to insert any other disks.

Double-click the Install program to commence the installation process. Right away, you will be asked to personalize your copy of Spectrum. Enter your name and click OK.

Afterward, the usual Apple IIgs installer program will appear. If the destination disk is not listed at top-right, click the Disk button until it is. When ready, click the Install button. After a few moments, you will be prompted to insert the Spectrum.Extras disk. When the installation is finished (it will take about three minutes), choose Quit from the File menu. You must then restart the IIgs. In the Finder, choose Shut Down from the Special menu. Select the Restart radio button, and click OK.

After the IIgs has restarted, launch the Spectrum application from where you installed it. It should be located in a folder named "Spectrum" at the root level of the disk. Insert the Spectrum.Extras disk. After a few more moments, you will be prompted to follow on-screen instructions. You will need to click the Extract button in the following dialog box in order to extract more files needed for Spectrum. The entire process may take up to seven minutes.

Afterward, you will be asked to install optional support files. If you are not short on disk space, you may as well install all of them. Installing all of the files will take about six to seven minutes. When finished, you will be treated to a dialog box that presents a rather odd choice of buttons: reboot and restart. Though usually the two terms mean practically the same thing, in this case, "reboot" means restart the Apple IIgs, and "restart" means quit and re-launch Spectrum. If you already rebooted the IIgs earlier, you should need only restart Spectrum.

Using Spectrum

While Spectrum can be used as a traditional telecommunications program with a direct serial or modem link to a remote system, this section will cover Spectrum's use with TCP/IP and telnet. If Marinetti is active when Spectrum is started, Spectrum will automatically switch into TCP/IP mode.

To connect to a telnet server, you must first define it as a Service. To do so, choose Services... from the TCP/IP menu. A dialog will open showing two predefined services for Compuserve and Delphi. If there is no TCP/IP menu, ensure that Marinetti is installed and active by following the instructions presented earlier in this chapter.

Click the New... button at the top-center. Enter a name by which to refer to the service, then enter in the service's Internet address, either an IP address or a hostname.

Spectrum has a number of ways of formatting the display screen. For telnet connections, the most appropriate display is usually VT100, which uses the simple IIgs 80-column text screen. Since most telnet services use just ordinary ASCII characters, this display screen will suffice. Otherwise, you may leave the selection at Default Display.

Spectrum supports a powerful scripting language. For example, if the telnet service requires you to enter a login username and password, you could have this procedure automated by script. For now, leave the script field blank and click the Save button.

The new service is now added to the list. Select it by clicking its name. Ensure that the Telnet checkbox is checked, then click Login.

Spectrum will then attempt to connect to port 23 of the remote system. If all goes well, you should see the welcome message from the remote system printed on the IIgs screen. You may then proceed as usual with the telnet session.

If you chose to use the VT100 or Spectrum Text displays, press COMMAND-W to return the usual screen with menu bar. When you are finished with your telnet session, choose Disconnect... from the TCP/IP menu. Click the Disconnect button in the resulting dialog box.

Other Features of Spectrum

Spectrum's scripting language has been used to create fully-featured applications such as FTP clients, email programs, and even a web browser.

In particular, the Spectrum web browser will be covered next in this chapter.

Browsing the Web with SIS

Spectrum Internet Suite, developed by Geoff Weiss and Ewen Wannop, is "an all-in-one tool that provides Web Browsing, Email Sending, File Managing, and Telnet Connecting."

SIS requires Spectrum 2.1 or later, System 6.0.1, 4 MB of RAM, and a hard disk with at least 4 MB free. SIS will also work fine with only 2 MB of RAM, though it may not be able to display very large web pages. As of this writing, the latest version of SIS is v1.2. Originally a commercial product, SIS is now free software, released under the terms of the GNU General Public License. Refer to this book's companion web site for details on how to obtain SIS.

SIS has the basic features of a web browser, including: proxy server support, browsing history, HTML 3.2 support, color text, text styles and sizes, and a disk cache for speed.

Installing SIS

SIS is available both in source and binary form. The source requires the ORCA/M assembler, a commercial product. Therefore, this text will assume that you are using an already-assembled binary of SIS.

If you haven't already, use ShrinkIt to extract the contents of the SHK archive to a convenient location on your disk. There are two text files which explain the installation procedure. The first is Readme.build. If you are using the ready-made version of SIS, all of the instructions in this file should have already been completed for you. Otherwise, you will have to follow them in order to proceed.

The second file, Readme.Install, contains the second part of instructions concerning Spectrum. The first step is to launch Spectrum, then choose Run a Script... from the Script menu. In the Open dialog box, navigate to the SIS.1.2 folder, then select the Install.SIS file. Click the Open button.

A welcome message will appear. After clicking OK, you will be asked to choose a location to install the SIS scripts. The default location is within the Spectrum.Script folder. Unless you wish to install the scripts elsewhere, click the Install button to accept this location.

The dialog will disappear to be replaced with an installation progress indicator. The installation process takes about two minutes. When it is complete, you will be asked to restart the Spectrum program.

The Spectrum splash screen will appear for a few moments. When the Welcome to Spectrum v2.5.3! message appears on the screen, you are ready to start SIS.

The Time Zone CDev was installed if it did not already exist on your system. If you did not have Time Zone, you must open the Apple menu and choose Control Panels. Open the Time Zone CDev, then from the list, choose your time zone and close the window. Finally, restart the IIgs and open Spectrum again.

Starting SIS

There are two methods to start SIS. The first is from within Spectrum, the second is from the Finder.

To start SIS from Spectrum, choose Run a Script... from the Script menu. If you installed the SIS scripts in the default location, Spectrum.Script, then you should need only scroll down the list of files and select Start.SIS. Otherwise, navigate to the folder where you chose to install the SIS scripts and select the Start.SIS file. Click Open or press RETURN to continue; the SIS splash screen should appear.

A SIS launcher program is installed in the same place as the SIS scripts (usually the Spectrum.Script folder within the main Spectrum folder). This program has an icon depicting a globe and a hand. Drag it to a convenient location on your disk. Double-clicking this icon will automatically launch Spectrum and start SIS.

When SIS is started for the first time, the Preferences window will open after the splash screen is displayed. From the Network Access popup menu at the top-right, choose TCP/IP. Click OK to dismiss the window. After the preferences are saved, you will be notified that SIS must be restarted. Dismiss the dialog box, then repeat the procedure for starting SIS from Spectrum.

You are now ready to browse the World Wide Web with the Spectrum Internet Suite.

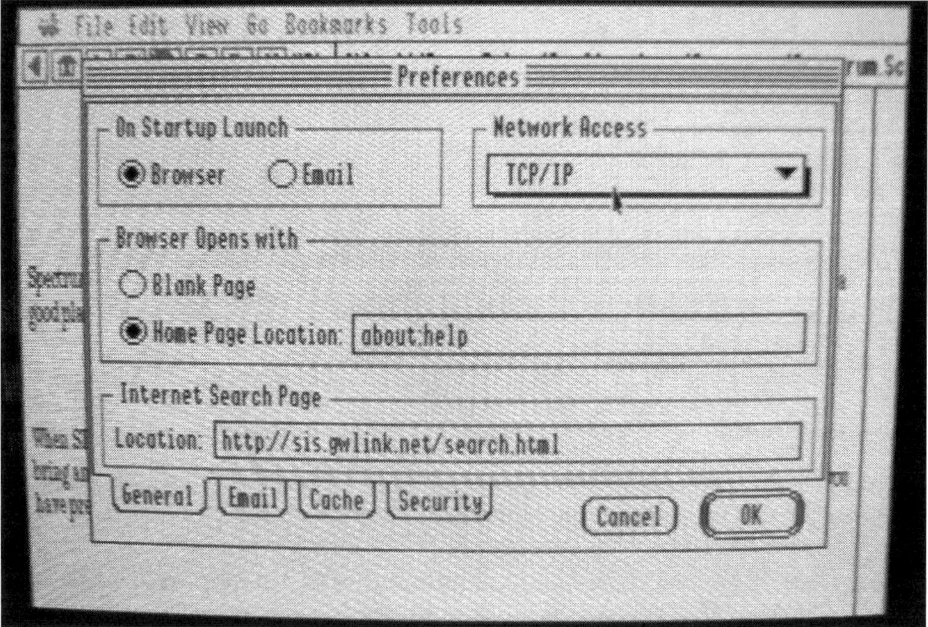

Figure 10-13. The SIS preferences window

Using SIS

Unless you configured it to do otherwise, SIS starts by opening the Home Page, which by default is a page containing some basic getting started information about SIS.

SIS can be operated by menu commands or by using the buttons located just below the menu bar. From left to right, these buttons are:

1. Back, which takes you to a previously-viewed page.
2. Home, taking you to the home page.
3. Forward, which takes you forward to a recently-viewed page.
4. Refresh, causing the current web page to reload.
5. Search, which takes you to a page for searching the Web.
6. Go, which causes SIS to load the URL in the address field.
7. Print, for printing the current page.
8. Find, for locating certain text on the current page.

To the right of the button bar is the URL or address field. Enter the URL to your favorite web site here, then click the green Go button to load it. You must click the Go button to load a page; unlike some web browsers, pressing RETURN will not load the URL. SIS will automatically complete some parts of the URL. For example, it will prepend http:// and www where needed. If you enter a domain name without a top level domain, such as apple, SIS will know to load http://apple.com.

SIS takes some time to download and display a web page on the Apple IIgs. On a standard, 2.8 MHz system, it may take as long as two or three minutes to display just one web page. Have patience.

Hyperlinks are displayed in yellow-highlighted, underlined style. Unlike conventional web browsers, SIS requires links to be double-clicked, not single-clicked, as you may be accustomed to. Double-clicking a link will take you to the web page in question. Once there, the back button will take you back to the previous page which contained the link.

Form fields such as text boxes, check boxes, and submit buttons are shown in green. In order to use them, you must double-click on them. To enter text into a form field, double-click the field and enter your text into the small window that appears. When finished, click the close box in the window.

Unfortunately, SIS does not have any way to display graphics on a web page. They are instead shown with a small placeholder image. Holding CONTROL while double-clicking this image will open a window showing the image location, as well as an option to download it to a file on the IIgs.

Other Features of SIS

SIS has many other features such as the ability to send email messages, store bookmarks, and use a proxy server. Fortunately, SIS comes with a built-in manual that explains these features and more. The manual consists of a series of HTML pages which can be viewed in SIS. To access it, choose Spectrum Internet Suite Help from the Tools menu, then double-click the yellow Table of Contents link.

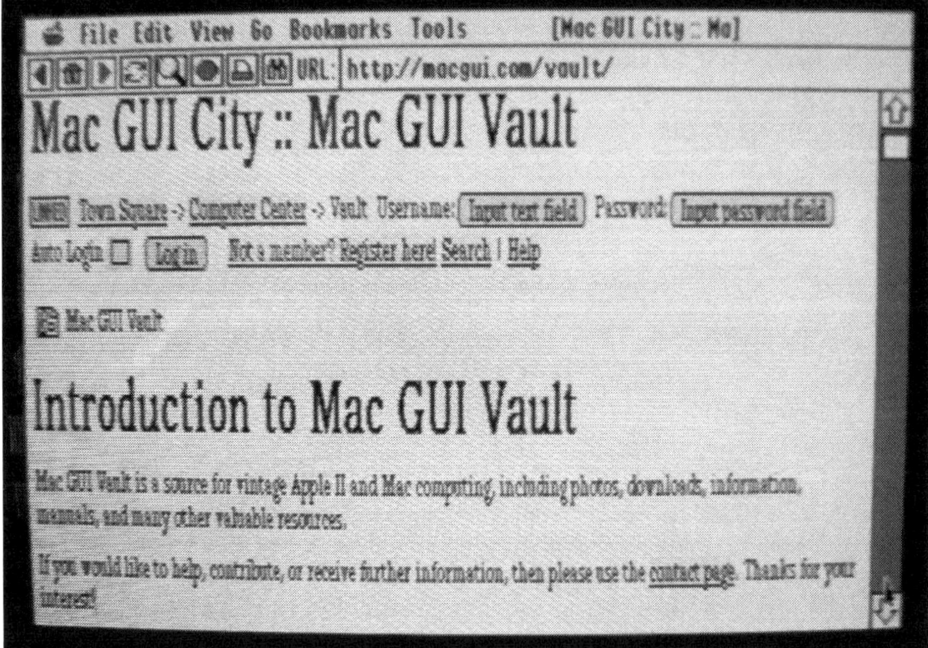

Figure 10-14. The SIS 1.2 web browser

Sending and Receiving Email with SAM2

If you have an email account that supports the POP3 protocol (and most accounts do), then you can send and receive email on your Apple IIgs using the SAM2 program, written by Ewen Wannop. SAM2 provides many features expected of a modern-day email client: support for multiple email accounts, an address box, mail filters, attachments, and support for HTML messages. The latest version of SAM2 is v2.0.2, which added spell checking when composing emails.

The minimum requirements to run SAM2 are System 6.0.1, Marinetti 3.0b3 or later, and 1 MB of RAM. Having more RAM and a hard disk will make using SAM2 more convenient.

Installing SAM2

SAM2 comes in a ShrinkIt archive. Unshrink it, then open the Read.Me.First file to read over the program description and installation notes. SAM2 requires two System Tools, two CDEVs, a sound file, and a number of fonts all to be copied to the System folder. Don't overlook the fonts that are in the HTMLTool folder. After copying these files to your System folder, you must restart the Apple IIgs.

When all of the necessary files are installed, double-click the Sam2 application to start it.

Configuring an Email Account

SAM2 requires a POP3 server in order to receive email, and an SMTP server to send email. To configure the two, choose Edit Accounts... from the Options menu.

The Account Configuration dialog box will appear. First enter a description for the email account, such as "Work Account." Then enter your full email address and name. The next three boxes are for the POP3 email server. Enter the server name (either as a hostname or as an IP address) and your username and password.

The next step is to configure access to an SMTP server. From the popup menu near the bottom of the dialog box, choose the only option listed, *Edit Server List*. If you have previously defined an SMTP server, then you could otherwise choose it from this popup menu.

If you choose Edit Server List, another dialog box, entitled "Server Configuration," will appear. Enter a description for this SMTP server, such as "Work SMTP." If the SMTP server operates on the standard port number, 25, then you may leave the Default port radio button selected. Otherwise, click the Custom port radio button and enter the port number in the text field to the right. Finally, enter the server address (either as a hostname or IP address) and the username and password, if required. If a password is required, choose Password from the Authentication popup menu. Click OK when finished, then answer Yes when asked to save changes, to dismiss the dialog box.

The Account Configuration dialog box will reappear, and the SMTP server that was just configured is now added to the Outgoing Mail Server (SMTP) popup menu. Choose it, click OK, then answer Yes when asked to save changes.

Reading Email

Once you have configured an email account, choose Check Mail... from the File menu. SAM2 will connect to the POP3 email server and download all of the email messages from the Inbox. Fetching new messages takes a fair amount of time. A standard Apple IIgs requires about eight minutes to download 50 messages. Downloading many messages with large attachments will take even longer.

Once the email messages are downloaded, they will be listed in a window, sorted by date and time in ascending order. Double-click any message subject to read its contents.

To view messages from a different mailbox, choose the desired mailbox from the Mailboxes menu. SAM2 will open a window showing the downloaded messages from that mailbox that are stored on the Apple IIgs.

If the email has any attachments, choose Extract Attached Files... from the Message menu to decode and download them. All downloaded files are placed in the SAM2 Downloads folder.

Sending Email

SAM2 allows for replies to existing emails, as well as sending new emails. Email messages sent from SAM2 are not sent immediately. Instead, they are all added to a message queue. Choosing the Send Queued Messages... command from the File menu will send them all in one batch.

To reply to a message, open the desired message, then choose either Reply To... or Reply To All... from the Message menu. The difference between the two is that the former will typically send the email to only one person, whereas the latter will send the email to multiple recipients.

The screen to compose the email message will appear. Compose your reply at the bottom, and set the From, To, Cc, and Bcc addresses as desired. You may also alter the subject line. To add an attachment, choose Attach File... from the Message menu. Select a file from the dialog box by highlighting its name and clicking the Open button.

When you are satisfied with your message, click the Queue button. After a moment, you will be returned to the original email message.

To send a new email message, you must close any open email, as well as the list of all emails. Choose Close from the File menu until there are no more windows on the screen. Then you may choose New E-Mail Message... from the Message menu.

Reading Usenet with SNAP

SNAP, written by Ewen Wannop, stands for Speccie's News Acquisition Program, and is a competent Usenet newsreader for the IIgs. As of this writing, the latest version of SNAP is v1.1.3. With SNAP, you can browse a list of newsgroups on a server, read articles, and post new articles and followups. SNAP is great for text messages, but cannot handle binary content, such as images or programs. This limitation is largely meaningless, as Apple II compatible binaries haven't been posted to Usenet in over 10 years.

SNAP functions as an online newsreader. That is, whereas most newsreaders save message headers and bodies to disk in order to speed up newsgroup access, SNAP does not. Instead, headers and messages are downloaded every time, making news reading a bit slower. There is an option to manually save individual articles to your Apple, but this is solely for your convenience. At a minimum, SNAP requires 1 MB of free memory and Marinetti 3.0b3 or later.

Installing SNAP

Unshrink the SNAP archive, then open the Quick.Start file in the resulting folder for installation instructions. You will need to copy two CDevs, two System Tools, and several fonts to the System folder. Restart your Apple, set the time zone using the Time Zone Control Panel, and then you can double-click the SNAP application icon.

If you get an error about missing required fonts, check to make sure that you copied the fonts from the Fonts folder within the HTMLTool folder too.

Configuring a News Server

You must enter the details for an NNTP (News) server in order for SNAP to be useful. To do so, choose Edit Servers... from the File menu, and click the New button in the resulting dialog box. In the Server Info dialog box, you must provide the details for the NNTP server, and optionally, a mail server. In the Menu Title field, enter a name by which to refer to the news server, such as the name of the service provider (this name must follow ProDOS file naming conventions: up to 15 alphanumeric characters and periods, starting with a letter). Enter the Internet address of the NNTP server in the News Server field. If the server requires authentication, enter your Username and Password. The Reply To field should be a valid email address, and will appear, along with your Real Name, on every message that you send with SNAP. The XPAT checkbox enables additional functionality, but is not compatible with all news servers; check with the administrator if you are unsure whether to use XPAT or not.

Click OK when finished. SNAP will verify the information that you entered. If everything was acceptable, the server will be added to the list, and you will return to the Servers dialog box. Click the Cancel button to dismiss the dialog box.

Building the Newsgroup List

Select your news server from the News Server submenu in the File menu. A new menu title will appear at the right with the name of your news server. Choose Rebuild Full Newsgroup List... from your news server's menu to download the full list of Usenet newsgroups. Click the Rebuild button. Depending on how many groups are on the server, this operation could take from 10 to 30 minutes. Downloading a list of 26,000 groups on a standard Apple IIgs takes about 14 minutes.

Most news servers have around 40,000 to 100,000 or more newsgroups, yet most people are only interested in just a few dozen. SNAP solves this problem by using a group subscription list. The subscription list contains just the groups that you're interested in reading. For example, you could create a group list that only contains the Apple II newsgroups.

To create a group list, choose Build Group Lists... from your news server's menu. Click the New button. In the resulting dialog box, enter a name for the list. In this example, the list will be called AppleII. The name for a group list may only contain letters or a period (it follows ProDOS file naming rules).

A new window will open on the screen, ready to receive the newsgroups that you wish to include in this group list. There are two methods of adding newsgroups. The first way is to click the Add Entry button and type the group name in the New Group List Entry dialog box that appears. This method is fastest when you want only to add a few groups, and you know the exact name of each.

The second method involves selecting newsgroups from the full list on the server. Choose Show Full Newsgroup List... from your news server's menu. The list is separated into pages. Click the double-arrows to move to the first, previous, next, or last page. To add a newsgroup from the full list, select its name by clicking on it, then click the Add to List button. When you are finished adding from the full list, choose Close from the File menu.

Some groups that you could add to your Apple II list include:

- comp.sys.apple2
- comp.sys.apple2.marketplace
- comp.sys.apple2.programmer
- comp.emulators.apple2

When you are finished adding groups to your group list, choose Close from the File menu. Finally, click the Close button in the Build Group Lists dialog box.

Reading Newsgroups

To start reading the newsgroups that you selected, choose your group list from the Open Group List submenu of your news server's menu. If you followed the previous example, you should see the AppleII list. SNAP will open a window showing the newsgroups in the list and will connect to the NNTP server to get the unread article counts.

Double-click a newsgroup name to open a window showing its articles. SNAP will download up to 200 articles by default.

Each article is displayed in ascending order of date. The figure in the leftmost column is the number of text lines contained in the article. Following is the date in month/year format, then the author name, and finally, the subject of the article. Click the More button to show later articles, if there are more than 200 (note that this number, 200, can be changed by setting the Article Limit).

To read an article, double-click its entry in the newsgroup window. SNAP will download the article and format it for display. Two shortcuts are available for moving to the previous and next article: COMMAND-< and COMMAND->, respectively. To return to the list of articles, choose Close from the File menu.

When you are finished reading the articles in a newsgroup, you may return to the group list by choosing Close from the File menu. Once you have finished reading a newsgroup, it is a good idea to mark the articles in it as having been read. Doing so will prevent SNAP from downloading them again, and will save time when reading the newsgroup again in future. Simply select the desired newsgroup, then choose Mark Read from the Messages menu. The unread message count will change to zero.

Alternatively, if the Mark Last Read box is checked for the newsgroup list, the last article that you read will cause all previous articles to also be marked as read.

To check for the arrival of new messages in the newsgroups, click the Update button.

Posting Articles and Replies

SNAP allows all of the traditional methods of replying to Usenet messages. One can either post a *followup*, which is a message sent to the newsgroup, or one may post a *reply*, which is an email message sent only to the author. In addition, there is also an option to forward a message by email to anyone.

To post a followup, reply, or forward a message, first open the desired message by double-clicking it in the newsgroup article list. The three options are all listed in the Messages menu.

Choose Followup... from the Message menu to post to the newsgroup. The original message will appear with an attribution line and quote marks (>). It is customary Usenet etiquette to remove irrelevant message content, that is, parts of the message to which you are not replying. One should also take care to type one's reply *below* the existing message, not above it.

You may alter the subject, list of groups to which the message will be posted, and followup group, all by changing the appropriate text boxes. When you are ready to send your message, click the Send button. Sending an article should take only a few seconds, and after one or two minutes, your message should have propagated to nearly every Usenet server in the world.

Replying by email and forwarding the message work much like posting a followup. Choose Reply by Mail... or Forward... depending on to whom you wish to send your message. Instead of specifying a list of newsgroups, you will instead see the standard To, Cc, and Bcc fields for emails.

To start a new discussion topic, choose New Posting from the Messages menu. At minimum, you must enter a subject and message body for your new article. Click Send when you're finished.

Other Features

SNAP has a few other features which were not covered in this text. Some of these features include a spell checker, message signatures, and importing of text files. The manual included with SNAP covers all of these features, and more, in fine detail.

Accessing an FTP Site with SAFE2

FTP is one of the Internet's oldest protocols for transferring files between computer systems. SAFE2 (which stands for Spectrum Automated File Exchange, version 2), also written by Ewen Wannop, implements this protocol on the Apple IIgs, allowing you to both upload and download files to and from any FTP server around the world. With SAFE2, acquiring new programs and software for the Apple IIgs becomes much easier. SAFE2 requires a minimum of 1 MB of free memory, as well as Marinetti 3.0 or later. As of this writing, the latest version of SAFE2 is v2.2.5.

Installing SAFE2

After unshrinking the SAFE2 archive, open the resulting folder, and follow the directions in the Read.Me.First file for installation. You will need to copy a font, a CDEV, and a System Tool to the System folder. Restart the Apple IIgs, then set your time zone from the Time Zone CDev (accessed from Control Panels in the Apple menu). Finally, SAFE2 should be ready to use. Double-click the application to start it.

Inside the SAFE2 folder is another folder called Link.Layers, which contains two Marinetti Link Layers. One is for the Uthernet (version 1.0.1b5), but you should already have the Uthernet Link Layer installed if you followed the instructions earlier in this chapter. The other Link Layer is for Sweet16, an Apple IIgs emulator for Mac OS X. You will not need this file unless you are using that emulator.

SAFE2 uses a two-pane interface. The left pane shows files on your Apple; the right shows files on the remote FTP server. When you start SAFE2 for the very first time, the left pane will show all mounted volumes, and the right pane will be blank. Later, you may define a list of favorite servers to quickly connect to; this list will be displayed in the right pane when you start SAFE2.

Connecting to an FTP Server

Clicking the Connect button in the lower-right corner of the screen will bring up an FTP server connect dialog box. Enter a name for your convenience, then enter the FTP host. The host can either be entered as an IP address (such as 169.254.170.90) or as a host name (such as ftp.example.com). If the FTP server requires authentication, be sure to enter the correct username and password. SAFE2 will attempt anonymous login if you do not supply a username. If you want to change to a specific directory after login, you may also specify it. Beware: if the directory you enter does not exist, then SAFE2 will immediately disconnect after login.

PASV mode may be required if your Apple IIgs connects to the Internet from behind a firewall. If you are able to connect to an FTP server, but do not see the contents of any directory, try checking or unchecking this box as appropriate.

If you have saved one or more servers as Favorites, they will appear on the right side and you can double-click the name to automatically connect. Alternatively, you may select a Favorite server, then click the Connect button to alter the previously-defined connection details.

Transferring Files

SAFE2 allows both uploading of files, that is, sending files from your Apple IIgs to the remote FTP site, and downloading, retrieving a remote file to your Apple. The Transfer window, shown in Figure 10-15, has three major areas. On the left are your files and folders on the Apple. The list on the right shows files and folders on the remote FTP server. You may enter a folder by double-clicking it. Return to the previous folder by clicking the Previous Directory entry (Remember that *directory* is another term for folder). Holding the SHIFT key while clicking will allow you to select multiple items.

To upload a single file from your Apple, you must select it, then click the left-hand Transfer button (whose arrow is pointing to the right). If you wish to upload multiple files, you must select them using the SHIFT key, then click the left-hand Transfer button. Downloading one or more files works similarly: simply select one or more files then click the Transfer button on the right-hand side to send the data to your Apple. You may also upload and download entire folders at a time.

During upload or download, a progress bar will show the current file being transferred, total bytes transferred, and transfer rate. The maximum transfer speed for a standard Apple IIgs is typically around 2 to 4 kilobytes per second.

The icons at the bottom of the screen deal mostly with the files and folders on your Apple and the FTP site. The trash icon is used to delete files or folders. The icons on the right side are used for renaming, deleting, returning to the home directory, and disconnecting from the FTP site, respectively.

There are two unlabeled checkboxes atop each other at the bottom center of the screen. The top checkbox enables encoding of files when uploading to an FTP server. Some files on the Apple may not survive being uploaded to a remote system. Encoding makes sure that the file format won't be changed. The bottom checkbox will automatically decode files downloaded from the remote FTP server, when appropriate to do so.

Tweeting with IItter

If you have an account on the popular social Web site, Twitter.com, then you may be amused to discover a IIgs program that will allow you to post Tweets. IItter is an NDA (New Desk Accessory) written by Ryan Suenaga, and will allow you to both post updates to your Twitter account, as well as obtain a list of the 20 most recent status updates of the people whom you're following on Twitter.

Since this book went to publication, Twitter may have changed their posting interface, potentially making IItter unusable. You will have to try it and see.

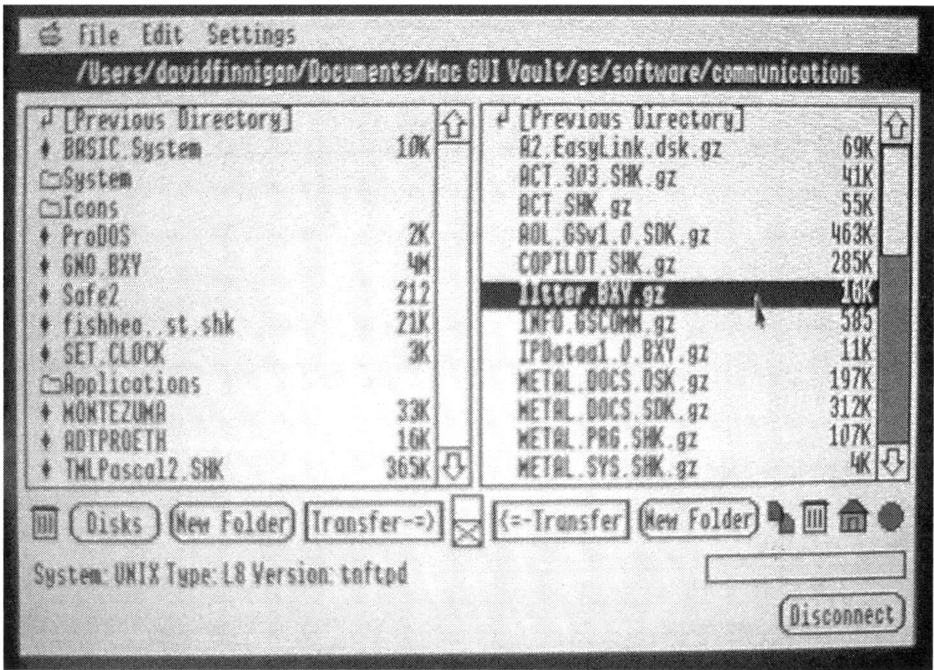

Figure 10-15. SAFE2 connected to an FTP site

NadaNet

Like the Uthernet, NadaNet is also a fairly recent development in the Apple networking world. NadaNet was developed by Michael J. Mahon in 2004, and it provides a method of connecting a number of Apple II computers via the 16-pin game I/O socket. NadaNet is a full peer-to-peer network, that is, each Apple can communicate with one another. Simple networking software interfaces with Applesoft BASIC, allowing the creation of networked games and other programs to be fairly straightforward. NadaNet also has parallel computing applications!

Mr. Mahon has provided a number of programs that you can examine and modify. One such program is a Pong demonstration in which two Apples bounce a pong ball back and forth using NadaNet. A ProDOS file server is also available, allowing any number of Apples connected to NadaNet to access shared files, even if the client computers are not running ProDOS. A message server allows jobs to be queued and run in parallel across the network.

NadaNet can be programmed from both Applesoft BASIC and assembly language. In particular, the NadaNet system adds additional commands to BASIC that allow PEEK, POKE, and CALL statements to be executed on other machines across the network. NadaNet makes it simple to run programs on other machines on the network.

Building a NadaNet system requires a special adapter for each Apple to be connected. You can either build the adapter yourself with parts and the schematic, or you can order as many pre-built adapters as you need from Mr. Mahon. Once the adapters have been built and connected, loading the networking software is simple: it is included on a two-sided DOS 3.3/ProDOS 5.25" disk.

Chapter 11 : Machine Language Monitor

Lurking below the surface of the friendly BASIC prompt is the world of the Machine Language Monitor, known as the *Monitor* for short. With it, you can tap the full power of your Apple by examining and modifying memory, and writing and executing low-level machine language programs. The absolute beginner will not make too much use of the Apple Monitor, but as his or her proficiency grows, so too will use of the Monitor.

The Monitor makes up the majority of the Apple's ROM (read-only memory) and it contains the critical software routines that your Apple needs in order to function. Written in 65C816 (on the IIgs) or 6502 (all other models) assembly language, the Monitor provides an interface to the hardware for Applesoft, Integer BASIC, and any other program on the computer. The Monitor is used any time that you type input for a program, or read output on the screen.

Although the Monitor is used without your knowledge, it can be accessed directly and used to control low-level aspects of the Apple. Among its abilities: writing and debugging assembly language programs, executing machine language programs, moving blocks of memory, altering the contents of memory, saving memory to cassette tape, and loading memory from tape.

What is Machine Language?

So far, you have used one language to communicate to your Apple, BASIC. However, even BASIC is not really the Apple's native language. The Apple is a digital computer, relying on streams of ones and zeros to do its work.

These ones and zeros form the basis of *machine language*, the instructions directly carried out by the Apple's microprocessor, either the 65C816 in the IIgs, or the 6502 in all other Apples. These instructions, of which there are around 60, are extremely simple. They mainly deal with adding and subtracting two numbers, manipulating bits and bytes, and loading and saving numbers to and from memory. As you can imagine, it takes tens or even hundreds of machine language instructions to accomplish even the simplest of tasks.

BASIC itself happens to be written in machine language. It serves as an interpreter, turning your English language instructions into those understandable by the microprocessor. BASIC makes programming the Apple much faster and more accessible for a wider range of users. However, this convenience comes at a price: namely, programs written in machine language are much faster than those written in BASIC.

Working in Hex

Up until now, the environment that you have been using on the Apple, BASIC, has always used the familiar base 10, decimal numbering system. The Machine Language Monitor however, does not use decimal. Instead, it counts using hexadecimal, or base 16. Whereas with decimal, one would start counting 1, 2, 3, 4, 5, 6, 7, 8, 9, 10; hexadecimal counts 1, 2, 3, 4, 5, 6, 7, 8, 9, A, B, C, D, E, F, 10. Hexadecimal is used as a shorter way to notate the base 2 numbers, the ones and zeros, that the Apple's microprocessor uses internally.

When using the Monitor, you will have to become familiar with hexadecimal. To help you out, Appendix E has a conversion chart between decimal and hexadecimal. It is customary to use a dollar sign ($) in front of a number to show that it is in hex notation. The Monitor does not follow this practice, but this book does.

Evolution of the Monitor

The Apple Monitor has undergone several enhancements and revisions throughout the ages. The later the model of Apple, the more features its Monitor has. For example, the earliest Monitors would only show memory in hex, while later versions show memory in hex and ASCII.

While all Monitors share the same basic set of features, this chapter will attempt to highlight the changes and additional features present in each Apple.

Accessing the Monitor

Unless you have the original model of Apple II, you need to explicitly command your Apple to enter the Monitor. The original Apple II with the Old Monitor ROM will always start up in the Monitor, and pressing RESET will also enter the Monitor. It is possible to have an original Apple II that has been upgraded with an Autostart Monitor, in which case, it will act like all later models.

For all other models of Apple, get to the BASIC prompt, then type:

```
]CALL-151
```

When you press RETURN, you should see the asterisk (*) prompt that signifies the Monitor. At this point, you now wield nearly full control and power over all aspects of your Apple II!

Newer versions of ProDOS BASIC.SYSTEM have a MTR command that has the same effect as CALL -151. If you get a SYNTAX ER-

ROR, then your version of BASIC.SYSTEM is probably older and does not have the MTR command, which was added in version 1.3.

Displaying Memory

One of the most common uses of the Monitor is to display the contents of the Apple's memory. If you have been following along with the instructions in this chapter, you should have just entered the Monitor. Press the RETURN key a few times. Your screen should look something like this:

```
]CALL-151

*
 FF
*

0080- FF FF FF FF FF FF FF FF
*

0088- FF 00 FF FF FF FF FF 03
*

0090- 4C FF 00 FF FF FF FF FF
```

The Monitor shows up to 8 bytes of memory on a single line. The beginning of the line indicates the address for the first byte of memory, separated by a dash and a space. In the case of the example above, memory location $0090 contains $4C, and location $0091 contains $FF. The Apple Monitor keeps a running pointer to show the next 8 bytes of memory every time you press RETURN.

Displaying a Single Byte

To show just a single byte of memory, just type its address, like this:

```
*FBB3

FBB3- EA
```

Recall that the monitor always uses addresses in hexadecimal format. This is contrary to BASIC, which always uses addresses in decimal format. Memory location $FBB3 is located in the Apple's ROM, and is the signature byte. It should be $38 for the Apple II, $EA for the II Plus, $06 for the IIe, IIc, and the IIc Plus, and $00 for the IIgs.

Displaying a Range

You may display a range of memory, using a period to separate the starting and ending address, as in this example:

```
*C600.C640

C600- A2 20 A0 00 A2 03 86 3C
C608- 8A 0A 24 3C F0 10 05 3C
C610- 49 FF 29 7E B0 08 4A D0
C618- FB 98 9D 56 03 C8 E8 10
C620- E5 20 58 FF BA BD 00 01
C628- 0A 0A 0A 0A 85 2B AA BD
C630- 8E C0 BD 8C C0 BD 8A C0
C638- BD 89 C0 A0 50 BD 80 C0
C640- 98
```

The Monitor displays the contents of memory starting at location $C600, and finishes at $C640. Coincidently, this range is the first few bytes of the ROM of the peripheral card in slot 6.

If you leave out the starting address, and instead only enter a period and an ending address, the Apple Monitor will display memory starting from the current location (most recently accessed) up to the ending address.

The Apple IIgs Monitor has an additional feature which makes the memory display more convenient: instead of just displaying the raw hex values, the corresponding ASCII characters are shown on the right. A period (.) is substituted for any unprintable ASCII characters. In a lot of cases, when you are looking at memory that is just machine language instructions, the ASCII output will be gibberish. However, it can come in handy. To cancel a large memory range display, press CONTROL-X.

In addition, the Apple IIgs Monitor uses something known as a bank number. Whereas the microprocessor in all earlier Apples could only address 65,536 memory locations, the 65C816 microprocessor in the Apple IIgs can access up to 256 banks of 65,536 locations. Wherever a bank number is entered or displayed, it is separated from the memory address by a forward slash (/). The bank number is always two hexadecimal digits, and the address is always four hexadecimal digits.

Specifying a bank number is optional, and the examples shown in this chapter will not show it. Just be aware that anywhere a memory location is entered, you may prepend the bank number and forward slash, if you so desire.

Modifying Memory

To modify memory, you must specify a starting address, separated by a colon, and the data to place there.

For example, entering:

```
*300:60
```

will insert the hexadecimal value $60 at location $300. You may enter more hex bytes, separated by spaces, and they will be entered into memory sequentially, beginning with the given address.

Additionally, you may omit the starting address, leaving just the colon and the hex bytes. Doing so will insert those values starting at the current memory location. Every time you display or modify memory, the current location is incremented.

Entering Literal ASCII

With the Enhanced Apple IIe Monitor came a new feature allowing an ASCII input mode. This will automatically convert any ASCII character into its hexadecimal equivalent. To do so, type a single quote, the desired character, and a space. For example, to enter the string “Dulce et Decorum est” at location $300 in memory, enter the following:

```
*300:'D 'u 'l 'c 'e '  'e 't '  'D 'e 'c 'o 'r 'u 'm '
'e 's 't
```

Simply separate each character with a single quote (') and a space. The very last character (the ‘t’, in the example) does not need a space after it; you may just end the line with RETURN.

The original Apple II, the II Plus, the standard IIe, and early revisions of the Apple IIc, do not have an ASCII input mode.

Literal ASCII with the IIgs Monitor

The Apple IIgs also supports the entry of literal ASCII, a feature which will automatically convert ASCII characters to their hexadecimal equivalents. To do so, enclose the desired characters within double quotes (") like so:

```
*300: "HELLO"

*300.304

00/0300:C8 C5 CC CC CF-HELLO
*
```

Here, the ASCII string “HELLO” is entered into memory starting at location $300. When asked to display the five bytes of memory from $300 to $304, the Apple shows the hex equivalent, followed by the ASCII representation.

To store a reversed ASCII string, enclose it in single quotes ('). The input string is limited to four characters. This feature is only available in the Apple IIgs Monitor.

Running Programs

After displaying and modifying memory, the next most common task for the Monitor to perform is that of running programs. To do so, enter a starting memory address, followed by G. The G is short for Go, and instructs the Monitor to start executing the code located at the given address. If you just type a G without an address, then the Monitor will execute code at the most recently-used memory location.

For example, type 3D0G to access DOS, providing that it is already in RAM.

When a machine language program finishes execution with a final RTS instruction, it will return control back to the Machine Language Monitor.

Copying Memory

If you ever need to move or copy a range of memory, you can do it in the Monitor with the Move command. First you specify the starting address at which the copy will be placed. Then you specify the range of memory that will be copied. An example looks like so:

```
*300<800.80FM
```

This command tells the Apple to copy the 16 bytes of memory from $800 to $80F to the 16 bytes of memory starting at $300, leaving the memory at $800 untouched. If you had a BASIC program in memory before you entered the Monitor, the first 16 bytes of it are now located at $300 too.

Filling a Memory Range on the IIgs

The Apple IIgs Monitor has a Zap command that will fill a range of memory with a given value. Zap uses the following syntax:

value<starting address.ending addressZ

The entire range of memory, including the starting and ending addresses, are filled with the specified value. Here is an example:

```
*FF<300.3EFZ
```

This will fill the memory range from $300 to $3EF with $FF. Again, only the IIgs Monitor has this command.

Filling Memory on Any Model of Apple

Only the IIgs Monitor has the Zap command, but its effect may be simulated on older models of Apple by using the Move command. Using the Move method even has the advantage of being able to fill memory with a byte pattern. To fill a block of memory, first place the desired byte(s) at the beginning of the block. Take the very first memory address, and add to it the total number of bytes in the fill pattern. Finally, take the ending location for the block, and subtract the total number of bytes. With the starting location of the block, you now have three values.

Use this syntax with the Move command:

```
*starting_addr_+_length<starting_addr.ending_addr_-_lengthM
```

The following example will fill the memory block from $800 to $80F with the byte $AA:

```
*800:AA

*801<800.80EM

*800.80F

0800- AA AA AA AA AA AA AA AA
0808- AA AA AA AA AA AA AA AA
*
```

The next example shows filling the same range with a 3-byte pattern, AA BB CC:

```
*800:AA BB CC
```

```
*803<800.80CM

*800.80F

0800- AA BB CC AA BB CC AA BB
0808- CC AA BB CC AA BB CC AA
*
```

In this second example, 3 was added to the starting address $800 to get $803, and 3 bytes were subtracted from the ending address $80F to get $80C.

This technique of using the Move command to fill memory with a single byte or pattern will work on any model of Apple.

Comparing Memory

If you want to compare two ranges of memory to see that they match, then the Monitor's Verify command will do just that. It will report any differences between two ranges of memory. Its syntax is similar to the Move command. One must specify the starting address of the first block, and the starting and ending addresses of the second block.

This example will command the Monitor to start comparing data at location $800 with location $900. The next 47 bytes will then be verified, finishing with $830 and $930:

```
*800<900.930V
```

If a difference is found in the two blocks of memory, the address and value from the first block is shown, followed by the equivalent value from the second block. If there are no differences at all, if the two blocks were identical, then there is no output.

To test the Verify command, follow these steps. First, enter two blocks of data like so:

```
*800:AA BB CC 11 DD EE FF
```

```
*900:AA BB CC 22 EE FF FF
```

Now tell the Monitor to verify these two 7-byte blocks of memory:

```
*800<900.906V

0903-22 (11)
0904-EE (DD)
0905-FF (EE)
*
```

The three differences are then displayed by the Monitor. In each of the three lines, the value in parentheses is from the first block starting at $800.

Searching Memory

The Enhanced Apple IIe Monitor introduced a search command that allows a search for one or two bytes in memory. These bytes may be entered either in hexadecimal or ASCII. One important thing to note is that two-byte hex or ASCII string sequences must be entered in reverse order.

For example, to search for the two-byte sequence $1234 between addresses $800 and $9FF, enter:

```
*3412<800.9FFS
```

and to search for the two-byte ASCII sequence “HI”, type the following:

```
*'I'H<800.9FFS
```

It is impossible to search for a two-byte sequence with a high byte of zero (meaning two leading zeros), such as $0030. The Monitor would search for just the low byte, $30.

The Monitor Search command does not allow searching for a sequence longer than two bytes. The original Apple II, the II Plus, standard IIe, and early revisions of the Apple IIc do not have a memory search command.

IIgs Pattern Search

The Apple IIgs Monitor has a command that allows for searching memory for a string up to 256 bytes long. The command is called Pattern Search, and it can accept either hexadecimal bytes, ASCII, or flipped ASCII (merely a reversed ASCII string).

The syntax is as follows:

**search value(s)*\<*starting_address.ending_address*P

When entering hexadecimal bytes, be sure to use leading zeros where appropriate. The following example will search for the byte pattern A9 01 in memory locations $2000 to $2FFF:

```
*\A9 01\<2000.2FFFP
```

To search for an ASCII string, enclose the string in quotation marks, as in this example:

```
*\"Apple"\<2000.2FFFP
```

If the pattern is found, each location of its first byte is displayed. For example, if ProDOS had been loaded into the IIgs, and the first search for A9 01 executed, the following may be displayed:

```
00/264E:
00/2915:
*
```

Redirecting Input and Output

Ordinarily, the Apple takes its input instructions from the keyboard, and shows its resultant output on the video screen. However, it is quite possible to send output to a serial card connected to a printer, for example, or accept input from a peripheral card. To do so, the Control-K and Control-P commands are used.

First, type a slot number from 1 to 7. Then, if you want to direct output to that slot, press CONTROL-P. Or, if you want to accept input from that slot, press CONTROL-K. Finally, press RETURN. Remember that CONTROL key combinations do not appear on the screen. You will only ever see the slot number that you typed.

If you type a slot number that does not contain a peripheral card, the Apple will freeze up. You must press CONTROL-RESET to regain control.

To return input and output back to the keyboard and video screen, respectively, enter 0 for the slot number. The next two sections offer two common scenarios involving output redirection using the Monitor.

Booting a Disk

With the Monitor, you can activate any card in slots 1 through 7. This includes being able to boot a disk with DOS on it. To do so, type the slot number, then CONTROL-P, then press RETURN, like so:

*6 (CONTROL-P, RETURN)

The disk drive should come to life and start loading the operating system.

Executing DOS 3.3 and ProDOS Commands

Any ProDOS command that is legal for immediate-mode execution may be given from the Monitor prompt. These commands include CATALOG, CAT, BLOAD, BSAVE, PREFIX, and others. Of course, the ProDOS operating system must first be loaded before any of these commands will work.

A limited subset of DOS 3.3 commands that are legal for immediate-mode execution at the BASIC prompt can be used from the Monitor:

- BRUN
- CATALOG
- CHAIN

- IN#
- INIT
- INT
- FP
- PR#
- RUN
- UNLOCK

Some DOS 3.3 commands are too similar to the built-in Monitor commands, hence, the DOS commands cannot be used.

Activating the 80-Columns Screen

The Monitor has its own equivalent of the BASIC PR# command. If you have an 80-column card in your Apple II or II Plus, or if you have a IIe or newer machine, type 3, then press CONTROL-P and RETURN:

*3 (CONTROL-P, RETURN)

This will activate the 80-column card in slot 3, and is analogous to typing PR#3 at the BASIC prompt. Warning: using this CONTROL-P command will disconnect DOS 3.3 or ProDOS.

If you are using an original Apple II or the Apple II Plus, and the cursor disappears, but the screen doesn't change otherwise, then you likely have to switch your TV set or video monitor over to the 80-column card in slot 3.

Leaving the Monitor

There are a few different ways by which one may escape the Monitor. The easiest method is to press CONTROL-C, then RETURN. This sequence should return you to BASIC.

Alternatively, you may type 6, then CONTROL-P and RETURN to boot a disk in slot 6.

Lastly, you could start a program running with the G command. 3D0G should take you back to BASIC with DOS intact.

Performing Calculations

You can easily perform simple arithmetic involving addition, subtraction, and multiplication in the Monitor. The one thing that you need to remember is that the input and output is all based in hex. The Apple IIgs Monitor can perform 32-bit addition, subtraction, multiplication, and division. Older models of Apple can perform some, but not all, of these mathematical operations.

Hexadecimal Arithmetic

All models of Apple II can perform hexadecimal addition and subtraction by separating the operands with a plus (+) for addition, or a minus (-) for subtraction, as shown in these examples:

```
*3+3
=06
*9+1
=0A
*2-1
=01
*10-A
=06
*
```

Computation takes place entirely in hexadecimal, with the result printed on the following line after the equal sign. Except for the IIgs, all models of Apple are limited to 8-bit computations ranging from 0 to 255 ($FF + $1 rolls over to $00). If the result of a subtraction is less than zero, the Monitor displays the one's complement result.

The Apple IIgs supports two additional operations, multiplication and division. Multiplication is done using an asterisk (*) and division with an underscore (_), identical to the previous examples shown:

```
*C_6
R-> $00000000   Q-> $00000002
```

```
*D_6
R-> $00000001   Q-> $00000002

*2*8
-> $0000000000000010

*
```

Division shows both the remainder, following the R, and the quotient, after the Q. The Apple IIgs may perform calculations with numbers up to 4,294,967,295.

Hex and Decimal Conversion

If you have an Apple IIgs, then your Monitor has a quite handy ability to convert between hexadecimal and decimal.

To convert a hex number to decimal, simply type the hex number followed by an equal sign (=), as shown:

```
*F=
Decimal-> 15 {+15}
```

The IIgs prints the conversion on the next line. To go the other direction, from decimal to hex, first type an equal sign, then the decimal number, like this:

```
*=256
Hex-> $00000100
```

Storing and Loading Memory

The Apple offers two methods to save and retrieve a range of memory onto an external device. These two methods are cassette tape and disk. You may find a number of times when you want to save an area of the Apple's memory: a shape table or a high-resolution screen are two examples.

Saving Memory to Tape

The Monitor's W command may be used to record a range of the Apple's memory to cassette tape. This command only works on the Apple II, II Plus, and IIe, since only those models of Apple have cassette ports.

First, ensure that your cassette tape recorder is properly attached to the Apple and is operational. The Apple has no way of knowing whether the recorder is working, has a tape, or indeed is even connected at all. Read the relevant section of Chapter 2 for instructions on how to connect a cassette tape recorder.

To save memory to tape, specify both the starting and ending memory addresses, separated by a dot. Then type a W for Write, like so:

```
*300.3FFW
```

As soon as you press RETURN, the Apple will send the data out to the cassette port. You should make sure that the cassette recorder has a tape in it, that it is plugged in to the Apple and the power, and that it is in record mode *before* you press RETURN. The above line will cause the contents of memory locations $300 to $3FF to be recorded on tape.

It is imperative that the tape be labeled with the memory range that it contains. Otherwise, it is too easy to forget, and the Apple has no way of knowing what the memory range should be. You must specify the same memory range when reading the tape back, otherwise it will not work.

The cassette tape format is fairly simple, consisting of three parts. First, a 10-second reference tone is recorded. This tone serves to both make sure that the nonmagnetic leader has passed, that anything previously recorded on the tape is eliminated, and to help the Apple read the tape back into memory later. Following the tone comes the actual data from memory. It is encoded as a sequence of high and low tones that represent the ones and zeros of memory. To your ear, it will sound like random noise (though it is, obviously, not random to the Apple). Finally, the Apple records a checksum byte on the tape. This byte is used by the Apple when it reads back the tape to ensure that the data was correctly read back.

If you are curious as to what the cassette recording sounds like, you can either play back a tape using earphones or a built-in speaker if it has one, or you could attach a speaker or earphones directly to the Apple's cassette out port and issue a cassette write command to listen.

Loading Memory from Tape

To get the Apple to listen to a cassette tape and place its contents into RAM, the R command, for Read, is used. One needs only specify a starting address and ending address, separated by a period, then followed by R, like so:

```
*300.3FFR
```

This command will instruct the Apple to start loading the cassette tape into RAM starting at location $300. If the cassette tape recording contains more or less memory than the given range, an error will occur. Loading memory from cassette can require some careful adjustment of the volume and tone controls on the play back device (typically, the cassette recorder). The volume should be loud, but not too loud. If you are having trouble loading cassette tapes, try with the volume adjusted to the middle setting, then slowly increase the volume each time until the Apple is able to successfully load the cassette tape recording into memory.

The Apple uses the reference tone at the beginning of the tape recording to lock on to the signal and identify when data is about to arrive. The Apple needs at minimum 3.5 seconds with this tone playing. Remember that the full tone is 10 seconds, as recorded using the cassette Write command. The Apple will wait forever until it hears the reference tone; this will allow you time to press the Play button after pressing RETURN. After the tone comes the data, which is altering patterns of ones and zeros, using high and low tones. To the human ear, it sounds like static. Finally, the checksum byte is read, and the Apple compares this checksum on the tape to its own checksum. If they match, then the Apple assumes that it has correctly and successfully "listened" to the tape. Note, however, it is still possible for the checksums to match, yet have the data be wrong. Because the checksum is just one byte with

256 possible values, it is possible for different data to have the same checksum.

If the checksums did not match, then the Apple will beep and print ERR. It is possible that some or most of the data read in from the cassette to RAM is good; the data that the Apple read from the cassette remains in memory whether the checksums matched or not.

It is possible, but not advisable, to read more or less memory than was originally recorded on the tape. Attempting either scenario may lead to partial success, but receiving an error message is also quite likely.

Saving Memory to Disk

To save memory to disk, DOS must first be loaded into the Apple's memory. Consult Chapter 7 for full details on how to boot DOS. To save memory to disk, the BSAVE command is used. Note that BSAVE should be used from a BASIC prompt, not from within the Monitor. BSAVE takes three arguments: a filename, a starting address, and a length. The filename determines the name on disk under which the memory will be saved. The starting address and length, both given in bytes, determine the range of memory that will be saved. In this example, eight bytes of memory from location $300 will be saved to a file named MEMORY:

```
]BSAVE MEMORY, A$300, L$8
```

Note that the address and length parameters, A and L, may be given in either decimal or hexadecimal format. The above example shows hexadecimal format, where the number is preceded by a dollar sign ($). When using decimal format, no dollar sign is needed. Following is the same BSAVE command, using decimal numbers:

```
]BSAVE MEMORY, A768, L8
```

Under DOS 3.3, the S, D, and V parameters may be used if so desired. ProDOS does not have need parameters, and can instead rely on the given path and file name to determine the correct disk.

Loading Memory from Disk

Memory is restored from a binary file on disk by way of the BLOAD command. You must first ensure that DOS is loaded into memory, and that you are at a BASIC prompt. The following command will load a file named MEMORY back into the Apple:

```
]BLOAD MEMORY
```

Ordinarily, BLOAD uses the starting address that is encoded in the binary file to determine where in RAM the file contents should be placed. For example, if the MEMORY file contained eight bytes of memory starting at location $300, then each subsequent BLOAD command would always place these eight bytes back at the same location, starting at $300. However, you may specify any starting address that you desire, using the A parameter.

As with BSAVE, the address parameter may be given in either decimal or hexadecimal form.

Changing Screen Display Mode

Using the Monitor, you may toggle the text screen display mode between Inverse and Normal. To activate Inverse mode, use the I command. All subsequent characters will be black on white. To return to Normal mode, white on black characters, use the N command.

Disassembling Machine Language Programs

Assembly language programs that are loaded into the Apple's memory are shown using hex values that represent the machine code directly executable by the 6502, 65C02, or 65C816 microprocessor in your Apple computer. While this format is easy for the computer to understand, it is inconvenient for human comprehension.

Therefore, the Monitor includes a feature known as a *disassembler*, a program that will convert machine language back into assembly language. While assembly language is no BASIC, it's easier to read than machine language. Each line of disassembled code will show the three-letter instruction mnemonic and its operand(s), if any.

Disassembly in the Monitor is performed using the List command, L. Typing L will disassemble the first 20 instructions from the most recently-accessed memory location. Or, you can specify a starting memory address from which to start the disassembly. Type L again to disassemble the following 20 instructions.

The following example disassembles part of the Monitor ROM starting at location $F800:

```
*F800L

F800-   4A          LSR
F801-   08          PHP
F802-   20 47 F8    JSR   $F847
F805-   28          PLP
F806-   A9 0F       LDA   #$0F
F808-   90 02       BCC   $F80C
F80A-   69 E0       ADC   #$E0
F80C-   85 2E       STA   $2E
F80E-   B1 26       LDA   ($26),Y
F810-   45 30       EOR   $30
F812-   25 2E       AND   $2E
F814-   51 26       EOR   ($26),Y
F816-   91 26       STA   ($26),Y
F818-   60          RTS
F819-   20 00 F8    JSR   $F800
F81C-   C4 2C       CPY   $2C
F81E-   B0 11       BCS   $F831
F820-   C8          INY
F821-   20 0E F8    JSR   $F80E
F824-   90 F6       BCC   $F81C
*
```

Typing L again would disassemble the next 20 instructions starting at location $F826.

Not everything in the Apple's memory is program instructions. Many areas of memory contain data or are linked to hardware peripherals. Unfortunately, the Monitor's disassembler cannot differentiate between code and data, and will try to interpret everything as assembly language code.

The Mini-Assembler

The Integer BASIC ROM of the original Apple II, and the Monitor in the Enhanced Apple IIe, IIc, IIc Plus, and IIgs contains a Mini-Assembler which can be used to write short assembly language programs. It is called "mini" because it is not a fully-featured assembler with macros and symbolic labels. However, it is quite convenient for writing short assembly language programs, and saves much effort over hand assembly and entry of machine code. Unfortunately, the technique of writing assembly programs is beyond the scope of this book; see Appendix A for some books from which you may learn assembly language.

Originally, the Mini-Assembler was part of the Integer BASIC ROM, and was therefore unavailable on the Apple II Plus or when Firmware Applesoft was in use. However, the ROM of every Apple since (and including) the Enhanced IIe contains the Mini-Assembler.

Entering the Mini-Assembler

On the original Apple II with the Old Monitor ROM, the Mini-Assembler is located at address $F666. Type the following line to enter the Mini-Assembler from the Machine Language Monitor:

```
*F666G
```

Or from the Integer BASIC prompt, enter the following command:

```
>CALL -2458
```

For all other Apples, you must type a single exclamation mark (!). The prompt will change from an asterisk (*) to an exclamation mark and the speaker will beep to signify that you have left the Monitor (or BASIC), and are now in the Mini-Assembler.

If you followed these instructions, yet the prompt did not change, then you probably have an Apple II Plus, an early revision of the Apple IIc, or an unenhanced Apple IIe which does not have the Mini-Assembler. One way to get the Mini-Assembler on these three machines is to load Integer BASIC into the Language Card. This should be done automatically when booting the DOS 3.3 System Master disk. Be sure to type INT to activate Integer BASIC before entering the Monitor.

Executing Monitor Commands in the Mini-Assembler

In the Mini-Assembler of the original Apple II (in the Integer ROM) and in the Mini-Assembler provided by loading the DOS 3.3 System Master with a Language Card, a Monitor command may be executed by prepending it with a dollar sign ($), such as $L to use the disassembler. This ability will save you time from having to switch between the Monitor and the Mini-Assembler. You can execute and debug your assembly language program entirely from the Mini-Assembler.

Unfortunately, when the Mini-Assembler was reintroduced in the ROM of the Enhanced IIe and later models, this functionality was not included. Attempting to use a dollar sign on these models will be met with a syntax error.

Leaving the Mini-Assembler

To leave the Mini-Assembler and return to the Monitor, press RETURN on a blank line. This technique will not work on the original Apple II, which has no intrinsic command to leave the Mini-Assembler; instead, you must press the RESET key. Alternatively, you may execute a Monitor command to get back to the Monitor, by using the dollar sign method as introduced in the previous section. The Monitor is located at address $FF69, so enter $FF69G to escape the Mini-Assembler and re-enter the Monitor.

Other Monitor commands, such as a dollar sign followed by CONTROL-C, should work on the Apple II Plus and some models of original Apple II as a way to leave the Mini-Assembler. Finally, on an original model Apple II without an Applesoft Firmware card, CONTROL-C will return you to Integer BASIC, $3D0G to disk-based Applesoft, and $0G to cassette-based Applesoft.

Instruction Formats

The 6502 microprocessor has six instruction formats used when programming it. These formats in turn correspond to the eleven addressing modes used by the 6502. The 65C02 introduced two new addressing modes as well as ten new instructions. However, only the Mini-Assembler on the Apple IIgs supports the new 65C02 instructions and addressing modes.

It is important to note that the Mini-Assembler, like the Monitor, does not require a dollar sign ($) in front of hexadecimal values. It merely assumes that all values are in hex notation. You may, however, enter a dollar sign if you so wish.

Absolute or *direct* addressing refers to a one- or two-byte static address at which memory will be loaded or stored. Following is an example:

```
! STA 300
```

Immediate addressing refers to a literal value that will be loaded into a microprocessor register. Here is an example:

```
! LDX #00
```

Note that the number sign (#) in front of the operand, 00, must be included, otherwise the Mini-Assembler will treat the operand as an absolute address, not a literal value.

By the way, immediate addressing in assembly language has nothing to do with immediate execution in BASIC. The term is the same, but the meaning is not, which can unfortunately lead to some confusion.

Indexed addressing adds the contents of either the X or Y register to the specified memory address, and uses the sum to load or store data. Following is an example:

```
! LDA 2000,Y
```

Pre-indexed indirect addressing takes the sum of the operand and a register to compute a zero page memory address. The contents of this address and the location immediately following it are used as the final address for the instruction. Here is an example:

```
! CMP (10,X)
```

Post-indexed indirect addressing takes the value at the given address, then adds the register contents to that value. This sum is then used as the final address to be used by the instruction. Here is an example:

```
! ORA (2F),Y
```

Indirect addressing is similar to indexed addressing, but is simpler because it does not involve any registers. In this mode, the operand specifies a memory location, and the contents of that location are used as the final destination, as in this example:

```
! JMP(3FE)
```

Such a location is known as a *vector*, an address that points to another memory address. In this example, the JMP instruction will cause a branch to whatever location is specified at $3FE and $3FF.

Syntax Errors

The Mini-Assembler will detect and alert the user of errors upon assembly language instruction entry. It will detect illegal mnemonics, addressing errors, out-of-bounds relative branching, and other mistakes. The speaker beeps and the incorrect line is printed again with a caret (^) beneath the erroneous character in the instruction. Simply correct the line by retyping it to continue.

Using the Mini-Assembler

Using the Mini-Assembler is fairly straight-forward. The Mini-Assembler only keeps track of one variable and that happens to be the program counter. Think of it like line numbers in BASIC, except that the program counter keeps track of the next memory address for each instruction. This is all done automatically for you, like using AUTO line-numbering in Integer BASIC.

To initialize the program counter, enter an address separated by a colon before entering any assembly language instruction. Further instructions will follow from this initial address, and it will be incremented as needed. Just type a space before the instruction to take advantage of this feature. You may change the program counter at any time by simply entering an address again.

As with BASIC programs, it is best to have a good idea, generally something written on paper, as to what your assembly language program will look like, otherwise you will spend a lot of time revising it by making space for more instructions or changing branch addresses.

Each line entered in the Mini-Assembler will be disassembled, thus showing the object code that the Apple will ultimately execute. The object code is shown on the left, and the assembly code that you entered is shown on the right.

Sample Session

The following illustrates as session with the Mini-Assembler to write and test a trivial assembly language program. This program will print the Apple's entire ASCII table. The source for this program is as follows:

```
300: LDX #$00
302: TXA
303: JSR $FDED
306: DEX
307: BNE $0302
309: RTS
```

First, enter the Mini-Assembler using any method described earlier.

```
*F666G
```

The first line of code should set the program counter:

```
!300: LDX #00
```

Remember that it is only necessary to enter the number sign (#) to indicate immediate addressing mode. The Mini-Assembler interprets all numeric values as hex, so entering a dollar sign in front of the 00 is unnecessary. As soon as you press RETURN, your line will be replaced by the assembled version, with the disassembly shown at right:

```
0300-   A2 00       LDX   #$00
!
```

Now the next line, TXA, does not need to have the program counter set. The Mini-Assembler knows what to do:

```
! TXA
0302-   8A          TXA
```

Remember that if you do not enter an address for the program counter, you must type a space instead. If you make a typing mistake and get flagged with a syntax error, just type the line again. The program counter does not advance when an incorrect line is entered.

Continue entering the rest of the program until you reach the final instruction, RTS. Your screen should look similar to this:

```
*F666G

0300-   A2 00       LDX   #$00
0302-   8A          TXA
0303-   20 ED FD    JSR   $FDED
0306-   CA          DEX
0307-   D0 F9       BNE   $0302
0309-   60          RTS
!
```

At this point, the program is assembled and ready to run. If your Mini-Assembler allows you to directly execute Monitor commands, type the following:

```
$300G
```

Otherwise, leave the Mini-Assembler (usually by pressing RETURN with a blank line), and enter this Monitor command:

```
*300G
```

You should be greeted with the Apple's full character set, both normal, inverse, and flashing.

When you are finished entering an assembly language program, it is a good idea to save it to disk or tape, as explained earlier in this chapter. You should also use the Monitor's List command to make sure that the program was entered accurately. Remember that on the original Apple II, you can do this by typing a dollar sign before the Monitor command. On other models of Apple, you will have to exit the Mini-Assembler to execute the program or list it.

If you are becoming more interested in learning assembly language, then as soon as you finish reading this section, take a look at Appendix A for some books to read on the subject.

Debugging Machine Language Programs

The Monitor includes three facilities for debugging machine language programs. These are: trace, single step, and CPU register display and modification. Unfortunately, the Monitor ROM of the Apple II Plus, IIe, and IIgs does not have the trace and single step features. Some early revisions of the Apple IIc also lack the trace and step commands.

Trace

Tracing a machine language program is the same idea as tracing a BASIC program (covered in Chapter 5). It is a debugging aid intended to help the programmer visualize exactly what a program is doing during its execution. However, since machine language programs don't have line numbers, the memory address of each instruction is printed instead. In addition, the hex code for each machine instruction is printed, the assembly language mnemonic for that instruction, and finally, the values of the CPU registers after that instruction was executed. All of this continues until a BRK instruction (hex code $00) is encountered.

To trace a program, enter its starting address, then T, like so:

```
*300T
```

That will trace the program starting at memory location $300 until a BRK instruction appears. If your program ends with an RTS (as is customary) and the Trace reaches it, then the Apple must be reset by pressing CONTROL-RESET, because the Monitor will go off tracing forever at that point. However, the Trace will return as usual from any subroutine called in the program. If you entered the short program shown in the Mini-Assembler sample session, try tracing it with 300T to see what happens:

```
*300T

0300-    A2 00         LDX    #$00
 A=FF X=00 Y=00 P=22 S=FD
0302-    8A            TXA
 A=00 X=00 Y=00 P=22 S=FD
0303-    20 ED FD      JSR    $FDED
 A=00 X=00 Y=00 P=22 S=FD
FDED-    6C 36 00      JMP    ($0036)
 A=00 X=00 Y=00 P=22 S=FD
FDF0-    C9 A0         CMP    #$A0
 A=00 X=00 Y=00 P=20 S=FB
 A=00 X=90 02          BCC    $FDF6
FDF2-    90 02         BCC    $FDF6
 A=00 X=00 Y=00 P=20 S=FB
FDF6-    84 35         STY    $35
 A=00 X=00 Y=00 P=20 S=FB
FDF8-    48            PHA
 A=00 X=00 Y=00 P=20 S=FA
```

Notice from the above output that Trace will follow all branches in the program, including branches to Monitor subroutines (in this case, COUT at $FDED).

Since Trace is designed to stop when it encounters a BRK instruction, it makes sense to insert such an instruction after the section of code that you wish to test, and start the trace at the beginning of that code section.

One additional advantage to tracing just small sections of code at a time is that the Trace command incurs a time penalty: tracing, disassembling, and reporting the register contents after every instruction takes longer to do than just executing the instructions as usual. Therefore, it is best to trace just a section of a program, rather than the entire thing. Executing the ASCII table program with the G command takes less than a second. Tracing through it with T takes several minutes (the author couldn't be bothered to wait around to find out how many).

Single Step

Single step execution means that only a single instruction of a machine language program is executed at a time. Each instruction results in the same diagnostic output as for the trace: address, hex code, assembly mnemonic, and register values.

To start single stepping a program, enter its starting address, followed by an S, as demonstrated:

```
*300S
```

This command will execute the first instruction at memory location $300, then return to the Monitor prompt. To step through each successive instruction, enter an S. Like the Trace command, the Single Step will stop at a BRK instruction.

As an illustration, here is what a few steps through the ASCII table program (from a previous section) looks like:

```
*300S

0300-   A2 00         LDX   #$00
 A=AA X=00 Y=FF P=22 S=F5
*S

0302-   8A            TXA
```

```
 A=00 X=00 Y=FF P=22 S=F5
*S

0303-   20 ED FD    JSR   $FDED
 A=00 X=00 Y=FF P=22 S=F5
*
```

Oftentimes, using the Step debugging aid is more useful than Trace, because it enables fine-grained control of the execution of the program. It is also easier to switch between Step and other Monitor commands, something that cannot be done with Trace.

Displaying CPU Registers

The microprocessor inside your Apple, be it the 6502, 65C02, or 65C816, has a number of high-speed, internal storage areas, known as registers. A *register* is commonly used to hold the input and results for a mathematical operation, as well as the index counter for a loop. When you program the Apple in BASIC, you do not need to worry about the registers, even though they are all being used. Assembly and machine language programmers deal with the registers directly in all of their programs.

Every model of Apple except for the IIgs has either a 6502 or 65C02 microprocessor with five registers each capable of holding a single 8-bit byte. These registers are known as the Accumulator (A), Index Register X (X), Index Register Y (Y), Processor Status (P), and Stack Pointer (S). The Apple IIgs uses a 65C816 microprocessor with considerably more registers (of which some are, to be technical, pseudo-registers or flags), some of which may hold a 16-bit, 2-byte value.

To display (examine) the registers, press CONTROL-E and RETURN. If you have just turned on the Apple, entered the Monitor, and used this command, you'll get a result like this:

```
A=FF X=FF Y=FF P=00 S=FF
```

This shows the current values of the five registers in the 6502 or 65C02. They are the Accumulator, the X register, the Y register, the Processor status, and the Stack Pointer. Each register can hold 8 bits of data, meaning that possible values range from 0 to

255 ($FF in hex). As always, the Monitor shows all numeric values in hex. These register values will be used the next time that the Monitor is used to step, trace, or execute a machine language program.

The Apple IIgs has more than just five registers. You will get a display such as the following:

```
A=0000 X=0000 Y=0000 S=01F4 D=0000 P=00
B=00 K=00 M=0C Q=88 L=1 m=1 x=1 e=1
```

Notice that the Accumulator, X, and Y registers are 16 bits long. The Apple IIgs is a 16-bit computer, meaning that its registers can handle larger numbers at a time, but it can also work in 8-bit mode for compatibility with older Apple software.

When you execute a machine language program with the G command, these are the starting register values that it will use.

Modifying CPU Registers

To change the values of the microprocessor registers, they must be on the last line displayed by the Monitor. Press CONTROL-E and RETURN to display them again if not. Then at the prompt, type a colon then one or more new values. These new values are applied to the registers from left to right. For example,

```
*: 3C
```

will set the Accumulator to $3C, whereas:

```
*: 3C 01 02
```

will set the Accumulator to $3C, the X register to $01 and the Y register to $02. Register values cannot be skipped; they are always applied from left to right. That is, to set the Processor Status register, for example, you must retype the three preceding register values, then a new value for the Processor Status register.

Type CONTROL-E again and you will see that your new values are displayed. These register values will take effect the next time that a program is stepped, traced, or executed from the Monitor.

Modifying a Single Register

In the Apple IIgs Monitor only, one may alter the contents of a single register by typing the new value, an equal sign, and the letter representing the register. The change takes effect as soon as the next program is executed. For example, to set the value of the A register to $FFDD, enter the following:

```
*FFDD=A
```

Pressing CONTROL-E then RETURN will verify that the change was made. Table 11-1 shows all 65C816 registers and their one-letter mnemonic.

Register/Flag Name	Mnemonic Letter
Accumulator	A
X Index	X
Y Index	Y
Direct Page	D
Data Bank	B
Program Register	K
Stack Pointer	S
Processor Status	P
Machine State	M
Quagmire State	Q
Accumulator Mode	m
Index Mode	x
Emulation Mode	e
Language Card Bank	L
Filter Mask	F

Table 11-1. 65C816 CPU Registers and Flags

Entering Multiple Commands

You may enter more than one Monitor command on a single line, and each command will be executed in sequence. For example, entering LLL will disassemble 60 machine language instructions. Single letter commands do not need to be separated by a space, but all other commands must be.

User-Defined Command

The Monitor may be programmed to execute a command of your choosing in response to CONTROL-Y being pressed. Such a command is called the User-Defined Command, and it will cause the Monitor to jump to location $3F8.

At location $3F8 there is enough room for three bytes of data: a JMP plus the address to a machine language routine. It is up to you to place the appropriate instruction code and address bytes.

The following example will cause CONTROL-Y to warm-start DOS (either DOS 3.3 or ProDOS) by jumping to location $3D0. First, one must know that the hex code for a JMP instruction is $4C. Secondly, one must know that an address must be stored "backward," with the low-byte first, and the high-byte second. With this information, the line that would be entered into the Monitor is as follows:

```
*3F8: 4C D0 03
```

Now, whenever you press CONTROL-Y and RETURN from the Monitor, DOS will be warm-started. The function of the User-Defined Command may be changed by merely altering the location for the JMP instruction.

Working with BASIC and Machine Language

There are some tasks for which BASIC is unsuitable, such as any application requiring precise timing or speed, or advanced animation or sound. Combining BASIC and machine language programs is certainly possible, but doing so requires some advance planning and forethought. The principal consideration is making sure that the programs do not try to occupy or use the same memory locations. The Apple has several large reserved areas of memory for the text and graphics screen, the operating system (either DOS 3.3 or ProDOS), and the BASIC program itself or Applesoft interpreter. Any machine language program you use must be strategically located so as not to interfere with any of these reserved areas of RAM. Secondly, if you will be using a subroutine that requires arguments or that provides output, your program must negotiate provisions for doing so.

A great source for machine language subroutines is the Monitor. Its advantages are notable: it is always resident in ROM, it has been thoroughly tested and debugged, and it is fully documented and accessible to the programmer. A full list of useful Machine Language Monitor subroutines may be found in Appendix H.

Integrating Machine Language Subroutines

Once you have identified a machine language subroutine that you wish to make use of in your BASIC program, you should ensure that it does not duplicate intrinsic functionality already present in BASIC. For example, the Monitor includes many high-resolution graphics routines which already exist in Applesoft, but are absent from Integer BASIC.

Next, you will need to know two important things about the subroutine: its entry point, and whether it accepts arguments. The entry point is the starting address of the subroutine, and will be used in the BASIC CALL statement. The arguments, or parameters, may pose a problem. Unless the machine language program was written with an interface to BASIC in mind, it will likely require that parameters be passed via microprocessor registers, and likewise, if it returns a value, will do so via one or more registers. BASIC has no way of accessing any microprocessor registers, so additional machine language code will have to be written to interface BASIC and the subroutine. Fortunately, most Monitor subroutines that require arguments already have an equivalent BASIC command, and many Monitor subroutines do not require any arguments at all.

After having made these preparations, you may finally include a call to the subroutine in your BASIC program. To improve readability of your program, it is a good idea to assign a numeric variable to serve as a label for the subroutine address. In this example, a BASIC program calls a Monitor subroutine located at $FF3A that beeps the speaker. One of the first lines of the program would read:

```
10 BEEP = -198 : REM ADDRESS OF MONITOR SUBROUTINE
```

and a later program line that calls this subroutine would look like:

```
100 CALL BEEP : REM ACCESS BEEP MONITOR SUBROUTINE
```

Now there will be little doubt as to what each CALL statement is doing.

Problems with Subroutines

Unless a subroutine is *relocatable*, containing no absolute references to itself, it must be loaded at an exact location in memory. Most of the time, it will not matter if a subroutine is relocatable or not if it does not conflict with BASIC or any other reserved area of memory. However, if a conflict does arise, an assembler or relocator can be used to automatically modify the program for use at a different address. If your only assembler is the Mini-Assembler, you will have to perform the task of relocation yourself. You may have to account for Apples with differing memory sizes, operating systems, the high-resolution graphics screen, or larger-than-usual BASIC programs. Another advantage of using Machine Language Monitor subroutines becomes apparent: they need never be relocated.

When programming in Applesoft, be sure to make use of USR whenever you need to pass arguments to a machine language subroutine. Unlike CALL, USR reserves locations $9D through $A3 to store the parameter that will be passed to the subroutine. Once in the subroutine, you can also use that area to pass results back to BASIC. In order to use USR, your BASIC program must use POKE to place a JMP instruction in locations 10 through 12 (decimal) to the beginning of the machine language program to be called by USR. See Appendix B for full instructions on how to do so.

Chapter 12 : The IIgs and GS/OS

If you have an Apple IIgs and have only been following the examples in this book so far, you've been missing out on a lot of potential that is realized in the Apple IIgs system. The GS is really two machines in one: it's a classic Apple II machine on one side, and it's an enhanced, almost Mac-like machine on the other.

There is so much to say about the Apple IIgs that an entire book could be written about it. In the interests of space, this chapter will go over the basics of the Apple IIgs and its operating system, and will cover some popular programs.

The IIgs Operating System

The latest version of the IIgs operating system, GS/OS, is 6.0.1, released in 1993. It is commonly referred to as System 6. Disk images may be freely obtained from Apple Computer's Web site, or you can order disks from Syndicomm. While this system is approaching 20 years of age, it still presents a remarkably usable interface.

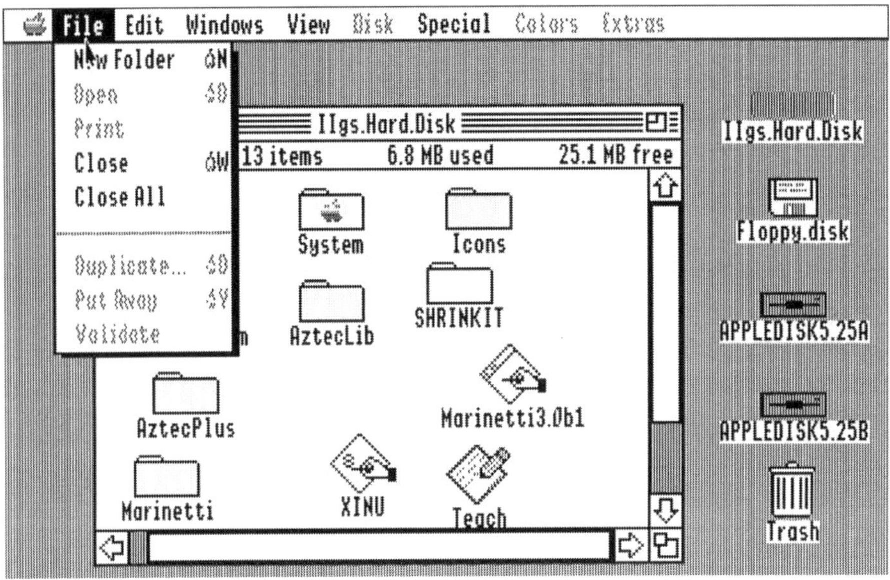

Figure 12-1. The IIgs System 6.0.1 desktop

System 6 presents the usual GUI (Graphical User Interface) metaphors of icons, windows, and menus. In case you are unfamiliar with using a GUI or the mouse, the next few pages of this chapter cover all of the basics, starting with the mouse.

In any case, some parts of the System 6 GUI may be new to you, so you are advised to at least glance over the material.

Starting System 6

If you have a hard disk system, your IIgs should start up System 6 as soon as it is turned on. Otherwise, you will have to insert the

System Startup Disk into the first 3.5" drive, then power on the Apple.

After a few moments, you should see the message "Welcome to the IIgs." A red progress bar will mark the advancement of the startup process, during which a few small pictures will appear at the bottom of the screen.

When the startup process is complete, the screen will change to show a white bar across the top with words. The rest of the screen below should be blue, except for some more small pictures at the right, which may include a hard disk, a 3.5" disk, and a metal trash can.

If you already know how to use the mouse, you may skip to the next section on Using the Finder. Otherwise, read on.

How to Use the Mouse

If you've never used the mouse before, getting proficient with it takes a bit of practice at first, but it becomes second nature after that. The mouse is meant to fit in your hand, either one, and be oriented with the cord pointing away from your hand.

On top of the mouse is a single button, used to issue commands with the mouse. Moving the mouse around on the table top should produce a similar movement of the black arrow pointer, also called the *cursor*, on the Apple IIgs screen. Whichever direction the mouse is moved, the cursor moves too. For example, if you roll the mouse to the left, the cursor moves left on the screen. This is because there is a ball underneath the mouse that rolls on the desk top that translates the physical mouse movement to the Apple IIgs. If it doesn't, then perhaps the mouse is positioned the wrong way. The cord of the mouse should come away from your fingertips. The only limits for the cursor are the four extreme edges of the screen.

Your mouse likely has a limited area of movement too. If you run out of room on your desk or work area for moving the mouse, simply pick up the mouse and move it to a better position. You will notice that the black arrow does not move when the mouse is suspended in air.

Using the mouse requires learning just four simple procedures: pointing, clicking, double-clicking, and dragging.

Pointing

The skill of pointing is fairly straightforward: it means to move the mouse so that the arrow, or cursor, on the screen (we'll call it the cursor from now on) is on top of some object on the screen. The tip of the cursor should be positioned squarely on the object to which you're pointing. This might be a menu, an icon, or a button (these terms will all be explained a bit later). Practice pointing at various features of your Apple IIgs screen (using the cursor arrow, not your finger).

Clicking

It is important that you learn the skill of pointing, because clicking is usually the second thing that happens afterward. When you point to an object on screen, you can click the mouse, by pressing and releasing the button, to make something happen. Try doing it now. Point your cursor at the Apple logo in the top left of the screen, then press the mouse button. If you did it right, by pressing and then releasing the mouse button, you should have seen something new appear on the screen for a moment, then disappear. Clicking the Apple logo made a menu appear.

The type of things that you could click include options from a list, icons, and buttons.

In many cases, clicking something on the screen will cause it to be highlighted, typically by inverting color from white to black. Doing so is known as selecting the item. The most common items which can be selected are icons, and items from a list. These will be explained shortly.

Double-Clicking

Double-clicking is the natural extension of clicking. Whereas a click means to press and release the mouse button just once, a double-click involves pressing and releasing the button twice in rapid succession.

To practice, point the cursor at any image of a folder, floppy disk, or hard drive. Then double-click it. If you did it right, a window will open, showing the contents of that object.

Dragging

The final mouse movement combines clicking and pointing into one. To drag means to hold the mouse button down while moving the mouse. To see what menu items are in the Apple menu, you must perform a dragging operation over the menu. Point to the Apple, then click and hold the mouse button. As you drag the mouse down the menu that appears, each menu item in turn will be highlighted. Releasing the mouse button when the cursor is on the desired command will execute that command. Or you can move the cursor off of the menu and release the mouse button. The menu will disappear and nothing else will happen.

Dragging is also used to move icons around the screen.

Using the Finder

The Finder is the program that presents the desktop metaphor of the Apple IIgs. It allows you to view windows containing icons that represent documents and programs. It then enables you to load programs, rename files, copy documents, initialize disks, and perform all sorts of other commands.

The difference from the disk operations presented in Chapter 7 is that with the Finder, you can use the mouse to select commands from a menu, instead of having to memorize and type in commands from the keyboard. If you do prefer using the keyboard, many Finder commands have an equivalent keyboard shortcut.

These shortcuts are marked with a hollow Apple logo and a letter. Pressing the COMMAND key on the keyboard in association with the letter will execute the menu command. For example, COMMAND-O will open the currently selected icon.

About Icons

The "small pictures" that you see on the screen are in fact icons. These *icons* represent the various types of items on a disk: application programs, documents, and folders. A folder, sometimes called a directory, is nothing but a container for more icons. Documents, of course, contain your work. Finally, applications are what allow you to accomplish some useful task with the Apple. These are the three main kinds of icons that you will encounter.

Icons can be acted upon, but first you must select one or more of them. When selected, an icon will change colors, becoming inverted. Figure 12-2 shows the three main types of icons, both unselected and selected.

Opening icons

Opening an icon will reveal its contents. There are two ways of opening an icon. The first method is simplest and most common: double-click the icon. The second method involves selecting the icon by clicking it, then choosing Open from the File menu.

If the icon represents an application, then it will start running. For most documents that you created, the application that was used to save that document will open, and the contents of the document will be displayed (you may come across some documents which cannot be opened by double-clicking; these typically require an application which you have not installed on the IIgs).

Folder icons open a new window showing the contents of the folder. A few icons can't be opened; instead, a dialog box will

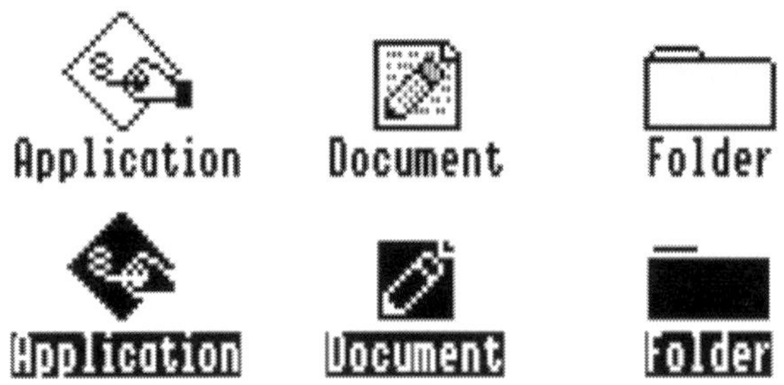

Figure 12-2. Three kinds of icons, unselected and selected

inform you of this situation. Most of the icons that can't be opened are part of the IIgs system, and you don't need to interact with them.

Moving Icons

An icon can be moved in one of two ways: either its position within a window can be changed, or the icon can be moved to a new folder. Both operations involve clicking and dragging. First click the icon to select it, then drag the icon to a new location by dragging the mouse. Release the mouse button when the icon has reached its final destination. When moving an icon to a new folder, you may either drag the icon into that folder's window, if it's open, or onto the folder icon.

Using Menus

Instead of typing commands on the keyboard, the Finder and other GS/OS programs use a system of menus for command-giving. Menus are located in the menu bar, a white strip running across the top of the screen. At the left should be a colored Apple logo, known as the Apple menu. Other words to the right, typically nouns, make up the remainder of the menus. These menus will change depending on what application is currently running, whereas the Apple menu is always available.

Each menu has a logical collection of menu items, or commands. Menu items are typically verbs, since they describe a particular action. The File menu has commands for working with files, such as opening a file, printing a file, and duplicating a file.

Choosing a menu item will instruct the Apple IIgs to execute it. To open a menu and display its list of commands, point to the menu title, then press the mouse button. The menu will appear as long as the mouse button is held down. Drag the mouse until the cursor is over the desired menu item. It will turn black to indicate that it's been selected. Finally, release the mouse button to choose that menu item. In Figure 12-3, the Preferences... menu item is highlighted. Releasing the mouse button will cause that command to be activated.

Just as menus change depending on what application is open, so too do the menus and menu items change. Menus and menu items are said to be context-sensitive. That is, they may only be chosen in certain circumstances. If these circumstances or requirements are not met, then the menu item will be dimmed (shown in gray). If all of the menu items in a menu are dimmed, then that menu's title will also be dimmed.

For example, if there are no open windows in the Finder, the Windows menu, and all of its commands, will be dimmed, since there are no windows to work with. Likewise, if no icon is currently selected in the Finder, the Icon Info... item will be dimmed in the Special menu. That command can only be used if one or more icons are selected.

Some menu items are followed by an ellipsis (...). This means one of two things: either the command will present a dialog box asking for additional input before the command is executed, or that a window will open. Some commands open an informational window, such as the About This Apple IIgs... menu item in the Apple menu. Other commands, such as Initialize... in the Disk menu, require additional input from the user.

Navigating Windows

Windows show you some sort of information or data. The Finder uses windows to show the contents of folders. Other applications, such as a word processing program or a drawing program, use a

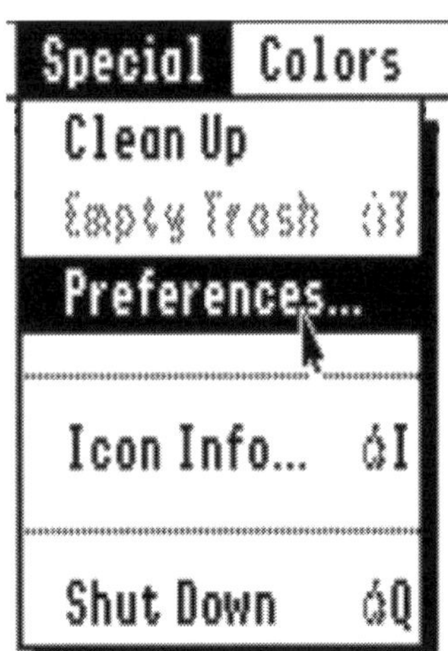

Figure 12-3. Choosing a menu item

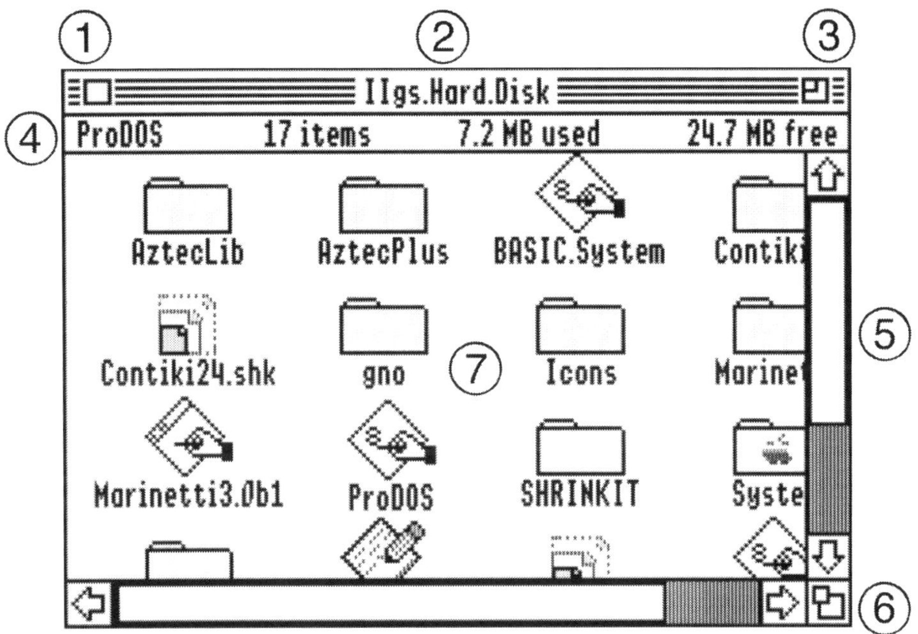

Figure 12-4. Parts of a window

window to show your work.

Finder windows are made up of seven major parts. Windows in other applications may have some, but not necessarily all, of these parts. Figure 12-4 shows a typical Finder window and its seven major parts.

1.) Close Box
Clicking the close box, the white square at the top-left corner of the window, will dismiss the window, making it go away.

2.) Title Bar
The title bar runs the full width of the window and has the name of the window in the center. The title bar has four lines running across it if the window is active, otherwise the title bar will be white.

Clicking and dragging the title bar will move the window around the screen. This is useful to do if the window is covering up some other icons.

Some applications may use a slightly different style of title bar, but it should behave similarly.

3.) Zoom Box
The window can be automatically resized by clicking the zoom box.

4.) Status Bar
Just underneath the title bar is the status bar. It shows information about the current folder window, as well as the current disk on which the folder is located. From left to right is the filesystem of the disk, typically ProDOS; the total number of items in the current window; how much disk space is used on the entire disk; and how much free disk space is left.

5.) Scroll Bar
Sometimes the contents of a window exceed the current size of the window, or even of the IIgs screen. The window may be thought of as merely a viewport onto its contents. Moving the scroll bar will reveal icons or other information that were previously out of sight. The concept is similar to that of rolling and unrolling a paper scroll. Most windows have at most two scroll bars: one for moving horizontally, the other for moving vertically.

A scroll bar is made of two parts. The first part consists of two arrows for scrolling the window contents upward or downward (or left or right, depending the scroll bar's orientation). Between the arrows is the scroll box, which is white. The scroll box moves between a gray field that represents the extent of the window. The size of the white scroll box is proportional to the amount of the window that is currently being displayed.

Scroll bars turn white when the entire contents of the window can be displayed at once.

6.) Resize Box
Clicking and dragging this area will make the window larger or smaller. Depending on the window's contents, resizing it may cause the scroll bars to become active, or the size of the scroll boxes to change.

7.) Window Contents
Finally, the rest of the window is devoted to showing its contents. In the Finder, that generally consists of icons.

Finder windows have two different methods of displaying icons. The first method, shown in Figure 12-4, is known as icon view, where every icon and its name is shown. The icons may be moved anywhere in the window, and they aren't necessarily sorted by any criteria. The second method is known as List view, where each icon is shown in a list, along with some other details about it, such as Size, Kind, and Last modified date. The list is sorted by either Name, Date, Size, or Kind. Use the View menu to change window views and sorting criteria.

When in List view, the status bar portion of the window will show another line with column headers. The column that is currently being used to sort the icons is shown in bold. Clicking any of the other column titles will sort the icons by its means. For example, clicking Size will sort the icons in descending order of file size (the largest sized files will be at the top of the list).

Renaming Icons

While almost any icon can be renamed, you should generally stay to renaming only the documents and folders that you created. Changing the name of system icons could cause your Apple IIgs to cease functioning correctly.

To rename an icon, click its name. The icon and name will turn black, showing that they're selected. The arrow cursor will change to an I-Beam, showing that you may now edit the name. Start typing the new name, then press RETURN when finished. If you change your mind, and decide that you want to keep the old name, delete the entire name, then press RETURN. Alternatively, you may press ESCAPE. Either way, the old name will reappear.

In GS/OS, filenames must follow the ProDOS naming convention, except that both upper and lower case letters may be used. Filenames are limited to 15 characters in length, and may only have letters and periods. The name must start with a letter.

To make things more confusing, there are times when an icon can fall under different naming regulations. The most common disk format that you will use with the Apple IIgs is ProDOS, but GS/OS knows about other disk formats too, such as DOS 3.3, HFS, and MS-DOS. Each of these formats has different rules for naming files. For example, icons on an HFS disk may have names up to 32 characters long, and can include spaces. Fortunately, the IIgs will let you know if the name that you've picked isn't suitable.

Deleting Icons

The Trash Can icon is used to discard other icons that you no longer want. These could include old folders, applications, or documents that you don't need. You may periodically need to delete files in order to make more room on the disk.

The Trash, located at the bottom-right of the Finder desktop, bulges to indicate that one or more icons have been thrown out. Icons moved to the Trash are not instantly deleted, but instead remain there for some time in case you change your mind and wish to retrieve them later. Emptying the Trash permanently removes the files within it, reclaims their disk space, and returns the Trash icon back to its usual, nonbulging state. The Empty Trash menu command in the Special menu is used to explicitly empty the Trash. At other times, the Trash is automatically emptied, such as when launching an application or starting up the Apple IIgs. Therefore, it is not a good idea to move an icon to the Trash unless you are fairly certain that you no longer wish to keep it.

Ejecting Disks

The Trash icon is also used to eject disks and remove shared network volumes. To do so, simply drag the disk or volume icon to the Trash. In this case, dragging the icon to the Trash signifies that you are done with the icon, not that you want it to be thrown out or erased. You may also select the disk's icon and choose Eject from the Disk menu.

Working with Compressed Files and Archives

Back in the days when disk storage was at a premium, various compression formats were devised. These compression algorithms sought out redundant data in a file and packed it in a more compact form. Still other formats were designed not to save space, but instead to facilitate transport of a file across foreign computer systems by encoding the file.

The most common compression format in the Apple II world is called ShrinkIt, and it will work on almost any model of Apple. ShrinkIt is both a compression and an archiving program in that it both reduces file size (compression) and can group multiple files and folders into one (archiving). The version of ShrinkIt for the IIgs is called ShrinkItGS. When ShrinkIt files are transferred across the Internet, they are often encoded with BinScii. This encoding ensures that the file and archive contents don't get mutilated when being sent across foreign (non-Apple) systems.

ShrinkIt for the IIgs can compress and decompress files as well as entire disks. Additionally, ShrinkItGS can handle StuffIt 1.5.1 archives, ARC files, ZOO files, Compress files, Binary II files, and ACU archives. Most of these other file types are compression formats used on Macintosh or UNIX-based systems.

ShrinkIt is fairly straight-forward to operate. To extract files from a compressed archive (known as unshrinking), either double-click the .SHK file in the Finder, or from ShrinkIt, choose Open Archive... from the File menu.

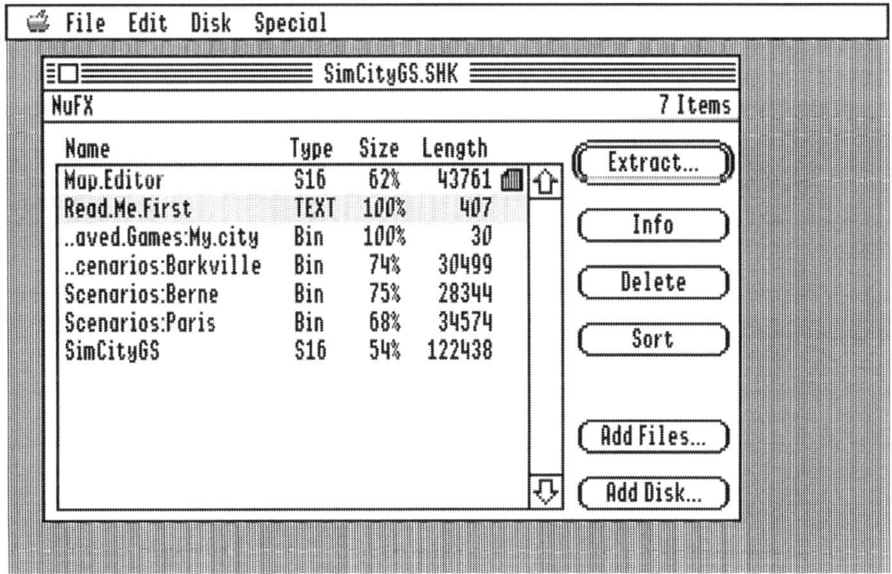

Figure 12-5. ShrinkItGS

Once the archive is open, a screen similar to that shown in Figure 12-5 will appear. Each file in the archive is listed with its file type, compression ratio, and file size.

To extract every file from the archive, press COMMAND-A, then click the Extract... button. Or to select just some of the files, click and select while holding the COMMAND key.

ShrinkIt can also be used to create new file archives. Simply choose New File Archive... from the File menu, and select the desired files and folders. Additional files may be added later using the Add Files... button.

Finally, in some cases, such as with older 5.25" disks, it may be desirable to make an archive of the entire disk. Such an archive has the extension .SDK. To make a new disk archive, choose New Disk Archive... from the Disk menu. Click OK after reading the informational dialog text, then select a disk drive.

The Control Panel

The IIgs has a number of customizable settings that are all accessible via the built-in Control Panel. Some of these settings include the current date and time, keyboard layout, mouse tracking, and slot configuration.

To access the Control Panel, press COMMAND-CONTROL-ESCAPE. This will cause a list of Desk Accessories to appear. Choose the Control Panel option, and press RETURN. You may also open the Control Panel by holding down the OPTION key when powering on the IIgs, and then pressing 1.

The Control Panel of the ROM 3 IIgs has some differences from the earlier revisions of IIgs. These differences are as follows:

- The ROM 01 has an Options section for the keyboard and mouse settings, whereas the ROM 3 does not.
- The ROM 01 has a setting for High Speed Mouse.
- The ROM 3 has two separate sections for Mouse and Keyboard settings.

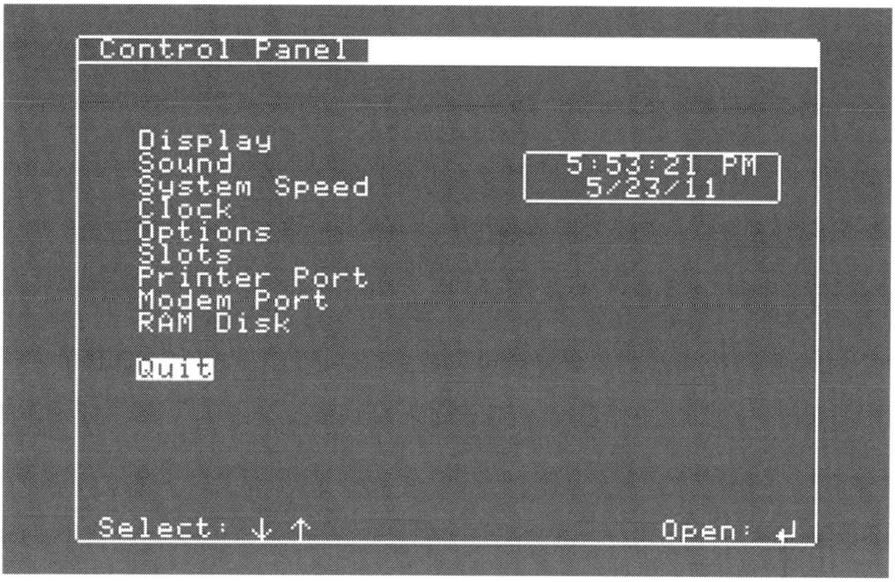

Figure 12-6. The ROM 01 IIgs control panel

- The ROM 01 has two size settings for the RAM Disk, whereas the ROM 3 has only one setting, and also a Resize after Reset option.
- The Slot settings for selecting AppleTalk networking work a bit differently.

Common Control Panel Settings

The default text screen settings for the Apple IIgs are white text on a bluc background in 40 columns mode. By choosing the Display option from the Control Panel, you can change the screen colors as well as default column mode. Many Apple IIgs users operate with 80 columns, white text, and black background and border.

The IIgs has a 65C816 processor that is capable of running both classic, 8-bit Apple II programs as well as newer IIgs programs at 2.8 MHz. In some cases, such as with games or other timing-critical programs, it may be desirable to have the Apple run at a reduced speed of 1 MHz. The System Speed panel has two settings: Fast and Normal, for 2.8 MHz and 1 MHz, respectively. In some situations, the speed change may not take effect until the IIgs is restarted with COMMAND-CONTROL-RESET.

The Apple IIgs is the only model of Apple to have a built-in clock and calendar which is maintained by a battery when the computer is off. To change the date, time, and display format of each, choose Clock from the Control Panel.

The volume of the internal speaker and the pitch of Apple IIgs beep are both controlled via the Sound control panel.

The Apple IIgs has dual-purpose slots. They can be configured either to accept a physical peripheral expansion card, or to simulate a virtual expansion card. Using the Slots control panel, you can enable or disable the virtual card for each slot. Additionally, you may enable AppleTalk networking support by changing two slot settings. On the ROM 01 IIgs, change slot 1 to Your Card and slot 7 to Built-in AppleTalk. For the ROM 3 IIgs, change slot 1 or slot 2 to AppleTalk and slot 7 to AppleTalk. Slot settings will not take effect until the Apple is restarted.

Every Apple will, by default, start scanning the slots from 7 down to 1 in search of a startup disk. Only the Apple IIgs has the option to change this behavior. Instead of scanning the slots, you may instruct the IIgs to try only one of the seven slots. In addition, you may also set the startup device to be an AppleTalk network (covered in Chapter 10), a RAM disk, or a ROM disk.

A RAM disk is a section of RAM that is reserved for use as a disk volume. While every model of Apple can be configured to use a RAM disk, the Apple IIgs is the only model with built-in support. A RAM disk is useful when high-speed access is required to a file or set of files. Just like any other RAM, the contents of a RAM disk are not permanent: they will disappear when the power is switched off. To create a RAM disk, open the RAM Disk panel. On the ROM 3 IIgs, there is only one setting for disk size. The ROM 01 IIgs, on the other hand, has both a minimum and a maximum size setting. It is recommended to set both size settings to the same value on the ROM 01 IIgs. Once set, the RAM disk will not appear until the Apple is restarted.

To remove the RAM disk, set its size to 0K, then turn off the Apple IIgs. The RAM disk will only be removed if the Apple IIgs is powered off then on again, not after a restart.

Replacing the Battery

These Control Panel settings are maintained even when the Apple IIgs is turned off in a special area of RAM known as the Battery RAM, or BRAM. The BRAM is kept powered by a 3.6V battery inside the IIgs. Unfortunately, the battery is only rated to last from five to 10 years, and it is quite likely that the battery inside of your IIgs is dead. This means that the settings will not be saved when the IIgs is turned off, nor will the clock keep time. It is possible to replace the battery, but depending on what model of IIgs you have, that may not be such an easy task.

In all models of IIgs, the battery is located underneath the power supply. The ROM 01 IIgs has a soldered-in battery, making replacement more difficult, whereas the ROM 3 has a much more convenient battery holder. There exists a modification known as the slide-on battery for the ROM 01, and your IIgs may have it.

Obtaining a Replacement Battery

The battery is an unusual type, a 3.6V Lithium 1/2AA, that one will not find so commonly in stores. The best places to look would be a camera store, a battery store, or an electronics store. There are some people and businesses who sell this type of battery online, but it is recommended to first check locally.

Accessing the Battery

You will have to partially disassemble your Apple IIgs in order to access the battery. First, make sure that your Apple is off, then unplug all of the cables from it, including the power cable. Second, push in the two plastic tabs on the back of the IIgs case, located at the left and right sides. Lift up the lid from the back. Remove the lid, and set it aside.

The interior of your Apple IIgs should now be exposed. With the front of the IIgs facing you, the large metal box known as the power supply will be on the left. The next step is to remove the power supply. First unplug the white connector that leads from the power supply. In the front of the power supply is one plastic tab holding it secure. Press back on the tab, and lift up the front end up of the power supply.

Figure 12-7. Location of the battery in the ROM 3 IIgs

Remove the power supply entirely from the IIgs. Finally, the battery will be visible at the back of the motherboard.

Installing the New Battery

If you have a ROM 3 machine, then the final step is simple: remove the black plastic battery cover, substitute the new battery for the old one, then replace the power supply and cover, and reassemble the IIgs.

However, if you have a ROM 01 IIgs with the original soldered battery, then you must face one final challenge. If you are familiar with a soldering iron, then you could desolder the old battery and substitute the new one. Or you could use clips to attach the new battery to the leads.

Once the new battery is in place, you should set the time and date on your IIgs. Test the battery by turning off the Apple IIgs, waiting 2 or 3 minutes, then turning it back on and verifying that it has retained the date and time.

Resetting the Control Panel Options

There may be a time when you wish to restore the Apple IIgs Control Panel settings to their original factory defaults. To do so, either power on the Apple while holding down the OPTION key, or press CONTROL-OPTION-RESET.

A menu will appear on the screen offering to either enter the Control Panel, set system standards, or continue booting the Apple. If you live in the United States or any other country that uses 60 Hz alternating current, press 2. Otherwise, press 3 for 50 Hz. All Control Panel settings will then be changed back to their original defaults.

The clock will not be reset; it will still retain the same date and time as always.

Disabling Access to the Control Panel

On the ROM 3 IIgs, it is possible to lock out the Control Panel in order to prevent tampering with the settings. To do so requires setting a jumper on the logic board.

The jumper is at location W1, near the power supply. Simply place a jumper block over the two pins of W1.

The ROM 01 IIgs does not have this jumper.

Using Desk Accessories

A Desk Accessory is an idea borrowed from the classic Macintosh system introduced in 1984: a small, self-contained program that performs one simple task, and does it very well. Some examples of Desk Accessories are a clock, a note pad, a file decompressor, and a calculator. A defining concept of the Desk Accessory is that it can be used while you are working in another program, without having to exit that program.

Desk Accessories come in two types: the Classic Desk Accessory, commonly abbreviated as CDA; and the New Desk Accessory, often shortened to NDA. The main difference between the two is that

CDAs are text-only, and are listed on the screen by pressing COMMAND-CONTROL-ESCAPE. Using any of these Desk Accessories temporarily interrupts the currently-running program. When you accessed the Control Panel earlier in this chapter, you were using a Classic Desk Accessory. On the other hand, New Desk Accessories belong to the graphical world of GS/OS and can operate alongside the currently-running program. NDAs are listed in the Apple menu for convenient access.

While you may only use one CDA at a time, you can have as many NDAs open and on-screen as the memory in your IIgs will allow. As an example, a clock NDA can show the current time as you type a letter in a word processing program.

Both CDAs and NDAs are installed in Desk.Accs folder inside the System folder. When installing a new Desk Accessory, you will need to restart your system for it to become active.

Mounting Disk Images

A popular way to provide software online is by way of disk image—a file that represents the complete contents of a floppy disk. The intended use is that one would use a program such as ADT (covered in Appendix D) to write out the disk image to a real floppy disk. However, doing so may be more trouble than it's worth.

The solution is Brutal Deluxe Software's MountIt program, which allows your Apple IIgs to use a disk image without having to make a physical copy of it. Up to 16 ProDOS disk images can be mounted on the Finder just like physical floppy disks. The disk images can be in any of three formats: .DSK, .PO, or .2MG. Once mounted, the disks act just like a real disk.

As of this writing, the latest version of MountIt is v1.4. MountIt requires System 6 or later, and at least 8K of free RAM. MountIt does not function under ProDOS 8; any mounted disks will disappear when a ProDOS 8 program is started.

To install, first unshrink the contents of the SHK archive to a folder on your disk. Then, open the folder where you unshrunk MountIt, and double-click the Installer program. In the Installer, if your startup disk is not displayed in the box in the top-right area of the window, click the Disk button until it is. Then click the Install button. When the installation is finished, click Quit, then Restart.

After the IIgs starts back up, you will now be able to double-click disk image files and have them mounted as disks in the Finder.

If you want to save any changes that you made to the disk image, be sure to choose Update disk images from the Extras menu.

Making Disks from Disk Images

Most software that is distributed online comes in the form of a disk image, a single file that represents the entire contents of a 3.5" or 5.25" disk. You have already seen that with MountIt, you can have a disk image appear on your IIgs desktop as if you had inserted a physical disk. However, you may want to instead create a real floppy disk from the image. DiskMaker, a shareware program written by Eric Shepherd, is one application to do the job.

DiskMaker is designed to work with ImageMaker, a program (also written by Mr. Shepherd) that can create disk images from real disks. The formats supported are raw, DiskCopy 4.2, DiskCopy 6, and Universal Disk Image (.2mg).

Using DiskMaker is fairly simple. First, double-click the DiskMaker icon. When the program is started, a file dialog box is presented. It is up to you to select a valid disk image file.

When you have chosen a file, another dialog box will appear, listing all disk drives connected to the Apple. In addition, a popup box allows you to specify the format of the disk image file. Select the destination disk drive, then click Make Disk. A disk drive will only appear on the list if it has a mounted disk. The first 3.5" disk drive, for example, is listed as ".APPLEDISK3.5A." If the target disk appears to already have data on it, you will be asked to confirm your selection.

To cancel the operation and return to the open file dialog, click the Skip button. To quit DiskMaker, click Cancel from the open file dialog.

Multitasking with GNO/ME

Up until now, you have only been able to run one thing at a time on the Apple. This is known as single-tasking: running just one program at a time. To switch tasks, you must quit the current program and load the next one. However, there are often situations where you may want to have two or more programs running at a time. This is known as multitasking. For example, you could have a telecommunications program downloading a file while you type up a report in a word processing program. Then you could have the printer print out your 10 page report while you work in another program. Every modern-day computer is capable of multitasking, and so is the Apple IIgs with the GNO/ME system.

Additionally, GNO/ME is capable of turning the Apple IIgs into a multiuser system, allowing multiple people to dial into the Apple from a modem or serial connection and run programs on it without having to be physically present in front of it.

GNO/ME, wherein the ME stands for Multitasking Environment (GNO/ME is often shortened to just GNO), was written principally by Jawaid Bazyar, and sold by Procyon Software in the early 1990s. By the late 90s, its status was changed to freeware, as it remains today. Many accompanying programs and utilities have been written by Mr. Bazyar and others. The latest beta version of GNO, 2.0.6, was released in 1997. However, this beta version still has some bugs and other issues. The latest stable release of GNO is 2.0.4, and this is the version that will be covered in this section. Neither version of GNO supports networking, though the final version of 2.0.6, when it is released, is expected to integrate with Marinetti to provide TCP/IP support.

GNO integrates with GS/OS to allow one ordinary desktop program to run, and many other text-only programs to run simultaneously. In addition, GNO is designed to integrate with the ORCA line of assemblers and compilers sold by The Byte Works. Most of the GNO source code is written in C.

Installing GNO

GNO requires a minimum of 1.25 MB of RAM, but more, at least 2 MB, is better. A hard drive with at least 5 MB of free space is required.

The GNO 2.0.4 installation comes on three disks. If you are installing GNO onto a dedicated hard drive partition, be sure to name that partition GNO. If you have done so, you may then double-click the kern program (you might need to scroll up in the window to see it) on GNO.Disk1 to begin installation. As the installation progresses, you will be prompted to insert disks 2 and 3, or if you have enough disk drives, you may insert them now.

If you have enough space on your hard drive, copy the contents of each of the three disks to your hard drive. Do this by dragging each floppy disk icon to the hard disk icon and clicking OK in the confirmation dialog box. After the disks are copied to the hard drive, you may put them away, since they are no longer needed. Proceed with installation by opening the GNO.Disk1 folder and double-clicking the kern program (you may need to scroll up in the window).

The installation process starts by asking two questions, one related to additional software compatible with GNO; the other about installing the Multi-User package. After you have read the notes in the introductory window, click the Install button.

The first question regards the ORCA series of languages available from The Byte Works. If you have them installed and wish to use them with GNO, click Yes. You will then be prompted to locate various programs and files in further dialog boxes. If not, click No. Clicking the Info button will present a screen with more information about using ORCA products with GNO.

The second question concerns installing the Multi-User package, which changes some of the fundamental operation of GNO. Installing the MU package adds a login prompt to GNO, as well as the ability for others to dial into the system via a modem or direct-connect serial line. Thirdly, the MU package adds some measure of protection between the users; for example, user Bob would not be able to access user Alice's personal files. If you want the full

GNO experience, click Yes. Otherwise, you can click No and install the MU package at a later date.

After answering this final question, the install program switches to a text screen and starts installing all of the GNO files to your hard disk. Finally, you will see an Installation successful message. After a few more moments, a percent (%) prompt will appear. Type exit and press RETURN to leave the install program.

Entering the Shell

The GNO shell, gsh, supports several useful features including command history and path expansion. At first glance, the shell appears to be quite similar to using ProDOS and Applesoft, except that the commands are different: cd instead of PREFIX, and ls instead of CAT. Further investigation, however, reveals that GNO is capable of much more than just these simple disk commands. The shell happens to be based on the Unix shell (Unix is a multitasking system for minicomputers).

Start GNO by double-clicking the kern program. You should see the screen change, and the message “GNO Kernel v2.0.4” with a copyright notice should appear. If you installed the MU package, a login prompt will appear. Type:

```
root
```

and press RETURN to login. A welcome message should appear, followed by a command prompt. The prompt will look something like this:

```
[3] 2:44pm root> _
```

The prompt conveys three pieces of information. First, in brackets, is the number of commands recently executed. Following is the current time. Lastly is the current directory where you are located, also known as the *current working directory*. Whenever you log in to GNO, you will be located in your home directory, which has the same name as your username. The *home directory* is your place to store documents, programs, and other files which only you will use and have access to.

Typing Commands and Arguments

At the prompt, try typing something, such as your name. When you press RETURN, you should get the following message:

```
[5] 2:50pm root> david
david: Command not found.
```

GNO is reporting that it was not able to find a program called "david."

For your first real command, try typing pwd (remember to press RETURN after every command, just as in BASIC):

```
[6] 2:52pm root> pwd
:gno:user:root:
```

GNO replied back with the full path for the current working directory. Pwd, which stands for "print working directory," is just one of many GNO programs, or *commands.*

As mentioned earlier, GNO uses the command ls, for list directory, instead of CAT. Try typing ls now. You will likely see two names, gshrc and history. These are the names of two files in your home directory.

Just as ProDOS commands used arguments to specify input, so too do GNO commands accept arguments. The arguments for a command in GNO are typically separated by a space and a dash, instead of a comma as in ProDOS. Try the following command:

```
ls -l
```

You should see something like the following:

```
[7] 2:56pm root> ls -l
total 0k
-rw-brd 0000 txt       485 Dec 22  2011 gshrc
-rw-brd 0000 non        99 Feb 11 14:50 history
```

The l argument is short for "long" and signifies that ls should display more information about each file in a directory.

Command History and Completion

To save typing, the shell has two handy features. One is called the command history, a list of all recent commands which you have entered. Press the UP ARROW key a few times. If you have been following along with these examples, you should see ls -l, ls, then pwd. Press the DOWN ARROW to cycle through commands in the opposite direction. Once the command is displayed on the prompt, you may execute it again by pressing RETURN, or modify it and then execute it.

The second time-saving feature is command completion, which is invoked using the TAB key. Simply begin typing the first few letters of a command, then press TAB. If only one command matches, its name will be completed on the prompt. Likewise, if you are typing the name of a file, pressing TAB will search the current working directory and fill in the filename if a match is found. If more than one name matches, the Apple will beep. You must type more letters from the name, then press TAB.

Putting Multiple Commands on a Line

Just like Applesoft and Integer BASIC allow more than one command or statement to be placed on a line, so too does the GNO shell allow multiple commands.

Instead of separating commands with a colon, as in BASIC, the semicolon (;) is used to separate commands. Each command will be executed in turn from left to right. The next command will not run until the previous command is finished. The shell prompt will return only when the final command has finished.

For example:

```
sleep 3;ls
```

will first execute the sleep command for three seconds, after which the ls command will run.

Running Commands in the Background

Some commands may take a long time to process, and do not require any further input from you. These commands can be run in the background, thus allowing you to accomplish other work while the command executes.

To run a command in the background, simply append an ampersand (&) to the end. For example, sleep is a command that pauses and does nothing for a specified number of seconds. Type the following command:

```
sleep 20&
```

When you press RETURN, the Apple will reply with:

```
[1]  +    56 Running sleep 20 &
```

In the mean time, you are free to enter any command that you wish. After 20 seconds, a notification appears indicating that sleep has finished execution:

```
[1]  + Done    sleep 5 &
```

Redirecting Input and Output

Every GNO command has what is known as standard input and standard output. Ordinarily, a GNO command receives standard input from the keyboard and sends its standard output to the screen.

Output of a program can be redirected to a file using the greater than symbol (>). If the named file already exists, its contents will be erased. Otherwise, the file is created anew.

Try the following example. Begin by typing:

```
cat > nonsense
```

Now type anything that you want. Make sure that you press RETURN a few times to make some new lines. When you're finished, press RETURN then CONTROL-D. The shell prompt returns. What you have done is executed the cat program and made its standard output go to a file named "nonsense." Everything that you typed, up to the final CONTROL-D, is now in that file. Try typing cat nonsense to see.

Redirecting input for a program is done in a similar manner, except that the less than symbol (<) is used instead. This example will use the wc command to count the number of lines in the nonsense file. Ordinarily, when one wants to count the number of lines in a file, one passes the filename to wc as an argument. However, wc also accepts standard input:

```
wc -l < nonsense
```

The -l argument for wc tells the program to return only the line count. You should get back a figure indicating the total number of lines in the nonsense file.

It is also possible to redirect both standard input and standard output at the same time, such as in:

```
wc -l <nonsense >lcount
```

This command causes the line count of "nonsense" to be placed in a file named "lcount."

Input and output redirection only work with *files*, not other commands. To redirect input and output to or from more than one command, see the next section.

Connecting Multiple Programs

It is possible to string two or more GNO commands together such that the output of an earlier command becomes the input of a later command. Doing so is called *piping*. GNO connects each program into the pipeline with a *pipe*: a one-way flow of data. Pipes differ from input and output redirection in that the programs are linked directly to each other; a file need not be used.

The vertical bar symbol (|) separates each command in the pipeline. Commands are always interpreted from left to right.

For example, here is a simple pipeline example:

```
cat history | wc -l
```

This pipeline involves two commands: cat and wc. The first command, cat, loads the file named "history" and sends its contents to standard output. The GNO pipe transfers this standard output to the standard input of the wc command, which in turn prints the number of lines to standard output. Since the pipeline ends here, the line count appears on the screen.

It is also possible to use output redirection. For example, to place the line count into a file, as in a previous example, the pipeline would look like so:

```
cat history | wc -l > lcount
```

After running this pipeline, the shell prompt will appear again. The file "lcount" now contains the final output of wc based on the input from cat.

Running Finder Desktop Programs

Under GNO, only one desktop program may be run at a time. However, all of the other GNO programs continue to run.

To load a program, simply type its name or full path. For example, to launch the Finder, type the following:

```
/IIgs.Hard.Disk/System/Finder
```

Be sure to type the name of the volume where the Finder is located (it's probably not called IIgs.Hard.Disk on your system). You may use the program as usual, and when you quit the program, control will be returned to the GNO shell.

Leaving GNO

To simply log out of your account, either press CONTROL-D, or type exit. The login prompt will reappear, allowing you or someone else to log in.

Some Common Commands

GNO and other UNIX-like systems all suffer from one drawback: it is difficult to find a comprehensive list and explanation of all possible commands. Furthermore, proficiency and speed with using the system requires memorization of the commands and each of their arguments.

GNO contains many more commands than just these. To find more commands, use the cd and ls commands to view the contents of the /bin and /usr/bin directories. That being said, here is a list of some of the most common commands that you will benefit from memorizing:

cat - concatenate and print files

The cat command will read one or more files sequentially and send their contents to the standard output.

Syntax: cat [*file1*] [*file2...*]

Example: cat some.file

cd - change directory

Analogous to PREFIX in ProDOS, cd is used for changing the current working directory. When used without an argument, cd will change to your home directory. Directories may be absolute or relative. An absolute directory starts with a /, and begins at the root of the file system. A relative directory starts with either a period, two periods, or a directory name. Specifying a single period refers to the current directory. Specifying two periods refers to the parent directory. See the examples for more explanation.

Syntax: cd [*path*]

Example: cd /bin

This is an absolute path, and will change to the bin directory at the root of the file system

Example: cd ..

This is a relative path, and will change to the parent directory.

Example: cd ./../work

This is another relative path. It begins with the current working directory, then changes in the work directory located in the parent directory.

cp - copy files

Using cp, one or more files, or even an entire directory hierarchy, may be copied to a destination location.

Syntax: cp [-riv] *target_file destination_file*

The -r option is required when copying an entire directory structure. To cause cp to verbosely print the name of each source and destination file, use -v. For interactive operation, use -i to cause cp to prompt if the destination filename already exists.

date - display current date and time

Use date -c to get a dynamic date and time display. Press CONTROL-C to return to the shell.

exit - log out of GNO

To log out of GNO so that another user may log in, either type exit at the command prompt, or press CONTROL-D.

init - change system run level

The system run level defines what mode GNO operates in. Typing init without any parameters will return the current run level, which is usually level 7.

Only the super-user root can change the system run levels, which are as follows:

- 0 - Shutdown the Apple IIgs
- 5 - Quit GNO and return to Finder
- 6 - Restart the Apple IIgs
- 7 - Local state (multi-user with no dialups).

There are other run levels, but they largely have no effect at all, and are intended for future enhancements and versions of GNO.

Example: init 5

ls - list files in a directory

One of the most oft-used commands, ls is frequently used immediately following a cd command. When given with no arguments, ls will list the names of all visible files in the current working directory.

Syntax: ls [-alsrR] [*directory_name*]

When provided with a directory name, the contents of that directory will be listed instead. The current working directory remains unchanged.

ls has several options, the most common of which are:

- a - Show all files, even invisible files (whose names start with a period)
- l - Show more information about each file in a list
- s - Show the size of each file in kilobytes
- r - Reverse the order in which files are listed
- R - List files recursively in a directory hierarchy.

Example: ls -la /usr/bin

man - command reference manual

Back in the 1970s, the manual for Unix systems was a hard-copy book. Later on, the man command allowed access to an electronic copy of the reference manual. Nearly every command for GNO has a man entry stating a brief description of the command, its parameters, and further information about operation of the command and parameters.

The manual is divided into sections, and the section name for a command is given in parentheses, such as ls(1) or init(8).

Syntax: man [*section*] *name*

Example: man wc

mkdir - make a new directory

Syntax: mkdir *directory_name*

more - show a file one screen at a time

More is used to "page" a long file, to show one screenful at a time. Press the SPACE BAR to advance to the next page, or press CONTROL-B to back up a page. Press Q to quit.

Syntax: more *filename*

mv - move files

The mv command is used to move one or more files or directories to a different location.

Syntax: mv [-vi] *filename destination*

The v parameter enables verbose mode, writing a line of output as each file is moved. To enable interactive mode, wherein mv will prompt if the destination file already exists, use i.

Example: mv nonsense ..

This example will move a file or directory named "nonsense" to the parent directory of the current working directory.

passwd - change account password

This command is used to change your user account password. First you will be prompted for your current password. Enter it and press RETURN. If your account currently does not have any password, simply press RETURN. Next, you will be prompted to type a new password.

pwd - print name of working directory

Pwd does not have any options. It always prints the full name and path of the current working directory to standard output.

rm - remove files or directories

To delete one or more files or directories is the purpose of the rm command. The v and i flags are supported for verbose output and interactive operation, respectively. The f argument attempts to force the removal of a file or directory, and overrides the i argument. When removing a directory, the r option specifies recursive removal: all files and directories within the hierarchy will be removed.

Syntax:

rm [-vif] *filename*
rm [-virf] *directory_name*

More than one file or directory name may be specified as arguments.

sleep - pause for some time

The sleep command is typically used to delay execution of some command. Sleep takes a single argument, a number of seconds, and waits until that duration of time has elapsed.

Syntax: sleep *seconds*

Example: sleep 3; ls

This example will wait 3 seconds before executing the ls command.

vi - screen editor

Vi is used for creating and editing text files. GNO actually uses a vi clone called stevie.

Syntax: vi [*filename*]

Vi operates in one of a few modes. It has a general command mode which is active when the program first starts. To return to command mode at any point, press the ESCAPE key. Most commands are a single letter, though some commands are two or more characters. Here are a few of the most common:

- :q   Quit vi
- :q!   Quit vi without saving changes
- :wq   Quit vi with changes saved
- :w   Save the current file
- a   Enter append mode for adding and editing text
- i   Enter insert mode for adding and editing text
- j   Move the cursor down one line
- k   Move the cursor up one line
- h   Move the cursor left one space
- l   Move the cursor right one space
- x   Delete the character under the cursor
- dd   Delete the current line where the cursor is located.

wc - word, line, and character counter

Wc is used to count the words, lines, and characters in one or more files. By specifying an option, one may receive just one or two of the totals instead of all three. By default, wc uses the standard input unless a filename is provided as an argument.

Syntax: wc [-lwc] [*filename*]

Example: wc -l nonsense

This example will return the line count in a file named nonsense.

Appendix A : Further Reading

This one book cannot possibly contain everything that there is to know about the world of Apple II. With that limitation in mind, this appendix contains several reference manuals and books which are highly recommended. Since these books are no longer published, obtaining copies of them is trickier than merely stopping at a bookstore.

It is recommended that you conduct a book search in the following order: first, check Amazon.com. There are several hundred used Apple II books for sale at reasonable prices. Secondly, you can check eBay, though you may find that the selection is narrower and the prices are higher. Finally, you might have luck looking through used bookstores in your area, especially larger ones.

All of these books are selections from this author's own personal library.

Manuals by Apple Computer

While these manuals are usually all authoritative and worth having, some are more essential than others.

Apple II BASIC Programming Manual, 1978

If you're using Integer BASIC, then this manual is the absolute beginner's guide to it. Written by Jef Raskin, this book takes a unique approach toward instructing the reader.

Apple II Reference Manual, 1979

This manual is the complete reference for the Apple II and II Plus computers. It contains schematics, source code, hardware implementation, and all other manner of details. As a reference manual, it is not quite so useful for the beginning

Apple user, but you will appreciate having it later as your knowledge increases.

BASIC Programming with ProDOS, 1983
This manual contains full coverage on using ProDOS with your Applesoft programs, especially the sequential and random-access disk files.

The Applesoft Tutorial, 1979
If you didn't learn Applesoft from this book, then try again with this tutorial.

The DOS Manual, 1980
An essential manual for working with DOS 3.3, especially the advanced features such as random-access files.

Books on Everything Else

These books cover a variety of subjects regarding the Apple.

The Apple II User's Guide
by Lon Poole, Martin McNiff, and Steven Cook
This book is highly regarded by many Apple II veterans. It contains a wide range of information on using and programming the Apple II Plus and IIe. If you can, try to get either the 2nd or 3rd edition, as they are rather profound improvements over the original 1981 edition.

The Apple User's Encyclopedia
by Gary Phillips, Joyce Conklin, and Donald J. Scellato
This book is a 460-page reference guide to everything on the Apple II, II Plus, IIe, and Apple III. Its entries include those relating to BASIC, machine operation, product vendors, software products, and hardware products. Needless to say, it puts the glossary in this book to shame.

The Easy Guide to your Apple II
by Joseph Kascmer
With fewer than 150 pages, this book is like a concise edition of the Apple II User's Guide, including sections on both operating and programming the Apple. This paperback focuses its

coverage on the IIe, but also includes the II Plus as well, to a lesser degree.

The Endless Apple
by Charles Rubin

This book is about extending the life of your Apple II system with add-ons and enhancements. It covers a wide range of peripherals and expansion cards.

Books on BASIC

While this book attempts to teach BASIC, it is not dedicated to the task, and covers many other topics as well. These books are in fact focused solely on BASIC, and therefore have much more coverage and many more example programs.

Applesoft BASIC for the Apple II & IIe
by Lois Graff and Larry Joel Goldstein

This book is suitable as both an introduction to using the Apple and programming in BASIC. Topics include elementary BASIC techniques, debugging, subroutines, programming with DOS, graphics, sound, games, and advanced BASIC techniques such as using PEEK and POKE. At least 15 example programs are included.

Basic Apple BASIC
by James S. Coan

This is a great introductory book that gives a brief background on operating the Apple II, then proceeds straight to teaching BASIC. It includes many example programs and coverage on disk files, high-resolution graphics, and shape tables.

Programming the Apple: A Structured Approach
by J. L. Campbell

This book attempts the impossible: turning BASIC into a structured programming language such as that of Pascal or C. It includes a lot of good programming techniques for writing longer BASIC programs.

Books on DOS and ProDOS

If you wish to do any in-depth programming with ProDOS or DOS 3.3, you will likely find these books to be invaluable references.

Apple ProDOS: Advanced Features for Programmers
by Gary B. Little

This book presents a detailed and thorough explanation of ProDOS suitable for both the Applesoft and assembly language programmer. The book first covers ProDOS basics, including file management and disk directory format. Then the internals of ProDOS are dealt with, including booting ProDOS, using the MLI, and how to write system programs. The remaining chapters deal with interrupts, disk drivers, and clock drivers.

Beneath Apple DOS
by Don Worth and Pieter Lechner

This book is the complete, unofficial reference manual to DOS. It covers everything from how DOS works, to how the disks are formatted. There are also several utility programs included. Make sure you get the newer edition which says "Updated for Apple IIe" on the cover, if you can.

Books on Graphics and Games

Applesoft and Integer BASIC can only do so much for game programming and graphics. These books focus mainly on using assembly language for the Apple, though some BASIC techniques may be included too.

Apple Graphics & Arcade Game Design
by Jeffrey Stanton

This book takes you through all of the steps of designing and programming a fast-paced arcade game in assembly language. All of the proven methods of joystick control, high-resolution and low-res graphics, trajectories, and effects are explained, with code examples. Experience with assembly language is recommended, but not required.

Apple II and IIe Computer Graphics
by Ken Williams

You will find a complete explanation of Apple II graphics, both low-res and high-res, in this book. Techniques such as plotting, shape tables, and animation are all covered. This book uses BASIC almost exclusively, as opposed to assembly language.

Hi-Res Graphics and Animation Using Assembly Language
by Leonard I. Malkin, Ph.D.

With the addition of double high-resolution graphics, the content of this book is much the same as that of "Apple Graphics" by Stanton. Likewise, no prior knowledge is claimed to be necessary, but absolute beginners would do well to follow along with a book devoted to teaching assembly language.

Books on Assembly and Machine Language

If you want to learn about programming your Apple at a lower-level, these books are highly recommended.

Apple Machine Language
by Don Inman and Kurt Inman

This book focuses on learning 6502 machine language, rather than assembly language, and it's done with the help of BASIC. For anyone who is looking for a low-level explanation of how to program the Apple, this book is satisfactory.

Assembly Lines: The Book
by Roger Wagner

Written by a veteran Apple II programmer, Assembly Lines is a beginner's guide to the 6502 instruction set and Apple II hardware. It covers all of the basics, and moves on to more advanced topics such as using the disk.

Programming the 6502
by Rodnay Zaks

This book is not specific to the Apple II, but the content is no less relevant. It covers programming techniques, the entire

6502 instruction set, data structures, addressing techniques, program development, algorithms, and sample applications.

What's Where in the Apple
by William F. Luebbert

Programming technique isn't actually covered in this book, instead it provides a memory map of the Apple, giving all locations and their functions. If you program in machine or assembly language, you will make good use of this reference guide. Try to get a newer edition with the blue or red cover, since those ones include additional material not present in the original green-cover edition.

Appendix B : Summary of Commands and Functions

This appendix lists all commands, functions, and statements shown in the many chapters throughout this book. The following information is contained in this appendix:

- Applesoft commands, functions, and statements
- Integer BASIC commands, functions, and statements
- DOS 3.3 commands
- ProDOS commands
- Derived mathematical formulas
- Reserved words
- Differences between Applesoft and Integer BASIC

Commands and Statements

All Applesoft, DOS 3.3, Integer BASIC, and ProDOS commands and statements are presented here in alphabetical order. Applesoft and Integer functions are listed after this section. Every command has a brief synopsis of its purpose or function, a line showing its syntax, and an in-depth description. In some cases, a brief example or two may be shown, meant to supplement the examples shown in Chapters 3 through 11.

Notation

All syntactic definitions in this appendix follow a common form of notation. The following is a list of conventions that are used.

Terms in brackets ([and]) are optional.

Braces ({ and }) hold a choice of terms separated by a vertical bar (|).

The ellipsis means that the previous item can be repeated as a series.

Terms in *italic* are described and their values must be supplied by the programmer. Table B-1 contains the most common italicized terms.

Words in UPPERCASE must appear as shown; they are the BASIC keywords.

Line numbers are not shown except when an example is provided. It is to be assumed that all programmed mode statements have a valid line number.

Common Term Definitions

The following table, B-1, lists the most common terms found in the syntax definitions given in this appendix. Terms not listed here will be defined in the description of the statement in which they appear.

Table B-1. Notation for command syntax

Notation	Meaning
address	Memory address, given either in decimal or hexadecimal. Hex must be prefixed with a $.
const	Any constant value.
drive	Drive number, either 1 or 2.
expr	Any legal expression.
expr$	Any BASIC string expression, variable or constant.
exprnum	Any BASIC numeric expression, variable or constant.

filename	Legal filename for either DOS 3.3 or ProDOS.
length	Length in bytes.
line	Any valid BASIC line number.
pathname	A ProDOS path.
position	Position number for EXEC or POSITION commands.
record	Record number for random-access files.
slot	Slot number, 1 through 7.
type	Any of the ProDOS file type codes, listed in Table E-7.
varname	Any numeric variable name.
volume	DOS 3.3 volume number, 0 through 254.

Table B-1. Notation for command syntax (*continued*)

APPEND

DOS 3.3 and ProDOS

Summary

Opens a sequential text file and prepares to add additional data to the end of it.

DOS 3.3 Syntax

APPEND *filename* [,S*slot*] [,D*drive*] [,V*volume*]

ProDOS Syntax

APPEND *pathname* [,T*type*] [,L*length*] [,D*drive*] [,S*slot*]

DOS 3.3 Description

Appending to a sequential text file requires a memory buffer of 595 bytes. It is not allowed to use APPEND with a random-access file. Append places the data pointer at the end of the file. Subsequent WRITE commands will store information starting at the first unused byte in the file, thus extending the length of the file.

If the file does not exist in the specified slot and drive, the message FILE NOT FOUND is displayed. If the volume number of the current disk in the specified slot and drive does not match V*volume*, then a VOLUME MISMATCH error occurs. Use volume number 0 (or none at all) to match any disk. APPEND will reopen the file (using CLOSE then OPEN) if it is already open.

The slot, drive, and volume numbers may be specified in any order. If omitted, the most recently used values take effect.

Very old versions of DOS, 3.2.1 and earlier, have a buggy APPEND that does not always start writing at the end of the file. Alarmingly, the data pointer will sometimes be set to the beginning of the file, meaning that a subsequent WRITE will obliterate the beginning of the file. The solution to this problem is to ensure that the DOS end-of-file marker is always written to the text file. The following machine language program shown in Table B-2 accomplishes the task in five bytes of memory. Simply POKE the decimal values into memory from locations 768 to 772 (or wherever else is convenient). Be sure to CALL the routine before closing the text file.

APPEND cannot be used in immediate mode; it is a DOS command requiring PRINT and CHR$(4) or CONTROL-D.

ProDOS Description

APPEND will create a new file if it does not exist. The command opens the file specified, moves the data pointer to the end of the file, then issues a WRITE to that file. A 1K memory buffer is required for this command; if the memory is not available, an error will occur.

Mode	Commands to Enter	Description
BASIC	POKE 768, 169 : POKE 769,0 : POKE 770, 76 : POKE 771, 237 : POKE 772,253	This subroutine calls a Monitor routine at $FDED to cause $0 (a null) to be sent to the current output device, the disk file.
Monitor	300: A9 0 4C ED FD	

Table B-2. Machine language routine for DOS 3.2.1 APPEND bug

All subsequent output from PRINT statements will be directed to the disk file after APPEND is used. Most other screen output, including error messages, will also be sent to disk, with one exception: the INPUT prompt is not sent. Any subsequent ProDOS command (including the null command, a CHR$(4) by itself) will cancel writing, but will not close the file (unless the CLOSE command was used).

The T*type* parameter allows writing to any file type other than text.

It is possible to append to random-access text files. The L*length* parameter specifies record length. If not provided, and the file exists, the file's original record length is used. Otherwise, if the file did not exist, a record length of 1 is assumed.

The slot and drive numbers may be specified in any order, and if omitted, are substituted with the ProDOS prefix.

APPEND cannot be used in immediate mode; it is a ProDOS command requiring PRINT and CHR$(4) or CONTROL-D when used in a program.

AUTO

Integer only

Summary

Activates automatic line-numbering.

Syntax

AUTO *line* [, *increment*]

Description

AUTO will start automatic line numbering beginning at the numeric *line* argument, which must be between 0 and 32767. Line numbers are incremented by 10 unless an *increment* is provided. The next line number will be shown after each press of the RETURN key, unless the previous line entered was blank or had a syntax error.

To cancel a line, type CONTROL-X. To cancel automatic line numbering, press CONTROL-X then type MAN.

AUTO is only legal in immediate mode.

BLOAD

DOS 3.3 and ProDOS

Summary

Loads a binary file from disk into memory.

DOS 3.3 Syntax

BLOAD *filename* [,A*address*] [,S*slot*] [,D*drive*] [,V*volume*]

ProDOS Syntax

BLOAD *pathname* [,A*address*] [,B*byte*] [,L*length*] [,T*type*] [,S*slot*] [,D*drive*]

BLOAD *pathname* [,A*address*] [,B*byte*] [,E*address*] [,T*type*] [,S*slot*] [,D*drive*]

DOS 3.3 Description

If the *address* is not provided, then BLOAD puts the file into memory at the same location where it was originally BSAVEd. Otherwise, if *address* is used, the file is loaded into memory starting at that location. Loading a machine language program at a different location than which it was saved may cause it to cease functioning.

If the file does not exist in the specified slot and drive, the message FILE NOT FOUND is displayed. If the volume number of the current disk in the specified slot and drive does not match V*volume*, then a VOLUME MISMATCH error occurs. Use volume number 0 (or none at all) to match any disk.

The slot, drive, and volume numbers may be specified in any order. If omitted, the most recently used values take effect.

This is a DOS command which requires PRINT and CHR$(4) or CONTROL-D when used in a program.

ProDOS Description

BLOAD places a disk file into memory starting at position B*byte* of the file, and stores it in memory starting at location A*address*. If A*address* is not provided, the file is loaded into memory at the same address from which it was saved. Loading a machine language program at a different location than which it was saved may cause it to cease functioning.

The E and L options are mutually exclusive; they cannot be used together. L*length* is the total number of bytes to read from disk, and E*address* is the memory address at which to stop transferring the file. If neither option is specified, then the entire file is transferred into memory.

Use T*type* to specify a file type other than binary (BIN).

The slot and drive numbers may be specified in any order, and if omitted, are substituted with the ProDOS prefix.

This is a ProDOS command which requires PRINT and CHR$(4) or CONTROL-D when used in a program.

BRUN

DOS 3.3 and ProDOS

Summary

Loads a binary file from disk into memory, then executes it.

DOS 3.3 Syntax

BRUN *filename* [,A*address*] [,S*slot*] [,D*drive*] [,V*volume*]

ProDOS Syntax

BRUN *pathname* [,A*address*] [,B*byte*] [,L*length*] [,S*slot*] [,D*drive*]
BRUN *pathname* [,A*address*] [,B*byte*] [,E*address*] [,S*slot*] [,D*drive*]

DOS 3.3 Description

BRUN should only be used with binary (B) files containing executable 6502 machine language code. The file is located into memory starting at A*address*. If A*address* is left out, the file is loaded at the same location from which it was BSAVEd. Loading and running a machine language program at a different location than which it was saved may cause it to cease functioning.

Once loaded, the program is started by executing a JMP to *address*. The program may return to Applesoft or DOS 3.3 by using the machine language RTS instruction.

If the file does not exist in the specified slot and drive, the message FILE NOT FOUND is displayed. If the volume number of the current disk in the specified slot and drive does not match V*volume*, then a VOLUME MISMATCH error occurs. Use volume number 0 (or none at all) to match any disk.

The slot, drive, and volume numbers may be specified in any order. If omitted, the most recently used values take effect.

This is a DOS command which requires PRINT and CHR$(4) or CONTROL-D when used in a program.

ProDOS Description

This command should only be used with binary (BIN) files containing executable 6502 machine language code. The file is read into memory starting at position B*byte* of the file, and stored in memory starting at location A*address*. If A*address* is left out, the file is loaded at the same location from which it was BSAVEd. Loading and running a machine language program at a different location than which it was saved may cause it to cease functioning.

The E and L options are mutually exclusive; they cannot be used together. L*length* is the total number of bytes to read from disk, and E*address* is the memory address at which to stop transferring the file. If neither option is specified, then the entire file is transferred into memory.

The slot and drive numbers may be specified in any order, and if omitted, are substituted with the ProDOS prefix.

This is a ProDOS command which requires PRINT and CHR$(4) or CONTROL-D when used in a program.

BSAVE

DOS 3.3 and ProDOS

Summary

Saves a range of memory to a binary disk file.

DOS 3.3 Syntax

BSAVE *filename* ,A*address* ,L*length* [,S*slot*] [,D*drive*] [,V*volume*]

ProDOS Syntax

BSAVE *pathname* ,A*address*, L*length* [,B*byte*] [,T*type*] [,S*slot*] [,D*drive*]
BSAVE *pathname* ,A*address*, E*address* [,B*byte*] [,T*type*] [,S*slot*] [,D*drive*]

DOS 3.3 Description

If *filename* exists, its contents are overwritten, otherwise, it is created.

The contents of memory starting at *address* and ending at *address* + *length* are stored in a binary disk file. The *length* must be in the range 1 to 32767. To specify an *address* or *length* in hexadecimal, prefix the value with a dollar sign ($).

If the volume number of the current disk in the specified slot and drive does not match V*volume*, then a VOLUME MISMATCH error occurs. Use volume number 0 (or none at all) to match any disk.

The slot, drive, and volume numbers may be specified in any order. If omitted, the most recently used values take effect.

This is a DOS command which requires PRINT and CHR$(4) or CONTROL-D when used in a program.

ProDOS Description

If a file at *pathname* exists, its contents are overwritten, otherwise, it is created.

The contents of memory starting at A*address* are written to the disk file. If B*byte* is specified, writing begins at that byte location within the file. Transfer stops when either L*length* bytes are transferred, or immediately after the value at memory location E*address* is transferred.

Use T*type* to specify a file type other than binary (BIN).

The slot and drive numbers may be specified in any order, and if omitted, are substituted with the ProDOS prefix.

This is a ProDOS command which requires PRINT and CHR$(4) or CONTROL-D when used in a program.

Example

```
BSAVE PICTURE, A16384, L8192
```

CALL

Applesoft and Integer

Summary

Transfers control to a machine language subroutine.

Syntax

CALL *exprnum*

Description

The CALL command is used for invoking a machine language program or subroutine. Perhaps the most famous CALL statement is CALL -151, which is used to enter the Monitor from the BASIC prompt.

CALL is typically used to execute code which makes up functionality lacking in BASIC. For example, in Integer BASIC, which has no command to clear the screen and move the cursor to the home position, CALL -936 is used. Several such routines are listed in Appendix H.

Examples

```
100 CALL 2000
```

```
120 LOC = 768
130 CALL LOC
```

CAT

ProDOS only

Summary

Displays a condensed, 40-columns catalog of a ProDOS directory.

Syntax

CAT [*pathname*] [,S*slot*] [,D*drive*]

Description

CAT shows an abbreviated form of the specified ProDOS directory. It shows only the following five pieces of information about each file (from left to right on the screen):

1. An asterisk if the file is locked
2. Name
3. File Type
4. Number of 512-byte blocks used
5. Last modification date (Mo/Da/Yr).

The ProDOS CATALOG command shows more information about each file. CAT shows for the volume directory the number of free 512-byte blocks, used blocks, and total number of blocks on the entire volume.

If *pathname* is not provided, the current ProDOS prefix is used instead.

The slot and drive numbers may be specified in any order, and if omitted, are substituted with the ProDOS prefix.

This is a ProDOS command which requires PRINT and CHR$(4) or CONTROL-D when used in a program.

CATALOG

DOS 3.3 and ProDOS

Summary

Displays a disk catalog of files.

DOS 3.3 Syntax

CATALOG [,S*slot*] [,D*drive*]

ProDOS Syntax

CATALOG [*pathname*] [,S*slot*] [,D*drive*]

DOS 3.3 Description

The volume number and a list of all files on a disk are shown. The type, number of disk sectors, and status (locked or unlocked) of each file is shown. If a file is locked, an asterisk is displayed to the left of the file type indicator. The file types are represented by the following single letter codes:

A	Applesoft program
B	Binary (machine code) file
I	Integer BASIC program
R	Relocatable machine code file
S	Reserved for future use
T	Text file.

If a file's length in sectors exceeds 255, the counter starts again at 0. Thus, a file whose length is 257 sectors will appear to be 2 sectors long. This display issue has no other effect on the file or its contents.

The slot, drive, and volume numbers may be specified in any order. If omitted, the most recently used values take effect.

This is a DOS command which requires PRINT and CHR$(4) or CONTROL-D when used in a program.

ProDOS Description

The directory catalog is shown in 80 columns. For each file, the following information is listed (from left to right on the screen):

1. An asterisk if the file is locked
2. Name
3. File Type
4. Number of 512-byte blocks used
5. Last modification date (Mo/Da/Yr Hr:Mn)
6. Date of creation
7. Logical end of file: number of bytes used, or for random-access files, the maximum size if every record were filled
8. Load address in hex of the file (if it is binary), or record length (in decimal) if the file is random-access.

CATALOG shows for the volume directory the number of free 512-byte blocks, used blocks, and total number of blocks on the entire volume.

If *pathname* is not provided, the current ProDOS prefix is used instead.

The slot and drive numbers may be specified in any order, and if omitted, are substituted with the ProDOS prefix.

This is a ProDOS command which requires PRINT and CHR$(4) or CONTROL-D when used in a program.

Example

```
CATALOG ,S6,D2
```

CHAIN

DOS 3.3 and ProDOS

Summary

Transfers execution to another BASIC program loaded from disk without clearing any variables or arrays.

DOS 3.3 Syntax

CHAIN *filename* [,D*drive*] [,S*slot*] [,V*volume*]

ProDOS Syntax

CHAIN *pathname* [,@*line*] [,D*drive*] [,S*slot*]

DOS 3.3 Description

This command should only be used from within an Integer BASIC program to load and run another Integer BASIC program. All variables and arrays remain intact.

If the file does not exist in the specified slot and drive, the message FILE NOT FOUND is displayed. If the volume number of the current disk in the specified slot and drive does not match V*volume*, then a VOLUME MISMATCH error occurs. Use volume number 0 (or none at all) to match any disk.

The slot, drive, and volume numbers may be specified in any order. If omitted, the most recently used values take effect.

This is a DOS command which requires PRINT and CHR$(4) or CONTROL-D when used in a program.

ProDOS Description

CHAIN should be used from within an Applesoft program. It loads and runs the Applesoft program specified by *pathname* with all variables and arrays intact.

If @*line* is specified, program execution begins at the indicated line; if the line does not exist, then the next highest line number is used.

The slot and drive numbers may be specified in any order, and if omitted, are substituted with the ProDOS prefix.

This is a ProDOS command which requires PRINT and CHR$(4) or CONTROL-D when used in a program.

CLEAR

Applesoft only

Summary

Resets all variables to default values.

Syntax

CLEAR

Description

Executing the CLEAR command causes all numeric variables and array elements to have the value 0 and all string variables to have a null (empty) value. CLEAR can be used in a program without any harmful side-effects provided that the program logic can handle it.

Integer BASIC has a CLR command that has the same effect as CLEAR.

Example

```
]A = 50

]B$ = "HELLO"

]PRINT A;B$
50HELLO

]CLEAR

]PRINT A;B$
0
```

CLOSE

DOS 3.3 and ProDOS

Summary

Closes an open file and flushes its buffer to disk.

DOS 3.3 Syntax

CLOSE [*filename*]

ProDOS Syntax

CLOSE [*pathname*]

DOS 3.3 Description

Closing a file ensures that the data in the memory buffer is written to disk. A program must close any files that it opens in order to avoid loss of data.

Specifying a *filename* will close only that file; otherwise, all open files will be closed (except for an EXEC file, if active).

Very old versions of DOS, 3.2.1 and earlier, have a bug that can cause APPEND to start writing at the beginning of the file instead of the end. The problem is caused when a sequential file exactly fills a sector when it is closed. The solution to this problem is to ensure that the DOS end-of-file marker is always written to the text file. The machine language program shown in Table B-2 accomplishes the task in five bytes of memory. Simply POKE the decimal values into memory from locations 768 to 772 (or wherever else is convenient).

This is a DOS command which requires PRINT and CHR$(4) or CONTROL-D when used in a program.

ProDOS Description

Closing a file ensures that the data in the memory buffer is written to disk. A program must close any files that it opens in order to avoid loss of data.

Specifying a *pathname* will close only that file; otherwise, all open files will be closed (except for an EXEC file, if active).

This is a ProDOS command which requires PRINT and CHR$(4) or CONTROL-D when used in a program.

Examples

```
CLOSE
CLOSE DATAFILE3
```

CLR

Integer only

Summary

Resets all variables to default values.

Syntax

CLR

Description

Executing the CLR command causes all numeric variables and array elements to have the value 0 and all string variables to have a null (empty) value.

CLR is only legal in immediate mode.

The Applesoft equivalent of CLR is CLEAR.

COLOR

Applesoft and Integer

Summary

Sets color of next low-resolution point to be plotted.

Syntax

COLOR= *exprnum*

Description

COLOR sets the low-resolution color for PLOT, VLIN, and HLIN commands. The color choice remains until it is changed again with COLOR. The default color, before COLOR is used, is 0 (black). A complete table of colors is found in Appendix E.

COLOR accepts an integer from 0 to 255. In Applesoft, real numbers are automatically converted to integers. The maximum COLOR value is 15. Values higher than 15 will "wrap around," that is, 16 is equal to 0, 17 to 1, and so on.

This command has no effect when high-resolution graphics mode is active. However, when using PLOT to print characters on the text screen, the current color setting has an effect. See the PLOT command for full details.

Examples

```
10 HUE = 5
20 COLOR = HUE

50 COLOR = 18
60 COLOR = 2
```

CON

Integer only

Summary

Continues program execution after being halted.

Syntax

CON

Description

CON is used to continue program execution at the next instruction following a CONTROL-C, and sometimes following a CONTROL-RESET. CON should not be used if a program was not running, as it will cause a system hang.

There are some situations where a program cannot be continued. If the program was halted in the middle of an INPUT statement, CON will not be able to continue the program. Furthermore, if the program was changed after it was halted, then it sometimes cannot be continued.

CON is only appropriate for immediate execution mode.

The Applesoft equivalent is CONT.

CONT

Applesoft only

Summary

Causes a program previously halted to resume execution at the next instruction.

Syntax

CONT

Description

CONT will resume program execution at the next instruction if the program was stopped with CONTROL-C, STOP, or END. If no program was running, CONT has no effect. CONT cannot continue a program that was halted by typing CONTROL-C at an INPUT prompt; doing so will display a ?SYNTAX ERROR message. Furthermore, if the program is modified in any way, it can't be continued with CONT, and a ?CAN'T CONTINUE ERROR will result.

The Integer equivalent is CON.

CREATE

ProDOS only

Summary

Creates a new ProDOS file or directory.

Syntax

CREATE *pathname* [,T*type*] [,S*slot*] [,D*drive*]

Description

If T*type* is not provided, a directory file is created.

The slot and drive numbers may be specified in any order, and if omitted, are substituted with the ProDOS prefix.

This is a ProDOS command which requires PRINT and CHR$(4) or CONTROL-D when used in a program.

Examples

```
CREATE SUBDIR
CREATE SUBIDR/DOTTY, TBIN
```

- (DASH)

ProDOS only

Summary

Loads and executes any type of file.

Syntax

– *pathname* [,S*slot*] [,D*drive*]

Description

This command, which is referred to as the Dash command, performs the job of RUN, BRUN, and EXEC depending on the file type in question. It is also the only command that can be used to execute a system (SYS) file.

The slot and drive numbers may be specified in any order, and if omitted, are substituted with the ProDOS prefix.

This is a ProDOS command which requires PRINT and CHR$(4) or CONTROL-D when used in a program.

Example

```
-HELLO
```

DATA

Applesoft only

Summary

Defines one or more data elements for use in a program with READ.

Syntax

DATA *const* [,*const* ...]

Description

All DATA statements are combined in sequential order as they appear in the program to form a list of elements for use with READ. The DATA statements may appear anywhere in the program; it does not matter if execution passes to them or not.

There are some restrictions for the contents of DATA statements. String and numeric values are allowed, but a quotation mark cannot be part of a data element. Strings need to be surrounded by quotation marks only if they contain one or more colons, commas, or spaces.

If a data element is blank (null), it is resolved to a zero for numeric assignment, and an empty (null) string for a string variable.

DATA may be used in immediate mode, but it has no effect; its data elements cannot be read by a READ statement.

Examples

```
50 DATA 1,5,3
60 DATA SUSIE,JENNY,MARY
```

DEF FN

Applesoft only

Summary

Declares a user-defined function.

Syntax

DEF FN *name* (*varname*)=*exprnum*

Description

A function identified by *name* is defined. The name must follow the rules for numeric variable names. Its name does not interfere with any other variable names in the program.

The function's mathematical operation is defined by *exprnum*. Up to one argument, *varname*, may be passed to be used in *exprnum*. The function definition *exprnum* must fit all on one program line, however since another user-defined function may be a part of *exprnum*, it is possible to create functions of various levels of complexity. One limitation of a user-defined function is that it may not refer to itself, either directly (in *exprnum*) or indirectly (as the result of calling another user function).

A function is called using FN *name*. The value of *varname*, an expression, constant, or variable, must be legal, even if it is not used in *exprnum*. A function definition must occur in a program before it may be used, otherwise an ?UNDEF'D FUNCTION ERROR message is displayed. If a function *name* is defined more than once, the most recent version will be used. See the entry FN in the Functions section later in this appendix for more details on invoking user-defined functions.

DEF FN may not be used in immediate mode, though user-defined functions from the most recent program may still be used.

A user-defined function may not operate on strings.

Example

```
200 DEF FN AC (Q)= SQR(Q) + (Q * 2)
```

DEL
Applesoft and Integer

Summary

Deletes a range of lines from a program.

Syntax

DEL *linenum1*, *linenum2*

Description

All program lines in the range of *linenum1* to *linenum2*, inclusive, are deleted. If *linenum1* does not exist, the next highest line number is used; likewise, if *linenum2* does not exist, the next smallest line number is used.

DEL must be used with two line numbers separated by a comma. Both line numbers must be greater than or equal to zero, and *linenum2* must be greater than or equal to *linenum1*. Specifing equal line numbers will cause no more than one line (if it exists) to be deleted.

Only in Applesoft may DEL be used in deferred execution mode, in which case the program will halt after DEL does its work. Since the program is modified, CONT will *not* serve to resume the program.

Example

```
DEL 50,80
```

DELETE

DOS 3.3 and ProDOS

Summary

Removes an unlocked file from a disk.

DOS 3.3 Syntax

DELETE *filename* [,A*address*] [,S*slot*] [,D*drive*] [,V*volume*]

ProDOS Syntax

DELETE *pathname* [,S*slot*] [,D*drive*]

DOS 3.3 Description

If the specified *filename* exists and is unlocked, it is removed from the disk. The file is closed if it was open.

If the file does not exist in the specified slot and drive, the message FILE NOT FOUND is displayed. If the volume number of the current disk in the specified slot and drive does not match V*volume*, then a VOLUME MISMATCH error occurs. Use volume number 0 (or none at all) to match any disk.

The slot, drive, and volume numbers may be specified in any order. If omitted, the most recently used values take effect.

This is a DOS command which requires PRINT and CHR$(4) or CONTROL-D when used in a program.

ProDOS Description

A file must be unlocked and closed in order to be deleted. Directories must be empty before they can be deleted; the volume directory may never be deleted.

The slot and drive numbers may be specified in any order, and if omitted, are substituted with the ProDOS prefix.

This is a ProDOS command which requires PRINT and CHR$(4) or CONTROL-D when used in a program.

Example

```
DELETE MYPROGRAM, S5
```

DIM
Applesoft and Integer

Summary

Dimensions an array (or string value in Integer BASIC) with room for elements ranging from 0 up to the given subscript.

Applesoft Syntax

DIM *var*(*sub*[,*sub*...]) [,*var*(*sub*[,*sub*...])...]

Integer BASIC Syntax

DIM *var* (*sub*) [,*var*(*sub*)...]

Applesoft Description

DIM reserves memory space for an array named *var*. An array can be dimensioned in any of the following ways:

var(*sub*)	Single-dimension
var(*sub1*, *sub2*)	Two-dimensions
var(*sub1*, *sub2*, *sub3*, ...)	Multiple-dimensions

An array can contain any of the three major variable types: integer, real, and string, though all elements of the array must be of the same type, as defined by the array name.

Subscripts in the array range from 0 up to *sub* as defined when the DIM statement was used for an array. When an array is first dimensioned, all subscripts are set to 0 for a numeric array, or "" (the empty string) for a string array.

No array may have more than 88 dimensions, however, arrays are more practically limited by the amount of memory available to Applesoft. Attempting to create an array that is too large for memory, or that has 89 or more dimensions will give an ?OUT OF MEMORY ERROR message.

If an array is used before it is dimensioned, it will have a maximum subscript of 10, allowing for 11 total elements.

Attempting to access an array element that is larger than the maximum subscript, or that uses a different number of subscripts, will result in a ?BAD SUBSCRIPT ERROR message.

An array may only be dimensioned once during the execution of a program. If an array is dimensioned again, the message ?REDIM'D ARRAY ERROR will appear.

Integer BASIC Description

Arrays in Integer BASIC are limited to one dimension. Only numeric arrays are allowed. The maximum length of a string variable is also set using DIM. Dimensioning an array reserves space for *sub* plus 1 elements, numbered 0 to *sub*. The array variable's simple name points to the first element in the array (for example, AR(0) = AR).

When defining a string variable, *sub* is the maximum length of the string, and must be in the range of 1 to 255. The contents of the string always have a null value after being dimensioned. Trying to use too many characters in a string, more than it was dimensioned for, will yield a *** STRING ERR message.

The maximum dimensions for an array tend to be limited by the amount of memory available to Integer BASIC. The elements of an array are not automatically initialized to zero after it is dimensioned.

Attempting to access an array element that is larger than the maximum subscript, or that uses a different number of subscripts, will result in a *** RANGE ERR message.

Examples

```
DIM AR(12)
DIM N$(5,20)
```

DRAW

Applesoft only

Summary

Plots a high-resolution shape on the screen.

Syntax

DRAW *exprnum* [AT *columnh, rowh*]

Description

The high-resolution shape corresponding to the integer value of *exprnum* is plotted on the screen in the color last defined by HCOLOR. Plotting commences at the coordinates specified by *columnh* and *rowh*. If these coordinates are not provided, the shape starts at the position most recently plotted with DRAW, HPLOT, or XDRAW.

The scale and rotation of the shape are defined by the SCALE and ROT commands, respectively, and must be executed before the shape is plotted.

The shape number, *exprnum*, must be in the range of 0 to the number of shapes in the shape table (which is limited to 255).

Examples

```
DRAW 2 AT 45,60
DRAW 1
```

DSP

Integer only

Summary

Displays the new value of a variable upon each change.

Syntax

DSP *var*

Description

Whenever variable *var* changes, its name and its new value are printed on the screen, mixed in with your program's usual output. Using RUN cancels the effects of DSP, forcing the programmer to use CON or GOTO when debugging a program with DSP in immediate mode.

DSP is also explicitly canceled by NO DSP.

END

Applesoft and Integer

Summary

Marks the end of a program, causing it to stop.

Syntax

END

Description

Program execution immediately terminates. No message is printed on screen.

END is optional in Applesoft; it is required in Integer BASIC. If the last statement executed in an Integer BASIC program is not END, then the message *** NO END ERR is displayed.

END may be used in immediate mode in Applesoft; it is forbidden in Integer BASIC.

EXEC
DOS 3.3 and ProDOS

Summary

Causes the contents of a sequential-access text file to be used in place of keyboard input.

DOS 3.3 Syntax

EXEC *filename* [,R*position*] [,S*slot*] [,D*drive*] [,V*volume*]

ProDOS Syntax

EXEC *pathname* [,F*field*] [,D*drive*] [,S*slot*]
EXEC *pathname* [,R*field*] [,D*drive*] [,S*slot*]

DOS 3.3 Description

An EXEC file is an ordinary sequential-access text file that contains one or more BASIC commands, program lines, or DOS commands. EXEC starts reading from the first line of the file, and each line is executed as though it had been typed into the Apple from the keyboard. Commands are executed, program lines are added to memory, and responses to INPUT statements are taken from the next line of the EXEC file.

An EXEC file can be used to perform many versatile tasks with BASIC programs, including entering them into memory, making changes, and merging program lines. EXEC files can even be used to create other EXEC files.

The option R*position* marks a number of lines (carriage return characters) to skip from the beginning of the EXEC file before starting to process the commands.

When the last line of an EXEC file is completed, the file is automatically closed. If an EXEC file causes another EXEC file to be opened, the first file is closed and all further commands in it are abandoned. The Apple switches to taking commands from the new EXEC file.

If the file does not exist in the specified slot and drive, the message FILE NOT FOUND is displayed. If the volume number of the current disk in the specified slot and drive does not match V*volume*, then a VOLUME MISMATCH error occurs. Use volume number 0 (or none at all) to match any disk.

The slot, drive, and volume numbers may be specified in any order. If omitted, the most recently used values take effect.

This is a DOS command which requires PRINT and CHR$(4) or CONTROL-D when used in a program.

ProDOS Description

An EXEC file is an ordinary sequential-access text file that contains one or more BASIC commands, program lines, or ProDOS commands. EXEC starts reading from the first line of the file, and each line is executed as though it had been typed into the Apple from the keyboard. Commands are executed, program lines are added to memory, and responses to INPUT statements are taken from the next line of the EXEC file.

An EXEC file can be used to perform many versatile tasks with BASIC programs, including entering them into memory, making changes, and merging program lines. EXEC files can even be used to create other EXEC files.

The option R*field* marks a number of lines (carriage return characters) to skip from the beginning of the EXEC file before starting to process the commands. F*field* has the same effect as R*field*.

When the last line of an EXEC file is completed, the file is automatically closed. If an EXEC file causes another EXEC file to be opened, the first file is closed and all further commands in it are abandoned. The Apple switches to taking commands from the new EXEC file.

The slot and drive numbers may be specified in any order, and if omitted, are substituted with the ProDOS prefix.

This is a ProDOS command which requires PRINT and CHR$(4) or CONTROL-D when used in a program.

Example

```
EXEC DOIT, R3
```

FLASH

Applesoft only

Summary

Changes text mode to flashing style.

Syntax

FLASH

Description

After FLASH is executed, subsequent text output to the screen will alternate between white on black and black on white (or, for the IIgs, whatever colors are defined in the Display Control Panel). Existing characters on the screen remain as they were.

Flashing text should not be used with DOS 3.3, for it causes the characters to have altered ASCII codes. If these characters are sent to a disk file, they will be incorrectly saved.

When an 80-column card is active, flashing characters appear as inverse style instead.

FLUSH

ProDOS only

Summary

Forces the contents of one or more ProDOS file buffers to be written to disk.

Syntax

FLUSH [*pathname*]

Description

This command causes the contents of a file's buffer to be immediately written to disk. Omitting the *pathname* flushes the buffers of all open files.

This is a ProDOS command which requires PRINT and CHR$(4) or CONTROL-D when used in a program.

FN

See Functions section later in this appendix.

FOR

Applesoft and Integer

Summary

Marks the beginning of a loop which will execute instructions for a specified number of times.

Syntax

FOR *varname* = *exprnum1* TO *exprnum2* [STEP *exprnum3*]

Description

First, *varname* is set to *exprnum1*. Then the statements following FOR are executed until a NEXT statement is encountered. The *varname* is then incremented by 1, if no STEP was included, or by *exprnum3* if STEP was given. Following, *varname* is then compared to *exprnum1*. If *varname* is greater than *exprnum1*, the loop is terminated and execution jumps to the statement following NEXT. Otherwise, the loop continues with the statement after FOR.

If *exprnum3* is less than zero, then the loop conditions differ. The loop is terminated if *varname* is less than *exprnum2*, and continued so long as *varname* is greater than or equal to *exprnum2*.

Since *varname* is compared at the bottom of the loop, the statements within the loop are always executed at least once.

Integer BASIC and Applesoft both require that *varname* be a number. Applesoft demands a real variable, whereas Integer BASIC requires an integer.

It is not possible to change the effective start, end, and increment values, *exprnum1*, *exprnum2*, and *exprnum3* once the loop has started. Even if these values are changed, the loop will not be affected. It is possible, however, to alter the value of *varname* within the loop, thus causing the loop to terminate earlier or later than it would otherwise. Loops started outside of a subroutine should not be terminated inside a subroutine.

FOR-NEXT loops may be nested several levels deep, but they must not "get tangled" with each other. Applesoft allows only 10 nested loops, while Integer BASIC permits up to 16.

Only in Applesoft may a FOR-NEXT loop be entered in immediate mode. The entire loop must be contained on one line. If NEXT is omitted, the loop will only execute once.

Examples

```
20 FOR N = 1 TO 10 STEP 2
30 NEXT N
```

```
100 FOR S = 100 TO 0 STEP -1
110 NEXT S
```

FP
DOS 3.3 only

Summary

Switches to Applesoft, clearing out any BASIC program in memory.

Syntax

FP [,S*slot*] [,D*drive*] [,V*volume*]

Description

This command checks several possible sources for the Applesoft interpreter. Depending on what model of Apple and what cards are installed, the source could be any of the following:

- On an Apple II Plus or any newer model of Apple, Applesoft is always loaded from the motherboard ROM.
- If the Applesoft Firmware card is installed in a standard Apple II, Applesoft is used from it, regardless of the switch position on the card.
- If the Apple Language card is installed and has Applesoft loaded into it, FP uses it.
- If no Firmware or Language card is installed, FP checks the specified disk for a file named APPLESOFT. If Applesoft is still not found, the message LANGUAGE NOT AVAILABLE appears.

Typing FP while in Applesoft will cause any program in memory to be lost.

If the file does not exist in the specified slot and drive, the message FILE NOT FOUND is displayed. If the volume number of the current disk in the specified slot and drive does not match

V*volume*, then a VOLUME MISMATCH error occurs. Use volume number 0 (or none at all) to match any disk.

The slot, drive, and volume numbers may be specified in any order. If omitted, the most recently used values take effect.

FP should be used only in immediate mode, though it will work in programmed mode.

FRE

ProDOS only

Summary

Removes old string values left over in memory from previous Applesoft programs.

Syntax

FRE

Description

The ProDOS command FRE is an enhanced version of the Applesoft FRE function. It operates much more quickly to remove old, unused data from the program string storage area.

This is a ProDOS command which requires PRINT and CHR$(4) or CONTROL-D when used in a program.

GET

Applesoft only

Summary

Assigns the next single character typed from the keyboard to a variable without displaying it on screen.

Syntax

GET *varname*

Description

GET halts program execution until a key is pressed or a device sends a character. If *varname* is a string variable, the character is assigned to it. If CONTROL-@ is entered, the null string is assigned to *varname*.

It is not recommended that GET be used with a numeric variable. Typing a colon or a comma results in an ?EXTRA IGNORED message, with the value being assigned as zero. Entering a plus sign, minus sign, CONTROL-@, E, or a space will also return the value of zero to *varname*. Entering a RETURN or any character other than the numbers 0 through 9 will result in a ?SYNTAX ERROR message.

Pressing CONTROL-C will not halt program execution, instead, it is treated as any other character.

GET can only be used in programmed mode.

GOSUB

Applesoft and Integer

Summary

Causes program execution to branch to a subroutine.

Applesoft and Integer BASIC Syntax

GOSUB *line*

Integer BASIC Syntax

GOSUB *exprnum*

Description

The GOSUB statement causes the program to branch to a subroutine on line number *line*. A subroutine's entry point is defined logically, by the programmer. In Applesoft, if the indicated line number does not exist, the message ?UNDEF'D STATEMENT ERROR is displayed.

Integer BASIC allows more flexibility in that the line number may be computed as the result of an expression *exprnum*. If *exprnum* does not evaluate to a legal program line, then the message *** BAD BRANCH ERR is printed. This form of GOSUB is similar to the ON-GOSUB syntax in Applesoft.

When a subroutine is complete, it should use the RETURN statement to branch back to the next statement following the initial GOSUB. In Applesoft, it is possible to use GOTO to safely branch out of a subroutine if a POP statement is first executed.

Subroutines may call other subroutines. Applesoft allows subroutines up to 25 levels deep, while Integer BASIC limits subroutines to just 16 levels.

GOSUB may not be used in immediate mode in Integer BASIC.

Example

```
10 GOSUB 30
20 END
30 PRINT "SUB"
40 RETURN
```

GOTO

Applesoft and Integer

Summary

Causes program execution to branch to the given line number.

Applesoft and Integer BASIC Syntax

GOTO *line*

Integer BASIC Syntax

GOTO *exprnum*

Description

The GOTO statement causes program execution to immediately jump to the line number indicated by *line*. If no such line number exists, the message ?UNDEF'D STATEMENT ERROR is displayed by Applesoft, while the message *** BAD BRANCH ERR is shown by Integer BASIC.

Integer BASIC allows more flexibility in that the line number may be computed as the result of an expression *exprnum*. If *exprnum* does not evaluate to a legal program line, then the message *** BAD BRANCH ERR is printed. This form of GOTO is similar to the ON-GOTO syntax in Applesoft.

GR
Applesoft and Integer

Summary

Activates low-resolution graphics mode.

Syntax

GR

Description

The screen is set to low-resolution graphics mode (40x40 blocks), and cleared to black. Four lines are left for text at the bottom, and the cursor is moved into this text window. The COLOR for plotting is set to black (0).

If issued while HGR2 is in effect, GR will clear its area of memory, but leave page 2 graphics and text on the screen. If HGR is in effect, GR behaves normally. To solve the problem with HGR2, be sure to issue the TEXT command to return to normal, then use GR.

To gain an additional eight rows of graphics area at the sacrifice of the four lines of text, issue the statement POKE -16302,0 after executing GR. If this command is in effect, typing in immediate mode will cause colored dots to appear at the bottom of the screen, but the commands will still work.

Use POKE -16301,0 to restore the text window.

HCOLOR

Applesoft only

Summary

Sets the high-resolution graphics color.

Syntax

HCOLOR= *exprnum*

Description

The color used for all HPLOT and DRAW statements is set to the value of *exprnum*. The color remains until changed again with HCOLOR. HCOLOR is not affected by HGR, HGR2, or RUN.

The high-resolution color codes are listed in Appendix E. The value of *exprnum* must be from 0 to 7, inclusive. Values outside of this range will cause an ?ILLEGAL QUANTITY ERROR message. Before the first HCOLOR statement is executed, the high-resolution plotting color is indeterminate.

If HCOLOR is used when low-resolution mode is active, the color being displayed is not affected.

Example

```
HCOLOR = 1
```

HGR

Applesoft only

Summary

Activates high-resolution graphics mode.

Syntax

HGR

Description

The screen is switched into high-resolution graphics mode (280 by 160 dots), leaving four lines of the text screen visible at the bottom. The rest of the screen is cleared to black, showing page 1 of memory (8K-16K). The cursor is not automatically moved down to the text window. HCOLOR is unaffected.

To gain full-screen graphics area (280 by 192), use the following POKE statement: POKE -16302,0 after issuing HGR. Any immediate mode commands will no longer display on the screen, but they will still work. To restore the text window, use POKE -16301,0.

High-resolution graphics are not available on models of Apple with less than 16K of memory. In order to use DOS 3.3 and HGR, at least 32K of memory is required. Applesoft on cassette or disk cannot use HGR, since the interpreter occupies the same area of memory used for high-resolution graphics.

Very long programs may extend into the area of memory used for high-resolution page 1. To avoid problems, use HIMEM: 8192. A side-effect of using this command is that the amount of memory available to the BASIC program is significantly reduced.

HGR2

Applesoft only

Summary

Switches the video screen into high-resolution mode, displays page 2, and clears it to black.

Syntax

HGR2

Description

HGR2 is similar to HGR in that it clears the display to black and shows a high-resolution graphics screen. The difference is that page 2 of memory (16K-24K) is displayed. Text screen memory is not affected, nor is HCOLOR.

HGR2 requires at least 24K of memory. On a 24K system, set HIMEM: 16384 before using HGR2 in order to protect the program and its strings from interfering with the graphics memory. DOS 3.3 and HGR2 cannot be used unless the Apple has at least 36K of memory.

There is no easy way to establish a text window. Using POKE -16301,0 will cause a text window whose contents are taken from page 2 to appear. BASIC commands only operate on text page 1, meaning that keyboard input and PRINT statements will be invisible.

HIMEM

Applesoft and Integer

Summary

Changes the highest memory location to be used for storing a BASIC program and its variables.

Syntax

HIMEM: *exprnum*

Description

HIMEM is used to protect upper memory regions from being clobbered, typically high-resolution graphics or machine language code. DOS 3.3 and ProDOS both reside above HIMEM and set it automatically when booted. Without an operating system, Applesoft automatically sets HIMEM to the highest memory address available. If an Applesoft program uses strings, they will be allocated starting at HIMEM, working downward.

Under DOS 3.3, increasing MAXFILES will adjust HIMEM down 595 bytes for each additional file buffer requested. When ProDOS requires a file buffer, it lowers HIMEM by 1024 bytes.

The memory location specified by *exprnum* must be in decimal, and it must be in the range -65535 to 65535 (-32767 to 32767 in Integer BASIC), otherwise the message ?ILLEGAL QUANTITY ERROR (in Applesoft) will appear. The value for HIMEM should not be set higher than the total amount of memory in the Apple, nor should it be set lower than LOMEM.

The current value of HIMEM in Applesoft may be obtained by checking two memory locations, 116 and 115 (decimal). Use the following two statements to return the value: PEEK(116)*256 + PEEK(115). In Integer BASIC, HIMEM is stored at 77 and 76. Use PEEK(77)*256 + PEEK(76).

HIMEM remains unchanged by CLEAR, RUN, NEW, and DEL. However, HIMEM is reset by pressing CONTROL-B RETURN from the Monitor, which also eliminates any program in memory.

Example

```
HIMEM: 16384
```

HLIN

Applesoft and Integer

Summary

Draws a horizontal line in low-resolution graphics mode.

Syntax

HLIN *col1*, *col2* AT *row*

Description

A horizontal line is drawn from *col1* to *col2* at the specified *row* on the low-resolution graphics screen. The color of the line is that last specified by the COLOR statement. When issued in text mode, or if the coordinates cover the text window, various characters will be printed on the screen. The exact characters are determined by the COLOR; see the description of the PLOT statement for full details.

Integer BASIC requires *col1* be less than or equal to *col2*, otherwise a *** RANGE ERR will occur.

HOME

Applesoft only

Summary

Clears screen and positions cursor at top-left corner.

Syntax

HOME

Description

Only the contents of the text window are cleared. The equivalent of HOME in Integer BASIC is CALL -936.

HPLOT

Applesoft only

Summary

Plots lines, dots, and polygons in high-resolution graphics mode using the last-specified value of HCOLOR.

Syntax

HPLOT *colh, rowh*
HPLOT TO *colh, rowh*
HPLOT *colh1, rowh1* TO *colh2, rowh2* [TO *colh3, rowh3...*]

Description

The simplest form of HPLOT places a color dot at the point specified by *colh, rowh*. The dot color is specified by the most recently issued HCOLOR statement.

The second form of HPLOT causes a line of color from the last dot plotted to the coordinates specified by *colh, rowh*. No dot will be plotted if there has been no HPLOT command yet issued. The line color is specified by the most recently issued HCOLOR statement.

The final form of HPLOT draws a line that may have more than one segment. A line is first drawn from *colh1, rowh1* to *colh2, rowh2*. A second line connects from *colh2, rowh2* to *colh3, rowh3*, and so on. The plotted line may be extended many times as long as the instruction will fit on a program line. The color of the entire line is specified by the most recently issued HCOLOR statement.

HGR or HGR2 must be used before HPLOT in order to avoid destroying the program or its variables.

If there is a text window present on the screen, attempting to plot into it will have no visible effect. However, switching to full-screen graphics with POKE -16302,0 will cause any dot or line plotted in the text window to be visible.

Examples

```
HPLOT 5,10
HPLOT 2,40 TO 6,30
HPLOT 0,0 TO 279,0 TO 279,159 TO 0,159 TO 0,0
```

HTAB

Applesoft only

Summary

Moves the cursor to an absolute column number, 1 through 40, on the current line.

Syntax

HTAB *col*

Description

HTAB moves the cursor left or right without affecting any existing characters on the screen. The columns are numbered from left to right, 1 to 40.

HTAB cannot be used to move the cursor past column 40 on a standard Apple II, II Plus, or unenhanced IIe. On these models of Apple, one must use POKE 36, *col* in order to move the cursor to the right half of the 80-columns screen. The Enhanced IIe and all later models allow the full 80-column range for HTAB. HTAB may be used with printers too.

The equivalent of HTAB in Integer BASIC is TAB.

Example

```
HTAB 25
```

IF-THEN

Applesoft and Integer

Summary

Causes a conditional branch to a program line, or a conditional execution of one or more program statements.

Applesoft Syntax

IF *expr* THEN *statement* [:*statement*...]
IF *expr* [THEN] GOTO *line*

Integer BASIC Syntax

IF *expr* THEN *statement*
IF *expr* THEN [GOTO] *line*

Applesoft Description

In the first form of IF-THEN, if *expr* is true, then the following statements on the program line are executed. Otherwise, none of the statements following are executed; program control passes on to the next program line.

In the second, conditional branch, form of the statement, the program jumps to line number *line* if the condition *expr* is true. Otherwise, the branch does not occur; program control passes on to the next program line.

If a GOTO *line* is included in one of the *statements* following THEN, the branch should be the last statement, for statements following it will never be executed otherwise.

IF-THEN is most commonly used with a relational expression. If a string is to be compared, each character of the string is compared by its ASCII value (listed in Appendix E). Strings are compared by each character until a mismatch is found. The character with the higher ASCII code is considered to be mathematically greater. If no mismatch is found, the longer string is considered greater. Applesoft is not capable of allowing string expressions with IF. If such an expression is executed more than two or three times in a program, the message ?FORMULA TOO COMPLEX ERROR will appear.

Any numeric expression whose result is nonzero is considered to be true. Only if the result is zero (false) does execution continue directly to the next program line.

If the letter A is used before THEN, Applesoft may mistakenly confuse it with the reserved word AT. To avoid this confusion, enclose the expression, including the A, in parentheses.

Integer BASIC Description

In the first form of IF-THEN, if *expr* is true, then the following statements on the program line are executed. Otherwise, the following statement is not executed; program control passes on to the next program line.

In the second, conditional branch, form of the statement, the program jumps to line number *line* if the condition *expr* is true. Otherwise, the branch does not occur; program control passes on to the next program line.

IF-THEN is most commonly used with a relational expression. If a string is to be compared, it can only be tested for equality or inequality with another string. Otherwise, *expr* may not be a string expression, anything that evaluates to a string value.

Any numeric expression whose result is nonzero is considered to be true. Only if the result is zero (false) does execution continue directly to the next program line.

If a FOR-NEXT loop is the *statement* following THEN, the entire loop must be contained on the program line. Further IF-THEN statements, if used as the *statement*, must also be wholly contained on the same program line.

Examples

```
10 IF A > 1 THEN GOTO 30
```

```
IF D = 5 THEN PRINT "PENTE"
```

```
IF (X + 5) <> (D - 3) THEN Q = Q + 1 : D = 0
```

IN#
Applesoft and Integer

Summary

Uses the specified slot number as standard input to the Apple.

General Syntax

IN# *slot*

ProDOS Syntax

IN# A*address*

Description

The most common form of IN# is when used with a slot number. IN# specifies which slot will provide input for subsequent GET and INPUT statements. When the Apple is first switched on, IN# is set to slot 0, the keyboard.

The special ProDOS format is used to assign input from a machine language routine in memory. It should be used with the memory location of an input device driver program. Some common input device drivers are listed in Table B-3.

If DOS 3.3 or ProDOS is active, this command requires PRINT and CHR$(4) or CONTROL-D when used in a program.

Examples

```
IN#2
```

```
IN#A49664
```

IN Number	Memory Location	Device
0	47182*	Keyboard
1	49408	Slot 1 (Serial or parallel card)
2	49664	Slot 2 (Serial or parallel card)
3	49920	Slot 3 or IIe Auxiliary slot (80-column card)
4	50176	Slot 4 (Mouse)
5	50432	Slot 5 (3.5" drives)
6	50688	Slot 6 (Disk II drives)
7	50944	Slot 7

* 64795 if ProDOS is disabled

Table B-3. Common ProDOS input device drivers

INIT

DOS 3.3 only

Summary

Prepares a disk for use with DOS 3.3 by clearing out any existing data and writing a startup BASIC program.

Syntax

INIT *filename* [,V*volume*] [,S*slot*] [,D*drive*]

Description

A 5.25" disk in the specified (or last accessed) slot and drive number is formatted for use with DOS 3.3. The program in memory is saved to the disk as *filename*, and runs every time that the disk is booted. The program must be an Applesoft or Integer BASIC program. There is no way to easily change the startup program name without running INIT again.

The disk is created as a memory-dependent slave disk. It may only boot under an Apple with as much or more memory than the Apple that was used to INIT the disk.

If V*volume* is provided, the disk will be initialized with that volume number. Otherwise, the default, 254, will be used.

The slot, drive, and volume numbers may be specified in any order. If omitted, the most recently used values take effect.

This DOS 3.3 command may only be used in immediate mode.

Example

```
INIT HELLO
```

INPUT

Applesoft and Integer

Summary

Reads a line of input from the keyboard or current input device.

Applesoft Syntax

INPUT ["*prompt*";] *var* [,*var*...]

Integer BASIC Syntax

INPUT ["*prompt*",] *var* [,*var*...]

Applesoft Description

INPUT accepts string or numeric input for one or more variables. If *prompt*, which must be string value, is provided, it is printed on the screen to notify the user. If no *prompt* is specified, only a question mark (?) appears. The prompt is only printed once, even if more than one variable is to be entered.

When an INPUT statement asks for more than one variable, the variables may be separated by a press of the RETURN key, or they may be entered on one line and separated with a comma.

INPUT does not accept arithmetic expressions as input, only a real or an integer may be entered for numeric input. Simply pressing RETURN when a numeric value is expected will result in a ?REENTER message. Numeric values may contain the digits 0 through 9, spaces, and a plus or minus sign. When entering real numbers or scientific notation, the decimal point (period), an E, and an additional plus or minus sign for the exponent, are also allowed.

If unacceptable entry is received, Applesoft will cancel all input, thus forcing the user to start over entering legal values. The message ?REENTER will appear if this is the case, and the INPUT prompt will be displayed again.

If a string value is entered, leading spaces are ignored. Entering a question mark anywhere counts as unacceptable entry, as described above.

It is possible to enter a string literal, that is, a string enclosed by quotation marks. If a string literal is not entered, all characters up to the next comma, colon, or carriage return are assigned to the variable. When two or more strings are requested, they may be enclosed in quotation marks and separated by commas. Pressing RETURN without entering anything will assign the null string ("") to the variable.

Unless the first character of a string input is a quotation mark, all characters after a colon are ignored.

INPUT must only be used in programmed mode.

Integer BASIC Description

INPUT accepts string or numeric input for one or more variables. If the first variable to be entered is a numeric variable, BASIC prints a question mark prompt. For string variables, BASIC does not automatically print any prompt.

If *prompt*, which must be string value, is provided, it is printed on the screen to notify the user. If the variable is an integer, the question mark mentioned earlier will follow the *prompt*. The prompt is only printed once, even if more than one variable is to be entered. It is not allowed for the *prompt* to be a string expression or string variable.

If an INPUT statement asks for more than one integer value in sequence, each value may be entered on a line, separated by a RETURN. Integer BASIC will display two question marks (??) on the second and following lines to indicate that more entries are requested. Optionally, all integer values may be entered on just one line by separating them with commas.

Numeric values must be entered using only valid numeric digits, 0 through 9, spaces, and a plus or minus sign. Entering nothing, that is, just pressing RETURN, will result in an error message.

When entering more than one string value, each one must be entered on a separate line. Most characters entered up until RETURN is pressed are legal and will be assigned to the string variables. The exceptions are CONTROL-C, CONTROL-H, CONTROL-M, CONTROL-U, and CONTROL-X, all of which affect either the cursor or the program itself. Pressing RETURN without entering anything at all will assign the null string ("") to the variable. Entering unacceptable characters, such as letters when an integer is requested, will result in *** SYNTAX ERR and RETYPE LINE messages appearing. If such an error occurs, all values for the INPUT statement must be reentered.

INPUT must only be used in programmed mode.

INT
DOS 3.3 only

Summary

Activates Integer BASIC.

Syntax

INT

Description

Using INT will eliminate any BASIC program in memory and switch to Integer BASIC. On the standard Apple II, Integer BASIC is accessed from the motherboard ROM. On an Apple II Plus, Integer BASIC must be present on an Apple Firmware or Apple Language card. For all other models of Apple, Integer BASIC is only available when the DOS 3.3 System Master disk is booted.

If Integer BASIC is not available, the message LANGUAGE NOT AVAILABLE is returned.

INT should only be used in immediate mode.

INVERSE

Applesoft only

Summary

Causes all subsequent text output to be of inverse style.

Syntax

INVERSE

Description

After INVERSE is executed, subsequent text output to the screen will appear as black characters on a white background (or, for the IIgs, whatever colors are defined in the Display Control Panel). Existing characters on the screen remain as they were.

Inverse text should not be used with DOS 3.3, for it causes the characters to have altered ASCII codes. If these characters are sent to a disk file, they will be incorrectly saved.

Lowercase inverse letters are available on the Apple IIe and all later models. The standard Apple II and II Plus models require a special accessory card or hardware modification in order to display lowercase inverse letters.

LET
Applesoft and Integer

Summary

Optional keyword for variable assignment.

Syntax

LET *var* = *expr*

Description

The LET keyword is optional, though it may enhance program readability. The variable *var* is assigned the value resulting from the expression *expr*.

Examples

```
50 LET X = 1
55 LET D$ = "ABC"
```

LIST
Applesoft and Integer

Summary

Lists a range of lines from the BASIC program currently in memory.

Applesoft and Integer BASIC Syntax

LIST *line1* [,*line2*]

Applesoft Syntax

LIST [*line1*] {- | ,} [*line2*]

Description

Given with no arguments, LIST will display all lines of a program, without pause. Pressing CONTROL-S may be used to pause the display, and pressing another key will resume listing.

If given a single line number as an argument, then only that line will be listed.

LIST may also accept a range *line1* to *line2*, separated by a comma (or in Applesoft, a hyphen), and then only the lines including and between the two line numbers *line1* and *line2* will be listed. In Applesoft, leaving off the starting line number *line1* will list all line numbers up to and including the second line number, *line2*. Likewise, giving a line number *line1* followed by a comma will start the listing from that line, and continue to the end of the program.

Both Applesoft and Integer BASIC add spaces to the program listing to enhance its readability. These spaces are not added when the text window is 33 characters wide. Use POKE 33,33 to resize the text window. (Entering POKE 33,40 or TEXT will restore the text window to its usual dimensions.)

In some cases, the spaces that LIST adds will make program lines too long to be easily edited or copied using ESCAPE and the arrow keys.

Examples

```
LIST 10,50
LIST ,50
LIST 20,
```

LOAD

Applesoft and Integer

Summary

Loads a BASIC program from tape.

Syntax

LOAD

Description

LOAD causes the Apple to start listening to the cassette in port for a program. Any program loaded from cassette will replace the current program in memory.

The cassette tape player should be playing as soon as LOAD is issued; there is no prompt to do so. When the Apple hears the reference tone on the tape, it beeps. When the program is successfully loaded from the cassette, the Apple beeps again. After this second beep, you must stop the cassette player.

If any error message appears, the tape must be stopped, rewound, and the LOAD reattempted. Typically, the volume of the cassette player needs to be adjusted if there is an error.

In Integer BASIC, LOAD is only allowed in immediate mode.

LOAD
DOS 3.3 and ProDOS

Summary

Loads a BASIC program from disk into memory.

DOS 3.3 Syntax

LOAD *filename* [,S*slot*] [,D*drive*] [,V*volume*]

ProDOS Syntax

LOAD *pathname* [,D*drive*] [,S*slot*]

DOS 3.3 Description

The file named *filename* is loaded from disk into memory. Any existing program lines, variables, and arrays are cleared.

If necessary, the Apple switches to the language necessary to run the program. If the requisite language is not available, a message to that effect is stated on screen.

If the file does not exist in the specified slot and drive, the message FILE NOT FOUND is displayed. If the volume number of the current disk in the specified slot and drive does not match V*volume*, then a VOLUME MISMATCH error occurs. Use volume number 0 (or none at all) to match any disk.

The slot, drive, and volume numbers may be specified in any order. If omitted, the most recently used values take effect.

This is a DOS command which requires PRINT and CHR$(4) or CONTROL-D when used in a program.

ProDOS Description

The file located at *pathname* is loaded from disk into memory. Any existing program lines, variables, and arrays are cleared. If there are any open files, they are closed. If the program does not exist on the disk, then the existing program, variables, and files are left alone.

The slot and drive numbers may be specified in any order, and if omitted, are substituted with the ProDOS prefix.

This is a ProDOS command which requires PRINT and CHR$(4) or CONTROL-D when used in a program.

Examples

```
LOAD HELLO, S6, D1
```

```
LOAD /USER.DISK/PROGS/MY.PROG
```

LOCK

DOS 3.3 and ProDOS

Summary

Prevents a disk file from being modified.

DOS 3.3 Syntax

LOCK *filename* [,S*slot*] [,D*drive*] [,V*volume*]

ProDOS Syntax

LOCK *pathname* [,D*drive*] [,S*slot*]

DOS 3.3 Description

When a file is locked, it may not be modified in any way, including by renaming, deletion, or other change. The UNLOCK command reverses this protection. The CATALOG entry for the file will show an asterisk by the file type to indicate that it is locked.

If the file does not exist in the specified slot and drive, the message FILE NOT FOUND is displayed. If the volume number of the current disk in the specified slot and drive does not match V*volume*, then a VOLUME MISMATCH error occurs. Use volume number 0 (or none at all) to match any disk.

The slot, drive, and volume numbers may be specified in any order. If omitted, the most recently used values take effect.

This is a DOS command which requires PRINT and CHR$(4) or CONTROL-D when used in a program.

ProDOS Description

When a file is locked, it may not be modified in any way, including by renaming, deletion, or other change. The UNLOCK command reverses this protection. The CATALOG entry for the file will show an asterisk by the file's name to indicate that it is locked.

The slot and drive numbers may be specified in any order, and if omitted, are substituted with the ProDOS prefix.

This is a ProDOS command which requires PRINT and CHR$(4) or CONTROL-D when used in a program.

LOMEM

Applesoft and Integer

Summary

Sets the lowest memory address to be used for storing a BASIC program and its variables.

Syntax

LOMEM: *exprnum*

Description

LOMEM is typically used to preserve a section of memory for use with a machine language program. It sets the lowest memory address that is used to store program lines and variables. Both DOS 3.3 and ProDOS use memory locations below LOMEM for their operation. Depending on what Applesoft interpreter is used (RAM versus ROM), LOMEM may also be set accordingly.

With Integer BASIC, LOMEM starts at 2048 when BASIC is started by pressing CONTROL-B. Firmware Applesoft sets LOMEM at 2051, and increments it whenever a program line is added. Applesoft resets LOMEM when NEW is used, and decreases LOMEM when program lines are changed or eliminated.

The value of *exprnum* must be between -65535 and 65535 (-32767 through 32767 for Integer BASIC), otherwise an error will occur.

The current value of LOMEM can be displayed in Applesoft by entering the following: PRINT PEEK(106)*256 + PEEK(105).

In Applesoft, if LOMEM is set lower than the highest memory address used by the operating system (as well as any BASIC program), an ?OUT OF MEMORY ERROR is displayed. Likewise, LOMEM is not allowed to be set higher than the value for HIMEM, otherwise the same error message is displayed.

LOMEM is not allowed in programmed mode in Integer BASIC, since it clears all variables.

Example

```
LOMEM: 3196
```

MAN
Integer only

Summary

Cancels the effects of the AUTO command and ceases automatic line numbering.

Syntax

MAN

Description

To stop automatic line numbering, first press CONTROL-X to cancel the current line, then type MAN.

MAXFILES
DOS 3.3 only

Summary

Specifies the maximum number of files that may be open at a single time.

Syntax

MAXFILES *limit*

Description

The parameter *limit* must be an integer in the range of 1 to 16; it specifies the number of files that may be opened concurrently. DOS 3.3 reserves 595 times *limit* bytes of memory for file buffers. When DOS is first booted, MAXFILES is set to 3.

All DOS 3.3 commands except IN#, MAXFILES, and PR# require a file buffer to execute. If no free buffers are available, the error message NO BUFFERS AVAILABLE is displayed.

Using MAXFILES causes HIMEM to be reduced. This change may cause parts of an Integer BASIC program or Applesoft strings to be eliminated. Therefore, MAXFILES should be used before RUNning a program.

This is a DOS command which requires PRINT and CHR$(4) or CONTROL-D when used in a program.

Example

```
MAXFILES 4
```

MON

DOS 3.3 only

Summary

Sends specified DOS 3.3 disk commands and data to the screen.

Syntax

MON [C] [,I] [,O]

Description

Under normal operation, data traveling between the Apple and the disk is not displayed. MON allows some or all of the information to be displayed on screen for debugging. The three parameters control what is shown: C for commands, I for input from the disk, and

O for output to the disk. These options may be specified in any order. If MON is used without any parameters, it is ignored.

To cancel MON, use NOMON.

This is a DOS command which requires PRINT and CHR$(4) or CONTROL-D when used in a program.

Examples

```
MON C
MON C,O
MON C,I,O
```

NEW

Applesoft and Integer

Summary

Clears the current BASIC program in memory.

Syntax

NEW

Description

This command resets some memory pointers to cause the Apple to forget about any program in memory. Effectively, all program lines are eliminated. Under Applesoft, NEW resets LOMEM, but does not change the settings for COLOR, HCOLOR, or HIMEM.

With Integer BASIC, LOMEM may only be used in immediate mode.

NEXT

Applesoft and Integer

Summary

Signals the end of a FOR loop.

Applesoft Syntax

NEXT

Applesoft and Integer

NEXT *varnum* [,*varnum*...]

Description

NEXT forms the bottom of a loop, causing *varnum* to be incremented or decremented according to the corresponding loop declaration (FOR statement). The program then either executes the statements in the loop again, or continues with the instruction following NEXT. See the FOR entry earlier in this appendix.

If *varnum* does not match the variable of any active FOR loop, a ?NEXT WITHOUT FOR ERROR will appear in Applesoft, and a *** BAD NEXT ERR is shown by Integer BASIC.

NEXT may specify multiple variables for nested loops. If so, the variables must be listed in the correct order (the outermost loop must be terminated last), otherwise an error will occur.

In Applesoft, using NEXT without a variable will automatically match the most recent loop. This method also results in a slight performance gain.

Integer BASIC does not allow NEXT to be used in immediate mode. In Applesoft, using NEXT in immediate mode may cause a branch back to the most recent FOR loop executed in programmed mode.

Examples

```
10 FOR I = 1 TO 10 STEP 2
20 PRINT I
```

```
30 FOR J = 0 TO 9 STEP 3
40 PRINT J
50 NEXT J,I

100 FOR V = 10 TO 20
110 PRINT V * V
120 NEXT
```

```
]10 FOR A = 1 TO 5
]20 PRINT A
]RUN
1
]NEXT
2
]NEXT
3
```

NO DSP
Integer only

Summary

Cancels the effects of DSP.

Syntax

NO DSP *var*

Description

DSP is used to show changes to a variable *var*. NO DSP will cancel this display.

NOMON

DOS 3.3 only

Summary

Cancels the effects of MON.

Syntax

NOMON [C] [,I] [,O]

Description

The NOMON command allows some or all of the debug information from MON to be disabled. The three parameters correspond like so: C for commands, I for input from the disk, and O for output to the disk. Executing NOMON C,I,O disables all output and returns the system to its usual state. These options may be specified in any order. If NOMON is used without any parameters, it is ignored.

Examples

```
NOMON I
NOMON O,C
```

NORMAL

Applesoft only

Summary

Causes all subsequent text output to be normal style.

Syntax

NORMAL

Description

After NORMAL is executed, subsequent text output to the screen will appear as white characters on a black background (or, for the

IIgs, whatever colors are defined in the Display Control Panel). Existing characters on the screen remain as they were.

NOTRACE
Applesoft and Integer

Summary

Cancels the effects of TRACE.

Syntax

NOTRACE

Description

This command will halt the display of program lines caused by TRACE. If TRACE was not active, then this command has no effect.

ONERR GOTO
Applesoft only

Summary

Causes program execution to branch to a user-defined error handler when an Applesoft, DOS 3.3, or ProDOS error occurs.

Syntax

ONERR GOTO *line*

Description

This command is used to override the standard Applesoft error reporting mechanism with your own subroutine. Using this command will cause the program execution to branch to *line* when an Applesoft, DOS 3.3, or ProDOS error occurs. Since the branch will only happen after ONERR GOTO has been used in a program, this statement should be used early on in the program.

Each possible error has an associated code number that can be accessed by your subroutine. This number is stored in memory location 222. Using PEEK(222) will return the error code. Appendix I lists and explains every possible error code.

If an error occurs inside a subroutine or a loop, the use of ONERR GOTO can cause some problems with program execution depending on how your error handling subroutine is constructed. The error handler must return to the initial GOSUB or FOR statement in order to restart the subroutine call or loop. If instead the error handler returns control back to a RETURN or NEXT statement, another error occurs. If there are two errors in a row with GET, and the error handler returns to the program with a RESUME, the Apple will freeze. The solution is to use GOTO in this case.

Furthermore, if a program uses PRINT statements (or has TRACE activated), the 43rd error that does not stem from an INPUT statement will cause the Apple to crash into the Monitor. If instead the error handling routine ends with a GOTO instead of RESUME, the 87th error with INPUT causes the Apple to crash into the Monitor.

A short machine language subroutine presented in Table B-4 provides a solution to these problems. Your program's error handling routine should CALL this subroutine. Use the POKE statements shown in the table to enter the subroutine into memory. Then, in the error handling code, use CALL 768.

Using POKE 216, 0 will return error handling control back to the built-in Applesoft error handler.

If your error handling routine resumes program execution with a GOTO statement instead of RESUME, you should issue a CALL -3288 to clean up the stack before executing GOTO.

ONERR GOTO may only be used in programmed mode.

Mode	Commands to Enter	Description
BASIC	POKE 768, 104 : POKE 769, 168 : POKE 770, 104 : POKE 771, 166 : POKE 772, 223 : POKE 773, 154 : POKE 774, 72 : POKE 775, 152 : POKE 776, 72 : POKE 777, 96	Change the 6502 stack pointer contents to the value contained in location $DF.
Monitor	300: 68 A8 68 A6 DF 9A 48 98 48 60	

Table B-4. Machine language fix for ONERR GOTO

Example

```
10 ONERR GOTO 1000
1000 REM ERROR HANDLING ROUTINE
```

ON-GOSUB

Applesoft only

Summary

Conditionally branches to one of many subroutines in a program based on an expression.

Syntax

ON *exprnum* GOSUB *line* [,*line*...]

Description

The expression *exprnum* should have a range of values from 1 to the total number of *line* entries, which should represent valid program line numbers. If the result of *exprnum* is 1, then the first line number will be selected for the subroutine branch, if 2, then the second line number, and so on. The subroutine should end with a RETURN statement that will cause the program to jump back to the next statement following the ON-GOSUB statement.

If the value of *exprnum* is not in the range 0 to 255, the message ?ILLEGAL QUANTITY ERROR is received. If the expression equals 0 or some value greater than the number of *line* numbers, then no subroutine branch will be taken; program execution will proceed to the next statement following ON-GOSUB.

While Integer BASIC does not have this command, Integer BASIC's GOSUB does allow the result of an expression to determine a line number, thus offering similar functionality.

Example

```
1000 ON (A * 2) / 150 GOSUB 2400, 3200, 3350, 4000
```

ON-GOTO

Applesoft only

Summary

Conditionally branches to one of many lines in a program based on an expression.

Syntax

ON *exprnum* GOTO *line* [,*line*...]

Description

The expression *exprnum* should have a range of values from 1 to the total number of *line* entries, which should represent valid program line numbers. If the result of *exprnum* is 1, then the first line number will be selected for the branch, if 2, then the second line number, and so on.

If the value of *exprnum* is not in the range 0 to 255, the message ?ILLEGAL QUANTITY ERROR is received. If the expression equals 0 or some value greater than the number of *line* numbers, then no branch will be taken; program execution will proceed to the next statement following ON-GOTO.

While Integer BASIC does not have this command, Integer BASIC's GOTO does allow the result of an expression to determine a line number, thus offering similar functionality.

OPEN

DOS 3.3 and ProDOS

Summary

Selects a file on disk for read or write access.

DOS 3.3 Syntax

OPEN *filename* [,L*len*] [,S*slot*] [,D*drive*] [,V*volume*]

ProDOS Syntax

OPEN *pathname* [,L*len*] [,T*type*] [,D*drive*] [,S*slot*]

DOS 3.3 Description

Opening a file allocates a 595 byte memory buffer for the transfer of data between the Apple and the disk. The value of MAXFILES, which is 3 by default, determines how many files are allowed to be open at any single time. OPEN will create a new file if it does not exist. Once a file is opened, the READ and WRITE commands may be used to retrieve and store information from and to the file, respectively. If the file was already open, it is closed and then reopened.

The presence of the L*len* parameter indicates whether the file is to be opened as a sequential-access file or as a random-access file. If not provided, the file will be opened as a sequential-access text file. Otherwise, *len* must be an integer between 1 and 32767 specifying a record length, and will cause the file to be opened as a random-access text file.

If the file does not exist in the specified slot and drive, the message FILE NOT FOUND is displayed. If the volume number of the current disk in the specified slot and drive does not match V*volume*, then a VOLUME MISMATCH error occurs. Use volume number 0 (or none at all) to match any disk.

The slot, drive, and volume numbers may be specified in any order. If omitted, the most recently used values take effect.

This is a DOS command which requires PRINT and CHR$(4) or CONTROL-D when used in a program.

OPEN may only be used in programmed mode.

ProDOS Description

OPEN will create a new file if it does not exist. The file must not be already open, otherwise an error will occur. A 1K memory buffer is required for this command; if the memory is not available, an error will occur.

Under ProDOS, the limit for simultaneously open files is eight. The EXEC command automatically opens a file, then closes it when finished. A BASIC program should use the CLOSE command when finished with a file.

The presence of the L*len* parameter indicates whether the file is to be opened as a sequential-access file or as a random-access file. If not provided, the file will be opened as a sequential-access text file. Otherwise, *len* must be an integer between 1 and 65535 specifying a record length, and will cause the file to be opened as a random-access text file.

The T*type* parameter allows opening any other file type than text.

The slot and drive numbers may be specified in any order, and if omitted, are substituted with the ProDOS prefix.

This is a ProDOS command which requires PRINT and CHR$(4) or CONTROL-D when used in a program.

Examples

```
OPEN RANDOM, L256
```

```
OPEN SESAME
```

PDL

See Functions section later in this appendix.

PEEK

See Functions section later in this appendix.

PLOT

Applesoft and Integer

Summary

Plots a point on the low-resolution graphics screen.

Syntax

PLOT *col, row*

Description

This command places a rectangular, colored block on the screen when in low-resolution graphics mode. The block color is determined by the value of the COLOR statement most recently used. Column numbers for *col* range from 0 to 39, left to right across the screen. Row numbers for *row* range from 0 to 47, top to bottom across the screen. If a block is plotted in rows 40 to 47, it will affect the contents of the text window at the bottom of the screen unless POKE -16302, 0 was used to remove the text window.

Using PLOT while in text mode, or by plotting a point in the text window, will cause an ASCII character to appear on the screen. One ASCII character takes the place of two vertically aligned graphics blocks, meaning that there are two coordinates for each possible character position. Both halves of the character position must be plotted in order for the character to appear. The COLOR statement executed before each half is plotted determines the character that appears.

To compute which character will appear, multiply the color number of the lower half by 16, then add the color number of the upper half. The result will be an ASCII screen code, listed in Appendix E. For example, if the color at column 15, row 30 is 5 and the color at column 15, row 29 is 9, the corresponding screen code is 89 (5 * 16 + 9).

POKE
Applesoft and Integer

Summary

Changes the value of a memory location.

Syntax

POKE *address*, *byte*

Description

The value of *byte*, which must be an integer from 0 to 255, is stored in memory at *address*. If *address* is a location greater than the total amount of RAM installed in the Apple, or if it specifies a location in ROM, or if it specifies an output device that is not ready, POKE will have no effect.

Careless use of POKE is capable of destroying the BASIC program or causing the Apple to freeze. One should take care to research each memory location and its use before using POKE with it.

See Appendix C for examples of useful POKE statements.

POP

Applesoft and Integer

Summary

Causes the most recent GOSUB statement to act like GOTO.

Syntax

POP

Description

POP causes the Apple to "forget" about the most recently executed GOSUB statement. In other words, the GOSUB statement is changed to behave like a GOTO. If a RETURN statement is encountered, it will cause program execution to branch back to the statement after the second most recently executed GOSUB. If there was no other GOSUB in effect, an error will occur.

POSITION

DOS 3.3 and ProDOS

Summary

Moves the file data pointer for the next READ or WRITE operation.

DOS 3.3 Syntax

POSITION *filename* [,R*position*]

ProDOS Syntax

POSITION *pathname* ,F*position*
POSITION *pathname* ,R*position*

DOS 3.3 Description

POSITION opens *filename* if it is not already open. It then scans through the file, starting from the current data pointer location, skipping over *position* fields (separated by carriage return characters). The data pointer is placed at the first byte of the field following *position* carriage returns. If, during the file scan, a byte is encountered where no data has been stored, the error message END OF DATA occurs. This error normally happens when *position* is beyond the last field in a file.

This is a DOS command which requires PRINT and CHR$(4) or CONTROL-D when used in a program.

POSITION may only be used in programmed mode.

ProDOS Description

POSITION scans through the file, starting from the current data pointer location, skipping over *position* fields (separated by carriage return characters). The data pointer is placed at the first byte of the field following *position* carriage returns.

The R and F parameters have the same effect; they are interchangeable.

This is a ProDOS command which requires PRINT and CHR$(4) or CONTROL-D when used in a program.

POSITION may only be used in programmed mode.

Example

```
POSITION APRIL.REPORTS, R20
```

PREFIX

ProDOS only

Summary

Sets or returns the base path that ProDOS uses for resolving relative paths.

Syntax

PREFIX [*pathname*] [,D*drive*] [,S*slot*]

Description

When used without a *pathname*, PREFIX reports the current ProDOS prefix. When used in a program, PREFIX will cause the first string variable of the next INPUT statement to contain the ProDOS prefix. See the example below for a demonstration.

When used with a *pathname*, the current ProDOS prefix will be changed to the string provided. The prefix is prepended to all ProDOS pathnames and simple filenames. The prefix string may be no longer than 64 characters, including slashes.

Use PREFIX / to clear the prefix.

The slot and drive numbers may be specified in any order, and if omitted, are substituted with the ProDOS prefix.

This is a ProDOS command which requires PRINT and CHR$(4) or CONTROL-D when used in a program.

Example

```
5 D$ = CHR$ (4)
10 PRINT D$;"PREFIX"
20 PRINT "PREFIX IS: ";
30 INPUT P$
40 PRINT P$
```

PR#
Applesoft and Integer

Summary

Switches output to a given slot number or device.

General Syntax

PR# *slot*

ProDOS Syntax

PR# A*address*
PR# *slot*, A*address*

Description

The most common form of PR# is when used with a *slot* number. All subsequent PRINT statements and other program output will be directed to a device connected to the peripheral card in slot number *slot*. When *slot* is a disk controller card, drive 1 of that card boots. PR# is set to slot 0, the TV screen, when the Apple is first powered on.

The first ProDOS-specific syntax assigns output to a memory location. A machine language subroutine (device driver) should exist at *address* to handle output. Table B-5 lists several standard ProDOS output device drivers and their memory locations. The second ProDOS-specific format assigns the specified *address* to the slot numbered *slot*. It does not redirect output.

If DOS 3.3 or ProDOS is active, this command requires PRINT and CHR$(4) or CONTROL-D when used in a program.

Table B-5. Common ProDOS output device drivers

PR Number	Memory Location	Device
0	47179*	TV screen
1	49408	Slot 1 (Serial or parallel card)
2	49664	Slot 2 (Serial or parallel card)
3	49920	Slot 3 or IIe Auxiliary slot (80-column card)
4	50176	Slot 4 (Mouse commands)
5	50432	Slot 5 (3.5" drives)
6	50688	Slot 6 (Disk II drives)
7	50944	Slot 7

* 65008 if ProDOS is disabled

Examples

```
PR#6

PR# A49920
```

PRINT

Applesoft and Integer

Summary

Causes the designated characters to be sent to the screen or current output device.

Syntax

PRINT [*expr* [{; | ,} ... [*expr*]] ...]

Description

The PRINT statement has several forms. The simplest form of PRINT is when it is used alone; it produces a carriage return character.

When used with any manner of string or numeric expression, the value of the expression is displayed. Many expressions may be displayed with a single PRINT statement, separated with commas or semicolons. Depending on the type of expression, as well as the type of separators used, the display of PRINT may vary.

Whereas positive numeric values are not preceded by any sign, negative values are always prefixed with a negative sign. In Applesoft, scientific notation is used for values with more than nine significant digits before the decimal point, as well as for values closer than ±.01 to zero. String values are displayed "as-is."

Spacing between expressions is governed by the use of commas and semicolons. Separating expressions with a semicolon ensures that no space is made between them. If the PRINT statement ends with a semicolon, no carriage return character is appended. The comma is used to align values with tab stops, each of which are several spaces apart. Only on the Enhanced Apple IIe and later models does the comma work reliably to space values across the 80-column screen.

Integer BASIC tab stops are all eight spaces apart, located at columns 1, 9, 17, etc. A tab stop is skipped over when any nonblank character is printed just before it, for example, at column 8.

Tab stops in Applesoft are wider than those in Integer BASIC: 16 characters apart. However, on the display screen, only the first two tab stops are 16 spaces wide; the third is only eight spaces wide on the 40-column screen.

If the PRINT statement ends with a comma, then the next PRINT statement will display its value at the next tab field.

Using the semicolon to concatenate values is optional in Applesoft; it is required in Integer BASIC. Omitting the semicolon in Applesoft will cause all values to be displayed end-to-end with no spaces in between.

When entering a program in Applesoft, the question mark (?) may be used as shorthand for the PRINT keyword. When a program is listed (with LIST), the word PRINT will appear in its place.

READ

Applesoft only

Summary

Assigns the next DATA element to a variable and increments the data pointer.

Syntax

READ *var* [,*var*...]

Description

READ is the companion statement to DATA. If a program contains one or more DATA elements, a pointer to the first item in the list is established when the program is first executed. Each successive READ statement returns the value indicated by the pointer, then increments the pointer to mark the next element. Eventually, the pointer reaches the last data element, and can advance no further. The RESTORE function is used to move the pointer back to the beginning.

The variable type of *var* should generally match the type of data in the list. It is acceptable to assign a numeric value to a string *var*. However, attempting the reverse, using READ with a numeric *var* when a string is returned, results in a ?SYNTAX ERROR and the line number of the mismatched DATA statement.

Attempting to read more DATA elements than actually exists is also a cause for error. In this case, the ?END OF DATA ERROR message appears, along with the line number of the READ statement that was used.

READ is permissible for use in immediate execution mode as long as more DATA elements are available. However, when DOS 3.3 or ProDOS is active, READ is assumed to be a disk command, and an error message appears.

Examples

```
200 READ IL$, SH
```

```
310 READ V
```

READ
DOS 3.3 and ProDOS

Summary

Takes data for subsequent INPUT or GET statements from a disk file.

DOS 3.3 Syntax

READ *filename* [,R*record*] [,B*byte*]

ProDOS Syntax

READ *pathname* [,R*record*] [,F*field*] [,B*byte*]

DOS 3.3 Description

The file *filename* is first opened if it is not already open. If the file is not located on the disk, a FILE NOT FOUND error occurs. READ causes all subsequent INPUT and GET statements to draw their input from the disk file named *filename* until another DOS command is issued.

If the file is a random-access text file, the R*record* parameter allows just that particular record to be read. The B*byte* option skips a number of bytes (characters) from the start of the file before reading. Both the B and R options must be integer values from 0 to 32767.

This is a DOS command which requires PRINT and CHR$(4) or CONTROL-D when used in a program.

READ may only be used in programmed mode.

ProDOS Description

READ causes all subsequent INPUT and GET statements to draw their input from the disk file at *pathname* until another ProDOS command is issued.

If the file is a random-access text file, the R*record* parameter allows just that particular record to be read. The F*field* option starts reading after skipping a number of fields (carriage return characters). The B*byte* option skips a number of bytes (characters) from the start of the file before reading.

This is a ProDOS command which requires PRINT and CHR$(4) or CONTROL-D when used in a program.

READ may only be used in programmed mode.

RECALL

Applesoft only

Summary

Recalls an Applesoft array from cassette tape to memory.

Syntax

RECALL *varnum*

Description

The variable *varnum* used with RECALL must be a numeric array, either real or integer, and it must already be dimensioned. As soon as RECALL is executed, the Apple starts listening for an array on the cassette tape. The only way to interrupt RECALL is by pressing CONTROL-RESET. There is no prompt to start the tape player; it should be playing as soon as RECALL is used. The Apple beeps twice: at the beginning of the array values, and when the array values are all recalled.

It is not necessary to use the same variable name as was used when the array was stored on tape, however the array should be of the same dimensions. If the stored array on tape exceeds the recalled array, an ?OUT OF MEMORY ERROR will occur. If the stored and recalled arrays have the same number of elements, but differ in dimensions, the message ERR results, but program execution will continue.

Problems occur if the recalled array has more elements than the stored array, resulting in some values being scrambled. If only the last dimension of the recalled array is larger than the stored array, then no scrambling will happen. If the recalled array has more dimensions than the stored array, there will be no problem as long as the earlier dimension sizes match.

RECALL cannot be used with string arrays. However, the CHR$ function could be used later on in the program to convert numeric values back to strings.

REM

Applesoft and Integer

Summary

Allows the rest of the line to be used for program comments.

Syntax

REM *comment*

Description

The *comment* can consist of any number of characters as long as the maximum program line length is not exceeded. When used on a multiple statement program line, REM should be the last statement, for it prevents any further statements on the line from being executed.

Though remark statements appear in the program listing, they are ignored at all other times. They exist purely for human convenience.

RENAME

DOS 3.3 and ProDOS

Summary

Changes the name of an unlocked file.

DOS 3.3 Syntax

RENAME *old filename, new filename* [,S*slot*] [,D*drive*] [,V*volume*]

ProDOS Syntax

RENAME *old pathname, new pathname* [,D*drive*] [,S*slot*]

DOS 3.3 Description

If the *old filename* exists on the disk, it is closed (only if it had been open) and renamed to *new filename*. No other changes are made. The file must be unlocked.

The RENAME command does not check if a file named *new filename* already exists on the disk. It is, therefore, possible to end up with two, three, or more files all sharing the same name.

If the *old filename* does not exist in the specified slot and drive, the message FILE NOT FOUND is displayed. If the volume number of the current disk in the specified slot and drive does not match V*volume*, then a VOLUME MISMATCH error occurs. Use volume number 0 (or none at all) to match any disk.

The slot, drive, and volume numbers may be specified in any order. If omitted, the most recently used values take effect.

This is a DOS command which requires PRINT and CHR$(4) or CONTROL-D when used in a program.

ProDOS Description

The RENAME command can only rename a file in the same directory; it cannot move a file to a different directory. The file must be closed and unlocked in order to be renamed. If a file already exists at *new pathname*, an error occurs. Only files in different directories may share the same name.

The slot and drive numbers may be specified in any order, and if omitted, are substituted with the ProDOS prefix.

This is a ProDOS command which requires PRINT and CHR$(4) or CONTROL-D when used in a program.

Example

```
RENAME CONSTANTINOPLE, ISTANBUL, S5,D2
```

RESTORE

Applesoft only

Summary

Moves the DATA pointer back to the beginning of the list.

Syntax

RESTORE

Description

The DATA pointer is reset to point to the first DATA element, affecting subsequent READ statements.

RESTORE

ProDOS only

Summary

Reads a list of Applesoft variables and their values from a file on a ProDOS disk.

Syntax

RESTORE *pathname* [,D*drive*] [,S*slot*]

Description

All Applesoft variables are cleared and replaced with those read from the disk file located at *pathname*. The file must be type VAR. The STORE command is used to create such a file.

The slot and drive numbers may be specified in any order, and if omitted, are substituted with the ProDOS prefix.

This is a ProDOS command which requires PRINT and CHR$(4) or CONTROL-D when used in a program.

RESUME

Applesoft only

Summary

Causes an Applesoft program to resume execution at the statement where an error last occurred.

Syntax

RESUME

Description

RESUME should only be used at the end of an error handling routine triggered by ONERR GOTO. Any other use of RESUME may cause undesirable effects.

RETURN

Applesoft and Integer

Summary

Exits a subroutine by returning control back to the statement immediately following the initial GOSUB.

Syntax

RETURN

Description

RETURN is a branch statement that sends program execution back to the statement that follows the most recently used GOSUB, unless POP was used.

If there is no active subroutine when RETURN is encountered, the message ?RETURN WITHOUT GOSUB ERROR is displayed.

ROT

Applesoft only

Summary

Sets rotation factor for a high-resolution shape.

Syntax

ROT= *exprnum*

Description

The rotational angle of the shape to be drawn by DRAW or XDRAW is set to *exprnum*, which must be a number from 0 to 255. A shape may be rotated in one of a total of 64 positions, but the number of positions depends on the SCALE used. An *exprnum* of 0 draws the shape upright as it was defined, 16 rotates 90 degrees clockwise, 32 rotates 180 degrees clockwise, and so on.

Only four rotation values are recognized when SCALE is 1, eight are valid when the SCALE is 2, etc. Rotation values greater than 64 repeat back at 0. An unrecognized rotation value will be replaced with the next smaller recognized value.

ROT is only parsed as a reserved word if the next nonspace character is an equals sign.

Example

```
20 ROT = 13
```

RUN

Applesoft and Integer

Summary

Starts execution of a BASIC program.

General Syntax

RUN [*line*]

Integer BASIC Syntax

RUN *exprnum*

Description

When used without a line number *line*, the BASIC program starts running from its lowest numbered line.

If the line number *line* does not exist, an error occurs. Otherwise, program execution starts at the given line number.

The starting line number may be the result of a numeric expression in Integer BASIC. Applesoft does not permit an expression.

RUN

DOS 3.3 and ProDOS

Summary

Loads and runs a BASIC program from a file on disk.

DOS 3.3 Syntax

RUN *filename* [,S*slot*] [,D*drive*] [,V*volume*]

ProDOS Syntax

RUN *pathname* [,@*line*] [,D*drive*] [,S*slot*]

DOS 3.3 Description

The file named *filename* is loaded from disk into memory and then run. Any existing program lines, variables, and arrays are cleared.

If necessary, the Apple switches to the language necessary to run the program. If the requisite language is not available, a message to that effect is stated on screen.

If the file does not exist in the specified slot and drive, the message FILE NOT FOUND is displayed. If the volume number of the current disk in the specified slot and drive does not match

V*volume*, then a VOLUME MISMATCH error occurs. Use volume number 0 (or none at all) to match any disk.

The slot, drive, and volume numbers may be specified in any order. If omitted, the most recently used values take effect.

This is a DOS command which requires PRINT and CHR$(4) or CONTROL-D when used in a program.

ProDOS Description

The file located at *pathname* is loaded from disk into memory and then run. Any existing program lines, variables, and arrays are cleared.

If the *@line* option is used, the program starts running at line number *line*. If that line number does not exist, the next highest line number is used instead.

The slot and drive numbers may be specified in any order, and if omitted, are substituted with the ProDOS prefix.

This is a ProDOS command which requires PRINT and CHR$(4) or CONTROL-D when used in a program.

SAVE

Applesoft and Integer

Summary

Saves the program currently in memory to cassette tape.

Syntax

SAVE

Description

The SAVE command places a copy of the current BASIC program on a cassette tape. The tape recorder should be running in record mode as soon as SAVE is executed. The Apple does not prompt the user to do so. The Apple beeps as it begins recording the program to cassette, and it beeps when the process is complete. After the second beep, you should stop the tape recorder.

In Integer BASIC, SAVE may only be used in immediate mode.

SAVE
DOS 3.3 and ProDOS

Summary

Saves the program currently in memory to a file on disk.

DOS 3.3 Syntax

SAVE *filename* [,S*slot*] [,D*drive*] [,V*volume*]

ProDOS Syntax

SAVE *pathname* [,D*drive*] [,S*slot*]

DOS 3.3 Description

A file named *filename* is created on the disk if it does not already exist. The current Integer BASIC or Applesoft program in memory is stored in that file. If the file exists, but is of a different language or file type, the message FILE TYPE MISMATCH is presented.

DOS does not provide any warning when it overwrites the old contents of *filename*. The original contents are lost.

If the volume number of the current disk in the specified slot and drive does not match V*volume*, then a VOLUME MISMATCH error occurs. Use volume number 0 (or none at all) to match any disk.

The slot, drive, and volume numbers may be specified in any order. If omitted, the most recently used values take effect.

This is a DOS command which requires PRINT and CHR$(4) or CONTROL-D when uscd in a program.

ProDOS Description

A file named *pathname* is created on the disk if it does not already exist. The current Applesoft program in memory is stored in that file. If the file exists, but is not a type BAS file, the message FILE TYPE MISMATCH is presented.

ProDOS does not provide any warning when it overwrites the old contents of *pathname*. The original contents are lost.

The slot and drive numbers may be specified in any order, and if omitted, are substituted with the ProDOS prefix.

This is a ProDOS command which requires PRINT and CHR$(4) or CONTROL-D when used in a program.

SCALE
Applesoft only

Summary

Sets the size of a high-resolution shape when next plotted by DRAW or XDRAW.

Syntax

SCALE= *exprnum*

Description

The size of the shape is determined by the value of *exprnum*. When *exprnum* is 1, the shape is drawn on a one-to-one scale, where each screen dot represents one vector. At a scale of 2, the shape is drawn twice its original size. A scale of 0 draws the shape 256 times its original size.

The value of *exprnum* must be in the range of 0 to 255, otherwise an ?ILLEGAL QUANTITY ERROR will occur.

SCALE is treated as a reserved word if the next nonspace character is the equals sign.

Example

```
200 SCALE= 34
```

SHLOAD
Applesoft only

Summary

Loads a high-resolution shape table from cassette tape into memory.

Syntax

SHLOAD

Description

The shape table is loaded into memory right below HIMEM and HIMEM is set below the shape table to protect it. The shape table starting address is also automatically set. To prepare a shape table, refer to Chapter 8. Instructions on saving a shape table to cassette tape are also detailed in Chapter 8.

SPEED
Applesoft only

Summary

Changes the rate at which characters are sent to the screen or another device.

Syntax

SPEED = *exprnum*

Description

SPEED affects output from PRINT statements, LIST, and error messages produced by the Apple. The speed rate *exprnum* ranges from 0 to 255: 0 is the slowest rate, and 255 is fastest. Supplying an out of range value will cause an ?ILLEGAL QUANTITY ERROR message to be displayed.

Example

```
SPEED= 240
```

STOP

Applesoft only

Summary

Halts the program and prints the line number that contained the STOP.

Syntax

STOP

Description

After the program is stopped, the message BREAK IN *line* is printed, where *line* is the line number containing the STOP instruction.

Example

```
]10 STOP

]RUN

BREAK IN 10
]
```

STORE
Applesoft only

Summary

Stores an Applesoft array on cassette tape.

Syntax

STORE *varnum*

Description

The array *varnum* is stored on tape. STORE immediately starts recording; it does not prompt the user to start the cassette player, no does it control tape movement. The tape player must be in record mode as soon as STORE is used. The Apple will beep once to signal that it is recording the array, then a final time when it is finished.

Only numeric (real or integer type) arrays may be stored. To store strings, they must first be converted to their ASCII values using the ASC function. The RECALL function restores an array from tape.

STORE
ProDOS only

Summary

Saves the names and values of all variables to a disk file.

Syntax

STORE *pathname* [,D*drive*] [,S*slot*]

Description

All variables and their values from the current program are put into a special format and saved to the file named at *pathname*. In addition, the STORE command also performs garbage collection, removing unused strings from memory. The RESTORE command loads a file with variables back into memory.

The slot and drive numbers may be specified in any order, and if omitted, are substituted with the ProDOS prefix.

This is a ProDOS command which requires PRINT and CHR$(4) or CONTROL-D when used in a program.

TAB

Integer only

Summary

Moves the cursor to a specified column on the current line.

Syntax

TAB *col*

Description

This is an Integer BASIC statement. The cursor is moved left or right across the current display line to column number *col* without affecting any characters on the line. The columns are numbered from 1 to 40, left to right. If 80-columns mode is active, TAB cannot be used to move the cursor to any column beyond 40. Instead, use the statement POKE 36,*col*. TAB has the same effect on printers as it does on the screen.

The Applesoft equivalent of TAB is HTAB. Applesoft also has a TAB function, listed in the Functions section of this appendix.

TEXT

Applesoft and Integer

Summary

Changes the screen to text mode.

Syntax

TEXT

Description

Unless the screen is already in text mode, the TEXT command switches from any of the three graphics modes to text mode. The prompt and cursor are moved to the last line of the screen. If the screen is already in text mode, TEXT has the same effect as VTAB 24.

If the dimensions of the text window are changed, TEXT resets the window to full screen.

When used in low-resolution graphics mode, the screen memory is not cleared, and graphics will appear as various characters in normal, inverse, and flashing modes.

TRACE

Applesoft and Integer

Summary

Prints the line number of each line as it is executed while running a program.

Syntax

TRACE

Description

TRACE should be used as a debugging aid, however it does cause the line numbers that it prints to be intermixed with your program's usual output. The effects of TRACE are disabled with NOTRACE.

UNLOCK

DOS 3.3 and ProDOS

Summary

Unlocks a file, allowing it to be modified.

DOS 3.3 Syntax

UNLOCK *filename* [,S*slot*] [,D*drive*] [,V*volume*]

ProDOS Syntax

UNLOCK *pathname* [,D*drive*] [,S*slot*]

DOS 3.3 Description

Unlocking a file removes its protection, allowing it to be changed, renamed, and deleted. A file is shown in the disk catalog with no asterisk before its file type if it is unlocked.

If the file does not exist in the specified slot and drive, the message FILE NOT FOUND is displayed. If the volume number of the current disk in the specified slot and drive does not match V*volume*, then a VOLUME MISMATCH error occurs. Use volume number 0 (or none at all) to match any disk.

The slot, drive, and volume numbers may be specified in any order. If omitted, the most recently used values take effect.

This is a DOS command which requires PRINT and CHR$(4) or CONTROL-D when used in a program.

ProDOS Description

Unlocking a file removes its protection, allowing it to be changed, renamed, and deleted. A file is shown in the disk catalog with no asterisk before its name if it is unlocked.

The slot and drive numbers may be specified in any order, and if omitted, are substituted with the ProDOS prefix.

This is a ProDOS command which requires PRINT and CHR$(4) or CONTROL-D when used in a program.

See Functions section later in this appendix.

VERIFY

DOS 3.3 and ProDOS

Summary

Checks that a disk file can be successfully read without any errors.

DOS 3.3 Syntax

VERIFY *filename* [,S*slot*] [,D*drive*] [,V*volume*]

ProDOS Syntax

VERIFY [*pathname*] [,D*drive*] [,S*slot*]

DOS 3.3 Description

The VERIFY command calculates a new checksum byte for *filename* and compares it with the checksum byte originally stored on the disk. If the two match, then no message is presented. Otherwise, the message I/O ERROR appears, indicating that there may be a problem with the file. Any file type may be used with VERIFY.

If the file does not exist in the specified slot and drive, the message FILE NOT FOUND is displayed. If the volume number of the current disk in the specified slot and drive does not match V*volume*, then a VOLUME MISMATCH error occurs. Use volume number 0 (or none at all) to match any disk.

The slot, drive, and volume numbers may be specified in any order. If omitted, the most recently used values take effect.

This is a DOS command which requires PRINT and CHR$(4) or CONTROL-D when used in a program.

ProDOS Description

The VERIFY command checks that a file exists at *pathname*. If no error message appears, the file exists. Entering VERIFY without a *pathname* will print a copyright notice.

The slot and drive numbers may be specified in any order, and if omitted, are substituted with the ProDOS prefix.

This is a ProDOS command which requires PRINT and CHR$(4) or CONTROL-D when used in a program.

VLIN

Applesoft and Integer

Summary

Draws a vertical line in low-resolution graphics mode.

Syntax

VLIN *row1*, *row2* AT *col*

Description

A line stretching from *row1* to *row2* is drawn in the column specified by *col*. The line color is determined by the last executed COLOR statement. When the screen is in text mode, or if the line extends past row 39 into the text window, various ASCII characters will appear instead of colored blocks. These characters are determined by the COLOR last used; see the explanation for PLOT.

With Applesoft, it does not matter which value, *row1* or *row2*, is greater. Integer BASIC requires that *row2* be greater than or equal to *row1*, otherwise a *** RANGE ERR will occur.

Example

```
VLIN 5,18 AT 23
```

VTAB

Applesoft and Integer

Summary

Moves the cursor to a different line in the current screen column.

Syntax

VTAB *row*

Description

The cursor is moved between screen rows without affecting any characters already displayed. The rows are numbered 1 to 24, top to bottom.

WAIT

Applesoft only

Summary

Pauses program execution until a certain bit pattern appears at a certain memory location.

Syntax

WAIT *address*, *exprnum1* [,*exprnum2*]

Description

The WAIT command is used to check some or all of the eight bits of memory location *address* for a binary bit pattern specified by the binary value of *exprnum1*. The *address* must be in the range of -65535 to 65535, otherwise an ?ILLEGAL QUANTITY ERROR will occur. Practically, the *address* is limited to the amount of RAM in the Apple.

The binary value of *exprnum1* is compared to the binary value of the byte in memory at *address*. Each bit is ANDed with the corresponding bit. If every resulting bit is zero, then the test is repeated. However, if any bit results in a 1, then the WAIT is over, and the program resumes execution.

If *exprnum2* is specified, its bits indicate the state (low or high) that is being waited for. A 1 bit means the corresponding bit must be low (0), and 0 means that the corresponding bit must be high (1). If *exprnum2* is not provided, 0 is used.

Only CONTROL-RESET will serve to interrupt a WAIT statement. The values of *exprnum1* and *exprnum2* must be in the range 0 to 255. It is possible to WAIT on a memory location whose bit pattern will never change or never match; in this case, the only solution is to press CONTROL-RESET or power off the Apple.

WRITE

DOS 3.3 and ProDOS

Summary

Prepares a disk file to receive data from the Apple.

DOS 3.3 Syntax

WRITE *filename* [,R*record*] [,B*byte*]

ProDOS Syntax

WRITE *pathname* [,R*record*] [,F*field*] [,B*byte*]

DOS 3.3 Description

The file *filename* is first opened if it is not already open. If the file is not located on the disk, a FILE NOT FOUND error occurs. WRITE causes all subsequent PRINT statements to send their output to the disk file named *filename* until another DOS command is issued. All other screen output, including error messages and INPUT prompts, will also be sent to the file.

If the file is a random-access text file, the R*record* parameter allows just that particular record to be written. The B*byte* option skips a number of bytes (characters) from the start of the file before writing. Both the B and R options must be integer values from 0 to 32767. Using the B*byte* option, it is possible to write past the end of a file. Doing so will work, but attempting to read the space where no characters were ever written will yield an OUT OF DATA error.

This is a DOS command which requires PRINT and CHR$(4) or CONTROL-D when used in a program.

WRITE may only be used in programmed mode.

ProDOS Description

WRITE causes all subsequent PRINT statements to send their output to the disk file named *filename* until another ProDOS command is issued. All other screen output, including error messages, but excepting INPUT prompts, will also be sent to the file.

If the file is a random-access text file, the R*record* parameter allows just that particular record to be written. The F*field* option starts writing after skipping a number of fields (carriage return characters). The B*byte* option skips a number of bytes (characters) from the start of the file before writing.

This is a ProDOS command which requires PRINT and CHR$(4) or CONTROL-D when used in a program.

WRITE may only be used in programmed mode.

XDRAW

Applesoft only

Summary

Draws a high-resolution shape using the complementary color of the background.

Syntax

XDRAW *exprnum* [AT *columnh*, *rowh*]

Description

The high-resolution shape corresponding to the integer value of *exprnum* is plotted on the screen in the color complementary to the dot already on screen. The complementary color pairs are listed in Table 8-7. Plotting commences at the coordinates specified by *columnh* and *rowh*. If these coordinates are not provided, the shape starts at the position most recently plotted with DRAW, HPLOT, or XDRAW.

XDRAW is used to draw and erase a shape without affecting the background. Using XDRAW an even number of times (two, four, and so on) with the same parameters will leave the screen as it was before XDRAW had been first used.

The scale and rotation of the shape are defined by the SCALE and ROT commands, respectively, and must be executed before the shape is plotted.

The shape number, *exprnum*, must be in the range of 0 to the number of shapes in the shape table (which is limited to 255).

Functions

A function accepts either numeric or string input, processes it, and then provides some output. Functions whose names end with a $ return a string value; all other functions return a number.

The nomenclature used for the syntax is the same as used in the previous section of commands, and is defined at the start of this appendix.

Integer BASIC lacks many of these functions, most notably the mathematical ones. Functions exclusive to Applesoft will be noted as so.

ABS
Applesoft and Integer

Summary

Returns the absolute value of a number.

Syntax

ABS(*exprnum*)

Description

The absolute value of a number is the number without a sign. See the examples for further explanation.

Examples

```
]PRINT ABS(-6)
6

]PRINT ABS(4.5)
4.5

]PRINT ABS(0)
0
```

ASC
Applesoft and Integer

Summary

Returns the ASCII code for a given character, in decimal.

Syntax

ASC(*expr$*)

Description

This function returns the ASCII code of the first character of *expr$*. The programmer should be aware that ASCII codes 0 through 95 are repeated in the range 96 through 255. ASC will not necessarily return the lowest possible ASCII code for a given character. Furthermore, differing ASCII codes, though they may appear to generate the same letter or symbol, are treated as different with the logical string operators (<, >, and =).

If a string is provided, it must be within quotation marks ("). Attempting to supply an empty (null) string will result in an ?ILLEGAL QUANTITY ERROR, while providing a null character (such as produced by CONTROL-@) will yield a ?SYNTAX ERROR.

For your reference, Appendix E contains an ASCII chart.

Examples

```
]PRINT ASC("A")
65

]PRINT ASC("PARTY")
80

]C$ = "N"

]PRINT ASC(C$)
78
```

ATN
Applesoft only

Summary

Computes the arctangent, in radians, of its argument.

Syntax

ATN(*exprnum*)

Description

The arctangent of *exprnum* is returned in radians. The function range is $-\pi/2$ to $\pi/2$ radians.

CHR$
Applesoft only

Summary

Returns the character represented by a given ASCII code.

Syntax

CHR$(*exprnum*)

Description

CHR$ performs the opposite function of ASC: it produces the character whose ASCII code is *exprnum*. Using this function, it is possible to generate special characters, such as control characters, which are not possible to type from the keyboard. Appendix E contains a table of all characters and their ASCII codes.

The value of *exprnum* must be in the range 0 to 255, otherwise an ?ILLEGAL QUANTITY ERROR will occur.

Examples

```
]PRINT CHR$(65)
A

]PRINT CHR$(07)


]PRINT CHR$(257)

?ILLEGAL QUANTITY ERROR
```

COS

Applesoft only

Summary

Returns the cosine, in radians, of the argument.

Syntax

COS(*exprnum*)

Description

The cosine of *exprnum* is computed in radians.

Examples

```
]PRINT COS(0)
1

]PRINT COS(3.14159)
-1
```

EXP
Applesoft only

Summary

Returns a power of *e*.

Syntax

EXP(*exprnum*)

Description

The value of *e* is raised to the power specified by *exprnum*. The value of *e* is approximately 2.71828, and it is used in natural logarithms.

FN
Applesoft only

Summary

Calls a user-defined function.

Syntax

FN *varnum* (*exprnum*)

Description

This function is used to invoke a user-defined function that was defined previously in an Applesoft program. The *varnum* is the name of the function as defined by DEF FN, and *exprnum* is the variable that replaces *varname* in the function definition. See DEF FN earlier in this appendix for further information.

A user-defined function may not call itself, either directly or indirectly (through another function).

If the program line that defines the function *varnum* has not been executed yet, attempting to use the function will yield an ?UNDEF'D FUNCTION ERROR message.

FRE

Applesoft only

Summary

Returns the amount of memory available to the program, in bytes.

Syntax

FRE(*exprnum*)

Description

The FRE function performs two actions: first, it returns the amount of free memory, in bytes, for variable storage in a program. This memory is located between the string storage and the array storage areas. If this value is greater than 32767, then "negative notation" is used. Simply add 65536 to get the true value.

The second purpose of FRE is to clear the string storage area of old, unused string values. Due to the way that Applesoft works, when the value of a string is changed, the old value is left in memory, and a new one added. Eventually, all of these old strings will fill up memory, preventing new strings from being created. The example below shows how to use FRE to clean up string storage. Only programs which make extensive use of strings should need to use FRE, and then only periodically.

Though the function takes an argument *exprnum*, this argument is never used. It must, however, be a legal numeric value. Using 0 is common.

Example

```
400 X = FRE(0)
```

INT

Applesoft only

Summary

Converts a real number to an integer.

Syntax

INT(*exprnum*)

Description

This function returns an integer that is less than or equal to the value of *exprnum*.

LEFT$

Applesoft only

Summary

Returns the leftmost characters of a string.

Syntax

LEFT$(*expr$*, *exprnum*)

Description

LEFT$ returns the leftmost *exprnum* characters from the string *expr$*. The string *expr$* must not be longer than 255 characters, and the value of *exprnum* must be from 1 to 255. If *exprnum* is greater than the total number of characters in *expr$*, the string is returned unchanged.

LEN

Applesoft and Integer

Summary

Returns the length of a given string.

Syntax

LEN(*expr$*)

Description

This function returns the total count of characters in *expr$*, including nonprinting and control characters. The length of *expr$* should not be greater than 255, otherwise a ?STRING TOO LONG ERROR message occurs. This message could only appear if *expr$* is a string concatenation.

LOG

Applesoft only

Summary

Returns the natural logarithm of a number.

Syntax

LOG(*exprnum*)

Description

The natural logarithm of *exprnum* is computed. If *exprnum* is zero or less than zero, an ?ILLEGAL QUANTITY ERROR is issued.

MID$
Applesoft only

Summary

Returns a substring.

Syntax

MID$(*expr$*, *exprnum1*, [*exprnum2*])

Description

The substring of *expr$* is returned, started by skipping *exprnum1* characters from the beginning of the string. If *exprnum2* is present, the string will be *exprnum2* characters in length. If *exprnum1* is greater than *expr$*, the null string is returned. If returning *exprnum2* characters would exceed the length of *expr$*, the value of *exprnum2* is ignored.

The length of *expr$* is limited to 255 characters. The values of *exprnum1* and *exprnum2* are limited from 1 to 255.

PDL
Applesoft and Integer

Summary

Returns the current value of the given paddle.

Syntax

PDL (*exprnum*)

Description

The value of game paddle number *exprnum* is returned. The value is a decimal between 0 and 255 that reflects how far the knob is turned (or how far the stick is moved for a joystick). The given argument *exprnum* must be between 0 and 3, otherwise the result will be unpredictable. If *exprnum* is outside of the range 0 to 255, an ?ILLEGAL QUANTITY ERROR message is presented.

Executing two PDL statements consecutively may cause the value of the second reading to be affected by the first. The solution is to allow a few program instructions to pass between readings, or even an empty FOR-NEXT loop with 10 or so iterations.

Example

```
]PRINT PDL(0)
128
```

PEEK

Applesoft and Integer

Summary

Returns the contents of the specified memory location as a decimal value between 0 and 255.

Syntax

PEEK(*address*)

Description

The function argument *address* must be a numeric variable. The byte located at *address* is converted to decimal before it is returned.

See Appendix C for some useful PEEK statements.

Examples

```
]A$=PEEK(1)

?TYPE MISMATCH ERROR
]A%=PEEK(1)
```

```
]PRINT A%
60

]B = PEEK(-151)

]PRINT B
169
```

POS
Applesoft only

Summary

Returns the current horizontal position of the cursor.

Syntax

POS(*exprnum*)

Description

The value that POS returns ranges from 0 to 39, corresponding to the location of the cursor on the current line. The leftmost edge of the screen is 0, the rightmost is 39. POS does not work correctly when the 80-column card is active.

Though the function takes an argument *exprnum*, this argument is never used. It must, however, be a legal numeric value. Using 0 is common.

RIGHT$
Applesoft only

Summary

Returns the rightmost characters of a string.

Syntax

RIGHT$(*expr$*, *exprnum*)

Description

RIGHT$ returns the rightmost *exprnum* characters from the string *expr$*. The string *expr$* must not be longer than 255 characters, and the value of *exprnum* must be from 1 to 255. If *exprnum* is greater than the total number of characters in *expr$*, the string is returned unchanged.

RND

Applesoft and Integer

Summary

Generates a random number.

Syntax

RND(*exprnum*)

Applesoft Description

RND returns a random floating point number greater than or equal to zero and less than 1. The behavior of RND is affected by the sign of *exprnum*. If *exprnum* is negative, a random number seed is started, meaning that all of the numbers returned by RND will follow a repeatable pattern.

If *exprnum* is positive, a different random number is returned each time. However, if *exprnum* is positive and a random number seed was started, all numbers will follow a pattern. This pattern is useful for testing programs that require random numbers.

The final behavior of RND is to return the most recently generated random number when *exprnum* is zero. This value is not affected by CLEAR or NEW.

Integer BASIC Description

RND returns a random number between zero and the given argument *exprnum* -1. Thus, RND(3) returns a mix of zeros, ones, and twos. Using RND(0) returns a *** >32767 ERR message. If *exprnum* is less than zero, a *** SYNTAX ERR occurs.

SCRN

Applesoft and Integer

Summary

Returns the color at a given low-resolution screen location.

Syntax

SCRN(*column*, *row*)

Description

The most common use of SCRN is to return the color code of the low-resolution block located at point (*column*, *row*), when *column* is from 0 to 39. However, if *column* is in the range 40 to 47, the color point of coordinate (*column* - 40, *row* + 16) is returned. If *column* is from 40 and 47, and *row* is from 32 to 47, the number returned by SCRN is unrelated to anything on the screen.

If high-resolution graphics mode is active, SCRN still returns a value related to the contents of the low-resolution graphics screen area. This means that SCRN does not have anything to do with the high-resolution display.

When the screen is in TEXT mode, SCRN returns a number from 0 to 15 related to the current character at position (*column*, *row*). The expression CHR$(SCRN(X-1, 2*(Y-1))+16 * SCRN(X-1, 2*(Y-1)+1)) returns the character at screen position (X, Y).

SCRN is counted as a reserved word only if a left parenthesis is the next nonspace character.

SGN

Applesoft only

Summary

Returns the sign of a number; whether it is positive, negative, or zero.

Syntax

SGN(*exprnum*)

Description

If *exprnum* is positive, SGN returns +1; -1 is returned if negative. Finally, if *exprnum* is zero, 0 is returned.

SIN

Applesoft only

Summary

Computes the sine of the given argument, in radians.

Syntax

SIN(*exprnum*)

Description

The sine of *exprnum* is returned, computed in radians.

SPC

Applesoft only

Summary

Prints one or more spaces.

Syntax

SPC(*exprnum*)

Description

The SPC function should be used from within PRINT statements to display *exprnum* spaces. If any characters are already on the screen, they will be eliminated if the spaces pass over them.

SPC always starts at the current column position of the cursor, and moves *exprnum* spaces to the right.

Example

```
500 PRINT SPC(3)
```

SQR

Applesoft only

Summary

Computes the square root of the given argument.

Syntax

SQR(*exprnum*)

Description

The value of *exprnum* must not be negative, otherwise an ?ILLEGAL QUANTITY ERROR will occur. The SQR function is faster than the equivalent expression (*exprnum*) ^ (.5).

STR$

Applesoft only

Summary

Converts a numeric argument into a string and returns it.

Syntax

STR$(*exprnum*)

Description

The value of *exprnum* is converted to a string in the form that it would appear if it were used in a PRINT statement. If *exprnum* exceeds the limits of real numbers, an ?OVERFLOW ERROR message is displayed.

TAB

Applesoft only

Summary

Moves the cursor rightward to the given column number.

Syntax

TAB(*exprnum*)

Description

The TAB function should be used from within PRINT statements to move the cursor right to column number *exprnum*. If the cursor is already at or past this column, no effect happens. TAB prints spaces over any existing characters on the line as it moves the cursor.

The column numbers for TAB are numbered 1 to 40, left to right. Only on an Enhanced Apple IIe and later models may TAB be used correctly on an 80-column screen. Use POKE 36, *exprnum* to move the cursor to columns past 40 on any model of Apple.

This function has the same name as the Integer BASIC TAB statement (explained earlier in this appendix), though the effect differs.

TAN
Applesoft only

Summary

Returns the tangent of the argument in radians.

Syntax

TAN(*exprnum*)

Description

This function computes the tangent of *exprnum*, and returns the value in radians.

USR
Applesoft only

Summary

Passes its argument to a machine language subroutine.

Syntax

USR *exprnum*

Description

USR places the value of *exprnum* in the Applesoft floating point accumulator (located in memory from 157 to 163, decimal; $9D to $A3, hex). The Apple then branches to memory location $0A with a JSR instruction. The three bytes starting at $0A should contain a machine language JMP instruction to the starting address of an assembly language subroutine. When the subroutine returns to

Applesoft (with an RTS instruction), the contents of the floating point accumulator are returned as a numeric real value from USR.

Appendix H contains a number of assembly language subroutines built into the Monitor. See also the CALL statement, explained earlier in this appendix.

VAL

Applesoft only

Summary

Attempts to convert a string to a numeric value and return that value.

Syntax

VAL(*expr$*)

Description

The first character of *expr$* must be a numeric character, otherwise zero is returned. The acceptable numeric characters include: all digits, an initial plus or minus sign, spaces, and a decimal point. For scientific notation, an additional plus or minus sign, decimal point, and the letter E are allowed. If any other character is encountered as VAL works its way across *expr$*, processing stops.

If *expr$* is longer than 255 characters (only possible through string concatenation), a ?STRING TOO LONG ERROR occurs. If the numeric value of *expr$* exceeds the limits of real numbers, an ?OVERFLOW ERROR message is displayed.

Derived Numeric Functions

The following functions use existing Applesoft functions and can be easily used with the DEF FN function.

Secant
SEC(X) = 1/COS(X)

Cosecant
CSC(X) = 1/SIN(X)

Cotangent
COT(X) = 1/TAN(X)

Inverse Sine
ARCSIN(X) = ATN(X/SQR(-X*X+1))

Inverse Cosine
ARCCOS(X) = -ATN(X/SQR(-X*X+1))+1.5708

Inverse Secant
ARCSEC(X) = ATN(SQR(X*X-1))+(SGN(X)-1)*1.5708

Inverse Cosecant
ARCCSC(X) = ATN(1/SQR(X*X-1))+(SGN(X)-1)*1.5708

Inverse Cotangent
ARCCOT(X) = -ATN(X)+1.5708

Hyperbolic Sine
SINH(X) = (EXP(X)-EXP(-X))/2

Hyperbolic Cosine
COSH(X) = (EXP(X)+EXP(-X))/2

Hyperbolic Tangent
TANH(X) = -EXP(-X)/(EXP(X)+EXP(-X))*2+1

Hyperbolic Secant
SECH(X) = 2/(EXP(X)+EXP(-X))

Hyperbolic Cosecant
CSCH(X) = 2/(EXP(X)-EXP(-X))

Hyperbolic Cotangent
COTH(X) = EXP(-X)/(EXP(X)-EXP(-X))*2+1

Inverse Hyperbolic Sine
ARGSINH(X) = LOG(X+SQR(X*X+1))

Inverse Hyperbolic Cosine
ARGCOSH(X) = LOG(X+SQR(X*X-1))

Inverse Hyperbolic Tangent
ARGTANH(X) = LOG((1+X)/(1-X))/2

Inverse Hyperbolic Secant
ARGSECH(X) = LOG((SQR(-X*X+1)+1)/X

Inverse Hyperbolic Cosecant
ARGCSCH(X) = LOG(SGN(X)*SQR(X*X+1)+1)/X

Inverse Hyperbolic Cotangent
ARGCOTH(X) = LOG((X+1)/(X-1))/2

A MOD B
MOD(A) = INT((A/B-INT(A/B))*B+.05)*SGN(A/B)

Reserved Words

Reserved words may not be used as the name of a variable. All mathematical operators, such as + and - are also treated as reserved words.

Applesoft

Table B-6. Applesoft reserved words

&	?	ABS	AND	ASC	AT
ATN	CALL	CHR$	CLEAR	COLOR=	CONT
COS	DATA	DEF	DEL	DIM	DRAW
END	EXP	FLASH	FN	FOR	FRE

GET	GOSUB	GOTO	GR	HCOLOR=	HGR
HGR2	HIMEM:	HLIN	HOME	HPLOT	HTAB
IF	IN#	INPUT	INT	INVERSE	LEFT$
LEN	LET	LIST	LOAD	LOG	LOMEM:
MID$	NEW	NEXT	NORMAL	NOT	NOTRACE
ON	ONERR	OR	PDL	PEEK	PLOT
POKE	POP	POS	PR#	PRINT	READ
RECALL	REM	RESTORE	RESUME	RETURN	RIGHT$
RND	ROT=	RUN	SAVE	SCALE=	SCRN(
SGN	SHLOAD	SIN	SPC(	SPEED=	SQR
STEP	STOP	STORE	STR$	TAB(	TAN
TEXT	THEN	TO	TRACE	USR	VAL
VLIN	VTAB	WAIT	XDRAW	XPLOT	

Table B-6. Applesoft reserved words (*continued*)

Integer BASIC

Table B-7. Integer BASIC reserved words

&	?	ABS	AND	ASC(	AT
AUTO	CALL	CLR	COLOR=	CON	DEL
DIM	DSP	END	FOR	GOSUB	GOTO
GR	HIMEM:	HLIN	IF	IN#	INPUT

LEN(	LET	LIST	LOAD	LOMEM:	MAN
MOD	NEW	NEXT	NOT	NOTRACE	OR
PDL	PEEK	PLOT	POKE	POP	PR#
PRINT	REM	RETURN	RND	RUN	SAVE
SCRN(	SGN	STEP	TAB(	TEXT	THEN
TO	TRACE	VLIN	VTAB	XPLOT	

Table B-7. Integer BASIC reserved words (*continued*)

Integer BASIC and Applesoft Differences

Integer BASIC is the first version of BASIC to be released with the original Apple II system in 1977. It was written by Steve Wozniak. Later that year, Applesoft BASIC, written by Microsoft, became available on cassette tape. Applesoft BASIC later received some changes and enhancements by Randy Wigginton in 1978, and was the standard BASIC for the Apple starting with the Apple II Plus in 1979.

Integer BASIC and Applesoft share much the same syntax, and quite a few of the commands and keywords are the same too. However, there are many differences between the two, both in how programs are entered and executed, and in which commands are available.

Differences in Commands

The following commands are exclusive to Integer BASIC:

- AUTO
- DSP
- MAN
- MOD

The following commands exist only in Applesoft:

ATN	CHR$	COS	DATA	DEF FN	DRAW
EXP	FLASH	FN	FRE	GET	HCOLOR
HGR	HGR2	HIMEM:	HOME	HPLOT	INT
INVERSE	LEFT$	LOG	LOMEM:	MID$	NORMAL
ON-GOSUB	ON-GOTO	ONERR GOTO	POS	READ	RECALL
RESTORE	RESUME	RIGHT$	ROT	SCALE	SHLOAD
SIN	SPC	SPEED	SQR	STOP	STORE
STR$	TAN	USR	VAL	WAIT	XDRAW

Table B-8. Commands exclusive to Applesoft

Some commands, operators, and constructs work differently in each version of BASIC, as shown in Table B-9.

Integer BASIC	**Applesoft**
CLR	CLEAR
CON	CONT
TAB	HTAB
GOTO N*20+200	ON N GOTO 200, 220, 240
GOSUB N*50+1500	ON N GOSUB 1500, 1550, 1600
CALL -936	HOME
POKE 50,127	INVERSE
POKE 50,255	NORMAL
X (variable name)	X% (integer variable)
#	<> or ><

Table B-9. Commands with different syntax

Other Differences

Values in Integer BASIC are constrained to the range -32767 to +32767, whereas real variables and constants (that is, numbers having a decimal point or an exponent) are only allowed in Applesoft.

Due to the number range restriction, CALL, PEEK, and POKE commands in Integer BASIC which reference memory locations greater than 32767 must do so using the two's complement negative number (where 65536 is subtracted from the number, sometimes called "negative notation"). Applesoft programs may use the full range (0 to 65535).

In Integer BASIC, program lines are checked for syntax errors upon entry (after pressing the RETURN key). Applesoft BASIC only checks syntax when a program is RUN and the statement is executed.

While Integer BASIC allows line numbers in GOTO and GOSUB statements to be computed with a variable or expression, line numbers must be constant in Applesoft.

Integer BASIC treats all characters in a variable name as significant. Only the first two letters of a variable name are considered in Applesoft, thus making, for example, MARS and MARCH the same variable.

String variables must be dimensioned before use in Integer BASIC. With Applesoft, only arrays are dimensioned. Furthermore, Applesoft allows multidimensional arrays. Integer BASIC arrays can only be one dimensional.

Applesoft initializes all elements in an array to zero upon a RUN, CLEAR, or CONTROL-RESET CONTROL-B RETURN. Integer BASIC does not automatically set any array elements; it is up to the program to do so.

Having an END on the last line of a program is optional in Applesoft, but required in Integer BASIC in order to prevent a *** NO END ERR.

If in Applesoft, an IF statement evaluates as false, program execution immediately moves on to the next line. With Integer BASIC, only the THEN portion of the IF statement is ignored.

The Applesoft TRACE command displays the line number of each individual instruction of a multiple-instruction line. Integer BASIC only displays the line number once.

In a FOR-NEXT loop, the NEXT must be followed by a variable name in Integer BASIC. Applesoft does not require a variable name after NEXT.

In Integer BASIC, an INPUT statement will always print a "?" with a numeric value, and will not print a "?" with a string value. In Applesoft, a "?" is only printed if an optional string is not present.

Appendix C : Peeks and Pokes

When programming in Applesoft, you may use a PEEK or POKE to either read a memory location, or modify a memory location. There are many functions of the Apple for which there is no BASIC command. A PEEK command reads a memory location, and assigns it to a variable if desired. The POKE command writes a value to a specified memory location.

Many of these memory locations are connected to the Apple hardware, or cause some setting to change. Merely referencing the address is enough to cause the switch. These addresses are known as toggles or *soft switches*, because they switch some aspect of the computer hardware based on a software command.

Due to the design of the Apple microprocessor, a PEEK will access a location just once, but a POKE will result in two accesses in rapid succession.

Scrolling Window

These POKE statements affect the text screen window.

POKE 32,L	Sets left side of the Scrolling Window (L=0 to 39)
POKE 33,W	Sets width of the Scrolling Window (W=0 to 40-L)
POKE 34,T	Sets top of the Scrolling Window (T=0 to 23)
POKE 35,B	Sets bottom of the Scrolling Window (B=0 to 23; B>T)

Table C-1. POKE statements for the text window

Text and Cursor Position

With these POKE statements, it is possible to move the cursor to any position on the screen.

POKE 36,CH	Sets horizontal cursor position +1 (CH=0 to 39)
POKE 37,CV	Sets vertical cursor position +1 (CV=0 to 23)

Table C-2. POKE statements for the cursor

Character Display

The current text style is affected by these POKE statements. It is also possible to select a character set on some later models of Apple.

POKE 50,255	White on Black (Normal)
POKE 50,63	Black on White (Inverse)
POKE 50,127	Flashing
POKE -16370,0	Select Primary Character Set (Only available on Apple IIe and later models)
POKE -16369,0	Select Alternate Character Set (Only available on Apple IIe and later models)

Table C-3. POKE statements for character display

Vertical Blanking Interval

Due to the way that television screens and display monitors work, the picture signal must be constantly refreshed at regular intervals to prevent the image from fading to black. On American systems, the refresh happens 60 times per second. At the end of each refresh cycle, there is a brief period of time when the Apple is not transmitting any signal to the TV monitor; the monitor is busy pulling the electron gun back up to the top left edge of the CRT.

Moving the gun takes some time, and programs on the Apple which require high-speed animations and graphics can use this time to prepare the graphics screen. Otherwise, if the graphics screen were updated indiscriminately, the image could change as the Apple was broadcasting it to the TV, thus resulting in a flickering image.

The solution, implemented on the Apple IIe and all later models, is for a program to wait for the vertical blanking interval, update the screen, and then continue. Doing so will ensure that there is no flicker, as long as the program is fast enough in updating the screen.

PEEK -16359	Read vertical blanking signal. If the value is 128 or greater, the refresh signal is being sent to the TV screen. Otherwise, if the value is less than 128, the Apple is in its vertical blanking interval.

Table C-4. PEEK statement for the vertical blanking interval

Graphics Mode Screen

The appearance of the graphics screen is controlled by a number soft switches. The PEEK statements for reading the soft switch statuses are only available on the Apple IIe and later machines.

Table C-5. Statements affecting the graphics screen

POKE -16304,0	Set graphics display mode
POKE -16303,0	Set text display mode
PEEK(-16358)	Read text switch (If > 127 then it is “ON”)
POKE -16302,0	Set full-screen graphics display mode
POKE -16301,0	Set mixed-text graphics display mode
PEEK(-16357)	Read mixed switch (If > 127 then it is “ON”)
POKE -16300,0	Turn page 2 high-res off (set page 1)
POKE -16299,0	Set display to high-res graphics page 2

PEEK(-16356)	Read page 2 switch (If > 127 then it is "ON")
POKE -16298,0	Turn high-res display mode off
POKE -16297,0	Set high-res graphics display mode
PEEK(-16355)	Read high-res switch (If > 127 then it is "ON")

Table C-5. Statements affecting the graphics screen (*continued*)

Keyboard

It is possible to bypass the BASIC INPUT and GET statements, and instead read the keyboard directly, one key press at a time.

PEEK (-16384)	Read keyboard. If > 127 then a key was pressed. Always clear the keyboard strobe before use.
POKE -16368,0	Clears the keyboard strobe.

Table C-6. Statements affecting the keyboard

Sound

Both the speaker and the cassette out port (if your model of Apple has one) are controlled by a certain memory location.

PEEK(-16336)	Toggles the speaker (1 click)
POKE -16336,0	Toggles the speaker (1 click, longer than PEEK)
PEEK -16352	Toggles the cassette out jack (1 click)

Table C-7. Statements affecting the speaker and cassette

Game Paddles

PEEK(-16287)	Read PDL(0) push button switch (If > 127 then switch is "ON")
PEEK(-16286)	Read PDL(1) push button switch (If > 127 then switch is "ON")
PEEK(-16285)	Read PDL(2) button (shift key) (If > 127 then switch is "ON")
POKE -16296,1	Clear Game I/O AN-0 Output (OFF-3.5V HIGH)
POKE -16295,0	Set Game I/O AN-0 Output (ON-.3V LOW)
POKE -16294,1	Clear Game I/O AN-1 Output (OFF-3.5V HIGH)
POKE -16293,0	Set Game I/O AN-1 Output (ON-.3V LOW)
POKE -16292,1	Clear Game I/O AN-2 Output (OFF-3.5V HIGH)
POKE -16291,0	Set Game I/O AN-2 Output (ON-.3V LOW)
POKE -16290,1	Clear Game I/O AN-3 Output (OFF-3.5V HIGH)
POKE -16289,0	Set Game I/O AN-3 Output (ON-.3V LOW)
PEEK -16272,0	Trigger strobe on pin 5 of the game IC socket, dropping voltage to 0 for half a microsecond.

Table C-8. Statements affecting the paddles and game I/O socket

High-Resolution Graphics

Table C-9. Statements affecting the high-resolution graphics screen

POKE 800,H	Set horizontal coordinate. H=MODULUS 256
POKE 801,H/256	H= 0 (left) to 279 (right) * Note: Both POKE 800 & 801 are required.
POKE 802,V	Sets vertical coordinate. (V= 0 (top) to 159 (bottom))
POKE 804,S	Starting address of shape table. S=MODULUS 256

POKE 805,S/256	Starting address of shape table. Both 804 and 805 are required.
POKE 28,C	Color of shape
POKE 812,X	Sets color for high-res
POKE 249,R	Sets rotation of shape (R=1 to 64; 0=Normal; 16=90° Clockwise)
PEEK (243)	Flash mask
PEEK (241)	Speed (256 - current speed)
PEEK (234)	Collision counter for shape
PEEK (232-233)	Shape table starting address
POKE 231,S	Sets scale of shape
PEEK (230)	High-res plotting page. (32=Page 1, 64=Page 2, 96=Page 3)
PEEK (224-226)	High-res GR X&Y coordinates
POKE 228,X	High-res GR color byte (X can be 0-255)

Table C-9. Statements affecting the high-resolution graphics screen (*continued*)

Errors

POKE 216,0	Resets error flag.
PEEK (216)	If equal to 127 then an error was detected.
PEEK (219)	Line number of error. Multiply by 256 and add to result from below.
PEEK (218)	Line number of error. See instructions above.
PEEK (222)	Returns error code in decimal.

Table C-10. Statements affecting the Applesoft error flag

Appendix D : Using ADT to Transfer Disks

It's a common situation: you have a working Apple, but no software for it. Unfortunately, Apple II disks use a unique format that renders them incompatible with all modern computer hardware. With *ADT*, which stands for Apple Disk Transfer, as long as you have some blank disks and a working Macintosh or PC computer, you can get software to your Apple and on to disk.

ADT is free software that can also be used to transfer all manner of games and software applications to and from the Apple. There are currently three major releases of ADT: MacADT, which supports 68K and PowerPC Macintosh computers running System 7 to Mac OS 9; ADTPro, which is written in Java and works on Mac OS X, Linux, and Windows; and A2V2, which is a modified version of ADTPro distributed with the Virtual][emulator program. Fortunately, all three versions operate in a similar manner.

Overall, the best release of ADT to use is probably ADTPro, which is at version 1.2.0 as of this writing. A2V2 has additional options to allow for transferring copy-protected disks. MacADT has the advantage of working on older Macintosh computers which have built-in serial ports.

ADTPro is written to take advantage of the ProDOS filing system, which requires 64 kilobytes of RAM. If you have an Apple II or Apple II Plus, then your Apple must have a Language Card or equivalent 16 kilobyte RAM card in slot 0. If not, then you will have to use the older version of ADT that only requires 48 kilobytes.

Getting Connected

Once you have obtained the ADT program for your PC or Macintosh, you next need to arrange a way to connect it to your Apple II. With ADTPro, there are three different options: audio, serial, and Ethernet. In terms of transfer speed, Ethernet is fastest, audio is slowest. However, Ethernet is not a common hardware feature on the Apple II, as it requires an expensive peripheral card.

From now on, the term "host" will be used in place of "PC or Macintosh."

Connecting with Audio

If you have no serial card in your Apple, or no way to connect to your host with a serial cable, then you will be forced to use the built-in cassette ports. Keep in mind that only the Apple II, II Plus, and IIe have cassette ports. If you have a PC, it must have working microphone input and speaker output jacks.

You will need to use two 3.5 mm, mini phono cables. It does not matter if they are mono or stereo. Connect the microphone port on the host to the cassette out jack on the Apple. Then connect the remaining two audio ports together.

The volume on the host computer should be set to half its maximum value.

Once you have the sound cables properly connected, proceed to the next section "Bootstrapping ADT."

Connecting with Serial

Using a serial connection is a bit trickier, but better than audio because the transfer speeds are much quicker. Every model of Apple may potentially have a serial connection, but some models do not have built-in serial ports. Consult the following table for the specifics on your Apple.

Model	Requires
Apple II Apple II Plus Apple IIe	A Super Serial Card or Apple Communications Card.
Apple IIc	An adapter for Din-8 to mini-din.
Apple IIc Plus Apple IIgs	Nothing; serial port is built-in.

Table D-1. Requirements for a serial connection

You may need a further adapter to match the serial port on your host computer. Macintosh computers with built-in serial ports (all those models manufactured before 1998) need no further adapter. If your host computer does not have any serial ports, then a USB-to-serial adapter may be used.

If you are using a Super Serial Card, you should set the DIP switches to ensure smooth operation during the initial bootstrapping process.

Table D-2 has the required switch settings. Recall from Chapter 10 that the terms "off," "down," and "open" all mean the same, and that "on," "up," or "closed" all have the same meaning too.

On the host computer, start the ADTPro program and choose Serial Configuration from the File menu. Choose a device listed from the Port pop-up menu for the serial connection. On Mac OS X and Linux machines, the serial port will usually be in the form of /dev/tty. Next, choose a speed. Most Apples should be able to handle at least 19200 baud.

SW	1	2	3	4	5	6	7
1	ON	OFF	OFF	ON	ON	ON	ON
2	ON	ON	OFF	ON	ON	OFF	OFF

Table D-2. Switch settings for the Super Serial Card

Early versions of the Apple IIc may have problems with high baud rates. The Apple IIgs with its built-in serial ports is easily capable of 115200 baud. Whichever speed is chosen here, remember it, for the same speed must be configured on the ADTPro client running on the Apple.

When you are finished configuring the host computer, click Ok to dismiss the dialog box, then click the Serial button.

If you do not have ADT on disk for the Apple, skip to the next section, "Bootstrapping ADT." Otherwise, on the Apple, boot the ADT disk, and choose Serial from the startup menu. At the main ADTPro screen, type G to configure the serial card. Use the LEFT and RIGHT ARROW keys to match the serial card or port being used. Use the SPACE BAR or DOWN ARROW key to select baud rate, then the LEFT or RIGHT ARROWs to change it to match the ADTPro host setting. Press RETURN to accept the settings and go back to the main menu.

To test the connection, press the D key on the Apple to get a directory listing. It should show three or four files from your host, such as ADTPRO-1.2.0.DSK. Meanwhile, the ADTPro program on the host should show the status "Request: directory contents." If everything happened as expected, you are now ready to send and receive disks to and from the Apple.

Connecting with Ethernet

In many ways, Ethernet is the most convenient connection mode, since it is ubiquitous on the computers of today. To use Ethernet with ADTPro, your Apple will need to be equipped with an Uthernet or LANceGS card. Refer to Chapter 10 for the installation of the Uthernet card. Both the LANceGS and Uthernet are 10 megabit per second interfaces, therefore, the Ethernet port on the hub, switch, or computer must be able to support that speed.

Start the ADTPro program on your host, and click the Ethernet button to start the ADT server. You should see your computer's IP address appear in the title bar of the ADTPro window. This address will be entered on the Apple II as the server IP address.

On the Apple, boot the ADT disk, and choose Ethernet from the startup menu. At the main ADT screen, press G to configure the

Ethernet card. You must set the slot in which the Ethernet card is installed, as well as provide the IP configuration. The server IP address is the address displayed in the ADTPro title bar on the host computer. The local IP address is the address for your Apple. The netmask determines which IP ranges should be sent to a router, while the gateway address should be the IP address of the router, if the network has one. If you are unsure about these latter two values, copy them from your host computer's network configuration, or ask your network administrator. If your network has a DHCP server, you can have most of these details configured automatically. Press RETURN when you are finished to go back to the main screen.

Now it is time to test the connection. On the Apple, press the D key to get a directory listing. It should show three or four files from your host, such as ADTPRO-1.2.0.DSK. Meanwhile, the ADTPro program on the host should show the status "Request: directory contents." If everything happened as expected, then you are now ready to send and receive disks to and from the Apple.

Bootstrapping ADT

If your Apple did not come with any system disks, then you can use ADTPro to transfer a copy of either DOS or ProDOS into your Apple's memory, where it may then be saved on to a disk. This task is known as ADT bootstrapping. Because additional software is required on the Apple to manage the Ethernet interface, you may only bootstrap over a serial or audio connection.

To begin, verify that the connection between the Apple and your PC or Macintosh is in place. On the host, launch the ADTPro program. It is a Java program, and will require a relatively recent version of the Java Runtime Environment (JRE). Consult the README file included with ADTPro if you need additional help in getting it started.

ADTPro will open a window featuring, among other things, four buttons. Three of these, labeled Serial, Ethernet, and Audio, represent the three connection methods to the Apple. Click the one that you're using. Remember that you cannot bootstrap the Apple from an Ethernet connection.

Bootstrapping with Serial

If you select the Serial connection, you will need to select a serial port on your computer. You will also need to set a pacing delay and transmission speed (baud rate). The pacing determines how long the host should delay after sending a line of data. This delay is required by the Apple to process the incoming line. The baud rate (speed) determines the rate at which the host sends characters to the Apple. If the rate is too quick, the Apple will not receive all of the data.

The default settings for pacing and speed are 150 and 9600, respectively. These settings should work on any model of Apple. With some models, these settings should be able to be increased to gain faster transfer times. The fastest settings that a standard Apple IIe was tested to handle were a pacing of 75 and a speed of 19200.

First, send ProDOS from the Bootstrap menu. A dialog box will appear, instructing you to enter two commands on the Apple. The first, IN#2, commands the Apple to receive input from slot number 2. If your serial card is in another slot, enter its number instead. Apple IIc, IIc Plus, and IIgs users, remember that the printer port is slot 1 and the modem port is slot 2.

The second command is to set the serial card's baud rate to match that of the bootstrapping speed setting on the host computer. Press CONTROL-I to get the serial card's attention. It should print APPLE SSC on the screen. If not, then the slot number may be wrong, or the card is in Communications mode where it expects a CONTROL-A instead. When the prompt appears, enter the command to set baud rate, for example, 14B for 9600 baud or 15B for 19200 baud.

After this step is completed on the Apple, press RETURN on the host computer to start the serial transfer.

When the bootstrap operation commences, the host computer will take control of your Apple. The first thing you should see on the Apple is CALL -151. Then many lines of hexadecimal digits will appear as the data are being transferred to the Apple. The transfer may take anywhere from two to four minutes. Table D-3 lists some bootstrap settings and transfer speeds.

Speed Settings	ProDOS Transfer Time	Serial Client Transfer Time
Pacing: 150 Speed: 9600	251 seconds	198 seconds
Pacing: 100 Speed: 19200	168 seconds	133 seconds
Pacing: 75 Speed: 19200	127 seconds	100 seconds
Pacing: 50 Speed: 19200	Too fast for the Apple to handle.	

Table D-3. ADTPro serial bootstrap speeds on a standard Apple IIe

If nothing appears on the Apple's screen, there is likely a problem with the serial communication link. If nonsense characters appear (typically accompanied by beeping and SYNTAX ERRORs), then the most probable cause is wrong baud rate.

When ProDOS is successfully transfered, you will see the usual ProDOS startup screen on the Apple for ProDOS 8 V1.9. An Applesoft prompt will also appear at the top of the screen.

The next step is to send the ADTPro Serial Client. Choose it from the Bootstrap menu on the host computer. Follow the on-screen instructions like before. The Serial Client may take from two to three minutes to transfer. When finished, the ADTPro main menu will appear on the Apple's screen. You are now ready to transfer disks.

If your model of Apple is too old to run ProDOS, you can send the older DOS-based version of ADT. The method is much the same as sending ProDOS. First choose to send EsDOS][Part 1. Follow the on-screen instructions, then wait until the message "NOW ENTER THE COMMAND INIT HELLO AND HIT RETURN" appears on the Apple's screen. At this point, you must insert a 5.25" disk into the drive. Type

```
INIT HELLO
```

to format the disk for DOS.

To send the DOS ADT client, first ensure that the bootstrap speed is at 9600 with the pacing at 100. Then choose Send DOS ADT Client from the Bootstrapping menu.

Bootstrapping with Audio

After clicking the Audio button, choose which program you wish to send to the Apple by opening the Bootstrapping menu and making a selection.

To start the bootstrapping, choose to send ProDOS. A dialog box will appear with instructions to follow. Do so, and the bootstrapping operation should commence without error. ProDOS will take about 114 seconds to send by audio. If the Apple successfully read all of the data, enter

```
2000G
```

from the Monitor to start ProDOS.

Next, send the ADTPro Audio Client which will allow you to send a disk image from which to make a bootable system disk. Another dialog box will appear with instructions similar to the first time. The audio client will take about 92 seconds to transfer. If it was successful, type

```
800G
```

from the Monitor to start ADTPro.

Transferring Disks

ADT was designed to transfer disk images quickly and efficiently. It supports bidirectional transfer: the Apple can send disk images to the host machine in order to backup and archive them, and the Apple can receive disk images from the host machine, allowing you to expand your software library with programs downloaded from the Internet.

Sending Disks to the Apple

Sending a disk image from the host to the Apple is a two-part process. First, ensure that the disk image is located in the ADTPro server's disks directory. Make sure that the server is started and connected.

On the Apple, boot the ADT client program that matches your connection type. From the main menu, type R for Receive. You will be prompted to type in the desired filename. You must enter the disk image's filename exactly as it appears on the host computer. When you press RETURN, the ADT client on the Apple will query the server. In a few moments, the screen should change to show a progress bar reflecting the status of the disk transfer. A 5.25" disk image should take about half a minute with most serial and Ethernet connections.

If the sound is on, the Apple will beep when the disk transfer is complete.

Receiving Disks from the Apple

Make sure that the host and the Apple are properly connected and configured. Start ADTPro on the host and choose the appropriate connection type. Likewise, start the matching ADT client on the Apple.

On the main menu of the ADT client, type S for Send. You will be prompted for a filename to save the disk image under. Enter a logical and legal filename (legal, according to the rules of the host machine's operating system). The ADT server will automatically append the extension ".dsk" to Apple disk image names. After you press RETURN, the Apple will confirm with the ADT host to see whether a file with that name already exists. If it does, you will be asked whether you wish to overwrite it or not.

Next, you will be taken to a screen that shows all currently-available disks on the Apple. Choose the one that you wish to send and press RETURN. The screen will change once more to show the status of the disk transfer. It should take less than a minute in most cases. The Apple will beep when the transfer is complete.

Errors when reading the disk will be marked with the letter X in the progress bar on the Apple's screen. Too many errors will cause ADT to give up and abort the transfer. Try cleaning the disk drive, using a different drive, or letting the disk warm up a bit before attempting the transfer again. Appendix G shows how to clean and adjust a 5.25" disk drive.

Appendix E : Tables and Conversion Charts

The first two tables in this appendix list low-res and high-res graphics colors. An ASCII chart is then provided, after which follows a chart for converting between binary, decimal, and hexadecimal. Lastly, two charts show DOS 3.3 and ProDOS file types.

Some of these tables appear elsewhere in this book; they are repeated in this appendix for convenience.

Colors

Code	Color	Code	Color
0	Black	8	Brown
1	Magenta	9	Orange
2	Dark Blue	10	Gray
3	Light Purple	11	Pink
4	Dark Green	12	Green
5	Gray	13	Yellow
6	Medium Blue	14	Aqua
7	Light Blue	15	White

Table E-1. Low-Resolution colors

Code	Color	Code	Color
0	Black 1	4	Black 2
1	Green	5	Orange
2	Violet	6	Blue
3	White 1	7	White 2

Table E-2. High-Resolution colors

ASCII Characters and Screen Editing

Table E-3. ASCII character chart

Dec	Hex	Char	Dec	Hex	Char
0	00	NUL	64	40	@
1	01	SOH	65	41	A
2	02	STX	66	42	B
3	03	ETX	67	43	C
4	04	EOT	68	44	D
5	05	ENQ	69	45	E
6	06	ACK	70	46	F
7	07	BEL	71	47	G
8	08	BS	72	48	H
9	09	HT	73	49	I
10	0A	LF	74	4A	J
11	0B	VT	75	4B	K
12	0C	FF	76	4C	L
13	0D	CR	77	4D	M
14	0E	SO	78	4E	N
15	0F	SI	79	4F	O
16	10	DLE	80	50	P
17	11	DC1	81	51	Q
18	12	DC2	82	52	R
19	13	DC3	83	53	S
20	14	DC4	84	54	T
21	15	NAK	85	55	U
22	16	SYN	86	56	V
23	17	ETB	87	57	W
24	18	CAN	88	58	X
25	19	EM	89	59	Y
26	1A	SUB	90	5A	Z
27	1B	ESC	91	5B	[
28	1C	FS	92	5C	\
29	1D	GS	93	5D	]

Dec	Hex	Char	Dec	Hex	Char
30	1E	RS	94	5E	^
31	1F	US	95	5F	_
32	20	SP	96	60	`
33	21	!	97	61	a
34	22	“	98	62	b
35	23	#	99	63	c
36	24	$	100	64	d
37	25	%	101	65	e
38	26	&	102	66	f
39	27	‘	103	67	g
40	28	(	104	68	h
41	29	)	105	69	i
42	2A	*	106	6A	j
43	2B	+	107	6B	k
44	2C	,	108	6C	l
45	2D	-	109	6D	m
46	2E	.	110	6E	n
47	2F	/	111	6F	o
48	30	0	112	70	p
49	31	1	113	71	q
50	32	2	114	72	r
51	33	3	115	73	s
52	34	4	116	74	t
53	35	5	117	75	u
54	36	6	118	76	v
55	37	7	119	77	w
56	38	8	120	78	x
57	39	9	121	79	y
58	3A	:	122	7A	z
59	3B	;	123	7B	{
60	3C	<	124	7C	|
61	3D	=	125	7D	}
62	3E	>	126	7E	~
63	3F	?	127	7F	DEL

Table E-3. ASCII character chart (*continued*)

Escape Code	Function
ESC @	Clears the entire text window and moves the cursor to the home position.
ESC A	Moves the cursor right one space.
ESC B	Moves the cursor left one space.
ESC C	Moves the cursor down a line.
ESC D	Moves the cursor up a line.
ESC E	Clears text from the cursor to the end of the line.
ESC F	Clears text from the cursor to the bottom of the text window.
ESC I	Enters escape mode and moves the cursor up a line.
ESC UP ARROW	Enters escape mode and moves the cursor up a line.
ESC J	Enters escape mode and moves the cursor left one space.
ESC LEFT ARROW	Enters escape mode and moves the cursor left one space.
ESC K	Enters escape mode and moves the cursor right one space.
ESC RIGHT ARROW	Enters escape mode and moves the cursor right one space.
ESC M	Enters escape mode and moves the cursor down a line.
ESC DOWN ARROW	Enters escape mode and moves the cursor down a line.
ESC R	Activates restricted-case mode.*
ESC T	Deactivates restricted-case mode.*
ESC 4	Switches to 40-columns mode.*
ESC 8	Switches to 80-columns mode.*
ESC CONTROL-Q	Deactivates the 80-column card.*

* only available when the 80-columns firmware is active

Table E-4. Escape codes

	Primary Character Set		Alternate Character Set	
Hex Values	**Character Type**	**Format**	**Character Type**	**Format**
$00-$1F	Uppercase letters	Inverse	Uppercase letters	Inverse
$20-$3F	Special characters	Inverse	Special characters	Inverse
$40-$5F	Uppercase letters	Flashing	Uppercase letters	Inverse
$60-$7F	Special characters	Flashing	Lowercase letters	Inverse
$80-$9F	Uppercase letters	Normal	Uppercase letters	Normal
$A0-$BF	Special characters	Normal	Special characters	Normal
$C0-$DF	Uppercase letters	Normal	Uppercase letters	Normal
$E0-$FF	Lowercase letters	Normal	Lowercase letters	Normal

Table E-5. Screen character sets

Number Conversion

Table E-6. Binary decimal hex conversion

Binary	Hex	Decimal
0000	0	0
0001	1	1
0010	2	2
0011	3	3
0100	4	4
0101	5	5

Binary	Hex	Decimal
0110	6	6
0111	7	7
1000	8	8
1001	9	9
1010	A	10
1011	B	11
1100	C	12
1101	D	13
1110	E	14
1111	F	15

Table E-6. Binary decimal hex conversion (*continued*)

DOS 3.3 and ProDOS File Types

File Type	Letter
Applesoft program	A
Binary	B
Integer BASIC program	I
ASCII text file	T
File is locked	*

Table E-7. DOS 3.3 file types

File Type	**Short Name**
Directory	DIR
Human-readable text	TXT
Applesoft BASIC program	BAS
Applesoft BASIC variables	VAR
Machine program or data	BIN
Relocatable machine code	REL
User-defined file type number *n*	$F*n*
ProDOS System program or data	SYS

Table E-8. ProDOS file types

Appendix F : Specs for all Apple II Models

This appendix contains details on all models of Apple II, as well as the various revisions within each model.

Identifying Apple II Models

All models of the Apple II family may be identified by checking two or more memory locations for specific values. These identification bytes are all listed in Table F-1.

The Apple IIgs is not listed because its identification bytes are the same as for the Enhanced Apple IIe. The only way to positively identify an Apple IIgs as an Apple IIgs is to use an assembly language routine.

The Apple IIe Card for Macintosh LC is also identified like an Enhanced Apple IIe. The only difference is that memory locations $FBDD and $FBB3 will contain $02 and $00, respectively.

Some Apple II models have additional locations which also serve to identify them. These additional locations and bytes are listed in the table for your reference only. They are not needed to identify the model; for example, the standard Apple II can be identified solely by verifying that location $FBB3 contains $38.

To use these locations and values in a BASIC PEEK statement, be sure to convert the hex values to decimal, and use negative notation (explained in Chapter 5) for the addresses if Integer BASIC is being used.

Machine	$FBB3	$FB1E	$FBC0	$FBBF
Apple II	$38		$60*	$2F*
Apple II Plus	$EA	$AD	$EA*	$EA*
Apple III (emulation)	$EA	$8A		
Apple IIe (original)	$06		$EA	$C1*
Apple IIe (enhanced)	$06		$E0	$00*
Apple IIc	$06		$00	$FF
Apple IIc (3.5 ROM)	$06		$00	$00
Apple IIc (mem. exp.)	$06		$00	$03
Apple IIc (rev. mem. exp.)	$06		$00	$04
Apple IIc Plus	$06		$00	$05

* These values do not need to be matched to identify the model

Table F-1. Apple II family identification bytes

The Original Apple II

The original Apple II computer, released in 1977, included Integer BASIC ROMs and the Old Monitor.

Popular firmware updates of the time were the Programmer's Aid #1 ROM, which was installed in socket D0, and the Autostart ROM, which replaced the Old Monitor ROM in socket F8. The Apple Language Card also adds the Autostart ROM functionality.

Though the Revision 0 Apple II motherboard lacks the power-on reset circuit, the addition of a Disk II controller card in any slot (except slot 0) adds this functionality. When combined with an Autostart ROM, a Revision 0 Apple II will scan the slots at startup for a disk to boot just like any other later model of Apple.

- RAM: 4K to 48K
- CPU: 6502A at 1.023 MHz
- Keyboard: uppercase only
- Slots: 7 general purpose, 1 special
- ROM: 12K, Integer BASIC

Revision	Description
0	Models with a serial number less than 6000 are typically Revision 0. Only four high-resolution colors are available: green, violet, black, and white. The speaker is wired to cassette out (this is a design mistake). On-screen text always has color fringes (due to color burst signal).
1	Two additional high-resolution colors are available: blue and orange. "Color killer" modification: removes color fringes on text. The Apple automatically does a reset when powered on. 50 Hz Eurapple jumpers added. Wirewrap video pin added. 20/24K RAM problem fixed. Two additional video signals available to slot 7.
3	Socketed memory select jumpers.
4	16K memory select jumpers soldered to board without sockets.
7	Memory select jumpers have been removed, 48K standard. Chip at motherboard location E2 removed.
RFI	Lid, base plate, and back panel changed to limit RFI. One 8304 chip replaced two 8T28 chips.

Table F-2. Apple II motherboard revisions

The Apple II Plus

The Apple II Plus, released around June 1979, has at least a Revision 1 motherboard, and also included the Applesoft and Autostart ROMs. Most models of Apple II Plus have a Revision 7 or RFI motherboard and 48K of RAM.

The *only* functional difference between an original Apple and the Apple II Plus is the firmware; the motherboard and every other chip is the same.

Externally, the only differences between the original Apple and the Plus were the name badge and the serial/model number sticker on the bottom of the case.

The final difference between the two models is the keyboard: only the oldest original Apple models have the early, one-piece keyboard. All Apple II Plus models should have the new, two-piece keyboard, and later original Apple models came with this keyboard too.

- RAM: typically 48K
- CPU: 6502A at 1.023 MHz
- Keyboard: uppercase only
- Slots: 7 general purpose, 1 special
- ROM: 12K, Applesoft BASIC

The Apple IIe

The Apple IIe, which superseded the II Plus in January 1983, was the first model of Apple to support lowercase display and keyboard characters. It has nine additional keys, totaling 63, and supports automatic key repeat with N-key rollover.

A Language Card is built-in, bringing the standard RAM configuration up to 64K. As with the Apple II Plus, Applesoft BASIC is standard in ROM. In addition, 80-column firmware is built into the system, but requires either an 80-Column Card or an Extended 80-Column Card in the Auxiliary slot. The Extended Card also adds an additional 64K of RAM.

The Apple IIe added one additional port on the back: a DE-9 connector for hand controls. The 16-pin DIP socket was also provided inside the case for older controls.

The earliest models of IIe had white-lettered keys. Later, the color was switched to black.

The last revision of the Apple IIe was released in 1987. It has the same Enhanced firmware as the previous revision, but with a redesigned keyboard, preinstalled Extended 80-Column Card, a reduced chip count, and a few other minor logic board changes.

- RAM: 64K or 128K
- CPU: 6502B or 65C02 at 1.023 MHz
- Keyboard: upper and lowercase
- Slots: 7 general purpose, 1 special
- ROM: 16K, Applesoft

Differences Between the Standard and Enhanced IIe

Hardware changes begin with the 65C02 microprocessor replacing the 6502B. The 65C02 is more power efficient and introduces new opcodes and addressing modes. The Enhanced IIe sports a new video ROM containing MouseText characters equivalent to those found in the Apple IIc. Furthermore are the new CD and EF Monitor ROMs with the Enhanced IIe firmware.

Revision	**Description**
A	No double-high-resolution. Supports only the Apple II and II Plus graphics modes.
B	Support added for double-high-resolution and double-low-resolution graphics. Video signal added to slot 7.
Enhanced	65C02 processor, MouseText characters, updated firmware.

Table F-3. Apple IIe revisions

The Machine Identification byte at $FBC0 distinguishes the Enhanced IIe from the standard IIe.

The Enhanced IIe firmware allows system startup from devices other than a standard Disk II or Apple 5.25 controller card.

The video firmware of the Enhanced IIe better supports 80-columns mode. In addition, lowercase input and display are supported. Two new Escape sequences control whether Control characters should be shown on the screen or not.

MouseText can be used to simulate a windows-based GUI on the Apple. These 32 characters take the place of the alternate character set.

Several Applesoft statements that did not work properly in 80-columns mode now do: HTAB, TAB, SPC, and comma tabbing in PRINT statements. Furthermore, Applesoft now recognizes keywords and variable names in lowercase.

Several new features are part of the Enhanced Apple IIe Monitor:

- Lowercase Input
- ASCII Input Mode
- Monitor Search Command
- Mini-Assembler.

Slot 3's behavior is changed with the Enhanced IIe. Whereas with the standard IIe, a card in the auxiliary slot would always disable the firmware of a card in slot 3, the Enhanced IIe allows the slot 3 card's firmware to be switched in to memory if the card's ROM has certain ID bytes.

The Apple IIc

The Apple IIc was designed as a compact, slotless version of the Apple IIe with the features of several common peripheral cards built-in. Many of the Apple IIc firmware changes appeared as part of the Enhanced Apple IIe system.

The Apple IIc has all the features of an Apple IIe, such as 80-columns capability and a full keyboard. A built-in disk drive with a port to attach another are included, as well as a port for attaching a mouse, a printer, and a modem.

The Apple IIc was the first model whose internal speaker has a volume adjustment. There is also a headphone jack that will cause the speaker to be disabled when headphones are in use.

While every revision of the IIc includes at least 128K of RAM, later revisions added a slot for memory expansion.

The revision number of the IIc is identified by the byte at location $FBBF. Type PRINT PEEK(-1089) from the Applesoft prompt to return the revision number.

- RAM: 128K
- CPU: 65C02 at 1.023 MHz
- Keyboard: uppercase and lowercase
- Slots: none
- ROM: 16K, Applesoft BASIC

The Apple IIc Plus

The IIc Plus debuted in 1989. It was then, and still remains today, the fastest stock model of Apple, featuring a 4 MHz processor that features accelerator technology and caching.

The IIc Plus is, as its name implies, an improved version of the IIc. It is built around the same form factor, but offers a redesigned keyboard like that of the IIgs and Macintosh, as well as a 3.5" drive instead of the 5.25".

Both the Apple 3.5" and UniDisk 3.5" drives may be connected to the IIc, in addition to the external IIc 5.25" drive. Unfortunately, the internal Memory Expansion Card connector will not accept the original IIc Memory Expansion Card.

While the original Apple IIc had an external power supply, the supply in the IIc Plus is built-in.

Revision	Description
255	The UniDisk 3.5 cannot be used. PR#7 can be used to boot the external drive. The serial port firmware does not mask incoming linefeeds, nor does it support XON/XOFF protocol.
0	The UniDisk 3.5 can be used. AppleTalk firmware is moved to slot 7, and PR#7 now returns an AppleTalk OffLine message instead of booting the external drive. The two deficiencies in the serial port firmware are fixed.
3	An internal slot is added to accept the IIc Memory Expansion Card. The AppleTalk firmware is removed; PR#7 has no effect. The Mouse firmware moved to slot 7.
4	A bug with keyboard buffering was fixed. When the IIc Memory Expansion Card is not present, the firmware provides correct information.

Table F-4. Apple IIc revisions

The serial ports on the IIc Plus are mini-DIN 8, matching those found on the IIgs and Macintosh.

The headphone jack was omitted, as was the 40/80 column switch from the original IIc. Instead of a volume knob, the IIc Plus features a slider switch located above the keyboard.

The internal revision number of the IIc Plus, located at the same address as that of the IIc ($FBBF), is 5.

- RAM: 128K
- CPU: 65C02 at 4 MHz
- Keyboard: uppercase and lowercase
- Slots: 1 Memory Expansion connector
- ROM: 16K, Applesoft

The Apple IIgs

Apple Computer released the Apple IIgs in late 1986. There are three major revisions of the IIgs, the ROM 00, the ROM 01, and the ROM 3. The ROM 01 revision is the most common model, and is compatible with the widest variety of software. The ROM 00 IIgs, typically found in the Woz Signature Edition case, is incompatible with some newer IIgs software and operating systems. The ROM 3 IIgs is incompatible with a small percentage of software, but is the most superior revision.

The IIgs knows how to act like an Enhanced Apple IIe for compatibility with existing Apple II software. Its processor may even be slowed down to 1 MHz for extra compatibility.

The ROM 3 IIgs began shipping in August 1989, featuring 256K of firmware and several other changes.

The GS stands for graphics and sound. The Apple IIgs has additional graphics modes offering much higher resolution with as many as 256 colors from a palette of 4,096. For sound, the IIgs has an on-board Ensoniq Digital Oscillator wavetable synthesizer chip with 64K of dedicated sound RAM. The Ensoniq is capable of true stereo and as many as 15 distinct voices.

- RAM: 256K or 1 MB built-in, expandable to 8 MB
- CPU: 65C816 at 2.8 MHz
- Keyboard: uppercase and lowercase detached ADB
- Slots: 7 general purpose, 1 special
- ROM: 128K or 256K, Applesoft

Table F-5. Apple IIgs revisions

Revision	Description
00	RAM disks limited to 4 MB. Firmware contains System 1.x Toolbox routines.

Revision	Description
01	Firmware changes, including bug fixes and the System 2.x Toolbox routines. RAM disks can be sized up to 8 MB. Startup screen displays copyright years and firmware revision.
3	1 MB of RAM soldered to the motherboard. Firmware updates, including some Control Panel changes and the System 5.x Toolbox in firmware. AppleTalk was moved from slots 1 and 2 to slot 7. Setting slot 4 to Your Card no longer disables the mouse in 16-bit (desktop) applications. Motherboard jumper to disable the Text Control Panel. Enhanced ADB controller. User-replaceable clock battery. Changes in motherboard to reduce electrical noise.

Table F-5. Apple IIgs revisions (*continued*)

Appendix G : Repair and Troubleshooting

Hopefully, you'll never need this appendix, but even though Apple computers are well-made and long-lasting, they can develop problems which you'll have to fix.

Some of the most common problems and solutions are covered in this appendix: unresponsive keys, chips making poor contact, disk drive speed and cleaning, and bad RAM chips.

Unresponsive Keys

When you first receive an Apple, or perhaps after a long period of disuse, one or more keys on the keyboard may not work. You press the key, yet nothing appears on the screen. Chances are, the key is not completely broken; instead, the key switch is not making good electrical contact.

To test if this is the case, try pressing the key many times in a row, up to 100 times. Use slightly harder force than you would ordinarily use to type a key. If the cause was bad electrical contact, then this procedure will often get the key to work again.

A slightly different problem stems from a similar cause: repeating keys on the keyboard of the Apple II Plus or original model Apple II. This keyboard is not an auto-repeating model. Thus, if a single key press causes multiple characters to appear on the screen, the cause is likely due to an intermittent contact caused by dirt or crud.

If you're so inclined, you may gently pry off the key cap, then spray electrical contact cleaner down into the key switch assembly. In a pinch, using a cotton tipped stick to place droplets of distilled water down into the key switch assembly will also work, since water is a mild solvent. Afterward, exercise the key by pressing it many times until it works correctly. Doing so will help ensure that the key remains in proper working order for many more years to come.

Cleaning and Reseating Chips

A quite common cause of strange behavior is that of chips making poor electrical contact with the circuit board. If you open the case of your Apple II, II Plus, or IIe, you will notice that most of the chips are not soldered directly to the circuit board; instead, they are in black sockets. The Apple IIgs only has a few chips in sockets; most are soldered. Most peripheral expansion cards also have socketed chips. While these sockets make replacing the chip easy, they can be the cause of loose contacts. Due to thermal expansion caused by the Apple heating and cooling, the legs of a chip may become loose, eventually failing to make a reliable contact with the rest of the Apple.

Loose chips are a common cause of failure and erratic behavior in the original Apple II and the II Plus, due to the large number of chips (over 100) all generating heat inside the case.

The solution is to gently press down on each chip to ensure that it is making a good connection in its socket. You will likely hear a light cracking as you press down on each chip. This is not a cause for concern, as long as you are not using too much force. Unfortunately, there isn't an easy way to identify the specific chip or chips which aren't making a good electrical contact. You'll have to press down on all of them.

Another cause of poor electrical contact is tarnish and oxide buildup, generally caused by airborne particulate matter (the very same that dulls your sterling). Tarnish builds up on the legs of a chip, breaking or weakening the electrical connection. To check for tarnish, examine the legs of each chip in your Apple with a good light. The metal should be a shiny silver color. If you have a very old Apple, some of its chips may have gold legs. Any legs which are blackened have tarnish, and should be cleaned.

To clean tarnish from the legs of a chip, first use a small flathead screwdriver or IC extractor to gently remove the chip from its socket. Pay attention to the orientation of the chip before you remove it; you will have to reseat it in the same direction. An ordinary pink pencil eraser will serve well to rub off the tarnish. Rub lightly so as not to bend the legs. When the legs have been restored to their shiny status, reseat the chip. Take care again to not bend the pins, and to correctly orient the chip as it was before you removed it. Repeat this procedure in turn for each chip that shows signs of tarnish.

Remember that the chips on peripheral cards can also suffer from poor connection in their sockets. Be sure to check them too. Tarnish on the chips on a Disk II controller card, for example, can cause the Disk II drive to not operate correctly.

Adjusting Disk Drive Speed

The 5.25" disk drive mechanism relies on the drive motor rotating the disk media at about 300 RPM. A small tolerance is allowed, but it is best to have the disk drive rotate at exactly 300 RPM. Disk drive speed issues typically manifest themselves in a drive that can read disks that it wrote or initialized, but not disks that were written or initialized in another disk drive. 3.5" disk drives rarely have this problem, and hard disks should never experience it.

The solution is to adjust the drive speed to get it as close to 300 RPM as possible. There are two methods: the first is to use a utility such as Copy II Plus that has an on-screen drive speed display. The second method is to disassemble the drive mechanism and manually calibrate the speed based on a strobe pattern. Both methods may require partial disassembly of the drive.

Disassembling the Disk II

Taking apart and adjusting the drive speed on a Disk II is fairly simple, only requiring the removal of eight screws in order to open the top and bottom halves of the metal case. If you are using a speed adjustment program on the Apple, then only four screws and the top case half need be removed.

Start the procedure by powering off your Apple, disconnecting the Disk II cable from the controller card, and ensuring that there isn't a disk inserted in the drive. Close the drive door, then turn the drive upside down.

Use a phillips screwdriver to remove the four black screws shown in Figure G-1. Then slide the top half of the case off of the drive. If you are using a speed tester program on the Apple II, then you are finished disassembling the drive at this point; you may skip ahead to the next section on Adjusting Speed.

If you will be using a fluorescent light to check speed, then there are four more screws, silver in color, which must be removed in order to release the bottom half of the case. Figure G-2 shows these screws.

Figure G-1. Bottom of the Disk II drive

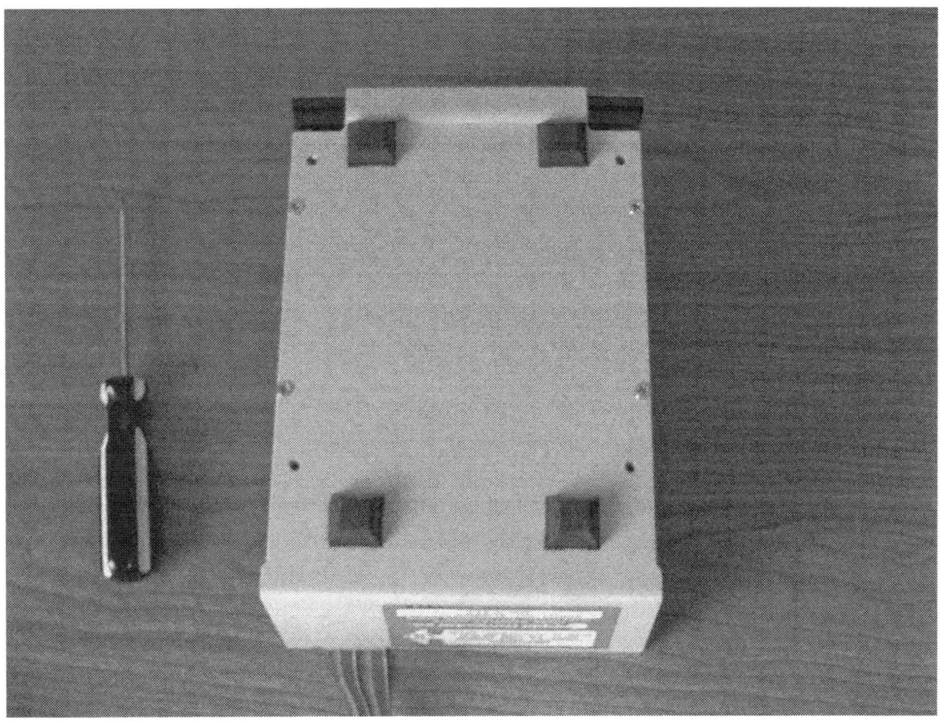

Figure G-2. Disk II with top half of case removed

When you have removed the four silver screws, flip the Disk II drive right side up, and release the plastic clamp holding the ribbon cable. This clamp is indicated by a white arrow in Figure G-3, where the cable has already been released.

The final step is to pull the bottom half of the drive case away, and turn the drive over so that its underside with the drive pulley and belt is visible, as shown in Figure G-4.

When you have finished disassembling the Disk II drive, you must reconnect it to the controller card in the Apple. Take additional care, for with the case removed, the components in the drive could be easily damaged.

Figure G-3. Location of cable clamp indicated by white arrow

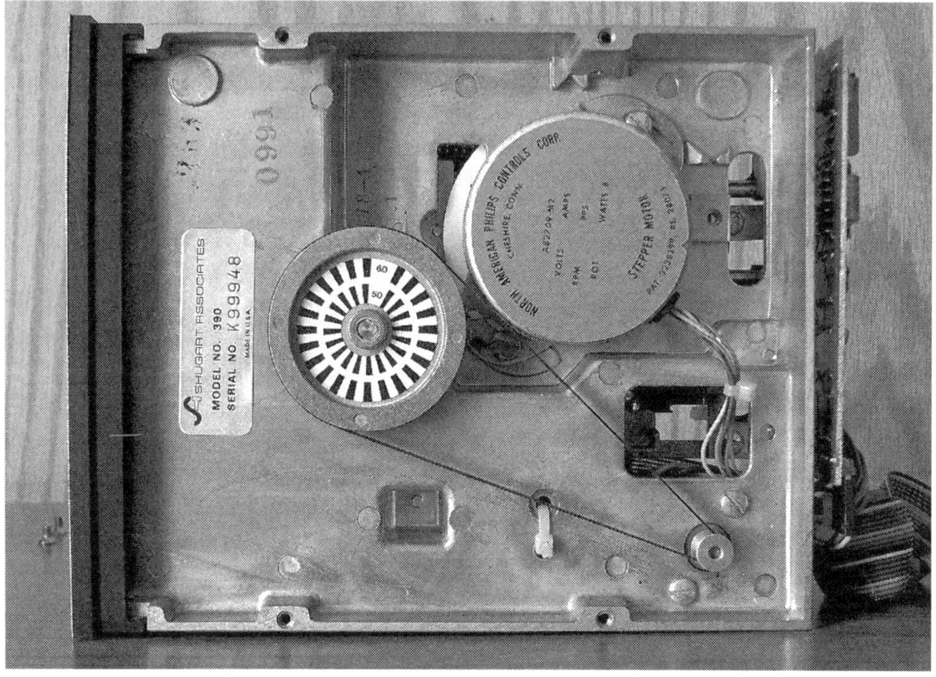

Figure G-4. Disk II belt pulley, showing speed adjustment pattern

Figure G-5. Speed adjustment control on the Disk II

Disassembling the Apple 5.25 Drive

The Apple 5.25 Drive does not require any disassembly if you are going to adjust its speed with the help of a program on the Apple. The speed adjustment control is accessible through a hole located on the underside of the drive, indicated in Figure G-6 with a white arrow. If you are using such a program, you may skip to the next section on Adjusting Speed.

Otherwise, power off your Apple, disconnect the drive, and remove any disk that may be inside it. Make sure that the drive door is closed, then turn over the disk drive. You must first remove the four silver phillips screws on the bottom of the case. Next, there are two more screws on the back of drive case, located on the left and right sides. When these six screws are removed, turn the disk drive right side up, and then remove the top half of the plastic case. Do so by pulling up from the back, where the cable comes out. You should see a metal enclosure that houses the drive mechanism.

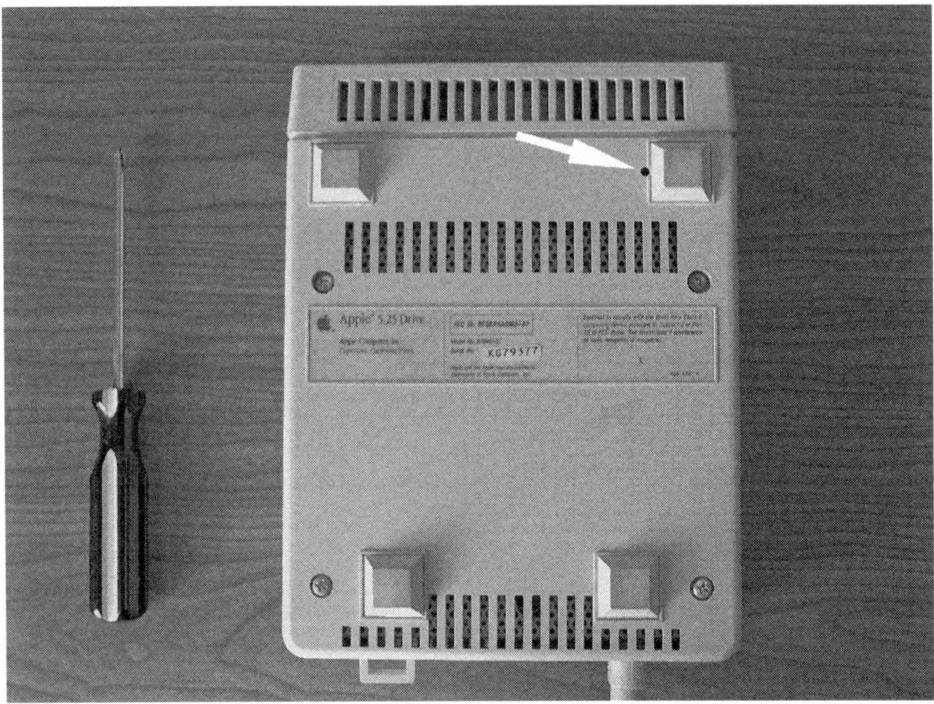

Figure G-6. Location of speed adjustment access hole

Next, the bottom half of the case must be removed. Pull up on the back of the metal enclosure, and pivot it on the bottom front edge of the drive. You may need to use two hands to do this: one hand holding the bottom of the plastic case, and the other hand pulling up on the metal enclosure. Take care not to apply too much force: the cable for the activity indicator LED is rather short, and it could become ripped. When the metal drive enclosure is free of the plastic case, carefully remove the indicator LED from the front of the drive by gently pulling on the cable as close to the LED as possible.

With the plastic case completely removed, there are now seven screws to be removed: two on each side, and three on the top. The four screws on the sides are each located within a metal circle. There are also additional screws on the side of the drive, near the front, but they *should not* be removed. These screws which should not be removed are indicated by the white arrow in Figure G-8. There are two on each side. Do not remove them.

Figure G-7. Removing top half of drive case

Figure G-8. Metal enclosure; arrow shows screws not to be removed

With the proper screws removed, use the screwdriver to carefully pry up the metal lid, working from the back (where the cable comes out). It may take a bit of force to get started. Once it has lifted, use your fingers to pull it completely off.

The disk drive's analog board should now be exposed. There are three cables to disconnect and two final screws to remove. First disconnect the gray cable that attaches to the Apple controller card. Then remove the two other cables that are attached near the back of the analog board. There is no need to disconnect the LED cable, which attaches at the front of the card. Next, remove the two silver screws located in the back corners of the analog card.

Carefully lift out the analog board and set it aside. A rectangular piece of cardboard and a metal plate are located beneath the analog board; remove them both. Then grasp the plastic front end of the disk drive, and carefully wiggle it out of the metal enclosure. There will likely be some resistance. The metal circles on the sides of the enclosure may pop out a bit; this is not a problem.

With the disk drive mechanism freed from the enclosure, turn it over so that the bottom side is exposed.

Figure G-9. Removing the analog card

The white arrow in Figure G-10 reveals the location of the speed adjustment potentiometer.

Now that you have disassembled the Apple 5.25 Drive to get access to the strobe pattern wheel, you will have to partially reassemble it in order to connect it back to the Apple. To do so, reattach the three cables which you disconnected from the analog board, making sure that you properly align the pins on the connectors. Lastly, connect the gray disk drive cable back to the Apple.

Adjusting Speed on the Disk II and Apple 5.25 Drives

The motor speed of the Disk II and Apple 5.25 drives is governed by a potentiometer. In the Disk II, it is mounted on the back of the drive, but oriented so that it is accessible from the side, as circled in Figure G-5. In the Apple 5.25 Drive, it is on the bottom of the drive. Turning the potentiometer clockwise will decrease speed; counterclockwise will increase speed.

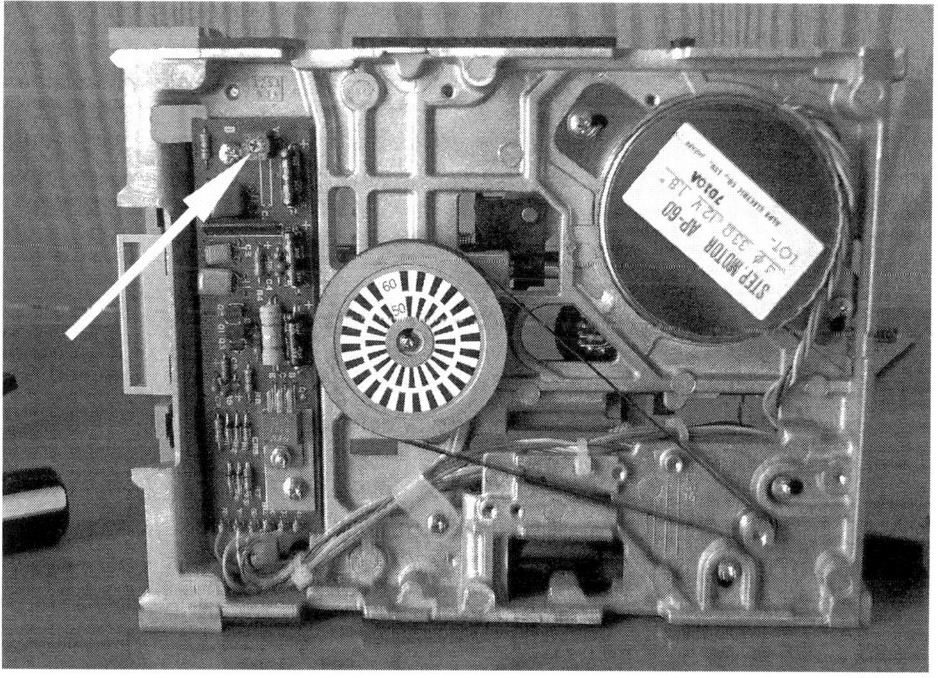

Figure G-10. Bottom of Apple 5.25 Drive, showing speed adjustment

If you are not using a program to adjust the speed, then you will have to watch the strobe pattern on the pulley under a fluorescent light. There are two patterns for 50 and 60 Hz alternating current. Only pay attention to the pattern that matches your local current; ignore the other one. Start the motor spinning by typing PR#6 (or the appropriate slot number) on the Apple. The pattern should not appear to be moving or flickering while the pulley is turning. Adjust the speed potentiometer until it is so.

If you are using Copy II Plus, insert it into a disk drive and boot it. From the main menu, select Verify, then select Drive Speed. At this point, you should remove the program disk for safety. Select the slot and drive number for speed testing. Insert a blank, writable disk into the target drive and press RETURN. This disk will be partially written-over, so be sure that it does not hold any important files.

An indicator on the screen will show drive rotational speed in milliseconds per rotation. The ideal speed is exactly 200.0 ms, which corresponds to 300 RPM. The value shown on the screen will likely be fluctuating slightly, ±.3 ms. Slowly turn the potentiometer with a jeweler's screwdriver until the speed reported is as close as possible to 200.0 ms.

A word of caution: if you have a number of disks that you know were written with this disk drive, and the drive speed was more than 2 or 3 ms off, then you may render them unreadable to the drive by adjusting the speed too much. In this case, it is best to adjust the speed by only 1 to 1.5 ms closer to 200.0 ms. This will ensure that those disks are still readable, and that disks from other drives are readable too.

Press the ESCAPE key when finished, remove the disk, power down the Apple, and reassemble the disk drive.

Cleaning the Disk Drive Head

If a Disk II or Apple 5.25 Drive is having problems reading disks, such as if you get frequent I/O errors, or disks that won't boot, there is likely a build up of oxide crud or dust on the disk head. Dirt and dust on the head often comes from using disks which were improperly stored in a dusty or otherwise unclean environment.

If you suspect that a disk drive has a dirty head, *do not* insert any more disks into it until you have cleaned it. Material stuck on the drive head has the potential to scratch the surface of any disk in the drive, potentially destroying the data stored there.

Follow the appropriate disassembly instructions for your drive, as given in the previous section, and take a look at the drive head. Figure G-11 has an arrow pointing to a build-up of oxide on the head. Ordinarily, the head should be a white rectangle with a thin black line running across it, all mounted on a circular platform. If there are any other markings on the white surface, they do not belong.

Use a cotton swab dipped in isopropanol for best results, or distilled water will work too, since it is a mild solvent. Rub the cotton swab on the drive head until the oxide crud has come off. Wait a few minutes for the liquid to evaporate before plugging in the drive and testing.

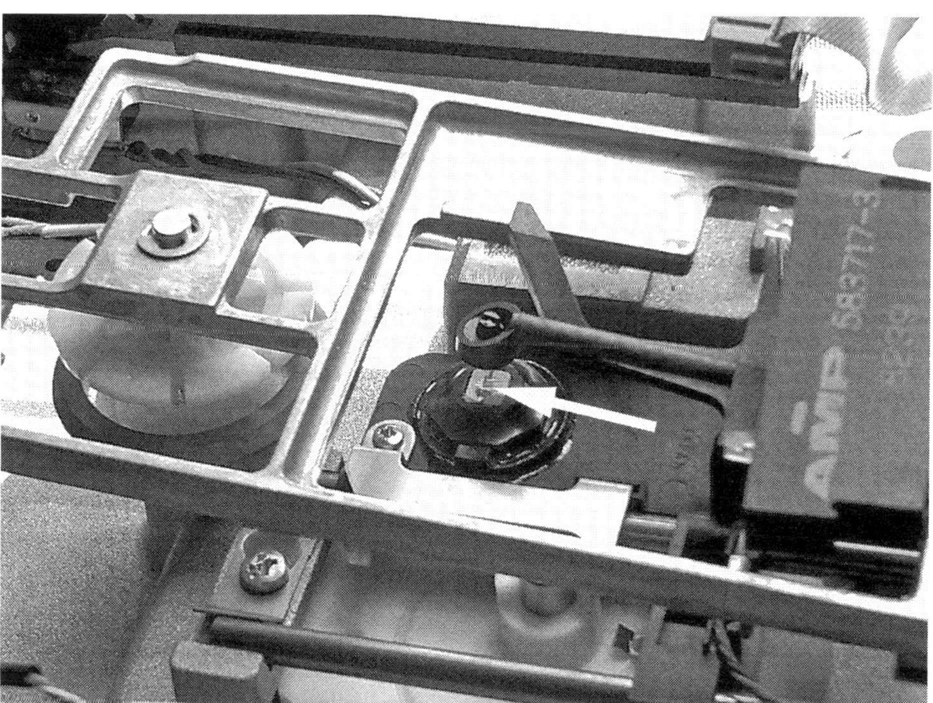

Figure G-11. Arrow indicating oxide buildup on the Disk II head

Testing and Replacing RAM

Faulty or failed RAM chips are another likely culprit behind "strange behavior" from your Apple. If you have cleaned and reseated all the chips, as described earlier, but are still having problems with your Apple, then RAM may be the problem. Bad RAM is detectable by programs that refuse to load, system crashes, or when random characters appear on the text screen.

RAM testing utility programs exist which can test RAM in all models of Apple, with one caveat: the defective RAM must not hinder the operation of the program! Some models of Apple include built-in RAM tests which will be described next.

When replacing the RAM in an Apple, be sure to get the right type. RAM chips come in varying speeds, and the Apple does require a minimum speed, but you are unlikely to get chips that are slower than this minimum, which is 200 ns. Faster chips, such as 120 ns, will also work.

The Programmer's Aid RAM Test

In 1978, Apple Computer released the Programmer's Aid #1 utility package. It consisted of a ROM chip destined for the D0 ROM socket on the motherboard of the standard Apple II. Accompanying it was a 96-page instruction manual that explained how to use the various routines which included: a music generator, tape verify routine, program relocator, BASIC line renumbering program, and a RAM test.

The RAM test will work on any model of Apple, but as it only tests the first 48K of RAM, and since the standard Apple II and II Plus lack a built-in test, it makes the most sense to use it only for these models.

The ROM chip is a bit obscure these days, due to the fact that it only fits in an Apple II equipped with the original Integer BASIC ROM set. However, it survives on the DOS 3.3 System Master. Boot the System Master disk, and type INT to switch to Integer BASIC. Another way to use the Programmer's Aid ROM is to install it on a ROM (Firmware) Card alongside the Integer BASIC ROM set for use in the Apple II Plus. Make sure that the red switch is flipped up to make the ROM on the card active.

To use the RAM test, first switch to Integer BASIC, and type CALL -151 to enter the Monitor:

```
]INT
>CALL-151

*
```

Verify that the Programmer's Aid ROM is loaded by checking the byte at memory location $D000. It should be $A9:

```
*D000

D000- A9
*
```

Once you have verified that the Programmer's Aid ROM is available, you must initialize the RAM test. The test program is implemented as a User-Defined Monitor Command, activated by CONTROL-Y. See Chapter 11 for full details on using CONTROL-Y in the Monitor.

Type the following command to initialize the RAM test:

```
*D5BCG

*
```

The Monitor prompt will return again, and it will appear as though nothing happened. In fact, the RAM test is now active and awaiting your input.

The RAM test uses the Monitor prompt for input, and it takes the following syntax:

starting address . number of pages CONTROL-Y

The *number of pages* times 100 must not be greater than the *starting address*. Recall that a *page* of memory is 256 bytes in length. To test the screen memory, the starting address would be 400. Since the screen memory takes up 1,024 bytes of RAM, that equals 4 pages. Therefore, enter the following:

`*400.4` (CONTROL-Y)

Typing CONTROL-Y will not cause anything to appear on the screen. Remember to press RETURN as usual afterward.

The screen should flash for a few seconds, then the Apple will beep and the Monitor prompt should return. The beep means that the test is complete. If no message is printed on the screen, then the test was successful.

To thoroughly test all 48K of RAM, enter the following lines:

`*400.4` (CONTROL-Y)
`*800.8` (CONTROL-Y)
`*1000.10` (CONTROL-Y)
`*2000.20` (CONTROL-Y)
`*3000.20` (CONTROL-Y)
`*4000.40` (CONTROL-Y)
`*7000.20` (CONTROL-Y)
`*8000.80` (CONTROL-Y)

This complete test will take over two minutes to run.

If there is an error, the word ERR and a chip location will be printed on the screen. For example, if the chip location is C-2, then the RAM chip in row C, in second position from the left, is faulty.

The Apple IIe Self-Test

The Apple IIe has a built-in self-test that will check the RAM chips for errors. The Apple IIe will test both the 64 kilobytes of main RAM on the motherboard, as well as the auxiliary 64 kilobytes of RAM on an Extended 80-Column Card, if it is installed. In addition, several unique LSI components such as the ROMs, MMU, and IOU are tested.

AA Code	Meaning
01	ROM failure (or RAM failure if last two digits are 01)
02	RAM failure or ADB tool call error
03	Soft switches and state register
04	RAM address failure or ADB tool call error
05	FPI Speed error
06	Serial port failure
07	Clock failure
08	Battery RAM failure
09	Apple Desktop Bus failure
0A	Shadow register failure
0B	Interrupt failure
0C	Sound failure (Ensoniq or RAM access)

Table G-1. Apple IIgs diagnostic error codes

To activate the IIe self-test, power on the Apple while holding the SOLID-APPLE key. The self-test takes about 30 seconds, and should end with the message KERNEL OK (for the standard, unenhanced IIe) or SYSTEM OK. Faulty RAM will be indicated with a logic board coordinate, indicating the location of the failed chip.

The Apple IIc and IIc Plus Self-Test

Starting with the UniDisk 3.5 ROM revision of the Apple IIc, a self-test program is included with the system. The Apple IIc and IIc Plus self-test is invoked in the same manner as, and performs nearly identically to, the Apple IIe test. If the test passed successfully, the message SYSTEM OK will be printed on the screen.

The Apple IIgs Self-test

The IIgs tests only the RAM installed on the motherboard, and not any installed on a Memory Expansion Card.

The Apple IIgs self-test is invoked by holding the COMMAND and OPTION keys while powering on the computer. The IIgs test runs for about 35 seconds, and should display the message SYSTEM GOOD when finished.

If the IIgs test fails, then the message SYSTEM BAD with an error code is displayed. The error code is of the format AABBCCDD, and is repeated several times on the screen in case of bad RAM causing a video display error. As a last resort, the error code is also sent to the printer port, and should appear on an ImageWriter II, provided that the printer is powered on, has paper, and has the Select light on. In the code, the AA represents the test type that failed, and the BB, CC, and DD portions indicate the specifics of the failure. When AA is 04, that means that the RAM test failed. Table G-1 lists all possible codes for AA and their meanings.

The presence of some Apple IIgs accelerators, such as the Zip GS, may cause the diagnostic to fail.

RAM in the II and II Plus

The Apple II and II Plus most commonly use the 4116 DRAM chip, a 16 kilobit 16-pin DIP. You may also use the 4 kilobit 4096 chip in the original Apple II and early models of II Plus, but you will be limited to 36 kilobytes or less of total RAM.

The motherboard of the II and II Plus can hold a maximum of 24 chips, divided into three rows of eight. Since these two Apples use the 8-bit 6502 microprocessor, a single byte of memory stores each of its eight bits in one of the eight RAM chips in a row. Because all eight chips are used, they must be all of the same type, either 4K or 16K.

The three rows of RAM chips are labeled C, D, and E, on the motherboard, located within a large white rectangle. Row C is the row closest to the keyboard, and it absolutely must be filled with eight RAM chips. Row E may only be filled if row D is also filled.

The standard Apple II and early models of the II Plus have memory configuration blocks located to the left of each row of RAM. These blocks dictate which type of RAM must be installed in each respective row. If your Apple II does not have any configuration

Total RAM	Row C	Row D	Row E
4K	4K		
8K	4K	4K	
12K	4K	4K	4K
16K	16K		
20K	16K	4K	
24K	16K	4K	4K
32K	16K	16K	
36K	16K	16K	4K
48K	16K	16K	16K

Table G-2. Possible RAM configurations of an Apple II or II Plus

blocks, then it likely is a newer model that requires 16K chips be installed in all three rows. There are nine possible RAM configurations, all shown in Table G-2.

If an Apple Language Card (or compatible) is installed in slot 0, it will add an additional 16K of RAM, bringing the total to 64K. It requires that the left-most RAM chip in row E be removed. A cable from the Language Card plugs into that socket instead.

An Apple II with a Revision 0 motherboard should not be configured with 20K or 24K of RAM due to a design mistake on the motherboard. This design mistake causes a range of RAM to be duplicated, thus making it appear as though there is more memory available than actually exists. This problem has been resolved on Revision 1 and later boards.

RAM in the IIe

The Apple IIe takes eight of the 4164 chip, a 64 kilobit chip. This same chip is also used on the Extended 80-Column Card.

RAM in the IIc and IIc Plus

The RAM chips in the Apple IIc and IIc Plus are soldered to the logic board, therefore making them more difficult to replace. They are of the same type as the Apple IIe RAM.

RAM in the IIgs

The ROM 01 Apple IIgs uses 256 kilobit DRAMs, whereas the "1 Megabyte" ROM3 IIgs uses 1 megabit chips. The RAM in the IIgs too is likely to be soldered instead of socketed.

The chips used on the Memory Expansion board must be 150 ns, 256k x 1 bit, and CAS before RAS.

Appendix H : Built-in Subroutines

Built into BASIC and the Machine Language Monitor are several indispensable subroutines which may be used in both BASIC and assembly language programs.

Most Monitor subroutines may be accessed from BASIC by using the CALL command, as taught in Chapter 5. You may recognize that a few of these subroutines have direct equivalents in Integer or Applesoft BASIC.

Some of the subroutines may be difficult to work with from BASIC because they require specific microprocessor registers to be set. Neither Applesoft nor Integer BASIC provides any functions for working directly with the registers. However, there is a method in Integer BASIC. First, CALL -182 to save the current registers to memory. Then POKE the desired register values in the following locations:

- A register - 69
- X register - 70
- Y register - 71

Then CALL -193 to load these values from memory into the registers. Finally, call the desired subroutine. Unfortunately, this method will not work in Applesoft. You will have to write your own assembly language program that will set the registers based on reading a known set of memory locations and then execute a JSR to the desired subroutine.

Following are the built-in subroutines, sorted into categories based on function. The decimal addresses are in the Applesoft format. To use them with Integer BASIC, subtract the decimal address from 65536. You will get a negative number that can be used with PEEK, POKE, and CALL in both Integer BASIC and Applesoft.

Text Output

Name	Hex Address	Decimal Address
COUT	$FDED	65005
Send a character in the accumulator to the current output device defined by CSW.		
COUT1	$FDF0	65008
Send a character in the accumulator to the screen.		
SETINV	$FE80	65152
Set text style to inverse.		
SETNORM	$FE84	65156
Set text style to normal.		
CROUT	$FD8E	64910
Print a carriage return using COUT.		
CROUT1	$FD8B	64907
Clear the screen from the current cursor position to the top edge of the text window, then call CROUT.		
PRBYTE	$FDDA	64986
Print the accumulator byte as two hexadecimal digits using COUT.		
PRHEX	$FDE3	64995
Print the lower nibble of the accumulator as a hexadecimal digit using COUT.		
PRNTAX	$F941	63809
Print the contents of the A and X registers as a four-digit hexadecimal value.		

Name	Hex Address	Decimal Address
PRBLNK	$F948	63816
Print three spaces using COUT.		
PRBL2	$F94A	63818
Print one or more spaces using COUT. The X register controls the number of spaces. When X is 0, 256 spaces will be produced.		

Keyboard Input

Name	Hex Address	Decimal Address
RDKEY	$FD0C	64780
Place a flashing cursor on the screen and jump to the routine specified by KSW (hex locations $38 and $39).		
RDCHAR	$FD35	64821
Get a character from the standard input, also interpreting the 11 escape codes.		
KEYIN	$FD1B	64795
The standard keyboard input routine that waits for a key press, stores it in the A register, and randomizes the random number seed in the mean time.		
GETLN	$FD6A	64874
Show a prompt and get a line of input from the user. The line is stored starting at $200 and the length is stored in the X register. The prompt character is stored at $33.		
GETLNZ	$FD67	64871
Issue a carriage return to COUT then call GETLN.		
GETLN1	$FD6F	64879
Call GETLN without a prompt.		

Low-Resolution Graphics

Name	Hex Address	Decimal Address
SETCOL	$F864	63588
Set the current low-resolution graphics color to the value as passed in the accumulator.		
NEXTCOL	$F85F	63583
Add 3 to the current low-resolution color.		
PLOT	$F800	63488
Plot a point on the low-resolution screen. The accumulator holds the Y position; the Y register the X position.		
HLINE	$F819	63513
Plot a horizontal line on the low-resolution graphics screen. The accumulator holds the vertical position of the line, Y register the left edge of the line, and location $2C the right edge of the line.		
VLINE	$F828	63528
Plot a vertical line on the low-resolution screen. The Y register holds the horizontal position of the line, the accumulator the top of the line, and location $2D the bottom of the line.		
SCRN	$F871	63601
Return the color of a point on the low-resolution screen in the accumulator. The arguments are the same as PLOT.		
CLRSCR	$F832	63538
Clear the entire low-resolution graphics screen to black.		
CLRTOP	$F836	63542
Clear only the top 40 rows of the low-resolution graphics screen.		

Sound

Name	Hex Address	Decimal Address
BELL	$FF3A	65338
Sends a CONTROL-G to the current output device.		
BELL1	$FBDD	64477
Cause the Apple speaker to beep for .1 seconds at 1 KHz.		

Miscellaneous

Name	Hex Address	Decimal Address
PREAD	$FB1E	64286
Return the position of a game paddle. The X register should hold a value of 0 through 3 to select the paddle. The reading is returned in the Y register.		
PRERR	$FF2D	65325
Print the word "ERR" and a bell character to COUT.		
IOSAVE	$FF4A	65354
Save the 6502 processor registers in locations $45 to $49 in the order A, X, Y, P, S.		
IOREST	$FF3F	65343
Restore the 6502 processor registers saved in locations $45 to $49.		
WAIT	$FCA8	64680
Do nothing for an amount of time specified by the accumulator. The delay is $(26 + 27A + 5A^2)/2$ microseconds.		

Appendix I : Error Messages

Applesoft, Integer BASIC, DOS 3.3, and ProDOS each have their own error messages and manner of displaying them. This appendix lists each error message and its associated code (if any). The messages are sorted into categories based on the environment that produces them.

Table I-1 shows how each environment formats its error messages.

Format	Environment
SYNTAX ERROR	DOS 3.3
SYNTAX ERROR	ProDOS
?SYNTAX ERROR	Applesoft
*** SYNTAX ERR	Integer BASIC

Table I-1. Error message formats

Handling Errors from Applesoft

Most Applesoft errors, and all ProDOS and DOS 3.3 errors, have an associated numerical error code. The Applesoft ONERR GOTO statement can be used to catch and resolve errors as they arise.

Error codes are stored in memory location 222. Using a statement such as

```
EC = PEEK(222)
```

will assign the code to a variable named EC. The line number of the program where the error occurred is stored at locations 218 and 219. The following statement:

```
EL = PEEK(218) + PEEK(219) * 256
```

will assign the line number to the variable EL.

DOS 3.3 Error Codes

Table I-2 lists DOS errors in numerical order. Following is an explanation of each error.

Language Not Available (Code 1)

The version of BASIC required was not found. Four commands may change the version of BASIC used on the Apple: FP, INT, LOAD, and RUN.

If a request for Applesoft is made, DOS makes checks in the following order: ROM, Applesoft firmware card, Apple Language card, RAM, the current disk drive.

When looking for Integer BASIC, DOS only checks ROM and RAM.

Range Error (Code 2 or 3)

The value for a DOS command option was too large or too small. For example, the value for slot number must be in the range 1 to 7.

Write Protected (Code 4)

DOS tried to write data to a disk that was write-protected. Refer to Chapter 7 for instructions on how to enable 5.25" disks for writing.

End of Data (Code 5)

A BASIC program has reached the end of a data or text file. Any byte beyond the end of the last field in a sequential text file or the

Code	Meaning
1	Language Not Available
2, 3	Range Error
4	Write-Protected
5	End of Data
6	File Not Found
7	Volume Mismatch
8	I/O Error
9	Disk Full
10	File Locked
11	Syntax Error
12	No Buffers Available
13	File Type Mismatch
14	Program Too Large
15	Not Direct Command

Table I-2. DOS 3.3 error codes and meanings

last record in a random-access file contains a value 0. This value represents null, and attempting to read it triggers this error.

The most likely cause is a program that uses INPUT or GET one too many times. Refer to Chapter 7 for suggestions on writing programs that can detect and avoid this error.

File Not Found (Code 6)

The specified file was not found on the current disk. Check the name for accuracy, or check that the correct disk is being used.

If this error occurs every time a disk is booted, then the startup program is missing. Check for a BASIC file named HELLO. Otherwise, you may have to INIT the disk to set the startup program.

Volume Mismatch (Code 7)

The volume number of the current disk does not match that specified by a DOS command. Use CATALOG to see the disk's volume number.

I/O Error (Code 8)

This error occurs when DOS is unsuccessful after 96 attempts at reading or writing a block of data from a disk.

This error can be caused by one of several circumstances:

- The disk drive door is open.
- The disk drive contains no disk.
- The disk is not formatted for DOS.
- The Drive option (D) for a command specified a nonexistent drive.
- A 13-sector DOS disk is being used.
- The Slot option (S) for a command specified a slot that does not contain a controller card.

Less commonly, the disk media may be physically damaged or the disk drive may need to be cleaned.

Disk Full (Code 9)

DOS ran out of room on the disk when trying to save a file. The file may have been partially saved; you should delete it immediately, since it does not contain all of its intended data.

Afterward, you should either delete some files from this disk to make room, or use another disk to save your data.

File Locked (Code 10)

An attempt was made by one of the following commands to modify a locked file: APPEND, BSAVE, DELETE, RENAME, SAVE, or WRITE.

Check the catalog listing for an asterisk (*) next to the file's type, indicating that it is locked. Locked files may not be modified in any way.

To avoid this error, either unlock the file, or perform the operation on a different file.

Syntax Error (Code 11)

A DOS command had a syntax error such as a missing option, missing separator, illegal value, or illegal characters.

If all DOS commands, such as CATALOG, return a Syntax Error, it is possible that DOS is disconnected from BASIC. To attempt to correct this problem, issue the command 3D0G from the Monitor prompt. Otherwise, you will have to reboot the disk to reload DOS.

No Buffers Available (Code 12)

Each open file and most DOS commands require a memory buffer. This error means that either too many files are open or not enough memory is available.

Try closing open files or use the MAXFILES command to increase the number of files which may be opened concurrently.

File Type Mismatch (Code 13)

The expected file type for a command was not encountered.

For example, only Applesoft and Integer programs (type A or I) may be used with LOAD, RUN, and SAVE. CHAIN can only be used with Integer BASIC files. BRUN must be used with B type files, and EXEC must be used with the T file type.

Program Too Large (Code 14)

This error occurs when DOS finds that a BASIC program or other disk file is too large to be stored in the Apple's memory. A possible cause is that HIMEM was set too low for the new program to fit in memory.

Another solution is to use MAXFILES to decrease the number of files which may be open, thus allowing more memory for programs.

Not Direct Command (Code 15)

One of the following commands was used in immediate mode: APPEND, OPEN, POSITION, READ, or WRITE. These commands can only be used in PRINT statements from an Applesoft or Integer BASIC program.

ProDOS Error Codes

Table I-3 lists ProDOS errors in numerical order. Following are an explanation and probable causes for each error message.

Range Error (Code 2)

The value for a ProDOS command option was too large or too small. For example, the value for slot number must be in the range 1 to 7.

No Device Connected (Code 3)

A program tried to use a slot that doesn't contain a card, or the card does not have any devices connected, or the disk drive contains no disk (not detectable on all drives).

A common cause of this error is trying to access a 3.5" disk controller that either has no drives connected or that does not have a disk inserted in a drive.

Write Protected (Code 4)

ProDOS tried to write data to a disk that was write-protected. Refer to Chapter 7 for instructions on how to enable 3.5" and 5.25" disks for writing.

Code	Meaning
2	Range Error
3	No Device Connected
4	Write Protected
5	End of Data
6	Path Not Found
7	Path Not Found
8	I/O Error
9	Disk Full
10	File Locked
11	Invalid Option
12	No Buffers Available
13	File Type Mismatch
14	Program Too Large
15	Not Direct Command
16	Syntax Error
17	Directory Full
18	File Not Open
19	Duplicate Filename
20	File Busy
21	File(s) Still Open

Table I-3. ProDOS error codes and meanings

End of Data (Code 5)

A BASIC program has reached the end of a data or text file, or an attempt was made to read data from a place where none had ever been stored. Any byte beyond the end of the last field in a sequential text file or the last record in a random-access file contains a value 0. This value represents null, and attempting to read it triggers this error.

The most likely cause is a program that uses INPUT or GET one too many times. Refer to Chapter 7 for suggestions on writing programs that can detect and avoid this error.

Path Not Found (Code 6 or 7)

A valid pathname was specified, but no file existed there, or an invalid pathname was used. There are two common causes: either the pathname is erroneous (it contained a typo or an illegal character), or the file never existed.

I/O Error (Code 8)

This error occurs when ProDOS is unsuccessful after 96 attempts at reading or writing a block of data from a disk.

This error can be caused by one of several circumstances:

- The disk drive door is open.
- The disk drive contains no disk.
- The disk is not formatted for ProDOS.
- The Drive option (D) for a command specified a nonexistent drive.
- The Slot option (S) for a command specified a slot that does not contain a controller card.

Less commonly, the disk media may be physically damaged or the disk drive may need to be cleaned.

Disk Full (Code 9)

ProDOS ran out of room on the disk when trying to save a file. The file may have been partially saved; you should delete it immediately, since it does not contain all of its intended data.

Afterward, you should either delete some files from this disk to make room, or use another disk to save your data.

File Locked (Code 10)

An attempt was made by one of the following commands to modify a locked file: APPEND, BSAVE, DELETE, RENAME, SAVE, STORE, or WRITE.

Check the catalog listing for an asterisk (*) next to the file's name, indicating that it is locked. Locked files may not be modified in any way.

To avoid this error, either unlock the file, or perform the operation on a different file.

Invalid Option (Code 11)

An invalid or inappropriate option was specified for a ProDOS command.

No Buffers Available (Code 12)

Every file that is opened in ProDOS has a 1K memory buffer reserved for it. No more than eight files may be opened at a time. Some ProDOS commands also require a buffer to operate.

If this error occurs, it could be that eight files are already open, or that not enough memory is available.

This error also occurs if a file is BLOADed above HIMEM or below LOMEM.

File Type Mismatch (Code 13)

The expected file type for a command was not encountered.

For example, only Applesoft programs (type BAS) may be used with LOAD, RUN, SAVE, and CHAIN. BRUN must be used with BIN type files, and EXEC must be used with the TXT file type.

Program Too Large (Code 14)

This crror occurs when ProDOS finds that an Applesoft program or some other disk file is too large to be stored in the Apple's memory. A possible cause is that HIMEM was set too low for the new program to fit in memory.

One workaround is to split the program into sections and use CHAIN to transfer control from one section to another in the program.

Not Direct Command (Code 15)

An attempt was made to use a command in immediate mode that may only be used in programmed mode. The following ProDOS commands may only be used in a PRINT statement from an Applesoft program: APPEND, OPEN, POSITION, READ, and WRITE.

Syntax Error (Code 16)

A ProDOS command had a syntax error such as a missing option, missing separator, illegal value, or illegal characters.

If all ProDOS commands, such as CAT, return a Syntax Error, it is possible that ProDOS is disconnected from BASIC. To attempt to correct this problem, issue a CALL 1002 from the Applesoft prompt. Otherwise, you will have to reboot the disk to reload ProDOS.

Directory Full (Code 17)

All ProDOS directories except for the volume directory may store an unlimited number of files. The volume directory, however, is limited to only 51 files.

To resolve this error, either use a different disk, delete some files from the volume directory, or use the ProDOS Filer to move some files to a different directory.

File Not Open (Code 18)

Some ProDOS commands only work on an open file. This error occurs when one of the following commands is used on a file that is not open: POSITION, READ, and WRITE. The solution is to open the file in question before attempting to use one of these three commands on it.

Duplicate Filename (Code 19)

A file at a given pathname already exists when trying to use CREATE or RENAME. Use a different name or path.

File Busy (Code 20)

Some ProDOS commands only work when a file is closed. CAT, CATALOG, DELETE, and RENAME cannot be used on a file that is open. Close the file, then use one of these commands.

File(s) Still Open (Code 21)

This message occurs after a program is suddenly interrupted while one or more files are still open. You must issue the CLOSE command to close all open files before you can LOAD or RUN an Applesoft program.

Applesoft Error Codes

Applesoft signals errors with a beep and a message in the form of ?XX ERROR, where XX is the particular error message. If the error occurs during the execution of a program, the line number is also printed on the screen.

Most Applesoft errors do have a code; a few do not. Those with codes are listed in Table I-4. As mentioned at the beginning of this appendix, errors with codes can be handled with a user-defined routine in a program.

Bad Subscript (Code 107)

A statement tried to access an element outside of an array's boundaries.

Code	Meaning
0	?NEXT Without FOR
16	?Syntax Error
20	Reset Key
22	?RETURN Without GOSUB
42	?Out of Data
53	?Illegal Quantity
69	?Overflow
77	?Out of Memory
90	?Undef'd. Statement
107	?Bad Subscript
120	?Redim'd. Array
133	?Division by Zero
163	?Type Mismatch
176	?String Too Long
191	?Formula Too Complex
224	?Undef'd. Function
254	?Re-enter
255	CONTROL-C Interrupt

Table I-4. Applesoft error codes and meanings

Can't Continue

The CONT command cannot be used to continue a program when none exists in memory, after an error, or after the program is changed.

Division by Zero (Code 133)

Division by zero is mathematically undefined, and therefore is not allowed. The most common occurrence is that a variable being used as a divisor is assigned the value 0 at some point in the program.

Formula Too Complex (Code 191)

More than two attempts were made to use a string with an IF statement, such as IF "FOO" THEN. Strings should not be used alone in IF-THEN statements.

Illegal Direct

Some Applesoft commands may not be used in immediate mode. These commands are as follows: DEF FN, GET, INPUT, ONERR GOTO, READ, and RESUME.

Illegal Quantity (Code 53)

A function argument or statement had an out of range value. Some examples are: a negative array subscript, LOG with an argument less than or equal to zero, and SQR with a negative argument.

NEXT Without FOR (Code 0)

The variable used in a NEXT statement would have caused an improperly-nested loop, or a NEXT was used before a FOR statement. This error is sometimes caused by branching into the body of a loop.

Out of Data (Code 42)

The data pointer for DATA statements was already at the end, and another READ statement was issued. This problem is usually caused by too many READ statements being executed as part of a loop, or when a RESTORE statement is mistakenly left out.

Out of Memory (Code 77)

The Applesoft interpreter ran out of memory. There are several reasons that could have caused this error:

- The program is too large

- The program has too many variables
- An array was dimensioned too large
- FOR loops nested more than ten levels deep
- LOMEM was set too high
- HIMEM was set too low
- An expression was too complicated
- GOSUB calls nested more than 24 levels deep
- Parentheses nested more than 36 levels deep.

Overflow (Code 69)

At some point during a mathematical calculation, the value was too large to be manipulated by Applesoft.

Redim'd Array (Code 120)

This error is caused by an attempt to define an array more than once. This error can also be caused by attempting to use an array before dimensioning it.

To avoid this issue, dimension all arrays at the beginning of the program, then ensure that no branches are ever made to those beginning program lines.

RETURN Without GOSUB (Code 22)

A RETURN statement was encountered before a GOSUB. The most common causes of this error are by unintentionally branching into a subroutine, or by having program execution lead to the body of a subroutine by leaving out an END or GOTO statement.

String Too Long (Code 176)

If a concatenated string ends up being longer than 255 characters, this error will occur.

Syntax Error (Code 16)

Some statement in a program is syntactically incorrect according to Applesoft's rules. There are many causes for this error, such as a typographical mistake, missing punctuation, or illegal characters.

Type Mismatch (Code 163)

An attempt was made to assign the wrong type of data to a variable. For example, trying to assign a string to an integer variable, or a real number to a string variable.

Undef'd Function (Code 224)

A call was made to a user-defined function that was never defined.

Undef'd Statement (Code 90)

An attempt was made to branch to a program line that does not exist. This error can be the effect of changing program lines, such as by deleting or renumbering them, and then forgetting to update references to those lines in GOTO and GOSUB statements.

Integer BASIC Error Messages

Integer BASIC has the least formal error messages, as they have no code number, and Integer BASIC lacks any built-in method for allowing the program to handle errors. Integer BASIC errors are always prefixed with three asterisks (*).

*** >255 ERR

Some value, such as one of the arguments for a PLOT statement, was out of range. Use a value that is in the range 0 to 255.

*** >32767 ERR

Integer BASIC cannot work with numbers less than -32767 or greater than 32767.

*** 16 FORS ERR

Integer BASIC allows no more than 16 nested loops.

*** 16 GOSUBS ERR

Integer BASIC allows no more than 16 nested GOSUB calls.

*** BAD BRANCH ERR

A GOTO, GOSUB, or IF-THEN statement specified a line number that does not exist in the program.

*** BAD NEXT ERR

A NEXT was encountered without a preceding FOR.

*** BAD RETURN ERR

A RETURN was encountered without a preceding GOSUB.

*** DIM ERR

An array was dimensioned more than once. Redimensioning an array is only allowed under one specific scenario explained in Chapter 4.

*** MEM FULL ERR

Not enough memory was available for the program. Either the program is too long, it uses too many variables, or an array was too large.

*** NO END ERR

The last line executed in the program did not contain END.

*** RANGE ERR

This error is typically caused by an array subscript that is less than zero or larger than the array's dimensions. Supplying arguments too large to HLIN, VLIN, PLOT, TAB, or VTAB will also cause this error.

RETYPE LINE

The wrong type of input was encountered from an INPUT statement, such as a string being entered instead of a number.

STOPPED AT *X*

This message occurs usually after an error message. The *X* is the line number where the error occurred. Pressing CONTROL-C to halt a program will also cause this message to appear.

*** STRING ERR

Some illegal operation involving a string was attempted.

*** STR OVFL ERR

An attempt was made to put more characters into a string than are allowed by its dimensions.

*** SYNTAX ERR

The Apple was not able to understand a program line. The statement likely contains unknown commands, typographical errors, or missing punctuation.

*** TOO LONG ERR

More than 128 characters were entered in response to an INPUT statement, or there were more than 12 sets of nested parentheses.

Glossary

#

8-bit Apple

A term for any model of Apple that is *not* the Apple IIgs. So-called because all other Apples utilize an 8-bit microprocessor, either the 6502 or the 65C02.

6502

The 8-bit microprocessor used in the original Apple II, II Plus, and IIe. Compare with *65C02*.

65C02

An enhanced version of the original 6502 microprocessor, used in the Enhanced IIe, IIc, and IIc Plus.

65C816

The 16-bit microprocessor utilized in the Apple IIgs. It can also operate in 8-bit mode for compatibility with older Apple software.

A

accelerator

Any type of replacement CPU or expansion board which allows the Apple to operate at an enhanced rate of speed. Using an accelerator will make your programs run faster.

active 40

The state of the text display screen when the 80-column firmware is active, but the screen is only showing 40 columns per line.

active 80
The state of the text display when the 80-column firmware is active and the screen is showing 80 columns per line.

address
A number used to identify a memory location.

ADT (Apple Disk Transfer)
A popular program for transferring disks to and from the Apple II computer. ADT is a two-part system: a server operates on a PC or Macintosh computer, and a client runs on the Apple.

Apple
1. The company that manufactured the Apple II computer series.
2. A generic name for any Apple II series computer.

Apple key
The name for the COMMAND key on older models of Apple.

Apple menu
In GUI-based applications on the Apple IIgs, the Apple menu appears at the left end of the menu bar. It contains any new desk accessories (NDAs) currently installed in the system folder.

Apple II
Apple Computer's second personal computer, first released in 1977. It was one of the most popular personal computers in the world at the time.

ADB (Apple Desktop Bus)
A system of connecting keyboards, mice, joysticks, and other input devices to the Apple IIgs.

AppleShare
Networking software that allows one or more Apple II and Macintosh computers to access a common hard disk or printer over an AppleTalk network.

Applesoft
The most common dialect of BASIC used on the Apple.

AppleTalk

A networking system for Apple II and Macintosh computers that allows them to connect and transfer data.

application

A software program that performs a certain task on the computer, such as word processing, and that is usually dependent on an operating system.

array

A program data structure representing a group of related values, such as integers or strings.

ASCII (American Standard Code for Information Interchange)

The system used on the Apple II for encoding and displaying letters and numbers both from the keyboard and on screen.

assembler

A program that takes an assembly language program and coverts it to machine language.

assembly language

A programming language which uses mnemonics to represent machine language instructions.

Autostart ROM

For users of the original model of Apple II, the Autostart ROM makes some useful changes: BASIC loads automatically when the power is switched on; if a Disk II drive is connected, it will automatically boot; new cursor control keys and line editing functions are available. The Autostart ROM may be obtained in three different ways: as an IC in the F8 socket on the motherboard, on a ROM card, or on the Language Card.

Aux (Auxiliary)

1. The eighth slot on an Apple IIe or IIgs, commonly used for memory expansion.
2. An additional 64 kilobytes of RAM available on the IIe or IIc.

auxiliary slot

See *Aux, definition 1*

B

BASIC (Beginners' All Purpose Symbolic Instruction Code)
A type of computer language that is based on English and that is easy to learn. It comes built into all Apple computers, in the form of either Integer BASIC or Applesoft.

baud
A rate of transmission between two computers or a computer and a peripheral device.

binary
Having only two states, on or off, or 1 or 0. At its lowest level, the Apple is a binary computer.

bit
Short for a binary digit, the smallest unit of information which a computer may store. A bit is either on or off, 1 or 0.

bit map
The term for a collection of bits which constitute an image, such as an on-screen graphic.

block
The smallest unit of information addressable on a ProDOS or HFS disk; usually 512 bytes.

Blue Book
A colloquial term for the Applesoft II Reference Manual of 1978.

boot
To start up a computer or computer program.

buffer
An area of computer memory used to hold information temporarily, typically while the information is being transferred somewhere else.

branch
(n.) A specific point in a program where execution may jump to a different area of the program.

(v.) When executing a program, to jump to a different section.

bug
A programming error in a program.

byte
A collection of bits, typically eight.

C

card
See *peripheral card*

catalog
A listing of all files present on a disk, or in a certain directory on a disk.

CDEV
An abbreviation for *Control Panel Device*, a module that appears in the graphic Control Panel on the IIgs and that allows you to change some function of the system, such as the time, keyboard, or slot configuration.

character
A letter, number, or symbol, typically representing using ASCII.

classic desk accessory
The name for a miniature program that can be used without having to exit out of the current application. Classic desk accessories (CDAs) are accessed on the Apple IIgs by pressing COMMAND-CONTROL-ESCAPE.

Clipboard
An area of memory on the Apple IIgs that holds the last piece of information that was cut or copied. The Clipboard contents can be pasted into other documents, even in other programs.

Closed-Apple key
A special-purpose key found on the Apple IIe, and later models where it is labeled OPTION, typically used for keyboard commands.

cold start
The process of starting up a computer when the power is first turned on. Compare with *warm start*

Command key
A key on the keyboard of the Apple IIgs and IIc Plus that when pressed, changes the behavior of another key. It is marked with a hollow Apple symbol.

compiler
A program which converts human-readable source code to machine language. Compilers exist for various languages such as BASIC and C.

control character
Any ASCII character which does not appear on the screen or on any printout; they are typically generated on the keyboard by pressing the CONTROL key in association with another key.

Control Panel
A program on the Apple IIgs that allows you to change system settings. There are two control panels: the text control panel, which is built into all IIgs computers, and the graphic control panel, which is a part of System 5.0 and later.

constant
A value in a program that never changes. Compare with *variable*

CPU (Central Processing Unit)
The CPU is responsible for fetching instructions from memory and executing them. The CPU in an Apple II is typically either a 6502, 65C02, or 65C816.

crash
When a program unexpectedly terminates, often resulting in the loss of data.

cursor
A flashing character on screen which marks where the next character will appear when typing.

D

daisy-chain
To connect a peripheral device to a computer system by connecting to an existing device, thus forming a chain.

debug
To remove programming errors and bugs from a program listing.

decimal
Any number represented using base 10 notation. Both Applesoft and Integer BASIC work with numbers in decimal.

desk accessory
A miniature program that can be used by temporarily interrupting the main application program. See *classic desk accessory* and *new desk accessory*

directory
An area of the disk that DOS uses to store a listing of all files stored on it, including name, size, and location.

disassembler
A program that will convert machine language instructions back into assembly language.

disk
A square object with a magnetic recording surface inside that is used in conjunction with a disk drive to store data, such as programs, text, and images. Compare with *hard disk*

disk drive
A device connected to the Apple that is responsible for storing and retrieving information on the surface of a disk.

Disk II

The first 5.25" disk drive system for the Apple II, released in 1978; the latest version is capable of storing 143 kilobytes of data on a single disk side.

Disk Operating System

A system program which is responsible for managing a disk, including loading and storing files, presenting a catalog listing, and taking care of other housekeeping tasks.

dragging

The mouse movement wherein the mouse button is held down while the mouse itself is moved across the table.

E

eject

To remove a disk from its drive.

escape mode

A typing mode, activated and deactivated with the ESCAPE key, that allows the cursor to be moved anywhere on the screen without affecting the current input line.

expansion slot

Any of a number of slots in the Apple II, II Plus, IIe, and IIgs wherein an expansion card may be plugged. All Apples with slots have eight of them.

expression

Any number of mathematical symbols or operations that yield a given result.

F

file

A named collection of data stored on a disk.

filename
The label assigned to a disk file, intended for human convenience and identification.

File Transfer Protocol (FTP)
A method of transferring files from one computer to another across a network.

Finder
The program on the Apple IIgs that is responsible for managing information on disks and launching application programs.

firmware
Software that is permanently embedded in the Apple's memory; also called ROM.

flippy disk
A colloquial term for a 5.25" disk which has had a notch cut on the other side, thus allowing data to be written to that other side when the disk is flipped over.

floating point number
A real number consisting of a whole number, a decimal point, and a fractional part.

folder
Another term for a directory. A folder collects a group of documents on a disk.

function
A self-contained unit of a larger program, designed to accept a given input, perform a task, and then return a value or output.

G

game paddles
A set of hand-held input devices, typically used for gaming, consisting of a large knob and a button.

game port
A 9-pin port on the back of the Apple IIe, IIc, IIc Plus, and IIgs into which a joystick or game paddles may be plugged. Earlier models of Apple had only a 16-pin DIP socket on the motherboard.

graphic Control Panel
The new desk accessory version of the old text Control Panel on the Apple IIgs. It was introduced in System 5.0 and is made up of one or more CDEVs.

graphics mode
A screen mode of the Apple in which graphics are displayed instead of text. There are three main graphics modes: low-res, high-res, and super high-res.

GS/OS
The operating system used exclusively by the Apple IIgs.

GUI
An acronym that stands for Graphical User Interface: a way of communicating with the computer through the use of icons, windows, and other metaphors of common objects. A GUI typically accepts input from a mouse.

H

hand controls
Either a joystick or a pair of game paddles used to provide input to the Apple, typically for games.

hard disk
A high-capacity, sealed disk storage system, which may be located internally or externally to the Apple.

hardware
The physical components of a computer system such as the keyboard, display, disk drive, and mouse.

hexadecimal
A numbering system which uses 16 as its base.

HFS (Hierarchical File System)
The file system commonly used on Macintosh computers.

high-resolution
An Apple II graphics mode which allows for 6 colors and an array of 280 x 160 dots, typically with 4 lines of text at the bottom of the screen.

I

icon
A symbol in a GUI that represents a folder, document, application program, or any other thing that can be selected.

ImageWriter
Apple's dot-matrix printer.

infinite loop
A loop that will never terminate, typically due to a programming error, but it may also be used to wait for user input.

initialize
To prepare a disk for storing data by dividing it into sections.

insertion point
In a GUI system, the insertion point takes the place of a cursor. It is a blinking vertical line that marks where the next character will appear when typing. See also *cursor*

integer
A whole number, lacking any decimal part.

Integer BASIC
The first dialect of BASIC available for the Apple II; it is not very common now.

interpreter
A program which converts instructions written in one language into another, "on the fly," meaning that the program must be interpreted each time that it is run. Applesoft and Integer BASIC are both interpreters. Compare with *compiler*

IWM (Integrated Woz Machine)
The name for the disk controller chip inside the Apple IIc, IIc Plus, and IIgs that is responsible for handling 5.25" and 3.5" disk drives.

J

jacket
The vinyl covering that protects a 5.25" disk.

joystick
An Apple input device, typically used for games, that provides two-axis input, and typically two buttons.

K

keyboard buffer
An area of memory that stores keystrokes until the Apple is ready to process them.

kilobyte
A unit of measurement equal to 1,024 bytes.

L

language
The established set of commands, syntax, and protocol with which the computer communicates with a human operator. Some common languages for the Apple are BASIC, Pascal, Logo, C, and assembly.

Language Card
An expansion card made for slot 0 of the Apple II and II Plus which added an additional 16K of RAM as well as the Autostart ROM; for the IIe and later models, its functionality is built-in. Its name stems from its original purpose of storing a programming language, such as Pascal.

Language System

An early system offered by Apple Computer which included a Language Card and Apple's own version of the UCSD Pascal P-System.

load

To place data, such as a program or file, into the Apple's memory.

local printer

A printer that is connected directly to the computer as opposed to being on a network.

log off

To terminate a work session with a file server or other multi-user system.

low-resolution

A graphics screen mode that offers a wider color selection at the expense of fine detail.

M

machine language

The most basic instructions which the Apple II can understand. Machine language works at the CPU level and contains instructions for loading and storing data in memory, and performing arithmetic operations.

Mega II

A custom chip in the Apple IIgs that emulates most functions of the Apple IIe.

megabyte

1,024 kilobytes, or 1,048,576 bytes.

memory

An area where the Apple stores information: either program instructions or data with which it is working. There are two main types of memory. See *RAM* and *ROM*

menu
A list of commands in an application.

mode
The state of a computer program that defines which commands it expects to receive and how it will act upon them.

Monitor
A system program that resides in the ROM of every Apple, allowing one to examine and modify memory, run programs, and perform other low-level tasks.

mouse
A small, hand-held device that is used to provide input to the Apple by moving an on-screen cursor and making selections with a button.

MouseText
A set of alternate screen characters, introduced with the Enhanced Apple IIe and included in all later Apple models, that can be used to simulate a GUI with the text screen.

N

network
A system of connected computers and peripheral devices that can communicate with each other and share information.

new desk accessory
A desk accessory on the Apple IIgs that uses the GUI. See *desk accessory* and *classic desk accessory*

nibble
Four bits out of a byte.

nonprinting character
A character, typically a control character, that does not appear on the screen.

notch

A cutout made on the edge of a 5.25" disk which enables write access. Covering the notch makes the disk read-only.

O

Old Monitor ROM

Refers to the original Apple II Monitor ROM that was part of the Integer BASIC package. The Old Monitor is characterized by its lack of enhanced line editing commands, and the fact that it does not automatically boot from a Disk II drive on start up. Compare with *Autostart ROM*

Open-Apple key

A special-purpose key found on the Apple IIe, and later models where it is labeled COMMAND, typically used for keyboard commands.

Option key

A key on the Apple IIgs and IIc Plus that when pressed, causes another key to produce a different character. On older models of Apple, this key was called the SOLID-APPLE key.

operand

A value supplied to an operator.

operating system

A program which handles low-level, common operations of the computer such as memory management, I/O, loading programs, and executing programs.

output

The results of a program or operation.

P

paddles

See *game paddles*

parallel

A method of communication in which data are transferred one byte (typically, 8 bits) at a time.

Pascal

A high-level, structured language that was used to teach programming concepts.

paste

To insert the contents of the Clipboard into a document.

pathname

The complete name of a document on a volume, made up by the volume name, and any directories in which the document is located.

peripheral card

Any of a number of small circuit boards that plug into a slot in an Apple and provide additional functionality, such as disk storage, input, or communications.

pointer

The on-screen indicator, moved with the mouse, used to make selections and execute commands.

pop-up menu

A menu of options wherein only the selected option is normally visible. Pressing the mouse button causes the other options to appear.

port

A socket on the back panel of the computer to which peripheral devices are connected.

prefix

In ProDOS, a pathname that is prefixed to all filenames and paths in disk commands.

printer

A peripheral device that produces output on paper.

printer buffer

An area of memory located either on the printer card or in the printer itself, used to store the document to be printed so that the Apple can be used to perform other tasks during the printing process.

processor

The main unit inside the Apple which is responsible for executing program instructions. See also *CPU*

ProDOS

An advanced disk operating system that superseded DOS 3.3. ProDOS allows for variable volume sizes, hierarchical storage, loadable device drivers, and many other features.

program

To write instructions for a computer, or the set of instructions that the computer follows to accomplish a task.

Programmer's Aid #1

A ROM chip containing a collection of utilities including a renumbering program, RAM test, high-res graphics subroutines, and sound routines useful for programmers.

programming language

The particular syntax and rules for programming a computer.

prompt

A symbol on the screen that indicates that the computer is ready to accept input from the user. The prompt also typically identifies the computer's mode.

R

RAM (Random Access Memory)

A type of memory whose contents are dynamic and disappear when power is removed.

RAM disk

An area of memory reserved to work like a high-speed hard disk, but whose contents are lost when the power is removed.

read

To cause data to be loaded from secondary storage, such as disk or tape, into main memory.

real number

A number having no imaginary part; in Applesoft, a number which may or may not have a decimal fraction.

record

A logical unit of a random-access data file.

recursion

The process of having a function or subroutine call itself. Recursion is not allowed in Applesoft BASIC.

Red Book

A familiar term for the Apple II Reference Manual of January 1978, one of the first manuals for the Apple II.

register

An internal, high-speed area of a CPU which is used for calculations and executing instructions. The CPU in the Apple has several registers which may store either one or two bytes.

reset

1. (n.) - A key that when pressed will cause the Apple to stop whatever it was doing and return to the command prompt.
2. (v.) - To cause the Apple to abort its current operation by pressing the RESET key.

return address

The address (or line number, in BASIC) to which a subroutine returns after completing its operation.

ROM (Read Only Memory)

A type of memory whose contents are static and remain even when power is removed.

routine

A discrete component of a software program that performs a certain task. A routine is typically superordinate to a subroutine. See *subroutine*

run
To start the execution of a program that is loaded into memory.

S

save
To place the specified contents of memory onto disk or tape.

sector
The smallest unit of storage on a formatted disk.

serial
A method of communication in which data are transferred in order, one bit at a time.

shape
A high-resolution graphic, defined by a series of vectors, able to be rotated, scaled, and positioned on the screen.

shape definition
A series of one or more plotting vectors that defines a shape.

shape directory
See *shape index*

shape index
A block of memory forming the start of a shape table, containing the total number of shapes and their starting offsets.

shape table
A block of memory that includes both a shape index and one or more shape definitions.

SmartPort
The port on an Apple IIgs to which up to two 3.5" disk drives and two 5.25" disk drives may be attached.

slot
See *expansion slot*

slot 0

This is a special slot which only exists in the original Apple II and the Apple II Plus. Typically, a Language Card is installed in slot 0.

soft-switch

A way to change a mode or function of the Apple by referencing a memory address.

software

The components of a computer system that define what instructions the computer performs.

startup disk

A disk with an operating system capable of starting up the computer with the operating system.

startup drive

The drive which the Apple checks for a startup disk. This is always drive 1 of each slot.

stack

An area of memory that is used to pass function parameters, as well as hold the return address for each subroutine call.

statement

A building block of a BASIC program that includes a command and one or more arguments used to carry out a specific procedure.

string

A sequence of zero or more characters, such as letters or numbers. An empty string, one with zero characters, is called a null string.

subroutine

A smaller, self-contained segment of a program that is called upon to perform one specific task.

SuperDrive

A high-density, 1.4 MB external floppy disk drive that can read and write any format of disk: ProDOS, Macintosh, MS-DOS, in both single-density (400K) and double-density

(800K). It requires a peripheral expansion card in order to work on the Apple.

Super High-Res
A graphics mode exclusive to the IIgs that can display information in 640 by 200 pixels with four colors or 320 by 200 pixels with 16 colors.

Super Serial Card
The most common serial communications card for the Apple.

syntax
The rules of the particular language that you are using.

T

terminal
A device used for interacting with a computer system, usually consisting of a keyboard and display screen.

text Control Panel
The version of the Control Panel that is built into all models of the Apple IIgs, accessible from the classic desk accessory menu.

text mode
An Apple screen mode in which text is displayed in 24 lines with either 40 or 80 columns per line.

text window
An area on the Apple text screen in which text is displayed and scrolled.

track
A concentric ring on a magnetic disk, consisting of many sectors. A typical 5.25" disk has 35 tracks of 16 sectors.

Trash
An icon on the Finder desktop responsible for holding discarded folders and documents for a short period of time.

U

unary operator

An operator that applies to only a single operand, such as the minus sign (-) for a negative number.

UniDisk

Apple's first 3.5" disk system, originally released for the IIe and IIc. It is an "intelligent" device, meaning that it has an on-board microprocessor, RAM, and ROM.

user

The human operating the computer.

user-friendly

A program that is written to be easy to use, with informative prompts and error messages.

Uthernet

A popular Ethernet expansion card for the Apple, manufactured by A2RetroSystems. It may be used with the ADT program, as well as Contiki and Marinetti.

V

variable

A value that may change in a program, and that is referred to by a name. Compare with *constant*

vector

1. A memory address that holds the location of another address.
2. A component of a high-resolution shape that tells whether or not to plot a point, and in which direction to move.

volume

Another term for a disk. In most cases, a volume takes up an entire disk. However, it is common for large-capacity hard drives to have more than one volume, thus appearing to be more than one disk.

warm start
The process of restarting a computer when the power is already on. See *cold start*

Winchester disk
An older type of hard disk used with the Apple II. See *hard disk*

window

1. A rectangular container on the screen for some type of information. A window might contain icons, a letter, or a drawing.
2. A quick means of escape from an upper story of a building.

Wozniak, Steve
The inventor of the Apple II, including much of its early software and peripherals.

write
To commit data from memory into a secondary storage system, such as a disk or tape.

write-protect
To cause a disk to be prevented from any write operations, whether intentional or accidental. 5.25" disks have a notch which must be covered; 3.5" disks have a hole which must be exposed.

Z

zero page
A term for the first 256 bytes of memory available to a 6502 or 65C02 microprocessor. This range of memory may be accessed at a higher speed than other memory in the Apple.

Index

This index contains just under 2,000 entries and was entirely created by a human person. To help you use this index, here is some information about how it is arranged.

The terms in the Glossary are not indexed since they are already in alphabetical order. Likewise, the command and function entries in Appendix B are not indexed for the same reason.

When alphabetizing, numbers are alphabetized according to the spelling of the most common pronunciation. For example, the entry for 6502 is alphabetized as if it were "six-five-oh-two."

If an entry title is not entirely clear, then clarification is provided in parentheses. These parentheses and their contents are ignored when alphabetizing the entries.

Integer BASIC error messages which are prefixed by three asterisks and Applesoft error messages which begin with a question mark are all alphabetized as if those symbols were not there. For example, ?SYNTAX ERROR is under S.

Example BASIC programs of any significance (more than just a few lines) are indexed, as are most photos, illustrations, and screenshots.

Entries are capitalized according to the most common convention. Therefore, error messages and BASIC keywords are in all caps, whereas generic terms such as "disk" and "semicolon," are not capitalized.

About the Author

David Finnigan is a relative newcomer to the Apple II, having only eight years' experience with the machine. In his spare time, Mr. Finnigan enjoys eating bugs, chasing hens, and crowing. He lives on a country estate in Illinois.

Made in the USA
Lexington, KY
16 December 2016